INTRODUCTION TO EARLY CHILDHOOD EDUCATION

Preschool through Primary Grades

Third Edition

Jo Ann Brewer

Salem State College

ALLYN AND BACON

Boston   London   Toronto   Sydney   Tokyo   Singapore

To all the teachers
who have helped me over the years,
but especially to
Barbara Simmons and John Nevius

Vice President, Education: Nancy Forsyth
Series Editor: Frances Helland
Editorial Assistant: Cheryl Ouellette
Senior Marketing Manager: Kathy Hunter
Production Administrator: Annette Joseph
Production Coordinator: Susan Freese
Editorial-Production Service and
Design/Electronic Composition: Karen Mason
Composition Buyer: Linda Cox
Manufacturing Buyer: Megan Cochran
Cover Administrator: Linda Knowles
Cover Designer: Studio Nine

Copyright © 1998, 1995, 1992 by Allyn & Bacon
A Viacom Company
160 Gould Street
Needham Heights, MA 02194
Internet: www.abacon.com
America Online: keyword: College Online

Library of Congress Cataloging-in-Publication Data
Brewer, Jo Ann.
    Introduction to early childhood education : preschool through primary grades / Jo Ann Brewer. — 3rd ed.
        p.   cm.
    Includes bibliographical references and index.
    ISBN 0-205-26774-2 (alk. paper)
    1. Early childhood education—United States.   2. Early childhood education—History.   3. Child development—United States.
    I. Title.
    LB1139.25.B74   1998
372.21—dc21   97–17754
                                                                      CIP

Printed in the United States of America
10 9 8 7 6 5 4 3 2 1   02 01 00 99 98 97

Brief Contents

Contents

7
Planning and Assessing Learning Activities 190

8
Language: Celebrating the Magic 224

12
Encouraging the Creative Arts 368

13
Living Together: The Social Studies 406

Preface

I n the prefaces to the two previous editions of *Introduction to Early Childhood Education,* I said that teaching young children was a very complex task. Now, as I am writing the preface to this third edition, I believe that statement even more strongly. Teachers of young children today must have a solid foundation of knowledge on which to base the many educational decisions they have to make, and their understanding of how best to work with diverse individuals and families must continually evolve. Nothing is more important than our children; thus, they deserve the very best of teachers.

The challenges of early childhood education are enormous: teaching more children who are poor, who are homeless, who live in dysfunctional families, and who endure the social upheaval in American cities. But as the challenges increase, so do the rewards for helping children develop in a safe and supportive environment.

This book defines *early childhood* as the period from birth through age eight and focuses on the school experiences of children in this age range. The early childhood years are more important than any other eight-year period in the life of a human being in terms of the learning that occurs, the attitudes about learning and school that develop, and the social skills that are acquired that will enable the individual to succeed in today's world. The problems of the future will only be solved by today's children if they value learning, know how to cooperate with others, and value a democratic way of life. Teachers can help young children develop these attitudes and skills.

The primary goal of this text is to provide a knowledge base for teachers of young children so they can make decisions that are founded on more than educational traditions or their own experiences as students. This text is also designed to encourage early childhood teachers to consider the child, the family, and the community when planning experiences for each individual. Finally, this text will help readers prepare for the National Teachers Exam, which some states require teachers to pass before they can become certified.

FEATURES OF THE TEXT

The changes in this third edition reflect some of the challenges faced by teachers of young children in today's world. Each chapter has several new features. Short "Parents" boxes throughout the text provide suggestions for teachers on communicating with parents of children in their classrooms. Although this has always been the responsibility of teachers, it can no longer be discharged simply by sending home report cards every six weeks. These boxes offer innovative ways to help parents understand what is happening at school and why.

Throughout each chapter, there are also short exercises to help readers apply the information in the text to real-world experiences. These "Theory into Practice" features are intended to encourage teachers in training to connect with both practicing teachers and available teaching materials. To strengthen further the connection to real practice, a section written by a practicing teacher, called "A Teacher Speaks," is included at the end of each chapter.

Another section, "Celebrating Diversity," has been added to most chapters to encourage teachers of young children to think about the positive benefits of diversity in their classrooms and to assure that they are sensitive to the diversity in their schools and communities.

The text begins with a brief discussion of child development (Chapter 1), which is intended to serve as an overview for readers. The focus in this chapter is on the relationship between child growth and development and planning appropriate activities. Chapter 2 provides a "slice of life" look at three different approaches to organizing school experiences for young children. Chapter 3 offers guidelines for making good decisions when planning learning environments for children. Chapter 4 is devoted to the topic of play and its importance in the learning of young children. Chapter 5 explores the topic of discipline and managing children's behavior in school settings. Chapter 6 is designed to help teachers promote parent involvement and work well with paraprofessionals and volunteers in the classroom. Chapter 7 provides guidelines for planning and assessing learning experiences and activities in early childhood classrooms.

Chapters 8 through 14—the content-area chapters—provide goals and activities for language development, the development of literacy (reading and writing), mathematics, science, the creative arts, the social studies, physical education, and wellness. Although each content area is discussed in a separate chapter, the focus throughout the book is on integrating the curriculum. To demonstrate this focus, the theme of *change* is developed in each content-area chapter in a feature called "Integrating the Curriculum." The purposes of doing so are to show that any well-chosen theme can incorporate all the content areas and to reinforce the idea that young children learn best when the experiences and activities planned for them are not divided into discrete subject-matter areas.

The last chapter, Chapter 15, examines assessment and reporting. This discussion aims to help teachers make good decisions about assessing the results of their planning and programs and reporting their assessments to parents.

Included at the end of the book are a number of appendixes, which provide useful resources on topics such as educational technology and child safety (see the "Contents"). In addition, a "Glossary" lists key terms (which are bolded in text), along with their definitions. Finally, a "References" section lists the professional works and children's literature cited and discussed in the text as well as selected sources of information for parents.

In this edition, as well as in previous editions, the goal has been to help readers view *developmentally appropriate practice (DAP)* as the process of choosing learning experiences that are individually appropriate for each child, that recognize the strengths of each learner, and that involve children actively in their own learning. In each chapter, readers are presented with a "Developmentally Appropriate Practice" box that asks them to respond to questions or statements designed to help build a strong understanding of DAP and what it means when implemented in classroom settings. Other comments about DAP appear throughout the text in relevant discussions.

Many activities appropriate for children of various ages are recommended throughout the text. These activities have been tried by real teachers in real classrooms. They are presented not as isolated units or events (something to do on Monday) but as applications of theory. When teachers understand theory, they can design their own learning activities and evaluate other activities presented in the many publications aimed at teachers of young children.

Several supplementary materials are also available to adopters of this text: an instructor's manual (prepared by Sharon Milburn of California State University of Fullerton) and a computerized test bank. I am sure these materials will be of use to teachers in education programs who want to make their classes as meaningful as possible for the students they teach.

Every teacher makes important decisions every day. This book is designed to help teachers of young children make wise decisions that will benefit the children they teach and, therefore, all of us.

ACKNOWLEDGMENTS

No book can be completed without the work of many people, and this one is no exception. Many teachers and students have helped me with ideas and offered me opportunities to be in their classrooms. I wish that I could list all their names, but I cannot. Judith Kieff and her early childhood education students at the University of New Orleans are among those who offered ideas and suggestions. I also want to thank all my students, who push me to think of new ways to explain concepts and see applications of theory in the classroom.

This edition was only possible because of the success of the first two editions, so I continue to be grateful to Colleen Dyrud, who helped create the first edition and continues to be supportive. I also appreciate all the comments and advice I have received from people who have used the text in their classes.

The editorial staff at Allyn and Bacon also have provided support and encouragement at every stage of producing this book. I wish especially to thank Frances Helland and Cheryl Ouellette for their work in guiding and supporting the publication of this third edition.

Several individuals reviewed the first edition and helped shape the second edition by making invaluable suggestions for improvements. I want to thank Donna M. Banas (Moraine Valley Community College, Illinois) and Joan Isenberg (George Mason University) for their reviewing help and also Julie K. Biddle (University of Dayton), Sheila M. Cole (Garden City Community College), Mary-Margaret Harrington (Peabody College of Vanderbilt University), Carol R. Foster (Georgia State University), Kathy Lake (Alverno College), Donna L. Legro (University of Houston), Betty Mason (Ohio University), Nancy Russell (Texas A & I University), Sandra L. Starkey (West Virginia Graduate College), Beverly Tucker (Valdosta State College), Betty Watson (Harding University), Deborah Webster (Mount Mary College), and Nancy Winter (Greenfield Community College), for their insightful answers to the questionnaires that helped shape this edition.

I would also like to thank those individuals who reviewed the second edition and offered helpful suggestions for this third edition: Tabitha Carwile Daniel, Western Kentucky University; Carol S. Huntsinger, College of Lake County; Marilyn McWhorter, Marshall University; and Marilyn Moore, Illinois State University.

In previous editions of this book, I have noted that my husband and colleague, Bill Harp, has been incredibly supportive of my work. As I have worked on this edition, he has been even more supportive. I would not have believed it was possible for anyone to do more, but he has. He has made sure that our household has kept running and that we have had meals to eat and clean clothes to wear, as well as given me encouragement all through the writing process. For all that he has done, I thank him!

Introduction
to Early Childhood
Education

1
YOUNG CHILDREN GROWING, THINKING, AND LEARNING

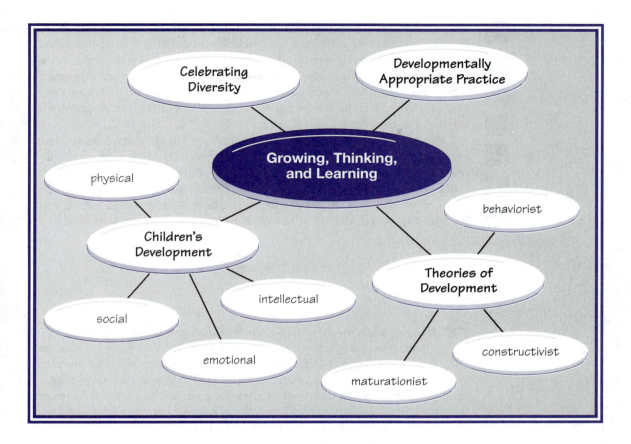

When you enrolled in the teacher-education program, you knew that you had much to learn about teaching and the other things that teachers do. You also knew that you had a lot to learn about children and what behavior is typical for children of different ages. So you were excited when your first observation for the year was focused on children's growth and development.

You chose to visit a child-care center that provides full-day services for infants and preschoolers as well as after-school programs for school-aged children. Physical development was easy to observe: You saw children crawling, walking, skipping, running, jumping, walking backward, and exhibiting numerous other examples of physical development. You also found many examples of social development: children sharing

toys and playing peacefully in the sand; helping each other complete puzzles; and taking turns on the outside equipment. You also noticed that some children were reading books, others were writing on a chalkboard, and others were explaining to the teacher what happened when they dropped a series of stones into a container of water. You saw one child tell the teacher how angry he was that he did not get a turn on the tricycle.

When you talked with the lead teacher at the child-care center, she explained that the materials, equipment, and activities were carefully selected to meet the developmental needs of the children. Given what you observed at the center, you realized that learning about the development of children is critical to your success as a teacher and you became eager to know what to expect of the children you will teach.

This chapter is meant to be a review of the principles of child development, not a comprehensive treatment of the topic. A basic knowledge of child development is critical to appropriate planning, teaching, and evaluating in programs for young children. Just as we would never plan a meal or vacation without knowing something about the ages and tastes of the participants, we cannot plan curriculum without knowing what children of a given age will likely be able to do and interested in doing.

The National Association for the Education of Young Children (NAEYC) defines *early childhood* as the period from birth to age eight (Bredekamp 1987). Some child-care programs serve infants and toddlers as well as preschoolers (three- and four-year-olds) or primary children (five-, six-, seven-, and eight-year-olds). Most of this chapter will discuss normal growth and development. Keep in mind that to determine the average age when a child is able to perform a task or behave in a certain way, some of children must perform that task earlier than the average and some, later than the average.

You will meet many children in your teaching career who have special needs, ranging from severe mental or physical challenges to slight delays in the development of language. You also will meet children who are gifted and talented in a variety of ways, who have attention deficits, and who are wise beyond their years in relating to people. Children come in all sizes, colors, and places on the developmental continuum. Our job, as teachers, is to recognize each child's abilities and growth and plan for the next steps as she grows physically, intellectually, socially, and emotionally.

DEVELOPMENTALLY APPROPRIATE PRACTICE

The term **developmentally appropriate practice (DAP)** will be used throughout this book to mean practice that is age and individually appropriate for each child in a program. Planning a developmentally appropriate curriculum means that teachers have to know each child—where he is developmentally and what his individual talents and interests are. DAP also requires that teachers think about children's basic needs for play and rest, that they focus on children's development in all areas, that they plan an inclusive program that honors the cultural differences each child brings to school, and that they work to support parents and families (Bredekamp 1987).

The chapters that follow will provide more detail about developmentally appropriate practice and ask you to reflect on what makes one choice developmentally appropriate and another, inappropriate. Please remember that although there are some basic guidelines that define DAP, in classrooms across the United States, it looks quite different. DAP requires that teachers and children work continuously to determine the best practice for a group of children at a given time. DAP is dynamic, not static. It cannot be the same for all children or all groups of children.

The purpose of this chapter is to review briefly some theoretical lenses through which child development is seen and to outline typical patterns of development. This knowledge is most useful when it can be consciously applied to selecting and organizing curriculum experiences. Often, teachers

Children's development in all areas is often reflected in play episodes.

choose activities or organize those activities in ways that can be traced to the different theories of child growth and development, but they are unaware of these connections. As a teacher, you need to recognize why you choose one activity over another or one organizational scheme over another.

THEORIES OF DEVELOPMENT

Children's growth and development can be described from several theoretical points of view. Each of these points of view has its supporters among practitioners in early childhood education, and each offers explanations of human growth and development. These theoretical positions include behaviorism, maturationism, and interactionism. Throughout your career, as you read and think about children and about planning programs that will be beneficial to them, reflect upon the points of view expressed by authors of articles and reports and notice how their suggestions differ depending on what they believe about children's development.

Behaviorist Theory

Behaviorist theory suggests that behavior can be shaped by the response that follows any particular action. John B. Watson (1878–1958), Edward Thorndike (1874–1949), and B. F. Skinner (1904–1990) are well-known behaviorists. Skinner is the best known of the modern behaviorists. He wrote extensively about learning as controlled by a system of rewards and punishments. His name is synonymous with the terms **stimulus-response theory** and operant conditioning (Hill 1977). The basic elements of stimulus-response theory include reinforcements, punishments, operant conditioning, and extinguishing behavior.

In classical conditioning, a learner is presented with a stimulus and a reward and learns to expect the reward whenever the stimulus is presented. This type of conditioning is exemplified by the classic Pavlovian experiment of ringing a bell and immediately presenting a dog with food until the dog salivates at the sound of the bell. Operant conditioning differs from classical conditioning in that the behavior precedes the reinforcement. For example, a pigeon may learn to push a lever to get a food pellet. Presenting a reward after a response provides positive reinforcement of the behavior. Negative reinforcement can also be used to elicit behavior. If the floor of the pigeon's cage were electrified and pushing the lever stopped the shock, the pigeon would learn to press the lever to avoid an unpleasant stimulus; that is negative reinforcement. Behavior can also be punished rather than reinforced. A pigeon might be punished by an electric shock for failing to push a lever on a set schedule.

In the classroom, reinforcements are often used to shape behaviors. Reinforcements in the classroom can be positive or negative. A positive reinforcement is something that is viewed by the learner as desirable. If a child completes a task or exhibits a behavior that is desirable, the teacher may positively reinforce that behavior by verbal praise, a token such as a sticker, or some other treat. Negative reinforcement involves allowing a child to avoid or escape from an undesirable consequence or situation if certain behaviors are exhibited. For example, the teacher might give a child the option of leaving the "time-out" chair more quickly if she does not talk at all for five minutes. Finally, punishment in the classroom need not necessarily be corporal (physical) punishment but can be "time outs," exclusion from the group, withdrawal of privileges, and so on.

In a classroom, **operant conditioning** might be used to shape children's performance on an academic task. For example, suppose a class of second-graders has been assigned the task of completing twenty arithmetic problems. Those children who complete the task promptly and correctly get a token, which can be redeemed for objects in the class store on Friday. With those children who do not complete the task either promptly or correctly, the teacher may take one of several approaches. If he knows that three of the children have never completed twenty problems, he may choose to reward their performance if they complete more than they have completed before. He may choose to provide neither positive nor negative reinforcement to children who complete the same number of problems they have completed in the past. If he believes that some children deliberately did not attempt the task for some reason, he might punish them by reducing their recess time.

Operant conditioning can be used to shape behavior by providing reinforcements when the learner's behavior moves closer to the target behavior. Shaping behavior involves the following components (Pellegrini 1987):

1. targeting the desired behavior
2. fixing a behavioral baseline
3. selecting reinforcers
4. analyzing the task and sequencing the segments
5. systematically applying the reinforcers (p. 113)

In the classroom example just discussed, by rewarding a child who completes more problems than in previous assignments the teacher is rewarding closer approximations to the target behavior of completing twenty problems. Teachers often use such techniques to help children gain control of their classroom behaviors. If a child is hitting other children, for example, the teacher will first collect baseline data through observations to determine how often the child is hitting and then provide rewards as the hitting behavior decreases.

Behaviors can be extinguished by failing to provide reinforcements for them. If a child is behaving in ways the teacher deems inappropriate, then the teacher can ignore the less desirable behaviors while consistently rewarding more desirable behaviors.

The goal of employing behavioristic techniques is for the desired behavior to become rewarding to the child so that the teacher or parent need not continue to provide extrinsic rewards. Most teachers, even those who believe strongly in other theories of development, employ some behavioristic strategies, as they ignore some behaviors and praise others. Most teachers have had experience with children who prefer negative attention—that is, punishment—to no attention; the usual strategy for dealing with such children is to make every effort to ignore their misbehavior and to reward their appropriate behavior.

Behaviorist theory does not say much about physical development, since most authorities agree that physical development is genetically determined and thus does not affect a child's behavior, at least in an optimal environment that includes good nutrition, lack of disease, and safety. Behaviorists are more concerned with how children develop socially, emotionally, and intellectually.

Maturationist Theory

The roots of the **maturationist** point of view are found in the work of Jean-Jacques Rousseau (1712–1778), who believed that children should be allowed to "unfold." A child is like a seed that contains all the elements to produce a wonderful apple if given the proper amounts of nutrients from the soil and water along with sunshine and an ideal climate. The modern maturationist point of view is most often associated with the work of the Gesell Institute (Ilg and Ames 1955). The Gesellian literature describes growth and development in terms of children's maturity. Experience plays a much less important role in development in the maturationist point of view than it does in the behaviorist point of view. Maturationists believe that each child's physical, social, emotional, and intellectual development follows an individual schedule that is basically predetermined. They believe that a child will develop to his potential when placed in an optimal environment and that his development will be slowed or retarded if the environment is not optimal.

Maturationists believe that a child's developmental level is the most important determiner of social and intellectual success, especially in school settings. They suggest that the child will have difficulty in school if he is "overplaced," that is, placed in settings where the requirements do not match his developmental level. Maturationists emphasize the child's own schedule of maturation rather than rewards and punishments, experiences, or interactions with the environment. Experience, in the maturationist point of view, is always filtered by the child's maturation level.

Even though this theoretical position has been criticized, many schools continue to screen children for entry into programs on the basis of developmental tests developed by the Gesell Institute (Meisels 1987).

Constructivist Theory

The **constructivist,** or developmentalist, point of view is founded on the work of Jean Piaget (1896–1980) and Lev Vygotsky (1896–1934). Modern interactionists, such as Jerome Bruner, George Forman, and others, continue to refine the theories of Piaget and to clarify concepts about children's development.

Piaget believed that children create knowledge through interactions with the environment. Children are not passive receivers of knowledge; rather, they actively work at organizing their experience into more and more complex mental structures. Piaget and Inhelder's (1969) descriptions of children's thinking include the concepts of assimilation, accommodation, and equilibrium. *Assimilation* is fitting information into existing schemas or categories. If a child has developed a schema for "dog" and is presented with a new example of a dog, such as a St. Bernard, the new example can be assimilated, or included, in the existing schema. If presented with a cat, the child may create a new schema for "furry pets that are not dogs." Creating a new category is the process of *accommodation.* Through a series of repeated assimilations and accommodations, the child eventually creates a mental structure that will account for all animals.

Equilibrium is the balance achieved whenever information or experience is fitted into a schema or a new schema is created for it. This balance is very short lived, as new experiences and information are constantly being encountered by the child. *Disequilibrium* describes the mental state in which there is an imbalance between assimilation and accommodation. Disequilibrium is motivating in that it drives the learner to achieve equilibrium. *Equilibration* is the process of moving from disequilibrium to equilibrium. Equilibration allows the learner to employ assimilation and accommodation as tools for achieving equilibrium (Piaget 1985). In the "dog" example, if the child is presented with a Basenji, a dog that rarely barks, disequilibrium may result as the child is confronted with a dog that does not exhibit one of the usual dog behaviors. The child must then assimilate this dog into her schema of dogs. Some researchers (for example, Flavell 1985) agree that equilibration is one process that contributes to cognitive growth but question the idea that one process can account for all cognitive development.

Piagetians categorize knowledge as physical, social, or logico-mathematical. Forman and Kuschner (1983) postulate a fourth kind of knowledge: knowing what one knows. The term used in the literature to describe this category of knowledge is **metaknowledge.** If a child knows about the number system, for instance, then his knowing that he knows the system is another type of knowledge that is not social, physical, or logico-mathematical.

Wadsworth (1989) describes the definition of *learning* in Piagetian terms as follows:

> Two usages or meanings of the word *learning* are differentiated by Piagetians. The first usage can be called learning in the broad sense, and it is synonymous with development. It is appropriate to talk about the development of, or the learning of, physical knowledge, logical-mathematical knowledge, and social knowledge. The second usage of learning is narrower. It refers to the acquisition of specific information from the environment, learning that is assimilated into an existing schema. Most content learning is the second kind. Both forms of learning imply comprehension.
>
> Rote memory, or memorization, is not considered learning because it does not involve assimilation and comprehension. Some theories, such as behaviorism, consider rote memory as a form of learning and do not differentiate between it and the two kinds of learning defined here. For Piagetians, learning always involves construction and comprehension. (p. 156)

Wadsworth goes on to explain that even though rote memory is not considered by Piagetians to be a kind of learning, it is valuable. Rote memory is certainly useful for knowing one's address or telephone number, for example, but comprehension is not necessarily a component of memorization. A child who comprehends place value is intellectually different from one who has simply memorized the algorithm for solving addition problems that require regrouping.

Theoretical Influences

THEORY INTO Practice

Observe a group of three-year-olds and a group of eight-year-olds at play. Make a list of what you consider the most obvious changes in children between three and eight years old.

The different theories provide points of view through which to interpret observations of children as they grow and develop (see Table 1.1). Depending on our theoretical orientation, we would look at examples of children's development differently. If a child were observed throwing a ball at a target, a behaviorist might point out the reinforcements that make the child seek closer approximations to the most effective throwing techniques. The maturationist observing the same child might focus on the child's physical maturity, as indicated by her ability to grasp and release the ball appropriately. The interactionist would view repeated attempts to

TABLE 1.1   General Overview of Different Theoretical Orientations

	Behaviorist	Maturationist	Constructivist
Physical Development	No special attention	Indicator of readiness for social and intellectual tasks	Internally motivated; influences other areas of development
Intellectual Development	Learning is achieved through reinforcement and rewards; is incremental	Learning is unfolding of child's potential if in optimal environment	Learning is a continuous process of assimilation and accommodation; results in changes in thinking rather than incremental growth of facts
Social Development	Shaped by reinforcements	Dependent on optimal environment	Learned through process of testing hypotheses; same as learning in other areas
Emotional Development	Shaped by reinforcements	Dependent on optimal environment	Learned through internal process; developmental
Motivational Development	External; rewards and punishments	Internal; child follows own program	Internal; child is active in own development

hit the target as evidence that the child was actively seeking information about velocity and angle of release in order to hit the target (although the child would not be expected to be able to verbalize these concepts).

A child develops as a whole. Development in one area certainly influences development in other areas. For example, when a child becomes mobile, he opens up many more possibilities for exploration and learning about the environment. Children who feel that they are learning successfully or who feel confident about physical abilities develop more positive self-esteem. Children who learn to control their impulsive behaviors may be able to sustain interactions with people and materials longer than children who do not, which affects their intellectual development. A child's social, physical, emotional, and intellectual development are always interrelated.

PARENTS AND **DEVELOPMENT**

- Create a parent library that provides selected books and articles on the typical growth and development of children.

CHILDREN'S DEVELOPMENT

This section provides very brief overviews of patterns in children's physical, social, emotional, and intellectual development. Table 1.2 on pages 10 and 11 summarizes and gives examples of these patterns.

TABLE 1.2

Overview of Patterns in Children's Development

	Birth to Three Years Old	Three to Four Years Old	Five to Six Years Old	Seven to Eight Years Old
Physical Development	Physical skills develop rapidly Sits and crawls Walks and begins to run Fine motor skills develop; can stack and pick up small objects Manages spoon or fork for feeding Grasps and releases objects	Physical skills increase Rides a tricycle Walks up and down stairs, alternating feet Runs Jumps with both feet Walks on balance beam Climbs on playground equipment Undresses and dresses self Catches ball with arms extended Walks backward and on tiptoe Holds crayon with fingers	Skips on alternate feet Rides two-wheel bike Skates Throws fairly accurately Catches ball with hands Turns somersaults Participates in games requiring physical skills Small muscle development increases; eye-hand coordination develops Fine muscle control increases; can use hammer, pencil, scissors, etc. Copies geometric figures Cuts on lines Prints some letters Pastes and glues Begins to lose teeth Handedness is well established	Physical skills become important in self-concept Energy levels are high Rate of growth slows Fine muscle control is good; can form letters well Permanent teeth appear Body proportions, facial structure change
Social Development	Responds to others Enjoys company of other children Can maintain involvement with another for a very short period Is unable to share without coaxing Shows very little ability to postpone gratification Imitates actions of others Begins to engage in parallel play	Becomes more aware of self Develops more altruistic feelings Becomes aware of racial/ethnic and sexual differences Is able to take direction, follow some rules Has strong feelings toward home and family Shows a growing sense of self-reliance Parallel play is common; cooperative play begins Imaginary playmates are fairly common	Expresses rigid ideas about sex roles Has best friends but for short periods of time Quarrels often but anger is short lived Is able to share and take turns Is eager to participate in school experiences Considers teacher very important Wants to be first Becomes possessive	Is more competitive with peers Depends on parents for expansion of interests, activities Is influenced by peer opinions Plays with opposite sex less often Needs teacher approval Is able to share Wants to please Is more independent at work and play Forms more enduring friendships Peer groups begin to form

TABLE 1.2

Overview of Patterns in Children's Development *(continued)*

	Birth to Three Years Old	Three to Four Years Old	Five to Six Years Old	Seven to Eight Years Old
Emotional Development	Cannot tolerate frustration Cries easily Is often unable to control impulses Begins to express affections Needs routines and security Begins to perceive emotions of others Expresses self, sometimes emphatically	Can tolerate some frustration Develops some self-control Appreciates surprises and novel events Begins to show sense of humor Needs overt expressions of affection Fears the dark, being abandoned, strange situations	Expresses and labels feelings Controls aggression better Expresses less concern when separated from parents Expresses sense of humor in jokes, nonsense words Learns right from wrong Develops a conscience	Expresses reactions to others Is sensitive to ridicule and criticism Expresses more worries: war, loss of parents Shows more persistence Expresses more empathy; is able to see others' viewpoints
Cognitive Development	Sensorimotor investigations of environment is predominate Development of concepts is rapid Develops a sense of object permanence Develops language May use some number and color words but may not understand them	Follows instructions of two commands Makes impulsive judgments and frequent mistakes Develops vocabulary rapidly Uses numbers without understanding Has difficulty differentiating fantasy and reality Begins to classify, especially by function Begins to use some functional abstract words "Why" questions are constant Thinking is very egocentric	Shows a growing attention span Is able to seriate objects Is able to group objects Is more deliberate, less impulsive in judgments Differentiates between fantasy and reality Uses language aggressively, in categorization Is aware that words and pictures represent real objects Becomes interested in numbers and letters Knows names of colors Does not spontaneously use rehearsal in memory tasks Follows three unrelated commands Some children begin to conserve number, length	Differences in reading and language abilities widen Transition to concrete operational thinking begins Talking and discussion are important Is able to plan Can sustain interest over long periods of time Begins to understand cause and effect Develops a growing understanding of time, money Uses slang and profanity Understands and uses more abstract terms Expresses more awareness of community, world

Sources: Association for Supervision and Curriculum Development 1975; Berk 1996; Tudor 1981.

Physical Development

Patterns of Development

Physical development is orderly, not random. Infant development is marked by the change from undifferentiated mass activity to controlled activity. It is easy to observe undifferentiated mass activity in an infant. If she is excited, her whole body moves and her arms and legs flail. Gradually, the baby becomes more capable of differentiated movements, such as deliberately reaching for and grasping a rattle. Movements that become controlled and deliberate also become organized into patterns, such as pulling oneself to a standing position, releasing the hands, and moving the legs and feet to walk. The patterns then become available to the child as possible responses to different situations. If the child wants a toy that is across the room, at first, the only option for getting there is scooting and rocking. As development progresses, crawling and finally walking and running become patterns of physical movement available to the child. The physical development of children in the infant stage proceeds very rapidly. The child learns to control head position, to grasp objects, and perhaps to stand and walk in the first year. As children grow, the development of their motor skills is not quite as rapid as it is in infancy, but it continues throughout childhood.

Observations of physical development reveal that growth is *cephalocaudal* (it proceeds from head to tail) and *proximodistal* (it proceeds from the cen-

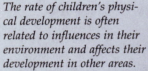

The rate of children's physical development is often related to influences in their environment and affects their development in other areas.

ter of the body outward) and that gross motor movements are developed before fine motor movements. Control of head and arm muscles is achieved before control of leg muscles. Similarly, children are able to control the muscles of their arms before they can control the fine muscles in their hands that are needed for tasks such as writing and cutting with scissors.

The rate of children's physical development is variable and related to environmental features such as nutrition and the freedom to practice movements. Some behaviors, such as walking, tend to emerge at about the same time in children, even if they have been confined as infants; others, such as throwing, seem to depend more on practice opportunities. Most children are encouraged to practice their developing skills through interactions in daily life. The parent may encourage the child to progress from letting go of support, to standing alone, to walking a step or two, and finally to walking several steps across the room. Children give their caretakers clues about what to encourage at any given time by attempting the behaviors. Thus, for example, most caretakers would not attempt to encourage walking in children who are not yet showing they are ready to walk by pulling themselves to a standing position.

By the time they are three, most children can walk backward and on tiptoe and can run. They can throw a ball and catch it with their arms extended. They can also ride a tricycle and hold a crayon or pencil with their fingers rather than their fists. Four-year-olds continue to refine their skills; they can bounce a ball, hop on one foot, climb ladders, alternate feet while walking downstairs, and jump from a standing position. Some five-year-olds can skip, and some learn to jump rope. By the time children are six, most can throw fairly accurately, and many learn to ride a two-wheel bike.

Children seven and eight continue to refine the skills that they have acquired and learn new skills. They are physically active, running, skipping, hopping, and climbing—rarely just walking. Their fine motor abilities increase so that they can draw, write, and learn to play musical instruments. Practice in motor skills is important in this period, especially for newly acquired skills such as swimming. Age and practice have more effect on the development of motor skills in this period than does sex. Girls can run as fast and throw as far and as accurately as boys during this period.

Implications for the Curriculum

It is important during the preschool and early elementary school years for children to have many opportunities for engaging in physical activities. Three-year-olds are in a constant state of motion, and it is important that teachers and parents provide opportunities for safe physical activity and not expect motor control that is beyond what the child can achieve. Fours and fives still need much more movement in their programs than sitting, although they can sit still for short periods of time for such activities as storytime.

Teachers and parents need to think carefully when planning activities for young children. For example, writing on a line requires excellent fine motor control, and most fives and sixes cannot perform this task without considerable difficulty. Children who engage in organized sports such as tee-ball and soccer when they are very young may face the same sort of difficulties. Some parents and coaches expect coordination beyond what five- to eight-year-olds are capable of. If children do participate in organized activities, parents and coaches need to be aware of the abilities that the activities require and to match their expectations to children's capabilities.

All young children need vigorous physical activity every day, and no child should be deprived of the opportunities for such activities because he must complete other tasks or because he is being punished. There is a growing concern that children in the United States are less physically fit than previous generations of children (Berk 1996). This trend seems to reflect the time that children spend in passive activities, such as watching television and sitting quietly at desks, and the lack of vigorous exercise in their daily lives.

The following suggestions may help teachers plan activities that encourage the physical development of children:

- Provide outside play every day that it is possible. Equipment should encourage climbing, running, jumping, and so on.
- Make sure children have access to an inside play area that contains a tumbling mat, Velcro balls and targets, and other materials to encourage movement.
- For very young children, indoor equipment for physical development can include rocking boats, steps, and low slides and tunnels. As children mature, appropriate equipment includes more complex climbing apparatus, balance beams, and so on.
- Provide balls that are age appropriate. For very young children, balls should be large and made of soft materials such as foam and yarn. As children learn to catch and throw more easily, they can use balls made of soft rubber. Durable rubber balls should be provided for children of about five and six who are learning to kick a ball.
- Beginning around five years of age, children can use jump ropes and hula hoops for experimenting with movement and control.
- Many classroom activities help children gain fine muscle control: painting, cutting with scissors, manipulating clay, stringing beads, sewing cards, using pegs and pegboards, and so on. Teachers must encourage these activities as the children's development indicates.

Social Development

Patterns of Development

As noted in the section on physical development, the child's first physical actions are not differentiated—she moves all over all at once when excited. The infant's social and emotional development is also undifferentiated, in the sense that responses to stimuli such as being cold or hungry evoke crying behaviors that are not specific to the stimuli. In a matter of weeks, the child's crying becomes differentiated so that the primary caregiver can distinguish between the cries that indicate that the child is hungry, bored, or in pain. By six weeks or two months, the infant is able to respond to an adult by smiling and begins to imitate behavior such as sticking out her tongue or closing her eyes. By eight months or so, the child has developed a strong attachment to the primary caregiver and is anxious about separation from him or her. Toddlers begin to develop attachments to their families. Two-year-old children are trying to establish their own identities, and "me do it" is one of their most frequent statements.

By the time they are three, children have established relationships with their families and with others outside their families. They have also developed some strategies for achieving what they want and some ideas about sex-role identification.

Development of Personality   One element of social development is development of personality. Erik Erikson (1902–1994), a psychoanalytic theorist, concentrated on studying the development of the ego—a sense of self (Ambron 1978). His description of stages in ego development are especially useful to teachers. Erikson viewed the child's developing identity as a reflection of relationships with parents and family within the broader context of society.

Teachers who think about children's behavior in Erikson's terms will plan programs that provide many opportunities for children to build trust and to make choices and feel successful in the choices that they make. Buzzelli and File (1989) suggest that building friendships is important in building trust. Helping children recognize their own needs and the feelings and emotions of others are important steps in building trust. The child must feel that her ideas are good ideas and that others respect those ideas. If too much of the time spent in school or child care is directed by the teacher, children will begin to feel that their ideas are unacceptable. Older children need to be able to participate in activities in which their achievements are obvious and celebrated. For example, four- and five-year-olds need to know that if they suggest activities, the teacher will listen and help them carry out their ideas, if possible. If the activity cannot be incorporated

Basic Trust versus Basic Mistrust (first year of life)

Experiences and sensations that give the infant a sense of familiarity and inner certainty provide him with a sense of self. He feels that the world is benevolent or at least reliable, and he likewise trusts himself and his own capacities. He has established basic trust. If the individual develops basic mistrust instead, he may tend to behave irrationally or to withdraw into schizoid or depressive states in later life.

Autonomy versus Shame and Doubt (second year of life)

During the second year of life, the infant develops muscular control; she moves about and begins toilet training. She needs firmness now, as a protection against the potential anarchy of her own impulses. The sense of self-control (autonomy) learned at this stage leads to a lasting sense of goodwill and personal pride. A failure to achieve well-guided autonomy can lead later in life to compulsive neurosis (a pervasive sense of shame before the world) and compulsive doubt of the self and others.

Initiative versus Guilt (the preschool years)

During the preschool years, the child has a boundless supply of energy, which permits him to learn all kinds of activities and ideas quickly and avidly. He concentrates on successes rather than failures and does things for the simple pleasure of the activity. Autonomy becomes more focused and effective. The child becomes "more himself." The danger in this period is that the child's exuberant and aggressive explorations and conquests may lead him into frustration. His new physical and mental strengths encourage ambitions that may turn out to be beyond his abilities—inevitably, he sometimes fails or is defeated. Unless he can come to terms with

into the classroom, the teacher will still treat the idea with respect and perhaps help the child modify the idea or accomplish some part of the activity.

Development of Self-Esteem　Another element of the social development of the young child is the development of self-esteem. The concept of self is developed gradually; the young child develops a concept of himself as a separate individual over a period of years. Through interactions first with the parents and family and then with peers and others outside the family, children gradually develop a concept of who they are and what they are like. In a classic study of children's self-esteem, Coopersmith (1967) found that children, especially boys, with high self-esteem had parents who were accepting, affectionate, and genuinely concerned about their child. The parents also enforced rules carefully and consistently and insisted on high standards of behavior but used noncoercive methods of discipline. They also demonstrated more democratic interactions with their children.

Teachers of young children often plan experiences in which improving self-esteem is the primary goal. However, such plans for activities

these disappointments he may be overwhelmed by resignation, guilt, and anxiety.

Perhaps the best way to help the child at this age is to encourage him to play constructively, to do some chores around the house, or to help care for younger children. In this way, the conflict between initiative and guilt may be resolved by the establishment of a constructive moral sense; it can set the individual on the road to goals that are not only possible for him but also deeply satisfying. If the conflict remains unresolved, in adult life, the individual may be inhibited or impotent (socially as well as sexually), or he may overreact by compulsive showing off.

Industry versus Inferiority (middle childhood)

Building on the previously developed trust, autonomy, and initiative, the child can achieve a sense of industry. In school, she learns the basic tools of literacy and cooperation that will enable her to become a productive member of society, and a sense of achievement becomes important to her. She learns the satisfaction of persisting at a task until it is completed and of using her skills to perform according to her own and others' expectations. In a culture like that in the United States, in which achievement is often measured in terms of doing better than someone else, she also learns to compete and to measure her productivity in relation to that of others.

The dangers of this period are twofold. On one hand, the child may learn to value achievement in work above all else; she may alienate her peers by excessively competitive behavior. On the other hand, she may feel unable to perform the tasks required of her and develop a sense of inferiority that prevents her from trying. Experiences of failure may lead to the child's feeling that she is inadequate, that she cannot be successful as a worker. In extreme cases, this sense of inferiority can affect the child's attitude toward work for life.

Source: Adapted from Erikson 1963.

often ignore the pervasive nature of the development of self-concept. Katz (1986) discusses the futility of planning an activity based on "me" (a booklet about my favorite food, my pet, my favorite dress, my best skill, and so on) as a means of improving self-esteem. Such an activity might contribute to the child's self-esteem if it is conducted in the context of a classroom environment in which children have choices and opportunities to participate in a variety of activities in which they can feel successful and in control. But if the classroom environment is generally structured so that children feel unable to be successful, then even a series of self-esteem lessons will not be effective.

Kostelnik, Stein, Whiren, and Soderman (1993) state that "fifteen-minute activities or the adult's gushing remarks will not infuse children with a sense of well-being or inoculate them against negative self-perceptions. Because esteem-influencing experiences pervade all aspects of children's lives and are ever-present, authentic esteem enhancing efforts must be pervasive too" (p. 78). Therefore, a teacher who wishes to build self-esteem in children will consider how children are treated all through the day. The kinds of experiences regularly provided for them are much more

Children's social and emotional development are important to teachers in developmentally appropriate classrooms.

important in the process of building self-esteem than isolated lessons or activities designed to focus on positive feelings about oneself.

The Role of Play   Play experiences are very important in the social and emotional development of young children. Children can "play" various roles and behaviors and get feedback about the appropriateness of the behaviors in play. They can play "bully" or "baby" and find out what kinds of responses their behavior elicits in nonthreatening situations. They can also play various adult roles. Young children often play the roles of family members, and with experience, they begin to play roles of those outside the family. They might play "grocery clerk," "filling station attendant," "dentist," or "garbage worker" and explore the behavior patterns that they believe are appropriate for those individuals.

Because play is so important in the lives of children, an entire chapter will be devoted to the topic of play (see Chapter 4).

Social Skills and Social Relationships   Research continues to emphasize the importance of fostering children's social development in the early childhood years. Ullmann (1957) found that unpopular children were more likely to drop out of school; Roff, Sells, and Golden (1972) found that unpopular children were more likely to have emotional problems as adults; and Roff and Sells (1968) found that unpopular children were more likely to engage in delinquent behavior as adolescents. In a review of the research on unpopular children, Roopnarine and Honig (1985) reiterated the importance of helping young children gain social skills. Yespo and O'Connor (1989) also examined children's social abilities and concluded that the late-preschool years are critical for intervention in social development.

These studies underline the importance of helping children learn to participate in social relationships. Children who are unsuccessful in social relationships are not capable of analyzing the situation and determining which behaviors need to be altered. It is then the teacher's responsibility to help a child break an unsuccessful cycle and implement new behaviors that will lead to success in establishing social relationships.

Rogers and Ross (1986) describe *social skill* as the "ability to assess what is happening in a social situation; skill to perceive and correctly interpret the actions and needs of the children in the group at play; ability to imagine possible courses of action and select the most appropriate one" (pp. 14–15). Children who are popular and most successful socially demonstrate these abilities, but children who lack social skills may need direct instruction through modeling, role-playing, or the use of puppets to help them develop these abilities. Roopnarine and Honig (1985), in a review of research on the unpopular child, add that teachers can help children become more popular by helping their families focus on more positive discipline techniques and making sure that positive social development is a major program goal.

Teachers and parents are concerned with the development in young children of prosocial behaviors: helping, cooperating, and empathizing. Kostelnik et al. (1993) report that prosocial behavior increases quite rapidly during the preschool years. In the classroom setting, teachers can help children develop these behaviors through modeling the desired behaviors, setting up situations that require cooperation, and suggesting specific ways that children can be cooperative or helpful. Some play equipment should be selected that can be used by more than one child, such as telephones, jump ropes, and board games. Teachers can model caring and empathy for each child and discuss with the children how some actions make others feel. Teachers can also demonstrate how to be cooperative by helping build a block construction or helping dig in the garden.

Honig (1982) found that prosocial behavior was most likely to develop under certain conditions, namely, when:

1. Children had consistent contacts with nurturing, individually attentive adults.
2. Children were able to identify feelings (their own and those of others).
3. Children were exposed to adults who modeled prosocial behavior.
4. Children had opportunities to respond to real situations in which prosocial behavior was appropriate.
5. Children were encouraged to think of possible alternatives to actions.

Aggression Another aspect of social development that receives attention is aggression. Teachers and parents are concerned with children's aggressive behavior. The results of studies indicate that aggressive behavior in the classroom can be reduced by providing enough space and materials so that children do not have to compete with each other. These studies also suggest eliminating toys that lend themselves to aggressive themes and not allowing children to benefit from aggressive behavior by either controlling the victim or getting the teacher's attention. It is also important to model cooperative behavior and discuss and demonstrate solutions to problems other than aggression (Potts, Huston, and Wright 1986; Yarrow 1983).

Kostelnik et al. (1993) recommend the following strategies for helping reduce aggression:

reducing the frustration in children's lives, . . .
helping children feel more competent, . . .
teaching children prosocial behaviors, . . .
helping children recognize instances of accidental aggression, . . . and
rechanneling children's expressive aggression. (p. 253)

Although some authors believe that aggression with inanimate objects is not appropriate (Masselli et al. 1984; Gray 1981; Fagot and Hagan 1985), others, including Kostelnik and her co-authors, believe that channeling aggressive behavior (hitting, kicking, and so on) so that it is focused on inanimate objects and does not pose a threat to the safety of others is a useful strategy. These authors do caution against letting aggressive behavior get out of control under these conditions.

Sex-Role Identification Sex-role identification is yet another important element of social development. Before they are three, children begin to identify themselves as boys or girls, and at around three years of age, they can identify others as boys or girls. They continue to develop their concepts of sexual identity and their attitudes about appropriate roles for males and females. In fact, preschoolers may be quite rigid about what is appropriate play or an appropriate task for males or females.

Teachers will want to structure the classroom and activities so that both boys and girls have equal opportunities and encouragement to participate. The literature selected for use in the classroom should contain models of behavior that is not stereotyped by sex, and teachers should avoid assigning tasks in a stereotypical manner (consistently having boys do heavy work and girls do verbal or artwork). Bigler and Liben (1990, 1992) have found that direct instruction can help children broaden their ideas about what comprises appropriate behaviors for boys versus girls.

Implications for the Curriculum

Teachers do not usually plan activities whose sole purpose is social development; instead, they think about social development as one facet of children's participation in a variety of classroom experiences. Teachers who want to help children develop socially will be aware of children's social abilities and take advantage of the classroom routine to further their development. Activities should encourage children to cooperate, to develop their self-esteem, and to gain skill in interacting with other children. The following are only a few suggestions of ways to promote growth in social abilities:

THEORY INTO Practice Observe in a preschool or a primary grade. Make a list of the activities or tasks you observe that are designed to stimulate a specific aspect of child development through either their content or their structure.

- Provide dress-up corners where children can take on a variety of roles. Simple costumes such as aprons and hats can help children explore new roles. Threes and fours need more family-oriented props; older children need more props for roles found in the larger community. Sixes, sevens, and eights may respond to props that help them reenact stories from literature.
- Involve primary children in solving social problems in the classroom through role-play and discussions of how to find alternative solutions, how to disagree without being aggressive, and how to make changes in rules they believe are inappropriate or unfair.
- For threes, popular play materials should be plentiful so that fewer arguments arise and children do not have to wait long for a turn. As children mature, teachers may help them work out approaches to taking turns and sharing toys and equipment, such as using waiting lists, a timer, and so on.
- Use puppets to model appropriate techniques for entering a play group. For example, the teacher could use a puppet to demonstrate how a child might ask a group playing with blocks if she could play, too.
- Encourage children to make as many decisions as possible. In free play, allow children to choose activities and experiences. In more directed times of the day, such as music or storytime, encourage children to choose songs or stories.
- Model empathy and caring behaviors, and encourage children to display these behaviors.
- Role-play solutions to problems in social interactions. For example, children might role-play how to make an introduction when a guest comes to the classroom or how to ask another child to share materials.

Emotional Development

Patterns of Development

Emotional development, like physical and social development, follows fairly predictable stages of growth (Berk 1996). The infant responds to any emotion with undifferentiated crying. As the baby grows, this crying becomes differentiated to reflect various emotions. By the time the baby is a few months old, he may scream in anger but produce none of the tears that accompany crying caused by physical pain. Infants have almost no capacity to wait for someone to attend to their needs; their reactions to feelings are immediate. Some researchers (Thomas and Chess 1977) have found that children have distinct temperaments early in life and that temperament tends to be stable over time. Other researchers (DeVries and Sameroff 1984) believe that temperament is responsive to environmental influences. If a baby is difficult and irritable, for example, the parents may not handle the baby as much as they might have handled a more responsive or easy-going baby—and this, in turn, will further affect the baby's temperament.

Toddlers are very compulsive in their behaviors. They have little control of their impulses and are easily frustrated. By the time children reach three years of age, they have developed some tolerance for frustration. They can wait for short periods of time. If their mother explains that dinner will be ready very soon, they can manage to wait for it. They are also developing some self-control; they do not respond to every impulse. Three-year-olds have been observed talking themselves out of doing something that they would have done without thinking a year earlier.

Threes and fours like surprises and novel events. They need the security of knowing that there is structure to their day—that they are going to play, have a snack, and so on—but they respond well to some surprises in the day. When someone dressed as Mother Goose stops by the classroom to share some nursery rhymes, they can handle the change. Three- and four-year-olds are also beginning to develop a sense of humor. They often laugh when they hear a word that sounds funny to them or when they see something incongruous. They are not embarrassed when they laugh at inappropriate moments because they cannot analyze their own behavior in order to determine that it was inappropriate.

By the time children are in kindergarten and first grade, they are able to express and label a wide variety of emotions. They can describe their own sad, angry, or happy feelings and can describe situations that produce given emotions in others. These children become more capable of controlling their aggressive feelings and, with some guidance, can learn to work out their frustrations with other children using words rather than hitting. Five- and six-year-olds also begin to develop a conscience and a sense of right and wrong.

Fives and sixes express their sense of humor in jokes or nonsense words. They often tell jokes without punch lines and still laugh at their own stories. They repeat jokes they have heard, often without understanding them. "Knock-knock" jokes are favorites, and children frequently make up their own versions. They also have great fun creating nonsense words or making rhymes with other words. These tend to be especially funny if they are a little naughty.

Children in the primary years, seven- and eight-year-olds, continue to gain even more control of their emotional responses. They are much less impulsive than younger children. They have strong responses to other individuals and usually like or dislike them immediately. Children in this age group are quite sensitive to criticism or ridicule. They demonstrate embarrassment at their own behavior. They tend to have more worries than younger children as they become more aware of world conditions and attend more to news stories they see on television or hear being discussed by adults. They worry about war, about things happening to their parents (death or divorce), and about accidents.

Seven- and eight-year-olds demonstrate persistence in trying to achieve their goals. This often drives their parents mad, as the child asks to do something over and over after it has been denied. Children this age develop much more empathy for other people and feel badly when someone else is hurting, either physically or emotionally. They offer comfort to family or friends without being prompted to do so.

Implications for the Curriculum

Emotional growth can be encouraged through typical classroom experiences if the teacher is aware of the child's level of development and what can be done to encourage development. The following are examples of classroom activities that can help children:

- Have children dramatize situations in which anger or frustration are handled appropriately.
- Use puppets to model appropriate responses to emotions. For example, with younger children, the teacher might use puppets to model the use of language rather than hitting to express anger. With older children, the teacher might model different responses to frustrations such as not winning a race or a game.
- Help children learn to acknowledge and label their feelings as they participate in classroom activities.
- Choose literature in which the characters respond to emotions appropriately, and discuss how they felt and how they acted.
- Provide empathy for children's fears and concerns. They are real to the child and should not be belittled.
- Allow children to share their humor; appreciate the growth in their sense of humor.
- Primary children may be helped to express their feelings through writing. Select examples from literature that illustrate how children have written about their frustrations or

> **PARENTS AND DEVELOPMENT**
>
> ■ Make sure that your program goals reflect your interest in children's growth in all areas of development. Communicate this interest in parent meetings, conferences, and narrative reports.

Sensorimotor Period (birth to two years)

The sensorimotor period is characterized by inter-actions with the environment based on the child's reception of sensory input and muscular reactions. The period begins with reflexive actions, which are gradually controlled by the child, and ends with the child's having developed a concept of separateness from others and the beginnings of symbolic think-ing. The task of this period is to develop the concept of *object permanence,* the idea that objects exist even when they cannot be seen or heard.

Preoperational Period (two to seven years)

The beginning of the preoperational period is char-acterized by emergence of the ability to represent objects and knowledge through imitation, symbolic play, drawing, mental images, and spoken lan-guage. One outstanding characteristic of preopera-tional thinking is lack of conservation. *Conservation* is defined as the knowledge that the number, mass, area, length, weight, and volume of objects are not changed by physically rearranging the objects.

Children whose thinking is preoperational are egocentric in that they cannot easily take the points of view of others. A preoperational child believes that everyone thinks as she does and that everyone thinks the same things she does. *Egocentrism* is not exclusive to the thinking of preoperational chil-dren but is most prominent then. Egocentrism is a factor in the child's reasoning at this stage because children do not question their own thinking and therefore do not change schemata readily.

Another characteristic of preoperational think-ing is *centration.* The preoperational child tends to pay attention to one element of a problem at a time and cannot coordinate information from multiple sources. Centration is related to classification, seri-ation, and other such tasks. The following anec-dote describes an example of centration:

> *A child was visiting with a family friend, and they were going out in a boat. The friend's boat was beside an identical boat at the dock. One boat was tied up about three feet further in the slip than the other one. The child walked up and down the pier several times, observing the two boats. After a few minutes he remarked, "Your boat is longer on this end, and that boat is longer on the other end."*

A fourth characteristic of preoperational think-ing is the difficulty a child has in trying to reverse

stresses and learned to cope more effectively with them through the writing process.

Intellectual Development

Patterns of Development

Cognitive development refers to the development of the child's thinking and reasoning abilities. Malkus, Feldman, and Gardner (1988) define *cog-nitive development* as "the growing capacity to convey and appreciate meanings in the several symbol systems which happen to be featured in a given cultural setting" (p. 29). These symbol systems include words, pic-tures, gestures, and numbers.

thinking. *Reversibility* is defined as the ability to follow a line of reasoning back to the beginning point. In the problem of conserving number, a child is presented with two rows of eight plastic chips and observes that they are equal. When the space between the chips is lengthened, the preoperational child believes that the number has been changed because the row is longer. When the child is able to reverse the reasoning process, she will be able to determine that moving the chips does not affect the number. A child may be able to reverse an operation physically before being able to reverse operations mentally.

Preoperational children have difficulty in reasoning logically about transformations. The child tends to concentrate on the elements of change and not on the transformations of objects or materials from one state to another. Piaget found that children had difficulty thinking about successive changes in states and about the relationship of one event to another. Piaget made this observation when walking with a child through the woods and drawing the child's attention to the snails that could be seen at various points along the path. The child could not determine if the snails were all the same snail or different snails. Children can observe the beginning point and the ending point of transformations, but they often have difficulty following all the points in between. If a child is asked to draw what happens to a pencil as it falls off a table, he can draw the pencil on the table and on the floor but not all the steps between the table and the floor.

Concrete Operational Period (seven to eleven or twelve years)

Children begin making the transition from preoperational thinking to operational thinking at various times. In most kindergarten classrooms, a few children will be beginning to think operationally. In the primary grades, more children will be operational thinkers, even though many may still be preoperational on some tasks. Piaget and Inhelder (1969) described the operational thinker as one who employs "identity or reversibility by inversion or reciprocity" (p. 99) in solving problems.

Concrete operational thinkers are able to solve problems of conservation and reversibility. They can *decenter*, or coordinate information from more than one source, in solving problems. They are not as egocentric in their thinking. Because they are aware that others may come to conclusions that differ from theirs, they are much more likely to examine their own conclusions.

Sources: Piaget and Inhelder 1969; Wadsworth 1989.

The cognitive development of young children is described by different theorists in different terms. The behaviorist point of view is that children grow intellectually through accumulating more and more information. Most measures of intelligence are based on this idea of accumulating knowledge. Another point of view is that of the constructivists, or developmentalists, who describe knowledge as being constructed from children's interactions with the environment. According to this viewpoint, intellectual development is influenced by both maturation and experience (Piaget 1969). Cognitive development is indicated by a growing ability to plan, to employ strategies for remembering, and to seek solutions to problems.

Piaget and Inhelder (1969) described the cognitive development of children as progressing in several stages, including the *sensorimotor stage,* the *preoperational stage,* and the *concrete operational stage.* The stages evolve with the child's growing maturity and experience. Although approximate ages have been attached to these stages, the rate at which individuals pass through them is variable; the sequence of stages, however, is invariant. In other words, a child must pass through each stage, but different children may pass through the stages at different ages. The transition time between stages is lengthy. Children do not move suddenly from one stage of thinking to another—changes may take months or years, as the child constructs and integrates knowledge. A child may be performing some tasks in ways that indicate preoperational thinking while performing other tasks in very stable operational ways.

More recently, early childhood educators have been influenced by two theories of intellectual development. One is that of Lev Vygotsky (1978), who described learning as the construction of knowledge within a social context. He believed that development could not be separated from its social context and that learning could lead development. Vygotsky viewed the learner as an active participant in constructing his own learning within the context of interactions with caregivers, a family or community, and a society. For example, a child in a society that depends on technology will learn to think differently than a child in a society that depends on agriculture.

Vygotsky also believed that language plays a central role in cognitive development, as learning language influences the way a person thinks about the world. For example, a child who learns the scientific language of classification will think differently about classification tasks than one who has not learned such language. Vygotsky agreed with Piaget that learning is dependent on the child's development, but he believed that learning new strategies (when presented at the appropriate level for the child) could lead to increased development. Bodrova and Leong (1996) describe a three-year-old child who is learning to classify objects but cannot keep the categories straight. When the teacher helps her by providing two boxes, one labeled "big" and one labeled "little," the child is able to keep the categories straight. Learning to classify in terms of *big* and *little* will aid the child's development of categorical thinking. As summarized by Bodrova and Leong (1996):

> The highest level of development is associated with the ability to perform and self-regulate complex cognitive operations. Children cannot reach the level through maturation or the accumulation of experiences with objects alone. The emergence of this higher level of cognitive development depends on the appropriation of tools through formal and informal instruction. (p. 19)

For early childhood educators, one of the most significant elements of Vygotsky's theory is the **zone of proximal development (ZPD).** The ZPD is the gap between what the child can do independently and what he can-

THEORY
INTO
Practice

Compare two articles about cognitive development written from different philosophical perspectives. List the points of agreement and the points of disagreement in their descriptions of how children think.

not do even with the assistance of someone (such as an adult or peer) who is more skilled than him. For example, if a child can independently solve arithmetic problems involving regrouping, then he does not need instruction in solving these types of problems but could learn to solve subtraction problems that require regrouping. However, he probably would not be able to solve problems that involve long division, even with assistance. The skill range in which the child *can* work successfully with some assistance is the ZPD. Clearly, it is a waste of time to teach children what they already know as well as what they cannot do, even with assistance.

Piaget and Vygotsky agreed that learning involved "major, qualitative transformations in thinking" (Berk and Winsler 1995, p. 111). And even though Piaget and Vygotsky did not agree on other points, both of their theories are valuable to the early childhood educator. Namely, both can help us understand that teachers must recognize the development of individual children, provide activities and experiences that will enhance children's thinking, and remember that all learning takes place in a social context.

Another theory of cognitive development that has only recently begun to be applied to early-childhood education is that of Howard Gardner (1983, 1995). Gardner believes that intellectual capacity does not develop as a whole but as different intelligences. So far, Gardner has identified seven intelligences that meet the strict criteria for being labeled as such: linguistic, logical-mathematical, spatial, bodily-kinesthetic, musical, interpersonal, and intrapersonal. He does not believe that these are necessarily all the intelligences possible, but they are all that he has identified at this time.

Gardner's work is not a shallow or superficial examination of the development of intelligence; however, teachers must be aware that many other authors have used Gardner's work and developed rather shallow approaches to supposedly testing and teaching the intelligences. What is most significant about Gardner's theories to the early childhood educator is (1) the support for offering a variety of activities and experiences so that every child can learn and (2) the focus on the fact that every person possesses a unique combination of strengths in the intelligences. Every child has abilities that can be recognized and honored. If Gardner's work helps change schools so that the focus is not solely on the acquisition of academic knowledge, he will have contributed greatly to the lives of young children.

Implications for the Curriculum

Planning for the intellectual growth of children is dependent on the knowledge of children's intellectual development. A child who is preoperational, for instance, would not be expected to solve problems in the same way that an older child would solve them. Also, children need chances to learn in ways that are active and that provide opportunities to learn in ways that suit their individual techniques for organizing and remembering information.

Knowing the child or the learner is absolutely necessary for planning a developmentally appropriate program. Several questions about DAP are directly related to children's development:

- Are the activities planned usually of interest to children of the age for which the activities are intended?
- Can most children complete the activities successfully?
- Will some children be allowed to choose more challenging activities?

- Will some children be allowed to choose activities that require less skill without being censured?
- Will expectations for performance reflect knowledge of child development?

One challenge for teachers is to avoid what Lilian Katz (1986) describes as "learned stupidity," which occurs when children are given tasks that they cannot do and, through failure at those tasks, learn to believe that they are stupid. No young child would have the life experience to evaluate an inappropriate task and determine that it was the task that was at fault, not the learner.

Young children learn best through manipulating objects and being reflective about those manipulations, not through passive experiences where they listen to someone tell them how something works. Young children need the stimulation of their peers in solving problems, and they need to be able to use what they already know in learning new information. Throughout this book, you will find suggestions for encouraging the intellectual growth of children; the following suggestions are merely a small sample of the endless possibilities:

- Provide old machines (toasters, TVs, radios, and so on) that children can dismantle and explore. (Be sure to remove the electrical connections and any springs that could be unsafe.)
- Set up problems to be presented to the class in ways that encourage divergent thinking and multiple right answers. For example, ask children how many different ways they can sort the blocks rather than ask them to sort the blocks by color.
- Give children the opportunity to choose as many of their own activities as possible. Children can learn to classify by playing with blocks, leaves, keys, items from the supermarket, and articles of clothing. When children are given a choice, they are more likely to learn.

THEORY INTO *Practice*

Select a specific age from two to eight. Prepare a brochure that summarizes typical child development in each of the following realms: physical, intellectual, social, and emotional. Beside each summary, list examples of activities that will encourage further development or are developmentally appropriate for the given age. For example, if the children can cut on a line, then art that encourages more detailed cutting would be appropriate.

- Provide materials that are open ended so that the challenge and complexity can be increased as the children grow. For example, given beads, children at different ages can string them, use them to create patterns, or use them to create models and designs.

- Encourage children to follow their interests. Jacque Wuertenburg (1993) calls it "leading through life." If a child is interested in spiders or snakes or computers, use that interest to help build skills and concepts.
- Assist children in understanding the application of what they are learning in school to real life. Learning without a purpose is difficult.

CELEBRATING DIVERSITY

The work of Vygotsky supports the notion that children from different cultures learn different things at different ages. Teachers need to recognize that children learn to use language in ways that are appropriate for their own culture and to perform tasks that are significant in their culture. For example, some Asian children can manipulate chopsticks successfully long before their European counterparts have the fine motor control to do so.

In celebrating the diversity of the children in their classrooms, teachers must also think about the expectations that children's families have for them and for their behavior and learning in the school setting. While it is not acceptable for teachers to engage in practices they feel are inappropriate for children, teachers must always respect the parents and their culture. For example, corporal punishment of children is advocated in some cultures. Suppose some parents suggest that if their son does not attend to task or misbehaves in school, you, the teacher, should hit him. Of course, you should not hit the child, but you should respect the parents' desire for their child to be successful in school. In addition, you should make sure that you keep the parents informed about their child's progress and behavior as well as what you are doing to help him.

The time you spend learning what parents expect of their children in terms of social and emotional development will benefit you in planning activities and experiences. For example, if a child's family encourages cooperation rather than competition, then they need to know that you are also interested in using cooperative behavior to solve problems and that you will not try to change their child.

CHAPTER SUMMARY

- Development can be described in different terms, depending on one's philosophical point of view. The major philosophical orientations are represented by the behaviorists, the maturationists, and the constructivists.

- Development is an orderly process of moving from undifferentiated movements and reactions to finely differentiated and controlled movements and specific responses.

- Physical development is most rapid in infancy but continues quite rapidly through the preschool years. Children in the primary grades continue to develop their physical abilities, but the rate is not as rapid as it is with younger children.

- Ideally, as their social development progresses, children become capable of successful interactions with others, develop prosocial behaviors such as helping and cooperating, learn to control aggression, and develop a positive concept of themselves.

- Emotional development is observed as children evolve from expressing undifferentiated responses to emotions to being able to express their emotions in socially acceptable ways and to control their impulses. Children grow more capable of understanding how others feel and develop a sense of right and wrong.

- Cognitive development describes the changes that take place in children's thinking and reasoning. Very young children learn best from handling objects; preschoolers need to manipulate objects and reflect on the outcomes of their manipulations; and elementary school children still need to use concrete materials in their reasoning processes. Young children do not employ adult logic in making sense of their environment nor can they reason in abstract terms.

- The different stages of child development have implications for planning a curriculum for young children. Teachers need to think about children's physical abilities and the cognitive requirements of different tasks when they select learning experiences. They also need to plan activities that will help children develop social skills.

LINDA SUE
ALLMAN
East Clayton
Elementary School
ELLENWOOD, GEORGIA

Brain-Based Learning in a Real Classroom

Five-year-old Susan clenches her tongue between her teeth as she focuses on the paper in front of her. The marker has smeared slightly, but the letters *spdr* are still legible. Susan has now completed her portion of a cooperative project on the study of spiders. Tomorrow, her group will not only report to the class information and observations about spiders but also will demonstrate social and group skills in working together toward a common goal.

This class project demonstrates how to put into practical use many of the theories put forth by brain researchers about how the brain electrically and chemically processes, stores, and retrieves data. Translating this information into manageable classroom practice can seem daunting. However, when blended with the principles of good teaching, this information is an important component of *brain-based education.* The basics of brain-based education are security, novelty, time, variety, and meaning.

Susan needs to feel safe in her environment in order to become a risk taker. Allowing her to make mistakes, flounder, and try again satiates the basic emotional system of the brain. This will trigger her attention system and allow her to focus on the content, opening her brain to all kinds of possibilities to sort, compare, and extend information. Teachers can build this safe and secure environment by providing encouragement, affection, positive reinforcement, and gentle guidance.

Once this element of security is in place, the teacher should provide an enriched environment with meaningful content. This environment needs to include enough novelty to provide constant stimulation to the child's attention system. The brain seeks novelty; it also seeks to understand the environment. Meaningful content connects the learner to real-life experiences through the use of concrete activities.

Developmentally young children need consistent schedules and daily routines; however, within that structure, unusual topics, captivating activities, humor, and interesting content provide enough novelty to commit content to memory. This enriched environment also includes adequate time for students to reflect on their learning. How often do teachers rush through instruction of one topic to get to something else? Time should be allotted to decision making, cooperative learning, planning, and reporting. Time to *think* is required in a brain-based classroom.

When the brain-based teacher sets up the learning environment, she must give a great deal of thought to ways of honoring different learning styles. Some children learn best working alone; some, in groups; some, while talking; some, while quiet. By providing a variety of learning activities, the teacher programs success into the day while also encouraging students to learn in different ways. Moreover, young children who are taught to honor each other's learning styles become more tolerant and accepting of others.

Susan's group project on spiders took several days to complete. The group's final report did not reflect the time spent making false starts, errors, messes at the art table, and trips to the library, nor did it reflect redirection by the teacher, some giggling, and even one argument. However, the report did show careful thought, divergent thinking, cooperation, planning, content, and four children who learned.

2

SCHOOLS FOR YOUNG CHILDREN
Choices in Design

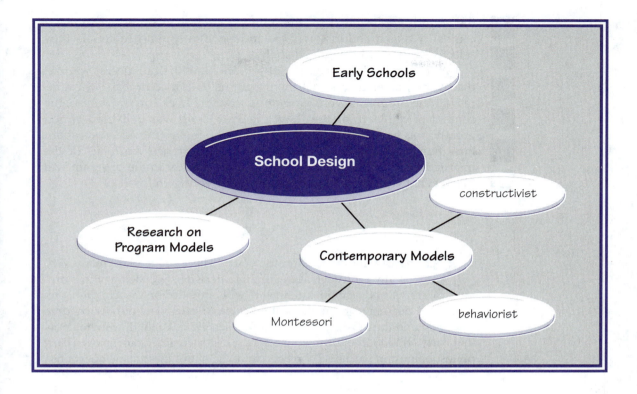

When you entered the kindergarten classroom in which you observed this week, a child asked, "Do you want to see my book?" You admired the child's book and were then invited to observe other children's accomplishments: a replica of the fire station they had visited several days ago; a painting of a bird's nest; a melody played on bells; and a plant along with a growth chart, starting from the day the seed was planted. Everybody in this busy classroom seemed to be doing something interesting, but you did not see anyone doing the lessons you had expected to see.

When you shared your observations with members of your class, you found that the school settings your peers had observed varied a great deal. Some had observed lessons in which small groups of students were learning the alphabet and the sounds represented by the letters. Others had observed in classrooms in which children worked independently with materials they selected from neatly arranged shelves.

When you finished sharing observations with your peers, you did discover some elements that the programs had in common. For example, all the programs were promoting learning in children. Even so, the content of the learning and how the instruction was delivered varied greatly. You have many questions now: Who makes the decisions about how the programs are organized? Who determines the focus of the instruction? Who determines what role the teacher in the program will play? What is the best kind of program for young children?

As an early childhood educator, you will be asked to make many decisions in your career. Many of those decisions will be about the programs and activities that you will provide for the children you teach. The decisions you make will reflect your own view of how children learn best and the most effective ways to teach them. You will want to know that early childhood education has a long history and that for many years, philosophers and teachers have been thinking about these same questions.

EARLY SCHOOLS FOR YOUNG CHILDREN

Early childhood programs today can trace their development back to early philosophers. For example, Martin Luther (1483–1546) believed that all boys should be educated (a radical thought in his day) and insisted that music and physical education should be an integral part of the curriculum (Frost and Kissinger 1976). A century later, John Comenius (1592–1670) suggested that all children should attend school, and he recommended an integrated, hands-on curriculum. He believed that children should learn to speak by speaking, to write by writing, and to reason by reasoning (Comenius 1642; reprinted 1969). Later educators, such as Dewey, Montessori, and Piaget, have echoed Comenius's call for active learning.

Two other philosophers, Jean-Jacques Rousseau (1712–1778) and Johann Pestalozzi (1746–1827), also made important contributions to early childhood education. Rousseau thought that educational decisions should be made on the basis of the child's nature. He also developed a stage theory of child development based on his belief that children from birth to age five learn best from physical activity and that children from five to twelve learn best by direct experience and exploration of the environment (Rousseau 1780; reprinted 1950). When educators advocate hands-on learning, they are agreeing with Rousseau. Pestalozzi wanted to rid the schools of cruel punishment and rote learning. He believed in having children participate in real, meaningful activities and in grouping children of various ages so that the older ones can help the younger ones (Pestalozzi 1885, 1894).

Friedrich Froebel

Friedrich Froebel (1782–1852) is credited with founding *kindergartens:* "children's gardens." He studied with Pestalozzi but believed that Pestalozzi did not go far enough in matching teaching to the nature of the child. Froebel began his school for young children in Blankenburg, Germany, in 1837. He believed that everything in the universe functions in relationship to God and that each person has a specific purpose to fulfill in this life. He wrote, "Education should lead and guide man to clearness concerning himself and in himself, to peace with nature, and to unity with God" (Froebel, 1826, ch. 5). The importance of the individual and the respect that must be accorded to each person is central to Froebelian thinking.

Froebel believed that play is the foundation for children's learning and envisioned the kindergarten as the child's bridge between home and school. He believed that appropriate play helps children think about the interactions between "life and self-activity, thought and action, representation and cognition, and ability and understanding" (Ransbury 1982, p. 104). Froebel believed that materials in forms found in nature—spheres, cubes, cylinders, squares, triangles, circles, and lines—help children explore the properties of matter and understand the relationships in the universe. He called these materials "gifts." He also designed sequences of activities that he called "occupations"; they included folding paper, drawing, and weaving. Froebel distinguished between what he called "thoughtless copying" and "deliberate imitation." He believed that when children perform the occupations, they restructure their own ideas and do not merely copy actions without thinking about them.

In Froebel's school, children often learned verses to accompany the occupations. Froebel encouraged these "Mother rhymes," which were what we would call *fingerplays* today. Children said the rhymes while they performed actions with their hands or bodies. Froebel believed that to teach young children, it was necessary to arouse and maintain interest and attention, use the child's curiosity, and plan for motivation to learn.

Although Froebel's structured approach to kindergarten instruction has been discarded, modern teachers of young children do employ fingerplays and play materials designed to encourage learning. Modern teachers also recognize the value of play as a mode of learning and the importance of recognizing the individual child. All these ideas can be traced to Froebel and his kindergarten.

The Child-Care Movement

The earliest **child care** was established in the settlement houses of big U.S. cities at the turn of the twentieth century "to provide a shelter for the children of mothers dependent on their own exertions for their daily bread; [but] also to rear useful citizens among the class represented by the children we reach" (Steinfels 1973, p. 29). Even though most working mothers worked because they had to for economic survival, the belief persisted that mothers should take care of their own children, so the availability of child care declined as the century progressed.

Other efforts at providing child care have been in response to national emergencies. During the Depression, the Works Progress Administration created nursery schools to provide teaching positions for unemployed teachers, and during World War II, the Lanham Act established nursery schools so that mothers could participate in the war effort. At the end of each of these periods, the federal funding ended, and so did the programs (Grubb 1989).

During the 1970s, there were repeated efforts to pass legislation to support child care. Progress on child-care legislation stalled during the 1980s, but there have been some positive steps, in the 1990s, such as more federal funding for programs that benefit children.

CHANGES IN EARLY CHILDHOOD EDUCATION

Head Start

The charity schools of the early 1800s (nursery schools supported by philanthropists to save children from poor families from disadvantaged environments) and the settlement house programs of the early 1900s shared the goal of trying to change the lives of young, poor children. Modern-day programs continue this effort.

One component of the War on Poverty in the early 1960s was **Head Start,** a compensatory program that was a major feature of the plan to break the cycle of poverty in the United States. Head Start provides educational, social, medical, dental, nutritional, and mental health services to low-income preschool children. In 1990, Head Start celebrated its twenty-fifth anniversary, and although its funding is expected to increase, the program continues to be able to serve only a portion of the eligible children. Since the beginning of the Head Start program, over 14 million children and their families have been served. Currently, about 750,000 children are enrolled in Head Start programs, and appropriations have been increased over previous years. In the 1994 Reauthorization Act, money was set aside for comprehensive child and family development programs (Administration for Child, Youth, and Families 1995). Many different programs have been developed and evaluated as part of Head Start, and much research in early childhood education has been undertaken in Head Start programs. Thus, Head Start has been beneficial not only to the millions of children who have attended programs but also to the profession of early childhood education.

Because some of the positive effects of Head Start did not last once the children were in elementary school, Project Follow Through was developed. Follow Through attempts to maintain the gains made in Head Start by continuing family education and health care and by emphasizing success. Follow Through programs have never been as widespread as Head Start programs, however.

Programs for Children with Special Needs

The education of children with special needs has undergone radical changes in the last few decades. Early in the twentieth century, children with disabilities were often excluded from school experiences. Later, they were identified but segregated into special classes in schools. Often, all children with disabilities from a given school district were housed in a special school so that they had no contact with other children.

In 1975, Public Law (PL) 94-142, the Education for All Handicapped Children Act, was passed in the United States. This law is often called the "mainstreaming law," but it does not mention the word **mainstreaming.** What the law does say is that every child is entitled to an education in the **least restrictive environment (LRE).** Separate schools or classes are appropriate only when the "nature or severity of the handicap is such that education in regular classes with the use of supplementary aids and services cannot be achieved satisfactorily" (PL 94-142 20 U.S.C. 1412, 5, B).

Public Law 99-457, enacted in 1986, reauthorized PL 94-142 and extended its provisions to younger children. The intent of the original law had been to provide services to children with disabling conditions from birth to school age, but the law had been written so that states were not required to provide services to children younger than school age. PL 99-457 extended the services to children from ages three to five and added incentives for states who served children from birth to age two, as well. Services can be provided by public or private agencies, but providers must demonstrate quality and integration. Key elements in PL 99-457 are its emphasis on the role of parents and its recognition of the importance of the family in the child's development.

Recognizing that labeling young children can be a very harmful practice, PL 99-457 does not require or emphasize categorical labels. Safford (1989) states the following reasons for avoiding labeling:

Young children's needs are difficult, if not impossible, to categorize with traditional labels.

Especially during the early years, these needs change rapidly.

Categorical labels have no utility for young children, since categorical programs may not be appropriate.

Early labeling of children may limit and restrict them, since others may respond to these labels in limiting and restricting ways.

Labels tend to follow the child, even after they are no longer applicable or appropriate. A label is a hard thing to lose!

Least restrictive services for young children, required by P. L. 99:457, are intended to foster the interaction of handicapped and nonhandicapped children. Labels tend to impede that interaction. (p. 10)

Federal law also requires that a minimum of 10 percent of the children enrolled in Head Start programs be children with disabilities and that services be provided to meet their special needs (Head Start, Economic Opportunity and Community Partnership Act of 1974, PL 93-644, 1974). To meet enrollment quotas, children who are disabled but not otherwise eligible for Head Start may be admitted (Safford 1989).

PL 94-142 was updated in 1990 and is now known as the Individuals with Disabilities Education Act (IDEA). IDEA expanded the categories of children eligible to receive special education services to include those with autism and traumatic brain injury. The new law continues to mandate parental involvement in educational decisions, education in the least restrictive environment, and individualized education programs (Hardman et al. 1993).

CONTEMPORARY MODELS

Today, many models describe goals, materials, teacher roles, and appropriate instructional practices for early childhood education. Roopnarine and Johnson (1993) describe fourteen models, including home-based models, models for children with special needs, and center-based models. These authors also admit that models in early childhood education have never had the same impact as models in other areas of education.

Models can serve as guidelines for planning and organizing experiences, but they are rarely, if ever, implemented totally. Uncritical acceptance of any model certainly does not encourage the professional growth and development of teachers and curriculum planners. As teachers use models and theories, they construct their own understanding of the teaching-learning processes and should be able to incorporate their experiences into any model to make it a more cohesive or complete explanation of how children develop and learn.

Most knowledge of models in early childhood education grew out of work done in the late 1960s and early 1970s in Head Start programs. Financial support for developing and testing models has been much more difficult to obtain since that period; therefore, fewer models have been developed. Of the fourteen models described by Roopnarine and Johnson (1993), the center-based models fall roughly into three categories: Montessori models, behaviorist models, and constructivist models. In this chapter, we will describe each of these three basic approaches to early childhood education. Although some of the models have been extended to address both younger and older children, for the sake of comparison, each program in this chapter will be described as it applies to four- and five-year-olds; notes about applying programs to younger or older children will be included.

Each section will include a description of the theoretical foundation of the model and the beliefs about teaching and learning on which the model is based, the goals of the model, a typical day in a school based on the model, and a brief evaluation of the model.

The Montessori Model

Maria Montessori (1870–1952) opened her school in Italy for institutionalized children in 1907, and her successes with these children quickly attracted the attention of the educational community. Over the next few years, Montessori schools spread throughout Europe and the United States. Montessori schools, at both the preschool and elementary levels, are now common in most U.S. communities. Although most Montessori schools are private, some public school systems offer Montessori programs as alternative schools.

How Children Learn: Montessori

Some key elements of Montessori philosophy include the ideas of the absorbent mind, the prepared environment, autoeducation, sensitive periods, and the principle of freedom for the child. Each of these elements is a factor in explanations of how children grow and develop.

The concept of the **absorbent mind** is important in Montessori philosophy. The prevailing idea in Montessori's time was that children do not do anything mentally during infancy. Montessori, however, believed that infants unconsciously absorb all that is around them and that gradually this process becomes conscious. As the child becomes conscious, he begins to organize experience and make generalizations. For example, after several experiences with cups of various kinds, the child comes to understand "cup" as a category that includes not only all existing cups but also all possible cups. Montessori philosophy also holds that the child's construction of a sense of self is accomplished if he is free to develop the pattern inherent in him (Standing 1962).

In a Montessori program, the teacher is responsible for the **prepared environment:** that is, for selecting and arranging the materials that make learning possible. Materials for learning must be carefully chosen and dis-

The educational philosophy of the teacher is reflected in the activities and experiences offered to the children.

played to catch the child's interest. The tables and chairs must be child sized and lightweight so that a child can arrange them in the way that is most comfortable for her. The environment must be orderly so that the child develops a sense of order and control. It must also be attractive so that the child develops a respect for beauty. Most Montessori classrooms are decorated with plants and objects from nature as well as colorful displays and tasteful pieces of art.

The teacher is responsible for sequencing the child's experiences so that he learns concepts logically. The materials for instruction are arranged so that the child can select from among them the ones in which he is interested, but it is the teacher's role to bring out and demonstrate new materials at the optimal time in the development of each child. Once the teacher has demonstrated the procedures for using materials, the child can choose to work with them. It is within this carefully planned framework that **autoeducation**—the organizing of information into logical patterns—takes place. Children learn to clarify their perceptions and organize their experiences through certain activities. The teacher's role is not to present information through direct instruction but to demonstrate the materials and guide the child's selection of materials and activities.

A basic premise of the Montessori philosophy is that the child copies reality rather than constructs it. From watching and then doing activities, the child organizes the world and her own thinking. One of the primary roles of a Montessori teacher is to demonstrate how materials are to be used and tasks are to be completed. These demonstrations are very specific in that there is an exact procedure for using each set of materials; children are not allowed free expression with the materials until they have mastered the exact procedures (Montessori 1914).

Most Montessori materials are self-correcting. They are designed so that the child gets feedback on the correctness of his actions from the materials. An example of self-correcting material is the Pink Tower, which is a set of cubes of graduated sizes. The child begins building the Tower by placing the largest cube on the bottom; each additional cube is placed on the Tower in order by decreasing size, such that the smallest cube is placed on the top. In demonstrating how to use the Tower, the teacher first shows how it is constructed; then he takes it apart and allows the child to construct it. The teacher does not supply information or cues to the child while she is attempting this construction. If the Tower is constructed correctly, each cube will be used and every cube placed on the Tower will be smaller than the preceding cube. If the child makes an error in construction, one or more cubes will be left over or will not fit properly. The purpose of the Pink Tower is to help the child develop abilities in seriation. Once the child has mastered the Tower, other materials are introduced in a careful sequence to aid her in transferring the ability to seriate from one situation to another and to further her thinking and reasoning abilities.

Montessori materials and exercises are basically divided into four categories that promote the development of daily-living skills and sensorial, academic, and cultural and artistic abilities. *Daily-living exercises* involve the physical care of oneself and the environment and include tasks such as washing a table or polishing shoes. The purpose of these tasks is not simply to develop a skill but also to aid the "inner construction of discipline, organization, independence, and self-esteem through concentration on a precise and completed cycle of activity" (Lillard 1972, p. 71).

Sensorial materials are designed to encourage refinement of the senses for the purpose of aiding the child in developing intelligence. Montessori believed that intelligence is developed as the child organizes and categorizes perceptions into a mental order. An example of sensorial materials is a collection of seven different fabric samples: velvet, silk, wool, fine linen, coarse linen, fine cotton, and coarse cotton. The teacher is to take care that these samples are pure. The child is encouraged to play with the samples, to learn the names of the fabrics, and then to identify a given sample by touch.

Academic materials include the moveable alphabet, sandpaper letters, and plane geometric insets. After the child has learned to recognize the individual letters of the alphabet and to compose some words with help from the teacher, he is presented with the moveable alphabet. There are several duplicates of each letter, and the child is encouraged to compose words with them. The child is freed from the difficulty of forming letters by hand and so can progress more quickly in composing and recognizing words.

Artistic or cultural materials and exercises are designed to help children learn to love and appreciate music and to learn to control movements of their hands and feet in preparation for dance. Rhythm and then harmony and melody are introduced. Children are taught how to use musical instruments

THEORY INTO *Practice*

Interview a Montessori teacher and a teacher from another type of program about their educational backgrounds. What elements of their educational experiences influenced them to make the program choices that they made?

and to recognize musical sounds through the sensorial exercises. Although drawing is never taught directly, children are taught about line and color before painting is introduced.

Freedom to choose activities and when to change activities is very important in Montessori education. The teacher may guide the child by demonstrating new materials he thinks might interest or challenge the child, but the child must choose which materials to use. The choice of materials is the child's, but how the materials are used is clearly defined. If the child chooses to use materials in unacceptable ways, the teacher may remove the materials and ask the child to make another choice. Freedom of choice is related to the concept of *autoeducation;* the child must educate himself. Standing (1957) summarizes this concept in the following statements:

1. The child must learn by his own activity.
2. He must be granted a mental freedom to take what he needs.
3. He must not be questioned in his choice—since the "teacher should answer the mental needs of the child, not dictate them." (p. 364)

Another important concept in Montessori education is that of **sensitive periods,** which are periods when a child is capable of and interested in learning specific things. This concept is much like that of *readiness.* For example, if a child is in a sensitive period in which she is fascinated with details, the teacher might supply materials that have many small parts to put together. Montessori teachers are trained to observe these sensitive periods and provide experiences appropriate for each period.

Montessori believed that young children want to be obedient and that they desire order in their environments. If a child becomes agitated or experiences "brainstorms" of activity, then he is to be removed silently and gently from the environment and encouraged to rest quietly until he has calmed down. Teachers in a Montessori school maintain discipline by expecting children to respect each other's work and workspaces and by removing children who lose control of their impulses.

Goals of Montessori Education

The most important goal of Montessori education is development of the individual. The facts a child learns are not as important as her mental or intellectual development. Therefore, the goals of Montessori programs emphasize development of general intellectual skills and general, rather than particular, subject-matter concepts. As stated by the American Montessori Society (1984), the goals of Montessori programs include development of:

*   Concentration
*   Observation skills
*   An awareness of order and sequence

- Coordination
- Perceptual awareness and practical skills
- Mathematical concepts
- Language skills
- Writing and reading skills
- Familiarity with the creative arts
- Understanding of the world of nature
- Experience with and understanding of the social sciences
- Experience with critical-thinking skills through problem-solving techniques

Montessori programs are concerned with children's development physically, socially, emotionally, and intellectually. The importance of physical development is reflected in an emphasis on outdoor play and participation in rhythmic activities. Social development is emphasized in discussions of appropriate behavior on the playground and in the focus on respecting the individual's work and space in the classroom. Intellectual development is achieved through activities designed to help children organize, classify, seriate, and heighten their perceptual awareness.

In the classroom described in the panel on pages 44 and 45, some children are developing perceptual abilities by matching pictures or completing puzzles. Others are learning the difference between lakes and islands by constructing models with clay. The outcomes expected from each of the experiences differ. Not all children share the same experiences, but all are guided to learn some concepts and to develop some abilities. Subject-matter concepts, such as the vocabulary to describe islands and lakes or the names of the letters of the alphabet, are conveyed through group or individual instruction. Content areas, such as science and social studies, are included in the program in the form of materials or equipment such as scales and maps. Math concepts are also developed through materials such as the Tower and beads. Literacy is promoted through materials such as alphabet letters of different textures and the moveable alphabet. Some activities, such as listening for syllables in names, are also designed to promote the development of literacy. Stories are read daily to encourage children's interest in books.

When children younger than three are accepted in Montessori programs, they usually attend two or three mornings each week and the programs are modified by having smaller groups and fewer choices for the children. The Montessori approach also includes elementary programs (and a limited number of secondary programs). Programs for children in the primary grades are fundamentally the same as preschool programs in that children are presented with materials and allowed to work with those they select. In the primary grades, there is much more emphasis on literacy, as children create words from the moveable alphabet. They begin writing

9:00 – 9:20	Arrival, group time
9:20 – 10:20	Choice time
10:20 – 10:45	Outdoor play
10:45 – 10:55	Group time, preparation for snack
10:55 – 11:10	Snack
11:10 – 11:30	Story time, one group in rhythms

In Susan's group, there are twenty-eight children, a head teacher, and two assistant teachers. The children in this group are between three and five years old. As Susan enters the light and airy classroom, she goes immediately to the area with open cupboards containing hooks and hangs up her coat while her mother signs her in for the day. Susan waves good-bye to her mother and joins the children who are gathered on the "blue line," a line of blue tape that forms a square in the middle of the largest room in the building. Susan is greeted by her teacher and says hello to her friend, who is already sitting on the line.

When all the children are gathered, the teacher sits at a small table containing a plastic mat, blue and brown clay, a rolling pin, and two identical trays about 5 by 8 inches in size. The teacher tells the children they are going to learn about the words *island* and *lake.* She tells them that an island is land surrounded by water and that a lake is water surrounded by land. She then asks about the colors of water and land, and the children respond "blue" and "brown." She makes a model of a lake by rolling out some of the blue clay and some of the brown clay and placing the brown clay around the blue clay on one of the trays. She repeats the process to make an island on the other tray. Then various children are called on to come up and point to the representations of the island and the lake. At the conclusion of the lesson, the teacher tells the children that this material will be available in the art room so that they can construct their own lakes and islands today.

The head teacher then tells the children that they may choose to work today in the solarium, the art room, or the large room. One of the teachers will be in each of these areas. The head teacher asks the children to go one at a time and choose their favorite things to work on and to get started working. All the children go immediately to an area and choose an activity.

One boy chooses a carpet square, places it on the floor, and selects from the shelves a tray containing a corkboard, a small hammer, and small wooden shapes, each with a hole drilled through it. Using the pegs on the tray, the child begins to attach each shape to the corkboard.

Susan takes a circular felt mat from a stack and places it on a nearby table. She then selects a basket containing a wooden board divided into six squares, with a picture of an animal on each square. She finds small squares with matching pic-

by copying words and then move on to writing sentences and stories. Instruction in reading often emphasizes a phonetic approach. Many Montessori materials are available for helping children develop concepts in mathematics, social studies, and science.

Two publications offer additional information about Montessori education: *Montessori Life,* a journal published by the American Montessori Society, and *Public School Montessorian,* published by Jola Publications (2933

tures and places one on each square. When she has completed this task, she places the pieces back in the basket, places the basket on the shelf, places the mat back on the stack, and chooses a carpet square, which she puts on the floor. She selects a puzzle from the shelf and begins to work on the carpet.

Meanwhile, some children have chosen to work in the solarium, where many science-oriented activities are available. Some children are working with the teacher using a scale to weigh various objects and find out whether they are heavier, lighter, or the same weight as other objects. Other children are filling containers with water from a tub; some are sorting objects based on the materials they are made of. In the art room, some children don painting smocks and paint at easels; one works with the clay to make islands and lakes; and other children choose paper and clay for drawing and molding experiences.

A few children in the large room are working with the teacher on recognizing letters. The teacher places white letters (upper- and lowercase) on a black background and tells the children the name of each letter and its sound. Then they look at a small set of pictures of objects whose names begin with that sound and name each one, emphasizing the sound. Another teacher moves around the room, working with individual children, for example, asking them the names of colors after they have matched color strips. Each child works with an activity as long as she chooses.

The children work with their activities for about an hour and are then instructed to put their materials away and get their coats for outdoor play. They play outside for about twenty minutes on swings, a climber/slide, and balance beams and also with some large outdoor toys. Susan walks the balance beam several times. One of the teachers holds her hand the first time, and then she walks with the teacher walking beside her but not touching her. Then Susan joins a group playing on the climber/slide and plays there until it is time to go inside.

As the children return to the room, they are instructed to wash their hands for snack and to sit on the blue line again. As the children are washing up, one of the assistant teachers beats the rhythm of a child's name on a drum, and then all the children clap the rhythm. Each child called on is asked what name to beat—some supply only their first names, some their full names. When all the children are on the line, the head teacher discusses a problem that occurred outdoors: Someone threw a rock. She asks the children to explain why they cannot throw rocks and concludes by having them think of things that they can throw outdoors. The children are dismissed to have their snack by getting up one by one as the teacher describes their clothing.

After the snack each day, one group stays in the large room for movement exercises. Susan goes with a small group to one of the small rooms for story reading. The small groups are selected on the basis of maturity and experience in listening to stories. The teachers read the stories and ask questions about them. They then read stories selected by the children, if there is more time.

By this time, parents are beginning to arrive. Susan's father signs her out, helps her collect her coat, and takes her home.

North 2nd Street, Minneapolis, MN 55411). Montessori Internationale also publishes a small journal once a year.

The Behaviorist Model

The behaviorist model of schools for young children is based on the learning theories of Edward Thorndike and B. F. Skinner (described in Chapter 1).

Basically, these theories explain behavior in terms of a stimulus and a response and operant conditioning. Three other key components in the behaviorist model—also known as **direct instruction**—are reinforcement schedules, shaping of behavior, and extinction of behavior. A *reinforcement schedule* is established after a specific response has been achieved; at that point, the learner is rewarded on a schedule rather than for every response. The learner might be rewarded for every two responses, then every four responses, and so on; eventually, the learner will not need a reward to continue the response. *Shaping of behavior* is changing behavior by controlling the rewards and punishments. If a child is disruptive to the group, the teacher might decide to change the child's behavior by ignoring all disruptive behavior and rewarding more appropriate behavior. Even calling the child's name when she is disruptive can be rewarding to a child seeking attention. Behaviors can be *extinguished* just as they can be encouraged. For instance, if a child throws a temper tantrum in order to get something that has been denied, the teacher can ignore that behavior until it is no longer exhibited. If a behavior does not result in the child's getting what she wants, she will try another behavior.

How Children Learn: Behaviorist

In the behaviorist view, a child acquires knowledge as the result of repeated interactions with the environment. The consequences of the interactions—reward or punishment—determine whether the interaction will be repeated. The most effective teaching presents a carefully selected stimulus and then controls the rewards or punishments connected with the child's response to the stimulus. The behaviorist view is that a child accumulates knowledge through repeated exposures to stimuli and that the learning process is directed by the adult who controls the sequence of stimuli and the reward system. The best known behaviorist, or direct instruction, model is the program developed by Bereiter and Engelmann (1966) and marketed under the trade name DISTAR. This program was developed in the 1960s as one model for achieving school success with children who are disadvantaged. Another behaviorist model is the Behavior Analysis Model, developed by Don Bushell (Roopnarine and Johnson 1993).

In the direct instruction model, the focus is on achievement of academic goals, especially in reading, arithmetic, and language. The lessons presented to children are designed to be conducted in small groups and are carefully sequenced. Each lesson includes an activity designed to motivate students and attract their attention. Following this part of the lesson, new information is presented and responses are elicited from students. If their responses are correct, the students are rewarded. If their responses are incorrect, the students repeat the lesson until the correct responses have been elicited and then rewarded.

The children's behavior is also controlled by a system of rewards and punishments. For example, when a child comes into the room in the morning and hangs up his coat without being reminded, the teacher might reward the child by giving him a token. Tokens can be redeemed later for extra play time or special activities or used to purchase items from a class store. Children who fail to follow the rules may receive no tokens or have tokens taken away.

Teachers who follow direct instruction models are expected to understand and be able to use reinforcement schedules, shaping of behavior, and extinction of behavior in achieving academic and behavioral goals. Bereiter and Engelmann describe the hallmarks of their methods as follows:

1. *Fast pace.* During a twenty-minute period as many as 500 responses may be required of each child. Usually five or more different kinds of tasks are presented during a single period.
2. *Reduced task-irrelevant behavior.* The teacher controls the session relying only incidentally on spontaneous exchanges to dictate the direction of instruction. Efforts of both teacher and children are focused on the tasks being studied.
3. *Strong emphasis on verbal responses.* These are often produced in unison, so that each child's total output can be maximized.
4. *Carefully planned small-step instructional units with continual feedback.* The teacher is not receptive to irrelevant exchanges but is very sensitive to possible areas of difficulty, possible ambiguities that arise from her presentation. She quickly corrects mistakes. She tries to anticipate and avert them.
5. *Heavy work demands.* Children are required to pay attention and to work hard. They are rewarded for thinking; half-hearted or careless performance is not tolerated. (in Spodek 1973, pp. 177–178)

With the direct instruction model, the classroom is simplified and the number of activities is limited. The rationale given by Bereiter and Engelmann (1966) for these limitations is that

an object-rich environment stimulates a culturally deprived child to attend to a glitter of superabundant stimuli. He darts from one object to another, treating each only in terms of sensory gratification. When the toy no longer "feels good," another one is selected. By minimizing the inducement of noise in the environment, the preschool can be far more effective in directing the child not to the vehicle of the concept but to the concept itself. Sterilizing the environment is a firm requirement of the work-oriented preschool. Toys should be limited to form boards, jigsaw puzzles (which are usually favorites with the children), books, drawing and tracing materials, Cuisenaire rods (to be handled during free time under the direction of the teacher), and a miniature house, barn and set of farm animals. Paper, crayons, and chalk (but no paint) should be available for expressive play. Motor toys, such as tricycles and wagons, and climbing equipment are not necessary for the program. (p. 72)

More recently, Neisworth and Buggey (1993) have summarized the basic procedures of the teacher in a behaviorist program:

- Reward constructive behavior; ignore undesirable behavior. The best rewards are those that are natural or intrinsic to an activity. Add-on, contrived rewards (e.g., tokens, extra praise) should only be used when necessary, much as crutches should be used.
- Teach skills in simulated settings or in the actual circumstances in which the skills are expected.
- Practice what you teach. Children will imitate teacher behavior.
- Behavioral teaching is by definition individualized. Plan developmentally appropriate sequences for each child.
- Choose rewards that are appropriate and motivating to the child. Children's preferences differ; not all children enjoy the same activities, rewards, or circumstances.
- Learning occurs when the child is interacting with the environment; maximize interaction.
- Plan for generalization; use shaping and stimulus-control. Evaluate acquired skills across settings, time, and persons.
- Make sure that children have opportunities to practice (and experience reinforcement for) learned skills periodically to maintain them. Optimally, what children learn at one time is used as part of more sophisticated behavior learned later. (p. 130)

Goals of Behaviorist Models

The most important goals of behaviorist models are achievement of academic competencies in language, reading, and arithmetic. Children are also expected to learn to answer questions from the teacher articulately and in complete sentences and to perform on cue. The developers of direct instruction models believe that children who are academically capable will have improved self-concepts. Motor development is not among the primary goals of direct instruction models.

In the description on pages 50 and 51 of a typical day in a behaviorist preschool, the children are engaged in activities designed to teach content knowledge or facts and to help them develop the skills necessary for success in school settings, such as answering questions posed and responding to cues provided by the teacher. Other activities are included to accomplish specific academic goals, to complement the teacher's instruction, or to reward performance.

The behaviorist models focus primarily on *intellectual development*, which is defined as the learning of content and facts, not as the development of generalized intellectual abilities. Physical development is not a primary goal of this type of instruction nor are social and emotional development. Behaviorists believe that children will achieve more positive self-esteem if they feel that they are successful learners. Children are assumed to develop emotionally as they learn to control their impulsive behaviors and respond appropriately in school settings.

Subject-matter content in language, mathematics, and reading is broken down into small, discrete steps, which children must master before going on to the next step. These subject-matter areas are emphasized because they are considered basic to the children's success. The curriculum is tightly sequenced but not integrated. Children learn each subject without regard for what is being learned in other subjects. Science and social studies are rarely included in the curriculum, and the arts are included in a very limited fashion as part of the choice activities.

When implemented with older children, the fundamental behaviorist model remains intact. Basically, the changes for older children are found in the content of the lessons presented in subject-matter areas.

Many elements of the behaviorist models are evident in current elementary programs. Specification of limited objectives, emphasis on the sequence of materials or activities, and mastery of small steps as a method of achieving larger goals are all behavioristic in origin. In many elementary schools that do not claim to be behavioristic, tokens or stickers are used as reinforcers, and grades are often viewed as rewards or punishments.

PARENTS AND SCHOOL DESIGN

■ Provide parents and other visitors to your school with references for articles or books that support your program philosophy and perhaps explain the differences between your program and others.

The Constructivist Model

Constructivist models are based on the learning theories of Jean Piaget (1896–1980) and Lev Vygotsky (1896–1934). Examples of constructivist programs include the School for Constructive Play, developed by George Forman; the High/Scope program, developed by David Weikart; and the Bank Street College of Education, developed by Lucy Sprague Mitchell. There are points of agreement among constructionist programs as well as some differences. Among the points of agreement are the following:

1. All contend that a basic objective to be drawn from Piaget's work is to foster structural change in children's reasoning in the direction of operational thought.
2. All emphasize the fundamental importance of the child's action for learning and development.

9:00 − 9:15	Arrival, group time
9:15 −10:00	Rotating instructional groups
10:00 −10:25	Outdoor play
10:25 −10:45	Snack
10:45 −11:10	Instructional groups
11:10 −11:25	Choice of activities
11:25 −11:30	Dismissal

The school Alan attends has separate classes for fours and fives. The classroom in which five-year-old Alan works each day is a large room with three smaller rooms that open off it. For Alan's group of thirty children, there is a teacher and two assistant teachers.

The teacher greets Alan at the door with a smile and tells him how glad she is that he is at school. As Alan hangs up his coat, the teacher slips him a red token, and he puts it into his pocket with a grin. Alan joins the other children sitting in a circle on the floor. In a few minutes, when all the children are present, the teacher joins the group and calls the roll. Alan responds to his name with "I am present." Then the teacher reviews the days of the week and the months of the year. Alan raises his hand to say the days of the week. He repeats the names successfully and receives another token. He also gets a smile and praise from the teacher. After a child is selected to pin the correct numeral on the calendar and move pointers on the weather chart to indicate today's weather, Alan is instructed to go to the language room with his group. Alan's group membership is based on his ability level. There are high, middle, and low groups.

One of the assistant teachers conducts Alan's language lesson for twenty minutes. Alan and the other members of his group sit on small risers to be as close as possible to the teacher and to facilitate their choral responses. The first part of the lesson is a warm-up in which the teacher tells the children that when she taps her pencil three times, they should clap their hands. Some children do not clap on cue, and the exercise is repeated. The children are reminded that paying close attention and responding quickly are very important.

Today's lesson is on the use of pronouns: *I, he, she, we.* The teacher opens a paper bag and removes a comb. She says, "I comb my hair." The children are instructed to pretend combing their hair and to repeat, "I comb my hair." Each child who responds correctly is rewarded with a token.

3. All borrow ideas from the child-development tradition in early education for materials, equipment, and activities that permit children to be active (for example, painting and other art activities, blockbuilding, pretend play, singing, and sand and water play).

4. None of the . . . Piagetian programs is just "Piagetian." Each recognizes certain limitations in using Piaget's theory alone as a basis for educational practice. (DeVries and Kohlberg 1987, p. 51)

Programs differ in their definitions of action, the extent of emphasis on logic in language, the extent of reliance on child development traditions, and how cooperation and interest are fostered. Some developmentalists define *action* as physical action; some broaden the definition to include mental action. Some programs place more emphasis on children's being

The teacher then goes through sentences using the pronouns *he, she,* and *we* with descriptions of other self-care actions, such as brushing the teeth, washing the face, and so on. When the lesson is completed, Alan and his group leave their room and walk with the teacher to the next room for their arithmetic lesson.

In this lesson, Alan's group is learning to recognize and complete simple addition equations. As the teacher holds up flashcards showing equations such as 3 + 1, the group responds, "Three plus one equals four." Today, the teacher repeats combinations whose sums do not exceed 6. When the children have reviewed these sums, they are given a worksheet, listing the same equations, and asked to complete it. Alan mumbles something to Brad, who is sitting beside him at the table. The teacher quickly reminds him that this is work time and that talking to friends is not appropriate now. She tells Alan that a token will be taken away if he talks again. Alan writes the answers to the problems and is rewarded when he does them correctly.

For the next twenty-minute period, Alan and his classmates play outside. The playground has swings, climber/slides, tire swings, and climbers. Alan chooses to swing and takes turns with Brad.

When the children return to the classroom, they are instructed to wash their hands before snack. The snack today consists of apples cut into fourths and crackers scored into fourths. The teachers introduce and reinforce the use of the fractional terms as the children eat their snacks.

After snack, Alan's group goes into a small room for the reading lesson. Again, the teacher gets the children's attention with a warm-up exercise, and when all have responded correctly, he begins the lesson. Today's lesson is on the sounds represented by the letters *b, m, l,* and *d.* The teacher presents a letter on a card and says, "This letter is *b* and its sound is 'buh.'" The children repeat the name and the sound several times. They already know the long vowel sounds, and today's letters are combined with each of the vowels in succession and pronounced.

When the reading lesson is finished, Alan and his group return to the large room, where all the children are gathered. They now have the opportunity to spend their tokens on some special activities. Alan chooses to spend three of his tokens for drawing with paper and markers. When he completes his drawing, he spends three more tokens to play with the jigsaw puzzles. Then he and the assistant teacher build some sets with the Cuisenaire rods. The teacher blinks the lights to indicate that it is time to put away all the materials and get ready to go home.

In a few minutes, the room is clean and orderly, and the children have put on their coats and are out the door.

able to articulate their understanding; others place more emphasis on performance. Some programs allow more time for free play and free expression than others. Some programs rely on free-play activities to help children develop cooperative behaviors; others specifically plan for interventions in behavior cycles.

How Children Learn: Constructivist

Recall from Chapter 1 that Piaget and Vygotsky described learning as a process that is under the control of the learner, or intrinsically motivated. According to Piaget, not all knowledge is acquired in the same way. Some kinds of knowledge, such as the concept of *hot,* can be learned only by experience with objects. We don't learn *hot* until we are burned. Thus, the properties of objects—texture, shape, function, and so on—are learned through experiencing them. Language and social customs, however, cannot be learned from experience but only from other people. Logico-mathematical knowledge—which includes what we know about mathematics, seriation, classification, and so on—can only be acquired by interacting mentally with physical objects.

For example, if you let a three-year-old loose in your classroom, he would explore everything about the desks. He would soon know that they have hard, smooth surfaces; that they balance on four legs; that they are heavy; and so forth. However, no amount of exploration would help the child discover the label *desk* that we apply to this piece of furniture. He would have to learn the word from someone in his social group who knows what we have agreed to call this thing. You might also put more than one desk at the front of the room and tell the child they are a *set* of two desks. But to the child, the desks physically remain separate, one and one. To understand that they are a set of two requires a mental construct beyond the normal abilities of a three-year-old.

Vygotsky (1986) recognized that children learn a great deal about their environments from manipulating objects; he called this kind of learning *spontaneous.* He also identified another kind of learning—what we typically think of as school learning (the freezing point of water, for example)—as *scientific* learning. Vygotsky believed that all learning is mediated by the social group, so if counting is important in the social group, then the child will learn to count. Recall from Chapter 1 that Vygotsky also believed that children are only capable of learning certain things, even with assistance, at given ages or skill levels; this notion is the foundation of the **zone of proximal development (ZPD).** An application of the ZPD is shown in the description of a typical day in a constructivist school (see pages 58 and 59), when the teacher sends two children to the library to find information about the praying mantis. The teacher must know whether these children can use materials from the library to further their own learning. If they cannot use printed materials or other library information, then this strategy will not be appropriate for them.

Constructivists believe that children want to learn and are, in fact, always learning. They also believe that children construct their own understandings and are continually refining them in terms of new experiences and knowledge. For example, at age two, most children have no concept of *maps.* By age four, however, most can draw a map, even if it appears to be a mass of scribbles to an adult; most four-year-olds know the functions of a map, some of the elements it contains, and perhaps some of the symbols. By age six, most children's idea of a map has developed so that it is much more specific. For example, children may draw their own houses, use lines (not scribbles) to represent roads, and add specific symbols, such as four-way stop signs. Even older children may add more conventional symbols and eventually understand the meaning of scale in maps.

A variety of activities and experiences help children develop skills and abilities.

Instruction in a constructivist program is provided primarily to individual children and to small groups; whole-group instruction occurs less frequently. Also, instruction rarely involves the teacher giving information to the students. More frequently, the teacher has arranged an experience in which to engage the learners and then asks them questions as they participate in the task. Supplying students with answers is not the goal in a constructivist program; in fact, unanswered questions are important in terms of continued interest and continued learning.

In a contructivist program, curricula are planned and learning experiences are selected to follow children's interests or expose them to new areas in which their interest might be aroused. The process of finding information, analyzing data, and reaching conclusions is considered more important than learning facts. An emphasis on process does not mean that content is lacking, however. Children learn a great many facts and concepts, but they are always embedded in meaningful contexts. For example, children who are learning about trees might "adopt" a tree and visit it on a regular basis in order to record changes over time. They might learn to identify and classify leaves of various trees and participate in experiments to discover the function of leaves. The children might examine the rings in a tree stump, draw conclusions about their observations, and so on. They might locate books about trees in the library, and the teacher might read to them about trees. In other words, the curriculum experiences would focus on children's learning how to find, analyze, and evaluate information, but facts would be presented in the process.

Constructivists believe that it is important to select curriculum experiences containing content that can be acted on in various ways. Teachers must also consider the developmental stage of the learner and the complexity of the tasks required to be successful in learning the material.

Goals of Constructivist Programs

The goal of any constructivist program is to stimulate children in all areas of development. Physical development, social and emotional development, and cognitive (intellectual) development are all important. Language development and an emphasis on the process of learning are also important. Programs attempt to keep a balance so that all areas of development are addressed and none are neglected. Encouraging children to become actively involved in their own learning and developing children's desire to continue to learn are also important goals.

Piaget on Early Education   Kamii and DeVries (1977) state that education must be based on the long-term objective of developing the entire personality, with particular emphasis on intellectual and moral autonomy. Their emphasis on intellectual development is based on Piaget's own statements:

> The principal goal of education is to create [people] who are capable of doing new things, not simply of repeating what other generations have done—[people] who are creative, inventive, and discoverers. The second goal of education is to form minds which can be critical, can verify, and not accept everything they are offered. The great danger today is of slogans, collective opinions, ready-made trends of thought. We have to be able to resist individually, to criticize, to distinguish between what is proven and what is not. So we need pupils who are active, who learn early to find out by themselves, partly by their own spontaneous activity and partly through material we set up for them; who learn early to tell what is verifiable and what is simply the first idea to come to them. (Piaget 1964, p. 5)

In the short term, constructivist programs also strive to help children achieve the following socioemotional goals:

1. To feel secure in a noncoercive relationship with adults
2. To respect the feelings and rights of others and begin to coordinate different points of view (decentering and cooperating)
3. To be independent, alert, and curious; to use initiative in pursuing curiosities; to have confidence in his ability to figure things out for himself, and to speak his mind with conviction. (Day and Parker 1977, p. 393)

Finally, such programs encourage children to achieve cognitive objectives:

1. To come up with interesting ideas, problems, and questions

2. To put things into relationships and notice similarities and differences. (Day and Parker 1977, p. 394)

Despite their general similarities, the goals of different constructivist programs can vary. The descriptions that follow will help clarify some of the differences in programs based on Piagetian theory.

• *The School for Constructive Play:* In George Forman's program, the goals are to help children develop cognitively through activities selected specifically to help them with the ideas of correspondences (identity and equivalence), transformations, functional relations, and changing perspectives. Forman (1993, pp. 143–144) recommends that teachers find ways to induce conflict in children's thinking. For example, in a game called Wedges and Wheels, the teacher plays with a set of wheels attached to a single axle and two wedges that form a ramp. When the child becomes interested in the game and wants to play, he is encouraged to do so. After a few experiences of rolling the wheels down the ramp, the teacher moves one of the wedges so that the wheels no longer fit on the wedges. She then watches to see how the child solves the problem of fitting the wheels on the wedges.

• *High/Scope:* The High/Scope program, developed by David Weikart, is known for emphasizing careful and systematic observations of the child and for organizing the curriculum around key experiences. *Key experiences* have been identified in the categories of social and emotional development, movement and physical development, and cognitive development.

> Key experiences provide a composite picture of early childhood development, are fundamental to young children's construction of knowledge, take place repeatedly over an extended period of time, and describe the concepts and relationships young children are striving to understand. They occur in active learning settings in which children have opportunities to make choices and decisions, manipulate materials, interact with peers and adults, experience special events, reflect on ideas and actions, use language in personally meaningful ways, and receive appropriate adult support. (Hohmann and Weikart 1995, p. 299)

The categories of key experiences are creative representation, language and literacy, initiative and social relations, movement, music, classification, seriation, number, space, and time.

Most activities lend themselves to several key experiences. For example, a child might choose to paint. Such a choice would give the teacher the opportunity to observe how the child was able to understand the routine of getting paper, paint smocks, and so on and then putting away the paper when he was finished. If the child needed instruction, it could be provided.

Painting would also be an activity that allowed the teacher to observe how the child represented objects and related to other children involved in the same task.

Key experiences provide teachers with a basis for planning and organizing the curriculum so that activities are not random. Through observing individual students, teachers are also able to assess how children are growing in their abilities, as categorized by key experiences (Bredekamp 1996).

• *The Bank Street College of Education:* The Bank Street Program grew out of the work of Lucy Sprague Mitchell, who had been a student of the famous educator John Dewey. Mitchell began a school for young children in which play would be taken seriously—namely, one in which children could play and researchers could study them doing so in a naturalistic setting. The Bank Street program is dedicated to fostering children's development, not simply to promoting specific learning. The following principles are the framework of the program:

1. Development is not a simple path from less to more; and it is not an unfolding, like the unfolding of a flower. Development involves changes or shifts in the way a person organizes experience and copes with the world, generally moving from simpler to more complex, from single to multiple and integrated ways of responding. The concept of stages of development is crucial, and is also a convenient way of talking and thinking about developmental change and growth. Stages are approximate and are only loosely related to age. . . .

2. Individuals are never at a fixed point on a straight line of development, but operate within a range of possibilities. Earlier ways of organizing experience are not erased, but become integrated into more advanced systems. While people will want to function at the highest possible level, they are also able to use less mature ways appropriately. (Even after a child knows how to hop and jump, there are times when it is a good idea to crawl; even adults find moments when it is appropriate to be silly.) . . .

3. Developmental progress involves a mix of stability and instability. A central task for the educator is to find a balance between helping a child consolidate new understandings and offering challenges that will promote growth. . . .

4. The motivation to engage actively with the environment—to make contact, to have an impact, and to make sense of experience—is built into human beings. The growing child gradually adds more ways of actively engaging with the world as she develops. Generally, the progression is from more physical, body-centered ways of responding to perceptual and then more conceptual, symbolic ways. . . .

5. The child's sense of self is built up from his experiences with other people and with objects; knowledge of the self is based on repeated awareness and testing of one's self in interaction. . . .

6. Growth and maturing involve conflict—conflict within the self, and conflict with others. Conflict is necessary for development. The way conflicts are resolved depends on the nature of the interaction with significant figures in the child's life and the demands of the culture. (Mitchell and David 1992, pp. 16–17)

Overview of Constructivist Programs

Although the goals or emphases of these constructivist programs are not identical, they are all concerned with the development of children's thinking and reasoning abilities and their abilities to represent experiences in meaningful ways. Each program depends on children's active involvement with materials and teachers' guidance in helping children reflect on their experiences.

In examining the activities of a typical day (see pages 58 and 59) in a constructivist classroom, we find that playing with blocks offers children opportunities to develop concepts in mathematics, such as length and equivalence. The addition of the pulley provides opportunities for developing concepts related to simple machines. Representation of experience is achieved through building the model of an apartment building. Several activities offer children opportunities to use their developing skills in literacy (signing in on arrival, recording comments about the painting, recording observations on the walk in the neighborhood) and to represent understandings. In exploring the numerical patterns in the room, the teacher attempts to aid children in the development of number concepts. Other activities require children to solve problems (taking apart the toaster, deciding who can play in the new area) using reasoning.

Constructivist programs focus on development of physical, social, emotional, and intellectual competence. The curriculum is based on children's interests and is integrated so that content is not arranged by subject-matter areas. Many activities and experiences are selected to help children think about solutions to social as well as cognitive problems. The interrelationship of all areas of development is important in developing the *whole child*. The content areas of science, social studies, mathematics, the arts, and health and safety are all integrated into themes of interest to the children. Literacy is taught in the context of children's other activities, as they extend their language to reading and writing. Constructivists assume that literacy skills are best learned within a context in which they can be applied.

Because the selection of materials and experiences is based on the children's developmental level, extending the program to younger or older children requires adapting materials and experiences; nonetheless, the basic tenets of choice, intrinsic motivation in learning, and a balanced program remain constant. With younger children, the choices of activities are more limited and the guidance of the teacher is more apparent. Projects for older children are selected so that in-depth explorations of topics is possible.

9:00 –10:00	Arrival, choice time
10:00 –10:15	Group time
10:15 –10:40	Outdoor play
10:40 –10:55	Snack time
10:55 –11:10	Group time for optional activities
11:10 –11:30	Story time and dismissal

Michelle bounces into her classroom, carrying a milk carton with a praying mantis in it. In Michelle's class of four-, five-, and six-year-olds, there are twenty-four children, a teacher, and an assistant teacher.

The classroom she enters has only one area large enough for all twenty-four children to sit down at once. The rest of the space is filled with areas arranged for different explorations or interactions. There is a large area for blocks; an area for dramatic play that contains dolls, child-sized kitchen equipment, dress-up clothes, and costumes; an area that contains easels and many kinds of art supplies; an area that contains a water table and sand table; an area that contains puzzles and games; an area for reading books that is furnished with two rocking chairs and some floor pillows; an area with many kinds of paper and writing utensils; an area that has baskets of math manipulative materials; an area that, at the moment, is filled with a large collection of old clocks and other small appliances; and another area where there is a table, which today is covered with paper and has some blocks and cardboard milk cartons on it.

Michelle's teacher notices her entry into the classroom and smiles a greeting. She notes that Michelle has signed in on the clipboard by the door and that she has hung her coat in the cubby labeled with her name. The teacher is helping two girls find a way to remove the levers and springs from an old toaster but turns her attention to Michelle and her box when Michelle approaches. The teacher listens while Michelle tells how she and her brother caught the praying mantis and made a container for it. She suggests that Michelle place the container on a display table near the door for other children to observe, if they choose.

Michelle does so and then decides to spend some time in the block area. She selects a tagboard circle with her name on it and places it on one of the pegs beside a picture of blocks on a pegboard near the door. When she gets to the block area, she tells her friend Amy that she would like to build an apartment building. They decide to work on it together and find that it needs a strong base to support the ten stories that they want to add to it. The teacher observes their construction and offers them a pulley, a small box, and some cord so that they can make an elevator for their building.

After about thirty minutes of animated block building, the girls put away the blocks and Michelle checks on her praying mantis. She finds three children at the table and tells them about catching the insect and making the milk carton container for it. She takes her name from the "block" peg and moves it to the "art" peg. She gets a friend to help her fasten her paint smock and attaches paper to an easel. She paints a picture of her praying mantis. When the teacher observes her painting, she suggests that perhaps Michelle would like to write about the insect. After Michelle has cleaned the painting area, she goes to a table where there are many kinds of paper, pencils, and markers. She finds her own journal in a basket and writes about the insect and draws pictures of it. The teacher helps her date her paper and her painting. The teachers have been moving from area to area in the classroom, asking questions, providing needed guidance, and suggesting activities to individual children.

The teacher rings a little bell, which is the signal for the children to finish their work and clean up the areas. After that has been done, the children meet on the rug, where the teacher is leading some fingerplays and songs. When all the children have gathered, the teacher asks them to think about some of the things they learned this morning. A few children tell about the parts they found in the appliances. Others tell about how they solved some problems in their play. The teacher says that she noticed that not everyone who wanted to do so could play in one of the areas where a new set of materials was available. She asks if they can think of some ways to solve the problem. The children finally decide to take a survey to determine who has already had a turn with the new materials and to make a sign-up sheet for those who have not yet had a turn. Some children make comments about the praying mantis and ask questions about it. The teacher asks how they could find out more about these insects. Two children decide that they could go to the library and ask the librarian for help in locating information. The teacher suggests a good time later in the morning for them to go.

Next, the children review the calendar for any special celebrations that are coming up and for the symbol that indicates the day the eggs in the incubator are expected to hatch. They recall their trip to the bakery last week and their plans for sharing time the next day.

After these activities have been finished, the children go outside to play. They can choose riding toys, swings, climber/slides, climbers, and some large blocks and tunnels for play. Michelle and a small group of friends climb and swing, shouting joyfully most of the time.

After about twenty-five minutes, the teacher signals the children to return to the room. As the children enter, each is asked to choose a snack: apple juice, orange juice, apple slices, or orange slices. They wash their hands and begin to help serve the snack. When they have finished their snack, the children construct a graph of their snack choices with help from the teachers and discuss all the relationships that are illustrated on the graph.

After the graph has been finished, the children get their coats again because today, they are going on a walk around the neighborhood. Each child has a clipboard and pencil and chooses something to look for. Some will observe the number and kinds of houses they pass; others will observe the number and kinds of businesses. A few children want to record the number and kinds of plants they see, and some will look for all the printed words that they can find. They know that tomorrow they will begin to transfer the information they collect to the map of their immediate neighborhood that they are building on the table.

When the class returns from the walk, the children gather on the rug again for singing and movement. Two children go off to the library to get praying mantis information; the others learn some new songs and review the lyrics to other songs that are printed on large charts. The children also use some little books in which they have illustrated a few of the songs.

The teacher then shares a story from a "big book," with large illustrations and type so that all the children can see while the teacher reads. As the teacher reads the story a second time, some children join in on the words that they recognize. The teacher tells them that they may choose to write their own stories tomorrow.

The two children return from the library with several books and some posters. The teacher places these books on the display table with the praying mantis. Several children are really interested in the insect, and the teacher promises that they will have time to observe it and read about it tomorrow.

As the children gather their coats and papers and get ready for dismissal, they review patterns and arrange themselves in line according to their coat colors. It takes some time, but they form a pattern of red, blue, green, and yellow coats; then they add the children who do not fit that particular pattern. Michelle has on a red jacket and gets in line to help complete the pattern. She has her painting in her hand and hurries to share it with her mother when the teacher dismisses the class.

When teachers select activities, they should consider the goals of the program and the needs of the children.

Teachers make conscious effort to teach subject-matter content in meaningful contexts and to select experiences in which children can apply skills being learned.

Summaries and Comparisons

The program models described in this chapter have some common goals, but each has a different view of what is the best and most appropriate learning environment for young children. One goal common to all three models—Montessori, behaviorist, and constructivist—is for children to learn. The models differ, however, on the means used to reach this goal. Educators who follow the Montessori philosophy believe that children learn best through interactions with materials in a prepared environment; there is little child-child interaction. Behaviorists believe that children learn best in a highly structured environment in which the information presented is carefully sequenced and the rewards are controlled. Those who hold a constructivist view of learning also believe that children learn through interactions with objects and people but that children must reflect on their actions, as well.

Other goals of the programs also vary. An additional goal of Montessori programs is to develop the child's intellect and control. Constructivist programs focus on development in all areas: physical, social,

PARENTS AND SCHOOL DESIGN

■ In the school's entry or main hallway, post each teacher's certification accompanied by a short statement of her philosophy of teaching.

emotional, and intellectual. Behaviorists generally focus on academic knowledge and place less emphasis on physical and social development. These differing views of how children learn (and the varied program goals based on these views) translate into very different experiences for children who attend these programs.

RESEARCH ON PROGRAM MODELS

Attempts to compare the effectiveness of different program models have been inconclusive. It is not an easy task to control all the variables that influence such research. For example, we could argue that it is invalid to compare the academic achievement of children who attend preschools based on the different program models described above because the focuses of some of the programs are much broader than academic achievement. Proponents of such broadly focused programs would argue that even if their children did not score as well on standardized tests as children from more academic programs, they learned other things that such tests do not measure. It is difficult to assess the academic achievement of young children accurately. It is also difficult to control for family involvement, teacher effectiveness, children's motivation, and so forth in studies that compare different program models.

Attempts to find differences between program models have produced mixed results. Children who show initial gains in skill levels as the result of a particular preschool experience may later show declines. Lilian Katz (1988) suggests that educators attend to the long-term, cumulative effects of programs, as evidenced by children's interest in learning. Not many long-term studies have been done, but one of the most significant research

THEORY INTO Practice

Visit at least two different programs that seem to have different emphases. (Check their advertisements in a newspaper or the Yellow Pages of the phone book, or call the principal of a public school.) Find as many common elements and as many differences as possible between the two programs.

studies on the effects of preschool experience is the Perry Preschool High/Scope research, conducted by Schweinhart and associates (1986).

The High/Scope curriculum used at the Perry Preschool was based on a developmentalist approach. The research compared High/Scope to traditional and direct instruction (behaviorist) preschool experiences. When children were studied in 1988 at the age of fifteen, those who had either a High/Scope or a traditional nursery school experience reported engaging in about half as much delinquent behavior as children who had experience in a direct instruction program. This study also found that children from constructivist and traditional programs exhibited much more prosocial use of time (holding offices in school, participating in sports) than those from the direct instruction group. Another long-term study (Karnes et al. 1983) compared five preschool curriculum models and found that students who had direct instruction did poorly on several measures of school success by the end of high school. None of these differences was statistically significant, although 70 percent of the nursery school students completed high school compared to only 47 percent of the direct instruction group.

The conclusion we can draw from research is that much remains to be learned about the development and learning of young children. Teachers and parents must think carefully about program choices and expectations for children. And researchers must continue to attempt to solve the complex problem of evaluating different approaches to instruction for young children.

CHAPTER SUMMARY

- Three models for early childhood programs were described in this chapter: Montessori, behaviorist, and constructivist.
- The key concepts in the Montessori program include the absorbent mind, the prepared environment, sensitive periods, autoeducation, and the importance of self-correcting, didactic materials. Montessori philosophy assumes that children need freedom to make choices and that they desire order and beauty in their lives.
- The behaviorist model of instruction is based on stimulus-response learning theory and operant conditioning. The instruction is primarily teacher directed and academic in focus.

- The constructivist, or developmentalist, model focuses on the child's development physically, socially, emotionally, and intellectually. Key elements include opportunities for the learner to construct knowledge and active manipulation of objects accompanied by reflection on that activity.
- The results of research that has attempted to compare the models of early childhood programs are very mixed. It is extremely difficult to control all the variables that impinge on children and their school experiences in order to actually compare the programs. The long-term effects on children's interest in learning must be considered when examining research findings.

A TEACHER SPEAKS

NANCY BIRKENMAYER
Christa McAuliffe
Elementary School
McALLEN, TEXAS

Individual Growth in a Mixed-Age Classroom

Our K–1 classroom is deep in the heart of Texas, only seven miles from the Mexican border. Our enrollment is predominately Hispanic and Anglo children from all socioeconomic backgrounds. My team teacher and I decided to try mixing my kindergarten class and her first-grade class the year before we were scheduled to mix the two grades completely in two K–1 classes. Doing so convinced us both that Vygotsky's social learning theory (1978) is indeed correct: *Children grow into the intellectual lives of those around them.* As the result of seeing the progress made by the younger children as well as the development of self-esteem in the older ones, we have now mixed our two classrooms, such that we have K–1 in both. Most of our kindergartners from the first year were promoted into our first grade, so we have been able to see the continuity of learning over a two-year period. The younger students benefit from observing what they will be able to do next year, and the first-graders benefit from being the role models of that learning. Another benefit is that rapport with parents and students was well established during our first year together; thus, we can take up where we left off at the end of the previous schoolyear.

Although the mixing of ages makes for a wide range of ability, individual children do not feel stigmatized if they are not able to do what others may be doing. They know that they are not the only ones—others are learning, too. As a result, they are less likely to compare themselves to their classmates. We celebrate the progress of each child at his or her own developmental rate.

Since the children in our classes are together for two years, we have seen traditions established in which the younger ones look forward for their own "rite of passage." Each of our classrooms is more like a family than a school. We share in each other's successes and struggle with each other's problems. The children establish relationships with each other and with their teachers, which are nurtured by a two-year involvement.

Perhaps the greatest reward of teaching in a mixed-age classroom has been watching the kindergartners mature into first-graders and observing the learning that takes place over a two-year period. We would not want to do it any other way.

3

CREATING AN ENVIRONMENT FOR LEARNING

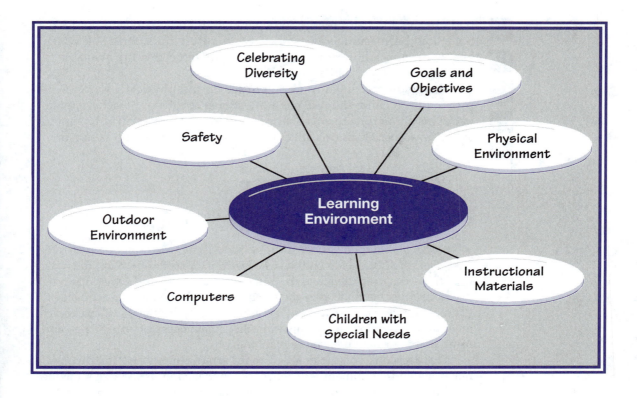

Your assignment this week was to focus your observations on the physical environment of the classroom. To do so, you needed to sketch the arrangement of the furniture and list the materials and equipment available to the children. When you went to the second-grade classroom where you were to observe, you found about what you had expected: The children all had desks, which were arranged in a U shape around the classroom. There were shelves along one wall, where materials such as art supplies and books were stored. The teacher's desk was at the front of the classroom and to one side. There were chalkboards on two walls and bulletin boards on the other two.

When you got back to your own class and heard from your classmates, you found that the physical environments everyone had observed varied greatly. Some had tables and chairs and no desks. Some had been arranged in work areas for art, blocks, sand and water, and so on plus a library. Some had many materials readily available to the children; others had almost none.

Now, you are much more interested in the physical environment provided for children. You have questions about how teachers make decisions about furniture and room arrangements, and you also want to know how such decisions affect the children's learning and behavior.

Some planning decisions can be made before the children arrive. Teachers can decide on the basic learning areas to be set up, the basic materials to be used, and the initial room arrangement. Other planning decisions must be made after the teacher and children become acquainted. Planning is never really finished. It is a continual cycle of making and implementing plans, observing, evaluating the effectiveness of your plans, and using that information for more planning.

The decisions you make about **room arrangements** and **instructional materials** and equipment will reflect your goals and expectations for the children. It is fairly common during an interview for a principal to ask a prospective teacher of young children to sketch a room arrangement that she would use. Much of what a principal wants to know about a candidate's curriculum priorities is reflected in how the prospective teacher chooses to arrange the room. If your program goals include encouraging children's exploration of a variety of materials and investigation of the phenomena around them, then you will not choose to set up your room with a desk for each child and the teacher's desk as the focal point of the classroom.

GOALS AND OBJECTIVES

Environmental decisions reflect the philosophy and goals of the teacher. Thus, you will find contrasts among the instructional materials and room arrangements designed to accomplish various sets of objectives. For example, assume that one of Teacher A's beliefs is that children become more literate through participating in a broad range of activities that include read-alouds, journal writing, exploring books, playing games such as Go Fish, and reading interactive stories on the computer. Given this belief, this teacher will make sure that her classroom has a comfortable library area, that the children can access many materials without asking for them, and that they have table space for playing games. Suppose that Teacher B, on the other hand, believes that children need to have lessons on various skills. His classroom might be arranged in a more traditional way, with a separate desk for each child, a space where a small group could sit for instruction (horseshoe tables were once common in primary classrooms), and fewer spaces open to the children.

The general goals of many programs include helping children to:

1. Learn that they are capable learners, that they can make choices, and that their ideas are respected
2. Learn and apply skills in a meaningful context
3. Explore a variety of materials
4. Become able to communicate their needs and feelings
5. Learn to use and appreciate many sources of information—people, printed materials, visual materials
6. Become able to express themselves creatively

In order to meet these goals, teachers have many decisions to make. Be aware that decisions you make about the learning environment can either foster or hinder achievement of these goals.

STRUCTURING THE PHYSICAL ENVIRONMENT

Often, many of the physical characteristics of the classroom in an early childhood program do not reflect the choices of the teacher—the room may be too small for the number of children, have a sink that the children cannot reach, have a bathroom down the hall, have chalkboards on every wall, or have only one electrical outlet. However, teachers can make other decisions about the physical environment, including how the furniture is arranged. Although teachers may not be able to choose the furnishings for the room at the outset of a program, they may be able to make changes over time. Teachers should also keep in mind that children need to be involved in planning the space, as well. The teacher should make preliminary plans and arrangements, but they must always address the needs of the children, once they are working in the classroom.

The furniture selected must be of appropriate size for children and should be easy to rearrange to meet changing classroom needs. The most flexible furniture includes tables and chairs and shelf units on wheels. Rarely will every child need to sit at a table at once, so there need not be places at tables for everyone. Every child does need a space for her own things; this could be a cubby or a portable tub of some kind. Figure 3.1 on page 68 shows one design for storage cubbies.

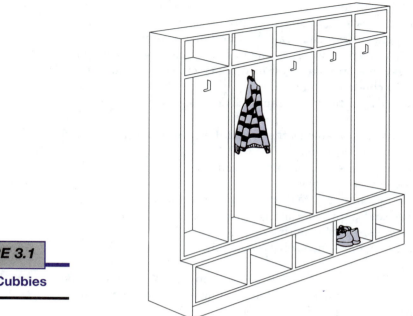

FIGURE 3.1

Storage Cubbies

Room Arrangement

Room arrangement is one way of communicating to children how they are expected to behave in the classroom. An open, stimulating arrangement invites children to participate and explore. A sterile, restricted environment says that the most important considerations in the classroom are obedience and order. "A stimulating environment provides the teacher with many opportunities to observe where a child's interests lie as well as those areas the child may be tentative in exploring" (Greabell and Forseth 1981, p. 71).

Furniture (or the lack of it) gives all of us information about how we are to act in a given setting (Heyman 1978). Think of the furniture in a bank lobby, a college classroom, or a living room. Arrangements of furniture and materials are effective predictors of the quality of early childhood programs. Prescott, Jones, and Kritchevsky (1967) determined that one element of program quality was the physical environment. They found that as the quality of the physical environment (amount of empty space, complexity of play areas, and so on) decreased, the amount of teacher restriction and control increased, the teacher's manner became less friendly, the children became less interested and involved, the number of rules increased, and the amount of conflict among the children increased.

Weinstein (1979) found that the research on classroom environments was not definitive with regard to the effect of environment on achievement but that it clearly showed that nonachievement factors (attitudes, behaviors) are related to environmental factors. Classrooms that are aesthetically pleasing and comfortable make those who live in them for hours each day feel better, regardless of their effect on achievement (Hill 1989). In summarizing the importance of the physical environment, Taylor and Vlastos (1983) state that "the physical setting of the learning environment does make a difference in, and directly contributes to, a child's behavior and learning" (p. 25). Vergeront (1987) recommends "softer" spaces that convey the message that "this place is for people." Softness can be achieved through the use of fabrics, cushions, color, curves, and surface textures.

One study (Grangaard 1995) and one anecdotal report (Schreiber 1996) both report that light in the classroom affects children's physical responses and academic achievement; children displayed much less off-task behavior in classrooms with full-spectrum lighting as opposed to those with fluorescent lights. Other researchers (Dyck 1994) are working on classroom designs that are more amenable to the active, project-oriented curricula of modern schools.

Trawik-Smith (1992) recommends that teachers who are faced with inappropriate classroom behavior, poor social interaction, or other behavioral problems consider the furnishings and arrangements of the classroom as potential causes of the problems. Possible corrective measures include the following:

Adding color, warmth, or softness to a classroom can foster security and happiness; creating private spaces nurtures emotional well-being. Organizing children in small groups and providing cozy, intimate places for them to play enhances positive social interaction. Rearranging learning centers can promote persistence and cognitive development. In short, physical design changes can resolve classroom problems and enhance program outcomes. (Trawik-Smith 1992, p. 30)

Caples (1996) agrees that the physical surroundings are important and suggests that adding "'ethnic' color palettes can be a source of pride and connection to the child's home community" (p. 18).

In choosing how to arrange furniture in the classroom, the first consideration—beyond the locations of doors and windows—is the locations of electrical outlets. In new schools, outlets are usually plentiful; outlets are often in short supply in older buildings, however. Areas that require electricity obviously must be located next to outlets. Usually, this means that videocassette recorders (VCRs), record players, tape recorders, aquariums, and other items that use electricity must be placed in the classroom first. Teachers should keep in mind these general guidelines for room arrangements:

1. Space must accommodate multiple uses. Few classrooms and centers have enough space for each activity to have its own area; therefore, areas must serve more than one purpose. For example, blocks can be placed in a corner that is also used for storytime during another part of the day.

2. Areas in which water is used should be as close to the water supply as possible. These include art, science, and water table areas.

3. Quiet areas should be close together so that children who want to work quietly can do so. *Quiet* does not mean that children cannot talk, but activities in such areas as the library, the writing table, and a listening station are quieter by nature than activities in some other areas.

4. Noisy areas, such as the blocks and dramatic play areas, should be grouped on the other side of the room from quiet areas.

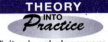

THEORY INTO *Practice*

Visit a local classroom. Measure the room and make a sketch of it, marking the doors, windows, electrical outlets, and water sources. Design a room arrangement for this classroom that you think would be workable.

Vertical space is often overlooked in classrooms for young children. The backs of room dividers, walls, and other vertical surfaces can be used for interactive activities, such as matching activities, in which children match dresses to dolls or cookie monsters to cans; dressing activities, in which children lace, tie, zip, and button various pieces of clothing; flannelboard or magnetic story activities, in which children create and retell stories; and so on. By using vertical spaces, teachers can provide an extra activity or two in areas that would otherwise be decorative or perhaps even wasted (Readdick and Bartlett 1994/1995).

Figure 3.2 shows an example of a room arrangement for a preschool or kindergarten classroom, and Figure 3.3 (on page 72) shows one for a primary-grade classroom. Evaluate these plans in terms of use of space, how well they would accommodate your objectives, and what traffic patterns you think would develop.

Assessing the Environment

One method of assessing the learning environment is to examine activity areas in terms of their simplicity or complexity (Kritchevsky and Prescott 1969). A *simple unit* for play or activity has one obvious use and does not have subparts for children to manipulate or improvise with; examples include rocking horses, swings, and vehicles. A *complex unit* has subparts made of two essentially different play materials that children can manipulate or improvise with. A sand table with tools is a complex unit; art activity tables with paint or clay and tables with books are also classified as complex. A *super unit* has three or more play materials juxtaposed. Examples include a tunnel with movable boards and boxes, a sand table

FIGURE 3.2

Room Arrangement for a Preschool or Kindergarten Classroom

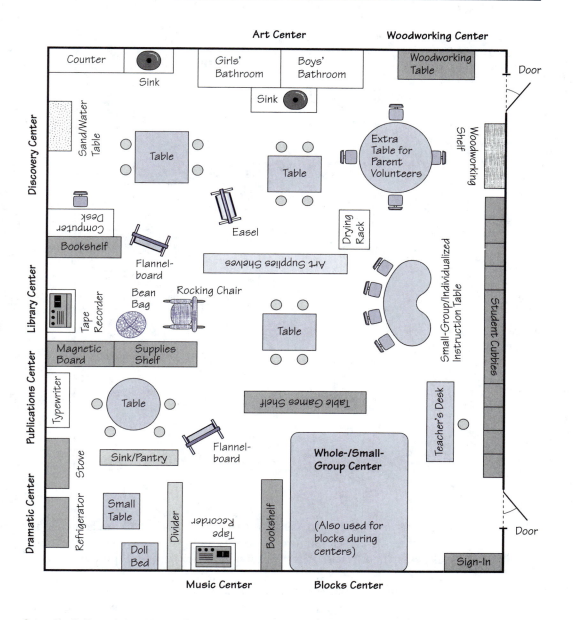

Source: Used with permission of Irasema González, Macario Garcia Elementary School, Pasadena, Texas.

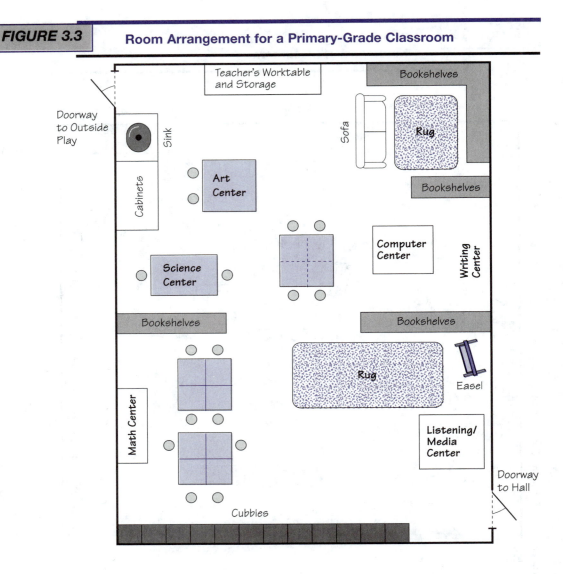

with tools and water, and a block area with hollow blocks, unit blocks, and block accessories. A super unit is about eight times as effective in holding children's attention as a simple unit; a complex unit is about four times as effective.

In analyzing your own room plans, count the variety of possible activities and the amount of things to do per child. Table 3.1 may help you analyze your own space. It shows Kritchevsky and Prescott's (1969, p. 13) analysis, in which the number of play spaces represents the number of children

TABLE 3.1

Analysis of Play Spaces

Number of Play Units	Type of Unit	Number of Play Spaces
12 vehicles	Simple	12
1 rocking boat	Simple	1
1 tumble tub	Simple	1
1 jungle gym with boxes and boards	Complex	4
1 dirt area plus scoop trucks	Complex	4
1 equipped sand table with water	Super Unit	8
	Total Play Spaces = 30	

Source: Kritchevsky and Prescott 1969, p. 13.

who can comfortably play in a given unit. Divide the total play spaces by the number of children to find the ratio of play spaces to children. If there are at least two play spaces for each child, children will be much more likely to find play spaces for themselves without teacher help than if the ratio were smaller. If the number of play spaces is less than the number of children, children will have difficulty finding something to do, other than grabbing something from someone else. An analysis of your room will provide information about whether there are adequate activities for the number of children and how you might rearrange the environment to make it more complex, if you need to add play spaces.

Harms (1970) suggests that, in addition to assessing the environment for the complexity of play spaces, teachers should consider the following questions:

- Can quiet and noisy activities go on without children disturbing one another? Is there an appropriate place for each?
- Is a variety of material available on open shelves for the children to use when they are interested? Are materials on shelves well spaced for clarity?
- Are materials stored in individual units so that children can use them alone without being forced to share with a group?
- Are activity centers defined so that children know where to use the materials?
- Are tables or rug areas provided for convenient use of materials in each activity center?
- Is self-help encouraged by having materials in good condition and always stored in the same place?
- Are cushioning materials used to cut down extraneous noise—rug under blocks, pads under knock-out bench?

- Are setup and cleanup simple? Are these expected parts of the child's activity?
- Is the children's work displayed attractively at the child's eye level?
- Do the children feel in control of and responsible for the physical environment? (pp. 305–306)*

In assessing the environment for a primary-grade classroom, the teacher must think about adequate space and materials for completion of projects such as a study of animals or birds. Some questions to ask about a primary environment include:

1. Can a child or small group get materials (paper, markers, scissors, and so on) and find a space to work comfortably?
2. Is it possible to move around the room without disturbing the work of others?
3. Is there a quiet place for a child or small group to read or think quietly?
4. Is the furniture arrangement flexible enough to allow moving from large group to small group to individual instruction without major disruptions and loss of time?
5. Are necessary items (such as a pencil sharpener) placed in the room so that a child needing to use them can do so without disturbing others?
6. Have the children been involved in solving the problems they encounter in getting their work done?

INSTRUCTIONAL MATERIALS

Materials for the classroom can be quite expensive. In addition to purchasing materials, most teachers ask for contributions from parents, go to garage sales, and scrounge materials from community sources. For example, some teachers get boxes and scrap paper from businesses that generate numerous computer printouts or wood scraps from local construction sites or cabinet shops.

The following guidelines will be helpful when you are selecting materials for the classroom:

1. Choose materials that can be used for more than one experience. Single-use materials like windup toys do not invite children to use them over and over, each time in a new or creative manner.
2. Select materials sturdy enough to withstand use by many active children.

* From Thelma Harms, "Evaluating Settings for Learning," *Young Children* 25 (May 1970): 304–309. Used with permission of NAEYC.

3. Select materials that serve many instructional purposes, such as small blocks, which can be used for constructing, for counting, for sorting by color, for arranging into patterns, and so on.

4. Select materials that can be used by children of varying ages and abilities. Sand, for example, can be used by very young children, who like to feel it and pour it from container to container. Older preschoolers can use sand to compare quantities and to measure. Primary-age children will be more sophisticated in their sand play. Barbour, Webster, and Drosdeck (1987) report observing one group of second-graders creating a desert environment after listening to their teacher read *The Desert Is Theirs* (Baylor 1970).

5. Choose safe materials; those with broken parts or rough edges should be discarded.

Learning Areas

One common technique for organizing instructional materials in classrooms is to place materials into learning centers or **learning areas.** Use of the phrase *learning centers* is sometimes criticized because it seems to imply that learning only takes place in those specific centers. The assumption underlying this discussion is that learning takes place all over and outside the classroom.

Some materials will not be appropriate for all age groups. The teacher must select those most appropriate for his group of students.

Basic furniture in any classroom should include tables and chairs of appropriate size, shelf units, storage units, an adult-sized rocking chair, sofas, child-sized rocking chairs, floor pillows, and a full-length mirror. The following lists include additional materials that teachers in preschool and primary grades have found to be useful. Teachers will also want to provide other materials to enhance the presentations of specific topics or themes.

Dramatic Play
- Child-sized kitchen equipment (with pots and pans)
- Dishes and silverware
- Tables and chairs
- Telephones
- Child-sized ironing board and iron
- Child-sized cleaning equipment (brooms, mops, dustpan, and so on)
- Assorted dolls
- Doll clothes
- Doll bed, carriage
- Doll house, furniture
- Assorted tubs, buckets, dishpans
- Assorted dress-up clothing and costumes

Blocks
- Blocks (unit and hollow)
- Block accessories (people, cars, safety signs, and so on)
- Small blocks (sets of cubes, small colored blocks)
- Sturdy wooden vehicles (cars, trucks, boats, planes, tractors, fire engines, buses, helicopters)

Art
- Adjustable easels
- Brushes (half-inch to one-inch widths)
- Liquid tempera paint (in a variety of colors)
- Painting smocks (purchased or homemade)
- Crayons
- Colored chalk
- Clay
- Scissors
- Glue, paste
- Paper (glazed for finger painting, newsprint, white drawing paper, construction paper in a variety of colors, tissue paper)
- Drying rack for paintings
- Miscellaneous supplies (fabric scraps, rickrack, yarn, ribbon, glitter, buttons, natural materials)

The phrase *learning area* will be used to indicate a specific location where related materials are arranged in a classroom. The basic learning areas in early childhood classrooms include areas for art, music, library/listening/writing activities, blocks, dramatic play, science/discovery activities, manipulatives/mathematics/games, woodworking, sand and water tables, and quiet activities. If space and equipment allow, an area for physical education is also important. These areas should reflect the children's ages, development, growing abilities, and changing interests; learning areas are not static.

See the box on these pages for an overview of what materials and equipment should go in the basic learning areas. The following sections will discuss these areas in more detail.

Library/Listening/Writing
- Computer and printer
- Typewriter
- Paper (various colors, sizes, shapes) and writing instruments (pencils, markers)
- Tape recorder, tapes, books with tapes
- Record player
- Flannelboard with stand and flannel pieces
- Books (professional and published by classroom authors)
- Magazines

Manipulatives/Games
- Hand puppets
- Puzzles
- Games (Lotto, checkers, chess, dominoes, Candy Land, Chutes and Ladders, Hi-Ho Cherry O, and so on)
- Beads and strings
- Sewing cards
- Manipulative materials (ranging from stacking rings to very complex materials)
- Tinkertoys (regular size and large size)
- Lego blocks, bristle blocks

Science/Discovery
- Aquarium
- Terrarium
- Magnets of various kinds
- Magnifying glasses
- Prism
- Metric measuring equipment, test tubes, slides, petri dishes
- Pattern blocks
- Pegs and pegboards
- Geoboards
- Geoblocks
- Base 10 blocks
- Unifix cubes
- Scales (balance and other types)
- Rhythm instruments
- Sandbox
- Water table with top
- Workbench with equipment

Physical Education
- Balance beam
- Tumbling mat
- Rocking boat
- Steps
- Walking boards
- Jungle gym
- Fabric tunnel
- Sawhorses (sturdy metal)
- Climbing ladder, climbing rope
- Balls of various sizes
- Ropes
- Hula hoops
- Bowling set
- Outdoor equipment (wheeled toys, gardening tools, sandbox)

Art

Teachers who want to encourage growth in art will think carefully about the materials and classroom environments that encourage participation in art activities. If the goals of an art program are to be achieved, materials for many art experiences must be readily available to children. In choosing a place in the classroom for art, consider sources of light and access to water. An area with a sink is ideal, so children can clean up easily, but a container of warm water will serve if no sink is available. Low shelves for storage of materials, easels for painting, and tables for working with other materials are also important. Traffic patterns must be considered when deciding where the art area will be located. If the area cannot be in a corner, other pieces of furniture can be used to isolate the space so that children do not walk through it to get from one part of the classroom to another.

Teachers can be creative in designing storage for supplies. Lasky and Mukerji (1980) report some creative storage solutions they have observed:

- Label cardboard or plastic shoe boxes and arrange them on bookshelves, windowsills, or counter tops that children can reach. Simple pictures can be labels for young children.
- Make adjustable shelves with cinder blocks to support lumber or heavy corrugated board (Tri-Wall).
- Place plastic dishpans or attractively covered cartons on top of children's coatracks for storing teachers' supplies.
- Cover a wall area with pegboard and suspend heavy shopping bags or see-through plastic bags from hooks inserted in the board. Hang smocks in the same fashion.
- Screw metal coat hooks into wooden moldings for suspending storage bags or smocks.
- Use the back of the piano or bookcase for hanging a shoe bag. Its pockets can hold many small items.
- Pierce an inverted small cardboard box or egg carton for use as a handy scissor or brush rack.
- Attach a roll of burlap, felt, or strip of cork to a vertical surface which children can reach. Keep a supply of needles threaded with yarn inserted in this oversize pincushion.
- Use divided frozen food trays or a revolving lazy Susan to hold miscellaneous small items.
- Make excellent containers for crayons or chalk out of discarded berry baskets or margarine cups. A label or clip clothespin painted the color of the contents helps children locate colors.
- Use small detergent or cosmetic bottles as dispensers for paint or glue purchased in quantity. (p. 30)*

Setting up an art area also includes deciding on smocks and floor coverings that will help children be most comfortable as they explore art materials. Smocks can be made from plastic or from old shirts. The point is to protect the children's clothing so that they are free from the worry of getting their clothes dirty. Floor coverings should be tile, if possible, so that floors can be cleaned easily (see Figure 3.4). Floors can be covered with newspapers to aid in cleanup. Materials for cleanup—water, sponges, a small broom and dustpan—should also be readily available to the children.

In selecting materials for art experiences, teachers must think about developmental appropriateness and possibilities for multiple uses. Chalk, markers, and crayons should be easy to grasp and should not break easily.

* From Lila Lasky and Rose Mukerji, *Art Basic for Young Children* (Washington, DC: National Association for the Education of Young Children, 1969). Used with permission of NAEYC.

Children should be allowed to use materials in a variety of ways. For example, some teachers only allow children to use crayons as they would pencils. But the wrappers can be removed from crayons so they can be rubbed across the surface of a paper on their sides. The fewer rules that are attached to materials, the more children will be encouraged to think for themselves and be creative in using them.

Just because art materials are arranged in one place in the classroom does not mean that art experiences cannot take place in other areas. Be open to a variety of places and possibilities for art activities. In nice weather, children might be offered the chance to do art outside; for example, they might do rubbings on outside surfaces. They might also choose to draw in other places in the classroom. On the other hand, even though art activities are not limited to one area of the room, it is convenient for all the supplies to be stored together in the art area so that children always know where to find

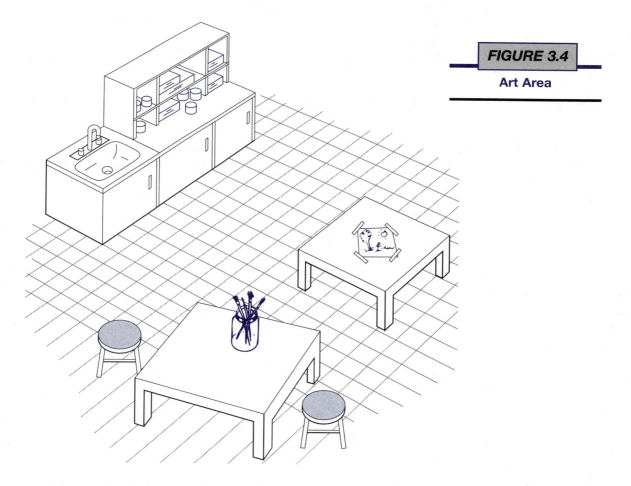

FIGURE 3.4

Art Area

what they need. Figure 3.4 on page 79 is a sketch of an art area that illustrates some of the suggestions in the preceding paragraphs.

Music

A piano is often the center of the music area. If you are lucky enough to have a piano and can play a simple tune, you can use it in many different ways to encourage children's music skills. Although a piano is still very valuable in an early childhood classroom, many teachers today use guitars and autoharps. These instruments are much easier to play and allow the teacher to face the children while playing. Still, many teachers like to have record players or tape recorders in the music area, to be used in group music experiences or by individual students.

Exploration of music can be encouraged by making a limited number of musical instruments available to children. If the classroom is equipped with a piano, a low shelf area near the piano is adequate for storing other selected instruments. A listening center with headphones gives children opportunities to listen to records and tapes without disturbing the rest of the class. Teachers should be aware that many children starting school today have no experience with records. They only know about compact discs and cassette tapes—a sign of the changing times!

The teacher might also keep a file of songs that children know, as well as charts of the lyrics. When these materials are made available, children can select songs for group singing or can review songs they especially like.

Usually, the space used for movement experiences is used for other purposes during other parts of the day. If possible, a space can be provided for movement during the time children choose their own activities. A shelf with scarves, hula hoops, large circles made of elastic (often known as *Chinese jump ropes*), a small drum, and ankle bells will encourage explorations of movement.

Library/Listening/Writing

An area for language arts activities should be located in a quiet part of the classroom and should have open shelves for storing books and a table for writing activities. Children may or may not need chairs for the listening center; sometimes the unit can be placed so that children sit on the floor to use it. It is better to display books standing up, with their covers showing, than to store them stacked on a shelf. Storing books standing up takes more space than stacking them, but children are much more likely to be enticed to choose a book if they can see its front cover. Since the number of books that can be displayed at once in this manner is limited, the books on display will need to be rotated frequently and selected to support topics of study.

In addition to a table for writing, a storage area for different writing papers and writing instruments is necessary. Pencils, pens, markers, and so on should be stored in small baskets or cans to make it easy for children to choose the ones they need. Paper in different colors and sizes should be available and can easily be stored in open boxes. Dictionaries should also be kept in this area. Picture dictionaries are especially useful for young writers. Children's personal dictionaries can also be kept in a basket in the writing area.

Typewriters and computers can also be housed in the library/listening/writing area. Children working with such equipment need the same supplies (word lists, dictionaries, and the like) that other writers need, so it is sensible to locate such equipment in this area. Use of typewriters and computers can generate quite a lot of talking and interaction, so they should be placed where students using them will disturb those in the quiet reading area as little as possible.

Blocks

Blocks require storage shelves and a large floor area for construction. A smooth carpet can help reduce the noise in this area and will not interfere with balancing the blocks. Larger blocks, such as hollow blocks, can be stored directly on the floor rather than on shelves. As Hirsch (1984) reminds us, the block storage area should be neither too neat nor too messy. If it's too neat, children will be intimidated and worry about cluttering the area when they use the materials; if it's too messy, children will find it difficult to locate the exact blocks they need, which is frustrating. Unit blocks should not be stored in carts or boxes. Such storage makes finding the needed block almost impossible and encourages children to toss the blocks back into the box, thereby denting them and reducing their useful life.

You will have to decide if you want to mark the block shelves (for example, with silhouettes of the blocks to be stored on each shelf) or if you want the children to determine the storage. Children do learn to recognize the shapes of the blocks and match them to the silhouettes, but they learn more about size relationships and classification when they are responsible for making storage decisions. Figure 3.5 on page 82 illustrates a block area.

Dramatic Play

The dramatic play area is often called the *housekeeping corner* or the *doll corner.* It is an area that will reflect the development and changing interests of the children as they grow. For example, threes and fours may need child-sized kitchen equipment, dishes and pans, dolls and doll beds, and other materials for acting out the roles in a family. As children grow and develop, they are able to assume the roles of people outside the family. Although they may still enjoy the kitchen equipment, they will often use the dramatic play area to act out roles of people in such locations as a grocery store, a gas station, a beauty or barber shop, a doctor's office, a hospital, an airport, or other areas that are part of their experience.

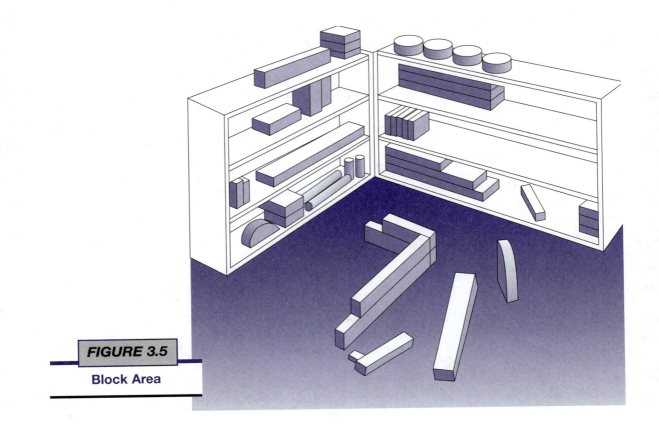

FIGURE 3.5

Block Area

The teacher will need to be flexible in providing the materials and assistance to support children's ideas. Primary-grade children often use this area for dramatizing characters in stories they have heard or read. They will need a variety of costumes, dress-up clothes, and props to support their play as their knowledge expands. If the dramatic play area stays the same throughout the year, then the teacher will need to take special steps to encourage children to develop and expand their interests.

Science/Discovery

Science activities do not take place only in the science or discovery area, of course, but the tools for investigations are kept on shelves in this area. Most teachers also like to have a table where interesting displays can be arranged and where children can explore materials—plants, soils, rocks, shells, leaves, or whatever. The area should be equipped with shelves that contain magnets, magnifying glasses, measurement containers, and other materials for investigating scientific topics. Teachers often include an invention corner in this area, where old appliances such as television sets, radios, toys, clocks, and toasters can be dismantled and reassembled, perhaps even using the parts to create new objects.

Manipulatives/Mathematics/Games

The math area is another area that will need to change to meet the needs and interests of children. This area should be the storage place for puzzles, beads, sewing cards, and other materials designed to help younger children develop fine motor skills. Older children will still be interested in puzzles and manipulative games and will also begin using pattern blocks, Unifix cubes, base 10 blocks, and other manipulatives used in mathematics. All ages will need construction toys and tabletop blocks. Games designed for individuals or small groups are often stored in this area. Playing cards, dice, and other game materials should also be available here; children will not only play with them but will use them for inventing games. This area needs shelves for storage and a table on which to work with the materials.

Woodworking

Woodworking areas require a workbench, storage areas for wood scraps, and shelves or a pegboard for holding tools. Young children who have not had much experience with woodworking are often satisfied with a sturdy log or other large piece of wood into which they can hammer nails. Children do not necessarily need to be able to make something until they have had more experience. Tools should be real tools designed on a small scale and sturdy enough to work well. Saws should really cut wood, and hammers should really drive nails.

Sand and Water Tables

Good-quality sand and water tables are available from supply catalogs, but they are expensive. A sand table can be constructed by adding a frame to the edge of a low table. Sometimes teachers substitute rice or cornmeal for sand in order to make cleanup easier. However, in addition to the fact that some teachers may be reluctant to use food in activities that render it inedible, neither of these materials has the same qualities that sand offers. For example, children cannot add water to these materials and mold them.

Many sand and water tables are equipped with covers so they can be used for other purposes when not being used for sand and water play. Accessories for sand and water tables depend on the developmental level of the children using them. Younger children may only pour and scoop, so precise measuring equipment is not needed. Older children will need materials to make measuring, comparing, and other investigations possible. Storage for accessories is often in boxes under the tables.

Water tables are more difficult to make than sand tables. The newest models of water tables are made of clear plastic and are often round with drains in the bottom that allow for easy draining and cleaning. Teachers often substitute a tub or a child's wading pool for a water table. These substitutes are better than not having water tables, but because children lean over them rather than stand around them and could easily fall in, even more supervision is required. The water in water tables should be replaced daily, so draining and filling conditions should be considered when purchasing a table. Water play accessories should include objects for filling and pouring, tubes and connectors, and materials that sink and float. Specific materials can be added to sand and water tables to help children explore topics in the curriculum.

Physical Education

An area where children can use a tumbling mat and engage in other physical activities is important. Some teachers like to place equipment that encourages gross motor development around the room, rather than in one area, because it takes up so much space. For example, balance beams and tunnels can be placed so that children can use them to get from one area of the room to another. Physical development is enhanced with bean bags, Velcro darts, Nerf balls, tunnels, bowling pins and balls, and so on. These materials should be stored on shelves or in a closet near an area large enough for children to use them without disturbing the work of others.

Quiet Area

Every classroom needs a small area where a child can go to be alone for a time. This area needs no special equipment—perhaps just a chair or a floor pillow. Some teachers like to make the quiet area inviting with flowers (nothing elaborate, just one or two), a piece of sculpture, or a drape of fabric. A child should be able to take a game or a book to this quiet area whenever she needs to.

Specialized Learning Areas

Some learning areas are set up for specific purposes and are not designed to be part of the classroom all year. Such specialized centers might be used for activities such as following up on stories, sorting and classifying objects, and demonstrating skills.

Activities to follow up on stories include placing pictures from the story in correct sequence, listening to a tape recording of the story while following along in the book, drawing a picture of a favorite part of the story, and so on. Sorting and classifying or problem-solving centers might offer collections to be sorted and explained (shells, keys, leaves, and so on) or materials to be grouped (paper and pencils, stamps and envelopes, keys and locks). Skill activities might be finding pictures of sets of objects whose names rhyme or finding the matching cylinders in a sound game. (Canisters from 35 mm film containing beans, rice, nails, stones, or other materials and having the lids taped on work well for this activity.)

Many magazines for teachers describe learning activities such as these. Teachers have to decide how they fit the program goals, if they suit the individual needs of children, and if so, where to locate the activities in the room.

Storage Areas

Each classroom needs an area in which materials not currently in use can be stored. A closet lined with shelves is ideal. If no storage facilities are built into the classroom, perhaps a storage unit can be purchased from a school supply firm. If the room contains no closet and a unit cannot be purchased, the teacher may have to improvise a storage area in one corner. Fabric can be used to cover the fronts of shelf units so that the contents are out of sight.

Beginning the Year

Teachers can begin the year by arranging materials in basic areas, knowing that they will make changes as soon as the children actually begin to work in the classroom. Teachers should try to simplify areas so that only the very basic materials and equipment are available for the first few days or weeks of the schoolyear. Materials that are easy to put away should be used until the children learn the routines of cleaning up work areas. Some materials should also be kept back initially and brought out later to add interest and novelty throughout the year; for example, large blocks and a few unit blocks can be put out in the block center right away, but other unit blocks and accessories can remain put away for use later.

For the first few days of school, activities in the art center should be limited to the use of crayons, paper, and clay. Unless classroom assistance

THEORY INTO Practice

Assume that you have the basic furniture for your classroom and that you have been given $1,000 to buy other materials and equipment for it. Check the prices in catalogs from supply houses that sell early childhood equipment. Make a list of what you would buy with your money. Compare your list with those of others in your group. How are your lists similar and different? Discuss reasons for your choices.

DEVELOPMENTALLY APPROPRIATE PRACTICE

Reflect on different classroom environments you have observed in terms of what you now know about planning a learning environment:

- Do any elements of the classroom environment indicate developmentally appropriate practice? Why?
- Can a classroom environment be developmentally appropriate when the desks are arranged in rows, with each child facing the teacher's desk in the front of the room? Why?

- Could a more flexible furniture arrangement fail to be developmentally appropriate? Why?
- In addition to furniture arrangement, what else in the environment would indicate DAP? Why?

is available—such as a parent volunteer or paraprofessional who can help children learn where to find paint smocks and paint, where to place their paintings until they dry, and how to clean up the art area—paint and easels should be brought out only after children have learned to handle the materials in other areas. Similarly, such areas as music, water tables, and carpentry can be set up when the teacher knows the children better and feels they do not require such close supervision.

Managing Learning Areas

More often than not, children will distribute themselves among learning areas without any problems of overcrowding. If new materials are added, the teacher may have to help children solve the problem of who has a turn first. If some areas do not attract children, the teacher's responsibility is to determine what the area needs and why it is not interesting to the children. The youngest children will need teacher guidance in choosing areas for play; older preschoolers may be able to plan their activities more independently, with the help of a few guidelines for managing the learning areas; and primary-grade children can take most of the responsibility for distributing themselves.

Many teachers have an activity time when children first arrive for the day; this allows children to choose an area and begin their activities without waiting for everyone else to arrive. Other teachers begin activity time after a group meeting, during which they have reviewed the calendar or completed other discussions with the group. To avoid having everyone trying to get to an area at once, many teachers use some scheme for deciding who chooses first and how choices are made during the play period. Some teachers group children randomly into two or three groups and rotate the group that gets to choose first. For example, the groups might be labeled red, yellow, and blue; if the red group has first choice today, the yellow group will have first choice tomorrow, and the blue group, the day after.

Teachers of very young children should try to allow them to play where they choose. When their choices cannot be honored, then the teacher should suggest another area and perhaps play there with the children for a few minutes. Some teachers of older preschoolers manage the number of children in each area by posting a number that defines how many can be in that area at a time. A child is free to join others in that area if the number of children allowed will not be exceeded. For example, if the block area will hold six children comfortably, a "6" is posted on one of the shelves. A child coming to the block area must decide if she can play with the blocks, given the number of children already in the area.

Other teachers like to use a pegboard system (see Figure 3.6). A pegboard is prepared such that the learning areas are displayed down the left

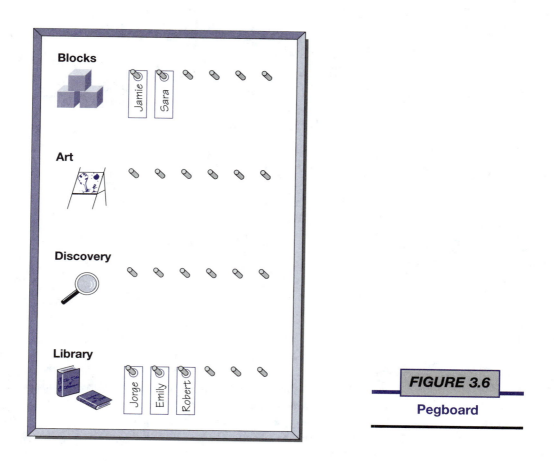

FIGURE 3.6

Pegboard

side. Pictures representing learning areas are added to aid the children in identifying each area. The number of pegs for each area is determined by the number of children that area can accommodate easily; pegs are placed in the row beside each picture to indicate how many children can use that area at one time. Again, if six children can use the block area, there will be six pegs beside the picture of blocks. Each child will have a tag with his name on it; he will place his tag on a peg when he wants to play with the blocks. If there are no empty pegs for the block area, he will have to make another choice. There should be more total pegs than there are children in order to give children as many choices as possible. And when an

PARENTS AND LEARNING ENVIRONMENT

■ To help parents understand the purposes of learning areas in the classroom, post a sign on the wall in each area that describes its goals. For example, in the block area, the sign could list intellectual goals, physical goals, and social goals that can be met through playing with blocks. Such signs can be useful to parents and other classroom visitors as they observe in the classroom.

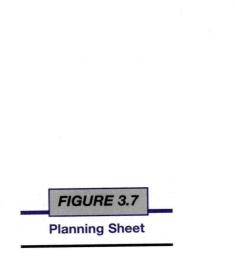

FIGURE 3.7

Planning Sheet

Name:_____
- ❏ Independent Reading/Writing
- ❏ Writing Conference with Teacher
- ❏ Reading Conference with Teacher
- ❏ Buddy Reading
- ❏ Special Activity
- ❏ Math Activity
- ❏ Outdoor Play
- ❏ Work on Project with Group
- ❏ Library
- ❏ Listening Center
- ❏ Games Center
- ❏ Special Lesson

area is not available for some reason, the pegs for that area can be removed for the day.

Such a pegboard system also allows some subtle guidance in helping children make new choices. For example, if a child always chooses the art area and the teacher feels that she has developed enough confidence to work in another area, the teacher might limit the number of art pegs so that the child will have to make another choice. The teacher should make sure that choices are available that will interest the child and perhaps go there with her to play for a few minutes.

Teachers may want to involve primary-age children in more formal planning. One way to do this is to provide each child with a planning sheet on which the scheduled events for the day are listed (see Figure 3.7). After reviewing the events, each child can check what he plans to do that day.

CHILDREN WITH SPECIAL NEEDS

Some areas and materials may need to be adapted for children with special needs, for instance, to make them wheelchair accessible or to add visual or auditory information to help all children work as independently as possible. Teachers should analyze the room arrangement and material storage areas in terms of the needs of all children in the class. Some spaces may need to be enlarged or more clearly defined to facilitate children's movement, some materials may need to be placed on more accessible shelves so they are within children's reach, or some materials may need to be organized so that children who have trouble hearing receive the maximum visual information.

Clutter may be distracting for children with perceptual difficulties. Some common supplies may need to be stored in several locations throughout the room so that children who have problems moving around have easy access to them. Room arrangements, materials, and schedules must be adapted for each group and for each individual child.

COMPUTERS IN EARLY CHILDHOOD PROGRAMS

In today's world, computers are a part of almost every early childhood program. Having a computer, or many computers, in the classroom may mean that the children are frequent and active users of computers, that children who are good get to use computers as a reward, that children use computers to reinforce skills lessons, or that the computers are gathering

Planning for the developmentally appropriate use of computers with young children is important.

dust because none of the adults feel comfortable using them. It is obvious that computers are not going away. So the question is: How will they be used in early childhood programs to benefit children?

The National Association for the Education of Young Children (NAEYC) has recognized that computers are common features in early childhood classrooms and thus issued a position statement on technology and young children. The statement assumes that computers can be misused, as can any other learning tool. The tenets are as follows:

1. A professional judgment by the teacher is required to determine if a specific use of technology is age appropriate, individually appropriate, and culturally appropriate. . . .
2. Used appropriately, technology can enhance children's cognitive and social abilities. . . .
3. Appropriate technology is integrated into the regular learning environment and used as one of many options to support children's learning. . . .
4. Early childhood educators should promote equitable access to technology for all children and their families. Children with special needs should have increased access when this is helpful. . . .
5. The power of technology to influence children's learning and development requires that attention be paid to eliminating stereotyping of any group and to eliminating exposure to violence, especially as a problem-solving strategy. . . .
6. Teachers, in collaboration with parents, should advocate for more appropriate technology applications for all children. . . .
7. The appropriate use of technology has many implications for early childhood professional development. (NAEYC 1996)*

The full text of the NAEYC statement can be found in Appendix A.

To maximize what the computer can contribute to the growth and development of children, Davidson and Wright (1994) suggest that "certain attitudes and assumptions about computers need to permeate the program" (p. 78). Namely:

1. Computer use is a social activity.
2. Computer use is a child-initiated and child-directed activity.
3. Computer software allows children to explore, experiment, and problem solve.

* From National Association for the Education of Young Children, "NAEYC Position Statement: Technology and Young Children—Ages Three through Eight" (adopted April 1996), *Young Children* 51(6): 11–16. Copyright © 1996 by NAEYC. Reprinted with permission.

4. Computers offer new learning opportunities when unexpected things happen.

5. Computers are one of many materials in a developmentally appropriate classroom. (p. 78)

Unlike adults, who usually work at computers alone, most children prefer to work at computers with other children. Language development is encouraged when a group gathers around the computer and the operator explains what she is doing. Of course, the nature of such interactions will depend on the options provided by the software. If the software is open ended and the user has many choices to make, then making and explaining those choices will encourage interchanges between children. Similarly, children using software need to be able to explore what will happen if they push this button or that button. Sharing discoveries is another avenue for children's communication. Kent and Rakestraw (1994) studied the language used by primary-grade children as they interacted with computers and found that "computers appear to be a valuable tool for facilitating language use within the classroom. When used appropriately, they can provide a genuine, real world context for children's exploration as we guide them through their journey to becoming competent literacy learners" (p. 336). Brett (1994) agrees that the computer could be a useful tool for developing both language and social skills.

Computers in early childhood classrooms should be one of many materials offered for children to explore and use as tools to accomplish their own goals. For example, children might spend some time in the library area, where there are many books from which to choose, but they might also spend time at the computer with some of the newer interactive storybook programs. A book presented on screen is not necessarily more abstract than a book held in the hand (except to those of us who have never read a book on computer). Children can use the computer to produce signs for their block play, just as they can write them with paper and pencil.

Computers are much more effective in a classroom than in a lab. A lab setting does not encourage the integration of computers into daily class activities nor does it encourage the use of computers to solve problems as children seek answers to their own questions (Shade 1996). If computers are best used in a classroom setting, then the question is, How many computers should a classroom have? That question can only be answered by the classroom teacher in terms of her individual children and curriculum goals. Is one computer enough? Is ten too many? In one second-grade classroom, the teacher chose five computers as optimum for her class. One of these computers is more powerful (and expensive) than the others and is available for all the children, if they need its particular capabilities to

THEORY INTO Practice

Observe for at least an hour in an early childhood classroom in which there is a computer. How many children used the computer? What did they do with it (games, drill and practice, problem-solving programs, graphics)? How did the teacher handle who could use it? Did equal numbers of boys and girls use it? What kinds of social interactions did you observe centered around the computer? From your observations, would you recommend that a center buy a computer? Why?

complete a project. The other four computers serve as "home" computers for designated groups of five children each, but in practice, any child can use any computer that is available. For example, a child might work on one computer but save his work to a disk and move it to his home computer when he is finished. This class also has a camera attached to the computer and portable keyboards for each group to use on field trips and so on.

Because the teacher of this second-grade class stresses collaborative work and projects chosen by individuals or small groups, this arrangement for using five computers seems to work beautifully. In classrooms for younger children, teachers often find that one or two computers are enough if units of computer time are made available as one of the choices for children. The optimal number of computers for each group is dictated by the program goals and individual differences in children.

Computers can be used in ways that are inappropriate for young children. For example, research has shown (Clements, Nastasi, and Swaminathan 1993) that the use of drill-and-practice programs can lead to children's loss of creativity. Some studies of such programs do show gain on measurements of reading-readiness skills (Clements, Nastasi, and Swaminathan 1993), but the importance of obtaining such skills is not consistent with a more wholistic view of how children learn to read and write. A better use of computers in early childhood classrooms is to create stories and pictures, as opposed to practicing discrete skills. Teachers can help individual children meet their own learning goals through adapting their interactions with computers (Samaras 1996).

Teachers will need to carefully evaluate software before purchasing it for their classrooms. Several guides and newsletters are available for helping teachers as well as parents make good decisions about their purchases. (Addresses of some of these resources can be found in Appendix B.) Isenberg and Rosegrant (1995, p. 29) suggest that teachers should think carefully about software that is purchased for classroom use. They recommend that teachers keep the following features in mind as they evaluate any computer program: *Technical features* include how function keys are used, how learners can manipulate the program, and whether learners' work can be saved or printed. *Learning features* include the voice or visual supports provided, the rate at which items are presented, and the amount and types of feedback available. *Content features* include what children learn—information, processes, or skills—and the level of difficulty within each area. *Developmentally appropriate features* include whether the program is suitable for the given children's ages, how complex the activities are, and whether children can be playful with the program. Teachers should use these evaluation criteria not only before ordering software but also after observing children actually using the programs.

PLANNING THE OUTDOOR ENVIRONMENT

Outdoor environments, like indoor environments, require planning if they are to achieve the best results for the children (Herlein 1995). Ideally, outdoor play areas should be adjacent to indoor areas, with easy access to toilet facilities. Outdoor areas should be securely fenced and should have covered sections for play on rainy or very hot days. Outdoor areas should include sections with different surfaces: grass, concrete, areas for digging, and sand. Play areas should include different terrains when possible; hills and inclines provide interesting terrains for riding toys, rolling downhill, and so on, as well as visual interest. Paved paths and large areas are ideal for wheel toys or riding toys. In addition to the physical exertion required by riding toys, they offer children many opportunities for dramatic play.

Apparatus for swinging, climbing, sliding, and crawling should also be provided in the outdoor environment. Some apparatus should have higher bars for swinging while hanging by the hands and lower bars for hanging by the knees or elbows. Studies have shown that children develop more upper-body strength when they play on playgrounds equipped with overhead ladders (Gabbard 1979). In selecting apparatus, the teacher should think about providing a balance of equipment so that children will use all the large muscles as they play. The hull of a rowboat or the body of an old car can stimulate dramatic play and offer something to climb on. Boards for walking and balance beams are also useful pieces of equipment.

Many playgrounds leave nothing for children to use in planning, arranging, or creating. Jones (1989) recommends that play areas have "loose parts" that children can move around and with which they can build and be creative. With movable equipment, children can construct their own play environment; boxes, boards, barrels, sawhorses, and short ladders work well. Tires and tubes are also useful for rolling around and stacking.

An outdoor play space should include a gardening area, a sandbox, a water play area or water table, a storage area for tools and toys, and tables or easels. (If need be, portable easels can be moved from the classroom for outside use.)

Having a gardening area does not mean that the entire area must be used for planting. At least some of the space should be reserved for impromptu digging. When children dig, they learn about the composition of soil, the differences between dry and damp soil, the insects and worms that

Planning for outdoor play is an important part of creating the best possible program for young children.

live in the soil, and the pieces of organic matter that decompose to produce soil. A garden that includes an area for planting and caring for the plants, in addition to a digging area, can extend many classroom experiences.

An outside sandbox has advantages that an indoor sand table cannot offer. Children can climb into a sandbox, sit in the sand while playing in it, and create play areas on a much larger scale. An outdoor sandbox should have a cover to keep the sand clean, preferably one that folds back in sections to make handling easier. In many areas of the United States, a sandbox also should have some kind of roof so that the sand does not get too hot or stay wet all the time. Baker (1966) observed that the sandbox was frequently the place children started playing while they watched the more vigorous play around them. When they gained enough confidence, they joined the more active play.

Opportunities for water play outdoors can be provided with a small wading pool or a water table. Pools of water must be carefully supervised. Children can use the water outside much as they do in the classroom—pouring, measuring, and comparing. The differences are that outside, much more splashing is acceptable, and water can be carried all over the play area. Practically everything outdoors can be "painted" with water. A few large paintbrushes and some buckets are essential water play accessories outdoors.

Finally, many fine arts activities can be provided outdoors if portable easels or tables are available for painting, creating collages, and other art activities. When the weather is pleasant outdoors, art experiences can be especially satisfying because children do not have to be as concerned about paint spills or drips. Cleanup is simple.

A shed for storing outdoor materials is a must. It can hold garden and digging tools, sandbox and water toys, riding toys, balls, and other materials used outdoors. Teachers tend to be much more relaxed about allowing children to dig in sand and mud when they know that the tools do not have to be clean enough to take back indoors when the play ends. A shed will also protect the toys and tools from exposure to the elements and prolong the life of materials.

Figures 3.8 and Figure 3.9 (on page 96) are illustrations of playground designs (Frost and Klein 1979). Analyze these playgrounds, employing the

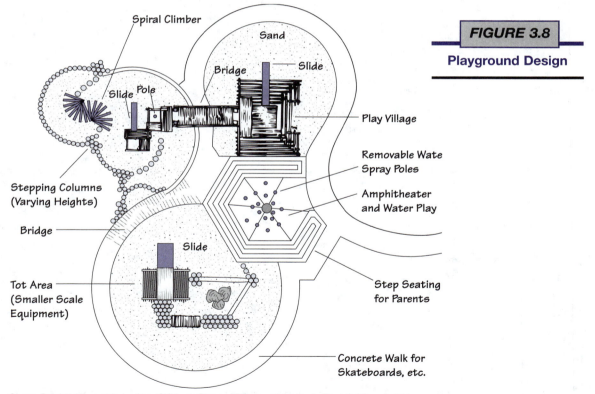

Source: Reprinted by permission from *Children's Play and Playgrounds* by Joe L. Frost and Barry L. Klein (Boston: Allyn and Bacon, 1979, p. 193; designed by Nan Simpson).

PLANNING THE OUTDOOR ENVIRONMENT

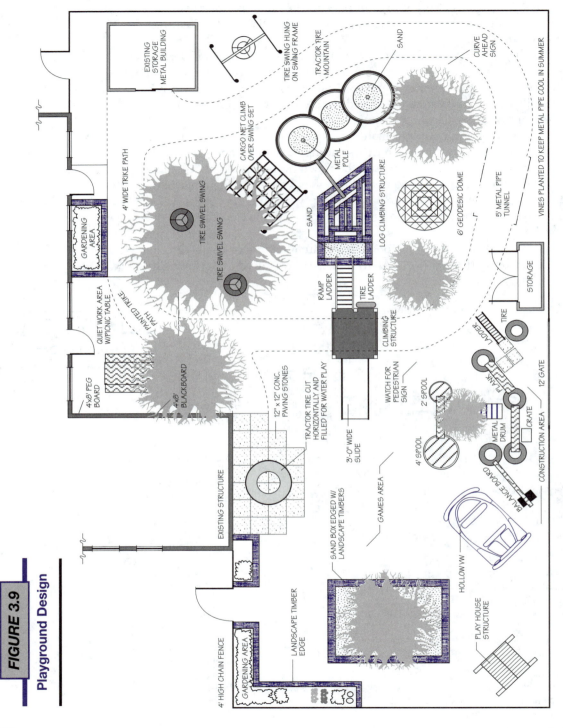

FIGURE 3.9

Playground Design

Source: Reprinted by permission from *Children's Play and Playgrounds* by Joe L. Frost and Barry L. Klein (Boston: Allyn and Bacon, 1979, pp. 94–95).

The following labels appear in the playground design:

- EXISTING STORAGE METAL BUILDING
- TIRE SWING HUNG ON SWING FRAME
- TRACTOR TIRE MOUNTAIN
- SAND
- CURVE AHEAD SIGN
- CARGO NET CLIMB OVER SWING SET
- 4' WIDE TRIKE PATH
- TIRE SWIVEL SWING
- TIRE SWIVEL SWING
- SAND
- METAL POLE
- LOG CLIMBING STRUCTURE
- 6' GEODESIC DOME
- 5' METAL PIPE TUNNEL
- VINES PLANTED TO KEEP METAL PIPE COOL IN SUMMER
- GARDENING AREA
- QUIET WORK AREA W/PICNIC TABLE
- PAINTED TRICE
- PATH
- RAMP LADDER
- TIRE LADDER
- CLIMBING STRUCTURE
- STORAGE
- 4×8' PEG BOARD
- 4×8' BLACKBOARD
- 12" × 12" CONC. PAVING STONES
- WATCH FOR PEDESTRIAN SIGN
- LADDER
- TIRE
- 12' GATE
- EXISTING STRUCTURE
- TRACTOR TIRE CUT HORIZONTALLY AND FILLED FOR WATER PLAY
- 3'-0" WIDE SLIDE
- 2' SPOOL
- METAL DRUM
- CRATE
- PLANK
- CONSTRUCTION AREA
- BALANCE BOARD
- 4' SPOOL
- GAMES AREA
- SAND BOX EDGED W/ LANDSCAPE TIMBERS
- HOLLOW VW
- 4' HIGH CHAIN FENCE
- GARDENING AREA
- LANDSCAPE TIMBER EDGE
- PLAY HOUSE STRUCTURE

same criteria that you used earlier for analyzing room arrangements. How well is the space used? What objectives will be met by each design? What traffic patterns do you predict?

PLANNING FOR SAFETY INSIDE AND OUT

In choosing any room arrangement or collection of instructional materials, one of the critical criteria is safety. Teachers must make every effort to provide a safe learning environment, both inside the classroom and on the playground. In addition to the safety considerations already mentioned for individual pieces of equipment, the following list will help you analyze the environment for safety:

A Safety Checklist

1. Check the environment, both inside and outside, for any hazards. Check electrical outlets and cords; make sure children cannot pull over any equipment (television sets, projectors, and so on); remove dangerous plants; cover sharp edges; make sure fences are sturdy and exit gates are childproof; and eliminate any other hazards to children's safety.

2. Practice emergency procedures on a regular basis. Children's and teachers' responses to fire drills (and in some areas, tornado and earthquake procedures) must become automatic.

3. Make sure that the classroom contains a fire extinguisher and that all staff (and children who are old enough) know how to use it.

4. All teachers and staff members should be trained in first aid and cardiopulmonary resuscitation (CPR). At minimum, one person with such training should be present at all times. Staff should be required to have special training for CPR with infants, if the program accepts children that young.

5. Post a list of the names of all children and a map of fire exit routes near each exit.

6. Keep a first aid kit adequately stocked at all times. Keep it in a specific place, so that any staff member can locate it quickly.

7. Keep an up-to-date list of emergency phone numbers (parents, relatives, doctors, and hospitals) for each child.

8. Keep the number for the nearest poison control center posted near the telephone.

9. Post a list of children's allergies (including reactions to wasp or bee stings), so that it can be checked before planning any food experiences or outdoor activities.

10. Keep a list by the door of the adults authorized to pick up each child. Do not release a child to any unauthorized person.

11. Make all posted information readily available to substitute teachers.

Teachers must consider a number of factors in assessing playground safety. Frost and Wortham (1988) devised the following checklist, which you may find helpful:

- A fence (minimum four feet high) protects children from potentially hazardous areas (e.g., streets, water).
- Eight to twelve inches of noncompacted sand, pea gravel, shredded wood, or equivalent material is in place under and around all climbing and moving equipment.
- Resilient surface is properly maintained (e.g., in place, noncompacted, free of debris).
- The equipment is sized to the age group served, with climbing heights limited to the reaching height of children standing erect.
- There are no openings that can entrap a child's head (approximately four to eight inches).
- Swing seats are constructed of lightweight material with no protruding elements.
- Moving parts are free of defects (no pinch, shearing, or crush points; bearings are not excessively worn).
- Equipment is free of sharp edges, protruding elements, broken parts, and toxic substances.
- Fixed equipment is structurally sound—no bending, warping, breaking, or sinking.
- Large equipment is secured in the ground, and concrete footings are recessed in the ground.
- All safety equipment (e.g., guard rails, padded areas, protective covers) is in good repair.
- The area is free of electrical hazards (e.g., unfenced air conditioners and switchboxes).
- The area is free of debris (e.g., sanitary hazards, broken glass, and rocks). (p. 24)*

The Americans with Disabilities Act (ADA) requires that playgrounds be accessible to children with disabilities and that schools and programs modify playgrounds to make them accessible. Sorohan (1995) suggests that the following elements should be considered when thinking about playground adaptations:

- *Support:* Some children need back supports to play in sandboxes or with spring toys.
- *Reach:* Avoid placing elements too high or too low for children in wheelchairs to reach.

* From Joe L. Frost and Sue C. Wortham, "The Evolution of American Playgrounds," *Young Children* 43 (July 1988): 19–28. Used with permission of NAEYC.

- *Diversity:* Think about materials that will enhance development of social and cognitive skills as well as gross motor skills. Materials that can be manipulated and those that require two or more children to play are both useful.
- *Cues:* Provide visual, tactile, and auditory cues to help children move around the playground safely.
- *Getting on and off:* Ramps and transfer platforms might be needed for some students. Think about equipment that will allow a child to return to his wheelchair without assistance after use.
- *Location:* Place playgrounds close to buildings for easier access.
- *Proximity:* Do not construct separate playgrounds for children with disabilities.
- *Independence:* Providing an aide to push a child in a wheelchair over an inaccessible surface does not meet the requirements for accessibility. The conditions must be provided that will enable the child to move independently, without assistance (adapted from Sorohan 1995, p. 30).

See also Appendix C, which presents a rating system for use in evaluating playgrounds for children ages three through eight (Frost 1996).

PARENTS AND PLAYGROUNDS

- ■ Invite parents to observe children playing on the playground. Provide a guide sheet that will help parents identify various kinds of play and activities.
- ■ Provide resources so that parents can read about what makes playgrounds challenging, fun, and safe for children of various ages.

CELEBRATING DIVERSITY

Teachers can show respect for the community and the cultures of children in their classrooms by asking for information and help from various school patrons and parents. Some special materials can be selected for learning areas that will help children feel more at home. For example, the dress-up center could include several pieces of clothing that are typical of that worn by certain ethnic groups in the community. Some traditional clothing may be too rare or expensive to use for children's play, but if it can be obtained, it will be valuable for the children. Pictures can be taken around the community and used as illustrations in student-made books or as posters for the classroom.

Play materials, such as puzzles and dolls, also need to reflect the various cultures of the community. If they are not available commercially, perhaps some members of the community would be willing to help make them. Sears and Medearis (1993) describe a project in which community members helped schools develop materials, art projects, science activities, and so on that were culturally appropriate for local Native American groups. With some effort, teachers could replicate the work of this project with their own local cultural groups.

CHAPTER SUMMARY

- Program goals and objectives are reflected in room arrangements and choices of materials and equipment.
- Basic learning areas in early childhood classrooms include art, music, library/listening/writing, blocks, dramatic play, science/discovery, manipulatives/mathematics/games, woodworking, sand and water, physical education, and quiet areas. These areas are designed to help children develop their interests; each should include storage areas for materials.
- Specialized learning centers are designed to help children master one activity or task. They are designed for temporary use in the classroom.
- Learning areas can be streamlined for the beginning of the schoolyear. Teachers must decide which areas and materials will be most important for children at the beginning of the year and which can be added later.
- Room arrangements help communicate to children what is expected of them and are related to attitudes and behaviors of the children.
- In planning room arrangements, teachers should consider multiple uses of space, the need for water, the need for quieter areas, and the need for areas where more noisy activities can take place.
- Environments can be analyzed in terms of the number of play spaces per child. This type of analysis will help teachers determine the complexity of the environment and what, if anything, should be done to change it.
- Teachers should try to select instructional materials that can be used for multiple experiences, can contribute to many instructional uses, are sturdy, and can be used by children of varying ages and abilities.
- Computers are increasingly likely to be included in programs for young children. Above all, teachers must think of computers as a tool for learning. Accordingly, software should be evaluated in terms of its appropriateness for the children and in terms of what is required of the learner in using it.
- Outdoor play environments require careful planning to ensure that the experiences and activities conducted outdoors will be as productive and satisfying as those conducted indoors.
- Regular classroom environments should be adapted as required to allow children with special needs to have access to different areas and materials.
- In selecting materials for their classroom, teachers must consider the diversity of the families represented in the schools. Instructional materials should reflect the variety of cultures in the community and also perhaps the world at large, regardless of the school population.

LANI L. HOLGATE
Oak Grove
Elementary School
MEDFORD, OREGON

Classroom Management Using Charts

In order to develop responsibility, help children recognize their names, provide a management system for using activities, and provide a meaningful reading experience, I use a pair of charts. One chart has all the children's names on it. The other one has the activities listed on it.

For the name chart, I write the names in two columns so all names are next to an edge of the chart. I put a sticker by any child's name who needs help recognizing his or her name.

On the other chart, I list the activities. I make this list color coded by writing each activity in a different color or combination of colors. I also cut out pictures of each activity from supply catalogs, or I draw a picture showing the activity. This way all children can "read" the chart.

My management system consists of color coding clothespins to coordinate with each activity. I limit the number of children who can use an activity by the number of clothespins I place on the chart. Each child chooses the activity he or she wants by taking a clothespin from the activity chart and placing it on his or her name. If the activity the child wants does not have a clothespin on it, he or she must choose something else. Responsibility for cleanup is also easier to manage because it is easy to see who participated in each activity. I do allow children to change activities, but they must clean up their first choice before changing their clothespin and their activity. Also, each child is responsible for his or her clothespin. No one can pick for someone else, and no one can take a clothespin off someone else's name.

This management system is easy and inexpensive, and it works. The main limitation is the size of the chart, but you can use more than one activity chart. I have also tried to eliminate the name chart by having children clip their clothespins on their shirts, but there are two drawbacks to this system: lost clothespins due to children forgetting to take off their clothespins, and my not being able to see readily who is using each activity.

4

PLAY
Learning at Its Best

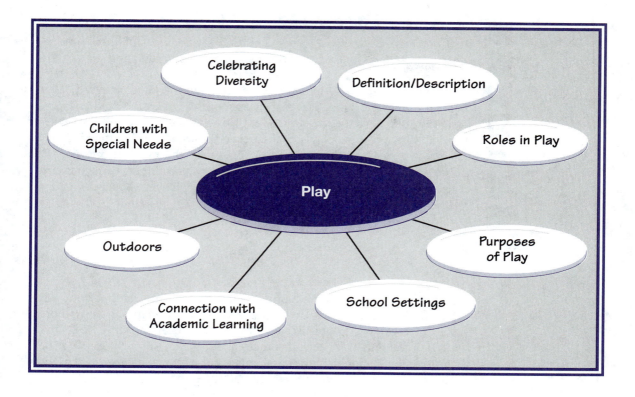

This morning, you are on your way to visit a local kindergarten to observe young children in a classroom setting. When you get there, you find that it is a warm and welcoming place and that the teacher is glad to have you visit. As you begin your observation, you see several children putting on costumes and pretending they are grown-ups. One child is playing the father, one the mother, and several pretend to be children in the family. When another child wants to join the group, she is asked to be the doctor for the sick child. You notice that several children have constructed a block structure in another part of the room. Another child is building a smaller structure without displaying much interest in the group structure. At a nearby table, three children are working with puzzles. Each child has a puzzle, and although the children are talking to each other about a variety of topics, each is completing his puzzle individually.

When the children go outside, there is more rough-and-tumble play than you expected. Many of the children spend most of their time in "chase" and "war" play. A few children dig in the garden and play in the sandbox, which is what you had expected to see.

You have many questions about the activities you have observed: Why does the teacher encourage play in the classroom? What are the children learning as they play? What is the purpose of play activities in the children's development? How are these play activities related to academic curriculum goals? You also wonder how the parents feel about their children "just playing" at school. The purpose of this chapter is to answer some of these questions and to help you make informed decisions about play in the school settings for which you will be responsible.

Teachers, parents, and administrators need continued support in their efforts to include play in the curriculum and to defend its use to those not as knowledgeable in early childhood education. Almy (1984) has published statements in several sources about the child's right to play. She writes that the distinguishing characteristics of play make it essential to the child's development. She believes that adults must provide opportunities for children to play and to learn from observations and actions as well as from being told things.

In a position paper approved by the Association for Childhood Education International (ACEI), Isenberg and Quisenberry (1988) state that "play—a dynamic, active and constructive behavior—is a necessary and integral part of childhood, infancy through adolescence." The ACEI also asserts that teachers must take the lead in articulating the need for play in children's lives, especially as a part of their school life.

DEFINING PLAY

Play in a school setting can be described on a continuum that runs from free play to guided play to directed play. *Free play* can be defined as play in which children have as many choices of materials as possible and in which they can choose how to use the materials (within bounds, of course; for example, they cannot hit others with the blocks). *Guided play* is defined as play in which the teacher has selected materials from which the children may choose in order to discover specific concepts. If the goal is to learn to classify objects as large or small, then the teacher will provide several sets of objects to play with that could be classified as such. *Directed play* is play in which the teacher instructs the children how to accomplish a specific task. Singing songs, engaging in fingerplays, and playing circle games are examples of directed play (Bergen 1988).

DESCRIBING PLAY

Social Play

Teachers who observe children playing will notice several different levels of involvement with other children in play episodes. In her classic study, Parten (1932) describes these levels as *solitary, onlooker, parallel, associative,* and *cooperative play.* Table 4.1 summarizes Parten's descriptions of levels of social play.

THEORY INTO Practice

Observe the play of three-year-olds, five-year-olds, and seven-year-olds. Record the play behaviors in the categories that Parten used (1932; see Table 4.1 below). Among the different age groups, do you observe differences in the number of categories of play and the amount of time spent in each category? Explain your answer.

TABLE 4.1
Levels of Social Play

Level	Description
Solitary Play	Play in which children play without regard for what other children around them are doing. A child may be constructing a tower with blocks and be completely oblivious to what other children in the room are doing.
Onlooker Play	Play in which the child who is playing individually is simultaneously observing those playing in the same area. The child may be talking to peers. Children who watch other children play may alter their own play behavior after watching. Children engaged in onlooker play may seem to be sitting passively while children around them are playing, but they are very alert to the action around them.
Parallel Play	Play in which several children are playing with the same materials, but each is playing independently. What one child does is not dependent on what others do. Children working puzzles are usually engaged in parallel play. They usually talk to each other, but if one leaves the table, the others continue playing.
Associative Play	Play in which several children play together but in a loosely organized fashion. Several children might decide to play "monsters," for example, and run around the playground, chasing each other. But there are no definite roles, and if one child does not run and chase, the others can continue to play.
Cooperative Play	Play in which each child accepts a designated role and is dependent on others for achieving the goals of the play. When children want to play "store," for instance, one child must accept the role of store clerk and others must be shoppers. If a child refuses to play unless she can be the storekeeper, the play episode will end.

Source: Based on Parten 1932.

Children of different ages exhibit different levels of social play. Very young children are not cognitively capable of assuming different roles and playing cooperatively. They do not possess enough information about roles or enough social skills to work together for a single purpose. Older children do not engage in cooperative play exclusively. They may engage in any of the levels of play; they simply have a much broader repertoire of possible play behaviors.

Play with Objects

There are levels of play with objects as well as levels of social play. Piaget (1962) and Piaget and Inhelder (1969) have described different types of play with objects, including practice play, symbolic play, games with rules, and games of construction. **Practice play,** or functional play, is play in which children explore the possibilities of materials. Even adults engage in practice play when the materials presented are new to them. For instance, children using dominoes in practice play would stack them and stand them on end. After playing with the dominoes for some time, children might begin to use them *symbolically.* They would use a domino to represent something else. Perhaps they would make a corral of blocks and pretend that the dominoes were cattle in the corral.

In a *game with rules,* children might play according to rules they have made up themselves or according to the rules that are generally agreed on

In their play, children explore the possibilities offered by objects and materials.

for playing the game. If the children were playing with dominoes, for example, they might decide that the rules were to match all the ends but not play the doubles across; if they know the conventional rules for playing dominoes and keeping score, they might follow those rules instead. Anyone who has ever tried to play a game with rules (such as Candy Land or Concentration) with a three- or four-year-old knows that a child this age will usually play the way she wants to and that following the rules is almost impossible.

Games of construction are described by Piaget as growing out of symbolic play "but tend later to constitute genuine adaptations (mechanical constructions, etc.) or solutions to problems and intelligent creations" (Piaget and Inhelder 1969, p. 59). Levels of object play depend on the children's maturity and experience. As children mature, they become more capable of using materials symbolically and of playing a game with accepted rules.

Vygotsky on Play

In their important work on the theories of Lev Vygotsky, Bodrova and Leong (1996) have summarized his views on play. In sum, play develops from the manipulative play of toddlers to the socially oriented play of older preschoolers and kindergartners and finally to games. Vygotsky would label as *play* behavior by toddlers in which they begin to use objects in imaginary situations and label the actions with words. For example, using a spoon to bang on a table is not play, but using a spoon to feed a teddy bear and asking the bear to eat is play. Most five-year-olds focus on the social roles of their play, rather than the objects. For example, they can pretend to have a pad of paper and pen for taking orders if they are playing "waiter" or "waitress." Games, as a type of play, emerge in children's play behavior around age five. Games involve explicit and detailed rules in which the imaginary situations are hidden. For example, soccer is a game in which the players agree not to use their hands, although they could use them (Bodrova and Leong 1996).

Vygotsky believes that play is extremely important in the child's development in three ways:

1. *"Play creates the child's zone of proximal development."* In a play setting, a child can control behavior such as attending to a task before she is able to control that behavior in another setting.
2. *"Play facilitates the separation of thought from actions and objects."* In play, the child can pretend that a block is a boat; this separation of object from meaning is critical to the development of abstract thinking.

3. *"Play facilitates the development of self-regulation."* In developing self-regulation, children in play are required to make their behavior match the role they have accepted. For example, a child playing "dog" can stop barking or sit still on command (quotes from Bodrova and Leong 1996, p. 126).

According to Vygotsky:

> Play creates a zone of proximal development in the child. In play, the child always behaves beyond his average age, above his daily behavior; in play it is as though he were a head taller than himself. As in the focus of a magnifying glass, play contains all developmental tendencies in a condensed form and is itself a major source of development. (1978, p. 102)

Sociodramatic Play

Sociodramatic play is of particular interest to researchers. Smilansky (1971) has studied sociodramatic play and methods for facilitating such play and observed that it has the following elements:

1. *Imitative role play.* The child undertakes a make-believe role and expresses it in imitative action and/or verbalization.
2. *Make-believe in regard to objects.* Movements or verbal declarations are substituted for real objects.
3. *Make-believe in regard to actions and situations.* Verbal descriptions are substituted for actions and situations.
4. *Persistence.* The child persists in a play episode for at least ten minutes.
5. *Interaction.* There are at least two players interacting in the framework of the play episode.
6. *Verbal communication.* There is some verbal interaction related to the play episode. (pp. 41–42)

Sociodramatic play is especially important in the development of creativity, intellectual growth, and social skills. Not all children will have had experience with sociodramatic play. Therefore, teachers may need to assume more responsibility in fostering such play with these children. Teachers can look carefully for the elements of sociodramatic play and encourage it by intervening and helping children achieve any missing elements.

Research findings support the value of sociodramatic play:

> A vast amount of research indicates that imaginative play (symbolic play) is a significant causal force in the development of a multitude of abilities, including creativity, sequential memory, group cooperation, receptive vocabulary, conceptions of kinship relationships, impulse con-

trol, spatial perspective-taking skill, affective perspective-taking skill, and cognitive perspective-taking skill. (Gowen 1995, p. 78)

The ability to take on the role of another person and to shift perspective are important basic skills for academic learning. For some children, sociodramatic play occurs if time is allowed for it; for others, the teacher may have to be much more involved to get children to participate. This can be accomplished by providing time and often props to get children started in sociodramatic play. The dramatic play area or housekeeping center are often settings that encourage sociodramatic play by providing costumes, furniture, and other props. If children have ideas about play themes, the teacher can help them carry out these ideas by providing needed props.

Teachers might consider asking parents to help them collect materials that could be used for any number of play situations. Materials for given situations might then be stored in individual boxes so that they are available when the children's interests dictate use. Such boxes might include materials for playing "repair person," "beauty shop," "office," and so on. Myhre (1993) suggests prop boxes containing materials to recreate a bakery, a flower shop, and a beach party, as well as a jewelry and accessory box and "dentist," "police," and "firefighter" boxes.

In addition to providing time and props, the teacher might have to model appropriate play behavior for children with little or no experience in sociodramatic play. He may have to assume a role and play it for a few minutes, at least long enough to demonstrate the behavior so that children will understand and be able to perform the behavior themselves. The teacher might also suggest roles others could play or ask questions to get the children started on a play episode. The line between assisting children and dominating play is a fine one. Teachers must develop skills in listening to and responding to children, following their lead, rather than imposing their ideas about what children should be playing.

Reifel and Yeatman (1993) urge teachers to think of play in broader categories than those described by Parten and Piaget. They note, for example, that rough-and-tumble play, word play, and jokes are not covered in either theorist's description of play, although these behaviors are certainly part of children's play experiences. A play episode may begin with one type of play, move to another, and then back again, so teachers need to think about how children are relating to materials and to each other throughout play episodes, rather than make quick judgments based on short, isolated observations.

Finally, teachers should look for opportunities to encourage sociodramatic play that stems from real events in children's lives. For example, suppose one of the children has been in the hospital. When she returns to school and tells of her experience, the children will likely be anxious to play "being in the hospital." The teacher might ask some questions to help the children think about what they need to play "hospital" and then help them find appropriate props, such as clipboards to use for patient charts, stethoscopes, boxes for furniture, and so on.

ROLES IN PLAY

Role of the Child

Children in free-play situations choose to become involved in the play, are active in their involvement, can suspend reality, have no extrinsic goals for their activities, and bring their own meaning to the play (Spodek, Saracho, and Davis 1987).

Play Is Personally Motivated

Interview several children (ages three to eight) about what they like to play. Also observe as many of these children playing at home or at school as is possible. How do children define play for themselves? Do their verbal accounts match what they actually do in play situations? What can you conclude about the developmental trends in play?

In order for an activity to be called *play*, the player must choose to participate. If a child chooses an activity, it is usually play, although what is being done may appear to be work. For example, a child may load up a wheelbarrow with sand, move it across the playground to a new sandbox, and dump it. Similarly, children often "work" for hours gathering materials and building forts. The difference between play and work is that a play activity is self-chosen: The child controls how long she will participate and defines the goals of the activity. If an adult assigns the task, he has control of the goals and the time frame; therefore, even if the child has fun doing it, the task is not play. Play is always pleasurable to the participants. The feelings may be the satisfaction of having achieved internal goals or the pure joy of running freely. The player experiences pleasure in play.

Play Is Active

All play experiences require some active involvement on the part of the player. Play is *not* a passive activity, such as watching television, although play does not require active physical involvement. Children are playing when they participate in a "tea party" or investigate the hardness of rocks. Children playing are engaged in thinking, organizing, planning, and interacting with the environment. If the involvement is passive, then the activity is probably not play.

Play Is Often Nonliteral

Children at play can suspend reality, usually with the magic words "let's pretend." Time, setting, and characters involved in play can be negotiated at the moment and are not tied to reality. They need not even be possible; children might pretend to fly, to be from outer space, or to be monsters.

Play Has No Extrinsic Goals

Suppose a child is arranging and rearranging a set of letters on a magnetic board. If this task has been assigned for the purpose of helping her learn alphabetical order, it is not play. If the child is arranging the letters to suit goals that are her own, then it is play. In playing, the process, or means, not the end result, is most important. The *outcome* of play is not as important as the *participation* in it.

Players Supply Meaning to Play

Children sometimes explore or use materials in ways specified by others, but when they play, they provide their own interpretations for materials. A child might use base 10 blocks to build models of numbers if directed to do so by an adult. But if allowed to use the materials freely during another portion of the day, the child might use the blocks to build houses or roads.

Play Has No Extrinsic Rules

If an activity is to be considered play, the players must be able to alter the rules of the activity as needed. In a game of tag, for example, the players negotiate where the "safe" areas will be. Similarly, children playing with blocks may establish rules about spaces for building, but these rules are negotiated by the players.

Roles of the Teacher

The roles of the teacher in play within the classroom setting are very important. The teacher must be an observer, an elaborator, a model, an evaluator, and a planner of play (Bjorkland 1978).

Observer

In *observing,* the teacher should watch children's interactions with other children and with objects. He should observe the length of time that children can maintain play episodes, and he should look for any children who have trouble playing or joining play groups. These observations should then be used in planning additional play experiences, in making decisions about whether to enter play situations, and in making assessments of the play of individual children. In a review of studies concerning the effects of the physical environment on children's behavior in preschool settings, Phyfe-Perkins (1980) concludes that if a setting is to provide support for developmentally appropriate activities, the teacher must engage in systematic observation of children at play.

Elaborator

Another aspect of the teacher's role is that of *elaborator.* If the children are playing "going to the hairdresser," the teacher might help them collect items that could be used to represent those found at a hairdresser's shop. She might find photographs or magazine illustrations that would help the children construct a beauty salon. The teacher might even join in the play briefly and ask questions that would guide the children in thinking through their roles or their conceptions of a trip to the hairdresser. If older children were involved in a study of insects, the teacher might supply a film or videotape of insects so that the children could recreate insect movement or sounds in their play.

Modeler

Teachers who value play are often *modelers* of appropriate behaviors in play situations. For instance, a teacher may choose to sit in the block area for a brief time and join children in building in order to model ways in which the blocks might be used. Or she might choose to join dramatic play in order to model behaviors that are useful in entering a play group and responses that are useful for helping play continue. Sometimes, the teacher might model play behaviors that will get a play episode started or back on track if it has gone in a direction she considers negative. For example, children playing characters from a television program might begin to chase and catch each other rather aimlessly. The teacher might ask some questions about the purposes of the characters and demonstrate how they might handle interactions without running and chasing inside the room.

Evaluator

As an *evaluator* of play, the teacher has to be a careful observer and diagnostician to determine how different play incidents serve the needs of individual children and what learning is taking place as children participate in play. It is the teacher's job to recognize the academic, social, cognitive, and physical growth that takes place during play and to be able to communicate these changes to parents and administrators. Evaluation means that materials, environments, and activities must be carefully considered in light of the curriculum goals, and changes must be made if needed.

Planner

Finally, the teacher has to serve as a *planner.* Planning involves all the learning that results from observing, elaborating, and evaluating. The teacher must plan for new experiences that will encourage or extend children's interests in topics. For example, a parent who was a shoe clerk could come to the classroom to share her occupation. She might measure the children's feet and demonstrate that part of her job is to show the customers several choices of shoes in the proper sizes and to help them try on shoes. In planning to continue the children's obvious interest, the teacher might do several things: gather a collection of many kinds of shoes, find a rack suitable for storing them, borrow several of the instruments used for measuring feet, and so on. The teacher's careful planning will result in days of active play involvement by the children, as they arrange chairs to make a shoe store, write up sales, and bag shoes to send home with the "customers." The teacher can encourage the children to talk about the different kinds of shoes and who wears them, to draw shoes, to create signs for their shoe store, and even to write stories about shoes. When the children tire of the shoes and no longer demonstrate interest in playing with them, the shoes should be removed. By that time, the teacher will have already planned other experiences that will pique the interest of the children and can be extended in play (Ford 1993).

In planning for play that contributes to development, teachers should consider the following guidelines:

1. Make sure children have sufficient time for play.
2. Help children plan their play.
3. Monitor the progress of play.
4. Choose appropriate props and toys.
5. Provide themes that can be extended from one day to the next.
6. Coach individuals who need help.
7. Suggest or model how themes can be woven together.
8. Model appropriate ways to solve disputes. (Bodrova and Leong 1996, p. 132)

DEVELOPMENT OF PLAY BEHAVIORS

The play of infants is *sensorimotor:* They explore objects and people and investigate the effects of their actions on these objects and people. At about the end of the first year, children begin to exhibit play behaviors such as pretending to eat or sleep (Rubin, Fein, and Vanderberg 1983). They are also able to begin playful interactions with others, such as playing peek-a-boo.

Preschoolers engage in practice play, but as they mature, the time spent in exploring new objects decreases drastically (Ellis 1979). Only about 15 percent of the play of six-year-olds is practice play. Most of the play of older preschoolers can be labeled *constructive play:* play involving building or making something (Rubin, Fein, and Vanderberg 1983). Children may build things at any of the levels of social play. The objects are usually used in symbolic games or games with rules.

The play of preschoolers is very vigorous. They like to chase each other, especially in "superhero" play. (See Kostelnik, Whiren, and Stein

[1986] and Levin and Carlsson-Paige [1995] for some specific strategies for managing "superhero" play.) As children mature, they are able to play without materials that resemble the real objects; older preschoolers can pretend that they have whatever they need. Children also grow more able to assume the roles of characters outside their families. Three-year-olds can play family roles; older preschoolers begin to play characters from the larger community. Pretend play for five-year-olds is very intense and may incorporate children's knowledge of story characters or employ their developing literacy skills (Garvey 1977).

As children move into the elementary years, sociodramatic play decreases considerably. Games with rules tend to dominate the play of children moving into the concrete operational years (six or seven to ten or twelve), and pretend play becomes less acceptable, except in more formalized versions such as theater. Play becomes more competitive and based on language or academic skills.

PURPOSES OF PLAY

Play contributes to cognitive growth, aids social and emotional development, and is essential to physical development. Many of the abilities required to succeed in school settings are gained through play experiences. Eheart and Leavitt (1985) state that play offers young children opportunities "to master many fundamental physical, social, and intellectual skills and concepts" (p. 18). Other researchers have come to similar conclusions about both younger and primary-age children (Garvey 1977; Sylva, Bruner, and Genova 1976).

Intellectual Development

Both *exploratory play*—play in which the child has no objective other than exploration—and *rule-governed play*—play in which the child has objectives such as finding solutions to problems or determining cause and effect—contribute to cognitive growth. *Cognitive growth* is defined as an increase in the child's basic store of knowledge (Lunzer 1959); it occurs as a result of experiences with objects and people (Piaget 1952). Many studies support the positive relationship between play experiences and the development of children's cognitive abilities. Cognitive abilities include identifying, classifying, sequencing, observing, discriminating, making predictions, drawing conclusions, comparing, and determining cause-and-effect relationships. These intellectual abilities underlie children's success in all academic areas.

As children play, they learn how to solve problems—socially, physically, and intellectually.

Play helps children develop organizing and problem-solving abilities. Children playing must think about organizing materials in order to meet their play goals. For example, a child who wants to play "visiting the doctor" must decide where the doctor's office and the waiting room will be, what will be used for a stethoscope, and so on. Children must also organize tasks, deciding how to move and arrange materials so that they can play. Some of these organization tasks require very fine discriminations, such as sorting by size, shape, or color. Children playing must also think about the other players involved. Older children playing the roles of characters in books they have read must think about the roles being assumed by other players and take those into consideration when creating their own roles.

Children playing are often engaged in problem-solving behavior. They might experiment with adding water to sand to make it the proper consistency for holding its shape when molded, or they might search the room to find suitable materials for something needed in play. Children playing "going on the bus," for example, might look for things to use for seats and perhaps something to be the steering wheel of the bus. They might also look for props to serve as tickets and baggage. They might find old purses in the dress-up area to be suitcases or a pie pan to be the steering wheel.

Because they will also need people to participate as passengers, the children playing "going on the bus" will have to solve the problem of how to persuade enough other children to join the play. Sylva, Bruner, and Genova (1976) found that children who played with materials were as capable of solving a problem as children for whom the solution had been demonstrated. Children who play with materials are more likely to assume that there are many possible solutions to a problem and to continue trying to solve a problem longer than children for whom a solution has been demonstrated. Older children as well as younger ones are actively engaged in problem solving when they attempt to create a structure to match the image they plan. For example, children learning about triangles might build structures supported with triangles and test their strength; children learning about hexagons might build dodecahedrons from Popsicle sticks.

Children at play certainly demonstrate creative thinking and creative problem solving. During play, children must put together information from previous experience, from the real world, and from other play participants. Frank (1968) concludes that play "is a way of learning by trial and error to cope with the actual world" (p. 436).

Social and Emotional Development

In the Piagetian view, play pushes children out of **egocentric thought patterns** (Piaget 1962). That is, children in play situations are forced to consider the viewpoints of their playmates and therefore become less egocentric. If Susan and Juan are pretending to cook dinner, each may have definite ideas about how the task should be done. They will each have to accommodate the other's thinking in order to continue their play. Children learn to cooperate to achieve some group goals during play. They also have opportunities during play to learn to delay their own gratification for a few minutes—for instance, while someone else finishes playing with a drum.

Children often play out their fears and concerns. One study reports the reactions of a group of children after they witnessed an accident on their playground and describes how they worked out stress through their play (Brown, Curry, and Tittnich 1971). Children in different age groups (threes, fours, and fives) incorporated the accident into their play differently, but each group revealed some fear and tried to relieve it through "hospital" play or other play involving someone being injured. In another instance, children who had experienced a tornado played various forms of "hiding from the tornado" or "the tornado is coming" for a long time after the experience. Barnett (1984) found that children who were anxious showed reduced anxiety after enacting their fears in play episodes.

Although most teachers are not trained to be play therapists, they can be aware of how children explore different emotions (anger, sadness, and so on) and different social roles in their play. For example, children might "try on" the role of "bully" in a play situation; after they get feedback about how other people react to them in that role, they can alter their behavior.

Physical Development

Children achieve both fine and gross motor control through their play. They can practice all the gross motor skills of running, jumping, and hopping while playing. Children at play can be encouraged to lift, carry, and walk or hop, spin, and move in response to rhythms. They can also practice fine motor skills as they string beads, fit together puzzles, hammer nails into wood, or paint at easels.

Not only young children need active play; older children should participate in this type of play, too. They can throw, catch, kick, bat, balance on two-wheel bikes, and skate. Today's children often spend a great deal of time in passive behavior, such as watching television or videos. These children especially need to have the chance to climb, swing, pull, push, run, hop, jump, and walk in order to gain control of their bodies.

PLAY IN SCHOOL SETTINGS

Play at school usually differs from play at home in several ways. Generally, there are larger numbers of children in play groups at school than in play groups at home. The materials at school are often different than those at home; only a few children would have access to unit blocks or easels for painting at home. Toys and play materials also differ in the degree to which they must be shared. In a large group, children must learn to work cooperatively with others.

Play is often more restricted at school than at home. Play activities at school tend to be more guided and more closely observed. Teachers are more likely to plan specific ways of enhancing play than are most parents. For example, if the teacher observes a group of children attempting to build a space rocket, he may collect materials from around the room, such as boxes or paints, that will assist the children in achieving their goals. He may also find books in the library, pictures of spacecraft, or filmstrips or videotapes to extend the play to other activities.

Teachers will select play experiences that match the goals of their programs. If program goals emphasize discovery, then free play is most appropriate. If objectives require children to explore concepts, then guided play is most appropriate. Finally, directed play experiences are best if the teacher wants children to demonstrate specific skills. In learning concepts about sound, a child in a free-play situation might discover that he can produce sound by striking a surface. The alert teacher would help the child verbalize his discovery and continue to explore sounds, if he still showed interest. Guided play would be appropriate for teaching children the concept that the pitch of sound varies with the length and size of the string that is vibrated. The teacher might display cigar boxes with rubber bands of various lengths and thicknesses stretched over them. Whenever a child expressed interest in these materials, he would be encouraged to discover the differences in sounds produced by the various rubber bands. In directed play, the teacher might have the children listen to sounds produced by various instruments and indicate with hand movements the changes in pitch.

Van Hoorn et al. (1993) describe play at school as instrumental or illicit. *Instrumental play* is that which the teacher plans and encourages, such as the sociodramatic scenarios of playing "hospital" and "shoe store," described earlier. *Illicit play* is not sanctioned and may even be expressly forbidden by the teacher. Examples of illicit play include children creating guns from Tinker Toys or passing secret notes behind the teacher's back. Although such play may make the teacher uncomfortable, Sutton-Smith (1988) reminds us that it also contributes to a child's developing social skills.

Should illicit play be banned from early childhood classrooms? There are no clear-cut answers to this question. Teachers who try to ban play with weapons, such as "war," realize that children find ways to engage in these activities anyway, which creates more tension and management problems. On the other hand, some educators believe that "war" play stimulates children to believe that violence is an acceptable means of solving problems. "Sociopoliticalists argue that war play and war toys glamorize fighting and killing, promote excessive materialism, and foster unnecessary aggression" (Isenberg and Jalongo 1993, p. 246).

Some teachers recommend redirecting "war" play or "superhero" play to focus on the positive things that soldiers or heroes can do, such as saving people who are trapped by natural disasters or building hospitals to help people who are hurt. Teachers must also help children learn to solve their everyday conflicts peacefully (Rogers and Sharapan 1991). Parents should be involved in making decisions about how to handle "war" toys and other types of violent play in the classroom so that teachers will have their understanding and support.

Play in the Primary Classroom

Most teachers are aware that play is much more acceptable in classrooms of preschoolers and kindergartners than it is in classrooms of primary-grade children. The expectation that only serious learning should take place in primary classrooms is prevalent among parents and also among some teachers. Others believe, however, that play can be serious learning for primary-grade children. Granted, the play of first- and second-graders does not look like that of preschoolers and kindergartners; nonetheless, many play experiences are appropriate for primary-age children.

For example, children in the primary grades enjoy exploring and building with various materials, creating new machines from old parts, inventing toys, building robots and models, and working out basic physics problems (such as dropping different materials from different heights and measuring the speeds with which they fall). Activities for primary-grade children usually must be based on the children's special interests in order to generate enthusiastic participation, which is not so much the case with preschoolers. Children in primary grades certainly continue to play, although that play may be illicit and behind the teacher's back.

Wasserman (1992) tells stories of the Wright brothers and Frank Lloyd Wright and their early play experiences, "messing about." Sadly, these ingenious and productive individuals, who contributed so much to our knowledge and our lives, often had to stay out of school in order to indulge their curiosities and play. Wasserman asserts that "messing about" is essential for developing children's creative-thinking and problem-solving skills. Teachers should encourage children to discover and explore what really fascinates them.

Primary children are also interested in games with rules and enjoy learning to play a variety of board games. Although this type of play may not provide as many opportunities for exploring problems and creating solutions as "messing about," playing board games can help children develop social and communication skills.

Benefits of Play at School

When play is accepted as a vehicle for carrying forward the curriculum, children can learn organizational skills, develop oral language skills, and learn to take risks in solving problems (Perlmutter and Burrell 1995). Play that aids children in their development can be achieved at school if teachers provide time, space, materials, and sanction for play activities. Obviously, children need time to plan and carry out play episodes if they are to develop knowledge and skills in play. No child can get organized and complete a satisfying block construction in the ten minutes allotted to play in some classrooms. Christie, Johnson, and Peckover (1988) and Christie and Wardle (1992) found that the play patterns of children in longer play periods were more mature than those of children in shorter play periods. Space and materials are also prerequisites for productive play. Materials such as sand, water, blocks, and paint take up large amounts of space. Teachers may have to arrange the classroom so that the same space is used for different activities during the day.

Sanctioning play is important, as children will pick up subtle hints from the teacher that play is important or not important. One way for the

- How does play contribute to a developmentally appropriate program?
- Would it be possible to have a DAP classroom without play? Why?
- Would it be possible to have a play session that was not developmentally appropriate? Why?
- If play is important in developmentally appropriate practice, what are the most effective means of facilitating it?

- Does all play contribute to DAP? What about rough-and-tumble play? solitary play? Explain your answers.
- What aspects of play that are developmentally appropriate for eight-year-olds would not be appropriate for four-year-olds? Why?

teacher to make sure the children feel that play is important is to join in the play. It is a real art to know when and how to join in without disrupting the play or changing it to meet adult definitions of appropriate play. Other ways a teacher might indicate that play is important are to talk about play when children evaluate their day and to share the products of play. Often, teachers share and display only the products of work activities, such as drawings or pieces of writing; as a result, children come to believe that play is unimportant in comparison. To validate the importance of play, a teacher might take photographs of block constructions or of children discovering the attributes of water and share these along with artwork and stories.

As children gain experience and maturity, play in the classroom should reflect changes in the children. Children of different ages and different developmental levels use materials in different ways, so teachers must be alert in providing materials that will challenge the children to develop more in their play. For example, if the housekeeping center for five-year-olds is exactly the same as that for four-year-olds, play in that area by five-year-olds may stagnate. It is the responsibility of the teacher to add materials that will stimulate new play or allow children to play out their fantasies.

Selecting Materials for Play

Teachers have many choices when selecting materials for play. *Open-ended materials*—those that allow multiple outcomes and unique uses in each encounter—are the most useful. Such materials may be fluid materials that have no inherent structure, such as sand and water, or structured materials, such as various forms of blocks. Blocks, sand, and water do not have built-in functions that limit the possible outcomes of playing with them. Therefore, they are conducive to creative thinking and problem solving in children.

Children playing with blocks can create structures that represent their own understandings of the real world or that represent their fantasy worlds. Players can reproduce known structures or design totally new ones; they can control the outcomes and determine when the structure is complete without fear that it will be criticized or rejected. Players with blocks are free to make discoveries about the relationships among the block shapes and sizes and about the physics of stacking blocks. These children can experience the aesthetic pleasure of the feel of blocks and the symmetry of their constructions.

Children playing with sand and water are free to explore the properties of the materials and to learn how the materials respond under different conditions. They are in charge of the outcomes and derive satisfaction from playing to meet their own goals. Sand and water allow for individual experimentation and also group interactions. Children using sand and water establish their own goals and feel satisfaction when those goals are met.

Materials that allow children to make play choices and allow multiple outcomes are necessary for the best play environments. Many materials can be considered open ended if it is possible for children to use them in different ways. For example, teachers might supply rollers, boxes, balls, and targets that will help children develop concepts in physical science (Kamii and DeVries 1978). These materials are open ended to the extent that children have choices in exploring the arrangements and outcomes that can be achieved with them. Many commercial materials, on the other hand, are limited in terms of what children are able to do with them, providing only one or two options. When dollars for purchasing materials are limited, open-ended materials are the best investment.

Play as a Teaching Strategy

Teachers have a choice when deciding how to present information or new concepts to children. Some information must be presented in a teacher-directed format. For example, safety rules, such as those about fire, cannot be explored; they must be stated firmly. But generally speaking, *telling* is the least successful strategy for presenting information to young children. Even the young child can repeat words or phrases, but verbal responses only indicate that she has learned the words; such responses do not measure the child's understanding at all.

Play is one of the **teaching strategies** available to teachers as they plan for children's learning. The following examples illustrate goals that could readily be achieved through play:

Plan a play experience that would help children learn a specific concept.

- To encourage children to learn about appropriate clothes for the weather, provide many different pieces of clothing in the dress-up area.
- To encourage children to learn how to create secondary colors, provide paints in primary colors.

Play provides insight into children's interests and abilities.

- To encourage children to demonstrate the ability to classify, provide leaves, shells, keys, buttons, and models of farm and zoo animals.
- To encourage children to learn the characteristics of three-dimensional shapes, provide the shapes in boxes, geoblocks, and regular building blocks.
- To encourage children to learn about water erosion on land forms, provide water in containers (so that the flow can be varied) in the sandbox or gardening area.

Using play experiences as teaching strategies requires that the teacher observe how children use materials and that he ask questions to guide children's thinking and reflections. Sutton-Smith (1986) reminds us that "although we use play in various ways in the classroom for our own purposes, we need to remember that the children have purposes of their own, and need to deal with purposes largely by themselves (even if under distant supervision), making use of this vital and universal kind of communication [play]" (p. 13). Teachers can make plans for play experiences, but children's needs must be honored and they must be allowed to use play for their own learning. In other words:

> Play, then, offers the child the opportunity to make sense out of the world by using available tools. Understanding is created by doing, by doing with others, and by being completely involved in that doing. Through play, the child comes to understand the world and the adult comes to understand the child. (Chaille and Silvern 1996, p. 277)

Vygotsky's belief that representational play includes rules for behavior is obvious even to untrained observers when they watch children who assign or accept roles and are then chastised if they fail to behave according to those roles. For example, the child playing "dog" cannot go to work nor can the "baby" watch TV. As summarized by Berk:

> From this perspective, the fantasy play of the preschool years is essential for further development of play in middle childhood—specifically, for movement toward game play, which provides additional instruction in setting goals, regulating one's behavior in pursuit of those goals, and subordinating action to rules rather than impulse—in short, for becoming a cooperative and productive member of society. Play, in Vygotsky's theory, is the preeminent educational activity of early childhood. (1994, p. 33)

Teachers have many opportunities to plan environments and materials so that learning goals can be achieved in playful activities. Observations of children at play will help teachers choose other play materials that will help children learn concepts and clarify and extend their understandings. Selecting guided play as a teaching strategy does not imply that play is assigned; it means that careful thought is put into the selection of materials and intervention in children's play. A teacher might put out an assortment of materials that she expects will invite children to explore a new concept. If children do not learn the concept from interacting with the materials, then the teacher must choose other materials or select a different approach. Assigning a child to complete a task means that he no longer has a choice and that the teacher has chosen a strategy other than play.

Thus, teachers must be thoughtful when intervening in children's play and avoid trying to force their own agenda on the children. For example, the teacher can begin to play with a small group and propose a theme for the play, but the children must be allowed to reject that theme or convert it to one following their own interests. The teacher can also assume a role in sociodramatic play, such as the "neighbor coming over for lunch," but such an intervention must be done carefully. Moreover, the teacher will need to think about how to leave the play so that the children can continue on their own (Ward 1996).

Communicating the Benefits of Play

Teachers have an obligation to explain to parents and administrators the benefits of the time children spend playing during the schoolday. Teachers are and should be accountable for children's learning. Part of that responsibility is to be able to provide specific information about individual children and their play experiences. The following section applies specifically

Observe one preschool child for a thirty-minute play period. Make a list of the intellectual, social, emotional, and physical developments that you observe (for example, learning a concept, learning to share, learning to assume the role of another person, and so on).

to assessment of play; a more comprehensive discussion of assessment is included in Chapter 15.

One form of data to be shared is the *anecdotal record.* With this type of record keeping, the teacher or another adult records the child's behavior and verbalizations for a brief period of time. Judgments about the child's intentions or motivations should be clearly labeled as such in the record and distinguished from descriptions of the child's overt behaviors. At the end of the day, these notes are placed in the child's file. Over a period of time, the notes should reveal some patterns that will help the teacher talk to others about the child's growth through play. For example, the teacher might have noted that Jennifer played alone with the blocks and made horizontal patterns with them. A few weeks later, an observer might note that Jennifer had started to use vertical patterns along with the horizontal ones. Later, Jennifer might be seen building a vertical structure with a friend. Still later, she might build a vertical and symmetrical structure. An observer might note that Jennifer had talked about her building before she began the construction and completed a structure that matched her plans. These records would clearly reveal Jennifer's growth in building more complex structures and in planning her activities.

Another technique for recording play is to record where the children are in the classroom at given time intervals. For example, every ten minutes, the teacher or an adult records on a grid which children are playing with blocks, in dramatic play, in art, or in reading. Over time, these records reveal children's patterns of choice and, in combination with anecdotal records, can be very useful in planning other activities. Figure 4.1 is an example of such a record.

A third technique is to keep several records scattered through the room. As an adult observes a child engaged in particular behavior, he notes it on the record. For example, the following behaviors might be listed across the top of the form: "Completes puzzles with ten pieces," "Strings beads in a pattern," "Plays cooperatively with at least 2 others," and so on. The children's names are listed down the side of the form. Whenever a child is observed completing a puzzle with ten pieces, the date is recorded on the form. Such records are helpful because they offer flexibility in selecting what to look for in observations and make it quick and easy to record information. Figure 4.2 (on page 126) is an example of such a record.

Finally, teachers can keep samples of products from some play activities. Selected paintings, for instance, can be kept in a file for comparison with previous artwork. Obviously, it is impossible to keep samples of block constructions or sand play. Some results of these activities can be recorded in photographs, but most will have to be described in anecdotal records. As children talk about their experiences each day, the teacher can record some of their own evaluations. The teacher will also want to add to the child's file her own insights and interpretations of the child's play.

	9:00	9:10	9:20
Unit blocks	Sara Carlos Hillary Jason	Sara Hillary Brian Michael	Sara Michael Brad Gretchen
Easels	Cheri Karen Phil Juanita	Dolores Cheri Juanita Jason	
Clay			
Dress-up			

FIGURE 4.1

**Sample of
Time-Activity Record**

Before a teacher can share what children are learning in play experiences, he must be actively involved while the children are playing. If the teacher is busy doing other tasks while the children are playing, he will miss chances for observations and insights. We cannot share what we haven't seen or heard; therefore, play time is a very busy time for the teacher of young children.

PLAY AND ACADEMIC LEARNING

Sometimes observers of young children think that children will not learn academic skills if they spend their time playing. The truth is that play contributes to the development of academic ability. Children who are ordering objects by length or size in free-play situations, learning rhymes and chants in directed play, or exploring rhythms or constructing with Legos in guided play are all involved in activities that contribute to reading ability. Reading is a complex process that involves eye coordination, visual and auditory

	Completes puzzles with 10 pieces	Strings beads in a pattern	Plays cooperatively with at least 2 others	
Geoffrey				
Judith				
Leslie				
Michael				

FIGURE 4.2

Sample Record of Behavior

discrimination, and the cognitive ability to work with parts of wholes. Play is an important means of developing such abilities. Collier (1983) found that play assists the development of representational skills and the formation of the symbolic foundations that are necessary for reading.

One of the most important goals in reading instruction for young children is oral language development. During play, children have a chance to talk, argue, explain, and persuade as well as to use language in imaginative ways. Also, children engaging in pretend play grow more able to take on the perspectives of others. They practice visual discrimination skills as they sort, classify, and compare objects in the classroom. They practice auditory discrimination as they listen to others, explore sounds made by a variety of materials, and engage in musical play. Some children will want to create stories at the puppet stage, others will want to make books related to their play, and still others will want to create signs or messages as part of their play. Pellegrini (1980) found that children's play was a better predictor of success in some aspects of reading and language achievement than IQ or socioeconomic status.

The development of beginning science skills is easy to observe in play situations. Children are observing, making predictions, gathering data, and testing hypotheses. For example, children constructing with blocks are learning about physics as they experience practical applications of stress, mass, and weight. They can also explore ramps and gears and the operation of simple machines. They learn about earth science as they play in the sand and observe the weather. They learn about biology as they observe classroom animals and their life cycles. They learn about chemistry as they mix colors in water and observe the melting of snow and the effects of salt on ice. Children working at easels are engaged in scientific investigation as they experiment with various consistencies of paint and the results obtained with different paints and papers.

Abilities in mathematics are also developed when children play. Children may use two half-unit blocks to fill a space left by removing one unit block from their construction. They learn about set theory as they group objects such as wooden cubes or buttons. They learn about geometry as they explore various shapes in planes or in three-dimensional forms. They learn about topology as they construct with blocks. Children playing have many opportunities to sort, group, and classify. They also learn to use mathematics to solve problems: How many places should be set at the table? How many forks are needed if we need one for each plate? Children engaged in play have opportunities to explore the mathematical relationships in their environment. Curiosity, divergent thinking, and motivation to learn are vital for success in math and science, and these traits are best fostered through play (Henniger 1987).

Writing requires fine motor development; therefore, any activity that contributes to developing control of the fine muscles is useful in writing. Children can paint, cut, work puzzles, build with Legos, manipulate clay, and use various kinds of pens, crayons, and pencils for developing the control needed to make letters. Writing itself can be a part of many play activities, as children write notes to each other, make signs to enhance their buildings, and write menus or tickets as part of play. These examples illustrate the support for academic learning that is provided by play. Many of the activities contribute to learning in several different subject-matter areas. For example, sorting and seriating contribute to abilities in reading, mathematics, and science. Play has multiple outcomes.

Primary-age children engaged in project work can be involved in play experiences that will help them consolidate their learning and explore possibilities in given topics. Children learning about seeds can sort, group, and classify seeds; pretend to be sprouting seeds; create board games with facts about seeds; create models of seeds from clay or other materials; paint seeds; use seeds in counting and other mathematics activities; and so forth. Play should not be limited to the preschool years, as it is also an important tool for teaching children in the primary grades (Stone 1995/96).

In planning for play experiences that enhance the curriculum, teachers must be careful to make play available, not to assign experiences that they perceive as playful. Many playful experiences can be offered that correspond with themes of instruction, such as sorting rocks to accompany a theme of rocks (Stone 1995/96). If such an experience is provided as a choice and children choose to participate, then it is play; however, if the teacher assigns the task, then it is not play. As mentioned earlier, one of the criteria for determining if an activity is play is the element of choice. If choice is not present, then by definition, the activity is not play.

Children understand this. Consider how often children classify what they do at school as "play" or "work." The usual definition is that *work* is something assigned by the teacher, although older children may say it was *play* if it was fun (Perlmutter and Burrell 1995).

PARENTS AND PLAY

■ If you assign family homework, make sure that it is playful and fun for both children and adults. Board games, treasure hunts, and so on can be used effectively.

OUTDOOR PLAY

THEORY INTO Practice

Observe children playing outdoors. What are the most common activities you observe? Can you identify differences in outdoor play and indoor play? If so, what? Do the playground and the equipment and materials available limit or encourage the play? How?

Outdoor play offers children the same opportunities for growth as indoor play. And to be productive, outdoor play requires the same planning, observation, and evaluation as indoor play. Henniger (1994) states that "children deserve the same diversity and richness in their outdoor play environments as they have indoors" (p. 89).

Outdoor and indoor play offer similar benefits to children in terms of physical activity; an added bonus of outdoor play is that it includes large muscle activity, which is usually restricted indoors. Gross motor activities such as running, jumping, rolling, pushing, and hopping should not only be available to children but encouraged. To encourage outdoor play, the teacher may need to use some of the same strategies that she would use to encourage any kind of indoor play. Recording and celebrating outdoor play activities, perhaps through photographs or video recordings, may be one means of promoting them. For instance, the first time a child is able to hang by her knees on the bars is certainly an event worth celebrating. Providing props that encourage dramatic play outdoors, such as old boats or cars on playgrounds, is another effective means of encouraging children to play outside.

A definitive advantage of outdoor play over indoor play is that the rules for voice levels and physical exuberance can be relaxed. When playing outdoors, children can shout without being reprimanded and they can run, dance, and climb without damaging equipment or endangering others. Of course, rules that ensure children's safety and provide for cooperation among them are still needed for outdoor play. In many settings, children are allowed to play outdoors only in groups, and outdoor play times are set by the teacher.

Careful observation of children engaging in outdoor play will reveal many examples of problem solving. Children planting seeds might try to determine how deep is "shallow" or "3 inches deep." The child riding a tricycle down a slope might try to determine what speed is fast enough to raise her level of excitement but not so fast that the tricycle will go out of control. Children playing "race car" might try several methods before they successfully attach a steering wheel to a box to create a "car" so that it can "turn." A group of children might try to persuade several more children to play Treasure Island. None of these problem-solving skills is enhanced solely by outdoor play, but it is important to be aware that outdoor play is more than children just running off excess energy (Hartle et al. 1994; Henniger 1993/94, 1994). Curriculum areas enhanced by outdoor play are summarized in Table 4.2 (Frost and Wortham 1988).

Children's social skills can be observed in play outdoors as well as indoors. Teachers will find it interesting to observe which children are able to organize peers to play games or participate in other activities. Children's developing roles as leaders and followers may be evident in these situations. Some children may need the teacher's guidance in learning and applying strategies for joining groups at play and for learning to share equipment outdoors.

Many indoor activities can be brought outdoors, given the right materials. For example, children might set up easels and paint pictures outdoors, or they might use water to "paint" buildings and sidewalks, using big brushes that encourage large, sweeping strokes. Children might enjoy block building outdoors when provided with large plastic or weatherproof

TABLE 4.2 Play and Curriculum

Communication	Cognitive Development	Motor Development	Fine Arts	Social/Emotional Development
PVC pipe telephone system	Sand play	Wheeled vehicles	Chalkboard	Sharing materials
Cooperative planning	Water play	Super-structure with many motor options	Clay	Planning activities
Group dramatic play	Gardening	Sliding	Fingerpaint	Testing abilities
Organized games	Building with tools	Swinging	Musical games	Playing out frustrations
	Weather awareness	Running	Musical instruments	
		Balancing	Textures	
			Dramatization	

Source: Joe L. Frost and Sue C. Wortham, "The Evolution of American Playgrounds," *Young Children* 43 (July 1988): 25. Used with permission of NAEYC.

blocks, ramps, ladders, and other equipment. Such materials lend themselves to building structures that are large enough for children to get inside.

Although teachers of young children often discourage or forbid rough-and-tumble play because they believe it turns into negative or aggressive behavior, research reveals that such play is age related. Specifically, the incidence of rough-and-tumble play increases as children move from preschool into kindergarten and the primary years and then decreases as children reach middle childhood (Kostelnik, Stein, Whiren, and Soderman 1993). Other research shows that children who are typically rejected by their peers are more likely to misinterpret rough-and-tumble play and to participate aggressively. Popular children, on the other hand, are more likely to participate in a playful, unaggressive manner (Pellegrini and Boyd 1993). Teachers should be aware that rough-and-tumble play is developmental in children's play lives. When such play becomes aggressive, teachers should intervene and help children modify inappropriate behavior (Bergen 1994; Carlsson-Paige & Levin 1995).

Ideally, children should be able to play either indoors or out. However, lack of supervision and the fact that few schools have outdoor play areas connected to classrooms make such choices difficult.

PARENTS AND PLAY

■ If you distribute a parent newsletter, try to include something about play in each issue—perhaps a photograph of a block structure or of children playing in sand or water.

CHILDREN WITH SPECIAL NEEDS

Planning play experiences for children with special needs may mean structuring the physical environment so that participation is possible. For example, a child in a wheelchair cannot use blocks if the blocks are on the floor. A child who is visually impaired might need more tactile clues attached to play materials; a child who is hearing impaired might need help communicating in some play situations. These adaptations of the physical environment are relatively easy to make. Planning play experiences for other children may require much more than physically rearranging or adjusting the materials to be used.

The play of children with developmental delays may be more similar to that of younger children than to that of age peers. Children with developmental delays may not be able to participate in cooperative play or to negotiate the rules of a play situation with other children. Some children need specific guidance in play skills. For example, they may lack the social skills necessary for joining a play group or for sharing materials (Rettig 1994; Winter, Bell, & Dempsey 1994).

However, children can be taught specific play skills (Peck et al. 1978). Cole (1986) compared the effects of direct verbal instruction, modeling,

Play is important in the life of every child. Teachers should plan for any adaptations needed to help all children play successfully.

and withdrawal of intervention in promoting play skills in children with and without disabilities. He found that withdrawal of intervention was the most effective approach to promoting play skills in children with and without disabilities. He also found that withdrawal of intervention was most effective in promoting play skills and that persistent teacher intervention had negative effects. In other words, letting children teach each other seems to be more effective than intervening. Some researchers have found that motor development can also be fostered through play programs (Roswal and Frith 1980).

Gunsberg (1989) reports that contingency play that is structured by a simple, repetitive format is very effective with young children who have been abused or neglected. With this approach, the teacher responds to the child's actions so that the child can become attached to an adult and trust the adult to respond. For example, if the child covers her head, the adult plays peek-a-boo; if the child claps her hands, the adult plays pat-a-cake. These are the kinds of play routines that most children normally experience with caregivers. In addition to fostering feelings of attachment, the goals of contingency play include helping children control their impulses, helping them feel more effective in relationships, and motivating them to initiate and sustain play.

Children who are gifted also need special planning to make their play experiences appropriate. These children may be more socially advanced and more physically active than their age peers (Barnett and Fiscella 1985). They need play experiences that help them relate to their age peers and give up some of their need for perfection (Roeper 1987). Helping children who are gifted use some of the products of their play for other learning experiences is one way for the teacher to indicate that play is respected. For example, a child who invents a vehicle from odds and ends on the junk table might be challenged to think of ways to use the vehicle or to write about it.

Teachers who appreciate the benefits of play for children will strive to involve children with special needs in play by making whatever adjustments seem necessary in the play environment and by planning specific instruction in play skills for those who need guidance (Bordner & Berkley 1992).

CELEBRATING DIVERSITY

To celebrate the diversity of children in play settings, teachers can provide many culturally appropriate items in the play environment—for example, items of clothing and play foods that are common in a particular culture. Teachers also need to know enough about children's cultures and experiences to be able to recognize play episodes that reflect cultural knowledge and to encourage children to play roles that are part of their experiences. Although some studies have found class differences in children's sociodramatic play, many variables other than class can be offered to account for these differences (Hughes 1995). The most positive approach for teachers is to accept the differences in individual children and help them achieve successful play interactions.

CHAPTER SUMMARY

- Play in the school setting can be defined on a continuum that runs from free play to guided play to directed play. *Free play* is defined as behavior that is personally motivated, active, and pleasurable and that has no extrinsic goals or rules that cannot be negotiated by the players; free play is often nonliteral, and players bring their own meaning to the play experience. *Guided play* is play in which the teacher has selected materials from which the children may choose in order to discover specific concepts. *Directed play* is play in which the teacher instructs the children in how to accomplish specific tasks.

- Play contributes to the development of gross and fine motor skills, to cognitive growth, and to social and emotional development. In playing, children strengthen many problem-solving abilities, learn to express emotions in socially acceptable ways, and learn the social skills necessary for success in groups.

- Play can be described in terms of how the player interacts with other people. Play can be solitary play, onlooker play, parallel play, associative play, and cooperative play.

- Observers of children's play have noted developmental trends in play behaviors. Younger children exhibit much more exploratory play, preschoolers engage in sociodramatic play and constructive play, and elementary-age children are most likely to be involved in games with rules.

- Play in a school setting and play at home usually differ in terms of the guidance offered, materials available, and number of children involved in the play situations.

- Play contributes to academic achievement. Teachers who are concerned with academic success do not have to force children to give up play in order to gain abilities in math, science, and reading.

- Teachers have a very complex role in children's play. Teachers must observe, plan, and evaluate play experiences. They must also plan learning experiences that are best achieved through play. Finally, they must learn to communicate the benefits of children's play to parents and administrators.

- Carefully planned outdoor play experiences can provide many of the same benefits of indoor play and often allow more freedom for children than play indoors.

- Planning play experiences for children with special needs may include adapting the physical environment; special instruction in play skills may also be necessary. Children who are developmentally delayed may exhibit play behaviors that are typical of much younger children.

A TEACHER SPEAKS

MEGBE HUGHES
Isidore Newman School
NEW ORLEANS, LOUISIANA

Respecting Children's Play

Respecting the complexity, the value, and form in children's play takes much more from adults than just making time in the daily schedule for play to take place. Respecting children's play implies that we, as teachers, do not know all of the answers and that children can be counted on for some of these answers. Respect also implies children's right to privacy.

> It is true that if we are interested in children we must look to them and listen to them as a matter of course. And as we pay attention to their play, we must never violate its complexity by presuming to "decode" or oversimplify it. (Koste 1987, p. 44)

In my pre-K classroom, children learn by playing. Watching four- and five-year-olds play allows me to expand on their interests, their knowledge, and their play. Watching children play on the playground and providing them with different balls, bats, and/or building tools enables me to facilitate learning and enables the children to build new knowledge on their existing knowledge. Watching children interact in the dramatic play center and providing new and different props allows me to extend students' language and play without "telling" them what to do. Being the audience in a library corner as children act out their favorite story using puppets, costumes, or flannelboard pieces allows children to demonstrate their knowledge in a playful manner and gives me the opportunity to talk with them about the story. Paying attention to my students, their individual interests, and their varied skills allows me to build on what they know in supportive ways, fostering a love of learning in every student.

Assessing children's play by observing, taking anecdotal records, videotaping, and taking photographs allows me to give parents accurate information about the nature of their children's play and opportunities to extend play in my classroom. I observe my students interacting with each other and often initiate games with them; then I back away and observe them continue to play these games. I take anecdotal records daily on computer labels that I can file in each child's folder. This enables me to look at each child every day and compile an ongoing record of the child's play behaviors. Using videotapes and photographs is the best way that I have found to bring the classroom home. Parents enjoy seeing their children in action, and often these forms of assessment provide insight into how much learning is accomplished through play. Assessment is key when it comes to helping parents value play as an avenue for learning in the classroom.

I feel that we must respect our children's play and trust them to learn from their play. I see it as my job as a pre-K teacher to show parents how important play is to their children, and the most effective way to do this is through sharing my observations and talking with parents about what their child is learning as he or she is playing.

5

GUIDING BEHAVIOR
Encouraging Self-Control

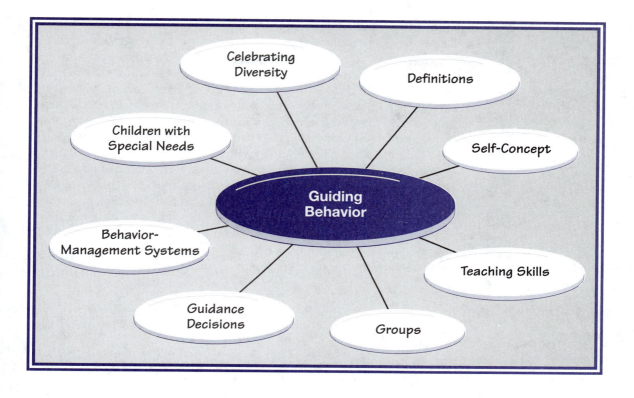

Your assignment as you visited a school yesterday was to observe the discipline techniques employed by teachers. You were in a first-grade class. When you entered the class, you could not find the teacher at first. She was on the floor in the back of the room, helping a small group plan a mural. You stayed in the room for most of the morning and observed only one interaction between the teacher and the children that could be categorized as discipline. The teacher asked two girls to find another place to do their work because they were disturbing a small-group discussion.

You thought all the talk about the difficulties of discipline was exaggerated until you got back to your class and discovered that most of your classmates had witnessed many more examples of teachers disciplining students. Some of your peers observed a system of discipline in primary classrooms in which the teacher wrote down children's names when they violated rules and added checkmarks for further violations. Each checkmark carried specific consequences. One classmate reported observing a first-grade class in which all the children's names were posted on a large chart; below each name was a pocket with a card in it, similar to those in library books. Each child who was "being good" had a card with a green dot on it; each child who had committed one transgression had a card with a yellow dot; and each child who had committed more than one transgression had a card with a red dot. A red dot meant that the child was excluded from recess and all activities other than academic work.

Obviously, discipline is an important topic. Parents continue to rate lack of discipline as the number-two problem in U.S. schools today (drug use is rated number one) (Elam, Rose, and Gallup 1996), and conferences and professional journals have sessions and articles about discipline and tips for teachers. You should understand that there are different points of view about how behavior problems should be handled and what strategies are most successful.

GUIDANCE, DISCIPLINE, AND PUNISHMENT

Discipline and **punishment** are not synonymous terms. Often, members of the public and even teachers use the word *discipline* when what they are referring to is *punishment* designed to enforce obedience to those in authority. Table 5.1 contrasts discipline and punishment.

The title of this chapter uses the word *guiding* because the best discipline consists of guiding children in developmentally appropriate ways to achieve self-control and eventually become self-disciplined individuals. Guidance is not punishment—it is helping children learn. Teachers must consider carefully how to guide and discipline children's behavior. Just as teachers would think about children's needs and developmental levels in planning for growth in literacy or any subject-matter area, they must think about how children can best learn to achieve self-control.

Corporal punishment is physical punishment; when the term is used in schools, it almost always refers to spanking. The Association for Childhood Education International issued a position paper supporting a ban on corporal punishment (Cryan 1987). The paper traces the historical and legal perspectives on corporal punishment and then briefly cites the research on the effects of such punishment. The effects are so negative, especially over the long term, that it is clear that corporal punishment is not an effective method of discipline and does not help children learn self-control.

TABLE 5.1
Discipline versus Punishment

Discipline	or	Punishment

Children are *disciplined* when . . .
they are shown positive alternatives rather than just told "no" . . .
they see how their actions affect others . . .
good behavior is rewarded . . .
adults establish fair, simple rules and enforce them consistently.

Children are *punished* when . . .
their behavior is controlled through fear . . .
their feelings are not respected . . .
they behave to avoid a penalty or get a bribe . . .
the adult only tells them what not to do.

Children who are disciplined . . .
learn to share and cooperate . . .
are better able to handle their own anger . . .
are more self-disciplined . . .
feel successful and in control of themselves.

Children who are punished . . .
feel humiliated . . .
hide their mistakes . . .
tend to be angry and aggressive . . .
fail to develop control of themselves.

Source: From *Helping Children Learn Self-Control* (brochure), (Washington, DC: National Association for the Education of Young Children, 1986). Copyright © 1986 by NAEYC. Excerpted by permission.

Punishment is not always corporal punishment, however. Children can be punished by being confined to their rooms, by having privileges restricted, or by a variety of other means. Some punishments are natural consequences of behavior. If a child breaks the crayons, then he will not have any when he wants to draw. If a child bullies her friends, no one will want to play with her. A later section of the chapter will discuss the use of natural consequences in a system of discipline (see "Dreikurs Model"). This section covers a punishment commonly meted out by early childhood teachers to control children's behavior: being confined to the "time-out" chair.

The original theory behind *time out* was sound: Taking time out gives children an opportunity to gain control of their own behavior and to choose when they are ready to return to the group. Unfortunately, that is not the way time out is used in most classrooms. In many classrooms, the time-out chair is clearly punishment that is overused to obtain obedience. Betz (1994) states that he has "seen it misused so often that it has become unbearably trivialized" (p. 11). He suggests that time out be used "either for fairly serious matters, such as when a child is wildly out of control and repeatedly hurting others, or when a child has exasperated you beyond endurance" (p. 11).

Miller (1984) also has concerns about the use of time out as a punishment technique. She recommends the following principles for using time out:

Time out is not a punishment. Children should not be threatened with or fearful of a time out.
Time out should not be humiliating. Consequently, there should not be a predetermined time-out chair or place.

Time out should last as long as the child feels is needed to calm down. If children underestimate the length of time they need, they can be asked to try to calm down again in time out.

Time out can be a time for the adult and child to talk about feelings—after the child has calmed down. An adult's presence can help calm an angry child, but only after calm has been restored will it be productive to talk. (pp. 17–18)

Punishment may stop a behavior temporarily, but it may also interfere with teaching children appropriate behavior (Schickedanz, Schickedanz, and Forsyth 1982). Punishment may reduce children's initiative if they do not know which behaviors will be punished, and it may result in children's avoiding new situations in order to avoid punishment (Clewett 1988).

Discipline is important—how teachers respond to children's behavior is crucial in helping them grow and feel competent. No one would suggest that discipline be ignored; chaos in the classroom is not healthy for children or for teachers. Neither would anyone be naive enough to suggest that discipline is easy.

There are no clear-cut rules to follow, because every situation and every child are different. The same behavior from two different children might (and probably should) elicit different responses from the same teacher. So much depends on the child's age, development, previous experience, and present situation that no rules will ever apply to all situations. Good discipline helps children gain self-esteem, learn to be cooperative, and gradually learn the skills necessary for taking responsibility for their own behavior.

PARENTS AND GUIDING BEHAVIOR

■ Make sure that parents are aware of your program goals in terms of developing appropriate social skills, and highlight the guidance strategies that lead to achievement of those goals.

TEACHERS AND DISCIPLINE

THEORY INTO Practice

Interview four different early childhood teachers about their discipline problems and solutions. What are their most common problems? What are their solutions to the problems?

Every teacher has faced or will face situations in which children's behavior is inappropriate or hurtful. It would be unrealistic to expect children who are still growing and learning to behave in ways that always please the other people around them. A professional teacher knows that some behavior management will be required when working with children and thinks about how different situations can be handled most successfully.

Teachers must consider the long-term effects on children's self-esteem rather than just the immediate results when making discipline decisions. Teachers must also think of discipline situations as teaching opportunities—opportunities to help children learn how to solve problems, how to negotiate differences, how to handle frustrations, and so on. Effective discipline requires thinking and planning, not only to prevent problems but also to prepare reactions that will be most appropriate when problems do occur.

A knowledgeable teacher also understands what is normal behavior for children of different ages and does not have unrealistic expectations. For example, very young children may scream or throw tantrums; four-year-olds may use foul language; five-year-olds may call each other cruel names; and eight-year-olds may form tight groups that gang up on outsiders. Children in one kindergarten class were often punished for lying. A sound knowledge of child development would have helped the teacher understand that many five-year-olds do not have well-developed concepts of truth and that most will deny any deed to protect themselves. Teachers have to think about what lying and other behaviors mean to the children they are teaching.

Guiding the behavior of young children is related to building self-concept, to curriculum planning and organization, and to teachers' beliefs about how children learn best. Guidance requires that teachers make decisions about individual and group behaviors. In some teaching situations, guidance may also require that teachers make decisions about discipline plans that are adopted by the school. The goal of all of this decision making is to plan carefully in order to prevent as many problems as possible.

GUIDANCE AND SELF-CONCEPT

Self-concept is a broad term usually referring to the "perceptions, feelings, and attitudes that a person has about himself or herself" (Marshall 1989, p. 45). Self-concept includes perceptions of our physical characteristics, gender, personality traits, ethnic identity, and so on. *Self-esteem* is a much more specific concept that refers to feelings of self-worth. Most of these perceptions are shaped initially by our parents and other significant adults. As children mature, their self-esteem is shaped more and more by their evaluation of the responses of their peers. High self-esteem is developed when children believe that significant people in their lives view them as valuable and worthwhile. Self-esteem is also increased when children feel competent, capable, and in control. High self-esteem is important; research has shown that low self-esteem is related to a number of problems, including lack of academic achievement, delinquent behavior, and poor mental health (Zigler and Finn-Stevenson 1987).

Social context is extremely important in children's development of self-concept. Caregiver responsiveness can help children learn that they are valuable and that they can influence their environment (Harter 1983). Freedom to explore the physical environment and materials that provide children with challenges and successes are also important (Bredekamp 1987). In a classic study, Sears (1970) found that children of parents who were authoritative (as opposed to authoritarian or permissive) had more positive self-

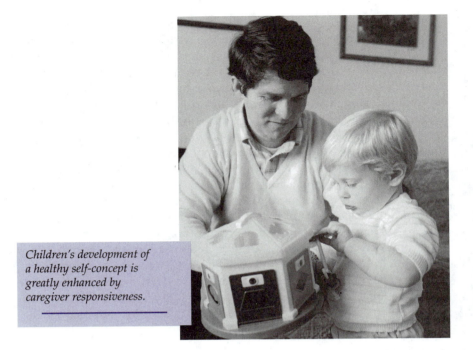

Children's development of a healthy self-concept is greatly enhanced by caregiver responsiveness.

concepts. *Authoritative* parents are in charge but do not make unreasonable demands; provide reasons for expecting given behaviors rather than asserting their authority; and help children make decisions about behavior. *Authoritarian* parents demand obedience because of their authority position, and *permissive* parents fail to set and enforce limits for their children.

For the early childhood teacher, several implications arise from the research on self-concept. One is that children need to feel competent; teachers must select materials and experiences thoughtfully to ensure both challenges and successes. Another implication is that children need to feel in control; therefore, as much of the day as possible should be spent in self-selected activities. Finally, teachers should approach discipline from an authoritative point of view, not an authoritarian or a permissive point of view.

PARENTS ᴬⁿᴰ GUIDING BEHAVIOR

■ Talk with parents about the growth of their child in terms of self-control as well as academics.

■ Help parents appreciate the positive qualities of their child's behavior.

GUIDANCE AND CURRICULUM PLANNING

Often, when teachers are having discipline problems, they look at the children to determine what is wrong with them. At times, teachers may need to look at the programs instead, to see if they are meeting children's needs—not just academic needs, but also social, emotional, and physical needs.

Preschool children need an environment in which they are safe to explore, in which they have enough materials to minimize conflicts, and in which they face very few demands to sit still or attend to teacher-directed instruction. Primary children also need to be able to move about the room and to have activities available that are interesting and appropriate for their level of development. Both age groups need a minimum number of rules. Nothing is harder than trying to make a group of children do something that is inappropriate for their level of development *and* be good while they are doing it. Appropriate curriculum activities, room arrangements, and routines will help prevent many discipline problems.

Curriculum activities need to be interesting and engaging for children. When caught in dull or boring situations, adults can play mental games, plan what they are going to do later, do something else (as when college students study for upcoming tests during boring lectures), or at least pretend not to be bored (as when employees chat politely with the boss at a dull office party). But children simply do not have the skills to look attentive while they are doing something else. When bored or frustrated, they pinch their neighbors, fall out of their chairs, or get out of their seats. In one second-grade classroom, two children were disrupting the teacher's lesson on the four food groups. Their behavior resulted in being removed from the classroom. Later, the teacher admitted that these boys were gifted and already knew all the information being presented. If the curriculum had been more individualized, these two boys would have done their own experiment involving food, which would have engaged them intellectually and eliminated their disruptions and the need for punishment.

In addition to examining curriculum activities for appropriateness, teachers also need to examine materials and classroom arrangements. If, for example, only two wheel toys are available for a large group of children, there will be disputes because of the unreasonable amount of time children must wait for a turn. Similar problems will arise if there are not enough blocks for several children to be building with them at one time. Children become extremely frustrated when they start a project and then find they do not have enough materials to complete it or when storage areas are so congested and unorganized that they cannot get the materials they need.

Room arrangements are also important in preventing discipline problems. If the blocks are in an area through which children must walk to get from one part of the room to another, the teacher will spend an inordinate amount of time mediating disputes over toppled structures. In primary classrooms, the pencil sharpener often seems to be a source of contention. The pencil sharpener should be located where users will disturb other children and disrupt the class as little as possible yet allow children to sharpen their pencils when needed. Nagging and making rules about such little

Many problems can be prevented with adequate materials and space.

things as using the pencil sharpener seems a waste of teacher energy in comparison to the time it would take to prevent the problem in the first place.

One technique to discover traffic patterns or areas of congestion is to make a map of children's movements. The teacher should make a copy of the floorplan of the classroom and draw lines to show the paths children take during given five-minute periods; observations should be repeated every thirty minutes to show patterns throughout the day. These traffic maps will help teachers make decisions about where to locate storage and program areas.

Once the teacher has examined the curriculum and the room arrangements in an effort to prevent problems, another step is to establish routines so that children feel safe and know what to expect. We would all be exhausted if we had to start from scratch to organize our time each day. We know that most of what we do is routine, and we do not have to put energy into deciding about most of our activities (eating, working, sleeping, and so on). Children also need routines in which activities are predictable but not rigidly set. Children need to know that there will be play time, snack time, outdoor play time, and other basic elements in their day. A mentally healthy person can change daily routines without undue stress. When they are secure about basic routines, children, too, can adjust to changes—the arrival of a guest speaker, a field trip, and so on. Complete lack of routine, however, leads to frustration, insecurities, and behavior problems.

Teachers might also need to examine their attitudes and feelings about autonomy and what constitutes obedient behavior from children. Kamii (1982) describes *autonomy* as the ability to make decisions for ourselves. She believes that schools generally reinforce children when they obey without thinking and therefore "unwittingly prevent them from developing autonomy" (p. 85). Having autonomy does not mean that children do not have to obey rules or respect other people and their property. It does mean that children learn to make decisions and think clearly about their behavior and their learning.

GUIDANCE AND BELIEFS ABOUT LEARNING

Teachers who advocate a constructivist approach in explaining how children best learn content material will also advocate a constructivist view of guiding behavior. That means that teachers will think about the role of errors in children's learning to control their behavior just as they would think about errors in children's learning to speak, read, and compute. Strategies such as providing demonstration, modeling, and giving specific feedback will be as appropriate in helping children learn self-control as they are in helping them learn content. And as with content material, teachers have to make decisions about what can be learned at the children's developmental stage and what teaching strategies will be most effective in achieving the desired behavior. For example, if a two-year-old grabs a toy from another child, the most appropriate reaction might be to offer the first child another toy, and explain gently that he cannot take things from others without their permission. However, if a four-year-old takes someone else's toy, then the teacher might suggest that the two children need to solve their problem. She might help them discuss their feelings and needs and guide them to come up with alternative solutions (Dinwiddie 1994).

Suggesting alternatives to aggressive behavior—such as how to use words in a conflict—is one of several effective guidance strategies (Wittmer and Honig 1994). Demonstrating and modeling prosocial behaviors can be accomplished through using puppets to role-play what is appropriate. Teachers can also provide direct instruction in skills such as

> **THEORY INTO *Practice***
>
> Make a list of the ways in which discipline must reflect the developmental level of the child in order to be effective.

DEVELOPMENTALLY **A**PPROPRIATE **P**RACTICE

Reflect on the connections between discipline and developmentally appropriate practice as you respond to the following questions:

- Can discipline be developmentally appropriate if it is not based on understanding the child and what is normal behavior for her given stage of development? Why?
- Should a system of discipline be instituted without considering the match between the child and the curriculum? Can discipline be appropriate if the curriculum is not? Explain your answers.

- Discipline must be considered as an opportunity for teaching. If it is not, can it be developmentally appropriate? Why?
- If you read about a conference presentation called "Developmentally Appropriate Discipline," what information would you expect to be covered?

using "nice talk," saying thank-you, and so on. Schickedanz (1994) also suggests that teachers emphasize what effects children's appropriate and inappropriate behaviors have on others.

GUIDANCE AND TEACHING SKILLS

In addition to thinking about children's developmental levels, professional teachers should respond to problem situations by analyzing what can be taught in them. Katz (1984) categorizes what can be taught as social skills, verbal skills, social knowledge, and dispositional learning.

Social skills include taking turns, negotiating, and coping. Taking turns is not limited to sharing toys but is important in all social situations. During language activities, for example, children must learn to read the signals from a speaker that tell them when they can have a turn talking—eye contact, body language such as inclining the head, and so on. Children must also learn when the speaker is not willing to give up the floor—when he says "ah, ah, ah," avoids eye contact, and so on (Wells 1981). A similar kind of reading of the situation is helpful when one child wants a toy that another child has. The teacher might suggest that the child who wants the toy observe the child who has it and look for signs that he is tiring of it and might be ready to give it up. The teacher might help by modeling language to be used in negotiation, such as "I'll pull you in the wagon later if you'll let me have the truck now." Children also need to learn coping skills because not every request that they make will be honored. The teacher might say "Well, perhaps you can play with the truck tomorrow. For now, you might want to listen to a record or draw a picture." We have all seen adults who cannot cope with not getting what they want, when they want it. Teaching children to cope gives them a valuable life skill.

Verbal skills that can be taught in problem situations include making appropriate assertive statements and talking about disagreements. For example, a child who has just had a toy snatched from her can learn to say firmly "I was not finished playing with that boat. Please give it back." Being able to be assertive without being aggressive is a skill that will serve the child well for the rest of her life. Carrying on conversations about disputes is often difficult for children because they lack the words to continue the discussion. Teachers may have to model the conversations by speaking for both children, as described by Katz (1984):

> Using this technique, the teacher might say to Leslie, "Robin really wants a turn," to which Leslie might grunt a refusal. The teacher might then say to Robin something like, "Leslie does not want to give up the tricycle yet." Robin might respond to this with a whining protest, in which case the teacher can paraphrase to Leslie what Robin is feeling by saying, "Robin really would like a turn now," and so on. In short, the teacher

keeps up the conversation, verbalizing to each child what she infers to be the feelings of the other. (p. 31)

Social knowledge includes the ability to put incidents into perspective and an initial understanding of the concept *justice*. If one child fails to get a turn on the swing, the teacher might say "I know that you are disappointed, but there are other things you can do." The tone of voice should be empathetic but not tragic. Children who hit learn about justice when they are restrained from hitting and told "I won't let you hit anyone. If anyone else hits, I will stop them from hitting, too." The child then begins to feel safer and to feel that the environment is a just one.

Dispositional learning in discipline situations includes learning to be more empathetic, to try different techniques, and to avoid negative dispositions (sulking, temper tantrums, whining, and the like). Children can be taught to be more empathetic (Honig 1985; Marantz 1988). One of the best strategies for teaching empathy is modeling accompanied by discussion. For example, if one child falls and hurts herself, the teacher can model appropriate empathy in her response. Concern for the feelings of others must be a priority in the early childhood classroom.

Children can also learn that problem-solving strategies can be applied in conflicts with others. The teacher might recommend a strategy to a child and then follow the recommendation by saying "If that doesn't work, come back, and we'll think of something else to try." Children must learn to accept that their first efforts may not always be successful while realizing that they can try again. Sometimes, a child may have adopted a negative behavior that the teacher would like to help him change—for example, tattling or complaining. The teacher must make a decision about how best to respond to a child's complaints to help him learn that complaining is not always successful and to learn when an adult should be told about an incident. Children are usually six or seven before they can understand the difference between tattling to get someone in trouble and telling the teacher about something that it is important for an adult to know.

GUIDING GROUPS

Children in groups must be given some rules. The fewer and more flexible these rules are, the better. As soon as children are old enough, they should have a part in making group rules. Some children as young as three can be involved in rule making.

Rules must be clearly stated. Leatzow, Neuhauser, and Wilmes (1983) observe that many early childhood educators have only one rule: "You may not hurt yourself or anyone else" (p. 83). This kind of rule covers many situations and is understood by the children. Other teachers add a rule that children cannot destroy property.

Sometimes, the teacher must manage the group in addition to guiding individual children. The younger the children, the fewer group-management techniques that should be needed. As children are able to participate in more group activities, group-management techniques will become more useful to the teacher. One rule for group management is not to call attention to an individual child. For example, a teacher might say "You all need to sit on your bottoms so that everyone can see the pictures while I read the story," rather than "Julian and Hope must sit down so that others can see." It also helps in this particular situation to reassure some children that they will get to see a book later if they are very excited about it. The teacher might say "You all need to sit flat on your bottoms now, but after I read the story, I'll leave the book here on the table if you want to look at the pictures more closely." With older children who are anxious to see something, the teacher might say "When you leave this table, put your name on the list if you want to see the book again later." Just as public criticism is to be avoided, so, too, is public praise inappropriate in group-management situations. For example, the teacher might say "Almost everyone is ready for the story; in just a minute, we will begin," rather than "Sara and Randy are sitting nicely, waiting for the story."

In using group-management strategies, teachers must be careful to preserve children's self-esteem and to use techniques that help children learn acceptable behaviors—the same concerns that apply when guiding individual behavior. Gartrell (1987b) acknowledges that learning these techniques takes commitment and practice on the part of teachers. Teachers must "deal with the young child's need to feel safe and secure, through personal acceptance, sensible limits, gentle correction, and genuine encouragement" (p. 55).

The same considerations of appropriateness of activity must be applied to group-management situations as to individual guidance situations. When children are in group situations too long or when group activities are inappropriate, behavior problems will result. One teacher of five-year-olds had a group lesson on the beginning sound of "r." The teacher had twenty-three children sit in a circle to listen to a recording about the letter *r*. The teacher held an inflatable figure representing *r*. During the thirty-minute lesson, the teacher had to discipline children many times— "Stop leaning back in your chair," "Don't pull her hair," "Pay attention," and so on. Clearly, this activity was inappropriate for five-year-olds, and the time spent on it was too long. The teacher could have saved much frustration for himself and the children by choosing other teaching strategies.

Planning for Key Points in the Schedule

Experienced teachers will agree that discipline problems are more likely at certain times of day than others, including arrival times, transition times, and departure times. Planning for these key times is essential.

For arrival time, the teacher might ask that children wait until everyone has arrived or until a set time has been reached before activities begin. The fact is, though, that children are not good at waiting. Alternatives to waiting might be to plan an activity to occupy children who arrive early or to allow these children to begin working in learning areas.

Music and fingerplays can be used to help children make transitions from one activity to another without nagging and reminding by the teacher. Often, children will put away toys and materials if the teacher helps and makes up a simple song ("This is the way we put blocks on the shelf" or "This is the way we wash the paint brushes"). Playing a record or tape of a march song will encourage the children to march around the room until they come to the area for group activities; while marching, they will have no time to become bored and get into trouble. If the children are old enough, one child can begin to lead either a song or a fingerplay, and each child can join when she is ready. Fingerplays led by the teacher can encourage children to do what is necessary without being reminded. For example, the fingerplay "Two Little Hands Go Clap, Clap, Clap" ends with the line "And one little child sits quietly down." By the end of this fingerplay, all the children will be sitting, and the teacher will not have nagged anyone to do so.

Departures also need to be planned. Teachers need to think about how to distribute notices and work at the end of the day so that children do not have to wait too long. A routine of getting coats, distributing materials to take home, and delivering some short closing message can help keep children on track during departures.

On occasion, an activity might be appropriate for most of the group but not for an individual child. If a child is having difficulty, it is usually appropriate to allow him another choice. The teacher might whisper to a child "You can stay here if you choose, or you may work quietly with the puzzles or books if you want." Individualizing curriculum means attending to the needs of different children. The sensitive teacher is usually aware of when a child may need to leave a group and tries to arrange for that before an incident happens.

In sum, many discipline problems can be avoided by anticipating when they are likely to occur and planning to circumvent them. Crosser (1992) uses the acronym BASIC to describe such planning:

Before school begins
Arrival and departure times
Schedule transitions
Interactions with equipment and materials
Conflict management (p. 23)

In other words, the teacher plans the environment, plans for special times in the day, plans to help children learn to work with classroom equipment and materials, and teaches children how to settle conflicts that arise.

GUIDANCE DECISIONS

When teachers are confronted with misbehavior, they must make decisions about whether to respond, how to respond, and how to evaluate the growth of the children involved.

Weighing the Situation

In some situations, the most effective response is no response at all. Children sometimes behave in ways that are not appropriate but are not harmful to anyone and are not disruptive if they are ignored. For example, suppose the teacher asks the children to come to group time and sit on the floor for a story. Jennifer comes to the group but stands instead of sits. The teacher comments to the group that she is almost ready to start reading and makes eye contact with Jennifer, who remains standing. Rather than call her name and force her to sit, the teacher should do nothing and begin reading, as if Jennifer were sitting quietly. Jennifer may soon sit down and join the group, or she may keep standing, but as long as she is not interfering with others, little will be gained from making her sit. If Jennifer continually refuses to do anything that she is asked, the teacher will need to take steps privately to find out what makes Jennifer feel so defiant.

Effective teachers know when to ignore behavior and when to deal with it. No rules determine what to ignore and when—only professional judgment provides the answers. In weighing a given situation, the teacher should ask herself these questions: What will be gained in terms of teaching and increased self-control by responding to the behavior? What will be lost in terms of the child's self-concept or feeling of autonomy?

Making the Choice to Respond

Once a teacher has decided to respond to a child's behavior, he must decide how. In this case, there are certain rules to follow:

1. The response should be private, if at all possible. A child who is hitting another child will have to be restrained immediately, but then he can be removed and the behavior can be dealt with privately.
2. The response should be developmentally appropriate—for example, redirecting a toddler; appealing to the empathetic feelings of a five-year-old; or explaining rationally to an eight-year-old.
3. The response should be aimed at helping the child increase her self-control. The teacher should express acceptance of the child's feelings and provide guidance in finding a socially acceptable way of expressing them.

THEORY
INTO
Practice

Write a description of a behavioral situation in which a teacher must decide whether to respond. Exchange descriptions among a small group of classmates, and discuss how you would respond to each situation and why.

4. The response should demonstrate caring for the child but firmness in rejecting the behavior: "I'm sorry that you are frustrated because you can't have the doll now, but you cannot spit on anyone. You can spit in the sink."

5. The response should involve as much knowledge about the child and her situation as the teacher can summon in the split second that is often available for making a decision. For instance, suppose that the teacher knows that Sylvia's father has just moved out and that her family is under stress. When Sylvia behaves in a way that is not typical for her, such as throwing sand on a friend, the teacher can quietly take her aside and explain gently that he knows that she feels like throwing something, that she can tell him how she feels if she wants to, but that she cannot hurt other children.

Withitness is a term that has become popular in the literature on discipline; it was derived from the work of Jacob Kounin, a well-known educational researcher (Charles and Barr 1989). Withitness is knowing what is

Good discipline offers children an opportunity to learn how to control their own behavior.

going on in the classroom at all times. If students observe that the teacher chooses to correct the wrong child's behavior, they will assume that the teacher does not know what is going on. Teachers with withitness also know to stop misbehavior before it spreads to others; timing such as this requires that teachers observe carefully.

Examples of Effective Responses

The following scenarios demonstrate effective responses to real-life problems in the classroom:

- You are reading a story to a small group. Several children start to whine that they do not like the story. One child puts her hands over her ears. Others notice and start to put hands over their ears. You could ignore the behavior and do a little editing of the story to finish it quickly. Or you could stop reading and say "I know that some of you like other books better. Perhaps we will read a book that you like better tomorrow. But some people like this book, so I'm going to finish reading it now. You can wait quietly for the few minutes that it will take."
- You find several children in the bathroom exposing themselves. You could say "I see that you are interested in the differences between boys and girls. Would you like to have me read this book to you that explains some of the differences?"
- One child pulls all the blocks off the shelf and refuses to help put them away. You might say "I know that it is much more fun to pull these blocks off the shelf than it is to put them away. We all have to do things that are not much fun sometimes. I'll help you begin, and you can finish." If the child still refuses to help, you could say "I'm going to put away these blocks now. Then you and I must talk about why you are not feeling like helping today."
- A child bites another child. First, you must restrain the child so that no more biting can occur. Then you might say "You cannot bite Sidney. You know that biting hurts very much, and the rule is that you cannot hurt anyone. I will not let you hurt anyone, and I will try not to let anyone hurt you. I know that you are angry, and I know that Sidney grabbed your toy. You must tell Sidney that you do not like it when he grabs your toy. Use words to tell him how angry you are."

Evaluating Growth

Evaluating children's growth in handling conflicts and in managing their own behavior requires that teachers keep anecdotal records of children's behavior over time and be able to document their growth in behaving in more acceptable ways. Gartrell (1995) relates the story of a child who said "you damm sunnamabitch" to another child. When the teacher got to the children, she comforted the second child briefly and then whispered "I'm proud of you" in the ear of the swearing child. She explained later to an observer that until last week, this child had hit or kicked others whenever he was angry; his teachers had been trying to get him to use words to express himself in these situations. When the teacher whispered in the boy's ear to congratulate him on his language use, she also supplied him with some words that would not bother people as much as the swear words.

Children's growth usually takes time and comes in little steps, but teachers need to be able to see the changes, even when they are small. Teachers must also evaluate their own growth in responding to children's behavior. Teachers must remember that both children and adults get tired and become angry. If teachers occasionally respond in ways that are less than professional, they should forgive themselves and learn from their experience.

BEHAVIOR-MANAGEMENT SYSTEMS

Several behavior-management systems have been designed to help teachers control children's behavior. The following sections will describe assertive discipline, the Glasser model, the Ginott model, and the Dreikurs model.

Assertive Discipline

Designed by Lee Canter (1976), *assertive discipline* is a system in which the rules for classroom behavior are established by the teacher and posted in the classroom. The consequences for breaking any of the rules are also posted. If a child breaks the rule against speaking out in class, for example, her name is written on the chalkboard. (In subsequent publications, Canter has recommended that the names be written on a clipboard or in a book, rather than on the board [Hill 1990].) Another offense results in a checkmark being placed after the child's name. Usually, the consequence of receiving two checkmarks is being sent to the principal's office or having the teacher call the child's parents.

Because disruptions prevent teachers from teaching effectively, Canter believes that use of the assertive discipline system enables teachers to be more effective and solves the management problems in any classroom. This system is in use in many elementary schools, which means that many early childhood teachers are required to follow assertive discipline.

THEORY

In a small group, discuss your own feelings about discipline. Do you feel comfortable about managing individual and group behavior? Have you had opportunities to observe many positive models of behavior management? Describe your observations.

Administrators who believe that the system helps teachers feel more comfortable about discipline are likely to promote its use.

One of the first things any teacher of young children must do is assess the validity of the assumptions of any behavior-management program. Canter based the assertive discipline system on the assumption that children want to disrupt the teacher and prevent teaching (Canter 1988; Hitz 1988). Teachers who believe that children have an inherent desire to learn and who have observed the eagerness with which young children approach learning will deem this an invalid assumption.

Another problem with assertive discipline is that it assumes that young children can operate according to rules. Experienced teachers know that young children can learn that some behaviors are acceptable at school and others are not. They also know that this learning usually takes time, guidance, and repeated experience. The assertive discipline system assumes that telling children that there is a rule and punishing them for breaking the rule will prevent unacceptable behavior. This approach may prevent the behavior at a given moment, but children will not know why the behavior is unacceptable nor will they learn to make better judgments about how to behave in future situations.

Behavior-management systems that enforce rules established by adult authority do not help children learn to be responsible. Such systems do, however, teach children to obey authority that is exercised through "power assertion" (Hitz 1988). There are situations in which adults must assert their power and demand instant obedience—for example, in order to prevent injury or cope with an emergency, such as a fire. Adults exert such control until children are old enough to learn rational reasons for controlling their own behavior in like situations. However, controlling children by power and demanding instant obedience should not be typical means of behavior management. Gartrell (1987a) expresses concerns that assertive discipline damages children's self-concepts and turns teachers into "managing technicians" (p. 11). Perhaps a larger concern is the danger that children will not be able to determine appropriate behavior and to develop a sense of responsibility for their actions.

The assertive discipline model also fails to examine the causes of disruptive behavior. The system is applied regardless of the curriculum, the room arrangements, or the schedule. No system of discipline should ever be applied without careful assessment of all the factors and individuals involved in a teaching situation.

Jones and Jones (1990) report that some schools that began assertive discipline programs several years ago have moved away from them, for several reasons:

Many teachers are frustrated because problem students seem to be relatively unaffected by the procedures, and students who do not need such repressive methods tend to find the method insulting or anxiety provoking. Our own concern is that too frequently the method creates a "sit down, shut up, or get out" philosophy in classrooms in which teaching methods are failing to meet students' basic personal and academic needs. Too often teachers use the Assertive Discipline procedures rather than examining their own teaching methods to consider how to prevent disruptive behavior. (p. 412)

Glasser Model

The Glasser model (Glasser 1985) is based on providing good choices for children and handling disruptions that do occur in a calm and logical manner. Glasser believes that good choices produce good behavior and bad choices produce bad behavior. He believes that behavior represents individuals' attempts to meet their needs and that if schools are to have better discipline, they will have to become places where fewer children and teachers are frustrated in getting what they need. Some of the important needs that Glasser identifies are the needs to belong, to be free, and to have fun. Schools in which children do not feel a sense of belonging or have no power to make choices are schools in which discipline problems are common.

Glasser recommends that teachers structure learning experiences so that children have high motivation to work on behalf of the group and that stronger students help weaker students, thus fulfilling the stronger students' need for power and the weaker students' need to contribute to the group. One of the hallmarks of Glasser's model is the class meeting, in which students discuss class rules and behavior. Although Glasser's model is used more often with older students than with young children, his focus on problem solving, on the choices provided by teachers, and on teachers' persistence in helping children with problems is appropriate for young children.

Ginott Model

The Ginott model (Ginott 1972) is based on setting up a classroom climate that is conducive to good discipline through effective communication between teachers and children. Ginott believes that discipline is an ongoing process that is achieved over time. One of the principles of his model is that corrective messages to children should attack the problem and not the child. Ginott uses the term *congruent communication* to describe responses that are in harmony with children's feelings about situations or themselves. He also advocates inviting cooperation, not demanding it. Teachers applying Ginott's recommendations do not label children and communicate their willingness to help children solve problems.

Charles and Barr (1989) report that even teachers who are sympathetic with Ginott's views feel that more structured management is needed in many teaching situations. Nonetheless, Ginott's emphasis on the ability to communicate well with children is of value to early childhood teachers. Another component of Ginott's model that is of value to early childhood teachers is its emphasis on the self-esteem of the child and the importance of the teacher's behavior.

Dreikurs Model

The Dreikurs model (Dreikurs 1982) is best known for its emphasis on logical consequences. Dreikurs defines *discipline* as teaching students to impose limits on themselves. He believes that all children want to belong and that their behaviors represent efforts to achieve a sense of belonging. Misbehaviors are the result of mistaken goals such as seeking attention, power, or revenge or wanting to display another child's inadequacy. Dreikurs suggests that the best method of discipline is encouraging positive behavior.

When teachers encounter behavior problems, Dreikurs recommends that they point out to students the logical consequences of their actions. In describing *logical consequences*, Charles and Barr (1989) use examples that apply to older children, but their explanation will suggest applications for younger children, as well:

> Logical consequences must be differentiated from punishment. Punishment is action taken by the teacher to get back at misbehaving students and show them who is boss. Punishment breeds retaliation and gives students the feeling that they have the right to punish in return. Logical consequences, on the other hand, are not weapons used by the teacher. They teach students that all behavior produces a corresponding result: good behavior brings rewards and unacceptable behavior brings unpleasant consequences. If a student throws paper on the floor, that student must pick it up. If a student fails to do work as assigned, that student must make up the work on his or her own time. (p. 83)

Gartrell (1995) believes that the terminology used can influence the mindset of the teacher toward guiding children's behavior; thus, he promotes using the term *mistaken behavior*, rather than *misbehavior*. *Misbehavior* makes teachers think of punishing, while *mistaken behavior* encourages thinking about guiding and teaching. Gartrell credits Dreikurs's thinking about behavior as the stepping stones that led to development of the concept *mistaken behavior*.

In evaluating different models for managing behavior, Charles and Barr (1989) state that "Dreikurs' views have the greatest potential for bringing about genuine attitudinal change among students, so that they ultimately behave better because they consider it the proper thing to do" (p. 85).

Assessing Behavior-Management Systems

It is the teacher's responsibility to assess any management system or discipline policy based on the following criteria:

- *Respect for children*—Not every teacher will love every child, but each child deserves respect as a human being. If it is hard to respect the child because of constant problems, the teacher should seek help from co-teachers, counselors, parents, or administrators. Using a behavior-management system that does not respect the individual child will cause more harm than it attempts to address.

- *Knowledge of individual children*—Discipline cannot be applied fairly if it is applied without knowledge of the individual child. For example, enforcing a rule against bad language with the child (discussed earlier), who swore instead of hitting would leave him without an acceptable way to express his frustration. As the child shows more growth, the teacher can continue to help him find more acceptable classroom words for expressing anger. Behavior-management systems often make it easy for teachers to gloss over the need to know each child.

- *Knowledge of normal growth, development, and behavior*—Children who are behaving in ways that are normal for their age may be helped to learn more acceptable responses to be used at school. But such behavior will not be irritating to the knowledgeable teacher because he will realize that it is a normal part of working with this particular age group.

- *Willingness to accept discipline as an opportunity for teaching*—Discipline is not punishment. Teachers sometimes have to work hard at helping children control their behavior in ways that teach them new strategies for interacting successfully in groups or with individuals.

- *Avoidance of judgmental words*—Calling children *good* or *bad* does not help them learn alternative ways of behaving. More appropriate descriptions of behavior guide children without judging them.

- *Limited but cooperative rule making*—Being well-behaved in a classroom where there are long lists of rules is difficult for children, because too many things are against the rules. As soon as children are old enough, they can begin to help teachers decide on rules that the group will follow.

CHILDREN WITH SPECIAL NEEDS

Many children with special needs require only guidance that is typical for their age, while others may require more support from the teacher. For

THEORY INTO Practice

Find additional information on the guidance systems presented in this chapter. Also try to find schools in which these systems are in use; observe in classrooms or interview teachers at these schools. What conclusions can you draw about the match between developmentally appropriate practice and each of these systems? Present your research in a paper, oral report, or video production.

many special-needs children, arranging the environment to facilitate their access to materials and equipment will greatly reduce their frustration and thus their inappropriate behavior, as well. Once children have equal access to materials and equipment, teachers can generally use the same guidance strategies they use with the children's peers. Some children, however, may require more support, so teachers may need to use guidance strategies that are usually more appropriate for younger children. For example, consider a child with a physical disability who is in a wheelchair; she is chronologically and developmentally age four. Given this, her teacher should be able to employ the same problem-solving strategies in guidance that are applied to other children of the same age. If the child needs additional support, such as having just one or two options rather than a more open-ended approach, then the teacher can provide that support.

Guidance for children with disabilities may focus on teaching them social skills. In addition to making environmental arrangements, Lowenthal (1996) suggests several strategies: using group affection activities, such as modifying games and songs in which children touch or hug each other in affectionate ways; teaching typically developing peers to initiate play with special children by offering toys or extending invitations to play; and using teacher prompts to help children recognize elements in social situations that they might not pick up on their own. Obviously, the strategies selected must be individually appropriate for the child.

Brown, Althouse, and Anfin (1993) found that guided dramatization was an effective strategy in encouraging children with disabilities to interact in positive ways with other children. These authors guided the dramatization of a familiar story by teaching it to a child with disabilities through interactive reading, telling the story with a magnetic or flannelboard, and then asking the child to choose someone else to help tell the story. As the children dramatized the story, the teacher took photographs and used them in retelling the story again. The target child was photographed playing with the other children and asked to tell about the play. These authors found that this sequence helped the child with disabilities learn how to interact with others and that the child initiated play experiences with other children based on the story.

CELEBRATING DIVERSITY

Guidance always entails values. We all select what is important to us and what is supposedly correct behavior through the lens of our own culture and family. Teachers must always keep this in mind as they make decisions about which behaviors are acceptable or appropriate and which behaviors are not. In addition, teachers must learn about the values and expectations

Teachers' choices about what is considered acceptable behavior may reflect their own cultural backgrounds.

that certain cultures have for the behavior of children and what children's families support within their cultural group. This learning is not supposed to result in teachers' feeling that they cannot make decisions about guidance. Rather, when teachers make decisions that conflict with children's cultural norms, they have an obligation to explain to the children (and their parents) why school behavior is different than home behavior. If parents understand the need for certain behaviors, they can help their children yet not feel that their own values and patterns are being ignored.

Gender differences in expectations for behavior in educational settings are also an issue when thinking about diversity. Gordon and Browne (1996) have reported that teachers typically pay more attention to boys, give them more positive feedback, and give them more attention and praise for achievement. The same study found that aggression is tolerated more in boys, that disruptive talking is tolerated more in girls, that teachers use physical discipline more with boys, and that teachers use more negative comments or disapproving gestures with girls. All these findings should strengthen the resolve of teachers to pay equal attention to all children, to base standards of behavior on developmental and cultural information rather than on gender, and to discourage dependent helpless and excessively conforming behavior in both boys and girls (Gordon and Browne 1996).

PARENTS AND GUIDING BEHAVIOR

■ All guidance decisions must be made with knowledge about and sensitivity to the individual child's family and culture. Working with families in an open and caring relationship is a prerequisite to guidance that is appropriate for each child.

CHAPTER SUMMARY

- Discipline is a major concern of teachers. It is perceived by the general public to be the most important problem in schools.

- The professional teacher views discipline as integral to the teaching process. Discipline must be based on knowledge of children's normal development, and the teacher must be aware of the effects of disciplinary decisions on children's self-esteem.

- The curriculum may contribute to discipline problems if activities are not appropriate for children. Children need both challenges and successes. They also need interesting, engaging activities that they select themselves.

- Room arrangements may be a source of discipline problems. Too little space to work, traffic through play areas, and spaces that are difficult to supervise may be sources of frustration to both teachers and children.

- Teachers who view discipline as a teaching opportunity can help children learn social skills, verbal skills, coping skills, and the disposition to use positive strategies in relating to others.

- Good group-management techniques require that the teacher avoid calling attention to individual children for either positive or negative behaviors.

- Often, teachers have the choice of ignoring inappropriate behavior. The decision to respond to behavior must be based on the teacher's professional assessment of the situation and what a child can learn from it.

- When teachers decide to respond to behavior, their responses should be private, developmentally appropriate, aimed at helping children achieve self-control, expressive of concern for children, and based as much as possible on knowledge of the individual children involved.

- In the last few years, many schools have adopted behavior-management systems that all teachers, even those in early childhood, must apply. In assessing any such system, teachers should examine the assumptions on which the system is based, its effects on children's self-esteem, and the cognitive requirements the system makes of young children.

- *Discipline* and *punishment* are not synonymous terms. Punishment often has long-term negative effects and does not teach children self-control.

- The goal of learning to control their own behavior must be set for special-needs children as well as typically developing children. Moving toward this long-term goal means that each child will learn problem-solving strategies that are developmentally appropriate.

- Teachers should respect children's cultural backgrounds when making decisions about behavior. In addition, teachers should help parents and caregivers understand the importance of having certain behaviors at school and the differences between what behaviors are acceptable at home versus school.

Setting Up a Positive Classroom Atmosphere

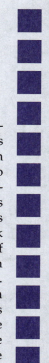

When I first began teaching kindergarten twelve years ago, I had a well thought out discipline plan in mind to use with my students. As the schoolyear went on and I implemented the plan, I noticed that the more I disciplined, the more discipline I needed. I was living with my grandmother, who had taught school for forty-one years, so I shared my concerns with her. Her advice to me was "Look for the good in children!"

Granny was my mentor, someone I knew I wanted to pattern my teaching after, so I gave her advice a try in my classroom. It didn't take long for me to realize that children responded much more positively to encouragement and praise than to consequences and punishment. The more I complimented, the less I disciplined! I adopted Granny's discipline plan as my own, and in looking for the good in children, I have found the most effective discipline plan for my students and me: Guide behavior in a positive direction, and most discipline problems will be eliminated. Setting up a positive classroom atmosphere by looking for the good in children is my main goal, from the first day of school to the last!

Looking for the good in children is not really a discipline plan at all. It is an attitude—an attitude that a teacher must truly possess before a positive classroom atmosphere can be achieved. The teacher must believe in it wholeheartedly before she can expect her students to believe in it, too. She must also be ready to accept unconditionally each child she teaches as the unique individual that he is and be able to ignore many behaviors labeled negative that are really developmentally appropriate characteristics and behaviors of children.

The achievement of full and unconditional acceptance of every child for whom we are responsible is essential to a positive classroom atmosphere. Accepting a child does not mean simply tolerating him but rather affirming his value as a person, not in relation to his achievements or behavior but simply because of his existence. Acceptance of a child does not happen automatically; rather, it is a goal for which to reach. It means being aware of the familial, cultural, and societal differences by which all of us are shaped. In many subtle and some obvious ways, adults show children their respect or lack of respect for them as people. One simple way of showing respect for a student is to address him in private, if possible, concerning discipline. Another way is to never use sarcasm against a student. Still another way is to respect students as you do other adults, while not expecting the behavior of adults from them. Teachers have the responsibility of building into a child's life those interactions and experiences that can contribute to a sense of pride in who the child really is.

In a classroom with a positive atmosphere, the teacher must ignore as much negative behavior as possible and recognize and reinforce as much positive behavior as possible. Although punishment cannot be ignored, I try to emphasize the good in children and only use punishment in extreme behavioral instances.

Looking for the good in children—really accepting them as they are—and positive reinforcement: These are some of the elements of a positive classroom atmosphere according to Karen Willis (and Granny). It all sounds pretty idealistic, but it really works if you can make the commitment to keep a positive attitude! Teachers are responsible for assuring that children will flourish in school. And although I think children learn in spite of inadequate classroom atmospheres, I do not believe they reach their full potentials in these situations. I challenge you to strive to obtain a positive classroom atmosphere so your students can reach their highest goals. You may find that achieving a positive atmosphere is beneficial to you as a teacher, too!

6

TEACHERS, PARENTS, AND PARAPROFESSIONALS

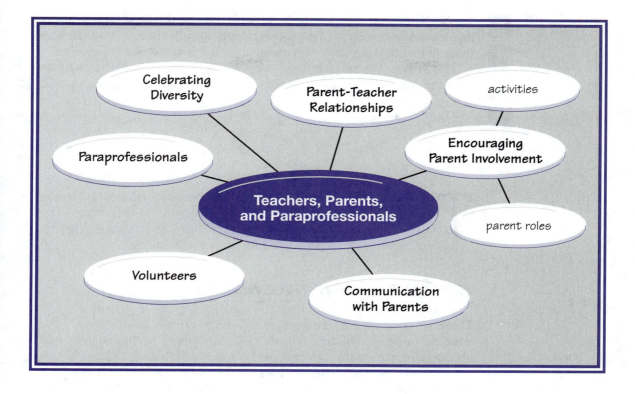

Your observation this week was not what you had expected. You went to a school for children from ages three to five or six. Some of the children in this school had been identified as having special needs and were entitled to services provided by the school district. You expected to see teacher aides with these children, and your expectations were accurate in some instances—for example, interpreters were working with deaf children and aides were helping children in wheelchairs. What surprised you were the number of classrooms in which the teachers and aides were working together as a team. You knew that the teachers were ultimately responsible for all instruction in the classroom, but you also saw aides busy instructing small groups and tutoring individual children. Your only previous experience with teacher aides had been with some who supervised the playground and lunchroom.

You were also surprised at the number of parents who were volunteering. You knew that today most mothers work outside the home, so you had thought that the days of "room mothers" and "room helpers" were over.

What does the teacher do to keep all these adults working together smoothly so that the children benefit from the extra hands, extra ears, and extra eyes?

This chapter will explore the relationship between families and teachers and address the theme of communicating with parents. The teacher's goal must be to forge a partnership with parents that results in the best possible educational experience for the children.

NEED FOR PARENT INVOLVEMENT

There are good reasons for teachers to want parents to be involved in the education of their children (Olson 1990). Greenberg (1989) believes that encouraging parent involvement aids teachers in building children's self-esteem, reduces discipline problems, and increases children's regard for themselves as learners. Parents teach their children much that cannot be taught in school. Teachers who view parents as important partners in the children's education will appreciate parents more and be more open to parental involvement.

Research indicates that children achieve more when parents are involved in their schooling. The major findings from the research on parent involvement have been summarized by Henderson (1988):

- The family, not the school, provides the primary educational environment for children.
- Involving parents in their children's formal education improves the children's achievements.
- Parent involvement is most effective when it is comprehensive, well-planned, and long-lasting.
- Involving parents when their children are young has beneficial effects that persist throughout the child's academic career.
- Involving parents with their children's education at home may not be enough to improve schools; a school's average level of achievement does not appear to improve unless parents are involved in the school.
- Children from low-income and minority families benefit the most when parents are involved in the schools, and parents do not have to be well-educated to make a difference. (p. 153)

When parents are involved in their children's school experiences, they are as likely to be affected positively as the children. A study of parents who worked in Head Start programs found that they "gained significantly in their positive attitudes about the importance of education" (Systems Development Corporation 1972). Leik and Chalkey (1990) report that Head Start parents who were involved in an enrichment program (involving more parental activities than the minimum required by Head Start) were more likely to see their children as competent than were parents who did not participate in the enrichment program. However, both groups of parents functioned more effectively after being involved in parental activities.

Parent involvement also affects the family, as the parent gains skill in interacting with all the children in the family, not just the child in school. Many parents who have become involved with their children's schools have even used the skills learned there to improve their job opportunities (Kagan 1982).

In reviewing what we know and do not know about parent involvement programs, Epstein (1991) offers these conclusions:

- Parents and teachers are more similar than different—they have many goals in common and a need to share information.
- Programs must continue through the elementary and high school years, not stop after the early childhood years.
- Programs must include all families.
- Programs make the teacher's job easier.
- Program development takes time.

REALITIES OF PARENT-TEACHER RELATIONSHIPS

Parent-teacher relationships are not as simple as many articles lead us to believe. New teachers could mistakenly come to think that parent volunteers are common and that all parents will attend parent conferences if they are invited to do so. However, as teachers of young children, you need to recognize that although parent involvement is very important, it is not always easy for the teacher, the school, or the parents to facilitate.

Pressures on parents today are tremendous. Changing family structures, economic conditions, and lack of support for the nuclear family contribute to the stress. Family structures have changed radically from the 1950s; only 5.9 percent of Americans have a "Dick and Jane" family (Cline 1990), in which the father works outside the home and the mother stays at home to care for the children. More and more children live with single parents, in two-parent working families, or in blended families created by remarriages. Many children also live with relatives other than their parents.

Families today may consist of stepparents, foster parents, grandparents, single mothers, single fathers, or any number of other configurations.

The plight of children in the United States continues to be serious. Even though the percentage of children under six who are living in poverty dropped from 25.6 in 1993 to 24.5 in 1994, the *number* of these children continues to be extremely high (Children's Defense Fund 1996, p. 77). Children living in poverty tend to live in families headed by women, to be children of color, and to have young parents.

More than half the mothers of children under six are employed outside the home, and that number is constantly rising (Children's Defense Fund 1996, p. 93). This enormous number of mothers in the workforce reflects economic conditions that make it ever more difficult for a family to survive economically. Many mothers work because they are the sole source of support for their children. These economic stresses in turn make it more difficult than ever before for parents to have choices about child care, to spend energy nurturing and educating their children rather than just trying to survive, or to become involved in the formal education of their children.

In addition to these pressures on the family, today's nuclear family does not have the support from the extended family that was available to past generations. Families often live long distances from other relatives and must depend on outsiders for child care and advice or support. Many parents are isolated; they have no one to help them cope with all the demands of caring for children and maintaining their daily lives.

In a review of research on changing demographic trends, Halpern (1987) found that:

1. families with young children are increasingly dependent on agencies outside their informal social networks for the emotional, informational, and material support underlying nurturant childrearing;
2. our sense of collective responsibility for other people's children, never strong to begin with, is deteriorating further;
3. the stress on parents of trying to provide both adequate economic support and adequate care and nurturance for children is likely to intensify; and
4. we as a society face the urgent task of renewing and redefining our social contract with each other, and with young families in particular; the early childhood care and education community has a central responsibility with respect to this task. (p. 34)

Implications for Teachers

One of the first rules for teachers who want to establish good relationships with all parents is to adopt a **nonjudgmental attitude** toward them. Most parents care desperately about their children. There are many reasons why parents do not get involved in school, but lack of concern about their children is usually not one of them. Some parents may have had negative experiences in school, so that any contact with the school revives their own feelings of inadequacy; others may be overwhelmed with the pressures in their lives and unable to cope with one more demand; still others may not know what they can do to help their child in school. For some parents, it would be culturally inappropriate to be other than passive in their involvement with the school. (In some cultures, teachers are highly respected figures of authority. For parents from such cultures to take an active role in school would be perceived as an infringement on the teacher's authority.)

There are many other reasons why parents may not get involved. The fundamental principle that should guide teachers in working with parents is that parents need help, understanding, and support, not criticism (Hranitz and Eddowes 1987). It is imperative that teachers persist in efforts to involve parents in their children's education.

New teachers must expect to be involved in major efforts to restructure family and school relationships. Expecting all families to meet middle-class standards for involvement in schools is unrealistic. It is also unrealistic to believe that only one model for family involvement is possible. Families and schools must learn new ways of interacting. Karr and Landerholm (1991) state the goal well: "Programs must meet the needs of the parents they serve rather than demand that the parents meet the needs of the program" (p. 6).

Teachers of young children must be especially sensitive to the needs of children from different family structures, and this sensitivity should be reflected in the language used to discuss families. The phrase *broken home*, for example, is inappropriate. A child's parents may be divorced and she may be living in a single-parent family, but there is nothing inherently wrong or deprived about such a family structure. Similarly, teachers must avoid planning activities in which the child is to make gifts for parents or events that are labeled "father-son" or "mother-daughter." Activities involving gifts or family events should be presented as opportunities to share with someone special in a child's life—a foster mother, a grandparent, or any other relative—rather than being specifically labeled for mothers and fathers. When using photographs of families, teachers should make sure that a variety of family structures are illustrated and that discussions are not limited to families made up of Mother, Father, and children.

Although it is not directly the responsibility of the teacher, it is important that all school employees treat parents with respect and consideration. There are many sad stories of the school secretary or other staff treating parents poorly when they come to school, such as when they enroll their children. If a problem with parental treatment is apparent, teachers should suggest that the school board of directors provide sensitivity workshops for all school employees.

ENCOURAGING PARENT INVOLVEMENT

Many educators have developed strong relationships with even hard-to-reach parents. Greenberg (1989) summarizes the characteristics of a teacher in a successful parent outreach program. Such a teacher:

- shows equal, warm welcome and respect to all parents;
- truly *listens* to parents, knowing that they don't always agree with teachers and that teachers aren't always right, . . . seeks to elicit from parents knowledge about the child, the child's culture, and the parents' views and values, and then customizes the child's school experience accordingly and works with parents, starting where they are;
- holds meetings at varying times of the day and evening to permit parents who work various shifts and parents who live far away to be able to attend;
- implements a regular policy of reaching out to hard-to-find parents through home visits; . . .
- provides a reason for low-income parents to bother to come to school [for example, by offering transportation and escorting to more specialized services or programs in which they can learn about childrearing or other subjects]. (p. 73)*

THEORY INTO Practice

Interview several parents of young children about how they prefer to be involved in their children's education. Try to determine if their children's schools have offered them chances to be involved and how they feel about what has been offered.

Teachers should encourage parents to visit frequently and to drop in without an appointment. Teachers can also provide guidance to parents in how to help young children learn at home. Parents can prove to be strong allies in supporting developmentally appropriate programs if teachers take the time to help them understand how activities are selected and why teaching decisions are made (Stipek, Rosenblatt, and DiRocco 1994). Sending home appropriate activities that will involve parents with their children is also useful in terms of helping parents understand that learning is not limited to drills on basic skills.

Teachers and schools must make the effort to work with parents. Teachers who have not worked with parents may think that those who have less than a high school diploma are unwilling or lack the ability to work with their children. Research indicates, however, that teachers who use home-learning activities are able to involve parents, regardless of their educational backgrounds. Reporting on the results of their research, Epstein and Dauber (1989) assert:

> If schools don't work to involve parents, then parent education and family social class are very important for deciding who becomes involved.

* From Polly Greenberg, "Parents as Partners in Young Children's Development and Education: A New American Fad? Why Does It Matter?" *Young Children* 44 (May 1989): 61–75. Reprinted with permission of the author.

Parents, teachers, and children all benefit from positive interactions through school programs and activities.

But if schools take parent involvement seriously and work to involve all parents, then social class and parents' level of education decrease or disappear as important factors. (p. 21)

Rosenthal and Sawyers (1996) suggest that educators check the "family friendliness" of their schools by asking the following questions:

- Are all school meetings with parents problem-focused?
- How easy is it for a parent to find out what is going on in a classroom?
- Are parents a source of information? Is parental input valuable and can you name a few specific instances when parental input had an impact on outcome?
- Do parents typically come to the school to discuss positive activities?
- Are meetings only held during the school day?
- Do school personnel usually discuss parents in a negative fashion?
- Are parents informed when their children are doing well?
- What percentage of parents were at the last school function?
- Do teachers and parents describe their relationship in an adversarial fashion?
- Did most of the parents struggle with school themselves? (p. 196)

The answers to these questions should help teachers and administrators determine their feelings about parents and what changes need to be made, if any.

ENCOURAGING PARENT INVOLVEMENT

FIGURE 6.1

Continuum of Parent Involvement

HIGH

- Parents, trained by teacher, assist in classroom in such learning activities as reviewing writing samples, assisting at learning centers, or helping with computer use.
- Parents in classrooms reinforce processes and concepts introduced by teachers.
- Parents in classrooms practice with children on vocabulary words, number facts; help them enter answers on computer cards.
- Parents read to children in the classrooms.
- Parents make classroom presentations or present hands-on activities in areas of expertise.
- Parents participate in committees that directly influence school curricula and policies. Committees consist of parents, teachers, and administrator(s).
- P.T.A. parents work on sponsorship and implementation of curriculum-related and family-oriented activities, e.g., cultural arts contests, displays, Family Fun Night.
- Parents make instructional materials for classroom use, as directed by teachers.
- Parents assist in school library, checking out and shelving books.
- Parents participate as room mothers or room fathers.
- Parents supervise on class trips or chaperone at school functions.
- Parents visit classrooms during American Education Week or Back-To-School Night.
- Parents attend classroom plays, presentations.
- Parents attend school assembly programs.
- Parents attend competitive games, athletic events at school.
- Parents attend promotion ceremonies.
- Parents attend parent-teacher conferences.
- Parents are encouraged to help children with homework at home.
- Parents are involved in P.T.A. fundraising activities.
- Parents are asked to join P.T.A.
- Parents are encouraged to read school's handbook for parents.

LOW

- No parental involvement.

Source: Harlene Galen, "Increasing Parental Involvement in Elementary School: The Nitty-Gritty of One Successful Program," *Young Children* 46 (January 1991): 19. Reprinted with permission of NAEYC.

Parent Roles

Parents may take on a variety of roles in the school. Figure 6.1 illustrates the levels of parent involvement along a continuum, from very passive to very active. At the "low" end of the continuum are parents who never participate in any school activities, although they are active in the sense of sending their children to school; one level higher are parents who participate in very passive roles that only require them to listen. Further along the continuum are parents who participate by attending events at school or volunteering their time to help teachers in the classroom; even further along are those parents who get involved in decision making at the school or district level and who assist in teaching. Parents of children in cooperative schools usually are at this point. Some parents take total responsibility for their children's education and make the commitment to educate their children at home.

Many parents do not see how their involvement at school could possibly benefit their children. Teachers need to supply specific information about why parent involvement is important. For example, teachers often suggest that parents read to their children but do not share with the parents why reading will help the children become more literate. Parents who have specific information are much more likely to become involved.

Parents who choose not to be involved in their children's school cite as reasons health problems, economic differences between themselves and teachers, and work responsibilities. Some teachers, on the other hand, believe that parents are not more involved because of their unrealistic expectations of the school's role; an attitude that school is not important enough to warrant taking time from work; jealousy of teachers; teachers' lack of trust of parents; and a lack of activities to draw parents to school (Leitch and Tangri 1988).

Swick and McKnight (1989) found a cluster of characteristics in kindergarten teachers that strongly supported parent involvement, including belonging to a professional association and adhering to a developmentally oriented philosophy; they also found that administrative support for parent involvement was vital. Galinsky (1988) found that teachers who had more education and were parents themselves were more likely to have positive perceptions of parents. She explained that it is not being a parent per se that leads to positive perceptions but "the ability to put themselves in the parent's shoes and to be empathetic" (p. 8). If teachers feel that parental involvement is important, they will work to overcome the barriers that they perceive are keeping parents out of the school.

Every parent who wants to be involved should have the opportunity to do so. Teachers need to find out from parents how they would like to be involved. The most direct way of determining how parents feel and what they would like to do is to ask them—during a home visit or during a

FIGURE 6.2 **Parent Interview Form**

1. Would you like to work with the children in the classroom?
2. What would you prefer doing in the classroom if you were to come?
3. Name something special that you can do or make or something you know about that you would be willing to share with the children.
4. I'm going to read a list of items to you. Tell me if you have ever felt a need to know more about any of these items by answering either yes or no. (Interviewer: Please check appropriate category.)

	Yes	No
a. How to teach my preschool children		
b. Whether my child is developing appropriately		
c. Services provided by community agencies to which I have a right		
d. How to communicate better with my children		
e. How to help my children interact better with others		
f. How to discipline my children		
g. How to make toys and other things for my children		
h. How to tell whether my child is progressing in school		
i. What to do when my children do things that I do not consider proper (temper tantrums, thumb sucking, bad manners)		
j. How to play with my children		
k. Where to take my children so they can have a nice time and learn		
l. How to help my children retain their cultural heritage		
m. How to use and develop the talents and skills that I know I have		
n. How to refrain from hitting my child		
o. How to guarantee that my child will succeed in school		
p. How to talk to teachers		
q. How to help my child learn a second language when I don't speak a second language		
r. How to extend language learning		
s. How to use my home environment as a learning experience for my children		

5. What is your opinion of preschool parents coming together at least once a month to talk and learn more about the areas to which you answered "yes"?
6. If you felt that this parent meeting is a good idea, how can we make sure that the meetings are worthwhile for parents?
7. Would you be willing to help organize the first parent meeting?
8. Are there other ways you might be willing to help with the parent meetings?
9. Name something special that you can do or make or that you know about that you would be willing to share with other parents.

Source: Mary Hohmann, Bernard Banet, and David P. Weikart, *Young Children in Action* (Ypsilanti, MI: High/Scope Press, 1979), pp. 328–329. Reprinted with permission of the publisher.

conference early in the year. Another way is to have them respond to a questionnaire. Figure 6.2 is an example of an interview form for teachers to use in determining the kind of involvement parents need or want.

In any case, teachers will want to have available lists of things that parents can become involved in and be accepting of their choices. Teachers might list a variety of things that parents can do at home and some that they can do at school. At home, for instance, parents might sew costumes for the dress-up area (teachers can supply the patterns and fabric), type a newsletter every two weeks, help collect materials needed for a project, tape record stories or poems for the children, and so on. At school, parents might supervise children during cooking, water play, or other activities that require extra supervision; read to individual children or small groups; talk to the class about their work; accompany the group on field trips; and so on.

Activities for Involving Parents

Many activities can be arranged to involve both parents who choose to be active and those who choose more passive roles. A number of levels of participation are possible:

THEORY INTO Practice

Interview several teachers of young children about how they involve parents in their programs. In their opinions, what are the most successful techniques?

1. Family reading, family math, or family science nights are evenings when the children and their families are invited to school and participate in reading activities or math activities that are developmentally appropriate and that help parents understand why such activities are provided in school.
2. Potluck dinners offer a way to celebrate holidays by inviting families to share social evenings together. If the children can make part of the meal to share, so much the better.
3. Parent education workshops can range from sessions in which outside speakers talk about child development, discipline, or some other topic of general interest to meetings of small groups who want to discuss specific issues, such as sibling rivalry, with other parents.
4. Formal organizations of parents such as Parent-Teacher Associations can provide programs for parents and teachers.
5. Committees of parents can discuss school issues, including curriculum decisions, school policies, and hiring of staff.
6. Parents can become members of teams involved in making recommendations for children with special needs.
7. Parents and teachers can attend workshops in which they make instructional materials for use in the classroom.
8. Chapman (1991) suggests that parents can help produce videotapes that focus on lessons and explain the "whys" of the lesson (why certain materials, teaching strategies, responses to wrong answers are

used) or that teach other parents specific techniques for helping their children, such as how to motivate them.

COMMUNICATION WITH PARENTS

It is the teacher's responsibility to keep the lines of communication with parents open. Communication with parents can be divided into two categories: communication *about the program* and communication *about the individual child* (Bundy 1991). Parent conferences, newsletters, and telephone calls are all avenues for communication, but they are used more to talk about an individual child than about the program. Home visits, parent visits to the school, school handbooks, letters and notes, and a teacher who is prepared with good written information about community resources will supplement the above-mentioned communication methods and keep parents informed about the school's program.

Cattermole and Robinson (1985) asked parents what they considered the most effective forms of communication they received from school. Their first choice was information they received from their children—followed by school newsletters, report cards, parent-teacher conferences, visits to school, notes or phone calls from teachers, and formal meetings and informal contacts with friends.

School Handbooks

School handbooks are especially useful for sharing basic information about programs. A handbook should include the school calendar; the hours of each session; school policies, such as procedures for getting refunds of tuition payments, celebrating birthdays at school, or handling sick children; a class list for each class; a list of the staff (with perhaps a short professional biography of each); and statements of the school's philosophy (Bundy 1991). The school handbook might also list the goals and objectives for the children, emergency procedures, bus routes, and other information useful to parents.

Home Visits

Although not as common as they once were, **home visits** are still an important means of establishing solid parent-teacher relationships. Some parents are much more comfortable in their own homes than at school. (However, teachers should be sensitive to the fact that some parents may find a home visit from the teacher uncomfortable or intrusive, for any number of reasons.) The information gained about the child, the parents, and the home environment are well worth the investment of time and energy required to complete home visits.

If a home visit can be arranged before school starts, the child and teacher can get to know each other individually before having to relate to each other in a group setting. Parents will also appreciate meeting the teacher before school begins and having a chance to ask questions about the program and discuss expectations for their child.

Home visits can be effective if teachers plan and prepare for them. The following suggestions may help in planning visits:

1. Schedule the visits well in advance. Send a written reminder of the visit. Let the parents know how long you expect the visit to last. Arrive and leave on time.
2. Make sure that parents know the purpose of the visit. Assure parents that they do not need to make any special preparations for your visit.
3. Be a gracious guest. If the parent offers something to eat or drink, accept it politely. Respect the parents and the home.
4. Do not make snap judgments about the home environment. If the physical surroundings do not match your image of a home, do not conclude that the home is not a good environment for the child.
5. Be prepared to talk about the program and your plans for the children in an informal manner. Listen, ask questions, and listen some more.

Often, teachers like to take something when they visit—materials for making a nametag for the child, a camera for photographing the child, a photograph album of activities from the previous year, a puppet, a wooden puzzle, a book that can be returned to the classroom later, or paper and crayons for drawing. Taking something can provide openings for sharing information and opportunities for observations (Johnston and Mermin 1995).

It is also helpful for the teacher to take an information sheet for the parents that gives his name and phone number, a school calendar with holidays and special events marked, information about snacks if parents will be providing them, and a list of rules for celebrating birthdays and for bringing objects to share at school. The teacher might also take along a list of materials that he needs at school. Teachers in one school district hand out a list of "beautiful junk"—egg cartons, oatmeal boxes, assorted nuts and bolts, baby food jars, old paint brushes, wood scraps, bottle caps, used magazines, and the like—that most households accumulate and that even families of limited means can contribute.

During a home visit, the teacher may want to discuss the special needs and interests of the child, any allergies or health problems that the teacher needs to be aware of, and the expectations the parents have for the child in the program. If it seems appropriate, the teacher can also discuss how the parents would like to be involved in the program. Parents may also want to know about the teacher's background, training, and experience. He should be prepared to discuss the program, how decisions are made about what to study, and how he plans to deal with discipline problems.

If the teacher is unable to visit two or three parents at home, he might try inviting them to a special meeting at school, where he shares the information he would have shared in a home visit. Kieff (1990) found that parents of children labeled "at risk" by their school district preferred meeting in small groups with the teacher. These parents did not feel comfortable in large, formal parent meetings.

It is important that all parents understand how much they teach their children and how important they are in their children's education. Hohmann, Banet, and Weikart (1979) suggest that teachers help parents "realize that . . . parenting *is* teaching, . . . they already know a lot about child development in general and about their own children in particular, and . . . teachers are not purveyors of knowledge but rather people who wish to support and extend the learning that's already going on at home" (p. 20).

If parents cannot or will not come to school and the teacher cannot visit them at home, the teacher might try inviting the family to meet at a park, library, or other public place. Meeting on neutral ground may help the parents feel more comfortable. If such a plan is impossible, then the teacher should try to contact the parents by phone or by letter to share the information. The teacher should make his contacts with them nonthreatening and nonjudgmental. It is vital that the teacher continue to reassure parents that he is interested in their child and will welcome their questions.

Parent Visits to School

Some parents can arrange to visit the school during school hours and should always be welcomed. Parents who come to observe the program and their children's participation in it should be invited to sit and watch or to join in activities, whichever they feel most comfortable in doing. Every parent who comes to observe should be invited to schedule a conference so that any questions or concerns can be discussed. One school sends special invitations to each parent to attend school on a given day, beginning a few weeks before regularly scheduled conferences. The invitations indicate that if parents cannot come on the stated day, they can come any time. With a little persistence, teachers in this school get almost 100 percent of the parents to visit the school, and conferences are much more successful after parents have seen the program in action.

Parents can be invited to participate in holiday celebrations that the children have planned or invited to visit when the children are involved in a group activity so that they can observe their child's behavior in a group setting. Rather than having children put on performances, it is advisable to

THEORY
INTO
Practice

Work with a small group of your classmates to plan a parent evening for math, reading, or science. Your plan should outline activities for the parents and children and include explanations of why these activities are important.

ask parents to visit when the children are involved in normal classroom activities, such as singing, playing musical instruments, or dramatizing stories. These activities do not require practice by the children but do allow the parent to feel good about their children's abilities.

The teacher might want to prepare an observation guide for parents so that they can see some of the important aspects of the program during their visit. Figure 6.3 on page 176 is an example of such a guide, which can be adapted to fit the teacher's own needs.

Sometimes, parents who cannot attend school during the day can be invited for an evening visit. The children can come, too, and get involved in some of their usual school activities, so the parents can learn more about what their children do at school.

A **parent place** in a corner of the classroom can help parents feel that they are important and needed. A table and a small bulletin board are all that is necessary to provide such a corner for parents. Parents can use the bulletin board to communicate with each other (notes about car pools, child care, and so on). The teacher can post photographs of parents working with the children or creating materials or games for the classroom, notices of special events of interest to families, lists of items that are needed in the classroom, and so on. The table can hold a small resource library for parents, providing copies of articles and books that parents might find helpful; pamphlets, magazines, and brochures such as those published by the National Association for the Education of Young Children (NAEYC) and the Association for Childhood Education International (ACEI) on a variety of topics; and other materials. Some larger schools provide "parent rooms" where parents can meet other parents, wait to pick up their children, or find information about parenting. Epstein (1991) lists making room (literally) for parents as an important component of parent involvement programs.

When parents cannot visit school or stay long enough to observe, notes and photographs of their children engaged in activities help communicate what is going on in class. A videotape of a day in the class that parents can borrow may also help to communicate with some parents. Greenwood (1995) reported very positive results when she created a video of children's activities that she circulated among parents. She made several videos during the year and also volunteered to make copies for parents, if they sent blank tapes. Another teacher wrote a daily log of activities, which she posted for parents to read as they picked up their child ("Prickly Problems" 1989).

Letters and Notes

Parents appreciate letters that give them information about school programs and their children, in particular. Instead of newsletters, some

FIGURE 6.3 | **Observation Guide for Parents**

Welcome to XYZ School!

We are always pleased to have parents visit our programs! This sheet may serve as a guideline for observing your child as he or she interacts with others in school. We encourage you to schedule an appointment with the teacher to discuss your observations. You may use any part of this form, or you may turn it over and write down some questions that you want to ask the teacher later. Please do whatever is most comfortable for you. Enjoy your visit!

Check or circle whatever items are appropriate.

Setting:
    Indoors
    Outdoors

Activity:
    Choice time (individual)
    Whole group
    Small group directed by teacher

Social Interactions:
    With other children
    With adults

Materials, Equipment, or Activities Selected:
List here

Did your child use material or equipment as it was designed to be used? or did he or she use the material or equipment to make up a game?

Time Spent in Each Activity:
Estimate here

Types of Interactions:
    Solitary activities (played alone)
    Small group activities (joined or formed a small group)

teachers like to send form letters that may include suggestions for things the parents could do at home to complement what the children are learning in school. Adding a personal note about the child at the bottom of each parent's letter makes this practice even more effective. Brief notes that communicate the child's progress are an important way of letting parents know that the teacher is aware of their child and her accomplishments.

Notes should always be positive. A note saying that "Sebastian succeeded in tying his shoes today" or that "Nancy read a complete book independently" will help parents feel that the teacher is staying in touch with them. Most teachers keep a list of parents and jot down the date when they send each parent a note. When all parents have been contacted, the teachers start over. Some schools even have notepaper printed with captions such as "Good News" or "Happygram."

D'Angelo and Adler (1991) suggest the following guidelines for preparing effective written communication for parents:

- Keep sentences short. Try to keep sentences to ten or fewer words, and never allow them to include more than twenty words.
- Keep paragraphs short. Try to keep paragraphs to an average of six lines.
- Use easy words. Let the short, familiar words bear the main burden of getting your point across. Use big words or technical terms when only those words will express a message accurately.
- Get to the point. State the purpose of your message up front and omit irrelevant information.
- Write things in logical order. The newspaper formula of "who, what, where, when, why, and how" is helpful as an organizing device.
- Be definite. Don't hedge. Be careful with such words as *seems, may, perhaps, possibly, generally, usually,* and *apparently.* Give a clear picture of what you want to say.
- Be direct. Speak to each reader. Say "you should" or "please do" instead of "parents should."
- Use the active voice more often than the passive. Put the subject at the beginning of the sentence. For example, write "Please sign and return the consent slip if you want your child to go on the trip to the zoo," rather than, "A consent slip must be signed by the parent in order for the child to attend the field trip to the zoo."
- Know your audience. Ask yourself, For whom is the material being written, and how well does the audience read? If you aren't sure, test your materials on a few people representative of the target audience. When in doubt, assume that there are at least some poor readers in your audience.
- Know yourself. Be yourself. Write as you would talk, and write to express—not to impress.
- Write and rewrite. Write a draft, then read it over. How long are the sentences? How many long words have you used? Have you used the pas-

sive voice a great deal? Are there unexplained technical words? Have you used jargon or abbreviations that your audience may not know? Can you say the same thing more clearly, more succinctly, or more interestingly? Ask someone else to read what you've written. Then rewrite it. (p. 354)*

Telecommunication

Some centers use technology to make communication with parents quick and easy. Bauch (1990) reports that one center uses a computerized calling system to call parents and deliver messages about the program. These systems allow the calls to be placed at the times that are convenient for parents and in the language the parents prefer.

A similar use of current technology is to equip each teacher's room with an answering machine on which the teacher records a short message like the following, which any parent can hear by calling:

> Today, we went to the zoo to look for patterns. We found patterns on the animals, in the enclosures, and in the pathways. You could help your child find patterns in your home. We printed patterns with junk items in art, and we read a patterned book, *Brown Bear, Brown Bear*. Your child has a copy of this book, and you could read it or let him or her read it to you. If you have a chance this weekend, encourage your child to look for patterns in numbers, such as the pattern of house or apartment numbers on your block.

Parents of Children with Special Needs

Parents of children with special needs are by necessity more involved in their children's education than some parents because legal requirements specify that they be consulted and informed about decisions made about their children. Meetings to plan educational programs for children with special needs must include the parents. Communication with these parents may take the same forms as it does with all other parents, but it may need to be more specific and more frequent. Teachers should check with their program administrators or principals about the legal requirements for communicating with parents of children with special needs.

Parents of children with special needs may themselves need support from the teacher. Spidel (1987) notes that the parent of a child who is exceptional often expects the child's teacher to:

---

* From Diane A. D'Angelo and C. Ralph Adler, "Chapter I: A Catalyst for Improving Parent Involvement," *Phi Delta Kappan* 72 (January 1991): 350–354. Reprinted with permission of the authors.

1. Understand his child's assets as well as his deficiencies.
2. Appreciate his child's accomplishments whenever and however they appear.
3. Help the parent (and the child) live without guilt or blame.
4. Tell his child how it really is (the truth about himself may be difficult for a child who is learning disabled but not as difficult as the bewilderments and heartaches he experiences from half-truths and evasions).

Shriver and Kramer (1993) found that most parents of students with special needs are satisfied with the services their children receive in the schools and with the teachers they have.

Community Resources

Finally, many parents need information about resources available to them in the community. Teachers are not expected to be child psychologists or marriage counselors, but they can help by keeping on hand a supply of brochures that describe the services offered by various community agencies with contact and referral information.

THEORY INTO Practice

Locate resources that might be needed by parents in the community where you hope to teach. Make sure that you know the procedures for referrals and whom to contact for each of these resources. Obtain copies of printed information that describes these resources and the services offered by each.

VOLUNTEERS IN THE CLASSROOM

Volunteers in the classroom are very important, especially as resources continue to shrink and schools cannot afford to hire enough adults to maintain adequate adult-child ratios. Volunteers can be parents or others from the community. Community volunteers can be recruited from colleges, service groups, senior citizen groups, church groups, and the like. These volunteers often bring many skills and abilities to share with children—talents in music, storytelling, woodworking, art, or other areas that can enhance the program. Many teachers are especially interested in recruiting older volunteers in order to promote the intergenerational contact that is so often missing in the lives of today's children.

Both community and parent volunteers must be screened and trained before working in the classroom. Some schools have volunteer coordinators who are responsible for interviewing prospective volunteers and determining their suitability for working with children. In other situations, teachers themselves interview volunteers. Whoever conducts the interviews should try to determine what the person has to offer the children, his expectations about volunteering, and his ability to communicate with and nurture children. If a volunteer seems unsuitable for working directly with the children, he can be asked to perform tasks that do not involve the

Parents and paraprofessionals can contribute immeasurably to school programs.

children, such as typing materials, mounting artwork, placing the children's work in their portfolios, and so on.

Training for volunteers should clearly describe the philosophy of the program, goals for the children, activities that are appropriate for volunteers, discipline in school, and school policies and procedures. Such training is important, as every person who works in the classroom models behavior for the children and teaches by example.

Volunteers should always feel that the work they do is of real benefit to the children. They must perceive that the tasks they are asked to do in the classroom are a value added to the regular program. For example, if volunteers are asked to correct papers, they may see that task as something the teacher would do anyway and believe that they are not really adding to the quality of the program. It would be more appropriate to ask volunteers to do tasks that the teacher simply could not do without their help. Any special experience that can be added because the volunteer is available to help will make it clear to the parent or community volunteer that she is needed to provide this experience for the children.

Some examples of appropriate activities for mature and well-trained volunteers include:

1. Reading to children (individually or in small groups)
2. Supervising small groups in outdoor play

3. Taking a small group for a walk around the schoolgrounds (looking for signs of changing seasons, collecting natural materials, observing surface differences, and so on)
4. Supervising children in an area that could not be used without additional help (cooking, water, music, tumbling, sewing, and so on)
5. Playing board games with children or helping them learn to play checkers, chess, or other such games

It is important to take the time to help volunteers understand what they can do in the classroom and how to do it most easily. Although many parent and community volunteers are quite able to work with one child at a time, they may not have especially good group-management abilities. Specific instructions allow those who are not specially trained in working with groups of young children to feel more secure. If a volunteer were going to supervise the art area, for example, the instructions shown in Figure 6.4 would be helpful. A planning sheet such as the one shown in Figure 6.5 on page 182 would guide a volunteer in supervising a cooking experience. Another approach is to develop a file of cards listing suggestions for different activities and to laminate the cards for durability.

Teachers should always take the time to thank volunteers for their help. Immediate positive verbal feedback is important. Written thank-you

➡ Children may choose to do art activities between 9:15 and 10:15.

➡ Choices available to the children: paint and easels, modeling clay, crayons or chalk and drawing paper, swatches of fabric for collage.

➡ Any child who chooses easel painting should wear a painting smock. The smocks are on the hooks beside the sink. Children should be encouraged to get their own smocks and to replace them when finished. Completed paintings are to be placed on the drying rack to the left of the sink. All children should be encouraged to clean up and put away the materials they use when they have completed their work.

➡ We are emphasizing the concepts of texture. Please use texture words such as *rough, smooth, grainy, splintery, nubby, bumpy,* and so on when talking to the children about their work.

➡ Some children will need help labeling their work with their names. You can write their names and the date in one corner of their work. If they want you to write something about their work, please write exactly what they say.

Thank you so much for your help. We could not offer so many choices to the children without it.

FIGURE 6.4

Instructions for the Art Area

FIGURE 6.5

Planning Sheet

COOKING PLANNING SHEET

Project _Fruit Salad_   **Date** _3/25_

Type: (Individual)   Small group

Purpose:

To help children learn about:

(new foods)   similarities and differences in color
  other cultures   similarities and differences in size
  texture changes   similarities and differences in weight
  changes in smell   effects of heat

To develop:

(small muscle skills)   eye-hand coordination
  other _____

Skills to be emphasized:

  pouring   sorting   dipping   mixing   spreading
  rolling   cracking   beating   juicing   grinding
  slicing   grating   peeling   (cutting)   other _____

Ingredients needed:

  _apple_____   _walnut_____
  _orange_____   _____
  _banana_____   _____
  _pineapple_____   _____

Procedure:

1. _Prepare stations for each step of the recipe._____
2. _Supervise children as needed as they complete_____
   _each step of the recipe._____
   _____
   _____
   _____

notes are also invaluable in helping volunteers feel appreciated. These need not be expensive—a small note that the teacher can send home with a child for his parent or mail to a community volunteer is appropriate.

More elaborate displays of appreciation for volunteers are often planned once or twice a year. Some schools like to have a tea, a luncheon, or a breakfast to honor those who have contributed volunteer time. If teachers can get publicity in the local paper for special contributions by volunteers, they should do so—public praise is always welcome. Articles in newsletters that go out to all the parents can note the work that volunteers are doing at home and at school.

WORKING WITH PARAPROFESSIONALS

Most classroom teachers are delighted to have **paraprofessionals,** or teacher aides, to work with in the classroom. Teacher aides can add immeasurably to the quality of the program; they can provide individual attention, increased supervision, scheduling flexibility, and assistance in instruction. (In most states, it is illegal for a teacher aide to *teach,* meaning that aides are not responsible for planning instruction and making instructional decisions.)

Paraprofessionals' levels of training and experience vary a great deal. Some will have completed programs of preparation to become paraprofessionals; others will have had no training at all. In most

Many activities in the classroom would not be possible without the help of paraprofessionals.

schools, paraprofessionals must at least have high school diplomas and be eighteen or older.

After the teacher knows about the background and experience of the aide, she can make plans for training or orientation. Pickett and others (1993) recommend creating written job descriptions for teacher aides. Such descriptions can help in defining the roles of paraprofessionals, in promoting job satisfaction, and in guiding evaluation. Teachers can help children by encouraging schools and school boards to offer needed training for aides. Love and Levine (1992) found that training increased the effectiveness of teacher aides, which should not be surprising.

Working successfully with an aide requires some planning on the teacher's part and some ability to communicate well with adults. The following guidelines will help:

1. Take the time to discuss your philosophy, the program, what you consider appropriate discipline, and other pertinent information with the aide. Even if the aide has training and experience, it is important that you agree on how the class should be handled.
2. If the aide lacks training, provide it. This is not always easy because the aide may be paid by the hour and may not be willing to stay longer or come earlier without extra pay. Try to arrange for your aide to be paid for the time spent in training. Provide written information, explain why you do things the way you do, and then model the behaviors that you expect in the classroom. Take a few minutes for discussion each day.
3. Do not assign the aide all the "dirty" chores in the classroom. No one wants to clean the gerbil cage and the painting area all the time and

DEVELOPMENTALLY APPROPRIATE PRACTICE

Think about all you have learned about DAP and reflect on those principles when applied to working with parents and teacher aides. Adults should be treated in developmentally appropriate ways, just as children should be. For example, adults need choices about what and how they will learn, and they need to be able to apply what they know to new information. When thinking about DAP, consider the importance of volunteers and teacher aides in programs:

- Are volunteers and aides given choices as much as possible?
- Are parents and teacher aides talked to and treated in ways that are respectful of their skills and abilities?
- Do the programs planned for parents allow choices and recognize the importance of parents as the first teachers of their children?

- Are parents' cultural and ethnic differences not only recognized but celebrated?
- Are the individual differences in parents considered when planning activities for parents?

never get a chance to do some of the more interesting classroom tasks, such as supervising a small group on a walk or in an art activity.

4. Provide positive feedback and praise for the work of the aide. It is important that he appreciate his contributions to the program.
5. Make sure that the children consider the aide as a teacher.

If the law states that aides are not to teach, what are they supposed to do? Generally, teacher aides can do almost everything that teachers do, with the exception of planning learning experiences and being responsible for assessment and reporting. However, aides can certainly contribute their observations of children or activities, which the teacher can communicate to parents and use in planning future activities. Assignments for aides should be determined by their level of skill and experience. A teacher could not expect an aide with no experience to work with the whole class during music time, for example.

Paraprofessionals can take on certain types of duties, including the following:

THEORY
INTO
Practice

Interview a teacher's aide to determine what she likes most and least about her work. Find out how she thinks her work situation could be improved.

Instructional Duties

1. Reading to individual children or small groups or listening to children read
2. Providing individual help for children completing tasks
3. Providing small-group instruction that is planned by the teacher
4. Teaching children a song or a fingerplay
5. Working with a small group with manipulatives for mathematics or with materials for science investigations

Supervisory Duties

1. Supervising learning areas
2. Supervising outdoor play experiences (some states require one certified teacher on the playground during recess)
3. Supervising children on field trips
4. Supervising children as they move from one part of the building to another
5. Supervising the children as they complete routines (hanging up coats, using the toilet, and so on)

Classroom Maintenance Duties

1. Preparing classroom displays and bulletin boards
2. Setting up and helping serve snacks
3. Helping to keep the classroom and materials clean and ready for use
4. Setting up and running audiovisual equipment
5. Gathering materials from the library or other resources

As the teacher and aide work together, it is important that the teacher maintain good communication with the aide, discussing what needs to be done and the priorities for the day. The teacher should be sensitive to adults' need to be involved in making decisions and should plan to involve the aide in choosing tasks to be done. The teacher and aide must also evaluate the process as they work together: Is the aide learning new skills so that different activities are now appropriate? Does the aide feel appreciated? Is the aide comfortable with the tasks that he does routinely? Do the teacher and aide agree on most issues? Does the aide want to learn new techniques for working with the children? Are both the teacher and aide satisfied with the communication between them?

Working successfully with aides requires that teachers provide frequent positive feedback and praise for a job well done. Notes of appreciation to aides, notes to principals or administrators or in newsletters specifically commending aides, and any other special recognition that is deserved can make teacher-aide relationships more positive and assure that good work continues.

CELEBRATING DIVERSITY

Families can serve as resources for helping all children learn about and respect cultures that are different than their own. For example, all the children's families could be invited to contribute to the classroom some play items that are significant in their cultural traditions. Even families of limited means can contribute items such as empty food containers from traditional meals (Clark 1995). Having children bring in cultural items for sharing time is also useful in terms of celebrating diversity (Neuman and Roskos 1994). Families can become resources as food, songs, and stories from different cultures are studied.

It is very important for the school and its teachers to acknowledge children's cultures and help their families feel comfortable in the school. Both parents and children need to understand that speaking a language other than English is not unacceptable, so they need not feel embarrassed. Community translators are often willing to help schools communicate with parents who do not speak English. Families respond well to activities such as potluck suppers, field days that include picnics or cookouts, and other activities that provide an atmosphere of acceptance and a chance to get to know other parents. Lee (1995) interviewed parents belonging to five Asian groups, who made suggestions for reaching out to reticent parents. Their suggestions are listed in Figure 6.6.

FIGURE 6.6 Reaching Out to Parents

Suggestions offered by parents who participated in the study about how to reach out to reticent parents who seldom take part in school activities:

1. Encourage active parents to stress the importance of participating in school activities.
2. Urge children to encourage and remind their parents to attend school activities.
3. Invite parents to visit school and observe their children any time, and reassure them that they will be given a friendly welcome when they come to school.
4. Clearly indicate to parents that a language difference need not be a primary concern for parents who are interested in getting involved at school.
5. Invite interpreters to come with parents for open-house and back-to-school-night activities, or encourage teachers to have interpreters present.
6. If two or more parents belong to the same Asian* ethnic group, reassure them that they are free to speak in their own language to each other during parent meetings. This way, Asian parents who are able to communicate in English may help others to understand the discussions.
7. Reserve some time to communicate with Asian parents alone after the parent meeting (e.g., on back-to-school night) so that Asian parents do not feel that they have been ignored.
8. Visit reticent parents in their homes. In general, Asian parents respect teachers and feel honored when their children's teachers visit. Asian parents also view that teacher's willingness to come forward as a sign of sincerity (Shen & Mo 1993). Parents are more willing to be educational partners when they learn that teachers make an effort to reach out to them.
9. Sometimes children inhibit parents' participation because they feel embarrassed by their parents' inability to communicate well in English. They sometimes wish their parents would not appear at school. Convey that a language difference is not a negative trait.
10. Provide an opportunity for parents in the same Asian group, whose children attend the same school, to get acquainted with one another.
11. Schedule parent-teacher conferences to enable parents from the same Asian group, with children in the same class, to visit school at the same time. This way, reluctant parents may not feel as threatened by the unfamiliar school environment and may be encouraged to communicate with the teacher.
12. Asian parents who speak English and are familiar with school procedures can give introductions regarding the following matters to reticent parents from the same Asian group: school registration procedures, immunization, school volunteer programs, parent-teacher conferences, school educational goals, grading and evaluation systems, etc. Holding meetings about these issues in a parent's home might provide a less threatening environment for the reticent parent. Schools may also conduct seminars in parents' native tongues to help them become familiar with basic features of the school system, such as educational services and programs, extracurricular activities, and procedures for assessment and evaluation of children (Yao 1988).
13. Send notes to parents from time to time. The note could be a one- or two-sentence progress report, or it may be something that would make parents smile, such as, "Do you know what your child did today that gave us a good laugh?" or "Would you like to know what interesting thing your child did today?"

Source: Fong Yun Lee, "Asian Parents as Partners," *Young Children* 50 (March 1995): 4–8 (p. 7). Published by the National Association for the Education of Young Children. Copyright © 1995 by NAEYC. Used with permission.

*Although the parents in the study were all Asian, the same guidelines could be applied to parents from other ethnic groups.

CHAPTER SUMMARY

- Parent-teacher relationships are very complex. Changing family structures, economic conditions, and isolation of the nuclear family all contribute to stresses on families that sometimes make parent involvement in the school difficult.

- A teacher must approach families with a nonjudgmental attitude and be sensitive to the needs of children from many types of family structures.

- Family involvement is important for children's self-esteem and achievement. Parents may choose not to be involved, to be involved only passively, or to be actively involved in their children's education.

- Activities for involving families include family nights at school, potluck dinners, parent education programs, meetings of parent organizations, and committee meetings.

- Home visits by teachers can provide a wealth of information about children, their families, family interactions, and how children learn at home. Home visits must be carefully planned if they are to contribute to establishing good parent-teacher relationships.

- Inviting parents to visit and observe the program in action can open lines of communication between parents and teachers. It is important to make arrangements for parents who cannot visit during the regular schoolday to visit at some other time and see how the program works.

- Setting aside a corner of the classroom for parents will communicate to them that teachers value their presence and believe that their involvement is important.

- Teachers should be prepared to offer assistance to parents who need help in meeting their basic needs; teacher must be informed about community resources, whom to contact for help, and the referral process.

- Parent or community volunteers in the classroom can enhance the program for children. Volunteers need to be screened and trained to be most effective and should be given tasks that benefit the children directly.

- Teacher aides can make vital contributions to programs for young children. Although they are not supposed to teach, aides can assume responsibilities for instruction, supervision, and classroom maintenance tasks. Teacher aides need carefully planned orientation and training.

- Everyone on the school staff should respect the cultural diversity of the students. Families can be wonderful sources of artifacts, food, clothing, and music that will enrich any program offered to children.

A TEACHER SPEAKS

MARGARET
EGENHOEFER
Dixon Elementary School
New Berlin, Wisconsin

The Relationship between Teachers and Teaching Assistants

I teach kindergarten in a suburban school district. During the course of my twenty-year career, I have had the opportunity to work with various teaching assistants. I have strived to make this a beneficial experience for both the children and myself.

The most important point is to establish a good working relationship with your assistant. You will want to set guidelines. While it is not imperative that you become social acquaintances, a sincere yet professional rapport should be created for a positive experience. This will also make it easier to resolve any difficulties.

Before school starts, meet with your assistant—perhaps for lunch or a cup of coffee. Ask about family, past work experiences, hobbies, trips—just as you would when meeting a new colleague, neighbor, or friend. Share some of your personal background, including some of your strengths as a teacher. Use this time to show a sincere interest in her as a person and discover interests or strengths that your assistant might share in the classroom at some point.

It is important to set a framework. If your district doesn't have a job description for your assistant, then you need to create one. Include the amount of time she will be working with the children versus doing clerical duties, delegation of authority in the classroom, work schedule, evaluation system, and confidentiality expectations. It is also wise to share your educational philosophy and style of discipline.

It is essential to show your assistant respect in the classroom:

• Notice the good things and give sincere compliments, when they are deserved.
• Share important school memos about upcoming events, policies, school newsletters, and the like.
• Create a working space in the room for your assistant to keep notes, binders, books, and other school-job-related materials. I have my assistant's name next to mine on the bulletin board in "our note corner," so that the children can see it and view her as part of the teaching team.
• Introduce your assistant to parents via your newsletter, open house, or other means.
• Include her when making class graphs, charts, or books.
• Make sure your assistant is part of the class photo for the school memory book.
• Keep the lines of communication open—ask about her weekend, share a humorous school anecdote, ask for an opinion about a classroom situation, and so forth.
• Share articles from professional journals pertinent to your educational beliefs or notices about upcoming conferences that might be of interest. You may want to attend a conference or workshop together and talk about your reflections and ideas.
• Be realistic in your expectations. If your assistant doesn't understand a concept or method, model the technique in a nonthreatening manner.
• Let your assistant know your daily plans for the classroom in an informal planning session or in a written memo.

If a problem does arise, be honest and set time to talk things over. State the problem and listen to her response, but make sure your views are known, too. If the problem cannot be resolved, call in a third party, such as your principal. In the rare circumstance that an aide performs an undesirable behavior that is harmful to the children, make sure to document it as accurately and objectively as possible.

If your district requires a formal evaluation of your assistant, discuss the procedure with her. Be sure to give reasons for your ratings and give your assistant a chance to respond.

I have been fortunate to have my present assistant for the past five years. The children see us as a unified team. It takes time and commitment to make our relationship work, but it is well worth the energy. It makes both of our jobs more satisfying. In turn, we feel that we are providing our students with the best teaching possible. And isn't that the point of education?

7

PLANNING AND ASSESSING LEARNING ACTIVITIES

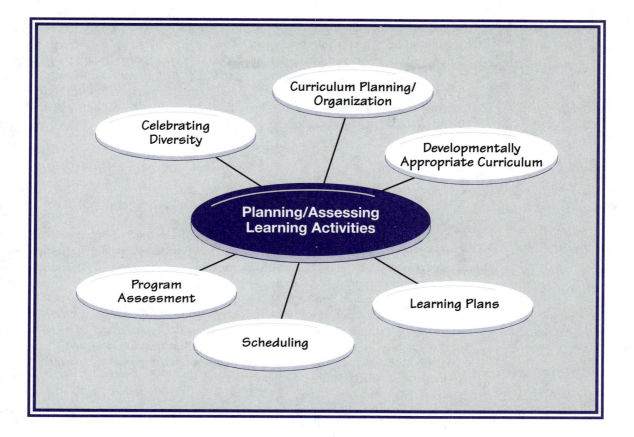

You observed in a kindergarten this week. You were amazed at the variety of activities the children had to choose from during most of the morning. You noticed that the teacher encouraged children to choose a project that interested them and that some children continued to work on the same activity for the entire time. One child built an elaborate block structure to represent the harbor the class had visited last week. She labeled all the parts with signs. She smiled happily when the teacher photographed her construction, asked the teacher for a blank book in which to mount the photograph, and told you that tomorrow she would write about the construction in the book. You wondered how building this block structure fit in with the teacher's goals and objectives for the class. Other children were involved in such activities as creating animals from cardboard boxes, painting at easels, observing and recording the behavior of a large frog, and following the directions in a book for making an appropriate home for a box turtle.

The teacher showed you his plan book, and you found lesson plans that did not follow the outline you learned in your first education class. How do teachers select learning activities? What does a lesson plan that includes many different activities look like? How does a teacher evaluate a program?

In planning a **curriculum** for young children, the teacher must select objectives, select and organize content, choose the appropriate learning experiences, determine the most appropriate sequence for the learning activities, and determine how to assess both children's growth and the program itself. *Curriculum* is a term that has many definitions: It can mean all experiences that happen at school; a written plan for learning; a syllabus that lists learning topics and the order in which they will be presented; or a program, such as a drug abuse prevention program, that specifies a sequence of activities. In this chapter, *curriculum* is defined as a written plan for learning experiences in which children will be involved.

CURRICULUM PLANNING

In designing a curriculum, the teacher must begin by thinking about the goals of the program. What will children know or be able to do when they finish the program? Will the focus of the program be on learning specific information or on learning how to find information? Will the focus be on academic learning or broader goals of development and growth as a whole child? If we assume that the program sets broad goals for development in all areas—physical, social, emotional, and intellectual—that will be the framework for the curriculum.

Next, the teacher should analyze the options for achieving the goals. For the broad goals described, the options would include taking field trips, having classroom visitors, conducting demonstrations and experiments, and participating in activities such as classifying, problem solving, reading aloud, doing hands-on projects, and others. Over the course of a year, each of these options might be selected several times. For example, suppose the children are learning about the life cycles of plants. A seed specialist might be invited to the class to share information about seeds with the children, or the children might take a field trip to a nursery or arboretum and clas-

THEORY INTO Practice

Examine a brochure for a preschool or a curriculum guide for a primary grade. Determine the long-term goals of the program. Choose one of the goals, and list two or three content topics that might help meet those goals.

sify seeds and plants in a variety of ways. The children might also plant seeds and care for the seedlings, or they might chart the growth of their plants and check the parts of their plants against a diagram provided on the computer. The outcomes of the study of plants would be intellectual development in learning facts about plants and seeds; physical development in planting and recording plant growth; social development in learning how to behave on a field trip or how to interact with a visitor; and emotional development in learning how to inhibit impulsive responses or develop control in a group setting.

For each part of a study of plants, the teacher would select objectives that would help achieve the purpose of the specific study and be related to the overall program goals. Objectives should not be too broad or vague (e.g., "The children will learn to love reading") nor should they be so narrow that they limit the possibilities for children's success (e.g., "Every child will learn to count to 10"). Suppose that our objective is as follows: "Children will develop increased skill in classification and in communicating their own criteria for classification categories." Assume that various classroom materials are usually available to the children for classification, such as buttons, keys, seashells, and so on, but for this experience, children also will be provided with collections of seeds that can be classified in a variety of ways. The children might also classify leaves; if they are responsive to the leaves, they might invite a botanist to explain how scientists classify leaves.

After choosing the content (knowledge of plants) and the objectives (increased skill in classification and communication), then the teacher should select possible activities that will help children achieve the goals of the program. Knowledge of the content area is critical here, as the teacher must decide the sequence of activities and experiences that will be most beneficial to the children. Will going on a field trip to get an overall view of plants be more beneficial at the beginning of the plant study, when children are introduced to the subject; in the middle of the study, when they will have had some experiences with plants; or at the end, when children may need help consolidating their knowledge? Some experiences must precede others. For example, children could not be expected to communicate their criteria for classifying leaves without having had some experience in actually classifying leaves.

In short, when planning the curriculum, the teacher is responsible for selecting the objectives and the content, determining how it is organized, selecting the learning activities, and then assessing the activities. The teacher must also consider the interests of the children when selecting curriculum experiences. If the teacher who selects plants as content finds, after a day or two, that the children have absolutely no interest in plants, she should select another topic. Suppose the children had expressed interest in the caterpillars they found on the playground. Caterpillars and other insects could be just as useful in helping children understand and apply

THEORY INTO Practice

Examine a brochure for a preschool or a curriculum guide for a primary grade. Determine the long-term goals of the program. Choose one of the goals, and list two or three content topics that might help meet those goals.

classification abilities as plants. Children should also be encouraged to choose what they would like to do from the many learning activities available and to make some choices about what they would like to learn about any given topic.

Although the sequence of planning a curriculum has been presented as a linear process, in reality, it is usually more recursive than linear: Teachers plan content and activities, adapt them for individual children, select other activities, evaluate, and plan again. All the steps are there, but the process is rarely a completely linear one.

CURRICULUM ORGANIZATION

When designing curriculum, teachers have several options for choosing how to organize the learning experiences. The most common approaches to organizing curriculum for young children are a facts approach and a skills approach. With a *facts approach,* experiences are arranged so that children learn a given set of factual information, such as the days of the week, the letters of the alphabet, or the names of colors. With a *skills approach,* experiences are selected and arranged so that children learn to cut on a line, to share, or to find information that they want in a selection of reference books.

In elementary schools, the most common organization has been the *subject-matter approach,* whereby children learn reading or math or social studies. Another approach is *thematic organization,* in which skills, facts, and subject-matter knowledge are integrated around a unifying theme, such as a study of whales. In the 1960s, Jerome Bruner (1960) and other curriculum leaders attempted to help designers of curriculum organize experiences around the key concepts of the various disciplines. In some curriculum guides, you might find key concepts and ideas in such objectives as "Children will recognize change as basic to understanding the social studies." The broadest organizers are the basic human needs shared by all people: friends, social responsibility as a citizen, and so on. The various types of curriculum organizers are summarized in Table 7.1.

THE DEVELOPMENTALLY APPROPRIATE CURRICULUM

In 1987, the National Association for the Education of Young Children (NAEYC) issued a statement defining *developmentally appropriate practice* in

TABLE 7.1
Types of Curriculum Organizers

Knowledge Sources	Content
Facts	Colors and shapes; number names in order; names of months and days of week; weather observations; stories of Columbus, the Pilgrims, George Washington, and Abraham Lincoln.
Skills	**Academic:** counting in sequence; letter recognition; phonics; number writing **Coping:** personal cleanliness; clothing management; eating; classroom cleanup **Social:** making friends; sharing; taking turns; using conventional rules of politeness **Process:** information seeking; problem setting; pursuing personal areas of curiosity; learning how to learn
Subjects Formal integration of subjects is referred to as an *integrated curriculum*.	Reading; social studies; math and science; language arts; music; arithmetic; health education; physical education
Themes A combination of subjects and skills is also referred to as an *integrated curriculum*.	**Historical and Current Events:** Columbus Day; Washington's birthday; Halloween; Spring; Circus **Topics:** transportation; community services; communication; families; nutrition
Structure of disciplines, key concepts	**Math:** sets, subsets, geometric shape, equivalent sets, greater than–less than, congruent length, longer, shorter **Physical Science:** force, energy, motion **Life Science:** adaptation if a factor in all plant and animal life **Economics:** key prices are determined in the marketplace largely by supply and demand
Holistic	Friendship: belonging and acceptance, approval, and respect; a sense of competence, independence, and autonomy; social responsibilities in the class, at home, and in the community; a healthful, nonpolluted environment; maintenance of personal well-being; survival skills

Source: Sidney Schwartz and Helen F. Robison, *Designing Curriculum for Early Childhood* (Boston: Allyn and Bacon, 1982), p. 35. Used with permission.

Developmentally Appropriate Practice in Early Childhood Programs Serving Children from Birth through Age 8 (Bredekamp 1987). In order to provide examples of what developmentally appropriate practice should look like in the early childhood classroom, two more volumes were published: *Reaching Potentials: Appropriate Curriculum and Assessment for Young Children,* volume 1 (Bredekamp and Rosegrant 1992), and *Reaching Potentials: Transforming Early Childhood Curriculum and Assessment,* volume 2 (Bredekamp and Rosegrant 1995). Furthermore, the original statement on developmentally appropriate practice has been revised and issued in *Developmentally Appropriate Practice in Early Childhood Programs,* revised edition (Bredekamp and Copple 1997). All of these titles are mentioned here so that you can appreciate the long struggle to define and explain frameworks for programs in early childhood education. Remember that the NAEYC represents a broad spectrum of professionals in the field of early childhood education; therefore, you should consider the following statements of guidelines as distillations of the thinking of all these people, not simply statements of single points of view:

Guidelines for Developmentally Appropriate Practice

A. Developmentally appropriate curriculum provides for all areas of a child's development: physical, emotional, social, linguistic, aesthetic, and cognitive.

B. Curriculum includes a broad range of content across disciplines that is socially relevant, intellectually engaging, and personally meaningful to children.

C. Curriculum builds upon what children already know and are able to do (activating prior knowledge) to consolidate their learning and to foster their acquisition of new concepts and skills.

D. Effective curriculum plans frequently integrate across traditional subject-matter divisions to help children make meaningful connections and provide opportunities for rich conceptual development; focusing on one subject is also a valid strategy at times.

E. Curriculum promotes the development of knowledge and understanding, processes and skills, as well as the dispositions to use and apply skills and to go on learning.

F. Curriculum content has intellectual integrity, reflecting the key concepts and tools of inquiry of recognized disciplines in ways that are accessible and achievable for young children, ages 3 through 8. . . . Children directly participate in study of the disciplines, for instance, by conducting scientific experiments, writing, performing, solving mathematical problems, collecting and analyzing data, collecting oral history, and performing other roles of experts in the disciplines.

G. Curriculum provides opportunities to support children's home culture and language while also developing all children's abilities to participate in the shared culture of the program and the community.

H. Curriculum goals are realistic and attainable for most children in the designated age range for which they are designed.

I. When used, technology is physically and philosophically integrated in the classroom curriculum and teaching. (pp. 20–21)*

* From Sue Bredekamp and Carol Copple (Eds.), *Developmentally Appropriate Practice in Early Childhood Programs,* rev. ed. (Washington, DC: National Association for the Education of Young Children, 1997). Copyright © 1997 by NAEYC. Reprinted with permission.

Guidelines for Developmentally Appropriate Assessment

A. Assessment of young children's progress and achievements is ongoing, strategic, and purposeful. The results of assessment are used to benefit children—in adapting curriculum and teaching to meet the developmental and learning needs of children, communicating with the child's family, and evaluating the program's effectiveness for the purpose of improving the program.

B. The content of assessments reflects progress toward important learning and developmental goals. The program has a systematic plan for collecting and using assessment information that is integrated with curriculum planning.

C. The methods of assessment are appropriate to the age and experiences of young children. Therefore, assessment of young children relies heavily on the results of observations of children's development, descriptive data, collections of representative work by children, and demonstrated performance during authentic, not contrived, activities. Input from families as well as children's evaluation of their own work are part of the overall assessment strategy.

D. Assessments are tailored to a specific purpose and used only for the purpose for which they have been demonstrated to produce reliable, valid information.

E. Decisions that have a major impact on children, such as enrollment or placement, are never made on the basis of a single developmental assessment or screening device but are based on multiple sources or relevant information, particularly observations by teachers and parents.

F. To identify children who have special learning or developmental needs and to plan appropriate curriculum and teaching for them, developmental assessments and observations are used.

G. Assessment recognizes individual variation in learners and allows for differences in styles and rates of learning. Assessment takes into consideration such factors as the child's facility in English, stage of language acquisition, and whether the child has had the time and opportunity to develop proficiency in his or her home language as well as in English.

H. Assessment legitimately addresses not only what children can do independently but what they can do with assistance from other children or adults. Teachers study children as individuals as well as in relationship to groups by documenting group projects and other collaborative work. (p. 21)*

---

* From Sue Bredekamp and Carol Copple (Eds.), *Developmentally Appropriate Practice in Early Childhood Programs*, rev. ed. (Washington, DC: National Association for the Education of Young Children, 1997). Copyright © 1997 by NAEYC. Reprinted with permission.

Although at times a content-area study might be appropriate, these guidelines support an integrated, **thematic approach** to curriculum. As explained in the next section, this approach is believed to be the most productive in helping teachers design a developmentally appropriate curriculum.

Rationale for an Integrated Curriculum

The idea of integrating curriculum is not a new one. At the turn of the century, John Dewey (1859–1952) (1902) advocated the organization of curriculum around projects that would interest and involve children. The most common approach to curriculum organization in schools in the United States, however, continues to be subject-matter organization, in which learning is segmented into math or science or language arts (Jacobs 1989).

You probably remember that in elementary school, you had reading first thing in the morning, math right before lunch, and science in the afternoon. Yet when children learn outside of school, they learn in wholes. For example, a child visiting tide pools could learn about many things at once: language arts (learning vocabulary for the animals and plants of the tide pools); physical skills (staying on top of the slippery rocks); classification (noticing which animals are related); the environment (noticing pollution or litter); family stories (hearing parents tell about when they visited these tide pools as children); and so on. A child's learning experiences outside school are not divisible into subject-matter areas.

An integrated curriculum can help a child make sense of the world more easily. If a child is learning the names of the letters of the alphabet, that knowledge must be placed in a context that makes sense to him. When the child learns the names of the letters by hearing the teacher read alphabet books and by exploring the forms of the letters in writing, he knows that the names of the letters communicate information about the printed form of language. He recognizes that this information is personally useful, not something learned to please an adult but that has no other utility for him.

An integrated curriculum provides opportunities for:

1. In-depth exploration of a topic and learning that is more than just superficial coverage
2. More choices and therefore more motivation to learn and greater satisfaction with the results
3. More active learning
4. An opportunity for the teacher to learn along with the children and model lifelong learning
5. A more effective use of student and teacher time

Organizing learning experiences around a theme can be productive, but if thematic teaching is to be successful, the theme must be carefully selected, activities carefully planned, and evaluation of the theme and of individual children's progress carefully monitored.

Selecting a Theme

In choosing a theme, there are several important considerations. Katz and Chard (1989) list the following criteria: relevance, the opportunity for application of skills, the availability of resources, teacher interest, and the time of year.

Relevance is defined as the applicability of a topic of study to a child's life. In other words, does what is learned have meaning for the child other than the fact that her learning it pleases the teacher? In considering the *opportunities for application of skills,* teachers must think about whether children will have opportunities to engage in reading, writing, and computation activities that have real meaning for them. Will the skills help children answer their own questions and solve their own problems? *Availability of resources* must be considered because theme studies require many resources—a textbook and a workbook are not sufficient. Are community resources (people and places to visit) available that will contribute to the topic? Can real objects be acquired to illustrate the topic? Is there adequate support from the library—posters,

THEORY *Into* **Practice**

Develop a list of possible themes for a given age group that meet the criteria listed in this chapter. Compare your list with those of others in your group.

In planning, teachers should design activities that are interesting to children and that allow them to become actively involved.

media, reference material? *Teacher interest* is a consideration because teachers will want to model interest and guide the children's explorations and investigations. There are too many appropriate themes to choose one that does not appeal to the teacher. *Time of year* is important not only because the teacher will want to be aware of seasonal topics (in the fall, for example, materials for study such as seed pods can be collected; in the spring, leaves are available to feed silkworm larvae) but also because the teacher must take into consideration that he will know the children much better later in the year. The first themes of the year should not be unfamiliar to children but should be topics that the teacher knows have been part of their previous personal experiences and that will interest them.

Katz and Chard (1989) group topics of study in the following way:

1. *The children themselves:* homes, babies, families, food, school bus, TV shows, toys, games
2. *The local community:* people, hospital, shops, building site, transport services, waterworks, fish market
3. *Local events and current affairs:* annual carnival or county fair, important anniversary, Independence Day, royal wedding, visit by a famous person
4. *Place:* neighborhood, roads, directions, landmarks, rivers, hills, woods, transport
5. *Time:* clocks, seasons, calendar, festivals, holidays, historical objects, historical events
6. *Natural phenomena:* weather, water, wind and air, plants, animals, mini-beasts, rocks, the sea, dinosaurs
7. *Content-free concepts:* opposites, pattern, color, symmetry
8. *General knowledge:* deserts, ships and other vehicles, inventions, space travel, rivers
9. *Miscellaneous:* hats, black holes, puppets, math or book week (pp. 65–66)

There are other ways of grouping topics, of course. The point is that many different kinds of topics are available for study, and teachers will want to balance the program by offering a variety of topics. Some teachers choose topics that are more scientific to alternate with topics that are focused more heavily on social studies. For example, studying plants or animals would involve more science (although social studies would not be excluded), and a study of festivals would involve more concepts in social studies.

One of the major reasons for selecting a thematic organization is to offer children the opportunity for in-depth rather than superficial study of various topics. Therefore, the theme selected must be one for which the activities are worthwhile. Thematic organization alone does not guarantee a well-planned, thoughtful curriculum. There are trivial approaches to thematic organization as well as to other types of curriculum organization. A teacher could decide to focus on mice as a theme and provide meaningful activities in which children learned about nutrition, training, building mazes, genetics, and so on. Or the teacher could choose mice as a theme and focus on it simplistically: covering the container where the children place their work with paper to represent cheese, decorating the bookmarks children use to mark their places in the reader with mice, using pictures of mice to enliven math worksheets, and having children make paper mice in art. A theme cannot be implemented solely by classroom decorations.

Implementing the Theme

Once a topic has been selected, the teacher (and the children, if they are old enough) will brainstorm areas of interest related to that particular topic. Older children will be able to see more relationships than younger ones.

After a topic and related subtopics have been chosen, the next step is to select activities that will help children learn content and apply their skills in meaningful contexts. What can be learned on a field trip? What can resource people share with the children? What play experiences can be facilitated? Are there construction possibilities? What skills can be applied in this study? What curriculum goals can be met through the study of this topic?

Let's assume that one of the teacher's curriculum goals is to help children become familiar with a variety of reading materials: narrative, poetry, expository writing, and so on. In studying corn, for instance, the children can read (or listen to the teacher read) information books about corn and perhaps stories and poems about the importance of corn to some Native American groups. Another goal might be for children to participate in the writing process on a daily basis. They could write records of the growth of corn plants, describe in writing what happens to corn when it is popped, or create their own informational books about corn. Yet another goal might be for children to increase their ability to recall and retell significant details. Participating in activities such as popping corn could be the basis for recalling and retelling meaningful details.

Once a theme has been tentatively selected, the teacher and children can create webs of things the children know and might want to know. Figure 7.1 (on page 202) is a web created by a teacher and children interested in corn. Figure 7.2 (on page 203) shows the web as it was expanded by the teacher to include other possible ideas and activities. Jones and Nimmo (1994) describe the value of webbing:

> It gives a staff of adults the chance to explore the possibilities of any material or idea in order to make decisions about use: Is it worth doing? Is it

THEORY INTO *Practice*

Select a developmentally appropriate topic and develop a theme around it. Include plans for learning experiences and materials that will be available in the various learning centers in the classroom. Your theme should be a topic that you believe will hold the children's interest for two to three weeks.

FIGURE 7.1   Web Created by Teacher and Children

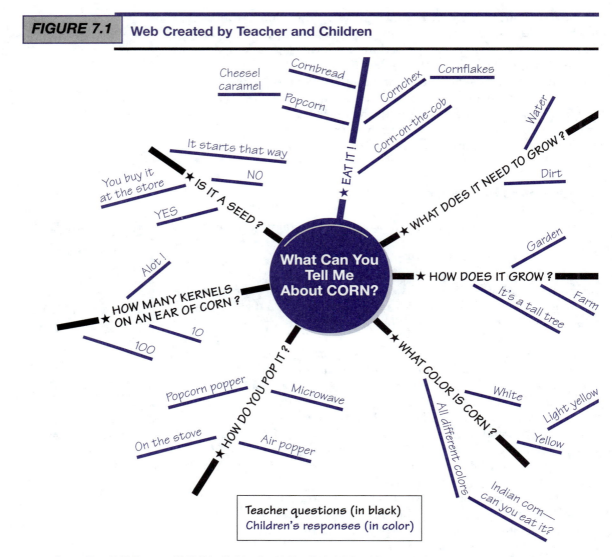

Teacher questions (in black)
Children's responses (in color)

FIGURE 7.2   Original Web Expanded by Teacher

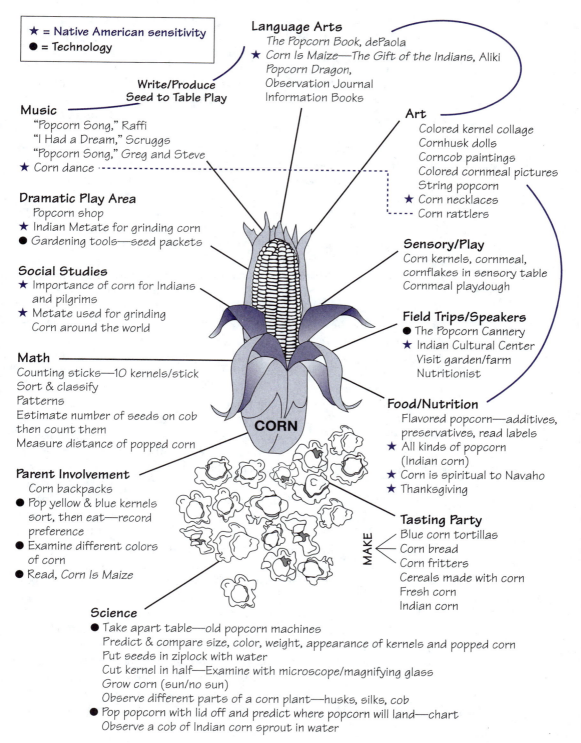

★ = Native American sensitivity
● = Technology

Language Arts
The Popcorn Book, dePaola
★ *Corn Is Maize—The Gift of the Indians*, Aliki
Popcorn Dragon,
Observation Journal
Information Books

Write/Produce
Seed to Table Play

Music
"Popcorn Song," Raffi
"I Had a Dream," Scruggs
"Popcorn Song," Greg and Steve
★ Corn dance

Dramatic Play Area
Popcorn shop
★ Indian Metate for grinding corn
● Gardening tools—seed packets

Social Studies
★ Importance of corn for Indians
and pilgrims
★ Metate used for grinding
Corn around the world

Math
Counting sticks—10 kernels/stick
Sort & classify
Patterns
Estimate number of seeds on cob
then count them
Measure distance of popped corn

Parent Involvement
Corn backpacks
● Pop yellow & blue kernels
sort, then eat—record
preference
● Examine different colors
of corn
● Read, *Corn Is Maize*

Art
Colored kernel collage
Cornhusk dolls
Corncob paintings
Colored cornmeal pictures
String popcorn
★ Corn necklaces
Corn rattlers

Sensory/Play
Corn kernels, cornmeal,
cornflakes in sensory table
Cornmeal playdough

Field Trips/Speakers
● The Popcorn Cannery
★ Indian Cultural Center
Visit garden/farm
Nutritionist

Food/Nutrition
Flavored popcorn—additives,
preservatives, read labels
★ All kinds of popcorn
(Indian corn)
★ Corn is spiritual to Navaho
★ Thanksgiving

CORN

MAKE

Tasting Party
Blue corn tortillas
Corn bread
Corn fritters
Cereals made with corn
Fresh corn
Indian corn

Science
● Take apart table—old popcorn machines
Predict & compare size, color, weight, appearance of kernels and popped corn
Put seeds in ziplock with water
Cut kernel in half—Examine with microscope/magnifying glass
Grow corn (sun/no sun)
Observe different parts of a corn plant—husks, silks, cob
● Pop popcorn with lid off and predict where popcorn will land—chart
Observe a cob of Indian corn sprout in water

likely to generate developmentally appropriate activities? What are the ways we might want to enrich the activity by being prepared with other materials or questions? How long might children's interest continue?

A web is a *tentative* plan. It doesn't tell you exactly what will happen or in what order. That depends in large part on the children's response. So, first you plan and then you start trying your ideas, *paying attention to what happens*, evaluating, and moving on with further activities. (p. 11)

Once curriculum goals have been reviewed, the teacher (and children) can determine activities that will be possible in this study. Not every child will participate in every activity; choices will be available to the children. The teacher must think about the objectives of each activity and the relationship of the objectives to the curriculum goals. If an activity cannot contribute to the curriculum goals, it should be eliminated as a choice.

Classroom learning areas should be used to enhance particular themes. For example, in a study of plants, materials such as flowers (not poisonous), leaves, and seed pods could be placed in the art center; books and computer software about plants could be available in the library; puzzles with plant content could be available in the manipulatives area; and accessories could be added to the block area so that the children could create a farm. Enhancing learning areas in these ways does not mean that children will be assigned to do certain tasks in the areas; rather, materials will be available to help children complete their investigations or follow up on their interests.

Many teachers try to follow the children's lead in planning curriculum. If the children are interested in a certain topic, then the teacher will help them explore that topic and develop their interests until their questions and activities lead them to another topic. Several authors have described this **emerging curriculum** approach and their own ways of implementing it (Byrum and Pierce 1993; Edwards, Gandini, and Forman 1993; Jones and Nimmo 1994). These teachers believe that the best curriculum is that in which the children are fully engaged and their interests are fully explored. The challenge, however, is to build a curriculum that not only follows the children's interests but also meets the goals of the program.

The most famous of the emerging curriculum schools are those of Reggio Emilia, which are municipal schools in a city of about 130,000 people in northern Italy. Much has been written about these schools and the project approach that they use (Bredekamp 1993; Edwards, Gandini, and Forman 1993; Gandini 1993; Kennedy 1996; Malaguzzi 1993; McCarthy 1995). These projects grow out of simple experiences, such as the children's visit to a poppy field. The children examined the flowers, drew them, painted them, sculpted them, discussed them, created murals of them, and otherwise continued to focus their activities on the poppies for a long period of time. The teachers continued to guide the children by asking questions, offering new materials, and helping the children refine and rethink their work.

The quality of the work that the Reggio Emilia children have produced is what has led to so much investigation of the processes employed in the schools. The teachers who implement this sort of emerging curriculum have support from colleagues and administrators. In Reggio Emilia, they also have support from parents, who often attend teacher planning meetings and feel comfortable making suggestions. (These parents also know how hard the teachers work!)

A child-centered curriculum that produces outstanding products while focusing on the process of learning and doing is the ideal in early childhood education. A teacher, especially a new teacher, who wants to implement a child-centered curriculum should find a colleague who also wants to implement such a program. That way, all of the questions, problems, failures, and successes can be shared with someone else struggling to achieve the same goals. A solitary teacher without support will find implementing such a program nearly impossible.

Evaluation

Teachers must use some method of recording each child's progress and the goals met by the activities focusing on a given theme. One method is to construct a record sheet for each child, with a list of curriculum goals down the side and columns across for each theme of study. As children complete activities, their work can be recorded on the list. Figure 7.3 on page 206 illustrates this format. (Note that in most state and district curriculum guides, goals are generally grouped by subject-matter content; that is, all the literacy goals, social studies goals, science goals, and so on are listed together. Thus, a teacher might have to use a checklist with a subject-matter organization scheme even if her classroom activities are organized thematically.)

In evaluating the children's progress, the teacher might use several different assessments, such as observations of the children's behavior, a checklist to record skill achievement, or a narrative that describes the child's growth. (Assessment possibilities are described in Chapter 15.) In evaluating the theme, the teacher would observe the children's interest and record the contributions of the theme to overall goals.

Although a teacher may choose to repeat a theme another year, rarely can a theme be repeated in the same form. The interests and experiences of different groups of children vary considerably, and some themes that work well with one group are not at all interesting to other groups. Even if topics are repeated, the activities chosen by the children are likely to vary so much that one year's implementation of the theme will not be the same as

FIGURE 7.3

Evaluation Checklist

CHILD'S NAME _Jamie_

	Plants	Insects	
Reads a variety of materials: reference materials, narrative stories, poetry	10/6	11/5 11/20	
Participates in writing process: personal writing, letter writing, narratives, expository writing	10/8	11/10 12/1	
Recognizes adaptation as a factor in all plant and animal life (habitat, camouflage, food chain)	10/12 10/15 10/16	11/20 11/23 11/24	
Uses computation to solve problems			
Uses the scientific process to solve problems			

a previous year's. When a teacher simply applies a theme to the children, it becomes mechanical, and the classroom routine fails to reflect children's interests and experiences. Theme studies require considerable investments of time and energy by the teacher, but the result—meaningful experiences for the children through which they gain not only knowledge and skills but the disposition to learn—is well worth the effort.

As you read the chapters in this book about language, literature, literacy, math, science, social studies, the arts, and health and physical education, remember that although these content areas are presented in discrete chapters, the underlying assumption is that knowledge of each subject-matter area will help you to integrate curriculum. You do need to understand the goals and objectives in each area in order to plan appropriately, but you should use this knowledge to plan meaningful and conceptually important themes. Throughout the content chapters of this book (Chapters 8 through 14), a theme of *change* will be the focus. So even though the discussion in each chapter will be about a discrete subject (math, science, music, and so on), the emphasis will be on an integrated curriculum.

However the curriculum is organized, teachers are responsible for developing the plans for learning experiences in their classrooms. The following section provides some advice on creating those plans.

LEARNING PLANS

A **learning plan** differs from a lesson plan in that often a lesson plan outlines only one lesson. In early childhood programs, however, learning experiences are not usually confined to single lessons. As Elkind (1982) reminds us, "Clearly children learn in many different ways and what mode of learning is employed depends very much upon what is to be learned" (p. 7). Learning plans involve long-term planning, unit or theme planning, and short-term goals. Each day's activities should contribute to the unit or theme goals, and each unit or theme should contribute to the overall goals of the program.

As the teacher of the program, you may not have much control over the program goals. They are often established by the administration of the center or school, hopefully, with the collaboration of the teachers. These are the kinds of goals that centers advertise on their consumer brochures or that are printed in the curriculum guides of school districts. However, goal statements do not define how goals are to be achieved. The "how" is

THEORY INTO Practice

Write a learning plan for a given group of children.

Successful learning experiences begin with careful planning.

Program Goals:
Improved problem-solving skills, increased language development, increased fine motor development

Theme: How Plants Change

Objectives:
- Children will be able to distinguish plants from nonplants.
- Children will learn the following vocabulary: *seed, stem, leaf, flower.*
- Children will learn the basic requirements for plant life (light, water, soil).

Activity Time:
- *Discovery:* Make available bean and pumpkin seeds for planting (have cups, soil, watering can in learning area).
- *Art:* Use leaves collected from local trees for printing (cover leaf with paint and press paper over it; Mr. Gonzales to help supervise here).
- *Library:* Put out information books about plants.

Small Groups:
Take a walk around the school to observe different kinds of plants. Gather plant materials for use in the collage. Provide each child with a small paper bag for collecting.

Cooking:
Mrs. Turner (parent volunteer) will help the children shell and cook green peas.

Read:
The Carrot Seed (Kraus 1945)

Movement:
Pretend to be trees swaying in the wind.

Evaluation:
The teacher will observe children's responses to the planting activity and will record evidence of plant knowledge on the walk (anecdotal records).

up to the teacher and should reflect knowledge of children's development, the children's abilities and interests, and the teacher's own interests.

A daily learning plan may indicate the materials to be placed in the learning areas, include notes about guiding specific children's learning, and suggest plans for evaluation of activities. If one of the daily goals is learning to use the concept "line" in talking about art, the learning plan would note the pieces of art to be displayed, specify that strings and strips of paper should be made available in the art area, and call for an emphasis on line in movement experiences. Teachers would work with individual children as they participated in art or movement to emphasize the concept of line and would talk with those who were looking at the art examples about how the artists had used lines. This plan would fit into the larger theme of lines and space being explored in a variety of areas and support the overall goals of increasing children's ability to communicate effectively and to explore a variety of materials.

Several daily learning plans for preschool and primary children are presented in boxes in this section. Take some time to review them, and as you do, keep this in mind: Learning plans should always be as complete as possible but should never be so rigid that **incidental learning** cannot be included in the day's schedule. For instance, if a child brings a pet rabbit to school, obviously time must be allotted to observing and discussing the rabbit. If the children are really interested in the rabbit, then the teacher might make some plans for additional experiences with rabbits in a few weeks. The point is to take advantage of what the children want to know now as you keep the overall goals in mind. When Alice came to the Cheshire Cat and asked which road to take, he told her that it did not make any difference, since she did not know where she was going. Teachers of young children need to know where they are going—and they need to plan which road to take but be prepared to take another one, if it appears to be better for the children.

Although learning plans are more appropriate in terms of planning for instruction than isolated lesson plans, lesson plans may sometimes be designed to teach specific elements of a broader learning plan. For example, the learning plan on plants suggests that children use leaves for printing. A lesson plan for that activity might look like that in Figure 7.4 on page 210.

Some plans will provide for whole-class activities, others for small groups, and still others for individual children. For example, from the learning plan for six- to seven-year-olds (see page 211), the whole class might listen to the teacher read *Tops and Bottoms* (Stevens 1995). After that, small groups might work on research projects about corn, and individuals might plant seeds and create art projects. In every learning plan, there should be a good balance of whole-group activities, small-group activities, and individual activities.

DEVELOPMENTALLY APPROPRIATE PRACTICE

Reflect on plans for learning experiences for children. Review the framework for developmentally appropriate curriculum as you think about these questions:

- Can a teacher of young children purchase a curriculum that is developmentally appropriate? Why?
- Given what you know about developmentally appropriate practice, can a teacher plan the topics of study for the year before meeting the children? Why?
- Can a teacher incorporate the topics/goals of the school curriculum guide into a developmentally appropriate curriculum? Why?

- If a first-grade teacher wanted to study transportation with her students, would that be developmentally appropriate? If your answer is no, under what conditions would the topic be appropriate? If yes, explain why the topic is appropriate.
- What qualities make any topic of study developmentally appropriate?

FIGURE 7.4 **Sample Lesson Plan for Activity on Plants**

Objective:	Children will participate in a printing activity.
Materials:	• Leaves gathered from local area
	• Tempera paint
	• Brushes or sponges
	• Newspapers
	• Paper towels
	• White construction paper
Procedure:	1. Cover the work surface with newspaper.
	2. Allow each child to select the leaves he wishes to use.
	3. Arrange the leaves on a paper towel with the veined side up.
	4. Cover the leaves with a light coat of tempera paint using a brush or sponge.
	5. Place white paper over the towel and painted leaves; then press all over.
	6. Lift off the paper.
	7. Repeat as the child desires.
	8. Place the finished paper on a drying rack, and help the child clean up (hang up smock, wash hands, and so on).
Alternative:	The child may wish to paint the leaf and then pick it up by the stem and place it on the white paper. Allow experimentation.
Evaluation:	Observe the child's interest and participation. Also observe the child's language. (Does he talk about leaves and perhaps even what kind of leaf he is choosing?)

Mandated Lessons or Goals

If the school district has **mandated goals** and corresponding materials to be used, the professional teacher must decide if the materials are appropriate for his particular group of children and if not, how the children could achieve the mandated goals in a more appropriate manner. For example, in one school district, kindergarten teachers were told that all kindergarten children should have mastered eighteen basic sight words from the adopted basal reader by the end of kindergarten. A professional teacher would be accountable for teaching the sight-word vocabulary to all the children for whom this goal was reasonable, but given his knowledge of emerging literacy, he would choose a meaningful context for helping children learn to recognize the sight words. These basic words (*boy, girl, I,*

Program Goals:
Increased ability to use print to solve problems and meet personal needs and increased skill in oral communication

Theme: How Plants Change

Objectives:
- Children will be able to describe the life cycle of a seed-bearing plant.
- Children will be able to locate information about plants in books and videos and on the computer.
- Children will create products to demonstrate their knowledge of plants.

Group Time:
The teacher will review the children's choices of activities for the day. She will read the poster with the directions for planting seeds and call the children's attention to the illustrations that can be used if they forget the words. She will demonstrate texture with several materials. The teacher will also ask the children to think about texture, if they choose the art activity.

Activity Time:
- *Discovery:* The children will be provided with containers, soil, seeds, and water. Following the instructions on a poster, each child will select, plant, and water three different seeds. Paper will be provided for recording the date, the kind of seed, and the amount of water for each container.
- *Art:* Wild seeds and seed pods will be provided for creating collages. Seeds or pods might also be used to print on paper, if the children are interested in doing so.
- *Library:* A variety of books on plants and seeds will be available for browsing. Computer programs will also be available for the children to access information about plants.
- *Language Arts:* Make paper, pens, pencils, markers, glue, and a blank model of an accordion book available to the children. They may each make a book that illustrates the life cycle of a plant with seeds, or they may choose another project.
- *Social Studies:* Read *Tops and Bottoms* (Stevens 1995). Then classify plants into the parts people eat: leaves, stems, roots, and seeds. Use real examples and then sample some of them at snack time. Trace the life of one plant from the farm to the table. Visit a farm where corn is grown; follow the corn to the cannery or the grocery store. Observe the produce section of the supermarket.
- *Movement:* Have children use their bodies to depict slowly unfolding as a plant growing, twining, turning, or swaying in the wind. Children can select or compose music to accompany these movements.

ran, look, and so forth) are common in children's writing and in the stories and poems that a teacher would use in the classroom. The teacher would use the words as they occurred naturally and help children recognize them in these contexts. Keeping good records of the children's work helps the teacher discuss the learning that is taking place and the reasons why the choice of instructional materials is important to the children's success.

The professional teacher of young children depends on assessment of program goals and the growth of individual children to make decisions about what instruction is most appropriate for them. Materials and programs must be carefully evaluated in terms of children's needs before they are used for instruction. Most goals can be reached by many routes; the teacher must choose the one that suits the children best.

SCHEDULING

THEORY
INTO
Practice

Interview several teachers about their daily schedules. How are the schedules similar? How are they different?

One professional chore that helps the teacher manage the activities of the class in an appropriate manner is setting up the daily class schedule. Like room arrangements, furniture, and choices of areas, the schedule can be planned before the teacher knows the children, but plans should be made with the knowledge that the schedule will change to reflect the needs of the group and of individuals.

A schedule must allow children to move around and select materials and activities as easily as possible. In planning a schedule, the teacher should begin by noting any fixed times, such as the time the class can use the outdoor play area, lunchtime, or time with specialists (music, physical education, or art). The teacher should try to arrange for a large block of the time that is left to be a period in which children have a choice of activities and materials. Other activities that the teacher wants to include can then be added: a story time, a music time, a group time, and a snack time.

The time allotted for these activities will depend on the children's ages. Threes and fours need much shorter story and music times than older children and probably do not need group time at all. Fives and sixes can benefit from longer story and music times and from group time, as well. Teachers in primary grades experience more intrusions in their schedules (fixed recess periods, visits from various specialists, and so on), but they still have long periods of time during which they can schedule activities. One source of tension in planning any schedule for young children is attempting to balance large-group times and times for self-selected activities.

One purpose of a schedule is to provide routine and structure for children so that they know basically what to expect each day (Lund and Bos 1981). Another purpose is to provide balance in the day. For instance, activities in which children are relatively passive should not be scheduled back to back so that children have to sit quietly for long periods of time.

Table 7.2 shows samples of schedules for younger children and older children on half-day programs, a full-day program for kindergarten children, and a full-day schedule for primary-grade children. Note that none of these schedules includes time for cleanup or toileting. Teachers should involve children as much as possible in cleaning up the room and putting away materials before moving to other activities. Ideally, all rooms for early childhood programs should have bathrooms attached so that children can just go to the bathroom when they need to. Teachers in some

TABLE 7.2

Schedules for Various Programs

Program	Times	Activities
Half-Day Program for Younger Children	9:00 – 10:00	Activity time
	10:00 – 10:10	Music time
	10:10 – 10:40	Outdoor play
	10:40 – 11:00	Snack time
	11:00 – 11:10	Quiet time
	11:10 – 11:20	Movement activities
	11:20 – 11:30	Story time
Half-Day Program for Older Preschoolers	9:00 – 10:00	Activity time
	10:00 – 10:20	Music and movement
	10:20 – 10:40	Group time (calendar, weather, discussions)
	10:40 – 11:00	Outdoor play
	11:00 – 11:10	Snack
	11:10 – 11:30	Story, poetry
Full-Day Kindergarten	9:00 – 9:15	Opening, singing, planning for the day
	9:15 – 10:15	Activity time
	10:15 – 10:45	Snack
	10:45 – 11:15	Outdoor play (gross motor play indoors in bad weather)
	11:15 – 11:45	Story time, literature study
	11:45 – 12:30	Lunch and recess
	12:30 – 1:30	Rest period
	1:30 – 1:40	Group time (discussions, planning for afternoon)
	1:40 – 2:15	Activity time
	2:15 – 2:45	Library music, art, or physical education
	2:45 – 3:00	Evaluations of activities, dismissal
Primary Children	9:00 – 9:15	Opening, singing, planning for the day
	9:15 – 10:30	Activity time (theme activities)
	10:30 – 11:00	Physical education
	11:00 – 11:30	Math activities
	11:30 – 12:30	Lunch and recess
	12:30 – 1:00	Literature activities (read-aloud, drama)
	1:00 – 2:00	Activity time (theme studies)
	2:00 – 2:20	Recess
	2:20 – 2:45	Library (alternating with art or music specialists)
	2:45 – 3:00	Sharing events of day, discussions, plans for next day, dismissal

older buildings (where this arrangement is often not the case) may have to arrange to take the class to the restrooms in groups. If possible, the teacher should send a few children at a time with an aide or volunteer while other children continue working.

SCHEDULING

Details of the Schedule

Activity Time

Experiences that are appropriate for children will be discussed in more detail in the content-area chapters (Chapters 8 through 14). Children usually participate in these experiences during activity times. For example, if the theme was a study of how insects change, children would work puzzles depicting insects in the manipulatives area; observe insects on display in the science area using a magnifying glass and record their observations; read (or look at pictures in) books about insects in the library; sort pictures of insects; examine sequence boards showing the life cycles of insects in the language arts area; and play with puppets and flannelboard cutouts of insects in the language arts area. Children might paint or draw insects or build insect homes in the art area. Whatever the theme, it would be incorporated into as many content areas as possible and reasonable. Activity times are scheduled so that children can participate in small-group and individual activities.

Group Time

Some traditional group time experiences are not especially meaningful to children. As noted earlier, threes and fours probably do not need group time at all. Trying to get them to learn about the calendar is not the best use of their time. Fives and sixes can review the calendar and daily weather, but these should be *brief* reviews, not extended drills. Other activities appropriate for group time for fives and sixes include planning and evaluating their experiences during activity time, participating in some short group experiences (such as viewing a videotape that relates to a theme topic), listening to a resource person, discussing a problem in the room, having specific instruction in fire safety rules, and so on. Whole-group instruction is not an appropriate teaching strategy for content areas; lecturing on a topic to children of this age is of little value.

Group time with primary children may be used for some of the same activities as those suggested for fives and sixes. It may also be used to help children recognize the choices they can make for their theme studies and to do more formal planning of their day. Some limited group instruction with primary children is useful. For example, the teacher may teach the whole group to recognize story structure or to recognize particular strategies that an author has used in a story the children are reading. Group discussions of books the children are reading are also important. Likewise, having children present work they have completed can be a valuable component of group time in the primary grades.

Show-and-tell, or sharing, is often a regular part of group time, especially with five- to eight-year-olds. Show-and-tell often becomes "bring-and-brag," as children bring their newest toy to show off. The teacher usually controls the audience for the speaker and directs the children while they speak or ask questions. If sharing time is to achieve the goal of promoting more effective communication, however, teachers must structure the time so that children do the talking and organizing, rather than the teacher.

One technique is to have the sharing focus on the children's work, rather than on objects brought from home. Children may also need to share something especially meaningful to them from time to time, but not every child needs to share something every day. Another technique is to organize sharing time into small groups so that children share with three or four others and do not have to sit while twenty-five children share, one at a time. It is important to evaluate sharing experiences on the basis of what the children are actually learning, rather than simply to state that sharing is an important means of children learning to communicate more effectively.

Snack Time

Very young children need a snack during the morning or afternoon. Snack time should be considered a teaching time, as children learn about new foods, learn to carry on conversations, and learn how to help prepare and serve the snack. Snacks should always be nutritious and help children learn about good nutrition.

Snack time for fives and sixes can be quite time consuming in a half-day program when time is so limited. By the time all the children have washed their hands, been served, eaten their snacks, and cleaned up, twenty to thirty minutes out of a two-and-a-half-hour day have been used up. Therefore, some teachers prefer to have snacks available on a table, so that two or three children can serve themselves and then go back to their activities. Other teachers prefer to incorporate snack time into the activity time by making food preparation one of the activities. In this way, the activity time can be extended.

Transitions

Transitions from one activity to another are the most likely times for behavior problems or disruptions in any program. What can the teacher do when one or two children are ready to begin a new activity and the others are still cleaning up their work areas? Or what can the teacher do when the class is ready to go the cafeteria for lunch and the principal asks her to hold her class for exactly two more minutes? The teacher can have children who have completed their cleanup help others finish. Those who have finished can then sit in the group area and listen to a tape recording of nursery rhymes, folk songs, or fingerplays; others will join as they finish. With older children, one child can begin a rhyme, the second can say the next line, and so on; the last child can begin another rhyme.

When moving children from one area to another, the teacher should try having them move in groups by color or kind of clothing (all children

Moving children successfully from one place or activity to another requires good planning.

wearing yellow, all children wearing sandals, and so on). Playing rhythms on a drum or piano also helps in moving children from one area to another; they can march around the room and then out the door to go outside or to the lunchroom. There are many memory games that children can play in line, such as Going on the Train, in which the first player takes something beginning with *a,* the second something beginning with *b,* and on through the alphabet. Children can also play guessing games, such as Twenty Questions or Who's in My Family? or they can listen to tapes of jokes or short pieces of poetry (Alger 1984).

The teacher should involve the children in solving transition problems. If it is time to go outdoors, the children might be asked to think of ways they can all get their coats without bumping into anyone or crowding. It is also helpful to have the activity that follows cleanup be something the children are anxious to do; dawdlers are not encouraged to finish their tasks when what they are going to do next is not exciting to them (Alger 1984).

Simplifying Routines

The routines of checking attendance, counting the children who will purchase milk, and so on can take up quite a lot of time. Some teachers choose to make these routines learning experiences for the children and as simple as possible for themselves. One way to check attendance is to have the children sign their names on a paper attached to a clipboard by the door. The teacher can see from the child's signature what he knows and is learning about writing.

Another technique is to divide a board in half, labeling one half "Present" and the other half "Absent." Nails or pegs are added below the label on each half, enough for all the children in the class. Each child is given a nametag with a hole in it, which he will hang on the board. As the children come in every day, they move their nametags from the "Absent" side to the "Present" side of the board. In preparation for the next day, the teacher reverses the "Present" and "Absent" headings.

Taking a count for milk can be accomplished by having each child who is purchasing milk place a marker with her name on it in a pocket marked "Milk." The same technique works for lunch counts.

Adapting the Schedule

For the first two weeks or so of the new schoolyear, the schedule may be adapted to help children make a more comfortable adjustment to school. Some schools have only half of the children assigned to each classroom come each day for the first week; the other half of the class comes to school the second week. This way, children have a chance to learn about school routines and get more attention from the teacher while they adjust. Some schools for younger children divide groups in half and ask each half to attend for half of each day for the first two or three weeks; other schools begin the year on a staggered schedule, so that there are five children the first two days, ten the next two days, and fifteen on the fifth day. Teachers should work with the administration and parents to make the beginning of school successful for all involved; sometimes, parents are willing to help more at the beginning to assure a good start for all children.

Teachers may also have to adapt schedules to fit the children's developing abilities. Children may not be able to sustain their play for as long as the teacher predicted at the beginning of school and may need two short play periods, rather than one long one. Children may need more rest than was predicted. They also may be able to engage in activities of their choice for longer than might have been predicted. Teachers, with input from the children, may need to adapt schedules to fit the individuals' needs.

PARENTS AND PLANNING

■ Make sure that parents are aware of your typical daily schedule. Invite them to come to class at different times of day so they can observe individual activities as well as small- and whole-group activities.

Kindergarten: Half-Day, Full-Day, or Alternate-Day Programs

This section applies specifically to kindergarten because there is so much debate about the values of different schedules for kindergarten children. The schedule for threes and fours is generally either a morning or an afternoon session of about two-and-a-half or three hours, whereas schedules for primary grades are usually set to match the full-day elementary school schedule. Some schools have two sessions of kindergarten each day. Because of transportation problems and the need for full-day child care, some schools have adopted an alternate-day schedule, so that kindergartners attend for a full day but only on alternate days. Other schools provide full-day programs for some kindergartners, especially those deemed at risk of academic failure. What does the research say about these different schedule patterns?

The research yields no conclusive results. Jalongo (1986) explains how difficult it is to control all the factors when trying to determine what is best for young children. Obviously, no child can attend a half-day program and an alternate-day program at the same time, so the effects of different schedules on the same population of children cannot be studied. Other factors involved in assessing what type of schedule works best include the skills of the teacher and the maturation and self-esteem of the children. To find that a group attending a half-day program scored higher on an achievement test than a group attending an alternate-day program would not be especially useful because of all the confounding factors. One study (Gullo et al. 1986) did attempt to control all the variables and found that children in all-day programs scored higher on achievement tests than children from half-day or alternate-day programs. The only significant difference in the social behaviors of children in these groups, according to teachers, was that children who attended alternate-day programs showed fewer negative behaviors. These findings are certainly not conclusive.

When evaluating schedules, the best approach is to determine what is best for the children involved, to plan for excellent experiences no matter when the children are in school, and to evaluate continuously. A full-day program that involves children in inappropriate activities is not beneficial to children, even though they are there longer than children in half- or alternate-day programs. Decisions should not be made on the basis of convenience; rather, the guideline should be to provide optimal environments for children.

Other Scheduling Issues

An ongoing problem for kindergarten and primary teachers is *pull-out programs,* in which children are removed from class at certain times for special lessons or activities, such as speech therapy. Removing children from the class makes it difficult to schedule large-group activities and also complicates having all children participate in small-group or individual activities.

One solution to the problem, which is being used in an ever-increasing number of schools, is to have the special teachers come to the regular classroom to work with individual students, rather than have the students go to the teachers. In schools in which this solution has not yet been implemented, the regular classroom teachers might approach the special teachers with the idea and agree to help solve any problems that arise. If this solution is not applied and pull-out programs remain a fact of life, regular classroom teachers should try to arrange activity time for that part of the day when the most children will be in the room. Classroom teachers should also try to work with the schedules of the special teachers in order to achieve a more reasonable day for the class. Regardless, there does not seem to be an easy solution to the problem of pull-out programs.

PROGRAM ASSESSMENT

When teachers evaluate an early childhood program, they are looking for evidence that the program is appropriate for the children enrolled and that it is effective in bringing about their growth. The following questions will help teachers evaluate their programs:

1. Would you like to be a child in your classroom?
2. Is there a balance of small-group, whole-group, and individual activities?
3. Do children spend more time in self-selected activities than in teacher-directed activities?
4. Do the children's interests influence activities and learning experiences?
5. Does every child find success and challenge every day?
6. Is there a balance of emphasis on intellectual, social, emotional, and physical growth?
7. Are skills taught in a meaningful context?
8. Can children withdraw from activities without penalty?
9. Are activities and experiences selected on the basis of their relationship to the goals of the program?
10. When planning activities, is the information from observations and assessments used to guide planning?
11. Do individual children show evidence of growth?
12. Are interactions with parents supportive of children's growth?

Answers to these questions will be derived from evaluating the schedule, the lesson plans, and the instructional materials and observations of

PARENTS AND PLANNING

■ Adapt the twelve questions listed on page 219 such that they ask parents about their activities with their children. For example, adapt question 1 to ask: Would you like to be a child in your family? (Note that parents might not be able to answer question 10.)

interpersonal relationships in the classroom. A teacher who respects children's interests will not determine a list of topics to be studied before getting to know the children. (This is not to imply that a teacher cannot make tentative plans for topics he predicts will be of interest to the children.) Further, in a good program, materials will be readily available to help children learn a variety of facts and skills in a playful manner. Finally, other evidence that the program is a good one is found in the attitudes of the children. If they see themselves as active learners who seek support for their own learning, rather than waiting for the teacher to tell them everything to do, the program is effective.

If you are interested in reviewing a much more detailed evaluation of a program, consult the *Accreditation Criteria and Procedures of the National Academy of Early Childhood Programs* (NAEYC 1984).

CELEBRATING DIVERSITY

To celebrate the diversity of the classroom, teachers should plan for experiences and activities that reflect the diversity of society. For example, in selecting themes, teachers should think carefully about the meanings of the activities for the children involved. For example, what will a two-week theme with a focus on St. Patrick's Day mean to a class of three- and four-year-olds who are Hispanic or Southeast Asian? On the other hand, St. Patrick's Day may be an important holiday to a child from an Irish household. Perhaps implementing a theme about this holiday could be justified if there were Irish children in the class and the theme focused on the holidays of all the ethnic groups represented in the class. In sum, the themes selected must be relevant to the lives of the children. Teachers should consider that by focusing on holidays, they may be denying children experiences with more interesting and relevant themes, such as those focusing on animals, insects, plants, and other children's interests.

Diversity can be celebrated in many of the activities and experiences that teachers plan for young children. For example, when planning cooking experiences, teachers can prepare foods that are typical of the various ethnic groups represented in the class. Members of the community can be invited to share special ethnic foods, traditional clothing, stories, and games. Community members whose work is nontraditional for their *gender* also can be invited to share information about their work with the class. Teachers should not advocate a curriculum that simply adds a "diversity feature." Rather, their goal should be the authentic integration of people and other resources that will help children explore topics in ways that diversity is naturally included.

Experiences with literature can enhance children's knowledge and appreciation of racial and ethnic differences, if they are planned carefully by teachers. Namely, teachers should select pieces of literature to add information or interest to themes, ensuring that the works of authors and illustrators of various racial/ethnic groups and both genders are included. Books, both fiction and nonfiction, and poetry that include a wide variety of characters should also be selected. In one second-grade boy's reading-response journal, he explained that he really liked a particular book because he was Hispanic and had never known about a book with Hispanic characters before. Children should be able to find characters like themselves in books that are part of the classroom experience.

Please note the items in the web in Figure 7.2 (on page 203) that are marked with stars to indicate sensitivity to Native American cultures as they relate to the topic of corn. These experiences are natural to the study of corn and illustrate how diversity can be an integral component of theme studies in the early childhood classroom.

CHAPTER SUMMARY

- *Curriculum* can be defined in many ways: as a program, as a written plan for learning experiences, as a syllabus listing topics and sequences of topics, or as everything that happens at school. In this chapter, *curriculum* was defined as the written plan for learning experiences.
- The steps in planning a curriculum include determining the purpose of the curriculum, analyzing the options that are available, selecting the features to be included, producing the design, and evaluating the design.
- Teachers developing a curriculum must select content and sequence activities so that children can use the information they have already learned to learn new information.
- Assessment of a curriculum must be appropriate for the age and level of development of the children and for the activity.
- A curriculum can be organized around facts, skills, subjects, themes, key concepts, or common human needs.

- A thematic organization of a curriculum provides learning opportunities that are not divided into segments and that better match children's learning experiences outside the school setting.
- In selecting a theme, the teacher must consider relevance, opportunities for application of skills, availability of resources, his own interests, and the time of year.
- Evaluation of themes and experiences is necessary. One technique is to record on charts the curriculum goals met by a theme and the goals met by the activities in which each child actually participated.
- A learning plan differs from a typical lesson plan in that a learning plan encompasses much more than one lesson. It may specify a variety of activities, long-term goals, theme goals, and short-term goals.
- When teachers are faced with mandated goals, they must use their professional judgment in meeting those goals and must document children's progress very carefully.

- A schedule is designed to offer children the security of routine and to add structure to the day. Teachers must create schedules that contribute to meeting the goals of the program.
- Findings of research on the effects of half-day, alternate-day, or full-day kindergarten programs have not been conclusive. Much depends on the goals and objectives of the program and the actual experiences of the children while at school.
- Teachers must evaluate the progress of individual children; they must also evaluate the program itself. Important areas for evaluation include teacher-child relationships, the opportunities for children to make choices, and the balance of activities provided for the children.
- Teachers who are planning activities and experiences should make sure that children are learning about their own culture and the cultures of others. Diversity can be addressed through experiences with literature, cooking, play, and various content areas.

BETH PETER
Neill Elementary School
BURNSVILLE, MINNESOTA

Planning for Success

My classroom is a multiage classroom that houses first- through fourth-graders who are constantly in different places on the continuum of learning development. However, meeting a wide variety of needs and matching different stages of development in the classroom is a challenge that is not unique to multiage. I've taught in single-grade classrooms where the needs of the students are also quite diverse.

I'm certain that there are many "teachable moments" that happen throughout my day, but the majority of my instruction is carefully planned ahead of time. I believe that planned instruction is a vital element in taking a student to his next learning step. This planning takes a variety of forms and a variety of time frames, but it all has a common thread of building upon a student's strengths in the area in which I want new learning to occur.

I plan on a daily basis. Each day, for as many students as I am able, I examine what he has done today to enable me to plan his instruction for tomorrow. Let me use writing as an example. My students write daily. As I look through their writing for that day, I record in a notebook what I see them doing successfully in regard to the content of their writing, the surface features like their spelling and structure, and their handwriting skill. I carefully examine their writing for evidence that they are attempting to gain control over these same areas. Common strengths, attempts, and needs can be seen, from which I plan writing conference groups, editing conferences, modeled writing lessons, spelling lessons, handwriting groups, and reading material that might take them to the next learning step. I also need to have a strong understanding of the writing process, the broad stages of writing develop-

ment, the reading process, and the stages that readers go through. My students become the guides of what will be next in my instruction.

I also use observation of their reading and writing behaviors to ask myself if there is a part of the process that needs instruction. I cannot wait until the teacher's manual tells me that it is time to teach contractions because I think teaching at the point of a student's need is where true learning occurs. You might think that it would be an impossible task timewise to meet individual learning needs, but I find that students naturally fall into groups with common needs. These groups change as fluidly as the needs of the learners change. Obviously, I do not have the time to meet with each of my students individually on a daily basis, but through small-group *and* individual instruction, I am able to see each of my students daily.

I use "running records" and the information I receive from their analysis to guide my reading instruction and to form groups for guided and shared reading experiences. The information from a running record allows me to meet the learner with a text that is at her instructional level and will allow her to build on what she is currently doing as a reader. Again, my students fall into groups that have common needs.

Even though the majority of my planning for instruction takes place on a daily basis, I still need to have a strong picture of where I want my students to go and how I am going to get them there. This planning is more global and is the umbrella for what I plan on a daily basis. I keep the skills that a life-long learner needs in mind as I plan and write down what I expect to see happening with a student as a result of my instruction.

8

LANGUAGE
Celebrating the Magic

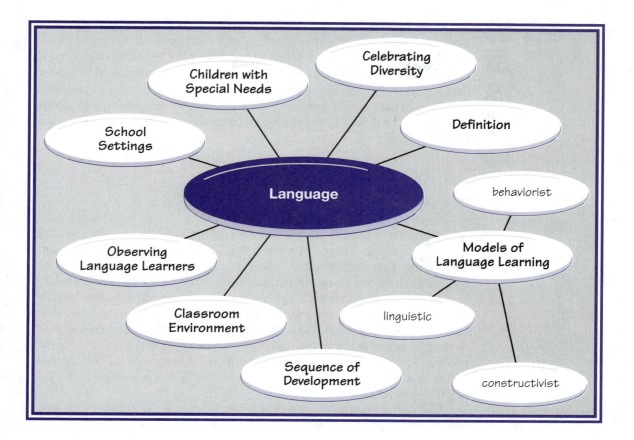

This week, your observation at a preschool focused on children's language. You observed a two-year-old, a three-year-old, and a five-year-old.

The two-year-old was a boy who was excited about dinosaurs and named several types of dinosaurs while showing you models of them. He also talked about dinosaur tracks; he rolled out a piece of Play Doh and pushed the feet of one of the dinosaur models into it to show you how tracks are made.

The three-year-old, a girl, was very quiet and did not initiate any conversation with you. You watched her play outdoors with the other children, but she never uttered a word; she just smiled and nodded when asked questions.

The five-year-old, another girl, was also quiet in the classroom, but when she was outdoors, she asked several children to play a game of tag with her and explained all of the rules to them. You noticed that she spoke Spanish and English and seemed quite competent in both languages.

When you returned to your classroom, you found that many of your peers had similar experiences. Now all of you have questions about the extraordinary variations found in children's language development. How do children learn language? What sort of program is best for helping them become more proficient users of language? Are published materials available to aid children in developing language abilities? What is the role of the teacher in planning for children's language development?

One of the most exciting moments in parenting is when Baby says that first word—when he puts together sounds that communicate meaning. Parents share that moment with all who are close or can be reached by telephone, and the word is dutifully recorded in the baby book.

One of the characteristics that makes us human is our language, which gives us the ability to share with others our ideas, thoughts, dreams, discoveries, and knowledge. That children achieve the ability to communicate so rapidly and seemingly so effortlessly is a marvel to all who observe the process. The ability to communicate with others is learned so rapidly that it almost seems magical. Come celebrate this magic, the wonderful world of children's language.

Two premises underlie this chapter and should be kept in mind as you read. One is the belief, articulated by Goodman et al. (1987), that language is not acquired externally but rather is part of a process of personal development and emerges in the context of social use (p. 38). That is not to say that language is not present in the child's environment but that learning language is a more complex process than simply adopting language that is outside oneself. Therefore, in this chapter, the term that will be used to describe the learning of language is *language development* rather than *language acquisition*.

The other premise underlying the chapter is that oral and sign languages are not developed in isolation; they are always related to cognitive development and to the development of other language abilities. We cannot separate spoken or sign language and written language. Each system of language contributes to learning language; one does not precede the other.

DEFINITION OF LANGUAGE

For the purposes of this chapter, *language* is defined as a system of communication used by humans, which is either produced orally or by sign and that can be extended to its written form. Language also has characteristics that define it further. One characteristic is that language is rule governed. The rules of a given language are learned intuitively by those people who speak it; only speakers who make a scientific study of the language are likely to be able to verbalize these rules. An example of one of these rules is the placement of words denoting number, color, and size in descriptive phrases. For example, in describing *one big red balloon,* we would never say "red one big balloon."

Another characteristic of language is that it is arbitrary. There are no logical connections between the sounds that we use to label objects and the objects themselves. Social groups merely agree to use a particular combination of sounds to represent an object. Actually, very few words sound like what they represent, such as *buzz* or *hiss.* Words like *table, chair, bottle,* and so on have no logical connections with their referents.

Language is also changing. New words are constantly entering our lexicon, and others are being discarded. Meanings, too, are changing. With a little thought, you could probably list thirty or forty words that have been added to the English language within the last five years and ten or so that have changed meaning. Even young children use words that were once uncommon (*rewind*), that did not exist a short time ago (*CD,* for *compact disc*), or that have changed meanings recently (*tape* or *videotape* as either a noun or a verb).

PARENTS AND LANGUAGE

■ Encourage parents to talk to their children and celebrate their language achievements. Suggest that parents keep journals of special words that their children enjoy.

LANGUAGE SYSTEMS

Every language is a set of systems: phonology, morphology, syntax, semantics, and pragmatics. *Phonology* is the system of sounds that make up the language; it includes the sounds that are used to make words, the rules for combining the sounds, and the stress and intonation patterns that help to communicate meaning. Different languages use different sounds and allow different combinations of sounds in words. In some languages, for instance, words can begin with the "ng" sound, but not in English. The task of the child is to learn to distinguish differences in sounds and intonation patterns that signal different meanings.

A second system of language is *morphology,* which deals with the meanings of sounds. A *morpheme* is the smallest unit of sound that carries meaning. Some words are morphemes; some are combinations of morphemes. *Tiger* is an example of a word that is a morpheme. The plural, *tigers,* is a combination of the free morpheme *tiger* and the bound morpheme *s.* The *s* is bound because it signals meaning but cannot carry meaning alone. Other morphemes signal changes of tense, person, and number rather than meaning. Mastering English morphology includes learning how to form possessives, plurals, and past and progressive verb tenses. For example, in English we say "one apple," but we must say "eight apples." Many other languages signal the number change with the number word only and do not require pluralization of the noun *apple*.

Syntax is a third system of language. In simple terms, the syntax of a language contains the rules for combining words into phrases and sentences and for transforming sentences into other sentences. Syntax provides information about word meanings based on their places in sentences. If you heard *A crad was zagging wickily,* you would know that the action described occurred in the past and that *wickily* described how the *crad* was *zagging.* You would also know that more than one *crad* existed because the article *a* signifies one of something. Children mastering syntax learn how to construct negatives, questions, compound sentences, passives, imperatives, and eventually complex sentences that include embedded clauses.

Semantics is the fourth system of language. Learning semantics means acquiring vocabulary and meanings associated with words. Some words are probably learned by repeated association, such as *bottle.* The word and the object are presented to the child simultaneously, over and over again. Other word usages reflect the child's growing ability to categorize. A very young child may begin by using *doggie* to refer to any four-legged animal but then learns more specific terms, such as *horse* and *cow.* A child's system of meanings is constantly developing and changing as a result of experience and maturation. Cognitive abilities are reflected in a child's speech. For example, a child will begin to use *gone* about the same time that she learns the concept of object permanence. Mastering the semantic system requires that a child learn word meanings and relationships between and among words.

In addition to learning all the other systems of language, the child must learn the rules for using language in social interactions. *Pragmatics* is the use of language to express intention and to get things done. Speakers must learn to adapt their language to achieve their communication goals in different situations and to do so in socially acceptable ways. Pragmatics includes the rules for appropriate language in church, on the playground, and at the dinner table. A speaker of any language would not be considered competent in its use until he had mastered the basic rules for language use in various social contexts. Children reflect their understanding of pragmatics when they learn to say *please* or when they speak more simply to a baby than they normally speak. Hymes (1974) describes the ability to use language and to use it correctly in various interactions as **communicative competence.**

Children become more proficient users of language as they use it with a variety of speakers and in a variety of contexts.

As an illustration of communicative competence, Dyson and Genishi (1993) describe a first-grade classroom in which the children have just taken a standardized test. When the children learn that the school board requires that they take such tests, they want to write to the school board. In the course of the discussion, the children talk about what kinds of things they can say to a school board and decide that their teacher should probably read the letters before sending them "cause they [the school board] might not be able to understand them" (p. 123). Communicative competence is learning to use language in different situations and for different purposes.

Sociolinguistics, the study of language in a social context, is closely related to pragmatics. Sociolinguists ask: "What are the key aspects of a communication encounter and how do they influence one another? How do we adapt the language to various social contexts? And how does the language style used affect the social context itself?" (Lindfors 1980, p. 6). A speaker's ability to produce language does not automatically include the ability to communicate effectively in a given social situation. Figure 8.1 on page 230 illustrates the relationship between linguistic competence and communicative competence.

Anyone who has ever studied a foreign language should be familiar with the concept of knowing more language than can be used effectively. Early lessons in Spanish, for instance, will include learning words for foods, places, colors, numbers, and so on. The learner's ability to communicate, however, will be quite limited until he knows some of the systems of that language (for example, that adjectives follow nouns) and has experience in applying them. Similarly, a child learning a first language will know words

FIGURE 8.1

Linguistic and Communicative Competence

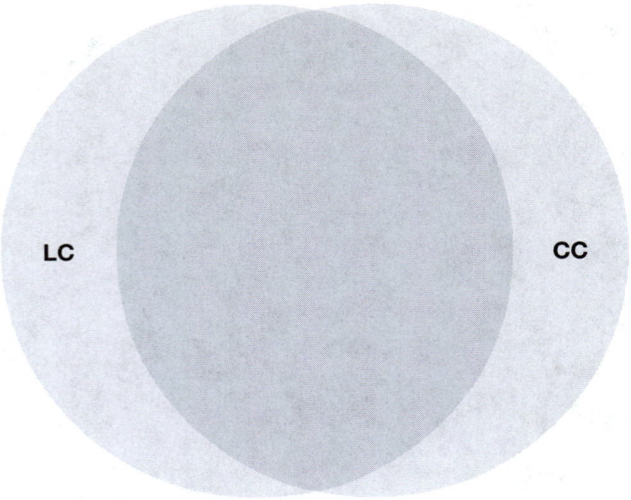

LC = Linguistic competence
CC = Communicative competence

Source: Celia Genishi and Anne Haas Dyson, Eds., *Language Assessment in the Early Years* (Norwood, NJ: Ablex, 1984). Reprinted with the permission of Ablex Publishing Corporation.

that she cannot use effectively; competence will come with experience. The learner's ability to communicate also will be quite limited until he knows some of the rules for putting together sentences and speaking in different situations. Children learning language may use phrases such as "Will you do me a favor?" or repeat patterns such as knock-knock jokes without fully understanding what a favor is or what makes a knock-knock joke funny.

MODELS OF LANGUAGE LEARNING

Three major theories attempt to explain the development of children's language: the *behaviorist* model, the *linguistic* model, and the *contructivist* model (Berko-Gleason 1985; Butler 1974; King 1987). Each theory will be examined briefly.

Behaviorist Model

The behaviorist model of learning language describes the process as consistent with the rules of operant conditioning, based upon a stimulus-response model. In the simplest terms, infants are presented with language, they imitate the language, they are rewarded for their imitations, and they continue to repeat what they have heard. Imitation does not have to be exact or immediate in order for children to make use of it in learning language.

Behaviorist explanations fail to account, however, for the fact that much of children's language is constructed in ways that have never been modeled by mature speakers. For example, a child may say "Higher the swing!"—a construction not used by any other speaker in the child's experience. Behaviorists also have difficulty explaining regressions in children's language. Typically, a young child will use the correct form of a past-tense verb, such as *went*. But as the child matures and generalizes the rules for constructing past-tense verbs, he replaces *went* with *goed*. Later, as the child learns that some words are exceptions to the general rules, *goed* is replaced by *went*.

The difficulty of modifying language through adult input is another problem for behaviorists. According to the stimulus-response model, the child should respond to adult correction of her language use. But as anyone who has attempted to correct a young child knows, this does not always happen. Literature on this subject contains many stories of adults' attempts to correct young children's language (McNeill 1966). The fact is, children do not change the forms of their language easily.

On the other hand, the behaviorist point of view does have some validity. Children obviously speak the languages of their homes. Any human child can learn any human language. No human language can be said to be more complex or more difficult than other languages. Children learn to produce the sounds needed in their native languages and to eliminate the sounds that are not required. Children also learn to repeat words and phrases that they hear around them, even when they do not know what they mean.

Linguistic Model

Another explanation for the development of language is the linguistic, or nativistic, model. Linguist Noam Chomsky (1965) was instrumental in developing this model. The theory holds that language is inherent in the child at birth and needs only be triggered by social contact with speakers in order to emerge.

When the linguistic explanation for language acquisition was developed, the study of language was dominated by behaviorist thinking. Some theorists began to question whether children could learn language as quickly as they obviously did solely through interactions based on stimulus and response. These theorists reasoned that language must be part of children's human inheritance. Chomsky (1965) theorized that humans were equipped with a *language acquisition device*—a structure in the brain that made possible the learning of language.

Evidence in support of this theory is that humans are the only species to acquire language, which they use to communicate ideas and pass on to other generations knowledge they have gained. Linguistic theorists also point out that language development is almost universal among humans. Only humans who have experienced severe trauma or mental retardation are unable to use language; the vast majority of humans use language at some level of competence. Linguistic theorists have contributed to the field of language development by forcing researchers to examine their models and more carefully observe what children actually do in learning language.

Constructivist Model

A third theory for explaining language development is that of the constructivists. This group of theorists—represented by Jean Piaget (1959), Jerome Bruner (1983), and Lev Vygotsky (1962)—believes that children learn language quickly because human brains seek patterns and order in language, just as they constantly seek patterns and order in the environment. For evidence, these theorists point to examples of language that is produced when there has been no previous model; to the uniqueness of language (the fact that except for clichés, we may never hear exactly the same sentence used in the same context more than once); and to the obvious reliance of the child on the so-called rules of language, which are never taught but which are abstracted from examples presented to the child.

Learning language is not an effortless process. Children make a conscious effort to learn the names of things, feelings, and actions. The constructivist model views the learner as vital in the process of learning language. The learner is active in seeking and constructing meaning and in seeking communication with others (Bruner 1983; Jaggar and Smith-Burke 1985; Shuy 1987). Learning to discriminate and correctly label a cat or a dog illustrates the active nature of language learning. If a child sees a dog and says "Doggie," the caregiver will likely respond "Yes, it's a dog." If the child labels the animal "Kitty," the response will likely be "No, it's a dog." The child is left on his own to determine the features of each animal that are distinctive, because it is difficult to describe the features verbally in a way that has any meaning for a very young child.

Children learning language produce hypotheses and test them with the speakers in their environments. They try different combinations of sounds and words in different situations. Constructivists believe that this problem-solving behavior is very important in learning language. They also believe that the errors in children's speech reflect new knowledge about language rules.

Constructivists also recognize the importance of social interactions in the development of language. Many of the words learned first, such as *bye-*

bye and *hi,* only have meaning as parts of interactions with others. For constructivists, many factors affect language learning. These factors (social, maturational, biological, cognitive) interact and modify one another as a child learns language (Berko-Gleason 1985). Many constructivist researchers believe that infants control much of their interaction with adults in their environments by smiling, making sounds, and repeating adult sounds to continue the interactions.

Bruner (1983) describes the language acquisition support system that adults create for children who are learning language. The support system is "scaffolding" that provides a framework and supports the child until she has mastered language forms at a given level; the scaffolding is moved to a higher level when the child's language forms become more complex. For example, when a very young child in a highchair drops a cereal bowl to the floor, her parent says "Uh-oh." When the child has learned to say that phrase each time she drops something, the parent begins to say "Down" or "Gone" each time. As the child's language abilities increase, the parent begins to use longer sentences when something is dropped, such as "Please don't drop your cereal bowl on the floor."

Whitmore and Goodman (1996) point out that the *functions* of language—why we use it—precede the *form.* For instance, children use sounds that are not recognizable as words to convey meanings such as "Turn the page," "Read," and "Pick me up."

SEQUENCE OF LANGUAGE DEVELOPMENT

Language development follows a sequence, which is fairly predictable even though there are many individual variations. Most children move from differentiated crying (crying that sounds different in response to different stimuli: being pricked by a pin, feeling cold or wet, and so on) through cooing and babbling to expressive jargon and one-word sentences. Some children learn the names of objects before other words. Nelson (1973) classifies children's language as *referential* or *expressive.* Common nouns are referential; social words are expressive. Many children develop *idiomorphs* (not real words), which they apply to objects that they evidently find related. For example, when shown flowers or pictures of flowers, the child may make a sniffing sound. For a period of time, this sound will represent anything to be smelled. Soon the child will develop longer utterances and learn to produce negatives and questions. Then the child's language consists of some mature forms and some immature forms. By the time children are eight to ten years old, their language is mostly mature. At the same time, the child's comprehension of language is developing rapidly.

Language development is not complete at the end of infancy; it continues throughout one's lifetime. Children continue to make rapid gains in

THEORY
INTO Practice

Tape record the language of a two-year-old, a four-year-old, and a six-year-old engaged in a similar activity—playing with clay or playing with another child outdoors, for example. Listen to the tapes several times, and compare the differences in the children's language in terms of vocabulary, length of sentences, use of adjectives, and so on.

vocabulary during the early childhood years. Three- and four-year-olds learn to construct questions and negatives. "Why he no go?" changes to "Why isn't he going?" and "Me no do it" becomes "I didn't do it." Children also begin to use and understand more complicated sentences, such as "The dog under the table is mine." By the time a child begins kindergarten, she will have mastered most of the basic forms in her native language, although some immature forms, such as "gots" and "goed," will be present in her speech. Even children of eight and nine can be confused by such sentences as "The boy was bitten by the dog," since they respond to sentences as if the first noun named is doing the acting.

Older primary children are learning vocabulary and learning to use more complex sentence forms correctly. They are also becoming more aware of their audience. Very young children assume that their listeners share their context; older children can take the point of view of the listener and not assume a shared context. They gain skill in giving directions and relating stories in a sequence. They also gain abilities to use language that is not context bound and to discuss objects, events, and some abstract ideas, such as love.

Language play begins in infancy as children play with sounds and continues as young children create rhyming words or make up preposterous names or other silly words. The play of older children usually depends on changes in form or word meanings. Children may create secret languages, such as Pig Latin, and a host of sayings for all types of situations, such as lying, cheating, name calling, begging, telling the truth, using table manners, and so on.

Older children and adults continue to learn language. People learn the vocabulary related to their professions and their hobbies, and they learn to use more formal speech when it is appropriate. Even the most literate person discovers new vocabulary words or new expressions as he listens and reads; language development does not end as long as a person is mentally active and an environment for learning is available.

PARENTS AND LANGUAGE

■ Be sure that parents understand that so-called errors in their children's speech, such as adding -ed to verbs, are signs of language growth. Giving children opportunities to learn vocabulary in meaningful ways is the most useful strategy for helping them develop their language abilities.

CREATING AN ENVIRONMENT FOR LANGUAGE LEARNING

Since almost all children learn language and can use it to satisfy their communication needs, observations of what parents and caregivers do naturally to encourage language development is helpful when planning for successful language learning. Parents or other caregivers teach language informally, focus on the intent or meaning of the child's utterances rather than on the form, expect success, recognize that language learning is wholistic, and celebrate the child's unique, creative uses of language.

Use an Informal Approach

Adults and older children in an infant's environment do not teach language formally. What they do is talk to the child about the environment and happenings in the environment. Long before an infant can produce language, speakers around the child will be talking to her: "Oh, are you thirsty? Here is a bottle of water" or "It's time for your bath now." They also make attempts to talk about what is interesting to the child. If the baby is looking at something, the adult will attempt to determine what has caught the child's interest and talk about it. As the child grows and becomes mobile, the parent's or caregiver's language is more controlling, but it is still closely related to the context (for example, "Play here with your ball. Roll the ball on the floor."). Parents do not plan language lessons each day. They just talk to their children as they make cookies, repair the sink, wash the car, cook dinner, and go through the daily household routines. Language is learned through meaningful interactions, not by talking about it or analyzing it.

In school settings, teachers can attempt to follow the child's lead in conversations and talk about topics that are meaningful and interesting to the child. Sometimes teachers are so determined to follow the given curriculum or their own agenda that they fail to respond to children's interests or to concentrate on topics that are actually important to children. It is not as easy to follow the child's lead at school as it is at home, where only one or two children are present, but teachers do need to think about children's needs and interests in communication experiences.

Focus on the Speaker's Intent

Learning language is a self-generated process. It is controlled by the learner and is not dependent on external rewards. Achieving communication with significant others seems to be reward enough to keep the child learning. Parents and other adults seem to know this intuitively, because the majority of their responses to a child's language are focused on the child's intent, rather than on the perfection of the utterance. Even parents who do correct their children's speech are much more likely to correct con-

THEORY INTO Practice

Observe an adult reading the same book on two occasions: once to a two-year-old and once to a four-year-old. How does the language of the adult differ in the two situations? Does he ask more questions or different kinds of questions of one child than the other? Does he expect more responses or different kinds of responses from either child? Explain your observations.

tent than form. If the child runs into the house and shouts "Daddy gots a new car!" the adult is more likely to respond "No, Daddy has borrowed that car" than to instruct the child to say "Daddy *has* a new car." In fact, if Daddy does have a new car, the response is likely to be "Let's go see it!"

In the early childhood classroom, teachers can make a real effort to focus on what children are trying to say rather than the form that they use. Teachers should concentrate on providing new objects and new experiences to help build the young child's vocabulary. Efforts to correct grammatical structures are relatively useless with this age group. A study that compared teachers trained to repeat the child's incorrect utterance in correct form and those trained to extend the conversation based on the child's utterance showed that extension is more useful in helping children achieve more language growth (Cazden 1965). If a child says "See red car," the teacher using extension would say "Yes, I see a red car and a blue car going down the street." These responses are much more closely related to what parents do in responding to the meaning rather than to the form of utterances. In primary classrooms, teachers can help children learn the vocabulary of topics that interest them, provide opportunities to express their own ideas, and continue to focus on children's meanings.

Expect Success

If you went to the local hospital and interviewed parents of newborn infants about their expectations of whether their babies would learn to talk, you would probably get emphatically positive answers (along with strange looks for asking such a question!). Parents expect that their children will become mature speakers. When the baby makes errors, they know that it is a normal part of the process in learning language. They do not expect that their child will be able to say "My bowl of cereal has fallen to the floor" when he drops his oatmeal off the highchair. They do know that their child's language will mature over time and that immature forms will be replaced by more mature and more complex forms.

In early childhood classrooms, teachers can also expect success as children are learning language. Teachers who view errors such as the use of irregular plurals (*mouses, feets*), adding *-ed* to form the past tense of verbs (*goed, runned*), and the use of incorrect verb forms as indicators of the child's growing mastery of the rules of English will treat those errors differently than teachers who view them as mistakes to be corrected. Language is learned through active exploration of the systems, not by direct imitation of models. Errors are indications of the active nature of language learning as well as growth and maturation.

Emphasize the Wholistic Nature of Language Learning

Children learn language, language functions, and how to use language in social interactions all at the same time (Halliday 1982). Parents do not set out to teach language to their children by limiting their children's learning to one piece of the complex system of language. They help their children learn language by conversing with them in meaningful contexts and in social situations. They present language as a whole, within a context, and within a social milieu. Few parents would drill their children by asking them to learn a list of nouns, followed by a list of verbs, and then some adjectives. They would not expect their children to practice language outside a real context. The idea of a parent's asking a child to go to his or her room and practice saying "I would like a drink of water" is ludicrous.

Teachers of young children can also preserve the wholistic nature of language learning by not breaking language into bits and pieces for study in school. Words in isolation—or worse, sounds in isolation—have no meaning that can be constructed. Children do not need to practice isolated elements of language; they do not learn the parts and then put them back together and use them. They do need to use language in a variety of situations and with a variety of speakers. They need to talk about topics of interest to them and to learn to adjust their language to meet the requirements of the speaking situation. Real talk provides young children a chance to practice their developing language.

Celebrate Creativity

Goodman et al. (1987) describe a child learning language as always creative or inventive and at the same time pulled back into conformity. Children are always creating new words and phrases, but when they find that their words fail to communicate what they intended, they conform more to the usual social forms. This inventiveness in language is important. We could not create new terms when they were needed if we lost our capacity to be inventive language users. Parents and others tend to celebrate some of the creative language of children. For example, many people have nicknames that were invented when they were children by younger siblings who could not pronounce their real names. Almost all families use special words that were either errors in pronunciation or words invented by their children.

In the classroom, teachers can celebrate children's unique expressions by recording them to share later or by posting them on a chart or bulletin board. Some of the expressions children use are very poetic. Teachers can also celebrate children's language by not changing it. If a child uses a dialect, these expressions can also be celebrated and recorded. There are appropriate times and strategies for helping young children develop skill in speaking effectively in different contexts, but for very young children, the focus should be on their unique ways of expressing that meaning. Children need to have their language accepted and valued.

Recognize Language Achievements

Children have made such amazing progress in mastering their native language before entering preschool that teachers sometimes fail to recognize how much they have accomplished. Children's linguistic competencies include the ability to select meaningful parts of a message, to recognize differences in linguistic contexts, and to use syntactic rules. If you say to a very young child "Your father has gone to the office to work," the child will respond "Daddy gone." Obviously, the child knows what is significant in the message. Children adapt their language to listeners when they are very young. This is particularly noticeable in children from bilingual families, who sort out which language they should speak with which people. Children also use correct syntactical rules from the time they begin to use sentences of more than one word. They say "More milk" as opposed to "Milk more," for example.

Daniels (1994) found that children learning sign language along with spoken language were more advanced than their age peers in language development and that they had no trouble with code switching (knowing when to use sign versus oral language). In short, children are efficient users of language and able to use whatever is in their environment to communicate.

In summary, children learn language when they are in environments where language is used and when they interact with others. They learn best when meaning, rather than form, is stressed. Parents set the stage for successful language learning by using language in real-life situations, by dropping specific intentions to teach language, and by accepting approximations that gradually become closer to adult models. Parents should also take delight in their child's progress and celebrate her imaginative and poetic uses of language.

PARENTS AND LANGUAGE

■ Invite parents to observe the language that children use in the classroom and to talk with you about the differences they observe between classroom language and that used at home.

OBSERVING LANGUAGE LEARNERS

Yetta Goodman (1985) has coined the term *kidwatching* to describe how teachers should pay attention to children—to what they are thinking and saying and how they are responding—which is extremely important in assessing language development. Teachers have to learn how to observe children's language and how they use it. Teachers must also learn how to provide the environments that foster children's growth in language abilities and what specific activities can be most helpful to a given child at a given time (Goodman 1985).

The following guidelines will be helpful as teachers observe the language of young children:

1. Always observe a child's language in a variety of contexts before drawing any conclusions about the child's abilities. Some children who are almost nonverbal in school settings will be extremely verbal on the playground. Some children will not contribute to conversation even in small groups but can communicate effectively one to one with a child or an adult.

2. Look for competence in using language for a variety of purposes. For example, how does the child share information, get what is needed or wanted, or use imaginative language? Can the child communicate both with adults and with other children?

3. Look for effectiveness in communication rather than for specific abilities, such as "The child speaks in complete sentences." Often, the most effective communication does not require the use of complete sentences. What teachers need to know is whether children can adapt their language to the requirements of different speaking situations.

4. Look for signs of growth in the child's knowledge of language systems. For example, are there changes in the child's use of inflectional endings and clauses?

5. Look for growth in vocabulary. As a child participates in the activities provided in the classroom, are labels for objects and actions becoming a part of his vocabulary?

Careful observation of children's language will provide insights that will help teachers plan activities and structure the environment to foster growth in language. The teacher who observes that a child does not know the language for expressing emotions, for example, will help by providing some of the labels for feelings when the child needs them. Other children may need more opportunities to recount incidents in sequential order. The teacher may guide by asking "What came first?" or "Then what happened?" and so on. Plans and guidance that meet children's individual needs can only be provided on the basis of careful observation. Without knowledge of children's language, effective instruction is almost impossible.

THEORY INTO *Practice*

Observe the home language of a child of five or six and the school language of the same child for the same amount of time. Do the numbers and kinds of verbal interactions differ in the two situations? Explain your observations.

LANGUAGE DEVELOPMENT IN SCHOOL SETTINGS

Commercial Programs

Encouraging the development of language is always one of the primary goals of teachers of young children. Toward this goal, various commercial programs are available, often consisting of a teacher's guide, pictures of objects in various categories, and sometimes plastic models of objects. These materials may also be accompanied by audiotapes or computer programs designed to allow children to practice repeating words or phrases.

Commercial programs designed to teach children language are objectionable for several reasons. One, of course, is that these programs ignore the interactive and active nature of language learning. Another objection is that most programs are designed for small-group instruction, yet it would be rare to find a group in which all the children needed to learn the same words or phrases. A third objection to commercial language programs is that most of the actual production of language is done by the teacher, rather than by the children. Finally, most of these programs are expensive.

Using a commercial program is not the answer for promoting children's language growth. Setting up an environment that encourages language growth and that is responsive to children's language *is* the answer. Language is learned best when children use it for meaningful purposes. In the best classrooms, children have many opportunities to talk with each other and with adults. Children playing with clay, sand, water, blocks, and other classroom materials are encouraged to talk about their experiences. As adults move around the play areas, they listen to the children's language, make observations, and expand on the children's language in meaningful interactions that are developmentally appropriate. If a three-year-old is playing with the sand, the adult might offer the language to describe what is taking place by remarking, for example, "You are making a tunnel in the sand." An eight-year-old playing with water and boats might be encouraged to use the vocabulary connected with boating: *deck, port, stern, aft, dock,* and so on.

Wells (1986) reached several disturbing conclusions following an extensive longitudinal study of the language of children in Bristol, England. For *none* of the children studied was the language used in the classroom as linguistically rich as that used at home, which was self-motivated, spontaneous, unstructured, and supported by adults. Wells concluded that several factors made language development at school much more difficult than it was at home: a large number of students per teacher, a curriculum dominated by norm-referenced tests, and the fact that many teachers did not believe that talking was important for learning.

Activities That Encourage Language Growth

Almost everything that happens in the early childhood classroom will contribute to children's language development. If children are arguing over a toy, the teacher can help them use language that is appropriate for disagreeing and for solving the problem. If an adult visits the class, the children can have opportunities for interaction with the visitor, who serves as another model of language use. If the children go on a field trip, they will have the opportunity to learn the vocabulary connected with what they are observing. Language development goes on all through the schoolday.

The activities described in the following sections are merely suggestive of the opportunities teachers have for helping children develop more competency as language users.

Literature

Language in children's books is very important. When an entire book contains three hundred words, an author cannot waste words but must choose the best ones to convey the ideas. Martin (1986); Harste, Woodward, and Burke (1984); and Blackburn (1985) point out that everyone stores up all the words, phrases, and story elements they hear and that this language becomes theirs after a time. Books help children fill up their storehouses of beautiful words. Even simple stories can do this.

Some classroom activities provide excellent opportunities for using language in authentic contexts.

In *Whose Mouse Are You?* (Kraus 1970), when the little mouse is asked about his brother, he replies, "I have none." That is probably not the way most children would respond nor is it the language most children would hear at home, but it is elegant. Sometimes we choose books or stories just because the words sound so wonderful. The elephant's child says, "Goodby. I am going to the great, gray-green greasy Limpopo River all set about with fever trees to find out what the Crocodile has for dinner" ("The Elephant's Child," in Kipling 1965, p. 132). We read such language because we love to hear the sound of it. Children, too, love the sound of language, whether they understand the meaning of every word or not. The language in books allows teachers to expand children's language in supportive and creative ways. Books with simplified vocabularies are somewhat useful for beginning readers, but for all other purposes, books should be chosen because they have beautiful language.

Narrative Stories Children's literature often serves as a focus for learning new vocabulary or new ways of expressing ideas and can provide the foundation for countless activities, including the following:

1. Compare the words used in different versions of familiar folk stories. For example, several words are used to label the woodcutter in versions of "Little Red Riding Hood." Children might discuss what they think is the best choice of words and what pictures the different words bring to mind.
2. Dramatize stories or rhymes. Actually speaking the words and performing the actions that go with them help children make vocabulary real and personal.
3. Have children retell stories in their own words and/or use puppets to recall stories.
4. Ask children to create new versions of stories by selecting words to fit the patterns in repetitive books. For example, in *Someday* (Zolotow 1965), the pattern is "Someday I'll _____." Children can think of what they will do "someday."
5. Encourage children to tell their own original stories and record them either in writing or on audiotape. Having children tell their own stories results in more complex language use and more detailed stories than is the case when children are asked to tell stories about a picture or wordless picture book (Hough, Nurss, and Wood 1987).

Storytelling Telling stories can also aid in children's language development. Storytelling has the advantage of being a direct communication between the listener and the teller. Children listening to a story are required to be active listeners. If they tune out, the story will go on; there will be no instant replay. Storytelling also invites children to become active by participating in the story, repeating phrases or words or creating voices or gestures for the characters.

Storytelling is also flexible. If the audience gets restless, the storyteller can add more drama to the voices, shorten the story, end the story immediately, or whatever is required to make the session successful. Of course, this requires that the storyteller pay close attention to the audience and respond accordingly.

Stories told to children should contain language that they can understand from context so that the storyteller will not have to stop for explanations. Stories for children should also be about topics and situations that appeal to them; if the children are not interested in what the story is about, they will tune out and become restless.

The storyteller should invite participation in the tale, especially after the first telling. Possible activities include the following:

1. Invite children to dramatize a story as you tell it. For example, "The Turnip," a Russian folk tale, works very well (Morgan 1990).
2. Provide materials so that children can retell stories during activity periods. Make available flannelboard pieces, wooden characters, finger puppets, or puppets, depending on the age and experience of the children.
3. Encourage children to tell their own stories. Older children can write and produce their stories in many forms: a skit for TV, a scroll story, a flannelboard story, and so on.
4. Encourage children to join the storytelling by repeating certain phrases or sounds.

Poetry/Chants/Rhymes   Finger plays and choral readings help children learn new vocabulary words and new sentence patterns that add to their repertoires. Teacher should plan activities such as the following:

1. Create new versions of song lyrics or rhymes by selecting words that fit the rhymes. For example, after learning *Alligator Pie* (Lee 1974), children can write or dictate new versions.
2. Dramatize rhymes or song lyrics. When children participate in drama, their actions indicate comprehension of the words. For example, the words of the various versions of "Bear Hunt" describe different actions; children can do the actions to demonstrate that they understand the words.
3. Dramatize concepts in science or social studies—such as the attraction and repelling of magnets or the arrival of a famous explorer—so that the language has real meaning for children.

Sharing Time

Sharing time can have many positive benefits for language development if managed appropriately. For instance, sharing time should be conducted in small groups so that children do not have to sit for long periods while each person has a turn. Objects should be displayed to the group, rather than passed around. Teachers should also help children learn how to begin and end presentations, and sessions should be structured so that children are not required to stand up or come to the front of the class in order to participate (Oken-Wright 1988).

Teachers should also control sharing time so that it does not turn into a session in which children show off their latest possessions. The following activities may help achieve that control:

1. Sharing can be organized so that children describe the details of the process for making objects they have created in class. For example, a child might share how a textile print or clay object was made. Cooking experiences and building with blocks are other activities that provide interesting topics for sharing.
2. Children can bring objects from home that are related to a theme or topic of study. For example, they might bring something square when the class is learning shape concepts.
3. Children can share personal experiences that are important to them. They might talk about a special trip or an exciting event that occurred at home, such as the birth of kittens.
4. Sharing time can be used as a brainstorming session for solving class problems and planning class activities.

Teachers must also consider children's ages in planning activities for sharing time. For instance, in considering the classroom, younger children might be asked to offer suggestions for classroom or playground safety, and older children might be asked to think about the room arrangement and how it might be altered for better traffic patterns. In planning themes and projects, older children might be asked to persuade others that a topic of study that interests them would be a good choice for the next class theme.

Classroom Centers and Activities

Classroom centers such as the block area, where several children work together, tend to encourage more language use than centers where the activities are more solitary. It follows that teachers who want to encourage children's language development and use will arrange learning areas so that children can talk to each other and will prompt children to work together.

Materials will also need to be interesting and novel enough that children will want to talk about them. Several recent research studies (Anen 1991; Dyson and Genishi 1991; Isbell and Raines 1991) have verified the common-sense knowledge that children who are encouraged to participate in active and interesting activities are more likely to use language and produce more language than children who are asked to complete skills activities. A classroom environment in which teachers and children use language for many purposes will contribute to the communicative competence of the children.

Language development also can be enhanced through thematic instruction (Bergeron et al. 1996). Themes that present real experiences and real materials to manipulate will certainly help children expand their vocabularies in meaningful ways.

Overview of Activities

It is obvious from these brief lists of suggested activities that almost every activity in an early childhood classroom can provide an opportunity for language growth. Teachers and children together can talk about personal experiences, classroom activities, feelings and emotions, and plans and expectations. A classroom in which children can talk with other children and with adults who respect and value their ideas as well as the way they are expressed will be a place where language flourishes.

CHILDREN WITH SPECIAL NEEDS

Most children learn to use language. For those few who cannot learn to use language in the usual ways, some specialized assistance may be required.

Children with disabilities may need special help in communicating effectively in the classroom. Many devices are available for assisting communication; some are very expensive, and others are inexpensive. Parette, Dunn, and Hoge (1995) describe some low-cost devices such as communication notebooks, communication vests, communication boards, communication aprons, and communication wallets. **Assisted communication** is becoming more commonplace for children with special needs. We can expect the technology in this field to continue to change, making such assistance more readily available.

Most schools offer programs for children with disabilities beginning at age three, and learning to communicate is a major goal of these programs. Full-inclusion classrooms (previously called *mainstreaming*) provide positive settings for promoting the language development of all children. Moreover, such classrooms provide the opportunity to include children with special needs in experiences that are not drill-and-practice sessions on words or phrases. For some children, teachers will need to ask for help from school language specialists to determine the most effective means of assisting the children in efforts to communicate.

Children with Language Delays

A **language delay** results in a child's using language that is noticeably deficient for his age (Dumtschin 1988). Sometimes, delays in language can be attributed directly to specific causes, including physical problems (such as loss of hearing or structural problems in the speech-producing organs) or disease (for example, cerebral palsy); mental retardation; or emotional problems (such as autism) (Cole and Cole 1989). Other delays in language have no apparent cause; the child seems normal in other areas, but his language is not typical for his age group.

One of the first steps in providing for the needs of a child with a language delay is to make a referral to diagnose or rule out any underlying cause for the delay. Some schools have speech and language therapists who can be consulted. If the center or school does not employ a therapist, the referral may be to a therapist in private practice. If no professional can be located, the National Association for Hearing and Speech Action can provide assistance. If a cause for the delay can be identified, the therapist will make recommendations for activities or strategies that will be helpful to the teacher and parents. If no cause for the delay can be identified, the teacher will want to provide as much support for the child's language growth as possible.

Research has shown that conversation between children and adults can be helpful in assisting children with language delays (Cross 1984; Lasky and Klopp 1982). As noted earlier, most adults respond to the meaning of a child's speech and continue conversations on topics introduced by the child. Children whose language is less mature than that of age peers may need even more conversation with adults that focus on their meanings and intentions. Teachers need to be especially careful not to assume that children cannot understand normal conversation just because they cannot produce language typical of age-mates. Restricting a child's language environment is not appropriate. While children with specific language impairments may use the same language patterns as younger children, they have more communicative competence. In other words, they are able to use what language they have more effectively (Rollins et al. 1994).

Researchers have also found that children with language delays have more interactions with adults who are critical of their language productions than do children who are making normal progress (Bondurant, Romeo, and Kretschmer 1983). Teachers should respond to children by supplying the correct labels for objects or actions without being negative. For example, if a child is looking at a book of zoo animals and mistakenly calls the tiger a lion, the teacher might respond, "This tiger is very large. Tigers and lions are both in the zoo."

Teachers should also be aware of their use of controlling language with children who have language delays. Cross (1984) found that children with language delays experienced more directive language from adults than did children whose language development was normal. Language that is controlling fails to help children develop positive interaction patterns or increase their vocabulary. For example, consider the message delivered by the command "Pick these up now!" with that of the direction "Please help me pick up the large blocks and put them on the top shelf."

Explicitly instructing children in the social uses of language and involving them in direct imitations have been found to be effective with children with language impairments but not with normally developing children (Connell 1987; Zirkelbach and Blakesley 1986). Such instruction must be geared to the observed needs of the individual child.

Jones and Warren (1991) make several suggestions for working with children with language delays. First, the teacher should follow the child's lead, establishing dialogue and planning novel activities that reflect the child's interests. The teacher should also provide support for the child's language by commenting on the child's utterances but not necessarily expecting a response.

Finally, teachers also need to be aware of the amount of talking by adults and the amount of talking by children encouraged in classrooms. If children are constantly involved in teacher-directed activities, in which listening and following directions are the accepted behaviors, then little time will be left for active language production (Hough, Nurss, and Goodson 1984). Children need to talk to adults and to other children if their language is to improve. Most of the children's day should be structured so that language is an integral part of activities. Teachers should make every effort to talk *to* children, not *at* them, and to accept children's language. All children need the same conditions in order to achieve maximum growth in language: an accepting environment, interesting things to talk about, and adults with whom to engage in meaningful conversations.

Ideas for the Classroom

Teachers who want to help all children develop their language abilities will encourage children to use language in classroom settings. This is especially true for those children whose language development is atypical. The following strategies may be useful in planning activities that enhance language development:

1. Encourage children to retell stories that you have read or told. A flannelboard may encourage older preschoolers to be more confident in their retellings.

2. Encourage children to use puppets to tell stories or to carry on conversations among puppet characters.
3. Involve children in learning finger-plays, song lyrics, chants, and choral readings.
4. Plan cooperative classroom activities in which children use language freely, such as card games or board games or building projects.
5. Be sure that children with language delays are not "talked down to" by anyone in the classroom and that their participation in activities is not limited.

CELEBRATING DIVERSITY

Language is one obvious and easily observable difference among the cultures of the children in any typical classroom. Suggestions for celebrating children's language in the classroom include the following:

1. Post signs and announcements in as many of the languages spoken in the class as possible.
2. Arrange for regular classroom use of books and recordings in the languages represented by students.
3. Encourage the parents of bilingual children to read to them frequently.
4. Share special words with children who speak other languages.
5. Share the feeling of accomplishment when children learn new vocabulary or forms in their native languages or new languages.
6. Buy good-quality books and computer programs that use the languages spoken by the children in the classroom.

Children Who Use Dialects

A **dialect** is a systematic variation of the common language spoken by a particular group. All of us speak dialects of some sort. There are regional dialects, social class dialects, and cultural/ethnic dialects. By definition, a dialect is rule governed and consistent.

Children who speak dialects are not merely making errors in their grammatical constructions; they are following the rules of their dialects. The most important thing for teachers to remember is that children who speak dialects are not less capable of learning language than other children, nor is the dialect less effective for communication than more standard English. When judgments are made about the correctness of children's speech, these judgments are usually social, not linguistic (Jaggar 1980).

Dialects may differ in terms of vocabulary, syntax, and morphology. Vocabulary differences include all the various terms used to describe, for example, the parts of a car, the seed in a peach, or an ice cream drink. Vocabulary differences may also include some verb usages, such as the use of *carry* for *take* (as in "He will *carry* you to town"). Syntactical differences often include deleting some words. In some dialects, the correct form of "He is working today" is "He be working," which indicates that the subject is presently working. Morphological differences include dropping some inflectional endings so that possessives are formed differently ("That girl shoes") or tense or number are indicated differently ("He go there yesterday"). The differences in dialects and more standard speech are usually only minor, surface differences.

Teachers of young children who speak dialects that are different from the dialect of the majority should be especially sensitive to each child's use of language and be prepared to honor the child's ability to learn language. The child's dialect is certainly effective for communicating in her home or neighborhood. Exposure to literature and to models of other, more standard dialects may give the child alternative ways of expressing needs and thoughts over a period of time, but the teacher's goal should not be eradication of the dialect.

DEVELOPMENTALLY APPROPRIATE PRACTICE

As you think about language development and developmentally appropriate practice, reflect on the following:

- Many children learn to use language differently than middle-class white children. These differences are not just dialectal but reflect culturally appropriate uses of language in telling stories or entertaining groups. In a developmentally appropriate classroom, what goals and standards should be set for children's language use? For example, should all children be expected to achieve the middle-class model of language use? Why?
- Language is best learned when it is used for a real purpose; thus, contrived activities to practice language skills are rarely effective. How

should real language be used in activities for children of different ages—say, preschoolers versus primary-grade children?
- The teacher must accept and respect the language of all children in a developmentally appropriate classroom. How can the teacher demonstrate acceptance and respect for an ESL student?
- The best environment for learning language includes the critical elements of DAP, such as choice, active involvement, age and individually appropriate expectations, and so on. How do these elements enhance learning language?

Ideas for the Classroom

Children who speak dialects need teachers who accept and respect their speech. The ideas that follow offer ways to help children develop their language skills in standard English while maintaining their dialect when it is appropriate:

1. Involve children in drama. They can dramatize stories and role-play various speaking situations.
2. Invite speakers to the classroom who are skilled in both the children's dialect and standard English.
3. Read children's books that use dialects.
4. Record the speech of several children saying essentially the same thing, and compare the words used.
5. Record what children say in standard spelling, but allow them to read what you have written in dialect.
6. Provide opportunities for children to talk to many different speakers.

English-as-a-Second-Language (ESL) Children

In the typical U.S. classroom today, many children do not speak English as their native language. To facilitate communication with these **English-as-a-second-language (ESL)** children,* a number of approaches may be used: Some schools offer special bilingual programs for students who do not speak English; other schools provide tutors whose goal is to help children learn English; and some schools expect classroom teachers to provide for ESL children in the regular classroom context. Since most teachers will have ESL children in their classrooms, they should be aware of some of the research on second-language learning and its implications for instruction.

To learn a second language successfully requires the same conditions that foster learning a native tongue (Krashen 1981). Specifically, the ESL learner needs someone with whom to talk and needs support for attempts at communication. Language is learned best within a social context in which success at communication is expected. Since second-language learners use the strategies of simplification and overgeneralization, which are also common in original-language development, they will benefit from encouragement rather than correction during the early stages of learning English. For example, ESL learners may simplify all verbs to one tense and depend on context to help communicate the real message. Finally, second-language learners pick up more details in order to make their communi-

---

* In some school systems, ESL students are referred to as having *limited English proficiency (LEP)*.

cation more effective. They learn to say "I went there yesterday in the afternoon" rather than "I go there." For young children, this process may take only a few months; for older children, it may take longer.

The following guidelines will help teachers of bilingual speakers be more effective:

1. Get as much information as possible about the child's language background. Try to determine if the child is a talker or shy at home. Find out what languages the child's playmates speak.
2. Be careful about the conclusions you draw from the information you gather. Assuming a child who does not speak much does not know much about language can be very dangerous.
3. Compare the child's language only to other similar bilingual children.
4. Understand that second-language learners will make grammatical errors. There are common generalizations made by second-language learners that are not made by first-language speakers.
5. Be aware that second-language learners may lose some of their competence in their first language. For example, a child may move away from the environment in which the first language was used regularly and therefore lose some ability to use that language.

6. Know it is normal for second-language learners to use both languages to communicate. *Linguistic borrowing* describes what happens when a word from one language is inserted into a sentence of the other language. *Code switching* is switching back and forth between languages, but not necessarily single words. Both are normal for bilinguals.

7. Learn as much as possible about the cultures represented in the classroom. Make sure this information is both for traditional and contemporary lifestyles. Use this information in order to determine if any test used to evaluate bilingual speakers is biased. (Piper 1993, pp. 210–211)*

Burnett (1993) stresses that appropriate assessment of ESL learners is crucial. He recommends setting up an assessment center that is more friendly than the usual testing office and conducting multiple assessments before decisions are made about any child.

In summary, the best environment for ESL learning includes support, encouragement, meaningful purposes for communication, and an expectation that children will talk with others who speak the language to be learned. "For a learner to be free to learn another language, the learner must be able to trust others to respond to the messages communicated and not be laughed at or singled out. In addition, a learner must be active in seeking people to talk with" (Urzua 1980, p. 38).

Ideas for the Classroom
Teachers who want to help ESL children achieve competence in English will be thoughtful about the classroom environment and activities that make learning English as much like learning a first language as possible. The following suggestions may stimulate teachers' thinking:

1. Plan for activities that require children who speak English and children who are learning English to work together (Hester 1987). This is one of the best strategies for helping children learn English. In the early childhood classroom, it is not difficult to arrange for such cooperative experiences.

2. Encourage ESL children to share their native language through songs, fingerplays, or books.

3. Share (or find someone to share) with the class stories or poetry in a foreign language and then in English.

* From *Language for All Our Children* by Piper, T., © 1993. Reprinted by permission of Prentice-Hall, Inc., Upper Saddle River, NJ.

4. Be careful not to separate non-English-speaking children or to exclude them from activities that you fear they will not understand. ESL children learn language by listening, watching, and following examples.

5. Writing and reading activities can be based on children's growing vocabulary in English. At first, children can make books of the words that they are learning. After only a few weeks, teachers will find that most children are learning too rapidly to use this technique.

PARENTS AND LANGUAGE

■ Arrange for parents whose first language is not English to share some of their native language with the class; children might like to learn greetings, counting words, or days of the week in another language. Also, ask bilingual parents to help you translate some favorite stories into their native language and then share them with the children. Finally, encourage parents to support their child's use of his first language and not to feel that it will be a detriment to his success.

CHAPTER SUMMARY

■ Language is composed of the systems of phonology, semantics, syntax, morphology, and pragmatics. Each of these systems offers a challenge to the learner.

■ Three different theoretical explanations were offered of the process of learning language: behaviorist, linguistic, and constructivist. The constructivist view is based most directly on observations of children learning language and using it to communicate.

■ Children all over the world learn language in a similar sequence, although with individual variations. The basic sequence begins with crying and moves through cooing, babbling, and echoing to the use of single words, multiple words, and then complete sentences.

■ Observations of children learning language reveal that it is learned informally; that adults should focus on the intent of the learner; that adults

should expect success; that language learning is wholistic; and that language is creative.

■ The language achievements of young children are quite remarkable. By the time children are five or six, they have mastered most of the basic forms of their native languages and have an extensive vocabulary.

■ Observing language development is important for planning activities and strategies that will help each child maximize language development. Observers should not merely look for discrete skills from a checklist but should observe children carefully in a variety of language contexts.

■ Activities that foster the growth of language take place in the classroom every day. Children need opportunities to talk with other children and with adults. They need something interesting to talk about, and they need teachers who celebrate their use of language.

■ Some children do not achieve language competence at the same rate as their peers. Children with language delays need teachers who are aware of the strategies that research has shown to be most important in helping them achieve growth in language.

■ Children who speak dialects other than the dialect of the majority and children for whom English is their second language (ESL) can be helped by knowledgeable teachers who structure supportive learning environments.

Teaching Content and Language Together

My kindergarten/first-grade classroom welcomes students who come from many backgrounds and who speak many different languages at home. In our classroom, English is the bridge language. It bridges my students to each other and their learning while, at the same time, their first languages are honored and respected. Because my students are at all levels of understanding and use of English, I need to establish language objectives for each lesson as well as content objectives. I do not teach English instead of content. I teach both together in meaningful, interactive ways.

A kindergarten classroom is the perfect ESL (English-as-a-second-language) environment. It is *language rich* and involves many opportunities for social interaction. *Language rich* means a classroom filled with hands-on materials that students are using daily; pictures tagged with written words all around the room; and poems, songs, and books that are repetitive and fun. It encompasses all of the things that children touch and experience with infinite opportunities for them to talk and draw pictures about everything in their own way, at their own pace. Students are learning language by using language—speaking, listening, reading, and writing.

Our current study of insects in the classroom is one example of my ongoing instructional strategy of teaching content and language together. Students rotate among three different activities called *centers*. During this time, I bring together objectives in math, science, social skills, following directions, reading, writing, and English. I assess students' counting skills, numeral recognition skills, and fine motor skills on paper as well as observe social skills and insect knowledge.

One *center* is an insect lotto game. The students at this center each have a board with nine insect pictures. One student holds a stack of cards with matching pictures; that student shows one card at a time. Students look at their boards to see if they have matches. The game is played until all of the boards are filled. Students are cooperating, matching, recognizing insects, and using the newly introduced vocabulary (insect names, *please, thank you,* and so on).

At another center, students use clay and various materials to create insects. Each must have three body parts, six legs, and two antennae. Students are introduced to and have knowledge of these characteristics of insects prior to the centers. Students make their insects and draw pictures of them to show their work. They are demonstrating their knowledge about insects by using new vocabulary (body parts, legs, insect names, antennae), using fine motor skills to draw, and having the opportunity for creative expression.

At the last center, I interact with students. We each have a sheet of paper with pictures of some insects (ladybug, butterfly, caterpillar, grasshopper, bee, ant). Next to each picture is a box. Together, we clap out the name of the insect. Each clap corresponds to a single syllable. Students record the number of syllables in the box. They are becoming aware of the sounds in words, counting, and using new vocabulary words.

People who can speak more than one language experience many advantages. They enjoy a rich understanding of language as a concept. Their opportunities are broad. Children who walk into our class speaking little or no English bring many gifts to share with us. They want to learn what we offer to teach, and we must deliver this in the most effective and meaningful ways.

9

THE DEVELOPMENT OF LITERACY
Reading and Writing

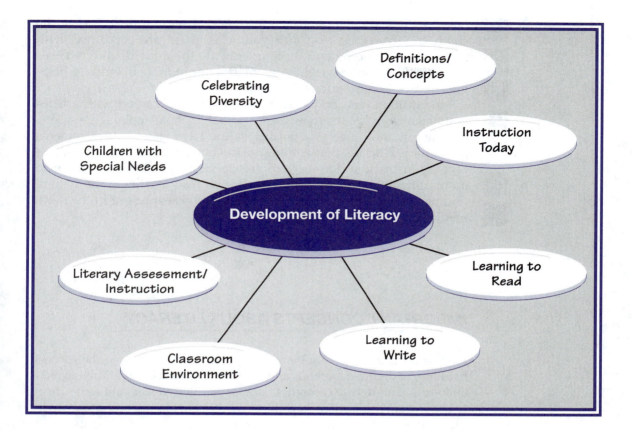

Development of Literacy

- Definitions/Concepts
- Celebrating Diversity
- Instruction Today
- Children with Special Needs
- Learning to Read
- Literary Assessment/Instruction
- Learning to Write
- Classroom Environment

Your observation this week was especially interesting. You visited a preschool program for three- and four-year-old children, and your assignment was to note any activities, behaviors, or lessons that focused on reading or writing.

You noticed several children who went to a shelf and got paper, crayons, and cellophane tape; they all made signs to label their block buildings and told you what their signs said. One little girl had four other children pretend to be her students as they played "school." Using a book she had made—in which one-word labels appeared under pictures of a tree, house, dog, and so on—the "teacher" asked the children in her group to "read" these words. Another small group played at the water and sand tables and did not attend to any of the other children as they read or wrote.

When you returned to your own class and discussed your experience with your peers, you found that everyone had observed vast differences in the reading and writing behaviors of the children. Given this, you and your classmates are concerned with instruction in reading and writing. How do the individual differences that were observed develop? And what is appropriate in terms of helping children become successful readers and writers?

In addition, you and your classmates are concerned with articles you have seen in the newspaper about "whole language"—some, attacking it and others, supporting it. You have also heard statements made by politicians that reading instruction in U.S. schools is failing because instruction does not emphasize phonics. There seem to be so many different opinions about learning to read and write that you're finding it very difficult to evaluate the opinions expressed in the news media. What should you believe?

IMPORTANT CONCEPTS ABOUT LITERACY

First, you must accept that there will always be debate about the success or failure of different methods and approaches to teaching children to read and write. This debate continues because learning to read and write effectively is vitally important to children's success in school and probably in life, as well. Certainly, parents are concerned about their children and want them to be successful readers. The debate also continues because children are so eager to learn to read and sometimes do so in spite of the instruction offered in school, which makes it more difficult to state definitive ideas about the quality of instruction.

Think about your own experience in learning to read. You probably were instructed in a small group of children; all of you read the same stories in the same book and at the same pace. But in addition to the instruction you got at school, you had other reading experiences. You learned how much fun it was to read the back of the cereal box while you ate breakfast. You might also have listened as your older siblings read their assignments to your parents. You might have played "school" with the children in your neighborhood. You probably read the funny papers on Sunday mornings or listened to books on tape. You read the signs in your neighborhood or city. Some children learned to read bus and subway schedules; others learned to read the directions for caring for a pet lamb. The point is that reading instruction is rarely limited to only that provided in a school setting.

Another important concept you should keep in mind is that how educators understand the process of reading and how children learn to read has changed a great deal in the last few years. When you were a child, most people believed that students come to school as basically "blank slates" in terms of reading and writing. As such, they know nothing about what is to be learned and must be taught everything. Based on this belief, the common approach to literacy instruction was to begin with what were considered the basics—the letters of the alphabet and the sounds related to them. After children had mastered this information, they learned to blend sounds to create simple words. For example, they would learn c-a-t and then say it fast to produce *cat*. Finally, they would get simple sentences to read and then more and more complex materials. If instruction did not focus on sounds, then it focused on learning to recognize words when they were presented repeatedly. Next, simple sentences were made from the words students could recognize, such as *See Dick run, See Sally run,* and so on. Although, many people were successful at learning to read through these methods, many were not. As a result, large numbers of children completed school without becoming truly literate.

A program of instruction that focused on either sounds or recognizing words on sight was based on the notion that a child would be ready for this instruction at a given point in time. Thus, *readiness instruction* consisted of activities to help children learn auditory discrimination (to recognize the differences in phonemes), visual discrimination (to recognize the differences in shapes or patterns), and instruction in such tasks as matching the uppercase to the lowercase of a given letter.

READING AND WRITING INSTRUCTION TODAY

Today, the conception of how to teach reading and writing is based on relatively new research that recognizes the vital relationship between the two and indicates that it is best to teach children both processes simultaneously. Other important research and observation helps us recognize the developmental nature of becoming literate (Harp and Brewer 1996). Children begin learning about language—and therefore literacy—at birth. Toddlers can make marks on paper and intend them to be messages. They can also recognize a great deal of **environmental print** in context. For example, most toddlers can pick their favorite book from a shelf holding many books or a selected box of cereal from the cupboard; similarly, they can recognize a stop sign or the "golden arches" of a fast-food restaurant. Many preschoolers can recognize and write their own names as well as some words such as *love,* and many can write some or all of the letters of the alphabet.

Clearly, these children are not "blank slates," waiting for instruction. Rather, they are active learners, seeking to make sense of written as well as spoken language. This concept of developing literacy, usually called

emergent literacy, is very nearly the opposite of the readiness concept, discussed earlier. Therefore, this concept is new to many people.

Given this background about past and present views of literacy instruction, let us examine what we know today about the processes of learning to read and to write.

LEARNING TO READ

We have learned a great deal about the process of reading in the last few years. In the past, researchers examined what actually happens when a reader reads. More recently, researchers have been trying to develop a model that would explain the process of reading and could then be used to help children engage in that process. *Reading*, by definition, means gaining meaning from print, not just pronouncing the words. As a reader tries to make sense of print, she predicts what the print will say, uses cues from the print to confirm or reject her prediction, and moves on if her prediction is confirmed. If it is rejected, then she must recycle through the prediction-confirming or -rejecting phase again, this time using more or different cues. At the same time, the reader is matching the meaning to what she knows about the topic. If what she knows matches, then she goes on; if it does not match, again she must reread (Goodman 1996, Goodman and

Burke 1980). Then the information is integrated into what the learner knows, and the cycle is repeated.

The true wonder of this process is that it happens so rapidly that good readers are not aware of doing it. Even beginning readers often apply several parts of the process simultaneously. What we know is that reading is not simply looking at the letters of the words, sounding them out, blending them together, saying the word, and then repeating that process. In addition, readers use cues in the reading process, including the print itself, their background knowledge, their knowledge of language, cues from the illustrations (if the material is illustrated), and any number of other signals that are personal to them.

Cues That Readers Use

The print itself offers cues, as there are many words that we recognize instantaneously (our *sight-word vocabulary*). However, print cues sometimes fail us. For instance, when we read the word *tear*, does it mean "water falling from our eyes" or "a rip in our clothing"? Nonetheless, sound-letter relationships do provide information as we read. For example, if we are reading a text about big cats and come to a word that we do not recognize, the *p* at the beginning of the word probably would cue us that the word is not *tiger* but *panther*. If we know that *mother* and other common words end with the sound represented by *-er*, that will also help us decode the word. We might also know the word *pan* and use that knowledge to determine the first part of the unknown word *panther*.

In addition to knowledge of sound-letter relationships, readers also use what they know about how language works. Language cues include *semantics*—knowledge of word meanings and the relationships between and among words. Meanings are rarely exact, but all language users have developed meanings for words. When several readers see the letters *c a t*, each may picture a different cat, but there will be enough shared meaning to communicate.

Another language cue is provided by the *syntax* of the sentence—the order in which the words and phrases are arranged. If, for example, the reader sees *the*, he will know that a noun will follow. Syntax is specific to a given language. In English, adjectives usually are placed before the nouns they modify, but in Spanish, adjectives are placed after the nouns.

Other cues include what we know about the world. If we read *A hurricane spawned a _____ when it came ashore*, we use our knowledge of weather to help us fill in *tornado*. We would not think that the word *spawned* had anything to do with laying eggs in this context.

Illustrations offer cues to readers if they correspond with the text and provide accurate information. Beginning or early readers often use pictures as cues to predict what new or unknown words are. Some readers develop other cues that are personal to them. For example, a smudge on a name card might help one reader recall the name on the card. Another reader might develop a cue such as color or the position of a word on a page or box to predict meaning.

In summary, readers use a variety of cues to create meaning. Moreover, readers bring to the reading process a wealth of information about language, topics, story structure, and words represented by squiggles.

PARENTS AND LITERACY

■ Plan a family literacy night, during which you use a "big book" demonstration to explain how you are helping the children learn to read. See Cairney and Munsie (1995) for ideas.

The Development of Literacy

Let's trace the development of literacy in Jeanann, who receives a book for her first birthday. She hugs the book and babbles something to her mother, which her mother interprets as "Pick me up and read this book to me." When Jeanann is comfortable on her mother's lap, she pays close attention as her mother reads and she touches the pictures of the objects she recognizes. We can assume that Jeanann already knows that books can be read, that someone can read them to her, and that they have pictures of familiar objects. She probably also knows that readers turn the pages as they read, and she may attempt to turn them herself.

A child's literacy can be developed through a wide range of activities and experiences.

By the time Jeanann is two, her books have simple stories rather than just objects and pictures, and she listens to longer, more complex stories as they are read to her older brother. She picks up some of the language of books and may "read" a book herself. She may use a special voice or even use "story" words, such as *Once upon a time* or *Once there was a miller who had a beautiful daughter,* when she reads to herself, her dolls, or someone else. *I read it* is a commonly spoken phrase.

At three, Jeanann can identify books on her shelf and can select the one she wants or the one requested by the reader. She can repeat more of the text of her favorite books and wants to hear some stories over and over again. She knows by this time that it is the *print* that is read, not the pictures, although she may use the pictures to tell her own version of a story. Once, when she asked someone to read a sticker book and was told that it had no words, she looked at it carefully and said, "Yes there are words"— and she pointed to the publishing information inside the front cover.

By age four, Jeanann can recognize her name in print along with the names of some of the letters of the alphabet. She likes to "read" to her toys and her younger siblings. She also has strong feelings about which books she wants to have read and can often repeat the words to familiar books exactly as they are printed (and will correct any reader who makes a mistake!). She has a good idea that books can have stories, information, pictures, directions, and so on in them. She also recognizes that people read many kinds of print—signs, cereal boxes, letters, maps, and so on.

As a five-year-old, Jeanann can recognize many letters of the alphabet; knows some familiar environmental print, even out of context (like the word *Stop* even without the red octagon); and is interested in a wide variety of books and other reading materials. She knows a few common words, such as *love* and *the end.*

By age six, Jeanann, like many other children, can read some easy-to-read materials and books with predictable print. As a beginning reader, her reading often sounds less fluent than when she reads familiar stories from memory. Beginning readers often pay so much attention to the print that they overlook other cues and read word for word. As they become more comfortable reading, they begin to use the other cues more frequently. By age seven or eight, many readers are ready to tackle chapter books and reference material.

As a mature reader, you probably rely more on the expectations that you have for the text than on the actual print. But if the material is difficult—say, a piece that requires background knowledge that you do not have—you may use print cues more. You may also find that you slow down the entire reading process and are aware that you are not comprehending.

Table 9.1 on page 264 provides an overview of the stages of reading. Readers at each stage have different expectations and understandings about print and what can be done with it. They also gain knowledge of the cueing

THEORY INTO Practice

Observe a class of four-year-olds and a class of second-graders. What are some of the developmental differences that you can observe in their reading behaviors?

TABLE 9.1

Stages in Reading Development

Stage	Parent/Teacher Role
Magical Stage The child is learning the purpose of books; begins to think that books are important; looks at books, holds books, often takes a favorite book with him or her.	Model the importance of reading; read to the child; talk about books.
Self-Concept Stage The child views himself as a reader; begins to engage in readinglike activities; may pretend to read books; imposes meaning from pictures or previous experience with books; uses booklike language, even though it does not match the text.	Read to the child; provide access to books the child knows; participate with the child in reading books.
Bridging Reader Stage The child becomes aware of actual print. He may be able to pick out familiar words; notices personally significant words; is able to read back stories that he has written; can read familiar print from poems, songs, or nursery rhymes. The child may believe that each syllable is a word and can be frustrated with attempts to match print and sounds; usually begins to recognize alphabet.	Read to the child; present words of familiar songs or poems on charts or in booklets; provide opportunities to write frequently.
Take-Off Reader Stage The child begins to use the three cueing systems (graphophonic, semantic, and syntactic) together. He is excited about reading; begins to recognize print out of context; attends to environmental print and reads everything (cereal boxes, signs, and so on). A danger in this stage is giving too much attention to each letter.	Read to the child; encourage reading in a variety of situations; do not force letter-perfect reading.
Independent Reader Stage The child is able to read unfamiliar books independently; constructs meaning from print and from previous experience and authors' cues; is able to make predictions about reading material. Material related directly to experience is easiest to read, but the child can understand familiar structures and genres and common expository material.	Read to the child; encourage age predictions about reading; select material that is relevant; provide instruction in story structure.

Source: Adapted from Orin Cochrane, Donna Cochrane, Sharon Scalena, and Ethel Buchanan, *Reading, Writing and Caring* (Winnipeg, Manitoba, Canada: Whole Language Consultants, 1984). Used with permission of the authors.

systems as they move through the stages and can integrate what they are reading with what they have learned in each stage. Of course, some children will move through these stages much more quickly than others. The point is to think about the individual child in terms of his understanding of the reading process.

The child who is learning to read is also learning about writing at the same time. It is almost impossible to separate the process of learning to read from that of learning to write. So as you read the following discussion

■ Send parents a newsletter that lists some of the children's favorite books, words to chants, and lyrics of songs that the children know by rote so that parents can enjoy reading or singing with their children. You should keep this newsletter short and make it reader friendly. Some teachers reproduce the covers of books, along with their titles, to help those parents who might not read themselves. Also encourage parents to tell family stories, and celebrate some of those in the newsletter (Buchoff 1995; Harding 1996).

of children learning to write, also keep in mind what is happening to them as *readers* and as *speakers*.

LEARNING TO WRITE

In the past, teachers and parents assumed that children would learn to write after they learned to read and that these experiences would take place primarily in a school setting. That view of writing dominated the instructional literature for years. Then in 1971, Carol Chomsky made a radical departure from the traditional view when she advocated that nonreaders should be writing and that reading instruction should begin with writing. Since that time, there has been a flurry of research activity focusing on young children and their writing. The resulting information has greatly expanded the view of writing—what it is, how it develops, and how best to teach it.

The more traditional view defined writing in terms that were mostly limited to handwriting. Children were expected to copy letters until they could reproduce close approximations of the teacher's model. Then they were expected to copy sentences. Teachers often gave children exercises in a handwriting text to copy or began the schoolday by writing a poem or a quotation on the board for the children to copy. Children's attempts at writing on their own were basically ignored or perhaps even punished—certainly not encouraged (Atkins 1984). In light of the research conducted since the 1970s, however, writing is generally defined more broadly today to include children's efforts at making marks on paper—beginning with scribbles.

Parents and teachers of young children have always known about young children's interest in writing. (They have been cleaning the results of that interest off walls and tables for years.) Children seem to be intuitively aware of the importance of their efforts. Goodman and Altwerger (1981) found that when they asked three-year-old children if they could write, the children would answer "Of course" and make marks on paper that they expected could be interpreted. (Interestingly, these same three-year-olds claimed not to be able to read because they had not been taught to do so.)

We now recognize that children construct their understanding of written language in a developmental sequence that is observable and very similar in all children. The stages of writing development have been described by Temple, Nathan, Temple, and Burris (1993); Clay (1975); and Ferreiro and Teberosky (1982). These stages are outlined in the following sections.

Development of Writing

Scribble Stage

As soon as children begin to make marks with writing instruments, they are beginning to learn about written language and how it works. The first stage in the development of writing is scribbling. Just as children babble before they use words, they scribble before they learn which forms are letters and which are not. Figure 9.1 is an example of scribbling.

Parents and teachers of scribblers should provide them with a variety of materials, such as paint, books, paper, and crayons. Parents and teachers should label the children's scribbling as "writing" and model writing just as they model reading for their children. Parents can model writing in

> The development of writing occurs in predictable stages.

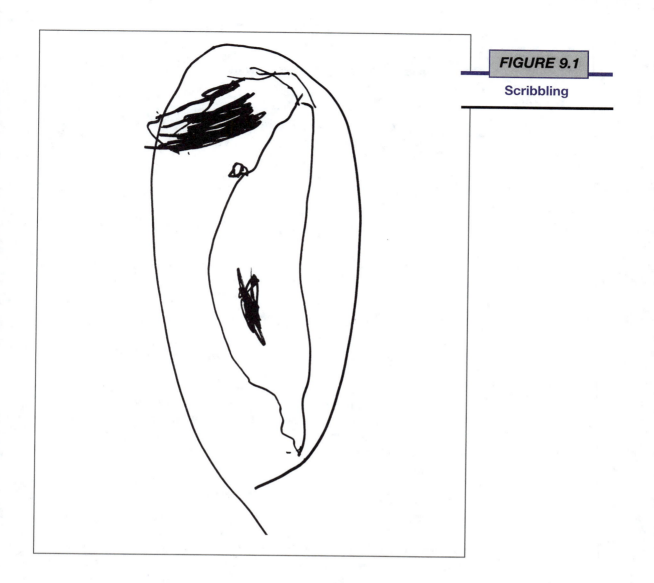

FIGURE 9.1

Scribbling

everyday situations, for instance, saying "We are almost out of milk. We should write it on our grocery list," or "I am writing a letter to Aunt Sue. Would you like to write something to her?" or "I am going to leave a note for Daddy so he will know where we are," and so on. Parents should also read aloud and encourage children to talk to each other and to adults.

Linear Repetitive Stage

The next stage in writing development is the linear repetitive stage. In this stage, children discover that writing is usually horizontal and that letters

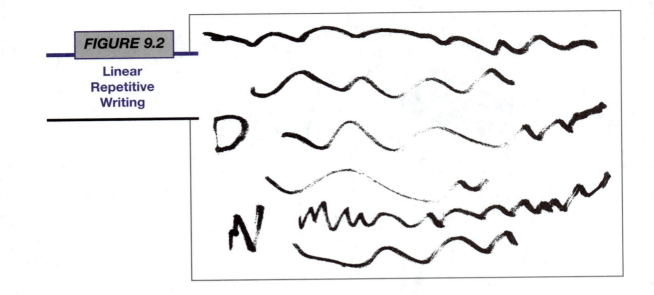

appear in a string across a page. Children in this stage think that a word referring to something large has a longer string of forms than a word referring to something small (Ferreiro and Teberosky 1982; Schickedanz 1988). In other words, children look for concrete connections between words and their referents. Figure 9.2 is a sample of linear repetitive writing. The child who did this sample mixed some letter forms with the linear scribbles.

Children in the linear repetitive stage need the same support that scribblers need from parents and teachers. Adults might also begin watching for the emergence of letter forms.

Random-Letter Stage

The next stage is a random-letter stage, in which children learn which forms are acceptable as letters and use them in some random order to record words or sentences. Children produce strings of letters that have no relation to the sounds of the words they are attempting to record. They may also include some forms that are not recognizable as letters because their repertoire of letters is so limited. Figure 9.3 shows an example of random-letter writing in which the message is "The 3 bears are so nice and cute." This sample illustrates clearly the inclusion of some forms that are not letters.

Teachers and parents should encourage children's attempts to write. Children need the adults around them to respond to the intent of their writing, not to correct their form. If the people around them honor their attempts to write and treat their writing as important, children's writing skills will grow. Just as we know that a child who is saying "goed" is actually making progress in learning language, we know that a child who has

"The 3 bears are so nice and cute."

FIGURE 9.3

Random-Letter Writing

discovered letters and understands that they stand for thoughts has made progress in learning about written language.

Letter-Name, or Phonetic, Writing

The next stage of development is that of early phonetic writing, in which children begin to make the connection between letters and sounds. The beginning of this stage is often described as *letter-name writing* because children write the letters whose names and sounds are the same. For example, they write the word *you* with the letter *u*. They begin to represent words with graphemes that reflect exactly what they hear. Figure 9.4 on page 270 is an example of phonetic writing in which the message is "Me and my family are going to Utah for 5 days." In this sample, it is easy to see that the child represented *my* with an *m, family* with *fa, going* with a *g,* and *Utah* with *UTO.*

Transitional Spelling

As children learn more about the written language system, they begin to learn the conventions of written language. They begin to spell some words in conventional ways, even though their spelling up to this point has been phonetic. A good example is the word *love.* Because children are exposed to this word so often, they begin to spell it in its conventional form very early. *The* is another common example.

This stage of spelling is called *transitional* to indicate that children are moving from phonetic spelling to more standard or conventional spelling.

FIGURE 9.4

Phonetic Writing

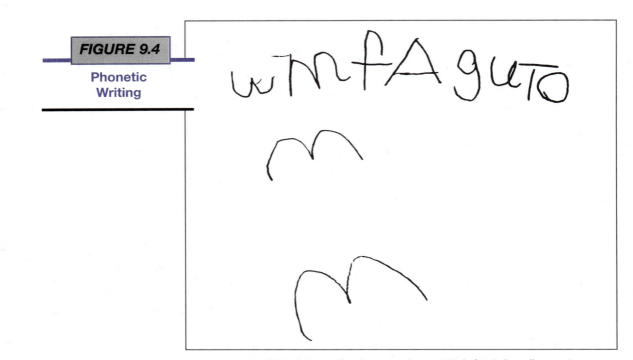

"Me and my family are going to Utah for 5 days."

Figure 9.5 is an example of such spelling. Beginning on the bottom left, this sample reads: "Once upon a time there was a tree. He had lots of friends, but very little friends. They were flowers. They were very nice flowers. They talked every day. The end." This child began her story on the left side of the page, but when she needed more space, she wrote the next line above the first line. She knew about the direction of written English but did not yet know how to place words on a page. (Consider all she *did* know about written English that allowed her to compose and record this story.)

Teachers and parents can foster independence in writing at this stage by asking children how they think words are spelled, by supplying needed information, and by encouraging children to help each other in the writing process. Instruction in spelling as an isolated subject is not necessary at this point. Children will learn to spell conventionally the words they need for writing. In Figure 9.5, much of the writing is correct. Teachers should focus on how much children know at this stage, rather than correcting spellings they do not yet know.

PARENTS AND LITERACY

■ Use examples from the children's work in class to explain the stages in writing development to parents. Also let parents know that you will send home a brief note when their child passes one of the developmental milestones in writing.

thay tokt evree bay The Enb.
flours thay wr.faree hlse flours
bot fary littl frans thay wr
a treeu he had lots of frends
wants apon a time thar was

FIGURE 9.5

Transitional
Spelling

Conventional Spelling

Finally, children achieve mostly conventional spelling. Just as children move slowly from babbling to adult speech, they need time to learn the conventions of written language. Adult speech is not mastered without considerable time and effort from the learner and support from sensitive adults. Children deserve the same support as they move from scribbling to mature writing.

Principles of Written Language

Marie Clay (1975) has been very influential in helping teachers of young children understand children's development in reading and writing. Her work, along with that of Don Holdaway (1980), has served as the basis for reading and writing instruction in all of New Zealand. Many U.S. schools and preschools have adopted the methods of instruction that these two researchers advocate.

Clay (1975) has observed the following principles that govern the development of written language:

1. *The principle of signs*—Children learn that objects or events can be represented with signs; they then move to learning letters as symbols that are arbitrary, that is, not related to their referents.
2. *The copying principle*—Children often copy models found in their environment, such as logos, or they copy their names, since their names are likely to be the print that they see most often.
3. *The flexibility principle*—Children discover that a letter can vary greatly in form and still be recognized as a letter. Children trying out this principle will create variations of letter forms and ask for feedback on the success

or failure of their variations. In this problem-solving approach, children learn to construct and to recognize various forms of the same letter.

4. *The inventory principle*—Children often take inventory of their own learning in a very systematic way. They may make lists of all the letter forms they know or all the words they can write. Although teachers might have a reason for asking children to write all the letters or words that they know, children also complete such inventories spontaneously.

5. *The principle of recurrence*—Clay describes *recurrence* as "the tendency to repeat an action," which contributes to the child's ability to form letters quickly and habitually. The child also begins to realize that the same letters or words can recur in different patterns. English-speaking children discover that letters can only be repeated twice in words and that words can only be repeated twice in sentences. For example, in words such as *Mississippi,* the same letter is repeated, and in sentences such as *He had had all he could eat,* the same word is repeated.

6. *The generating principle*—The generating principle causes children to use some of the elements of writing and some of the rules for combining them to produce new statements. Such behavior is basic to the development of oral language because children can never hear every sentence that they want to produce—they can only learn the elements and the rules for combining them. It is logical that children would use this same technique when attempting to master written language systems.

Conventions of Written Language

Children must learn other elements of written language that are not related to representing sounds with specific letters or combinations of letters. One of these elements is *directionality:* the **convention** that in English, writing begins on the left and moves to the right. Other conventions include the use of space around words and the use of abbreviations. Children must also learn to arrange words on a page and in a book. Children may temporarily ignore what they know about directionality if they cannot fit a word on a page or line. Through experience, they learn to carry words over to the next page or to put extra words on the backs of pages. Graves and Stuart (1985) observed that the space around words was negative space and that learning what to do with it was a difficult concept for young children. Some children attempted to fill up negative space by placing periods between the words. They recognized spaces but tried to make them positive rather than negative.

Only children with well-developed concepts of words will understand abbreviations. The use of abbreviations signals that children understand that the letters of abbreviations stand for words and could be expanded into the words for which they stand. Clay (1975) cites an example of a child who used abbreviations in squares to be colored a given color. The child marked each square with a *b* for *black, w* for *white,* and so on.

In order to make all these discoveries about written language, children need experience exploring writing, opportunities to make hypotheses about how print works, and feedback that verifies their guesses. Teachers and parents who recognize that children are exploring the flexibility of written language and constructing an understanding of what is possible will be able to foster growth in children's writing. They will offer many opportunities for writing, will recognize most mistakes as explorations of the written language system, and will be able to celebrate the growth that they can observe in the children's understanding.

The Writing Process with Young Children

Much has been written in recent years about the writing process and means of implementing it across the curriculum so that elementary children can achieve competence in writing. The work of Graves (1983) and Calkins (1986) has been helpful to teachers of older elementary children who want to create an environment that promotes writing skills and to take the time necessary to implement the process. The whole point of emphasizing the process of writing is to help teachers move away from giving children isolated bits and pieces of instruction in the conventions of printed language and toward helping children learn those conventions while engaging in relevant and meaningful writing activities.

Helping younger children write meaningfully requires providing the necessary tools (paper, writing instruments) and helping children appreciate the usefulness of writing. Even very young children should be encouraged to keep journals in which they can record their experiences and feelings. Young children may begin by drawing pictures and talking about them. As they participate in classroom activities, they may begin to use letters or words and phrases to aid in expressing their ideas. Gradually, the amount of writing will increase. Teachers of young children should be aware that not all children will choose to write in journals. Children are to be encouraged but not forced to write in their journals regularly. Figures 9.6, 9.7, and 9.8 (on page 274) are examples of journal entries from a kindergartner that were recorded over a period of a week.

Children should be encouraged to make use of print in play situations and in other activities. For example, a child was observed carefully writing a list, which he took home. The next day, his mother came to the classroom to ask for a copy of the recipe that had been used in a cooking experience. Her son had brought home a list of ingredients, but she didn't know what to do with them. From this experience, the child learned more about writing than would have been possible if he had completed a whole ream of work-

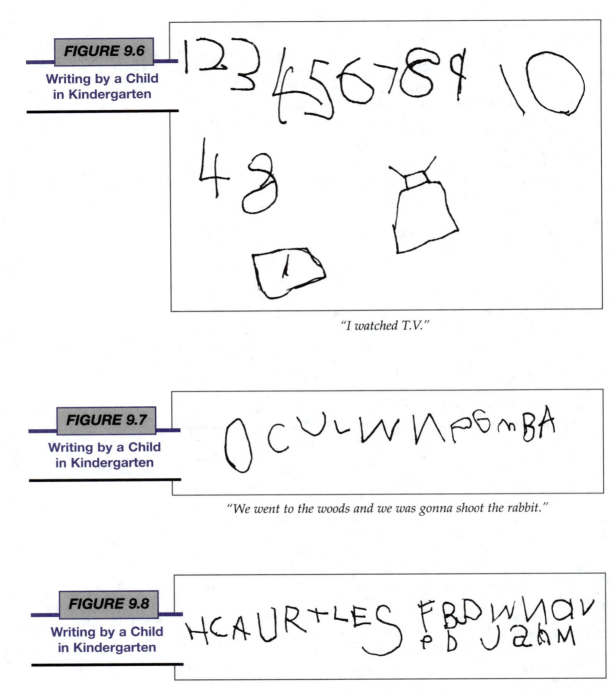

FIGURE 9.6

Writing by a Child in Kindergarten

"I watched T.V."

FIGURE 9.7

Writing by a Child in Kindergarten

"We went to the woods and we was gonna shoot the rabbit."

FIGURE 9.8

Writing by a Child in Kindergarten

"My dad is going to buy me a rifle. It's a deer rifle."

sheets. He learned that print is important in communication, that some lists require much detail, and that writing gets a response. Children might write dialogue for puppets or make signs to label the parts of the airport they have constructed with blocks. The teacher's tasks are to make sure that materials are available and accessible and to value and encourage what children do.

For younger children, the writing process will not include the usual steps that older children can complete, such as editing and writing revisions. Just writing for themselves, watching an adult write down what they dictate, and listening to well-written material being read is enough writing instruction for most young children. Primary-age children can be helped to edit their own writing and as they grow more skillful, the writing of their peers. By second grade, many children can look for capital letters at the beginnings of sentences, punctuation marks at the ends of sentences, and conventional spellings of familiar words. Children can also help each other by responding to each other's writing.

THEORY INTO Practice

Observe several young children as they write. How do they react to the opportunity to write? Do you find writing behaviors that you can now identify as part of the developmental process of learning to write? Explain your answer on the basis of your observations.

HELPING CHILDREN LEARN TO READ AND WRITE

As teachers of young children, our role in helping them learn to read and write successfully is a complex one. First, we have to learn what each child understands about reading and writing. Second, we have to plan classroom environments and activities that will help each child use printed language successfully. And third, we have to support the child in his efforts to make sense of print.

Goals of Literacy Instruction

The basic goals of literacy instruction for young children include (1) continuing their language development, (2) giving them personal knowledge of the functions of print, and (3) helping them learn about books and the importance of reading. This third goal can be divided further into several secondary purposes: to develop phonemic awareness, to learn about story structure, and to learn about what readers do. Children in the primary grades will continue language development, learn to apply reading strategies, and become independent readers.

None of these goals can be met by engaging a child in isolated practice activities that are designed to teach a specific skill. These goals are best met through an integrated curriculum in an environment that includes interesting play opportunities. Examples of activities that help children achieve these goals are described briefly in the sections that follow.

Developing Oral Language Skills

Oral language development is important for growth in literacy; both reading and writing are language skills (Glazer 1989). The more competent a child is in using oral language, the more she will know about how language works and the more able she will be to transfer this knowledge to the written language system. Oral language development will take place if children are provided with interesting activities in which to participate and are allowed to talk with each other and with adults. Dramatic play, for instance, allows children to "try on" the vocabulary and speaking mannerisms of various adults as they play "grocer," "shopper," "mechanic," "bus driver," "teacher," "cook," "parent," or "Superman."

Some children may need to learn the meanings of words they will meet in print later in school. Teachers can create opportunities for developing concepts by providing children with objects, activities, or experiences. When children play with lariats, classify leaves, or go on field trips to experience elevators, circuses, or restaurants, they are developing meanings. When they are expected to read words such as *lariat, maple leaf, elevator, circus,* and *restaurant,* they will have the knowledge to make the print meaningful for them. Language development activities can be extended to print as children observe the teacher recording their words as they dictate a story or see a chant or song they have learned printed on a chart. Young children need many opportunities to initiate and participate in verbal interactions with each other. They also need to engage in real conversation with adults rather than being limited to responding to questions posed by a teacher.

Learning about the Functions of Print

Children are not likely to be motivated to learn to read and write without some knowledge of the **functions of print.** Knowing that print can be decoded to reveal wonderful stories and secrets is strong motivation for learning to read. Children learn the functions of print by observing the teacher using a book to find information about the insects a child brings to school or by watching an adult follow directions for putting together a class incubator. Children learn about the pleasure print can bring by hearing the teacher read poetry and stories to them. They learn the usefulness of print for sending messages when they write thank-you notes to the clown who visited their class or when they see that an invitation to their parents to share a special event results in their parents' coming to school. Children learn that a shopping list can help them remember needed items. Using print all through the day and experiencing the pleasures of being read to are necessary activities for learning about the functions of print.

Of course, books also provide information and directions. Teachers can supply books that will enhance ideas developed in play. For example, children playing "going to the moon" would be interested in books about planets and space travel. Other children might be interested in books that

When children can manipulate print to meet their own needs, they become more skilled as readers and writers.

give directions for making an insect cage, that tell how to care for the classroom animals, or that provide information about snakes, dinosaurs, or monsters. An observant teacher will find many opportunities to share both informational books and stories. Children will unlikely exert all the effort it takes to learn to read if they do not know there are treasures to be found in print for those who can read.

Phonemic Awareness

Cunningham (1988) has defined **phonemic awareness** as "the ability to examine language independently of meaning and to manipulate its component sounds" (p. 516). Phonemic awareness is a cluster of skills at different ability levels, not a single skill that a child does or does not have. For example, recognizing rhyming words is one level of phonemic awareness, distinguishing the beginning sound of a word from the remainder of the word is another level of awareness, and completely segmenting the phonemes in a given word is yet an even higher level.

Phonemic awareness should not be confused with *phonics;* the two are not synonymous. Phonics involves teaching children sound-letter relationships through direct instruction (Griffith and Olson 1992). Phonemic awareness involves a broader range of skills and is achieved through less formal means (Chapman 1995; Richgels, Poremba, and McGee 1996).

Phonemic awareness is best achieved through children's daily interactions with print. For example, a child who wants to write a note might ask how to spell a certain word. The teacher might say the word slowly and ask what sound the child hears. When the child has identified that sound and recorded it, the teacher would repeat the whole word and ask what sound the child hears next. This pattern would be repeated until the child has spelled the word in full (or at least all the letters that have been sounded).

Children who write words using so-called invented spelling are well aware of the phonemic nature of language and do not need instruction in phonemic awareness. Teachers can also point out the phonemes of words in stories the children are reading. If the teacher was reading a "big book" about a greedy cat, he might remind the children that they can read the word *greedy* every time they see it because the *gr*, the *ee*, and the *dy* stand for the same sounds whenever they are printed together.

Several studies have found that phonemic awareness is a good predictor of reading success. For most children, the skills that constitute phonemic awareness will develop with repeated experiences in reading and writing. For those children who have difficulty developing these skills on their own, the teacher should offer guidance—for instance, regularly pointing out the phonemic nature of words. Eventually, the children's own phonemic skills will mature, and such specific help will no longer be needed.

Learning about Story Structure

Every time a reader chooses material to read—a magazine, a newspaper, a mystery novel, or a cookbook—he brings to that reading experience expectations of how the material will be written and what its structure will be. Knowledge of **story structure** is important because the more a reader knows about what to expect from printed material, the more likely he is to be successful in reading it. A skilled reader knows that a newspaper will be written in a distinctive style; that most of the information will be found in the beginning of the article, with details following; that certain types of articles will be in certain sections of the paper, maybe even on certain days; and so forth.

Children who are learning about reading are also developing knowledge of story structure and what to expect from various reading materials (Jensen 1985). Knowledge of story structure cannot be taught using skills worksheets. Such knowledge is developed through experience—reading many kinds of materials over a long period of time. For example, teachers can help children compare the structures of *The Greatest of All* (Kimmel 1991), *The Mouse Bride* (Cowley 1995), and *The Mouse Bride: A Chinese Folktale* (Chang 1992), three stories that have the same plot. Children can relate a cumulative structure to *The House That Jack Built* (Stevens 1985) and learn to recognize the characteristics of folktales (talking animals and magic objects) and realistic stories. When children have broad experiences with good-quality children's books, they will develop expectations for stories, which will help them become better readers.

Learning What Readers Do

Children learn what readers do as they observe people reading. Young children need to know that readers attend to the print of the text and that they think as they read. Even three- and four-year-olds begin to understand that it is the print that is being read, rather than the pictures, and that reading is constrained by directionality (Goodman and Altwerger 1981). Children who look at "big books" or class charts while the teacher reads them have the opportunity to develop this knowledge of directionality, as a hand or pointer moves from left to right under the print. Listening to "big books" being read aloud also gives children an opportunity to observe the changes in inflection indicated by punctuation.

Young children also learn what readers do when they engage in writing. As they record their own ideas, they become more aware that reading is the unlocking of an author's ideas, not just the pronouncing of words. Six-year-old Jason is a good example of a child learning to read by writing. He has "published" several books of his own and feels quite confident in his ability to read them and to write others. Jason reads the ideas from the books but certainly does not produce a word-perfect reading of the text. In fact, he pays little attention to the exact text. What is important is that he believes that he can read, that he is capable as a reader and writer, and that others value his ability. He is gaining in ability to recognize individual words and is becoming more aware of the importance of the text. Nothing in his reading experience is teaching him that he is not able to read.

This is the goal of an early childhood reading program for beginning readers. Not all children experience such success and support for their developing reading abilities. In a skills-based classroom, Jason might be placed in the low reading group because he cannot read the exact text yet. That placement would deliver a clear message to Jason each day: that he cannot achieve what his teacher and parents expect of him. He would learn that reading is a painful experience and one to be avoided, if at all possible.

Applying Reading Strategies

As children become more independent as readers, teachers can help them apply the strategies used by effective readers: sampling print, predicting what is coming, confirming predictions, and integrating new information with what is known (Weaver 1988). Children need opportunities to use what they know about language and how it works and to apply their own experiences to reading tasks. For example, children who know oral language can use their knowledge of semantics and syntax to predict the meanings of words, if the reading materials make sense to them. Materials for reading must be selected with the children's experiences in mind; children must be able to apply what they know about how the world works to their reading. A story about a caterpillar will not make sense if the reader has no concept of what a caterpillar is.

Which **cueing system** is used most depends on the skill of the reader and the nature of the material being read. For instance, as you read this textbook, you probably rely most heavily on the schematic system and pay least attention to the graphophonic system. You will realize that you do not look at every letter when you read if you think about how difficult it is to proofread your own work—it's nearly impossible. You know what you said, so to actually look at each letter is very difficult. Consider another demonstration of how little most readers use the graphophonic system: When you read an article that has been photocopied and the words on the edge of the page are blurred, you read over and fill in those words, usually without even thinking about them. A beginning reader, on the other hand, may focus so much on the print that she will fail to use the other systems. Reading will be more difficult for you when you are not familiar with the topic because you will not have adequate background knowledge. If you doubt the importance of background knowledge, pick up a biology journal next time you are in the library, and read an article or two.

A good reader coordinates the cues from all these systems through the use of learned strategies and does it so rapidly that she is unaware of even using the separate systems.

Becoming an Independent Reader

Teachers can help children gain independence as readers by providing reasons for them to read. In other words, reading should meet children's needs for gaining information or solving problems. If children are learning about spiders, the teacher should provide a wide variety of books about spiders. Children will need to read in order to obtain information and to write in order to share that information. Print can be used in the classroom to help children organize their activities, keep records, and make plans. The more reasons children have for using print for their own needs, the more easily they will become able to read independently.

> **PARENTS AND LITERACY**
>
> ■ Invite parents to share their favorite stories with your class. If they do not feel comfortable reading to the whole group, they could read to small groups or tell the story rather than read it.

CAMBOURNE'S CONDITIONS FOR LITERACY LEARNING

Brian Cambourne (1995) has studied the process of becoming literate for twenty years. Based on his observations, he formulated the model shown in Figure 9.9 on page 282. In this model, Cambourne stresses the importance of *immersion* and *demonstration*. This means that the learner sees and hears those people who are important in his life using reading and writing. *Expectation* that the learner can become a successful user of print is vital, as students usually learn what is expected of them. According to the model, the learner takes *responsibility* for her own learning in that she chooses the pieces to be attended to in any experience, not the teacher. To illustrate this point, consider that a child will sit in her crib and practice sounds and sound combinations, but it would never work to send a toddler to her room to practice sounds.

Employment means that the learner can actually use the information she is learning in real and meaningful activities—for instance, learning how to make cookies by reading the directions. *Approximations* in literacy learning are as necessary as they are in learning to speak. We would not expect a child to use the mature form of *cookie* on her first attempt to communicate the desire for a snack. Every literacy learner will also make mistakes, but these mistakes can be extremely useful to the teacher in uncovering what the child knows and can use about printed language. Finally, the learner must receive a *response,* or feedback from her efforts. Do not

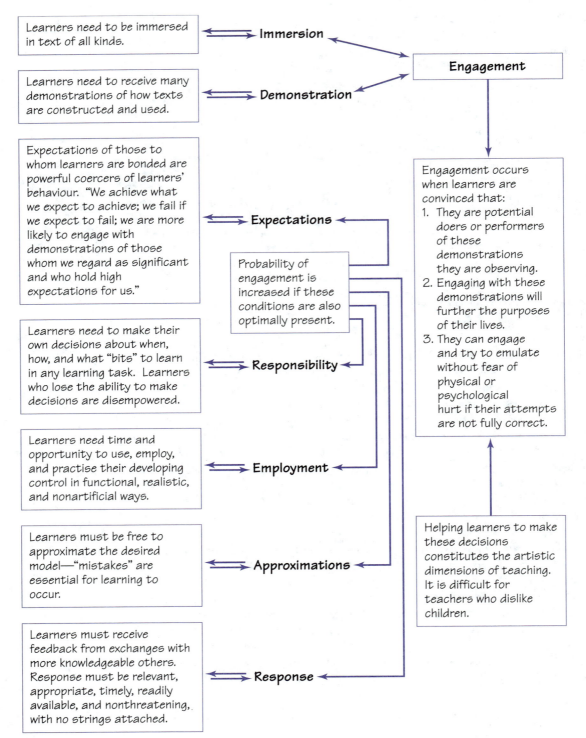

Learners need to be immersed in text of all kinds.

Immersion

Learners need to receive many demonstrations of how texts are constructed and used.

Demonstration

Engagement

Engagement occurs when learners are convinced that:
1. They are potential doers or performers of these demonstrations they are observing.
2. Engaging with these demonstrations will further the purposes of their lives.
3. They can engage and try to emulate without fear of physical or psychological hurt if their attempts are not fully correct.

Expectations of those to whom learners are bonded are powerful coercers of learners' behaviour. "We achieve what we expect to achieve; we fail if we expect to fail; we are more likely to engage with demonstrations of those whom we regard as significant and who hold high expectations for us."

Expectations

Probability of engagement is increased if these conditions are also optimally present.

Learners need to make their own decisions about when, how, and what "bits" to learn in any learning task. Learners who lose the ability to make decisions are disempowered.

Responsibility

Learners need time and opportunity to use, employ, and practise their developing control in functional, realistic, and nonartificial ways.

Employment

Learners must be free to approximate the desired model—"mistakes" are essential for learning to occur.

Approximations

Helping learners to make these decisions constitutes the artistic dimensions of teaching. It is difficult for teachers who dislike children.

Learners must receive feedback from exchanges with more knowledgeable others. Response must be relevant, appropriate, timely, readily available, and nonthreatening, with no strings attached.

Response

282

confuse *feedback* with *praise;* feedback can simply be recognition of the meaning that the child attempted. For example, the child who writes *pst* on the supply list at school will get feedback if the teacher responds "Oh, yes, we do need paste. I'll get some from the supply closet."

VYGOTSKY ON READING INSTRUCTION

Vygotsky's model of learning has been applied to reading instruction and is described by Mason and Sinha (1993). They list the following steps in the model:

1. Natural involvement
2. Mediated learning
3. External activity (child-directed learning and practice with the aid of props and occasional coaching by an adult)
4. Internal or independent activity

When applied to reading instruction for young children, Vygotsky's model provides that first, children are naturally involved in literacy activities: hearing stories read, observing others read, observing others write, attempting to write on their own, and so on. Next, children are engaged in mediated learning, such as having adults point out letters and words as stories are being read or as children are involved in writing activities. In the third stage, children begin to participate in such activities as rereading familiar stories (with books as props) and ask for adult assistance when faced with difficulties. Finally, children internalize the knowledge of print and how the "code" works so that their reading is independent.

To implement Vygotsky's model, teachers must plan appropriate classroom activities for the children. Appropriate activities are those that are useful, meaningful, flexible, shared, and wholistic.

This model seems to fit the early childhood classroom because the child is central at all stages and chooses the activities she wishes to complete. The teacher acts as a coach and helper to the child but does not dictate what the child will learn next or the strategies that the child will use in certain situations.

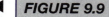 **FIGURE 9.9**   **The Conditions of Learning: A Model of Learning as It Applies to Literacy**

CLASSROOM ENVIRONMENT AND LITERACY

Classrooms that foster the development of literacy have several distinguishing characteristics: They are interesting and full of activity, they allow for participation in many different experiences, and they connect reading and writing to children's experiences. Classrooms where literacy emerges are also print rich: They contain a wide variety of reading, writing, and listening materials that are accessible to children.

In a stimulating, active environment, children will be encouraged to participate in a wide variety of experiences. Such a classroom will not be a quiet place! Children developing new concepts should want to talk about them, read about them, and write about them. For example, as a science activity, children might observe hatching silkworms. This activity would require research about when silkworms hatch, when the mulberry leaves that they eat are available, what will happen to the silk if the larvae are allowed to mature, and how to preserve some eggs so that another generation of silkworms can be grown. This activity might also involve gathering food for the larvae and observing the metamorphosis of the larvae into silkworms. Children involved in such experiences will be constantly talking about their observations, reading from a variety of sources, listening to others read, and writing about their experiences and feelings. Activities that encourage thinking, talking, reading, and writing should be part of every schoolday.

Several studies have found that adding selected materials to the play environment and guiding their use can encourage children to participate in more literacy activities in their play (Christie 1990; Morrow and Rand 1991; Neuman and Roskos 1993). Christie (1990) notes that giving children time to play is simply not enough. Teachers must also intervene to promote literacy activities, perhaps thinking about what literacy materials could be added to play areas, encouraging children to play in theme centers where literacy is a natural response to a theme, or modeling literacy behaviors in play areas. For example, a teacher might set up an office or a grocery store or invite children to write labels for their block constructions. Theme areas that involve literacy experiences include a doctor's office, a shoe store, a restaurant, a home (making lists, checking the TV guide, reading the newspaper, reading to babies, and so on), and a post office.

Neuman and Roskos (1993) recommend using real literacy objects rather than pretend objects. An office might be equipped with real file folders and forms. The materials selected should be familiar to the children from their real-world experiences. Morrow and Rand (1991) suggest that literacy materials be kept in clearly marked places, that they be changed frequently to keep children's interest in them high, that teachers model the uses of materials as needed or suggest possible uses when appropriate, and that all levels of development be accepted for the most positive results.

Planned Activities for Fostering the Development of Literacy

Language, including printed language, is a tool for communicating effectively. Teachers use all kinds of language to help children express their understanding and to help them gain new knowledge. The activities described in the following sections will help children connect concepts and oral and printed language.

Read-Alouds

Reading aloud to children—as individuals, in small groups, or as a whole class—is an absolutely essential part of literacy instruction. Not only does reading aloud provide children with a pleasurable experience, a positive emotional response to reading, and a means of getting "book" language in their heads, it also offers distinct opportunities to become more literate. Reading aloud also produces these benefits:

1. The teacher can demonstrate the nature, pleasures, and rewards of reading, which will increase the children's interest in books and their motivation to read for themselves.
2. Children learn the ways in which language can be recorded.
3. Children realize that some of their own experiences and thoughts are like those that have been recorded by the authors they have read.
4. Children who listen to stories can compose narratives in their own heads and want to create and record their own texts.
5. Children refine their understanding of the elements of language: patterns, sounds, rhythms, and styles.
6. Listening to stories they already know allows children to confirm their predictions about how the episodes are arranged to make the story work. Listening to known stories also allows children to discover new levels of meaning in a story.
7. Children who have had extensive experience in listening to stories are better able to edit their own stories in their heads.
8. Children need to be challenged by reading material that is beyond their independent reading level.
9. Reading aloud a variety of different texts throughout the schoolday helps children understand that reading goes well beyond any lesson or school activity (adapted from Mooney 1990, pp. 21–24).

Interactive reading aloud—in which children can ask questions, make comments, answer questions posed by the reader—is extremely valuable for young children but difficult to manage with large groups. Therefore, at least some read-aloud experiences need to be conducted with individuals or very small groups. Most teachers manage this kind of reading by using volunteers, teacher aides, or older children (Klesius and Griffith 1996).

Shared Reading

Shared reading—an instructional strategy in which the teacher takes primary responsibility for the reading but involves the children actively in the process—is another important experience that supports the young child's developing literacy. Shared reading is often done with books in a large format ("big books") and print, which all the group can see. While this approach certainly adds to the effectiveness, successful shared reading can be done with small groups and regular books.

In shared reading, the teacher introduces the book by reading the title, showing the children the front of the book, and asking them to predict what the story will be about. Once these predictions have been made and discussed, the teacher usually reads the name of the author and discusses other books by that individual (if appropriate). Then the teacher reads aloud the book, passing her hand or a pointer under the print as she reads it. On the second and other repeated readings of the story, the children can be asked to join in the reading of repetitive phrases. The teacher might then call attention to some elements of the print, perhaps capital letters, punctuation, illustrations that do or do not match the print on the page, the author's use of a specific word, the style of the story (folktale, realistic, personal narrative, and so on), or other features that will be meaningful to the children. Often, the children themselves call attention to features of the print on successive repeated readings. They may notice rhyming patterns, spelling patterns, page numbers, or any number of other features (Clements and Warncke 1994; Stewart 1995).

Eventually, of course, the children will have memorized the story and will be able to "read" it successfully. At that point, the teacher can suggest that the children write their own stories based on the pattern of the original, that they draw their own illustrations, that they write sequels, and so on, depending on the needs and abilities of the individual children. Some children may want to read the story independently, while others may want to play with the blocks and not do anything related to the story at the moment. Offering a choice of responses is extremely important (Fallon and Allen 1994). Thus, assigning every child to create a caterpillar from an egg carton after having read *The Very Hungry Caterpillar* (Carle 1969) would not be appropriate; however, making the materials available if children want to make caterpillars would be appropriate.

Journals

Providing journals and a time for writing in them is a strategy that will be successful for some four-year-olds and most five-year-olds. Journal writing may begin with drawing pictures and eventually move to writing messages and then to recording ideas. A journal in which the entries are dated and the teacher has sometimes recorded what the child has "read" from her writing will serve as an excellent record of the child's progress in writing. When milestones are reached, copies of significant pages can be made and sent home to parents. Some primary-grade children may want parts of their journals to remain private, and teachers should respect their wishes.

Examples of Literacy Activities

The activities described in the following list will help promote the development of literacy in children:

- The children construct an ambulance after they observe an ambulance go by while they are playing outside. The play grows into a need for a "hospital" and "patients" and "doctors." The teacher can contribute by offering books about ambulances or hospitals for browsing and by recording and reading back some of the children's statements about their play. The children might describe the ambulance and its sounds, and these descriptions could be recorded on a large piece of paper, to be reread several times as the play continues. Children might also choose to draw and write about their own hospital experiences.
- The children have learned to sing a song by rote. The teacher prepares a chart with the lyrics to the song printed on it. It is hung in the classroom, and children can follow the words as they sing. The words might also be printed on cards to be placed in a pocket chart; the children could then read the cards whenever they like. Children might be given copies of the lyrics in their own booklets. Primary children can write new lyrics to known melodies. As children engage in writing stories or song lyrics, they can get instruction in punctuation as it is needed, learn about editing, and decide about publishing their work. Barclay and Walwer (1992) suggest using song picture books to link the lyrics of songs to children's growing literacy abilities.
- The children have made some puppets. The teacher records the story that they tell with the puppets on a chart and places the chart near the puppet stage. Some children will be able to read it to others who want to play with the puppets. Some children might want to make their own books of the story. Other children might want to create new stories or sequels to the first. Older children can learn simple bookbind-

ing techniques and about the punctuation needed in the script for a puppet play.

- The children learn the text for a pattern book such as *Brown Bear, Brown Bear* (Martin 1970) and then write their own books using the same pattern. They might write "Jennifer, Jennifer, what do you see? I see Steven looking at me." *Brown Bear, Brown Bear* and *Whose Mouse Are You?* (Kraus 1970) are excellent models for helping children learn to use punctuation marks.

- The children visit the local fire station. The teacher arranges for photographs to be taken of the entire trip. The children might write about the trip and use the photographs as illustrations. The photographs and the children's writing could be bound into a book.

- The teacher reads a "big book" aloud to the children and explains what a reader does while reading (thinking, following along the lines of print, predicting, and so on). When the teacher rereads the book, the children join in when they recognize words. The teacher can plan any number of activities, depending on the needs of the group. Some children might write new stories based on the model in the "big book." For some children, the teacher might cover some of the words in the book with self-stick notes, print other words on them, and ask the children to read the new version of the story that is created. Other children might find all the words that begin with a given sound. Others will be able to read the student versions of the "big book" independently.

- The children dictate a report about their experiences catching tadpoles in the pond, and the teacher records their report on a large chart. This report might be reread and used as described in the "big book" example above. If older children have written their own reports about tadpoles, the teacher might help them compare their reports to those written by other authors. They might discuss what an author had to know to write the piece, what information might have been excluded, the expected audience of the piece, the point of view taken by the author, and the author's style.

- The children have listened to the teacher read *The Lion, The Witch, and the Wardrobe* (Lewis 1951). Several children might be interested in reading the other books in the series, *The Chronicles of Narnia*. Other children might write responses to the reading in their journals; some children might create wardrobes through which to enter the kingdom of Narnia; some children might adapt their favorite scenes for readers' theater; and some might create a board game based on the Lewis stories.

- A group of first-graders liked *Whistle for Willie* (Keats 1964) so much that the teacher decided to do an author study on Ezra Jack Keats. The class might read several more of his books, discuss the language used, read reviews of his books, study the art in his illustrations, create skits

As promised in the Preface, the theme of change will be illustrated in each of the content-area chapters of this book (Chapters 8 through 14). The point of these examples is to help you understand more clearly how any well-chosen theme could include any of the traditional subject-matter areas. Consider the following activities in promoting literacy:

➤ Chart the changes in characters in such books as *The Ugly Duckling* (Andersen 1990), *The Frog Prince* (Crane 1980), *The Crane Wife* (Yagawa 1979), *The Mixed Up Chameleon* (Carle 1984), and *Sylvester and the Magic Pebble* (Steig 1969).

➤ Find examples of illustrations that indicate changes. For example, in *Farmer Duck* (Waddle 1991), the beginning illustration is drab and cold, while the ending one is bright and cheery. Similarly, the endpapers in *Hey, Al!* (Yorinks 1986) are drab beige in the front of the book and cheery yellow in the end.

➤ Use *Round Trip* (Jonas 1983) and *Reflections* (Jonas 1987) to help children think about how the illustrations change when they are turned upside down. The illustrations in Gardner's *The Turn About, Think About, Look About Book* (1980) are also different images when turned to the side or upside down. *It Looked Like Spilt Milk* (Shaw 1988) is based on the changes in cloud shapes; children could spend some time observing clouds and thinking about what images they see and how they constantly change.

➤ Read *Changes, Changes* (Hutchins 1971). Build the structures with blocks; then take Polaroid pictures and create a book of the changes.

➤ Chart the changes in characters or in vocabulary used in multiple versions of one story, such as "The Three Bears," "The Three Little Pigs," or "Three Billy Goats Gruff." Read *Somebody and the Three Blairs* (Tolhurst 1990) and *The Three Little Wolves and the Big Bad Pig* (Trivizas and Oxenbury 1993). Compare the changes the authors made in the original versions of the stories.

➤ Compare multiple versions of the familiar rhyme "Over in the Meadow" (Galdone 1986; Keats 1971; Langstaff 1957). Record the changes noted among versions.

➤ There are several versions of the story "Stone Soup." Compare the changes in characters and settings: *Stone Soup* (Brown 1947), three French soldiers in a village; *Stone Soup* (McGovern 1968), one boy and an old woman; *Stone Soup* (Ross 1987), a fox and a hen; *Stone Soup* (Stewig 1991), a female character and a village; and *The Soup Stone* (Van Rynbach 1988), a soldier of the American Revolution.

for the characters in some of his books, read about how to put on a puppet play, or produce a play of their own.

• In response to her class's interest in the squirrels on the schoolgrounds, a teacher reads aloud *Nuts to You!* (Ehlert 1993). Those children who are still interested in squirrels might go through the card catalog in the library looking for other books on squirrels, use the CD-ROM to find entries about squirrels in the encyclopedia, or write their own stories and reports about squirrels.

These few examples illustrate how a teacher can use everyday class experiences to encourage children's developing abilities in reading and

Plan two or three classroom activities that will promote the development of literacy in developmentally appropriate ways.

writing. It is important to remember that not every child will be interested in participating in all these experiences. Some children will be just becoming aware of the print around them; others will be interested in making their own books. The teacher must not expect total participation by everyone. If a child is not interested in print, the teacher must discover things that do interest the child and then help him find ways to enhance that interest with print in a very personal way.

It is also important that the teacher not treat reading and writing as the only important activities in which children are involved. Children need to be involved in play, art, music, and so forth, and the teacher must value these experiences for themselves, without always tacking on a reading or writing component to supposedly legitimize the experience. To do otherwise would send children the subtle message that only reading and writing are important.

The communication triad—speaking, reading, and writing—should permeate all instruction in every subject. But each child's efforts in these areas should be natural—resulting from her own inclination and growing ability in each area. The artificial separation of learning into distinct instructional subjects must be avoided. When instruction is separated from experience, children develop the misconception that learning takes place only in school. Ideally, education is entering an era in which teachers will refocus on children's learning, rather than on defining education in terms of instruction.

ASSESSING LITERACY

As a teacher, you will not be able to plan activities that will support a given child's development of literacy without knowing what he understands about reading and writing now. In her book *An Observation Survey of Early Literacy Achievement,* Clay (1993) describes several strategies for observing the literacy development of a child in detail. Two of these techniques seem critical for teachers of young children: (1) observing the child's writing and (2) determining his knowledge of books and print.

Observing Writing

As a child writes, the teacher needs to observe the process the child follows on a regular basis and keep samples of his products on at least a biweekly basis. Observing the process will provide information about how many letters the child can use in writing, what he knows about the directionality of print, how he solves problems such as spelling unknown words, and how he works at writing. (Is it with pleasure, or does it seem to be a struggle?) Observing the products of writing can produce information about what the child knows about letters, letter-sound relationships, and punctuation and other conventions of writing (Button, Johnson, and Furgerson 1996). Such observations can help in judging the zone of proximal development for that child. For example, if a child spells *friend* as *frend,* then a little assistance will enable him to spell the word in the conventional way. If, however, the child spells *friend* as *frd,* then it seems likely that he is hearing the beginning and ending sounds of words and recording them accurately but trying to teach the conventional spelling of *friend* would probably not be useful at this time (Taylor 1996).

In observing how children handle books and what they know about print, the teacher may ask each child individually to show her the parts of the book (such as the front and back), where to start reading, what to do when finished reading one page, and where the top of the page is. The teacher might also ask the child to point to an uppercase letter, to point out a certain word, and so on. The teacher may also observe the children's behavior with books as they choose them from the classroom library shelves. Observing younger children will reveal if they know how to hold a book, which way is right side up, or how to turn the pages. Observing older children will provide information about how they determine which book to read and what they are interested in (Harp 1996).

Although it is beyond the scope of this chapter to describe in any useful detail good strategies for assessing children's reading behaviors, such strategies do exist. For instance, taking and analyzing running records or miscue inventories provide excellent information for determining how children apply reading strategies and what kinds of errors they make. These tasks can help teachers plan instruction geared to individual children's needs.

ISSUES IN LITERACY INSTRUCTION

Questions from parents or goal statements issued by schools often require teachers to think about what comprises the best practice in helping children develop literacy. Three issues in literacy instruction include (1) sound-letter relationships, (2) handwriting instruction, and (3) school or district requirements.

Sound-Letter Relationships

In some programs for young children, the reading curriculum centers around teaching sound-letter relationships. Teachers in such programs may feature a "letter of the week" and give children exercises in tracing or copying the selected letter. Teachers might require that objects brought for sharing time be objects whose names begin with the sound represented by the letter and that snacks be food whose names begin with the given letter.

There are several significant flaws in the "letter-of-the-week" curriculum. One is that a letter alone has no context and thus has no meaning. By themselves, letters have little value. Only when they are combined with other letters to represent sounds and words do letters have context and meaning. Focusing on an individual letter therefore means focusing on the most insignificant piece of information that is useful for real reading. Another flaw in the "letter-of-the-week" curriculum is that concentrating on sound-letter relationships leads children to believe that other strategies for reading are less important. But in fact, mature readers use sound-letter relationships much less frequently than other strategies. A third problem is that stressing sound-letter relationships tends to encourage parents to believe that mastery of this one aspect of reading is tantamount to mastery of reading, which is certainly not true. In addition, a focus on sound-letter relationships ignores what children already know about such relationships and may involve boring repetition of information for some children. In this sense, teaching a "letter of the week" violates the principle of good skills instruction that says such instruction should always be presented when it is needed by the learner.

These criticisms of the "letter-of-the-week" curriculum should not be interpreted to mean that learning about sound-letter relationships is unimportant. Understanding sound-letter relationships is one important skill in learning to read. To help children gain this skill, teachers should plan activities that are developmentally appropriate and designed for individual children. For children who are having difficulty with sound-letter relationships, alternatives to a "letter of the week" include focusing on a given letter in stories, charts, chants, poems, song lyrics, or other print. Reutzel (1992) recommends a number of activities: creating alphabet books from environmental print; creating an alphabet center in the classroom with wooden, magnetic, and sandpaper letters as well as stencils, chalkboards, and other writing materials; and using alphabet cookies and cereals, especially in pairs or small groups so that children can sort and eat the letters while talking to one another about which letters they have. Reutzel goes on to suggest that art experiences are also enjoyable and meaningful, such as compiling a collage of objects that begin with a given letter. Finally, he suggests the frequent use of alphabet books in the classroom. After repeated readings, children can create their own alphabet books.

Allowing children to write is the most sensible approach to teaching sound-letter relationships. When children write, they demonstrate their knowledge of such relationships. As they hear others read aloud; watch adults record their words; see the words to songs, poems, chants, and fingerplays on charts; and read books and messages, their knowledge of sound-letter relationships grows and is reflected in their writing.

THEORY INTO Practice

Role-play a conference in which you explain to a parent how you will teach phonics.

Handwriting Instruction

Instruction in the correct formation of letters should be part of the curriculum for young children only as it meets individual needs. The focus of all writing with young children should be the content of the message, rather than the formation of the letters. Children will explore the variability that is possible in producing letter forms and make judgments about the appropriateness of given forms based on the feedback they get when they use those forms for communication. Children do not need to be assigned practice in forming letters for no reason but some children may choose to copy models of print found in the classroom environment. Teachers can certainly allow or even encourage children to copy such print, but this must be the child's choice. When children have real reasons for writing legibly, they will want to learn to write letters that others can read. The desire to create letters, signs, displays, notes, invitations, and a multitude of other written forms is reason enough for children to practice legible handwriting.

In the beginning stages of writing, young children often produce letters that are backward. In a child's world, the orientation of most objects is not important—a chair is a chair, no matter which way it is facing. Children may not always attend to letter orientation, and backward letters are not indications of some sort of disability. Children may not only make letters backward; they may also begin writing on the right of the paper and produce whole words backward. Given many opportunities to engage in writing designed to communicate, children will correct these errors. A teacher should model correct grammar for children but without correcting their use of language. For example, if a child said "I goed to the store yesterday," the teacher would probably respond "Oh, what did you buy when you went to the store?"

School or District Requirements

If a school or district has established specific reading requirements for kindergartners or children in primary grades, teachers can use a variety of means in order to achieve those goals while keeping the children's contact with print appropriate and meaningful. For example, if the district requires mastery of a list of sight words, the methods for teaching those words will be determined by individual teachers. Teachers can point out those words in poems, stories, or chants and emphasize them on charts or "big books." Teachers can also focus children's attention on words from the list while taking dictation from them or when using language experience stories. Very few stories dictated by five-year-olds fail to contain *I, me, you, see, run,* or other common sight words. Teachers can then help children read those words. Multiple repetitions of such activities will usually result in chil-

TABLE 9.2

Stages in Different Aspects of Literacy

Stages in Oral Language Development	Stages in Writing Development	Stages in Reading Development
Babbling	Scribbling stage	Magical stage
Expressive jargon	Linear repetitive stage (with some scribbling)	Self-concept as a reader
One-word expressions, questions, negatives	Random-letter spelling	Bridging stage
Mature patterns mixed with immature forms	Letter-name, or phonetic, writing	Take-off stage
Mature speech	Transitional spelling	Independent reading
	Conventional spelling	Skilled stage
		Advanced skilled stage

dren's learning to recognize the required list of sight words, even when the words are presented in isolation. Teaching a sight-word vocabulary does not require drill and practice that is isolated from the children's experience or other practice that can cause some children to feel inadequate.

When reading is viewed as part of a developmental process, rather than as a set of discrete skills, both teachers and parents can place learning specific reading skills in better perspective and can celebrate a child's growth without pressuring him to perform a given skill at a particular time. Only then will our expectations be reasonable: growth for every child on a timetable set by the child himself.

ORAL LANGUAGE, WRITING, AND READING EQUAL LITERACY

Table 9.2 suggests a way of relating the development of oral language, writing, and reading: literacy. The chart is not meant to indicate that the stages coincide exactly but simply that children develop knowledge in each system simultaneously. The point is that achieving literacy is a developmental process, similar in nature to the development of oral language. Teachers and parents who view literacy in this way are much more likely to support children, wherever they are in the process, and to understand that it takes time to be a skillful user of language systems.

CHILDREN WITH SPECIAL NEEDS

Certain children may need special help in becoming successful users of printed language. Although some schools place all students with disabilities in very structured, direct instruction programs, more and more special educators are finding that these students respond to the principles of developmentally appropriate practice just like their classmates do. Special-needs students need choices, chances to follow their own interests, and opportunities for success as much as any other children.

One approach that may be helpful in teaching children with special needs is for the teacher to spend extra time with them in techniques such as assisted reading. Giving these children more specific strategy instruction in the context of authentic reading experiences may also prove beneficial (Sears, Carpenter, and Burstein 1994). Teachers must also use observational strategies to discover children's understanding of the reading and writing processes before attempting to help them learn successive steps.

Children with physical disabilities, such as sight or hearing losses, may need special materials to make their encounters with print successful. Teachers may need to provide materials printed in braille or very large print for children with vision limitations. Teachers may need to learn to sign or to have an interpreter present to take dictation from children who use sign rather than spoken language. Children who cannot hold ordinary writing instruments may need an adult or older child to act as a scribe for them; some children who have difficulty with controlling pens or pencils learn to use typewriters or computers to communicate.

Beyond these special materials and devices, children with sight or hearing challenges need teachers who assume that they will be successful, who determine what they know (even though it may take some outside help to do so), and who support their learning. It is important to remember that these children need to read and write about what is meaningful to them and to learn what they want to learn at the time, not what the teacher may have planned. Ruiz (1995) documented the stages her deaf child went through in learning to write. One of the outcomes of this study was to verify that children do not need a perfect, overlearned mastery of sound-letter relationships in order to be successful readers and writers. Ruiz's daughter learned to read and write with very little sound knowledge at all but in stages that roughly parallel those of hearing children.

Children who have not achieved the oral language skills typical of their age group may need more opportunities to learn and practice oral language forms. When words are introduced in print, some children may need more background experiences in order to develop meanings for these words. Teachers should arrange for children who have language delays to interact with other children as much as possible and to talk with adults, as well.

Some programs for children with multiple or severe disabilities help them become literate through the use of communication devices, a team effort involving speech and language specialists, and extra support in small groups (Erickson and Koppenhaver 1995). Additional information, current research, and other help regarding special programs is available from the Center for Literacy and Disability Studies, CB #8135, the University of North Carolina at Chapel Hill, Chapel Hill, NC 27599-8135.

CELEBRATING DIVERSITY

Most classrooms have some students who are bilingual or who represent various cultural and ethnic groups. Helping these children continue to develop as readers and writers is an extremely important task. Recall Cambourne's (1995) condition of expectation and the concept of engagement here, as discussed earlier in this chapter. Teachers must expect that all children are users of literacy in some way and try to discover what they know about print and how print is used in their homes. Teachers must also consider how to engage children and take steps to see that the classroom activities are appropriate and meaningful for all children, not just those from mainstream cultural groups or whose first language is English. As Schmidt (1995) states, "Schools may actually interfere with children's literacy learning if educators do not work to understand the diverse backgrounds of the children in their classrooms. Schools must take the first steps toward connecting with the children's cultures" (p. 411).

Activities that are arranged around meaningful themes may help children who speak English as their second language (ESL) become more skilled as readers and writers and speakers of English (Ernst and Richard 1995; Twiss 1996). For example, as children study houses, they can draw pictures of the houses they live in now and the houses they lived in before in their home countries. Sharing these children's pictures with the class provides opportunities for meaningful oral experiences and writing and reading experiences, whether in English or in students' native languages.

Learning to use what children know—such as how to recite street rhymes or classify grocery coupons—can help children feel that the literacy of their households is important and valued. Families can be encouraged to keep their own albums of literacy activities, perhaps using some materials provided by the school (Clements and Warncke 1994). Teachers can also use sharing time to help children present objects and events that are important to them and their families.

Teachers of children who speak dialects need to value the children's language and encourage them to develop their dialectal abilities while providing models of standard English when appropriate. For example, a child may communicate more effectively in his dialect on the playground but need a model of standard English when he has the opportunity to interview a guest speaker. Teachers who value children's language will not correct the use of dialects but will acknowledge them as an acceptable form of communication. When taking dictation from a child who speaks a dialect, the teacher should record the words in conventional spelling but not change the syntactical structure of the child's utterances. As a child reads from charts or books, the teacher should not correct the child who reads the text "My mother is going to work" as "My mama be going to work." Such a child has demonstrated an understanding of the printed text, and that is much more important than an absolutely perfect rendering of the text at this point.

ESL children need many opportunities to interact with English-speaking children and adults. The worst possible approach would be to isolate such children from the other children in order to give them special help in learning English. Children who play and talk with other children who speak English will learn the language quickly. Teachers should allow children to use their native languages when necessary for communication. In past years, schools often limited children's use of native languages in order to force them to speak English more quickly. That approach does not facilitate more rapid learning of English; rather, it does much harm to children's self-concepts and feelings of acceptance and actually hinders language development. The goal is not to eliminate children's first language but to help them achieve competence as speakers of a second language.

The concerned teacher will also learn enough about a child's native language to recognize where the child might have particular difficulties with English. For example, some sounds used in English, such as the *ch* at the beginning of *chair,* are rare in Spanish; there are differences in syntactical patterns between the two languages, as well. Chapter 8 mentioned the differences in placement of adjectives in Spanish sentences; Spanish also allows redundancy. A Spanish-speaking child might say "My mother, she," which is acceptable in Spanish. Some languages, such as Chinese, are not alphabetical; for Chinese children, teachers can provide experiences with sound-letter relationships in meaningful contexts. As a child begins to learn words in English, the teacher will record those words in print for the child and will make sure that the child has many opportunities to write and explore English (Brewer 1990).

Finally, using literature that represents the cultures of the children in the school in an authentic manner is an extremely effective means of celebrating diversity. All children need to be able to find positive images of themselves in books and other print media. Finding just the right book or story can help a child see the importance of his culture and its literacy.

CHAPTER SUMMARY

■ Literacy development takes place in observable stages, but the length of time a child spends in each stage is highly individual. Children exhibit some predictable behaviors as they move along the continuum of literacy, but each child does so at her own pace.

■ The beginning stage of learning to read is marked by the child's interest in books, followed by the child's developing a concept of himself as a reader. In the bridging stage, the child learns to attend to the print in the text, and in the take-off reader stage, he learns to use all the cueing systems simultaneously. The child then becomes an independent reader. Ideally, the ability to read continues to develop throughout one's life.

■ Long before formal instruction begins, children are doing important work in literacy development as they explore the world of print. Children need opportunities to write and to construct their knowledge of letters and the written language system.

■ The child's control of the form of written language progresses through a number of stages: scribbling, linear repetitive scribbling, random-letter spelling, letter-name spelling (or phonetic spelling), transitional spelling, to conventional spelling. The child's use of written language provides the teacher with an understanding of what the child knows about written forms that is invaluable in planning literacy experiences for her.

■ The development of literacy is best achieved in an interesting, active classroom where a wide variety of activities are available to the children. Children who are involved in interesting activities can be encouraged to use print in connection with these activities in meaningful ways.

■ Exercises in isolated skills are not appropriate for young children. Children cannot practice skills out of context and then apply what has been learned to actual literacy experiences.

■ Instruction in handwriting should be part of the curriculum for young children only as it meets individual needs to communicate more effectively.

■ In order to become literate, children with special needs should be offered choices in the materials they are expected to read, materials that match their interests, and opportunities for success in reading and writing.

■ Teachers should expect that *all* children will become literate. Being from a family who is poor or belongs to a racial or ethnic minority does not have to mean failure in school. All children need an environment that honors their knowledge of literacy and encourages their attempts to learn more about printed language.

ELTON KIKUTA
Jefferson Elementary School
CORVALLIS, OREGON

Teaching Reading through Writing

As someone who has been a primary teacher for the last twelve years, I can honestly say that the most commonly asked question by a first-grade parent is: How are you going to teach my child to read? One answer has remained a constant throughout the years: by teaching them to write. To me, writing is an effective and meaningful way to help children become familiar and comfortable with the written word.

Students come into a classroom with experiences that are unique to them. Learning how to write about these experiences empowers them to become true communicators of their knowledge. Learning how to write also helps students learn vocabulary, language patterns, and the beauty of words. Moreover, as students learn how to write, they gain the confidence that will allow them to take the risks needed to become effective readers and writers.

The students in my class have numerous opportunities to write. We have daily journals, in which students are free to write what they wish; most entries are about happenings at home and upcoming events. We also have a Writing Workshop time, in which the students have the opportunity to write, illustrate, edit, revise, and submit work to be "published" by our classroom publishing center. We often write in specific journals (e.g., math) and reflect on concepts being taught. Finally, we do theme writing, which involves the students in writing on a theme that I introduce. All these opportunities allow students to improve and apply their writing skills.

We have six steps in our writing process:

1. *Prewriting.* This is the time during which each student focuses on her topic, chooses her audience, selects her mode (poem, narrative, etc.), and decides the purpose of her writing. This step sets the tone for the entire process.

2. *Writing.* The students compose their work. During Writing Workshop time, I will often toss in a minilesson, which may involve using punctuation, making effective word choices, designing dedication pages, and the like. These minilessons give students skills and concepts to focus on as they compose their work.

3. *Editing.* We actually have three types of editing: Self-editing is done by the student who wrote the piece. Peer-editing is done by a classmate. Teacher editing is done by another adult or me.

4. *Revising.* The student corrects any errors that were found by the editors and may choose to revise parts of the story until she is satisfied. The student's work is then reedited, usually just by the teacher. The student may choose to add illustrations at this point.

5. *Publishing.* Once the student has finished her revising, her story is sent to the "publisher," who is usually a parent volunteer. The publisher laminates the covers and binds the book.

6. *Celebrating.* Once the book comes back from the publisher, the student shares her work with the class. I play fanfare music and introduce the author with gusto; the student stands in front of the class and reads her work. We also have author luncheons, in which authors from the class are invited to the room for lunch and to talk about past and future works.

Assessing children's writing is a very rewarding part of the job for me. It gives me an opportunity to see the progress that has been made and to establish goals with my students. Assessing also gives me the distinct pleasure of simply enjoying their work. Occasionally a parent is concerned with her child's writing—perhaps the handwriting is a bit askew, the use of punctuation is not quite right, or the grammar is incorrect. The parents' concerns are valid, and I let them know that their interest in their children's writing is appreciated. I also stress that learning to write, like learning to talk, is a developmental process that is unique to each child.

10

MANIPULATION
AND DISCOVERY
Mathematics

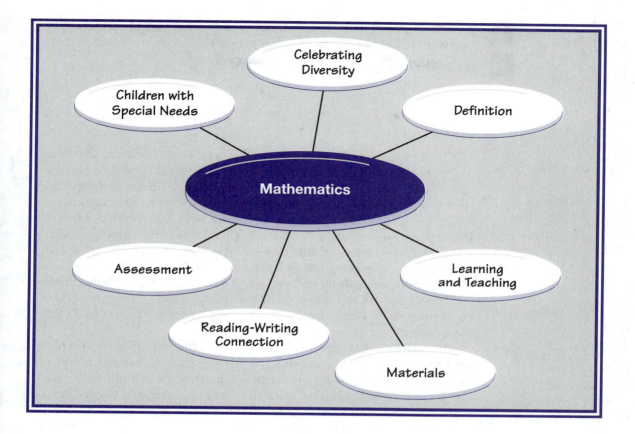

When you went to the primary school today, you found first- and second-graders using math in many more ways than you remember from your own school experience. Some children were building structures with geoblocks and seemed to be familiar with these three-dimensional shapes and their names. Other children were busily recording the scores of a game. Some were measuring objects in the classroom with a block from the block area; they were comparing their measurements with the results others had obtained.

You were very surprised to see all this activity during math time. You remember math as the period right before lunch, when the teacher taught how to solve a problem by demonstrating the steps on the chalkboard. After watching this demonstration, you worked pages and pages of similar problems on your own. In your experience, math always involved

paper-and-pencil activities. But that wasn't what you observed today. You want to know how that teacher gets her children interested in math and helps them learn concepts and algorithms.

This chapter and the next, on mathematics and science, are titled "Manipulation and Discovery" because young children learn mathematics and science from their manipulation of objects and their discovery of relationships and patterns in their environments. *Mathematics* means much more than just *arithmetic*. Perhaps when you were a child, math meant practicing arithmetic: working addition, subtraction, and multiplication problems on reams of ditto sheets. If you think of math for young children as limited to such simple equations as $1 + 1 = 2$, observe young children for a few minutes while they play. You will become aware of both their interest in mathematics and the scope of mathematics itself: "You got a bigger cookie than me!" "I am taller than you." "I have more clay than you." "I gots five pennies."

Many topics that seem relevant to mathematics activities are also relevant to science activities. As children learn to classify and group and as they think about functions and relationships, they are learning both math and science. In fact, it is often difficult to separate math and science in the early childhood classroom.

Children are mathematical thinkers outside of school. The challenge is to keep that interest, enthusiasm, and curiosity alive in the school setting. Teachers must make real efforts to make math easy for children to learn (Price 1989).

DEFINITION OF MATHEMATICS

The dictionary defines *mathematics* as "the science of numbers and their operations, interrelations, combinations, generalizations, and abstractions, and of space configurations and their structure, measurement, transformations, and generalizations." But for young children, mathematics is a way of viewing the world and their experiences in it. It is a way of solving real problems. It is an understanding of number, operations on number, functions and relations, probability, and measurement. It is much more than the pages of simple equations that you may remember working as a child.

As children grow and develop, their mathematical activities change. The youngest children explore, begin to group and sort objects, and make comparisons. As children enter school, they may be ready for labels for their mathematical thinking and for recording their discoveries using mathematical symbols. Through the early childhood years, mathematics should continue to be a manipulative activity (McCracken 1987).

The National Council of Teachers of Mathematics (NCTM 1989) calls for curricula that provide students with opportunities to **construct** their concept of mathematics across all grade levels. "Mathematics should be viewed as a *helping discipline,* not as a subject area that sorts and rejects students on their inabilities to perform" (p. 22).

HOW MATHEMATICS IS LEARNED

Piaget (1970) describes three ways that human beings can learn. They can learn from:

1. *The physical world*—Concepts such as "hot," "cold," "rough," "smooth," and so on
2. *The social world*—Concepts such as "language," "religion," "superstition," and so on
3. *The construction of mental relationships*—Concepts such as "counting," "seriation," "numeration," "conservation," and so on

Piaget calls the construction of mental relationships *logico-mathematical learning.* This type of learning will be our focus in this chapter (DeVries and Kohlberg 1987; Kamii and DeClark 1985; Kamii and Joseph 1989; Piaget 1970).

Logico-mathematical thinking requires the learner to create categories and hierarchies of objects without regard to their physical properties. For example, if you hold three yellow, wooden pencils in your hand, you will observe that they are made of wood and that they are inflexible. Those are physical facts. You cannot decide those characteristics. However, that there is a set of three pencils is a mental construct. They are physically separate objects, but their forming a set of three is a mental relationship. Think about the concept of "threeness." It is not dependent on the physical properties of the objects to which you are applying it. You could have three houses, three whales, three mustard seeds, three amoebas, and so on. In sum, the physical characteristics of the objects (including size, shape, color, texture, or temperature) do not determine that there are three; your placing them in a relationship is what makes that determination.

As learners, children abstract certain information from their experiences. For example, children learning color names learn to ignore other properties of objects and to focus on the property of color. Piaget (1970) calls this **simple abstraction** (also known as *empirical abstraction*). Although theorists do not agree on exactly how simple abstraction is accomplished, most believe that

Manipulatives aid children in constructing their understanding of concepts such as "number."

children abstract the rules that make language work from their experience with examples of language.

However, logico-mathematical concepts cannot be abstracted from experience. If, for example, a child plays with three dolls, he must reflect on the relationship he has created among the dolls; he cannot merely abstract the concept "three" because there are three dolls. We know that this is true because we can think about millions, billions, and trillions even though we have probably never had any experience with sets of this magnitude. We are able to think in these terms because we understand the hierarchical nature of the number system; that is, we understand that millions, billions, and trillions are comprised of thousands, hundreds, tens, and ones.

Piaget (1970) explains that we construct ideas via logico-mathematical learning by a process called **reflective abstraction.** This process works as follows: The learner manipulates objects and then reflects on the results. This reflection leads to reorganizing her mental constructs. Once this reorganization has taken place, it is impossible for the learner to think in exactly the same way again.

To illustrate the process of reflective abstraction, consider an example from mathematics. Most young children lack number conservation skills. Suppose a young child is presented with two identical sets of objects, such as plastic chips. In one of the sets, the chips are arranged in a row so closely that they almost touch each other; in the other set, the chips are arranged so that there are large spaces between the chips. Observing these two sets of chips, the young child will believe that the set that occupies the most space contains the most chips. After experience with manipulating sets and reflecting on the number of items in sets arranged in various physical configurations, the child will learn that the physical arrangement has no bearing on the number of objects in the set. This observation will produce a mental reorganization, so the child will never again think that physical configuration influences number.

Even very young children can recognize the difference between numbers of items in small sets—for instance, 2 cookies compared to 5 cookies. Piaget (1970) calls these *perceptual numbers.* But with numbers larger than 8 or so, perceptions are no longer reliable and a system of numbers must be constructed. This system must be based on the relationship among numbers: that 1 is included in 2, 2 in 3, and so on. When a child has created this system, he can begin to understand operations on numbers, such as addition, subtraction, multiplication, and division. Children can be taught that $2 + 3 = 5$, but *"they cannot be taught directly the relationships underlying this addition"* (Kamii and DeClark 1985, p. 14; italics in original). These relationships must be constructed by the learner, based on his observations.

When we count objects, we have to order them, so that each is counted only once. Creating that order is a mental operation. When we order objects from largest to smallest, for instance, we create a relationship among the objects. Concepts of size, time, and geometry must also be constructed by the learner.

Applied to mathematics, Vygotsky's (1978) view would prompt teachers to think about what children might be on the verge of discovering and to provide the materials and assistance that would enhance making those discoveries. Vygotsky's view would not support a step-by-step curriculum that fails to take into account the individual achievement of each child.

Think once again about your own experiences with math and math teachers. Most students have been in the situation of having a math teacher who truly understood geometry or calculus but could not teach students what he knew. If math could be taught directly from one person to another, then students could learn what was in the teacher's head. Obviously, that is not the case.

If we accept the thesis that mathematical concepts must be constructed by each learner, based on observations with real-life materials and situations, then what are the responsibilities of the teacher? One responsibility is to supply the language for the concepts that the child is constructing. A child can discover the concept "five" but must have the label *five* supplied. Teachers should use the language that mathematicians use, even with young children. It is no more difficult for children to learn the correct terminology than it is to learn some made-up version. Moreover, using the correct terminology from the start will eliminate the need to change terminology in the future (Monroe and Panchyshyn 1995/1996; Tracy 1994).

Another of the teacher's responsibilities is to arrange the environment so that the materials that best represent a concept are available for manipulation and to provide time for manipulation. When children are involved physically, the teacher must also involve them mentally by engaging them in reflective thinking; this can be accomplished simply through asking questions about what the children observe.

We can conclude, then, that mathematics instruction must be based on the hands-on manipulation of objects by learners and that symbols should be introduced after concepts are well in place.

HOW MATHEMATICS IS TAUGHT

Goals of Mathematics Instruction

The goals of mathematics instruction include:

1. Giving children opportunities to participate in many activities that encourage the development of mathematical concepts
2. Encouraging children to use mathematical knowledge to solve problems and understand relationships
3. Helping children develop a concept of mathematics as relevant to their own problems and environment, as opposed to viewing mathematics as something to memorize and repeat
4. Helping children view themselves as learners who are capable of succeeding in mathematics

These are very broad goals, and more specific objectives must be developed for introducing children to counting, measuring, grouping, adding and subtracting, and geometry. If the broad goals are achieved, no child will believe that she is not good in mathematics or that only adults know the answers and the only way a learner can know the answers is to be told them.

Mathematics in the Classroom

The curriculum standards established by the NCTM for kindergarten through fourth grade (K–4) are based on the following assumptions:

1. The K–4 curriculum should be conceptually oriented. . . .
2. The K–4 curriculum should actively involve children in doing mathematics. . . .

3. The K–4 curriculum should emphasize the development of children's mathematical thinking and reasoning abilities. . . .
4. The K–4 curriculum should emphasize the application of mathematics. . . .
5. The K–4 curriculum should include a broad range of content. . . .
6. The K–4 curriculum should make appropriate and ongoing use of calculators and computers. (NCTM 1989, pp. 17–19)

In the early childhood classroom, there are many opportunities for teaching mathematics that fit the NCTM standards. For example, most math in early childhood classrooms focuses on developing concepts rather than learning algorithms. A day in an early childhood classroom presents many problems that help children explore concepts: How many pieces of paper do we need for art? How many boys are here today? How many girls are here today? How many children are present? This is the ninth day of the month; what day will be next? How many days have we been in school this year? How many want to read Book A next? How much space will we need to store this game?

By asking questions such as these, the teacher can demonstrate to children the application of mathematics in the real world and cover a broad range of content. When learning mathematics is approached in this way, children will develop concepts as well as thinking and reasoning abilities. If children employed calculators or computers in finding answers to these questions, then all the standards would be met through answering the everyday math problems that arise in any classroom.

Greenberg (1993) explains the teacher's role as having four dimensions:

Procurement and management of appropriate materials; management of content offerings, inviting opportunities and choices.
Knowledge of the basic skills and concepts to be developed, of the process of spotting possible teaching moments, of how to converse with children, and of how to pose challenging questions.
Relationships with and knowledge of the individual child.
Knowledge of the nature of children in this age range—their emotional, social, physical, and intellectual needs, and their interests. (p. 78)

Children need to employ a variety of strategies to answer questions and solve problems. If the teacher supplies the strategy, it may not make sense to the child. For example, suppose that just before beginning an art activity, the teacher poses the question: How many pieces of paper are needed in order for every student to have one? Some younger children will need to get a piece of paper, bring it to a classmate, and repeat this

Observe two or three primary teachers as they conduct mathematics activities. What did you observe about the children's interests? their attitudes?

procedure until everyone has a paper. Others may be able to count the number of children in the class and get the corresponding number of papers. Some first- and second-graders will pass out the papers without counting the number needed in advance. Some children will be able to use the attendance figures to calculate how many classmates are absent from the class; others will need to count and may not know how to find the number who are missing. According to Schwartz (1995), authentic mathematics occurs in the classroom when children work like this with attendance figures, as well as with learning center choices and distribution of snacks or materials.

Kamii and DeClark (1985) cite an example of first-graders who were voting. The class included twenty-four students, and when the vote for the first choice was thirteen, one child said they did not need to vote for the other choices. Even after hearing the child's explanation of having a majority vote, the other children did not understand why this could be so and needed to continue the vote. Similarly, some children will be able to measure the size of a game and find an appropriate storage space; others will have to use trial and error. Children will be in many stages of understanding; they must use their own thinking to make sense of problems.

Mathematics in an early childhood program should not be scheduled for a specific period of instruction but should be an integral part of the schoolday. In the primary grades, math should be integrated into themes as much as possible, but if a theme is not appropriate for meaningful mathematics, then a math period should be scheduled.

Math instruction should also be part of the children's play time. Children can play games with cards, dominoes, or dice that help them think about math. (In some communities, such gaming materials might be unacceptable, and teachers will need to be creative in selecting other materials that encourage the same kinds of thinking.) Children in play also group, sort, classify, and seriate objects. They construct sets of blocks, beads, crayons, and other materials. Attendance records and weather charts provide many opportunities for thinking mathematically. As children play "grocery store" or participate in cooking activities, they can weigh, measure, and count in meaningful situations. Almost any topic of study lends itself to helping children develop mathematical concepts in addition to other knowledge. For example, if the class is studying shells or leaves, then classification, seriation, graphing, counting, and measuring will be integral parts of the study.

Andrews (1995) suggests that teachers who look for activities that meet the NCTM standards can find them in play activities with water, blocks, and art. Finding these activities, however, requires teachers to think much more broadly about mathematics than might have been the case several years ago. For example, young children learn very little about the calendar as it is typically taught in mathematics programs (e.g., days of the week: "Today is

_____; Yesterday was _____; Tomorrow will be _____"; date of the month: repeats similar sequence; months of the year: repeat months in order). Schwartz (1994) suggests that the calendar can be useful if it is used to record or plan for events. She suggests beginning with a daily plan (a schedule) and then adding a weekly plan and a multiple-week plan when doing so is necessary and will make sense to the children. For instance, a weekly plan would be needed to schedule for a field trip or classroom visitor, and keeping records of sprouting plants or hatching eggs would require a multiple-week plan. Teachers should try to think of how the children can really use the information from a calendar, rather than simply having them repeat words about concepts that mean nothing to them.

Instruction in mathematics should focus on providing experiences and activities for young children and asking questions to guide children's reflections. Children should be encouraged to think of mathematics as real problems to solve, not simply as calculations to complete. Burns and Richardson (1981) have identified the problem of teaching arithmetic first: "We teach the abstract processes of arithmetic first and then hope that children will learn to use these processes to solve problems. . . . The emphasis on problems must come first; it's the starting place for developing arithmetic understanding and for establishing the need for computation" (p. 39).

The Strand Model

The NCTM and several states have conceptualized the curriculum for mathematics in a *strand* model (see Figure 10.1 on page 310). (The word *strand* is meant to imply that the components of mathematics are all necessary and interrelated.) The strand model was developed to help teachers view mathematics as much more than arithmetic and to be an organizer for presenting information about mathematics. It is not a teaching model; rather, it illustrates that the real world of problem solving (through inquiry, exploration, investigation, questioning, discovery, and reflection) is the environment within which the different strands of math are used. The model is an artificial representation of mathematics because actually each strand is interrelated. Logical thinking is required to understand the nature of patterns and functions, that measurement is involved in geometry, that relationships are important in statistics, and so forth. The sections that follow will discuss each strand and offer some teaching suggestions for helping children develop concepts related to that strand.

As Figure 10.1 shows, each strand of mathematics is embedded in problem solving, as problem solving is the background for thinking in any area of instruction in math. Problem solving does not mean working word problems; it is an attitude of looking for real problems, finding ways of expressing those problems, and finding solutions to them through mathematics.

FIGURE 10.1

The Strand Model
of Mathematics

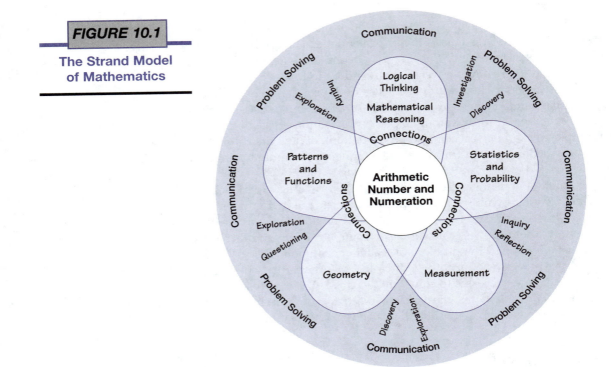

Source: Adapted from Karen Clark Smith, "Strand Model" (Corvallis, OR: Oregon State University, 1988). Used with permission.

Problem solving is not a set of standard procedures that children memorize and apply in given situations. Most real-world problems are not clearly defined; they do not lend themselves to solution by memorized strategies. Arithmetic is at the center of the model because it can be used to find and record solutions to real problems in all the strands of mathematics.

In a 1991 publication, the National Council of Teachers of Mathematics clarified the implications of teaching mathematics based on the standards established in 1989. The following principles should guide the teaching of mathematics:

- Help students work together to make sense of mathematics.
- Help students rely more on themselves to determine whether something is mathematically correct.
- Help students learn to reason mathematically.
- Help students learn to conjecture, invent, and solve problems.
- Help students to connect mathematics, its ideas, and its applications (pp. 3–4).

In addition to these principles of teaching, *communication* and *connections* have been added to the model. Note that communication of mathematical understanding crosses all the strands, which indicates that children should be able to use materials, diagrams, and pictures to relate mathematical ideas and know that learning to read, write, and discuss mathematics is important in learning mathematical concepts. Making connections indicates that teachers should help children understand the connections among the strands of mathematics. For example, when children solve problems about storage space in their classroom, the teacher may need to help them relate their solutions to mathematics.

Logical Thinking and Mathematical Reasoning

One of the strands in the model is logical thinking and mathematical reasoning. *Logical thinking* is sorting and classifying information. Any time children are faced with problems that require sorting and classifying, they must use logical thinking. Since *number* is one category of classification, sorting and classifying are important in creating mathematical categories. (Recall the three pencils mentioned at the beginning of the chapter; they can be classified as writing tools, wooden objects, painted objects, and so on as well as by number.) Some appropriate activities to help threes and fours learn to think logically include:

- Putting all the sand toys in one container
- Sorting the dishes in the housekeeping area into storage areas for plates, silverware, cooking utensils, and so on
- Classifying the unit blocks into different sizes for storage
- Sorting all the crayons, markers, and pencils into containers
- Comparing sets and using categories such as "more" and "less"

As you can imagine, this list could go on for pages and pages, as almost all the play materials in the classroom must be sorted and classified for storage each day. As children do these tasks or help teachers do them, teachers can talk to them about what they are doing and the criteria they are using for sorting and classifying. As children mature in their understanding, teachers should refine the criteria for classification so that items are sorted on the basis of increasingly complex criteria.

Fives and sixes engage in logical thinking when they sort materials, define the criteria for classifications, and seriate objects. Examples of problems for fives and sixes include:

- Sorting buttons, keys, or other objects into groups and then explaining the criteria by which the classifications were made—The teacher might then encourage children to think of other criteria by which the same objects could be grouped. If the children had already grouped buttons by color, then they might group them by size, by number of holes, by whether they are shanked or unshanked, or by what they are made of.
- Creating Venn diagrams with yarn circles—If one circle contains objects that are blue and the other contains objects that are square, the intersection of the circles will contain square, blue objects—yet another category.
- Sorting models of zoo animals and farm animals for storage—As each is placed in the container, the child makes a tally mark and then compares the sizes of the sets of animals. This is a meaningful and logical extension of classification into arithmetic.
- Going on a "circle hunt" to find as many circles as possible while on a walk—Groups record and then compare the numbers of circles they find. These numbers can be saved and compared to the numbers of squares or triangles found on other hunts.
- Playing card games (Old Maid, Rummy, Go Fish, and so on)

Sevens and eights can continue to classify objects and compare sets that are created. Tasks for sorting and classifying can be extended to sets of numbers; for most tasks, children can use arithmetic to record the operations. Teachers can stimulate sorting and classifying skills in the following ways:

- Asking questions—"If all these numbers are even numbers, can seven be included in this set?"
- Getting children to think about what pieces of information are needed to solve problems—"We know that our classroom is forty tiles long and thirty tiles wide and that it has eight windows. How many tiles cover the floor?"
- Posing "if-then" statements—"If you double your score and then find half of it, what will you have?"
- Asking children how many ways they can think of to get an answer to a problem
- Having children solve problems and defend their solutions

Seriation   Seriation tasks are inherent in the play experiences of even very young children. Seriation requires keeping in mind the characteristics of one element while comparing it to another element. Most very young children can compare two objects and determine which is larger and which is smaller. When asked to create a series based on size from a set of items, most four-year-olds will pick up two items at a time, compare them, determine the larger of those two, and then pick up two more items without considering the previous items. In their play, threes and fours will begin to place objects such as cans on the grocery store shelves in some kind of order, but seriating a large number of items is not an appropriate task. Appropriate seriating tasks for threes and fours include arranging dolls in the doll bed; arranging pairs of objects from the classroom (crayons, spools, spoons, plates, and so on) into sets of larger objects and smaller objects; arranging trucks in the block center by size; and arranging sets of three or four blocks into series.

Most fives can complete a simple seriation of more than three items. As children become more skilled, the numbers of objects to be seriated can be increased. Some classroom problems involving seriation for this age group include arranging stacks of paper by ascending size on the art shelves; arranging blocks in the unit block area by ascending or descending size; arranging strips of paper that represent the heights of each class member; and arranging stacks of blocks in ascending order (one block, three blocks, five blocks, and so on).

Sevens and eights can accomplish the following kinds of seriation tasks: arranging sets of numbers in order or in patterns (a seriation task similar to arranging stacks of blocks); finding missing items in a series; and creating double series (a set of balls to match a set of bats).

Statistics and Probability

Another strand in the model is statistics and probability. Statistics is an appropriate topic in the early childhood classroom when it is defined as comparing and analyzing information. Many activities in the classroom involve relationships that can be compared and analyzed. Some appropriate tasks for threes and fours include:

- Observing differences when snack choices are arranged on trays—If the children had a choice of orange juice or milk, the teacher could arrange the juice cups in a set and the milk cups in another set and then create a chart or graph with pictures of the snack choices to represent the information. If eleven children chose orange juice and nine chose milk, there would be eleven squares with pictures of orange juice and nine with pictures of milk.
- Observing and comparing the number of sunny days, cloudy days, snowy days, or rainy days marked on the calendar

Fives and sixes can carry out the following kinds of tasks:

- Creating graphs of information, such as their choices at snack time
- Graphing how many children walk, ride the bus, or come by private car to school

- Graphing how many children have on certain types of shoes
- Voting for their favorite books and recording the results with tally marks
- Collecting and analyzing data on such topics as birth dates (Curcio and Folkson 1996)

Sevens and eights can work with information that is important to them by:

- Graphing how many children eat the school lunch and how many bring their lunch each day for a month—Children can then try to determine why the choices were made. (Were there more children eating the school lunch when hamburgers were served as opposed to meat loaf?)
- Surveying the school to determine the students' favorite play equipment
- Tallying the number of books checked out of the class library, comparing the information for several weeks, and trying to determine the reasons for any variations

In the process of solving these problems, children use computation and logical thinking as well as statistics.

Children do not develop a firm concept of probability until they are in the concrete operational stage of thinking. However, sevens and eights can begin some interesting activities with probability involving small numbers. For example, they might flip a coin for a given number of times and record the number of heads and tails. Or they might draw colored cubes from a bag containing ten cubes: seven red and three blue. As each draw is completed, the child tallies the color of the cube and then returns the cube to the bag. After ten draws, the child predicts how many cubes of each color are actually in the bag. Drawing, tallying, and predicting can be repeated several times.

Measurement

Measurement is a third strand in the model. Measurement experiences for young children must be based on their ability to conserve length and area. Many children are interested in measuring, and some measurements are meaningful to them. For instance, children are usually quite interested in their own heights, weights, ages, and so on.

Threes and fours can take part in activities such as the following:

- Exploring measurement through materials such as balance scales
- Finding a block of the proper length to fill a given space
- Measuring each other for new shoes or new clothes

- Using different-sized containers in the sand and water areas—Children can use one container to fill another and thereby develop concepts of "larger" and "more."
- Using blocks to build walls or towers with lengths and heights equal to those of other objects

Fives and sixes still do not have stable understandings of linear measures, but they can begin to use nonstandard and some standard measures to measure objects of interest to them. Children of this age are still usually most interested in measuring themselves. The following kinds of measurement are appropriate:

- Measuring their heights with strips of paper or yarn and hanging the strips on the wall for comparison
- Measuring their tables with their hands or some other personal item such as their shoes
- Measuring the classroom by counting how many steps it takes to cross it
- Determining the number of pieces of paper that are required to cover their tables—If each group is given a different size of paper to use, the children can begin to recognize the need for standard measures.
- Measuring the cloth needed to cover the doll bed
- Using containers in the sand and water that are standard measuring cups or metric measures—The children can count how many cups are required to fill a quart or half-gallon milk carton.
- Measuring ingredients required in cooking experiences—Remember that a container that holds one-quarter cup is still one cup to the pre-operational child; therefore, a real understanding of fractions usually will not be gained from cooking experiences.
- Estimating the sizes of objects using strings—The children can cut strings that they think will fit around their heads or their waists and then try them out to check their predictions. They can use this same technique for estimating the girth of their Halloween pumpkins, a watermelon, or their teacher.
- Measuring the heights of their block constructions or determining how many tiles their constructions cover on the floor

Sevens and eights can continue to use nonstandard linear measurements. Some children may be able to make the transition to standard measures, especially when a task does not require repeated measures. Some appropriate measurement tasks for this age group include:

- Choosing the appropriate measuring device for measuring a piece of paper for a book cover or a piece of wood for something they are building in the woodworking area

- Accurately measuring given quantities of liquid, such as cups, pints, quarts, liters, and so on
- Using units (squares of paper or wooden blocks) to measure surface areas and making comparisons with arithmetical computations

As always, the emphasis should be on meaningful measurement tasks; the transition to standard measurements should be based on individual development.

Time   Time is a component of measurement that is often emphasized in programs for young children. However, children do not have the ability to quantify and integrate durations of time until about age ten (Levin, Wilkening, and Dembo 1984). Preschoolers are certainly aware of time, as they hear adults talk about time for snack, time for outdoor play, time to get ready to go home, and so on, but they believe that they can influence the passage of time.

One approach to assessing a child's concept of time involves first determining if she is familiar with an egg timer and then asking her to observe the flow of sand in the timer as she completes a task such as walking around a table. Most preoperational children will think that the flow is slow if they go slowly and fast if they move more quickly. Preschoolers can predict whether it will take more or less time for sand to flow out of containers of different sizes, but they do not have a stable understanding of the concept of time.

Teaching young children to tell time is not an appropriate goal. Preschoolers can be shown the clock face when it is time for certain events in their day, but they should not be expected to use that information. No one should expect to hear a preschooler say "It is ten minutes until time for snack." For a preschooler, a digital clock is easier to read than a clock with a dial because he only needs to recognize the numerals. A dial requires that the child translate the numbers 1, 2, 3, and so on to 5, 10, and 15 to indicate minutes, while also remembering that the numbers stand for the hour. Reading the time from a digital clock does not mean that the child understands time; it just means he can recognize the numerals and read them in two parts.

Fives and sixes may attach more meaning to the passage of time, but learning to read time is still only appropriate for individual children who are ready for the information. Some sevens and eights will begin to make the transition to a stable view of time and will need to learn to tell time. For other children, time still will not be a stable concept and they will need to know only the times that are important in their daily schedules.

Money   The money system is another component of measurement that is often included in curriculum plans. Remember that for young children, *bigger* means "more." Shel Silverstein (1974) describes the young child's idea of money very accurately in his poem "Smart":

Smart

My dad gave me one dollar bill
'Cause I'm his smartest son,
And I swapped it for two shiny quarters
'Cause two is more than one!

And then I took the quarters
And traded them to Lou
For three dimes—I guess he don't know
That three is more than two!

Just then, along came old blind Bates
And just 'cause he can't see
He gave me four nickels for my three dimes,
And four is more than three!

And I took the nickels to Hiram Coombs
Down at the seed-feed store,
And the fool gave me five pennies for them,
And five is more than four!

And then I went and showed my dad,
And he got red in the cheeks
And closed his eyes and shook his head—
Too proud of me to speak!*

It is very difficult for a young child to understand that a dime is worth more than a nickel when a nickel is physically larger than a dime. Money should be a topic in the curriculum only if children have a real use for the knowledge. Preschool children certainly do not have a concept of how much money is needed to buy objects. Some preschoolers think that if you need more money, you need only write a check. Preschoolers can begin to explore the ideas of money as they play "grocery store," "shoe store," or "riding on the bus." Teachers may make play money available for the children. Some fives and sixes may need more knowledge of money if they receive a small allowance and save money for special purchases. Sevens and eights can begin to use computations that involve money and change if the problems are real. For example, they might learn about change if some of them buy lunch at school: What amount of money did each student bring to buy lunch? Is it enough? Will there be change? If there is change, how much will it be? Can anyone buy an extra carton of milk today? How much more must the teacher pay for lunch?

Geometry

A fourth strand of mathematics is geometry. Geometry is more than Euclidean shapes. It includes topology (the connectedness of objects) and concepts of how shapes and forms are related to each other. The sequence of development of geometric concepts includes recognition of familiar shapes such as spoons, recognition of figures as open or closed, and recognition of Euclidean shapes such as squares and triangles (Copeland 1984). Very young children have difficulty recognizing the differences between shapes such as squares and rectangles. The emphasis for young children should be on experiences that help them develop concepts of space and the relationships of objects in space. Some examples of activities to encourage geometric understanding follow.

Threes and fours can use two- and three-dimensional objects of various shapes in their play and discover the properties of these shapes. At this age, children do not necessarily need to learn the names of shapes. They can build with blocks and begin to discover how space can be enclosed with lines and that objects can be inside or outside these lines.

Fives and sixes can do activities such as playing with blocks; playing with pattern blocks and exploring these shapes and their relationships; constructing a square from four smaller squares; and discovering that a regular hexagon can be divided into two regular trapezoids.

At any age, the emphasis should be on manipulation and on reflecting on what has been constructed, rather than on learning labels. Some children will be interested in labels and will want to know them, but drill and practice are not appropriate for children of this age.

Teachers can encourage sevens and eights in the following kinds of tasks:

- Continuing to explore both two-dimensional and three-dimensional shapes
- Exploring area and volume of different shapes—Children can fill hollow three-dimensional shapes such as cylinders, cubes, rectangular prisms, and spheres with sand or water and determine how they could compute the volume of each.
- Exploring spaces on a geoboard and constructing various shapes and repeating or rearranging them
- Using geometry and measurement in planning room arrangements that will fit everything, use space to the best advantage, and allow for the best movement patterns
- Applying their growing knowledge of geometry to problems in arranging the furniture in their rooms at home

The theme of change can be developed in mathematics programs for young children. The following are only a few of the possible activities for children of different ages:

➤ Create a shape using pegs on a geoboard; then change the shape, but use the same number of pegs to make it.

➤ Ask children in small groups to go outside and measure their shadows every thirty minutes from 9:30 in the morning until 2:00 in the afternoon. Record the results in a notebook.

➤ Create a chart to compare measurements of students' heights/lengths when they were born and now. Are the students who were the shortest babies now the shortest students?

➤ Weigh the children at the beginning of the year and then again in January and May. Compare the amount of change in weight at each measuring period.

➤ Fold a piece of paper in half, and count the number of sections created (two). Fold it in half again and count the sections again (four). Fold it in half again and count again (eight). If the paper is large enough, fold again and count again. Why does making a single fold produce more sections each time?

➤ Create a "change" game. Give each small group of children a set of Unifix cubes. Ask each child to change the set and then explain how it was changed. (Children can add cubes, subtract cubes, group cubes into more sets, and so on.)

Patterns and Functions

The fifth strand of mathematics is patterns and functions. Patterns are visual, auditory, spatial, numerical, or combinations of these. The base 10 system is organized in patterns of ones, tens, hundreds, and so on, and patterns are evident in all the strands of mathematics. Promoting recognition of patterns is extremely important in helping young children develop mathematical concepts (Burton 1982; Ditchburn 1982). Recognizing and creating patterns helps children learn to order, predict, and estimate. Children can make patterns with beads, blocks, tiles, pattern blocks, pieces of paper, shoes, their bodies, leaves, flowers, seeds, and numerous other materials. Children can be helped to recognize patterns on the calendar, in blocks, in games, and in art materials.

Functions are the patterns created when certain actions are performed on objects or numbers. When a piece of paper is folded once, the result is two sections of paper; when it is folded twice, the result is four sections; and so on. When preschoolers can begin to observe how many sections are created when they fold pieces of paper or that there are two shoes for every one person, that is functional thinking. Some ideas for encouraging functional thinking in threes and fours include having children observe the number of shoes per person when they take off their shoes for a movement experience; observe the number of crayons or pencils per person; and fold paper and observe the number of sections created.

Fives and sixes can record their findings about activities in function tables. For example, if every person has two shoes, a function table of this information would look like this:

People	Shoes
1	2
2	4
3	6
4	8

The children should be encouraged to find patterns among numbers in the table. Function tables could be created for a variety of activities.

Sevens and eights can work on creating more involved function tables. A child might create a table of a mathematical operation, such as multiplying by 4, and let a partner determine the function illustrated. Tables could be created for addition, subtraction, multiplication, or division problems from the children's experiences. (Note that this is *not* a suggestion to teach children mathematical operations formally.)

Guess the Function

2	8
3	12
4	16

Arithmetic

As noted earlier, arithmetic is at the center of the model, and like problem solving, it is a part of every strand of mathematical thinking. Young children can use basic arithmetic concepts in solving problems. Arithmetic includes the concepts of one-to-one correspondence, counting, number, place value, operations on whole numbers, and fractions.

One-to-One Correspondence   One-to-one correspondence is the concept that one object can be related to another object. Thousands of pages of workbook exercises have been filled with pictures of rows of dogs and rows of bones, with directions to the child to draw a line from one dog to one bone. Worksheets like these are supposed to help children recognize that if there is a bone for each dog, then the sets are equivalent.

In fact, these practice sheets are not very effective in helping children understand one-to-one correspondence because children need to create their own sets and construct their own understanding of equivalency. Providing them with sets that someone else has constructed does not allow them to develop the concept. For those of us who are no longer preoperational thinkers, it seems obvious that equivalency of sets can be established by counting. But for preoperational children who do not conserve number, counting is not a reliable strategy.

In one study (Kamii 1982), the researcher presented children with two sets of cubes, one set larger than the other. The experimenter told the children, "I will add cubes to the smaller set. Tell me when it has the same number of cubes as the large set." The researcher found that preoperational children continued to watch as blocks were added and spoke up when they believed that the set to which blocks were being added had more. The children failed to notice when the sets were equal.

Some teachers have tried to teach children one-to-one correspondence by having them physically attach one element of each set to an element in another set. Even these physical connections are not as effective in helping children develop the concept as are repeated experiences in creating sets of their own. What children must do is create sets and then think about the relationships that exist between the sets. Children create sets that help them understand one-to-one correspondence when they place one chair at the table for each person, put one brush in each jar of paint, pass out one sheet of paper for each person, or give each person a carton of milk. Teachers can help guide children's reflections by asking them if they had too few, enough, or too many chairs, brushes, papers, or cartons of milk. One-to-one correspondence also figures in seriation tasks, as children relate items in one series to items in another.

Counting   If you asked the next three or four people that you met on the street what young children should learn first about mathematics, it's likely they would all say counting. Some program goals include counting to 10 as appropriate objectives for fours and counting to 100 as an appropriate objective for fives or sixes.

Counting can be either rote counting or rational counting. *Rote counting* is naming the numbers in order without making any connection between numbers and sets of real-life objects. *Rational counting* is the ability to order and enumerate objects in sets. Rote counting is often encouraged by parents and teachers, but when children learn to count by rote it is *social knowledge* (that is, things children learn merely because they are told to do so by an adult) and not really related to mathematical understanding.

Learning to count proceeds in stages: The child knows that each object must have a distinct tag (counting word); the child knows that the list of tags must have a particular order; and the child makes the connection between counting and number. Teachers of young children can appreciate these stages, just as they appreciate stages in learning to walk or to write (Price 1989). Two-year-olds have a concept of counting and often attach number words to objects, even though it is almost impossible for them to count correctly. Researchers (Bullock and Gelman 1977; Gelman and Tucker 1975) have found that very young children can attach number tags to objects in ascending order (1, 5, 7) long before they can count accurately.

Counting is, of course, a very useful problem-solving strategy. It is best if the child discovers the strategy rather than has it imposed by the teacher or parent. For example, rather than saying "Count the plates and get a napkin from the cupboard for each one," a parent or teacher might say "Make sure that we have enough napkins for each plate." Discovery of counting as a problem-solving strategy takes some time, but it is worth it to the child.

Teachers will find many opportunities for helping children develop the concept of counting. Threes and fours are likely to be able to count only a limited number of objects correctly; therefore, counting activities should be individualized to match each child's abilities. Threes and fours can count:

- Pieces of paper needed for art
- Number of place settings needed in the housekeeping center
- Blocks used to build a structure
- Chairs or mats needed for the group
- Dolls in the doll center
- Trucks and cars

Most counting experiences for fives and sixes will involve larger numbers, such as the number of papers needed for the whole class, and will involve recording and comparing different numbers. Fives and sixes can become involved in:

- Counting the pieces of equipment taken outdoors and recording the number of items so that everything can be put away later
- Keeping score in games
- Counting the number of children absent each day and comparing the records over a month
- Counting the number of pieces of paper needed for a class project and multiplying to find how many would be needed for two projects
- Counting by twos, fives, and tens

Sevens and eights can continue to count, record, and compare numbers that have meaning for them in their daily lives and also learn to count by threes and fours.

Number Children's concepts of number develop fairly rapidly between the ages of about three and six. In their investigation of children's concepts of the magnitude of the first nine numbers in the counting string, Murray and Mayer (1988) found that most three-year-olds recognized 1 as a small number and other numbers as large but did not make other discriminations. Four-year-olds were able to discriminate between small and medium-sized numbers and small and large numbers, but they had trouble comparing medium-sized and large numbers. Five-year-olds could categorize all the numbers correctly.

Number can be explored without computation in many ways. Threes and fours can make books of numbers that relate to them: their measurements, ages, shoe sizes, clothing sizes, birthdates, number of teeth, and so on. Fives and sixes can explore how numbers are used in or on buildings. The teacher might ask the children to talk about what they learn from how the rooms are numbered, how seats in an auditorium are numbered, or how the houses on a street are numbered. The teacher might also have children look for as many other uses of numbers as they can find (Turkel and Newman 1988). Sevens and eights can continue to look for numbers in the environment and explore larger numbers.

Developing a sense of numbers and their relationships to each other (numbers can be less than, more than, or part of other numbers) is basic to being able to carry out operations on whole numbers (Van de Walle 1988). Primary children should have many opportunities to explore numbers and their relationships to each other before they are introduced to formal addition and subtraction exercises.

Place Value   Children obviously need to know that 12 and 21 do not represent the same number. Traditionally, place value has been included in the first-grade curriculum and again in the second-grade curriculum before children begin working on two-digit addition problems that require regrouping. Kamii and DeClark (1985) and Kamii and Joseph (1989) recommend that place value not be taught at all in first grade but that it be included in second grade when children use it to solve two-digit addition problems. They cite extensive research and classroom observations in which less than half the children below fourth grade understood that the 1 in 16 represents 10. In traditional mathematics texts, children are taught to write the answers to two-digit problems beginning with the ones column. Kamii believes that this is also social knowledge (as defined earlier). Real understanding of place value is not achieved until children are solid conservers and can understand the part-whole relationships involved in place value. Building an understanding of tens requires extensive experience in doing arithmetic; teachers cannot foster that understanding simply by supplying materials bundled into tens to help the child see the tens and ones in a problem.

Kamii and Joseph (1988) advocate major changes in instruction in two-digit addition. These researchers interviewed hundreds of children in grades one through three and found that almost all the children thought that the 1 in 16 was 1, even after hours and hours of place-value instruction. They encouraged children to work out solutions to two-digit problems and

then discuss how they achieved their solutions and provided the children with single cubes that they could use in solving the problems. Most of the children started with the tens column and worked through several solutions. They argued and debated with each other about their answers to the problems.

This problem-solving approach resulted in a much higher percentage of children knowing that the 1 in 16 represents 10 at the end of second grade. These authors are not suggesting that children should work math problems without manipulatives. What they are advocating is the use of materials, such as cubes or chips, that are not prearranged into sets of ten for the children. If the children discover that putting materials into sets of ten makes working the problems easier, then they can arrange the materials themselves.

Richardson and Salkeld (1995) relate the story of a class of five- and six-year-olds who could answer the question of how many days they had been in school that year by responding "fifty-seven"; they also could answer "5 tens and 7 ones" when asked how to write *57*. Yet when asked how many groups of ten could be made from the thirty-four cupcakes a mother had brought for a party, these same children guessed "six, eight, or ten." With this, the teacher was reminded that children can use words without understanding the concepts behind them.

This point is well illustrated in another story from Richardson and Salkeld (1995), this one about a child who was counting on his fingers to complete a sheet of addition problems. Observing the child, the teacher asked him how many cookies he would have if he had five and got three more; he answered "eight." When the teacher asked why he was counting on his fingers to solve problems that he knew, he explained, "These are my math problems. You asked me about cookies" (p. 28). It is easy for children to memorize what to do on paper-and-pencil tasks without having any understanding of what they are doing. The same can be said of many adults. For instance, you could say that to divide a fraction by a fraction, you invert the second fraction and multiply; however, you might not have the slightest understanding of why that algorithm works or what it really means to divide a fraction by a fraction.

The approach advocated by Kamii and her colleagues (Kamaii and Clark 1985; Kamaii and Joseph 1988, 1989) requires teachers to think carefully about what children can learn (as opposed to what they can do on paper) and to conduct research in their own classrooms to uncover the understandings of their children. A curriculum based on games and the children's arguing and debating their solutions to problems will involve teachers in planning, observing, and evaluating much more than a tra-

PARENTS AND MATHEMATICS

■ Invite parents to observe a group of students when they are negotiating the answers to math problems.

ditional program in which the teacher's job is to cover the material in the textbook.

Operations on Whole Numbers Threes and fours can begin to develop the concepts necessary for addition, subtraction, multiplication, and division, even though these problems are not presented to them symbolically or formally. Children can observe many meaningful examples of operations on whole numbers at home or in school settings:

- They see that when objects from two separate sets are combined, one larger set is created. While playing in the block center, children may put the blocks from two piles together and create one larger pile. They may pick up the crayons from each place at the table and put them together.
- They observe subtraction when they see a set reduced as elements are taken away. If a plate of crackers for snack is passed around, children see the number reduced as each child takes a portion. After they spend some pennies, they know that they have fewer.
- They observe multiplication when the teacher counts materials by sets or when they count groups such as place settings rather than individual pieces.
- They observe division when materials must be shared in equal portions. Often, it is a child's responsibility to determine how to divide food or play materials so that everyone has an equal share.

Instruction in addition and subtraction should not be attempted formally for fives and sixes until the children have achieved reversibility in thinking and understand subtraction as the inverse of addition. Instruction in multiplication and division should continue informally as they are needed to solve real problems; these operations can be presented as repeated addition or repeated subtraction. Fives and sixes can improve their arithmetic understanding by observing adults recording equations for arithmetic operations; recording the equations themselves; counting the sets of shoes worn by the children in the class; or passing out cards for a game by sets of two.

Sevens and eights will continue the use of addition and subtraction to solve problems. Teachers can begin more formal instruction in multiplication and division with children of these ages.

Each child should have numerous experiences working both multiplication and division problems with manipulative materials before she is asked to use the symbols. Children should not be asked to work problems without access to manipulative materials with which the problems can be solved. As addition, subtraction, and multiplication facts become familiar to children, they may not use the manipulatives on every problem, but they should always be available. Every child should view problems involving operations as something to be worked out, not as something that will be unsolvable if she forgets a fact.

Arithmetic is basic, but it should always be a tool for solving problems, not simply an end in itself. Achieving expertise in computation should be secondary to achieving the thinking and reasoning skills that are possible through all the strands of mathematics.

Fractions   As in other area of mathematics, the symbols for fractions should not be introduced until the concept is fully understood. Teachers of young children can use fractional terms (*one-half, one-fourth*) when they are relevant to children's experiences: one-half of a graham cracker, one-half cup of water, one-fourth of the paper, and so on. But the symbol $\frac{1}{2}$ should not be introduced until second or third grade. Fractions can indicate either how many of a set of equal-sized parts are being considered or a number. For children who are just developing a stable concept of whole numbers, formal fractions will be difficult.

Manipulatives for helping children learn about fractions include pattern blocks, fraction tiles, and teacher-made materials such as cardboard circles, squares, and rectangles cut into various fractional parts. Even for second- and third-graders, work with fractions should involve oral problem solving with manipulatives. Goals of instruction in fractions should include helping children know what halves, thirds, and fourths mean; know the difference between unit fractions (elements of a set) and nonunit fractions (parts of one whole); and recognize equivalent fractions.

MATERIALS FOR INSTRUCTION

Many excellent materials for helping children make discoveries about mathematical concepts are available today. Both commercial and teacher-made materials can be useful in good math programs. Commercial materials such as Unifix cubes, pattern blocks, geoblocks, and base 10 blocks are basic for a sound manipulatives-based program. Teacher-made manipulatives might include bean sticks, boxes of junk to be sorted and classified, glass beads on strings in sets from one to ten, geoboards, and so on. Most of these materials can be purchased as well as made by the teachers. When creating manipulative materials, teachers should ensure that mathematical concepts are presented accurately and that the materials do not distract from the concept to be learned. One does not bring in an elephant to teach the concept "gray."

Some materials—such as Cuisenaire rods, Dienes blocks, and Montessori rods—are not good choices for helping young children develop concepts of number. Remember that most of these children do not yet con-

serve number or length. When given a Cuisenaire rod that is supposed to
represent 5 because it is five times as long as the 1 rod, most preconservers
will say that this rod is one (and it is one rod). According to Piaget (1952),
"Cuisenaire rods . . . are open to the most totally opposed methods of using
them, some of them genuinely operative if the child is allowed to discover
for himself the various operations made possible by spontaneous manipulations of the rods, but the others essentially intuitive or figurative when
they are limited to external demonstrations and to explanations of the configurations laid out by the teacher" (p. 73).

Better representations of number are individual objects such as Unifix
cubes, chips, or beans. Once when observing a group of gifted kindergartners, the author saw a child build a square pyramid with Cuisenaire rods.
To determine how many units had been used to construct the structure,
she still counted each of the different-sized rods as one unit, even after several explanations by the teacher about how to count each rod.

Other materials may also prove less effective in helping children
develop concepts. For children who do not yet conserve length, a counting
line is not the best strategy for promoting understanding of addition and
subtraction. It is also important to be careful when choosing materials for
representing fractional parts of a whole. Objects that cannot be divided
accurately are not appropriate for developing fractional concepts. Pattern
blocks and fraction tiles are better representations of fractions than apples
and pies, which cannot be cut accurately into fractional pieces.

Some teachers continue to use worksheets and workbooks rather than
manipulatives. They may believe that manipulatives are too expensive,
that manipulatives take up too much time, or that parents expect to see

MATERIALS FOR INSTRUCTION

Materials should be provided that are the best possible models for the given concept to be learned.

paper-and-pencil evidence of children's work (Stone 1987). Some manipulatives are expensive, but materials of good quality will last indefinitely, and many manipulatives can be constructed by teachers for very little cost. Using manipulatives does take time, but covering the topics without achieving understanding is not efficient teaching. Taking the time initially to make sure that children understand will save time eventually because the same topics will not have to be taught over and over.

Calculators, Computers, and Young Children

Most young children have had some experience with calculators (Pagni 1987). Most households have one or more calculators that children have observed being used, and many young children have their own calculators.

It is reasonable for children to use calculators to solve arithmetic problems and to check their own and their peers' solutions to problems. But a calculator cannot substitute for real experience as a way of developing a concept of number or appropriate counting strategies. Thinking about the problem and how it can be solved should be the focus of instruction. Teachers should not be so concerned about developing children's basic skills that they do not use calculators. Calculators can be useful in computation.

Young children should be allowed to explore calculators. They may enjoy pushing the buttons and watching the numbers change. Older children can begin using calculators to solve equations and learn the importance of entering the numbers correctly. By the time children are seven or eight, they can use calculators in computation and for exploring functions and relationships among numbers.

Some computer programs can enhance a good manipulatives-based math program. Children who have had real experience with geoblocks and geoboards can extend their experiences with a software program called Logo, especially if they are able to manipulate the turtle. Yelland (1995) found that children using Logo worked in a collaborative environment to solve problems and that their reasoning and logic skills were enhanced. Other software programs are being developed almost daily. Many are simply drill-and-practice on arithmetic problems, but more and more programs ask children to interact with different situations and think logically about outcomes. Teachers should evaluate software carefully and choose programs that allow children to think, rather than simply practice algorithms.

THEORY INTO Practice

Write a paragraph explaining your beliefs about how computation should be taught to young children. Discuss your views with members of your group. Try to reach some consensus.

THE READING-WRITING CONNECTION

Teachers can help children use reading and writing to record their questions, their discoveries, and their solutions to problems. Many teachers (especially those in the primary grades) provide each child with a notebook in which to write his questions and solutions. The teacher responds to the child's work in the notebook, writes questions, and presents new problems to be solved. Children are also encouraged to read each other's notebooks and to discuss their solutions and discoveries.

In describing the reading and writing experiences of her class, Richards (1990) noted that children made books of ways they had solved problems and that their writing about mathematics was quite varied. They wrote summaries, descriptions, definitions, reports, instructions, notes, evaluations, explanations, and personal responses to math. Figure 10.2 is an example of writing about math.

Scott, Williams, and Hyssop (1992) suggest that mathematics is best conceptualized as communication and reasoning, not as a series of mysterious rules and symbols. They found that second-graders responded well to journal writing experiences in the math curriculum, including stories, pictures, and diagrams to explain their understandings.

FIGURE 10.2

**Writing
about Math**

$$\boxed{10} - \boxed{4} = \boxed{6}$$

Once opon a time ther was
ten cavemen four of them
went into a cave and got lost
the rest got very scared
and ran a way they only
came back to see if they
would come out but they never
did! So if you see a cave or six
cave men running dont ask them why
they are doing it!

by Melanie Kebler

Literature and Mathematics

Literature can also contribute to the instructional program in mathematics. The most obvious types of literature to use are counting books and rhymes. Many excellent counting books are available. In addition, problems in classification, ordering, and the basic operations can be introduced through literature. As described by Whitin (1994), "Books portray mathematics not as a sea of symbols and potentially frustrating mental tasks that have no meaning for children but as a tool for making decisions and solving problems" (p. 10).

Books that introduce addition and subtraction include *The Doorbell Rang* (Hutchins 1986), *Blueberries for Sal* (McCloskey 1948), and *Anno's Counting House* (Anno 1982). Having read these books, children can dramatize the stories and then write the equations from the stories or watch the teacher write them as they discover them.

Pat Hutchins's book *Clocks and More Clocks* (1970) is interesting for children exploring telling time. They can discuss what was wrong with the clocks in the story and try placing clocks in different parts of the building. *The Grouchy Ladybug* (Carle 1977) also illustrates the passage of time with clock faces. McMillan's (1989) *Time To . . .* uses photographs to record the daily events in the life of a kindergartner. Primary-grade children might enjoy *The Stopwatch* (Lloyd n.d.), especially if someone has a new stopwatch or a watch with a timer. Children can clock themselves participating in various activities and compare their times with those of their classmates.

One example of a book that introduces ordinal numbers (first, second, third) is *The Very Hungry Caterpillar* (Carle 1981). Children can review what happened to the caterpillar in sequence and then create their own stories of events that happened to them in sequence. *Freight Train* (Crews 1978) is another example of a book that encourages thinking about ordinal numbers. It can also be useful for classification; children can classify the types of cars illustrated (Harsh 1987).

Classification is also important in the story "The Lost Button" from *Frog and Toad Are Friends* (Lobel 1970). In that story, Frog and Toad go for a walk. When they return, Toad discovers that he has lost a button. As they retrace their path, they find several buttons, but none matches the description Toad gives until his button is found. In dramatizing the story, children can be encouraged to think about classifications from their own button collections. Tischler (1988) suggests a game in which one child plays Toad and rejects buttons by naming the criteria they do not meet. The child who has the correct button becomes the next Toad. Many different activities based on the buttons are possible.

Making pop-up books provides an opportunity for children to learn about angles, shapes, and estimation, as they fold origami figures and then create pop-up cards to hold them (Huse, Bluemel, and Taylor 1994).

THEORY INTO *Practice*

Find a children's book that includes some mathematical ideas. Remembering that children need real experiences with manipulatives, plan an activity following a reading of the book that involves using purchased or teacher-constructed manipulatives.

Younger children will need some assistance in creating figures and cards, but those in second grade and older should be able to work on their own. After making their own pop-up books, children can examine commercially published books in order to determine how the effects were created.

As discussed earlier, children learning mathematics concepts need to know the language to express the concepts, but knowing the language is not equivalent to understanding the concepts. Children may actually understand concepts before they are able to verbalize their understanding. Therefore, teachers must be sure to allow children to demonstrate their understanding with manipulatives rather than just writing their answers or telling what they understand.

ASSESSMENT

When assessing their knowledge of mathematics, it is not enough to find out what children can do—it is important to know what children understand. Historically, educators assumed that if children could do things such as counting and adding, they understood what they were doing. Research has proven otherwise.

Richardson (1988) found that children who could count often had no concept of number and some who could do place-value problems in their workbooks could not use place-value information to solve real problems. Labinowicz (1980) reported similar findings: Only about one-half the children who could work out equations such as 5 + 4 could work out the same problem logically when presented with real objects to add. In a later work, Labinowicz (1985) reported that children who had completed drills of number combinations could not automatically recall the correct answers. In interviews about how they solved problems, many children reported that they had taught themselves other ways of thinking about the number combinations in order to make sense of the problems. Children who can do tasks assigned by teachers but who do not understand them may not have enough time to engage in the experiences needed for them to develop the concepts. They may simply continue to do more tasks for which they memorize procedures.

The most effective type of assessment presents the child with a problem and has the teacher observe carefully the strategies the child uses in solving that problem. For example, to assess counting abilities, the child should be presented with real objects to count; the number of objects should be larger than the teacher estimates the child can count. To check a child's understanding of place value, the teacher should try to determine how she organizes objects in a large set for counting and question her about her strategies to try to reveal her thinking processes. Problems in creating patterns, in classification, and in basic operations should be presented with manipulative materials that the child can use to find solutions. Paper-and-pencil tests may help determine what a child can do, but only by giving a child real problems to work can a teacher uncover what he understands (Sgroi et al. 1995).

Teachers will need to assess children's abilities to conserve number and length in order to plan experiences. If children cannot conserve, it does not mean that the teacher must wait until they can before offering them mathematics instruction. Problems and tasks must be evaluated in terms of the kinds of thinking required to solve them; appropriate experiences can be selected based on children's levels of thinking. Children learn a great deal about mathematics before they can conserve number and length (McClintic 1988).

Teachers should not limit themselves to assessing children's computation abilities or problem-solving skills. Teachers should also assess how children feel as learners of mathematics, how children view mathematics, and what abilities children have to apply mathematical thinking to everyday problems.

CHILDREN WITH SPECIAL NEEDS

As in any other curriculum area, in mathematics, it is the teacher's responsibility to make sure that children with disabilities have access to the materials they need to help them understand the concepts as well as the time they need to explore those materials. Some materials may have to be modified, such as making tactile materials and providing braille numerals for students with visual challenges. Adaptations can make it possible for children with motor problems to roll dice or spin spinners—for instance, providing cups for the dice and easy-to-grasp handles on the spinners. Adaptations also may be needed for computers and calculators so that children can manipulate them easily. For example, some computers can produce very large print or can read aloud materials on screen.

CELEBRATING DIVERSITY

Most cultures employ the same concepts of number, counting, and the like that are employed in the United States. Thus, children who do not speak English as their first language often do very well in math because they know the concepts and have only to learn new labels for the numerals and operations. Teachers can take advantage of the knowledge these children have when planning working groups that will solve problems involving mathematics. These children should also be encouraged to write their own story problems in their native languages and to share what they know about math with their classmates. For example, a child could tell about the money used in his home country, and it could be compared to the money used in the United States. Counting words from the various languages represented in the class could be used for counting experiences or for labeling sets. Most teachers are aware that children like to learn how to count in other languages.

Teaching the history of mathematical learning in other cultures may not be appropriate for young children; it would be appropriate, however, for the teacher to mention contributions to mathematical knowledge made by cultures other than European Americans.

PARENTS AND MATHEMATICS

- Plan "homework" that includes solving math problems involving the family. How many people live in the household? How many windows are in the house or apartment? How many shapes can you find in one room?

CHAPTER SUMMARY

- Mathematics is more than just arithmetic. Mathematics includes classification, seriating, grouping, relationships, statistics, probability, fractions, geometry, and arithmetic.
- Mathematics is not a subject at which someone is innately good or poor. Neither is knowledge of mathematics transmitted from a person who knows to one who does not. Each individual learns mathematics by constructing understanding. Mathematical relationships are mental constructs.
- Mathematics in the classroom setting should be based on real problems that children are interested in solving. Some problems will involve the use of arithmetic; others will not.
- Instruction in mathematics should focus on helping children understand mathematical concepts before mathematical symbols are introduced.
- Writing down their questions, discoveries, and solutions can be very helpful to children learning mathematical concepts.

- Some mathematical concepts can be introduced through children's literature. Counting books and rhymes may interest children, and other books may introduce the basic operations, classification, or ordering.
- Assessment in mathematics should focus on the child's understanding, thought processes, and attitudes about mathematics.
- All children, including those with disabilities, need access to materials and time to explore them in order to understand mathematical concepts. Modifications may be needed for some materials in order for children to use them easily.
- Experiences that help children develop mathematical understanding do not usually depend on skill in language abilities. Thus, mathematics can be the subject area in which all children have an equal chance to succeed.

A Kindergarten Teacher's Approach to Mathematics Assessment

Mathematics filters into almost every aspect of the day in my kindergarten classroom. The children become mathematicians magically, without even being aware that it is happening. Positional and directional words are used daily in many situations. Sorting and patterning activities are part of play, calendar, and snack times. Adding and subtracting take place long before the children can put words to their actions. The mathematical activity adds excitement to the classroom and provides many opportunities for me to assess the learning of each student.

Assessment is an ongoing process, a collection of data that are then used for planning and instruction. Anecdotal records can provide useful information for planning instruction. One strategy for collecting these records is to use computer labels on which notes are recorded. When a label is full, it is transferred to a file for that child.

Another technique is to keep a growth-over-time piece for each child. The tasks completed should be fairly consistent so that growth can be demonstrated. Begin with a piece of paper divided into quadrants; write a direction in each square. Read the directions to the children. The four directions might include "Write your name," "Draw a picture of yourself," "Draw a picture of your house," and "Draw five things." As the year progresses, the last direction might change to "Show a set with one more/less than 5," "Write the numeral 5," or "Write an addition equation."

I call another activity *silent sorting*. I send two children with black shoes to one corner, two children with white shoes to another, and two children with sandals to another. Then each child in the remainder of the group tries to find where she belongs. The criteria for the sorting can be any number of factors.

Graphing is a skill that can be introduced to young children and that they generally enjoy. The most basic form of graphing is to use the children themselves, lined up according to some given criteria, such as height. Then objects can be used, like the children's shoes, if determining the most popular shoe color, or fruit, if determining the children's fruit preferences. The next step is to transfer the results to a paper or chart graph. Results should always be discussed and observations noted. Self-stick notes are wonderful for attaching children's observations directly onto the chart. Eventually, individual charts can be made. Children especially like manipulatives that are edible, such as cereal or candy. I use this type of activity to assess sorting skills, reasoning skills, and counting ability as well as the ability to create and interpret a graph.

Whatever the task, it is important that children explain how they came up with their answers. Their explanations provide insight into the approaches and ways of thinking they use to solve problems. Information from observations, tasks, daily activities, and explanations all help determine a child's strengths and what can be done to help her grow in mathematical thinking.

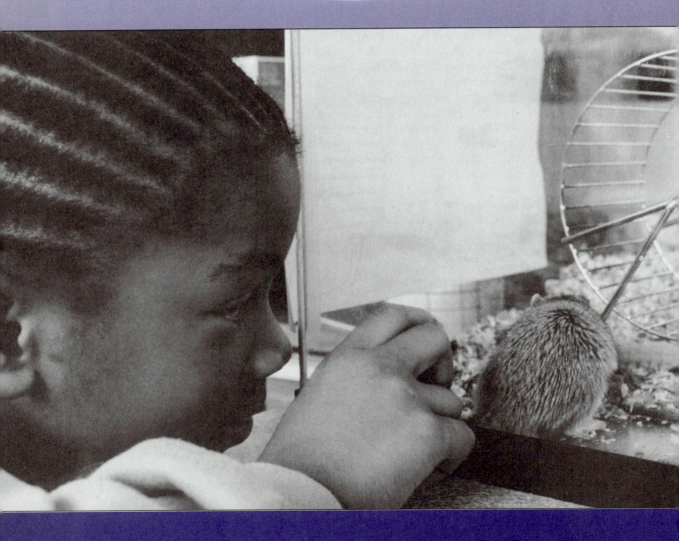

11

MANIPULATION AND DISCOVERY
Science

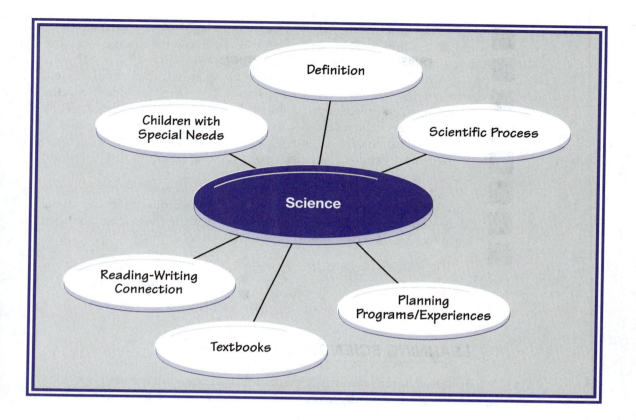

Your observation task this morning in the child-care center was to look for children engaged in scientific learning. You chose to observe a group of three- and four-year-olds for the first hour and a group of seven-year-olds for the second hour. In observing the younger children, you expected to see play and language learning, but you did not expect to see much "science." After all, threes and fours cannot really be expected to do experiments, can they?

Once you reviewed your notes, however, you found that children were engaged in many activities that could be labeled "science." Some children compared the textures of sand in different containers; other children tried to sink little wooden barges in water. You also found that many of the children's expressed interests were related to science. You overheard two children asking the teacher what had happened to the orange they had brought for snack several days ago—it was covered with mold. You noticed that the teacher did not throw the orange away but left it out for the children to see and smell.

In the second hour, you watched as seven-year-old children were instructed to take out their science books. They were provided with the materials to complete an experiment described in their textbooks: They were to observe the results of mixing unknown powders with water. At the end of the experiment, the teacher guided the children's discussion of their observations. Then they read the discussion in the text about dissolving.

After observing these two classrooms, you are left with the question: What is science? Is science the informal learning that was taking place in the class of younger children, or is it the more formal guided learning in which the older children were participating?

LEARNING SCIENCE

Just as children learn mathematics through manipulation and discovery, they learn science by manipulation, observation of the results of their manipulations, and discovery of relationships and effects. The role of experience in science is primary—science cannot be done without touching, tasting, feeling, smelling, pushing, pulling, rotating, mixing, comparing, and so on (McIntyre 1984).

Learning in the area of science involves primarily *physical knowledge* and *logico-mathematical knowledge*. When children explore the properties of materials, they are gaining knowledge from the materials themselves, which is physical knowledge. When they create relationships among materials, as in classifying leaves, their learning is logico-mathematical. As Chaille and Britain (1991) explain, "Constructivism is based on the idea that children are actively engaged—naturally and without the aid of direct instruction—in building theories about the world and the way it works. From a constructivist perspective, children are natural scientists and, given the opportunity, will engage on their own in experimentation and problem solving" (p. 23).

If a teacher believes that children must construct their own knowledge, then she will not make the mistake of *telling* them about concepts in science. Even so, believing that children must construct their own understandings does not free the teacher of the obligation to help children learn science. The teacher's role, then, is to plan appropriate activities, select appropriate materials, present challenges, provide time for experiences, and ask questions to guide children's thinking. Teaching science requires thoughtful planning and reflection.

DEFINITION OF SCIENCE

In general terms, *science* is the process of observing, thinking, and reflecting on actions and events. Kilmer and Hofman (1995) define science more specifically as the "knowledge about specific phenomena, . . . the processes used to collect and evaluate information, . . . and as a recently added aspect, [*technology* when defined as] the application of science to problems of human adaptation to the environment" (p. 43).

Children engaged in scientific thinking are constructing a framework of relationships within which factual information can be organized into meaningful and useful concepts. Science is an attitude exemplified by curiosity and interest in the world. Science is problem solving. Science is *not* learning facts and memorizing formulas.

Science in early childhood education is encouraging children to explore their environments and reflect on their observations and discoveries. Ideally, science is not a time set aside from other experiences; it is part of an ongoing integrated approach in which children think and construct basic understandings about the world. Broadly speaking, a child at the easel follows the basic scientific process when he hypothesizes (predicts

THEORY
INTO
Practice

Observe in a preschool program for threes and fours or in a primary classroom. Record all the activities that involve learning basic science concepts. Compare lists with your classmates. Do you agree on what could be labeled "science"? Why?

Science activities should use a variety of sources to help children learn about the world around them.

TABLE 11.1　Criteria for Defining Science

For Children 3 through 8, Developmentally Appropriate Sciencing . . .

Is	Is Not
Actively participating	Memorizing a lot of facts
Handling materials Controlling their own actions	Watching the teacher do most of the demonstrating and handling of objects
Investigating familiar phenomena	Studying content with no link to their knowledge or experience
Reflecting on teachers' open-ended questions	Being restricted by closed, single-right-answer questioning or being told what to expect
Observing the results of their own actions	Lacking opportunities to observe the results of their own actions
Experiencing both planned and spontaneous opportunities	Experiencing science only as teacher-planned activities
Investigating and working individually or in small groups	Participating in science activities only in a large group
Investigating the range of basic concepts	Learning about only one or two concepts
Exploring a variety of content from life, earth, and physical sciences	Learning only limited content
Having their knowledge and skills assessed in multiple ways	Having their knowledge and skills assessed only by written tests

Source: S. J. Kilmer and H. Hofman, "Transforming Science Curriculum," in *Reaching Potentials: Transforming Early Childhood Curriculum and Assessment,* vol. 2, edited by S. Bredekamp and T. Rosegrant, 43–63 (p. 62) (Washington, DC: National Association for the Education of Young Children, 1995). Copyright © 1995 by NAEYC. Used with permission.

that the paint is ready to apply to paper), collects data (paints), revises the prediction (determines that the paint is too runny or too thick), and draws conclusions about how paint reacts under given conditions. He may also discover the interactions of primary colors and explore those interactions very scientifically.

Kilmer and Hofman (1995) use the criteria listed in Table 11.1 to define *science,* identifying both what it is and is not. Raper and Stringer (1987) also have pointed out what science is not:

> Science is not book learning. We can learn a good deal from books, of course, and there is no other way that we can learn about the lives and discoveries of the great men and women of science except by reference to recorded information. But, fundamentally, the processes of science can only be understood by actively using them. Teachers need to be discouraged from seeing book learning as a substitute for practical activity. (p. 47)

As Holt (1989) explains:

Science is a way of doing things and solving problems. It is a style that leads a person to wonder, to seek, to discover, to know, and then to wonder anew. It is a style in which good feelings of joy, excitement, and beauty accompany these active mental and physical interactions with one's world. Not only children but adults can experience science. It is a way of life. (p. 181)

Perry and Rivkin (1992) suggest that teaching science requires some essential elements:

Time (playing and asking questions takes time), knowing something (some understanding of what can be learned from materials is vital), being open to one's own ignorance (teachers can look up information, consult with others, learn along with the children, but it is dangerous not to recognize what is not known), valuing one's own interests and interpretations (science is not right answers, but the asking of questions and thinking about what happens), valuing the symbolizing of experience and knowledge (recording, reworking and rethinking our ideas are as important in science as in any other area), and recognizing the need and being willing to collect and make available ample supplies for sciencing. (p. 16)

Many teachers report that they feel less prepared to teach science than any other subject-matter area (Wenner 1993). Perhaps such feelings are a result of teachers' misconceptions that science requires complicated materials and is a hard subject to master. This view of science is changing as more teachers at all grade levels are encouraged to think about science as explorating and inquiring rather than learning specific facts.

Sciencing, a term popular with early childhood teachers, implies not only the active nature of science experiences but the idea that both children and teachers are involved in the process of learning science—as opposed to having the teacher teach the children. *Sciencing* also implies that the whole classroom is used for learning rather than setting aside one area as a science area (McNairy 1985).

One of the most positive aspects of science as a field of study for young children is that it has not been affected by the trend to create readiness curricula. In some cases, this has meant that science has been ignored in curricula that focus on academic readiness; in other cases, children have been allowed to explore and investigate unhindered by a preconceived set of objectives that supposedly will make them ready to do science when they are older.

The fact is, science is easy to teach: Just supply children with an interesting environment, make the environment safe for exploration, and provide guidance as children do what comes naturally.

THE SCIENTIFIC PROCESS

The **scientific process** is a cycle of forming hypotheses, collecting data, confirming or rejecting the hypotheses, making generalizations, and then repeating the cycle. The basic skills used in the scientific process include observing, classifying and comparing, measuring, communicating, experimenting, relating, inferring, and applying. Because inferring and applying require more abstract thinking, young children should not be expected to be competent in these skills in a formal sense. Each of these skills, as it applies to an early childhood science program, is discussed in a following section.

Observing

Looking and *observing* are not the same thing. Teachers need to provide guidance in observation techniques. Children can be encouraged to look carefully for specific actions or information. For example, children can be encouraged to observe the behavior of a bird on the ground—does it walk or hop? Observation is certainly not limited to visual input; it should involve all the senses—seeing, hearing, smelling, tasting, and feeling.

Children need opportunities to explore materials using all of their senses.

Classifying and Comparing

Classifying is a basic process skill used in organizing information. In order to classify objects or information, children must be able to compare and contrast the properties of objects or information. Very young children begin to classify by function, color, or shape. Older children can classify on the basis of specific characteristics or properties, but multiplicative classifications, in which objects fit into multiple categories, are difficult for children in the early childhood years. Children must be able to think in concrete operational terms before they can think of objects as belonging to several categories at once, and most children are not concrete thinkers in the early childhood years. Teachers can encourage children to classify objects and to explain how objects have been grouped. Children can classify blocks by shape, group the materials that are stored in the art area, or sort buttons, leaves, shells, or other collections.

Measuring

Measuring is a basic process skill necessary for collecting data. Measurement does not refer only to using standardized measures. Children can measure the hamster's food by scoops, cut a piece of string the height of their bean plant, compare the sizes of seeds or rocks, or use a beaker to collect snow and observe the amount of water produced when the snow melts.

Communicating

Communicating is another basic process skill. Children can be encouraged to share their observations and their data collections through a variety of means. They can talk about their findings, make pictorial records, produce charts and graphs, or write narratives in order to share information, data, and conclusions. The communication process is important, as children begin to understand how knowledge is created in the field of science.

Experimenting

Experimentation is not a new process for young children. They have been experimenting since they first picked up a rattle or threw a cereal bowl off the highchair tray. In the scientific process, experimenting means controlling one or more variables and manipulating conditions. Teachers can help children think of their play activities as experiments by skillful questioning and encouraging children to reflect on their actions and the results of their actions. When children try to balance one block on a tower of blocks, drop food coloring into glasses of water, or plant several seeds in different soils, they can be guided to think of these activities as experiments.

Relating, Inferring, and Applying

Young children will use the process skills of relating, inferring, and applying only in very informal ways. *Relating* is the process of drawing abstractions from concrete evidence. For example, children who observe water freezing may not be able to relate that observation to the abstract idea that given liquids become solids at given temperatures. *Inferring* is the ability to determine cause-and-effect relationships or explanations for phenomena when the processes are not directly observable. Examples of such unobservable phenomena include electricity and magnetism. *Applying* is using information from experiences to invent, create, solve new problems, and determine probabilities. Children can be involved in applying scientific knowledge but not in a formal, analytical sense. For example, if children can observe the behavior of water when it is dropped on waxed paper, blown across waxed paper with a straw, or left outside on a winter night, they can apply some of these observations to other liquids and make predictions about what will happen to them under the same conditions. It is unreasonable, however, to expect children to analyze results and apply them without concrete experiences to think about.

PLANNING AN EARLY CHILDHOOD SCIENCE PROGRAM

A science program for young children should be based on broad goals and objectives that involve the children in processes, help them learn to think about problems, and help them learn more about the natural world. Table 11.2 lists the goals and objectives for sciencing with young children. Note that all these goals and objectives are very broad. None talks about learning specific scientific facts or being able to perform specific tasks because children participating in the scientific process—engaging in activities, reflecting on those activities, and learning about what other scientists do—are "doing science."

PARENTS AND SCIENCE

■ Help parents understand that children learn science when they wash a greasy dish, water a garden plot, ride their trike down a sloped surface, and so on. Some parents think science experiences have to be formal and difficult for learning to occur.

TABLE 11.2

Goals and Objectives for Sciencing with Young Children

GOAL: To develop each child's innate curiosity about the world

OBJECTIVES: Each child

- shows interest in and a willingness to investigate unfamiliar objects and events;
- shows respect for all living organisms, including humans; and
- shows appreciation for the beauty, balance, and orderliness of the environment.

GOAL: To broaden each child's procedural and thinking skills for investigating the world, solving problems, and making decisions

OBJECTIVES: Each child

- eagerly, actively participates in sciencing;
- uses senses appropriately to learn about unfamiliar objects and events;
- appropriately uses and cares for sciencing equipment (magnifiers, scales, etc.);
- quantifies observations (counts, measures, etc.);
- identifies similarities, differences, and changes in materials, events, and phenomena;

- classifies materials, events, and phenomena and explains rationale;
- records data;
- uses sequence of scientific method (prediction, data collection, drawing conclusions, generalization);
- readily shares information with peers and appreciates the perspectives of others; and
- shows familiarity with science processes terminology.

GOAL: To increase each child's knowledge of the natural world

OBJECTIVES: Each child

- actively participates in a variety of experiences exemplifying the basic science concepts of organization, cause and effect, systems, scale, models, change, structure and function, variations, and diversity;
- experiences activities from a range of science disciplines;
- shows familiarity with terminology related to basic science concepts; and
- represents and communicates knowledge.

Source: S. J. Kilmer and H. Hofman, "Transforming Science Curriculum," in *Reaching Potentials: Transforming Early Childhood Curriculum and Assessment,* vol. 2, edited by S. Bredekamp and T. Rosegrant, 43–63 (p. 45) (Washington, DC: National Association for the Education of Young Children, 1995). Copyright © 1995 by NAEYC. Used with permission.

Planning Content and Balance

Children's interest in biological science is so strong that teachers often emphasize it and fail to help children explore the areas of physical or earth sciences. But the basics of all areas of science can be developed in the early childhood years.

With guidance, children learn about botany as they sow seeds, eat plants, pull weeds, and smell flowers. They learn about zoology as they observe animals at the zoo, feed a puppy, hold a snake, and bury a goldfish. They learn about physics as they try to lift a heavier friend on the other end of the teeter-totter, observe the gears in a clock, watch someone jack up the family car, throw balls at targets, and feel the heat of a city sidewalk. They learn about chemistry as they watch sugar disappear in lemonade and feel the fizz when they place lozenges in their mouths. They learn about geology as they fill their pockets with stones, find fossils in rocks, pour water on sand, and mark the sidewalk with a rock. They learn about astronomy as they observe the sun, the moon, the stars, and the seasons.

The rule for planning a balanced science program for early childhood is simple: Do not try to teach children concepts about phenomena that cannot be touched, tasted, seen, or heard. If children cannot explore a concept through real materials, then the concept is too abstract and is not appropriate for the early childhood years. Children develop concepts over many experiences and explorations.

Vygotsky (1962) supports this notion, stating that "practical experience . . . shows that direct teaching of concepts is impossible and fruitless. A teacher who tries to do this usually accomplishes nothing but empty verbalism, a parrotlike repetition of words" (p. 83). Howe (1993) agrees: "The effort to teach concepts that are not accessible to children through their own experience and thinking is inappropriate in preschool and the primary grades" (p. 232).

Smith (1981) explains that "concepts of natural phenomena must be developed through manipulation of items within children's immediate environment and observation of children's reactions under varying circumstances. Abstract concepts outside the realm of immediate experience should not be included in an early childhood science curriculum" (pp. 5–6). Smith (1987) recommends that teachers ask the following questions in selecting science experiences:

Are the materials selected those that:
- children will naturally gravitate to for play?
- provide opportunities for the development of perceptual abilities through total involvement of the senses (perception of color, size, shape, texture, hardness, sound, etc.)?
- encourage self-directed problem solving and experimentation?
- children can act upon—cause to move—or that encourage children's observations of changes?

Do the experiences that evolve from children's play with the materials:
- provide opportunities for the teacher to extend the child's learning by asking questions or making suggestions that stimulate children's thinking?
- allow for additional materials to be introduced gradually to extend children's explorations and discoveries?
- allow for differences in ability, development, and learning style?
- allow children to freely interact with other children and adults?
- encourage children to observe, compare, classify, predict, communicate?
- allow for the integration of other curriculum areas? (p. 36)*

* From Robert F. Smith, "Theoretical Framework for Preschool Science Experiences," *Young Children* 42 (January 1987): 34–40. Reprinted by permission of the author.

Electricity is an example of a topic often presented in early childhood classrooms. However, the outcomes of experiences involving electricity usually reflect the child's preoperational thinking and often are not what is expected when the experiences are planned. Usually, children are supplied with batteries, small bulbs, and wires. The goal is to attach the wire to the battery and light the bulb. The expected outcomes are that children will develop an understanding that electricity is energy and that energy can be stored in a battery, channeled through a conduit (the wire), and released as the bulb lights.

What usually happens is that the teacher must verbalize these concepts. The children may learn to repeat them, but their explanations of why the bulb lights up include that "It wants to light up," that "It lights up because we want light," or that "It is magic." Electricity is a very abstract concept; even when children can be active in attaching the wires to the battery, what they learn from manipulating the objects is rarely what teachers expect them to learn (Good 1977). Unless an abstract concept can be made concrete, it is not appropriate for study by young children.

In planning experiences that will help children develop concepts, teachers must also examine the materials they select to make sure that the concepts children learn with them are not erroneous. For example, if all the tall containers in the water play area hold more than the short containers, children might assume that tall containers always hold more. The same sort of erroneous reasoning might result if children who are exploring floating and sinking find that all the materials that float are small and all that sink are large (Benham et al. 1982).

A science program, like a math program, consists of the children's everyday experiences supplemented by some planned experiences that will spark their interest and help them explore new materials and objects. Children's everyday observations will make them aware of what happens to milk when a carton is inadvertently left out overnight; to a carrot when it is left out in the room for a few days; to the volume of rice when it is cooked; to water left outdoors on a freezing night; to a snowball when it is brought into the classroom; and so on.

Planned experiences to supplement these observations require some preparation by the teacher. Planned experiences might involve bringing various animals into the classroom; bringing in assortments of natural materials for sorting and classifying; or providing levers and gears for children to explore. In each case, the teacher should help the children observe, hypothesize, collect data, and draw conclusions. A balanced science program, then, includes both types of experiences and activities to help develop concepts in the life sciences, physical sciences, and earth sciences.

In addition to thinking about the concepts that are appropriate for children to learn, teachers who are planning for science experiences must provide an environment that is safe for exploration, teach children how to explore and investigate safely, and encourage them to enjoy science and learn some basic concepts and attitudes that are not specific to any one experience.

Providing a Safe Environment

It is the responsibility of the teacher to examine the environment for any hazards to young children. As children mature and become more skillful, safety rules may change. The following are some general safety rules:

1. Equipment should be sturdy and in good repair. Although glass may be the best choice for some activities (such as making an aquarium), most materials provided for the children should be unbreakable. Metal materials should not have torn places or rough edges. Tubs and bins should not be cracked or torn.
2. Use of all heat sources should be well supervised. All electric outlets should have safety covers; electric cords should be taped against walls.
3. Plants in the classroom should be nonpoisonous.
4. Tubs and pools of water should be closely supervised.
5. Tools such as knives and hammers should be in good condition, and their use should be supervised carefully.

Teaching Children to Explore and Investigate Safely

Once the environment has been made safe, teachers need to think about rules to help children explore materials, objects, animals, and plants safely. The following general guidelines will help ensure safe explorations:

1. No material should be tasted or eaten unless the children know that it is edible or safe to taste. If, for example, the teacher provides powder for the children to explore, children must be taught not to taste the powder without instruction to do so. Children should be taught never to taste any unfamiliar substance.
2. Plants also should not be tasted or eaten unless the children know what they are or an adult says they are safe to eat. For instance, children should never eat leaves, berries, or roots unless they know they are safe. Children should be aware of safety precautions even when eating commercially obtained foods.
3. Children should be taught how to smell any unfamiliar substance. A child who plunges his face into a container will likely irritate his eyes

or nose. Teachers can demonstrate how to hold and sniff any substance without danger of inhaling the substance or burning membranes.

4. Children should be taught not to touch or handle unknown animals. Every child should know not to touch wild animals and how to hold any pet or classroom animal without hurting or frightening it.

The art is in teaching children to be properly cautious without dimming their enthusiasm. Teachers should make sure that children understand the necessity for these precautions while encouraging safe explorations and discoveries.

Encouraging Children to Enjoy Science

Children delight in their scientific discoveries. They may be cautious about touching a toad for the first time, but once they have, they will not be able to wait to share that experience with their families. Teachers of young children may need to relearn some attitudes about science themselves in order to enjoy and guide children's explorations.

Science should be nonbiased. Many adults feel that science is more appropriate for boys than for girls. In fact, all children should be encouraged to participate in a variety of activities and their interests should be respected, regardless of their sex or socioeconomic status. Children involved in a science-based curriculum gain observation skills and classification skills. They may also be encouraged to pursue careers in science. This encouragement is especially important for girls and children from ethnic and cultural minorities, who are underrepresented in the science professions (Iatridis 1981).

Science can be the hub around which other learning experiences are organized. One first-grader refused to read about hats and bears in his basal reader but would struggle to read anything about science. He dictated the following story:

> I like science. I'll tell about science. If you want to know about making sparklers. You need some aluminum filings and you need charcoal powder. You need sulfur and potassium nitrate. You buy these things at a pharmacy. You mix all these chemicals together to make sparklers. You put the stuff on wires like those in plant holders. You wait a night and a day.

This boy's story illustrates the interest many children have in learning about the world and the importance of building curriculum experiences around those interests. The point is not to make sparklers but to build on children's interests while teaching them literacy and other skills.

"Messing about" can be extremely important in developing scientific concepts. Not everything about science is neat and tidy. Sometimes, children's explorations do not end with neat answers. When a four-year-old beats the soap bubbles in a tub of water with a rotary beater until they get smaller and smaller, she doesn't necessarily come up with answers about how the bubbles get smaller, but her curiosity to try things out is sustained. Many discoveries have been made when specific outcomes were not planned.

Finally, teachers must be flexible in planning so that unexpected events can be appreciated. If a child brings in a pet iguana, the teacher should be able to leave his carefully planned study of tree rings for another day.

Teaching Basic Concepts and Attitudes

Some concepts and attitudes are important as children learn about science:

- *Conservation*—Children should begin learning early about the importance of conserving the world's limited resources. Most of this teaching can be done through modeling. For example, teachers should arrange for children to wash vegetables in a pan of water rather than under running water. By recycling all paper used in the classroom, teachers will help children learn not to waste paper. Lights should be turned off when they are not needed. Food should be used only to eat; use junk for printing, rather than potatoes or other vegetables. Collages can be made with inedible weeds rather than edible seeds (Holt 1989).
- *Respect for life*—Teachers can help children learn to respect life and not destroy it. For example, insects and spiders can be captured and released outdoors, rather than killed. Care should be taken that proper food and habitats are provided for any animal visitor to the classroom.
- *Respect for the environment*—Children can become aware of pollution, including litter. They can be taught not to litter and to recycle the materials used in the classroom.

Planning the Sequence of Activities

Kamii and DeVries (1993) have outlined some principles to follow in planning activities through which children can develop physical and logico-mathematical understandings. They suggest that teachers consider various levels of acting on objects when selecting activities.

- *Acting on objects to see how they react*—Young children engage in actions such as rolling, squeezing, and pushing objects. Teachers can ask children what will happen if they squeeze an object, and so on.
- *Acting on objects to produce a desired effect*—Children also act on objects not simply to explore them but intentionally to make things happen. They may pour the milk from their cup onto the highchair tray so they can splash it. The teacher might ask children to blow on a spool to move it across the floor and so on.
- *Becoming aware of how an effect is produced*—Many children can produce effects without knowing how they achieved the results. The teacher might ask a child to tell someone else how an effect was achieved. If the child is unable to do so, the teacher will know that the request was inappropriate for the child's level of development.
- *Explaining causes*—Most young children cannot explain the causes of many effects that they observe and should not be asked to give explanations.

Introducing the Activity

- *Principle I*—The teacher should introduce the activity in a way that maximizes children's initiative. An activity can be introduced by putting out material to which children will naturally gravitate; by presenting the material and telling them "See what you can think of to do with these things"; or by proposing a specific problem to be solved with the materials.
- *Principle II*—The teacher should begin with parallel play. Because teachers want children to do things with materials, they must make sure that each child has her own materials. (If, however, several children want to play together, they should of course be encouraged to help each other with questions, comparisons, and so on.)

During the Activity

- *Principle I*—The teacher should figure out what the child is thinking and respond sparingly in his terms. Figuring out what the child is thinking is sometimes quite difficult. The teacher may get clues from the child's actions or from his questions. The direction to "respond sparingly" may force the teacher to drop his own agenda and follow the child's, at least for the time being. Teachers can help children with practical problems to facilitate experimentation and observation, offer materials to encourage comparisons, or model new comparisons.
- *Principle II*—The teacher should encourage children to interact with other children.

- *Principle III*—The teacher should offer the child activities that increase her physical knowledge and that exercise her current social, moral, and motor abilities.

After the Activity

Teachers should encourage children to reflect on activities briefly after they have been completed. This can be accomplished through questions about what they did, the results of what they did, what they noticed, what other children did, the problems they encountered, and so on. The point is not to get all children to arrive at one right answer but to allow children to think about what they did.

Wasserman (1988) describes a model for science instruction that incorporates the same principles as the Kamii and DeVries model. She calls it *play-debrief-replay.* In this model, the children engage in investigative play with selected materials. Following the play, the teacher guides their reflection through questions and sets the stage for replay, in which the children play with the same materials again, either to duplicate their previous results or to explore further.

An example of these principles in action might be a bubble-blowing activity for young children. Since most children are fascinated by bubbles, just making the materials available will be motivational. To begin, each child should have his own bubble wand and access to bubble solution. As the children blow bubbles, the teacher should try to get them to think about the force needed to make bubbles. After a time, the teacher should offer the children bubble wands that are not round but square, triangular, or rectangular and perhaps of different sizes, as well. The children should be guided to observe the sizes and shapes of the bubbles blown with different wands and then to draw conclusions about those observations. To follow up, the children might make bubbles again but be encouraged to

---

DEVELOPMENTALLY APPROPRIATE PRACTICE

Think about what you have read and what you have experienced in regard to science instruction as you reflect on these questions:

- What elements of a science program are essential for DAP? Why?
- In comparison to traditional science programs, will developmentally appropriate programs produce more people who are scientifically literate? Why?
- Why are some teachers more successful at traditional science instruction than others? Is it motivation? intelligence? experience? Are any of the reasons for that success relevant to developmentally appropriate practice? If so, how?
- Should learning scientific facts ever be part of a developmentally appropriate program? If so, for what age group?

find different materials to use in the bubble solution—their hands, cheesecloth, and so on. In this replay activity, the children can apply what they learned from the first bubble activity.

An example of a play-debrief-replay scenario with primary-grade children might involve mechanics. Children could be invited to take apart an old toaster and observe the mechanical parts. As they worked, the teacher would try to determine what they were thinking about how the machine worked. After the children had a chance to examine the materials carefully, the teacher could provide other levers, springs, and gears for investigation. After reflection on the activity, the children could play with the materials again and perhaps invent their own simple machines.

PARENTS ᴬᴺᴰ SCIENCE

■ Prepare a set of activities based on kitchen science (things to do with common kitchen materials) or backyard science (things to do in the backyard or park) that can be sent home with children periodically.

SUGGESTIONS FOR EXPERIENCES IN THE CLASSROOM

Many science experiences can also be labeled math, art, or language arts experiences. In reading the following suggestions for appropriate science activities, keep in mind the discussion of an integrated model of curriculum in Chapter 7 and remember that science should not be separated from ongoing classroom experiences.

Biological Science

In a constructivist classroom, the teacher's role in helping children connect with nature will not be exactly the same as it is in teaching earth sciences or physical sciences. In those areas, the teacher may provide the children with materials and time so they can experiment in order to find answers to their questions. But as Chaille and Britain (1991) remind us, such experimentation is not possible with most questions about the natural world. Children cannot be allowed to experiment in ways that may harm other creatures, even if doing so will answer their questions.

Therefore, to help children learn about the natural world, the teacher will assist them in active observation, model respect for all living creatures, and serve as a resource person in answering questions. Wilson (1995) suggests bringing nature into the classroom. Adding materials in learning centers and taking children outdoors as often as possible (but with a focus on the beauty and wonder of nature, not in naming every plant and animal) are two ways of helping children gain appreciation for the natural world.

Threes and Fours

Science experiences for three- and four-year-olds should be playful. Teachers should be very alert to the discoveries that children are making as they play and should be ready to guide the children's thinking as they participate in the following kinds of activities:

- Observing animals—Small animals that can be held are ideal, such as rabbits, guinea pigs, or snakes. Teachers may want animals to visit for short periods of time rather than be permanent residents. Fish, birds, insects, spiders, and reptiles are also interesting to children.
- Observing simple ant farms or beehives—Some schools have specially prepared beehives that attach to windows so that children can observe the bees safely from inside the room.
- Observing spider webs, bird nests, or other animal homes
- Providing some care for classroom pets, such as feeding the fish or filling the rabbit's water container
- Collecting and observing tadpoles from the local pond
- Observing the life cycles of butterflies or moths
- Examining the different textures found in natural items such as tree bark
- Sprouting sweet potatoes, pineapple and carrot tops, grapefruit or orange seeds, and so on—With care (and a little luck), the children may actually be able to eat the results of their work.

Fives and Sixes

Science experiences for five- and six-year-olds should continue to be based primarily on play experiences. Teachers will want to record or encourage children to record their discoveries on charts and in reports. Many print materials can be provided to extend children's interests in science topics, and more planned experiences are appropriate as children mature. Activities for fives and sixes can include the following:

- Making a collection of seeds to sort—Most seeds sold commercially are treated with substances that are poisonous when ingested, so if the class uses commercially prepared seeds, the teacher should ensure that children do not put them in their mouths and that they wash their hands carefully after handling the seeds.
- Conducting an ongoing study of animals—During the course of the year, many different animals can be introduced into the classroom: hamsters, goldfish, lizards, gerbils, crayfish, turtles, garter snakes, and land snails. With some guidance (and some good library resources), children can help construct habitats for these animals, study their life cycles, and focus reading and writing experiences around these visitors. Teachers are cautioned not to use a human family analogy when

studying animals. The animals should be referred to as "male" and "female" rather than as "Mommy" and "Daddy." If a family analogy is used and the male gerbil eats the offspring, the teacher will have some explaining to do about what daddies do! The important concepts that children should learn are that it takes a male and female of the same species to produce offspring, that the amount of care animals provide for their young varies, and that each animal needs food, water, and protection in order to survive.

- Starting and maintaining a class garden—If creating one is possible, a garden plot outdoors is ideal. If weather and space limit outside gardening options, an inside garden can be planted in tubs or old wading pools. Children can help prepare the garden with pebbles or sand for drainage, soil for planting, and organic material for fertilizer. Children can learn about appropriate plants, plant seeds, and sprouts and care for the plants. They can also cook and eat the products of a garden.
- Conducting an intensive study of the life cycles of selected insects or amphibians—To learn about life cycles, children might study silkworms, butterflies, moths, frogs, or other creatures. The life cycles must be readily observable in the classroom, so that children can record changes and keep scientific records of the stages.
- Hatching eggs—Many classrooms hatch eggs in the spring. Ideally, eggs should be hatched by a mother hen at school, but an incubator is the next best choice. Hatching eggs can stimulate many reading and writing projects. Children can describe the development of the embryo or care of the eggs. Teachers should keep in mind that no hatching experiences should be undertaken without planning for what will be done with the baby animals after they have been hatched. It is not appropriate to teach children that life is expendable.
- Making collections of natural materials for sorting and classifying, such as leaves, pine cones, and seashells—What to choose depends on the environment and the children's experiences. Print materials such as posters, books, and magazines can be added to displays of natural materials, and experiences can be extended from these collections.

Sevens and Eights

Experiences for sevens and eights should continue to be based on their interests and their home and school environments. More of their experiences should involve experimenting and employing the scientific process. Activities for children of this age include the following:

- Studying plants—Children might learn the names and purposes of parts of plants and seeds and experiment with different conditions for sprouting seeds and growing plants while controlling environmental elements (light, soil conditions, amount of water, and so on). The teacher could introduce children to some plants that are not green (fungi, mushrooms) and plants that reproduce without seeds (ferns).

- Studying the life requirements of different animals—Children might carry out studies of animal growth and behavior, for example, by feeding two hamsters different diets (both healthy) and comparing their growth. The teacher can emphasize the importance of keeping careful scientific records and can extend children's interests to reading and writing experiences.

- Studying the characteristics of different animals and performing simple classifications based on these characteristics

- Studying birds in the local environment—Activities might focus on adaptations in feet, bills, wings, and so on to meet environmental demands and on the place of birds in ecosystems.

Physical Science

The value of children learning physical science comes not from memorizing specific concepts and facts but from having opportunities "to act on objects and see how objects react—to build the foundation for physics and chemistry" (Kamii and DeVries 1993, p. 12). For young children, activities in physics should meet these criteria:

1. Children must be able to produce the movement by their own action.
2. Children must be able to vary their action.
3. The reaction of the object must be observable.
4. The reaction of the object must be immediate. (Marxen 1995, p. 213)

Threes and Fours

Physical science experiences, like all school experiences for very young children, must be based on play experiences and everyday classroom activities. Some possibilities include:

- Manipulating modeling clay and observing its properties—Can it be rolled? stretched? pushed? Children can compare the properties of Silly Putty and Play Doh to those of clay.
- Using pull toys with removable wheels to discover the difference between moving toys with wheels and moving toys without them
- Painting with tempera paints—Children can observe how paint drips and runs, what consistencies paints have, and how colors mix.

- Playing with water—Teachers should provide a variety of containers, tubes, funnels, and so on for explorations with water (Bird 1983).
- Playing with blocks—Children learn about gravity, balance, and support as they build structures.
- Blowing activities with straws—Children can explore wind and air pressure (blowing) as forces to move different objects.
- Rolling balls toward targets from various distances and angles (Kamii and DeVries 1978)
- Using rollers and boards for moving materials, balancing themselves, and so on (Kamii and DeVries 1978)
- Observing light and shadows—Very young children often believe that shadows are parts of the objects that cast them. Activities need not include technical explanations of shadows.

Fives and Sixes

Teachers of fives and sixes can begin to introduce some activities to help the children develop specific concepts and can extend their experiences through reading and writing tasks. Children might share some of what they learn orally as a way of evaluating their daily activities in addition to recording some of their discoveries in their journals. Several activities are appropriate for this age group:

- Playing with water—Children can explore floating and sinking with a variety of materials. They can sort the materials into categories and then try to modify the materials that float so that they sink and vice versa. Modifications might include adding materials or making boats out of different materials.
- Moving objects across water by blowing on them through straws—Children can have races (Kamii and DeVries 1978).
- Blowing bubbles—Children can mix and compare bubble solutions and record the best mixtures. They can also experiment by dipping different shapes into bubble solutions and record their findings (shapes of bubbles, which bubbles last longer, which shapes produce the most bubbles, and so on).
- Finding gears, levers, and planes in the environment—Children can take apart old appliances to examine their parts.
- Learning about clamps, vises, and levers at the woodworking table (Schiller and Townsend 1985)
- Creating elevators during block play; using pulleys
- Experimenting with different weights in different positions on balance scales or teeter-totters
- Experimenting with sound using different materials and different ways of vibrating the materials

THEORY INTO Practice

Prepare a plan for a first-grade science activity using materials found in an average kitchen or home. This activity should involve no commercial materials.

- Controlling the variables for some physical changes in matter—Is there a way to make ice or snow melt faster or water evaporate more quickly?
- Making paper airplanes and paper helicopters—Do different folds in the paper produce different results?
- Cooking—Children can observe changes in matter (melting, hardening, expanding, shrinking, and so on).

Sevens and Eights

The physical science exploration of sevens and eights can be extended by reading and writing tasks associated with keeping careful records and recording discoveries:

- Playing with water—Experiences should be extended to exploring the properties of water and beginning activities that focus on water cycles. Children can record the results of rate-of-flow experiments on sand in the sandbox or changes in evaporation rates of water and other liquids.
- Dissolving and heating substances—Children can observe different reactions of matter by finding substances that dissolve in water or testing the effects of heat and cold on different materials.
- Changing states of matter (solid, liquid, vapor)—Children can observe matter in these states, record their observations, and form hypotheses about the causes of the changes.
- Inventing machines—Children can invent machines using gears, levers, inclined planes, or pulleys. Kuehn (1988) suggests that humorous inventions (balloon poppers, dog feeders, and so on) are appropriate because the children learn invention strategies without having to produce serious inventions.
- Exploring magnets—Children can explore magnets by creating structures with magnetic building pieces and testing which materials will or will not be attracted by magnets. They can also explore magnetic forces using different materials: Will iron filings be attracted through paper? plastic? wood? thin metal? (Harlan 1980)
- Studying sources of light and shadows—Children can measure the shadows of the same object at different times of day and record the results. Children can also create shadow plays or make silhouettes from shadows of children.
- Cooking experiences—More complex activities are appropriate, during

---

PARENTS AND SCIENCE

■ Have parents and children work together to create minimuseums that can be shared with the class when completed. Send each parent a letter explaining the goal of the activity, how it is related to work at school, and directions for creating the minimuseum. An example of such a museum might be a collection of items related to apples (Kokoski and Downing-Leffler 1995).

---

which time children can explore the reactions of different combinations of ingredients, temperatures, or other conditions of cooking. An example is separating biscuit dough into two portions, adding baking powder to one portion only, and then cooking and comparing the two portions.

Earth Science

Threes and Fours

As in other areas of science, basic concepts of scientific thinking about the earth and the universe are developed while young children play. For threes and fours, such concepts are developed when they play with different mixtures of sand and water and different textures and colors of sand; observe rain, snow, or other precipitation; or watch snow melt or water freeze or evaporate.

INTEGRATING THE CURRICULUM

Extending the theme of change, the following are a few of the many possibilities for science activities with young children:

➤ Observe the life cycles of insects or animals that undergo significant metamorphic changes, such as butterflies, moths, frogs, toads, and salamanders. Keep daily records of the changes that occur on a chart or in a journal.

➤ Observe the life cycle of an insect or animal that changes by growing bigger or by changing its skin rather than its shape. Examples include grasshoppers, cicadas, and some snakes. Keep daily records of the changes that occur on a chart or in a journal. Compare findings with those from observations of insects or animals that experience metamorphosis.

➤ Observe the changes in weather from day to day, season to season, and record them on a calendar. Point out that the changes in weather may not coincide with the official beginnings and endings of seasons.

➤ Observe daily changes in shape and appearance of the moon, and record them on a calendar. Keep the calendar for a full cycle of the moon.

➤ Observe the changes in light from day to night.

➤ Observe seeds before they are planted. Then plant them, and observe the changes as the plant grows. Record daily changes on a chart or in a journal.

➤ Make Jell-o and compare the liquid form to the solid form.

➤ Pop popcorn and record the change in volume. Measure the amounts of unpopped and popped corn.

➤ Boil water and capture the steam so that it condenses back to water. Then freeze it.

➤ Explore the changes in color that result when different colors of paint are mixed. Keep records of the findings.

Fives and Sixes

Earth science experiences for fives and sixes might include:

- Classifying rocks by size, shape, color, density, and hardness—Children can experiment with rocks by scratching them with nails, using eye droppers to drop vinegar on their surfaces, weighing rocks of approximately equal size, chipping rocks with a rock pick (if safety goggles are supplied), or comparing polished and unpolished rocks of the same kind. The teacher can read *Everybody Needs a Rock* (Baylor 1974).
- Making simple maps of the school property that show all the different surface coverings (grass, asphalt, gravel, and so on)
- Examining the different compositions of soil collected in the children's yards or from different places on the school grounds—Are there differences in color, smell, texture? What happens when water is added? Children can put each sample through a screen and compare what they find or plant seeds in each sample and record the results.
- Recording weather daily over the course of the year—What is the most common type of weather in any given month? Some children may be able to start taking some weather measurements with a large thermometer, a wind sock, and a rain gauge.
- Observing the change of seasons by noting the weather, plants, and animals in the local environment during each season
- Exploring the wind with kites, pinwheels, bubbles, and their own bodies

Sevens and Eights

The following activities are appropriate for seven- and eight-year-old children:

- Learning about air and air pressure through experiments such as blowing up balloons, creating bubbles in water, or moving materials with air
- Observing the weather—A simple weather station allows children to take their own measurements and record them. Weather studies can be extended into a study of light, air, wind, and clouds (Huffman 1996).
- Becoming familiar with the relationship of the earth, the moon, and the sun—Children might make models or observe the position of the moon in the sky for one complete phase.
- Learning about land features in the region—Children might observe land features such as ponds, lakes, mountains, rivers, or deserts and study the

PARENTS AND SCIENCE

■ Some teachers have been successful in using a "science backpack" that children take home on a rotating basis. The backpack contains a letter explaining the purpose of the activity, an information book and perhaps a narrative story that are related to the activity, and all the materials necessary for completing the activity (Kokoski and Downing-Leffler 1995; Patton and Kokoski 1996).

characteristics of these features as habitats for people and animals.

- Comparing temperatures in full sun and in the shade, holding other conditions constant
- Placing different materials in the sun and measuring their temperatures to begin understanding the differential heat absorption rates of different materials

USING TEXTBOOKS

Many science programs for primary children are based primarily on materials in textbooks. A more appropriate approach would be to organize science experiences for children and then use science textbooks as resources, much as we would choose other appropriate books to enhance study of a topic. For example, suppose a teacher organizes classroom activities around the theme of insects. If a science textbook included information about insects or photographs that could help children, then it should be used. But students should not study insects simply because the topic is in the textbook.

INTEGRATING SCIENCE THROUGH THE DAY

Science is so much a part of the youngest children's play experiences that teachers rarely need help in integrating science. Teachers of primary children are often required to teach a certain number of minutes of science each day and to document that they have planned and implemented science instruction.

One strategy for meeting the requirements for science instruction while integrating it with the other classroom activities is to plan thematic units that lend themselves to interesting science activities. Many themes that are appropriate for primary children emphasize science. In selecting a theme, the teacher must remember that it should be interesting to both the children and himself, important enough to be taught, and appropriate to the children's level of development and environment. Science themes include trees, fish, birds, minibeasts, patterns, and cycles, among others, as well as the traditional themes of senses, colors, and seasons. Table 11.3 on page 362 lists science activities for primary grades that revolve around the theme of changes in frogs and toads along with activities that can be used in other subject areas to complement the science activities.

Math and science are so closely related that it is often difficult to label activities as "math" or "science." For example, seriation activities may help children construct both scientific and mathematical concepts. Pearlman

THEORY INTO Practice

Develop a theme using a science topic that would be suitable for preschool or primary children. Discuss your reasons for including the amount of instruction in science that you recommend.

TABLE 11.3	Science Activities Based on Theme of Change, Subtopic: Frogs and Toads

Subject Area	Activities
Language Arts	• Read aloud a variety of narrative books and other sources about frogs and toads. What did the authors need to know to write the books? How did the authors learn what they know? • Write reports, scientific observations, and poetry about frogs/toads. • Emphasize the life cycles of frogs and toads and the changes they undergo as they grow. • Learn to use reference books and computer databases to find information about frogs/toads. • Look for other meanings of the word *frog* in the dictionary. Find as many of the objects mentioned as possible. • Discuss fairytales in which the prince or princess becomes a frog as the result of a spell. Why might a frog be used? What other animals could be used?
Science	• Study the characteristics of frogs and toads. • Chart the information needed to classify animals as amphibians. • Compare the life cycles of frogs/toads to those of lizards and other reptiles. • Construct a food chain that shows the place of frogs/toads. What do frogs/toads eat? What eats frogs/toads? • Find out how frogs/toads protect themselves (camouflage, poison in skin, and so on). • Construct an appropriate habitat for frogs/toads.
Social Studies	• Find out what frogs/toads contribute to the ecosystem. Many frogs have become endangered or have disappeared completely. Is this a problem? • Chart the benefits to people of having frogs/toads in the environment.
Arts and Crafts	• Compare the uses of drawings versus photographs in books about frogs/toads. Are photographs sometimes better? drawings? Why? • Try making some rubbings on smooth and bumpy textures. Relate these textures to the skin of frogs/toads. • Create illustrations of frogs/toads for reports, stories, or poetry about them.
Music and Movement	• Listen to recordings of frog calls. • Hop like frogs. • Play Leap Frog.

and Pericak-Spector (1994) suggest that learning about seriation should involve much more than ordering items by length. Activities should be provided that have children seriate by width, size, and thickness; by color; by texture; by sound; and by taste. Children with more experience in seriating can order a set of rubber bands by the pitch each produces when twanged or a set of containers by the estimated volume each holds. Measurement is another area in which science and math overlap. Children can explore materials and quantities that will balance on a double-pan scale or the volume of a given amount of popped corn and the amount of water needed to fill the spaces around it in a container (Lehman 1994).

THE READING-WRITING CONNECTION

As science is taught throughout the day, children will "learn to read for information, interpret graphs, compare charts, and keep journals as a natural part of their school day" (Fine and Josephson 1984, p. 29). Skills in language arts will be developed through meaningful activities, and children will learn science because it is interesting and exciting.

If teachers choose to organize science experiences around themes, reading and writing experiences can and should be integral parts of the theme. Many topics of interest will emerge from classroom incidents, classroom visitors, or trips. Teachers will want to extend the interests of the children through their developing literacy skills. Doris (1991) has developed some excellent guidesheets for helping children record their observations. On each sheet, the child records what she observed, draws a picture of it, and lists some things she noticed about it.

The following examples may give you other ideas of ways to help children use reading and writing in meaningful ways.

Class Pets

The class might acquire a pet when a child brings his turtle to the class for a few weeks. (Laws have changed about keeping and selling turtles. Check the laws in your area.) The teacher might incorporate some of the following reading and writing experiences into her plans in order to expand on the children's interest in the turtle:

- The children might learn "The Little Turtle" (a fingerplay).
- The teacher might find a large copy of the fingerplay, prepare a large chart, print the words to be used with a pocket chart, or find some other way to present the print in a large format. The teacher could read the words aloud several times, then the children could read chorally, and finally the children could read independently.
- After the children have read the words to the fingerplay many times, they might be given small booklets containing the words and then make their own illustrations. These booklets might be read independently.
- Children might write about turtles. The teacher could help children structure reports about turtles that contain factual information, records of observations of the class turtle, and narratives about personal experiences with turtles.
- The teacher might read aloud stories that feature turtles. "The Tortoise and the Hare"; *Timothy Turtle* (Davis 1940); *I Wish I Could Fly* (Maris 1986); *Turtle Tale* (Asch 1978); and *The Foolish Tortoise* (Buckley 1985) are all good choices.
- The teacher might read aloud information books about turtles and their habitats. Examples include *Green Turtle Mysteries* (Waters 1972);

THEORY INTO Practice

Prepare a "backpack activity." Include a letter of explanation, all the needed materials (nothing perishable), at least two books related to the activity, and instructions about what to do with the completed activity.

Nature's Children: Turtles (Switzer 1986); and *Turtle Watch* (Ancona 1987). The illustrations in Holling's *Minn of the Mississippi* (Holling 1951) might also be useful. *A Turtle in the House* (Navarra 1968) and *The Total Turtle* (Reeves 1975) supply information about the details of keeping a turtle as a pet. (Children might enjoy some of the illustrations in these latter two books, but the text is too complicated for reading aloud.)

- Children might keep a chart of the turtle's care. The chart should include columns for food, water, who cleans the container, who baby-sits on weekends, and whatever else is required in caring for the turtle.
- The children might dictate facts about turtles while the teacher records them (Laminack 1987).

Machines

For a study of simple machines, a teacher might plan reading and writing activities such as the following:

Choose a topic in science for young children, and find reference and storybooks related to the topic. Prepare a plan for reading and writing activities based on the topic.

- Read *Mike Mulligan and His Steam Shovel* (1939) and *Katy and the Big Snow* (1943), both by Virginia Burton.
- Read directions for putting together a simple household device. Discuss the structure of the directions. Children might write directions for putting together an invention of their own in two or three steps.
- If possible, take a walk to a construction site, and have the children write descriptions of one or more of the machines they see at work there.
- Have children write reports of what they find when they dismantle a household appliance.
- Have children write invitations to parents to come to class to talk about the machines they use in their work.
- Children might use Maccaulay's *The Way Things Work* (1988) as a reference book for finding information about machines.

Plants

For a study of plants, children might participate in the following activities:

- Find information about specific plants in references books.
- Read the planting directions on seed packages and the directions for plant care on tags from a florist.
- Keep records of plant growth, amount of water, fertilizers, and any other information that can be charted or graphed.
- Write reports of classification experiences with seeds or leaves.
- Invite someone who sells seeds or plants to visit the class and talk about her work.

- Invite a guest whose hobby is gardening to talk about plants and gardening techniques most suitable for the area.
- Write invitations and thank-you letters to these speakers. Write reports as a group or as individuals of the information gained.

Clearly, any topic in science can be expanded by reading and writing experiences that are real and meaningful to the children. Science experiences can also be extensions of literature experiences. Butzow and Butzow (1988) argue that scientific and technological literacy are becoming increasingly important and that the issues related to science and technology should be introduced early in a child's experience. Many issues can be introduced through literature experiences, and follow-up activities can be planned to help children gain information and develop problem-solving skills along with increasing literacy skills.

CHILDREN WITH SPECIAL NEEDS

Some adaptations of materials may be necessary to help children with disabilities develop concepts in science. Some possible adaptations include:

- Helping children with visual impairments sort and classify objects using tactile cues
- Helping children with hearing impairments experience sound through tactile means—For example, children can feel the vibrations of tuning forks, guitar strings, or rubber bands stretched across cigar boxes.
- Arranging materials so that children with physical disabilities can work with them easily and as independently as possible

As in other areas of study, teachers will want all children to participate fully and will adapt materials when necessary to make that possible. "Multisensory instruction with a variety of activities provides the experiential background necessary for concept formation for all students. It also allows students with sensory limitations to profit from more activities" (Cain and Evans 1984, p. 233).

Multisensory activities are also appropriate for children who are gifted. Follis and Krockover (1982) recommend that programs for such children be discovery based and designed to foster independent learning. Teachers of children who are gifted must be careful not to emphasize the verbal facility of these children so much that they fail to involve them in manipulative learning experiences.

CELEBRATING DIVERSITY

Teachers should be sure to include the contributions of various cultures when they discuss inventions and materials that make everyone's lives more safe and pleasant. When visitors are invited to the classroom to demonstrate or talk about science, they should not all be white males. Children need to know that people from both genders and all ethnic and cultural groups have contributed to the world's storehouse of scientific knowledge.

In addition, teachers should make sure they know enough about the cultures of students in their classrooms that they do not engage the students in activities that will be offensive. For example, people from some cultures would find playing with cornmeal on a sand table offensive. Others would be disturbed by studies of plants or animals that have symbolic meaning in their particular cultures. The key is to understand the various communities of the children well enough that you can avoid offending them.

CHAPTER SUMMARY

- Science *is* process, thinking, and an attitude of curiosity and interest in the world. Science *is not* memorizing facts and formulas.
- The scientific process is a cycle that includes forming hypotheses, collecting data, confirming or rejecting the hypotheses, making generalizations, and repeating the cycle. Process skills for young children include observing, classifying and comparing, measuring, communicating, and experimenting. Other process skills that are used less often by young children include relating, inferring, and applying.
- One goal of science instruction is to get children actively involved in exploring and manipulating a variety of materials or phenomena. Other goals include helping children acquire factual knowledge and encouraging their curiosity and interest.
- A balanced science program includes the everyday, playful activities of children that can lead to scientific understandings as well as experiences planned by the teacher. Science instruction should include activities that focus on biological science, physical science, and earth science.
- Concepts in science must be constructed by the

learner. Very little knowledge in science can be simply transmitted from teacher to learner.
- Teachers planning science experiences must provide a safe environment for exploration, must help children learn to investigate safely, and must help children enjoy science.
- Topics in science can easily be extended to promote literacy by having children create and read charts, reports, journals, and literature.
- Most topics in science can be the focus of a thematic organization; classroom experiences in all subject-matter areas can revolve around the science topic.
- Children with special needs can benefit from a multisensory, hands-on approach to teaching science. Teachers may have to make minor adaptations in materials to meet the needs of special learners.
- Children should be provided with examples of the work of scientists from many cultures to help illustrate the contributions these people have made to our daily lives. Teachers should ensure that no activities will be offensive to the cultural groups represented in the classroom.

CONNIE WESTHOF
St. Mary's Episcopal School
EDMOND, OKLAHOMA

Science for the Preschool Child

Science for the preschool child can be defined as opportunities for exploring, observing, discovering, predicting, and questioning. With this in mind, preschool teachers can capitalize on children's natural curiosity about their everyday world. Science need not involve elaborate experiments. Instead, take a child's-eye view of the world, and think about children's interests.

Animals and "critters" are usually of great interest to children. Keep a "critter" cage readily available for those caterpillars, insects, and butterflies that children catch on the playground. Provide magnifying glasses, pencils, and paper, and let children observe and then draw what they have observed. Ant farms and tadpoles are also interesting to observe. Some of the easiest animals to have in a classroom are hermit crabs. They are unusual, interesting, and require little care. Best of all, they are basically odor free.

Chromatography is an unusual yet favorite activity of children. Cut a coffee filter into quarters. Draw a solid line with a washable marker from side to side (black works best). Then fold the filter to look like an ice cream cone, and place it in a baby food jar with the point just barely touching the water (one-half inch of water). Observe as the water travels up and separates the black into different colors. Be sure to use pencil, not markers, if you write students' names on the filter. Once demonstrated, this makes a good center activity for children to choose again and again. Experiment with different-colored markers.

Cooking and making various concoctions are great ways to demonstrate physical changes and the properties of mixtures. My favorites are cooking green eggs and ham after reading the Dr. Seuss book. Children enjoy making Silly Putty, Creepy Clay, and Goop. Recipes for unusual mixtures can be found in *Mudworks*, by MaryAnn F. Kohl (1989; Bright Ring Publishing), and *Kid Concoctions* and *Kids Creations*, both by Robynne Eagen (1994; Teaching and Learning).

Sometimes it is appropriate to have young children record what they have observed through pictures (drawing ants) or through charts ("Which Is Heavier?" "Does It Sink or Float?").

Science can add fun and excitement to any program, so be adventurous. Choose one activity to try each month, and decide what works for you. Do not despair if every activity does not work according to plan. That is a part of science, too—figuring out what went wrong and what else to try. Persevere and you will establish in your students a love for science that will shape their future.

12

ENCOURAGING THE CREATIVE ARTS

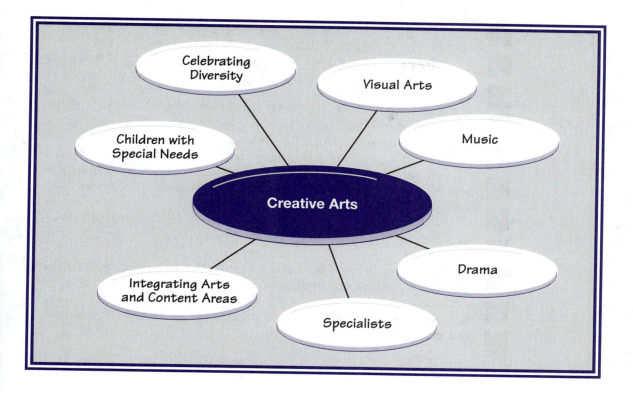

Today, you visited a school where there were a class of four-year-olds, a kindergarten, and a first grade. You were assigned to observe creative experiences in these different age groups. The four-year-olds sang to themselves as they played with blocks and rode on the tricycles. They also spent a short time listening to music, and one activity they could choose today was finger painting. Most of the children painted, but some chose to play with clay instead. In the kindergarten class, you saw some children painting at easels while other children were making vases from orange juice cans to give as gifts. The first-graders were scheduled to have a music lesson for thirty minutes. The teacher explained that they have music three times a week, art twice a week, and physical education daily with specialists. You chose to observe the music lesson. The children sang some familiar songs, moved to

369

various rhythms that the music specialist played on the piano, and listened for repeating melodic phrases in several pieces of music.

When you returned to class, you were surprised to find that many of your classmates' observations were not at all similar to yours. One visited a school where no art was taught; the teacher at that school explained that next quarter, the art teacher would come and the children would have art once a week for a nine-week period. In another school, one of your classmates found a kindergarten teacher presenting lessons on perspective. He was using the model of a children's book and trying to get the children to copy the illustrator's use of perspective. In another school, fine arts seemed to be the focus of the curriculum. Children were involved in arts activities for most of the day.

Now you have questions about planning and evaluating creative experiences. You also wonder how teachers ensure that the time spent with building specialists in art, music, and physical education and movement is most productive for a given group of children. What is the purpose of creative arts in the curriculum? Should teaching art be left to art teachers? Likewise, should only music and physical education/ movement specialists teach those subjects? How do teachers plan and evaluate creative arts experiences?

The arts are important in an early childhood program. Not only do they encourage self-expression and imagination, but they are pleasant for both children and teachers. In creative experiences, children reveal what they know and how they think. Children also learn problem-solving strategies as they create ways of moving or ways of representing what they have observed (Edwards, Gandini, and Forman 1993). The creative arts also provide opportunities for helping children learn content from the sciences, social studies, and other subject-matter areas.

In a position statement supporting every child's right to involvement in the expressive arts, prepared for the Association for Childhood Education International, Jalongo (1990) notes these benefits:

- The expressive arts foster "learning from the inside out," authentic learning that changes behavior and encourages reflection.
- The expressive arts enhance the child's ability to interpret symbols.
- The expressive arts are associated with growth in all areas of development, including academics.

- The expressive arts regard the child as a meaning-maker and constructor, a discoverer and an embodiment of knowledge rather than a passive recipient of someone else's ready-made answers. (p. 196)

An early childhood program would be much the poorer without music, art, and drama.

Definitions of **creativity** vary considerably. For the purposes of this chapter, *creativity* is defined as "the proactive, purposeful impulse to extend beyond the present, characterized by originality, imagination, and fantasy" (Edwards 1990, p. 8). To foster creativity, the teacher of young children must help them express themselves and avoid teaching them that their interpretations of their world are not "correct" or "good." Young children are willing to draw and sing and dance without self-consciousness. They do not worry that the colors they use are not the colors of the things they are representing in real life. Nor do they worry that what they have drawn does not look like what they say it is. They believe in themselves and their abilities. The challenge is to maintain their belief in themselves while working in a group setting.

The National Education Association (NEA 1990) passed a resolution stating that

artistic expression is basic to an individual's intellectual, aesthetic, and emotional development. The Association further believes that fine arts transcend cultural barriers and foster multicultural understanding. The Association therefore believes that every elementary and secondary school curriculum must include a balanced, comprehensive, and sequential program of fine arts. (p. 17)

The arts provide us with several more ways of seeing and of expressing ourselves; children are the poorer if their education does not include a wide diversity of experiences with art (Haskell 1979). Art is also a way of expressing feelings when other language is inadequate. Dancer Isadora Duncan was once asked what a dance meant. She replied that if she could tell what it meant, she would not need to dance it (Bateson 1977). Thomas Kean (1989/90), former governor of New Jersey, believes strongly in arts education. In addition to other reasons for including the arts in the curriculum, he believes that arts education contributes to success in the workplace:

Creativity and expressiveness will be valuable commodities in an economy that places a premium on adaptability. As a recent report on "workplace basics" put it, "Increasingly, skills such as problem solving, listening, negotiation, and knowing how to learn are being seen as essentials." The "frill" of art may well provide the best career training a solicitous parent could hope for. (p. 5)

INTRODUCTION

THEORY
INTO
Practice

Choose a topic usually taught in the primary grades, and plan several appropriate arts experiences to enrich the topic.

The arts can serve as an integrating force that helps children make connections with their experiences. The arts help young children put together what they know about topics in science, social studies, health, math, literature, and so on. The arts are also important for personalizing education. "There is an increasing awareness among educators that the development of instructional approaches that integrate the student's affect and unique personal experiences with course content can increase student motivation, participation, and learning" (Edwards 1990, p. 5).

As noted in Chapter 7, probably the most discussed early childhood programs in the world in recent years are the preschools of Reggio Emilia in northern Italy. Arts are the major focus of the school experience in these programs, and the curriculum is project based. Projects generally grow out of children's play and interests, although some are initiated by teachers in response to observed needs of the children. Children express what they are learning and observing in their environment through the arts. For example, children might be encouraged to create images of themselves using many different media. These images and the discussions about them might lead to explorations of body movements. The environment is also visually stimulating in ways that encourage pondering, wondering, and remembering.

The goal of these preschools is to enhance children's creative and intellectual development, and the arts are believed to be central to that development (New 1990). Gandini (1993) states that teachers in Reggio Emilia view art as only one of the child's means of expression: "Children's expression through many media is not a separate part of the curriculum but is inseparable from the whole cognitive/symbolic expression in the process of learning" (p. 8).

Even though many people and organizations have made statements about the importance of the arts, they are still neglected in many school systems. Moreover, the arts are the first area to be cut whenever schools have budget problems, and they were not even included in the National Educational Goals developed by the governors and the president (Horn and Sieder 1992). Engel (1995) suggests that the difficulty of assessing art skills and performance is one of the reasons the arts are not especially valued in schools.

VISUAL ARTS

The term *visual arts* usually refers to graphic arts, such as using crayons, chalk, and paint and creating sculpture or collage. From the constructivist point of view, as children grow and develop, their representations with graphic materials change in predictable and unvarying stages. Every child moves through the same sequence of stages, but every child moves through them at an individual rate. As teachers observe these stages, they can make inferences about the child's cognitive development and thinking processes. The following are brief descriptions of the stages in drawing.

Stages in Development

Many art educators have tried to describe the stages in the development of children's drawing. Lowenfeld and Brittain (1982) have identified these stages as scribbling, preschematic, schematic, and drawing realism. The first stage, *scribbling,* usually begins at about thirteen months of age. Before that age, children put the crayons or pencils in their mouths. At about thirteen months, children begin to mark with crayons and pencils. The first scribbles are generally zigzags, not distinct shapes. Kellogg (1970) has examined children's scribbles and concludes that they usually fall into distinct patterns, which can be identified by an educated observer. By around three years of age, children begin to include distinct shapes, mostly circles, in their scribbling. Figure 12.1 on page 374 is an example of scribbling.

At about four years of age, children begin to make attempts to represent objects that are familiar in their environment. This stage is the *preschematic* stage. Children in this stage typically draw human figures with very large heads and legs coming out of heads. Kellogg (1970) points out that these first drawings of humans derive from the circles and lines that children have created in their scribbles. Children may also draw other objects that are part of their experience, such as animals, using basically the same forms. Colors used in children's drawings are not realistic, and figures tend to be placed randomly on a page. Figure 12.2 on page 375 is an example of a drawing by a child in the preschematic stage.

At about seven years old, children move into the *schematic* stage, in which definite forms are developed, representing the child's environment. Children will repeat basically the same forms, again and again—drawing people or trees or birds with the same forms or symbols. Figures or objects are often arranged on a baseline, rather than placed at random on the page; however, the baseline itself may be placed randomly or at an angle to the edge of the paper. Children in this stage often represent objects in space from a point of view that is much different from the adult point of view. Children may use an "X-ray" perspective so that viewers can see the inside and outside of a house at the same time. They may also draw objects from different views in one picture. The drawing in Figure 12.3 on page 376 is representative of the schematic stage.

At around nine, children enter the stage of *drawing realism.* They begin to make their drawings much smaller and include much more detail; they are also no longer eager to share their work with adults. Some children in early childhood classrooms may be making the transition into this stage. The drawing in Figure 12.4 on page 377 is typical of the drawing realism stage.

THEORY INTO *Practice*

Observe a three-year-old and a primary child as they paint at easels. Record their conversation, if any. Compare the paintings created and the language used by the children.

FIGURE 12.1 Scribbling

Observe the large outline of the firefighter that has been partially erased and replaced with a person more in proportion to the truck and building.

Another approach to describing children's art development is that of Engel (1995, 1996), who believes that teachers can view children's drawings from two perspectives: one, a descriptive perspective and the other, a developmental perspective. In looking at children's drawings from a descriptive perspective, teachers should keep the following questions in mind:

FIGURE 12.2

Preschematic Drawing

1. *Materials, context:* What is it made of? And, if the information is available, when and under what circumstances was it made? . . .
2. *Basic elements, techniques:* What can the observer see? . . .
3. *Character of communication:* What does it represent? . . .
4. *Aspects of organization, meaning:* How is the picture organized? . . .
5. *Function, intent:* What is it about? . . .
6. *Sources, origins:* Where does the idea come from? . . . (pp. 31–34)

In viewing children's drawings from a developmental perspective, teachers should consider the descriptors outlined in Table 12.1 on page 378, which presents a developmental continuum.

FIGURE 12.3 | **Schematic Drawing**

The furry wope

How young children draw does not seem to reflect training. Brittain (1969) reported his experience in trying to teach nursery school children to draw squares. After many experiences with squares, the children began to draw them at around four years of age. As Brittain put it, "Those children who were not so lucky as to be taught square making abilities also accomplished the task successfully at the age of four" (p. 46).

Even though instruction may not result in changes in drawing, children can learn the vocabulary of art. Dixon and Tarr (1988) demonstrated that children could be taught to recognize elements of art. In a unit on lines, the children moved to music to create lines with their bodies; looked at examples of lines in art; and used lines in their own art with straws, strips of paper, and markers. After these experiences, the children could identify

FIGURE 12.4 **Drawing Realism**

lines as elements of art. Schirrmacher (1986) recommends that teachers point out the elements of color, line, mass or volume, pattern, shape or form, space, and texture when discussing art with young children.

Aylward et al. (1993) found that preschoolers were able to classify works of art by style after a course of study that specifically introduced abstract art and artists. In addition, the teachers observed that the children were more involved in their own art projects during and after this study.

Davis and Gardner (1993) suggest that teachers respond to children's art not by asking them to tell about their pictures and then writing on them (usually just labeling the components) but by demonstrating their own perceptions. For example, the teacher might say "Look at the action in this line; this figure is indeed scribbling around on this page" or "This is a

TABLE 12.1 Developmental Continuum in Children's Drawings

Preschool (ages 2–5)

- scribbles, loops, zigzags, wavy lines, jabs, arcs—often partially off the paper at first
- chance forms or shapes
- trying out different effects
- meaning in the act itself, not in results or product
- experimenting with leaving a mark, with colors and motions to leave a sign or have an effect
- reflecting motion of hand/arm
- separate lines, circlelike shapes, combined straight and curved lines
- other basic forms, controlled marks, first schematic formulae, mandalalike shapes

Sources: physical act of moving a hand and arm, basic concepts such as the circle, exploration of possibilities of line

Early Primary (ages 4–6)

- shapes combined, becoming schemas; intentional image repetition of schemas; development of preferred schemas
- beginnings of representation, often of people; letterlike forms; basic forms represented consistently—houses, flowers, boats, people; animals in profile
- meaning (subject matter) increasingly readable
- repertory or symbolic forms repeated, practiced, and new elements added
- beginnings of individual style (e.g., typical way of drawing a house)
- figures isolated, no context or baseline; each discrete (no overlapping of whole or of parts); size and details according to perceived importance or interest (e.g., long arms)
- several figures on the page; beginning representing of events or narratives; schematic figures placed in a larger concept, for example, knowing an elephant is a four-legged animal with a trunk, the child uses a well-established routine or schema, for drawing animals—cats, dogs, and so forth—and adds a trunk

Sources: child's concepts and knowledge about the world, which takes precedence over direct perception (as in the elephant example above)

Middle Primary (ages 5–8)

- elaboration and variation of schematic figures and experimentation; repetition of imagery, practicing "set pictures" (always drawn the same way), such as racing cars
- details often traditional or formulaic, such as windows with tie-back curtains, chimneys with smoke coming out at an angle, girls defined by skirts and long hair
- narrative, illustrative, inventive; baselines often multiple; "see-through" houses; most figures in own space, without overlapping

Sources: copying conventional renderings by other children, imagination, book illustrations, TV, cartoons, and so on

Late Primary (ages 7–10)

- increased differentiation—of kinds of animals, flowers, buildings, and so on; practiced drawing of favorite subjects—battle scenes, princesses, characters from TV, comics, books; pictures often telling detailed stories
- interest in drawing from nature
- figures sometimes in profile, with limbs bent, props added to indicate roles (e.g., cowboy hat and rope); increasing demand for looking real
- color more naturalistic; scenery, overlapping, shadows, beginning perspective, and shading; more realistic use of scale; distance, elevations, and perspective added
- backgrounds: landscapes, seascapes, sky, underground, under the sea; figures more logically interrelated; elevations, consistent viewpoints given
- action: eye still seeing one relationship at a time, the mind having to put them together on the page to solve problems; fine control of line

Sources: observation, imagination, book knowledge, copying, and so forth

Source: B. S. Engel, *Considering Children's Art: Why and How to Value Their Works* (Washington, DC: National Association for the Education of Young Children, 1995), p. 35. Copyright © 1995 by NAEYC. Used with permission.

nicely balanced drawing; see how you have placed these large figures over here; it makes your drawing very strong" (p. 202). Such statements help children realize that the symbols of art can indeed communicate and that the symbols need not be accompanied by words in order to be valuable.

Goals of Visual Arts Experiences

The expected outcomes of art instruction are much more process oriented than product oriented. In other words, goals are likely to be general—involving children in art experiences and helping children become aware of the elements of art—and are unlikely to include having each child achieve a certain product. Other important goals of visual arts experiences in the early childhood classroom include:

1. Encouraging children to explore a wide variety of materials
2. Providing activities that give sensory pleasure to the participants
3. Allowing children to make discoveries about color, shape, and texture
4. Helping children gain control of fine muscles and practice eye-hand coordination

Painting at an easel offers the opportunity to solve problems and to express oneself.

5. Helping children feel comfortable with their ability to express themselves through art
6. Introducing children to the work of the world's artists

Clearly, these goals are very broad; they do not focus on specific skills, such as mastering perspective. The purpose of art in the early childhood years is to help children express what they know and feel and to begin to recognize how others express themselves through art.

Colbert (1991) reminds us that "the goal of the visual arts in early childhood settings is not to make children into artists. The goal is to enhance those abilities children bring to us, their perceptions, memories, feelings and observations about their own worlds" (p. 25).

Suggested Visual Arts Experiences

Colbert and Taunton (1992) suggest that children need many opportunities to create, look at, and talk about art; they also need to become aware of art in their everyday lives. The activities described in the following sections will help achieve these objectives.

Graphic Art

Children can draw with pencils, crayons, chalk, and markers. A variety of papers of different colors, surface textures, and shapes can add interest to drawing activities. Patterns, dittos, or coloring books carry the message that the child cannot produce acceptable representations for herself; these should therefore be avoided. If the goal is for a child to learn to control the marker or chalk in order to fill in spaces, the child can fill in her own spaces, achieve the goal, and maintain a feeling of competence by drawing her own shapes and figures.

Painting

Young children can paint with tempera at easels or on tables, or they can finger paint. Children painting at easels have freedom to move their arms and can use more muscles than they can sitting at tables, where the muscular movements tend to be confined to the hands. When painting at easels, children can learn to control the paint drips, explore the results of using paints of different thicknesses, and stand back to look at their work from eye level more easily than when painting at tables. Finger paint invites children to explore texture and to risk the messiness. Children can be encouraged to use the sides of their hands and their palms as well as their fingers in the paint.

Teachers may want to offer other paint experiences such as rolling paint from a roll-on bottle; spatter painting; blowing paint with a straw;

dropping paint on paper; using objects other than a brush to apply paint (sponges, crumpled paper, aluminum foil, and so on); or rolling a small ball or marbles in paint and then on paper placed on the bottom of a box.

Printing

Printing can range from quite simple experiences, such as dipping a sponge or a piece of junk into paint and then pressing it onto paper, to complex projects, such as preparing a print form, rolling ink on it with a brayer, and then printing with it. Most kindergarten and primary children can make simple prints. Younger children tend to smear the paint when they try to press objects on paper. In addition to junk prints, kindergartners and primary children can make prints by gluing yarn, fabric scraps, or pieces of natural material onto cardboard or cylinders and then printing with these. Or they can combine media by doing a crayon rubbing and then printing over it.

Sculpture

Children enjoy sculpting with a variety of media; modeling clay is most commonly used. Clay should be available to children regularly. Clay experiences can be varied by using potter's clay that will harden; then children can paint their creations. Other variations include mixing clay with collage materials so that objects are embedded in the clay to achieve three-dimensional creations. Paper is another popular medium for sculpting—it can be folded, torn, crumpled, or glued into three-dimensional forms. Cardboard tubes and small boxes are useful, too. Wood sculpture is also popular; children can glue wood scraps to create extraordinary shapes and designs. (Cabinet shops will often save wood scraps for teachers. Hardwood scraps usually have interesting shapes.)

Collage

Collages can be made with tissue paper; natural materials, such as bark and seeds; fabrics; and a variety of found materials. Collage gives children opportunities to develop an appreciation for texture and appealing arrangements of objects that are not possible with other media. Another advantage of collage is the use of glue. Paste and glue offer unique sensory experiences, and children will want to explore the stickiness, adhesive qualities, and spreadability of different adhesives.

Sewing and Weaving

Very young children can sew on styrofoam trays with holes punched in them or on net stretched in a frame. Kindergartners can sew on burlap with yarn. If children have trouble tying knots, the ends of the yarn can be taped on the back of the burlap with masking tape. Older children can sew with a variety of fabrics, either to create soft sculptures or to decorate the fabrics. Primary children can produce simple projects on circular or straw looms. They can also weave paper or fabric strips into interesting designs.

Combining Techniques

Teachers will think of many other experiences that are appropriate for young children and many ways to combine basic techniques. For example, children might paint on fabric; dye fabric; create simple batiks using crayons and dye on fabric; create puppets using paper, clay, or fabrics; use yarn to create a string design on cardboard and then print with the cardboard; finger paint on a table top and then make a print of the design by covering it with paper and rubbing lightly; create a crayon resist by drawing with wax crayons and painting over the drawing with tempera; or color with crayons, cover the colors with black crayon, and then scratch a design through the black crayon. The list of ideas is almost endless. Keep in mind, however, that as Wachowiak (1977) notes, children often do not enjoy or appreciate a new process or media until they become involved in it.

Viewing and Talking about Art

Schiller (1995) describes her experiences with bringing examples of fine art into her preschool classroom. Although she received very little response from the children at first, over time, they began to discuss the artworks during group times and to choose their favorite pieces. Adding appropriate artworks that relate to topics of interest to the children is the key to getting them to talk about and look at art more closely.

Art versus Craft Activities

Art and craft activities are not the same. *Art,* as it is being defined in this chapter, is an opportunity for children to explore media with no external product goals. Although children may indeed create products as part of an art experience, they have control of their products, and the process of creating is more important than the products that result. *Craft* activities, on the other hand, generally require that children produce something, and most of the products will be very similar or even exactly the same. Some craft activities, such as making pencil holders for gifts, are acceptable if children have a choice about whether to participate. Such craft activities can be made more appropriate for children if the materials and designs for decorating the cans are selected by the children rather than dictated by the teacher. The planning, decision making, and self-expression that are so important in art are rarely found in craft experiences, in which the outcome is predetermined.

Many activities presented to young children as art are neither art nor craft. When children are given patterns for making owls or spiders at Halloween or flowers in the spring, what they learn from these cut-and-paste activities is to follow the teacher's directions, to wait until they are told what to do with materials, and to make their products look exactly like the teacher's model. Such activities meet none of the goals of art. Justifying these experiences with the claim that they teach children to follow directions is questionable—children can learn to follow directions in other activities. The negative learning and frustration that often accompany these projects outweigh any advantages in learning to follow directions.

Edwards and Nabors (1993) describe several examples of what is and what is not art. They describe *art* as becoming "absorbed in what the *process* has to offer rather than in how their *products* will be evaluated" (p. 79, italic in the original).

Both art and craft activities have important places in an integrated curriculum. When provided with needed materials, children can paint a mural of snow activities, build a birdhouse or bird feeder, or illustrate a class book on a topic that they have studied (Dever and Jared 1996). Certainly, it is not difficult for teachers to think of art and craft activities that might accompany certain topics of study. However, teachers must stay focused on allowing children to choose the activities they want to do and to express themselves as they participate in art and craft activities that enhance instruction in other areas.

Taking Art Seriously

Art education should be viewed as a serious undertaking for young children, not a curricular "frill" that can be omitted without harm. Teachers who believe in the value of art in the early childhood curriculum will offer "children sufficient experiential motivation so that they will have something to express and psychological safety so that they will feel free to do so" (Seefeldt 1995a, p. 44). These teachers will also believe that simply putting out materials is not enough—that teachers need to talk with children about their art and help them consider and reflect on their expressions, in the same manner that they would talk to children about their writing. In addition to providing an

PARENTS AND THE ARTS

- Plan a session to help parents look at and respond to their children's art products in positive terms. Make sure parents do not feel they have to be artists to be involved with the arts.

outlet for self-expression, art experiences encourage critical thinking when children are allowed to choose how to express themselves and communicate with others through their art (de la Roche 1996).

MUSIC

Music, like art, is a basic way of learning, experiencing, and communicating. All children deserve a rich musical environment in which to learn to sing, to play music, to move, and to listen. Music is also a valuable tool for helping children gain content knowledge and make sense of their experiences.

Music is a pervasive influence in our lives. We hear music when we worship, exercise, relax, drive, and attend baptisms, weddings, and funerals (Merrion and Vincent 1988). Planned musical experiences should not be delayed until children can participate in group singing or until they can keep an accurate beat. Since research indicates that children respond to music very early, McDonald (1979) suggests that "the starting time for learning about music is the same as the starting time for any learning. Music is one facet in the total education of the child. It must emerge with the nature and needs of the child, from birth onward" (p. 4).

Music is a joyful learning opportunity for children.

Goals of a Music Program

The goals of an early childhood music program should include:

1. Teaching children to sing tunefully
2. Encouraging children to experiment with tempo, volume, and quality of sound
3. Encouraging children to express themselves through singing, movement, and playing simple instruments
4. Giving children opportunities to listen to music
5. Exposing children to a wide variety of types of music

For very young children, music need not necessarily be a group experience, although very short group experiences may be successful. More frequently, music is an individual or small-group activity. As children go about the day's activities, they and their teachers can sing about what they are doing. Also, music need not be limited to actual songs—it is *sound* that brings pleasure and helps children express feelings or thoughts. A child crooning a lullaby while rocking a doll or splashing rhythmically in water is making music a part of everyday experience.

Singing

Children learn to sing tunefully over a period of time. Young children need a supportive and encouraging environment for singing. Their ability to sing is closely related to their growing abilities in other areas of development. McDonald (1979) distilled the following information from research on children's singing:

- By age two most children sing as we generally recognize the skill. Much of their singing is self-generated and spontaneous, occurring as individual exploratory experiences with melody or playing with language.
- The pitch range of their spontaneous singing can be quite extensive. From A flat below middle C to the C# an octave above middle C has been reported. However, when learning songs by imitation, a limited range from D to A (above middle C) seems to be their most comfortable, usable range.
- Many spontaneous songs grow out of motor activities or play with language and vocabulary, and language development may be enhanced by creating simple songs containing repetitive words or phrases.
- Their spontaneous songs frequently use the "teasing chant" melodic configuration (as in "Rain, Rain, Go Away"). Songs with large melodic

intervals are more difficult to sing than those with smaller ones. When melodies contain intervals larger than a fifth or sixth, young children often compress them so that they fit into their easily used pitch range.

- Very young children are not attentive to the necessity to match pitch or tonality when singing with others. Rather, they choose their own pitch range. You may match your pitch to those of the children and in this way introduce the concept of singing in unison.
- Two- and three-year-old children often sing only snatches of songs. Between the ages of two and three, there is considerable progress in the ability to reproduce songs in their entirety. Many three-year-olds are able to sing whole songs accurately and develop a large repertoire of songs.
- Many young children regard group singing experiences as opportunities to listen without joining in. When they do sing, they often lag behind a bit. Sometimes they begin participating by whispering the words. Often they sing only parts of songs—perhaps a repeated phrase that has caught their attention. They enjoy listening to favorite songs over and over and need many opportunities to listen before they become participants in group singing. (pp. 13–14)*

Primary children increase their repertoire of songs, continue to grow in their ability to sing in tune and to recognize the expressive qualities of a song, and may be able to sing an individual part while others sing related parts.

Research indicates that children learn songs in a predictable pattern, beginning with words and moving to rhythms, phrases, and contour (McDonald and Simons 1989). As children gain more control of vocal pitches, they become more able to produce melodies of songs. Beginning singing instruction should include rhythmic speech—chants and rhymes—to help children gain control of their voices. Older children who are not able to sing in tune can also be helped by speech-to-song instruction. Gould (1969) recommends that teachers focus first on activities that include tone-matching exercises. The teacher matches tones produced by the children and then introduces short melodic patterns that match individual children's pitch. When these melodic patterns are mastered, the teacher can introduce short melodic patterns in the singing range. Children's singing voices develop in response to the environment—opportunities and encouragement are very important.

Selecting Songs

In choosing songs for children, teachers must consider the pitch range, the intervals, and the subject of the song. The range must be one in which most

* From Dorothy T. McDonald, *Music in Our Lives: The Early Years* (Washington, DC: National Association for the Education of Young Children, 1979). Reprinted with permission of NAEYC.

children are comfortable singing, which includes approximately the A below middle C to the G or A above middle C. As children mature, the range can be increased; children in the primary grades who are comfortable singing can be introduced to songs with greater range. Songs with descending intervals and few wide skips in the melody are more easily sung by young children. Songs should also be repetitious, both in melody and rhythmic patterns. Children enjoy a wide variety of songs about animals, themselves or their friends, and some nonsense rhymes and jingles (McDonald and Simons 1989).

Gilbert (1981) lists the following points to consider when choosing songs to teach:

1. The song should *appeal to the children*. It may be the tune itself or the rhythm that is attractive; whatever it is, if children like the song and can remember it easily, they will enjoy singing it.
2. The song should *not be too* long and, in general, the younger the child the greater the need for repetition and for a predictable pattern within each verse.
3. Songs with *a chorus* encourage even shy children to join in.
4. Songs which lend themselves to *movement* often have greater potential with young children.
5. Avoid tunes with *very high notes* or *difficult leaps*.
6. Choose songs with words that the children *understand*. Sometimes it is necessary to explain a particular word; at other times it is better to substitute another word or phrase. Always try out new words to see how they "sing." (p. 16)

A surprising number of songs fit the criteria described above. Some examples include "Go Tell Aunt Rhody," "Twinkle, Twinkle Little Star," "Where Is Thumpkin?" "Baa, Baa Black Sheep," and many other nursery songs. Older children will enjoy folk songs ("Michael Row Your Boat Ashore" and "This Land Is Your Land"), humorous songs (such as the songs from *Mary Poppins*), and songs from other cultures. Teachers will know that songs are good choices if the children sing them spontaneously or ask to sing them in group music times.

Presenting Songs

Teachers who are not confident of their singing voices can begin by learning a few simple folk songs and singing them with individual children or small groups before singing with the whole group (Jalongo and Collins 1985). What children need most is a teacher who loves music and shares that interest and enthusiasm; young children are very appreciative of the teacher's singing and are not music critics. Jalongo (1996) believes that "teachers who have limited musical backgrounds can do as well in teaching music as do teachers with extensive musical backgrounds, but only if nonmusicians are conscientious and enthusiastic about following a daily musical curriculum featuring high-quality music" (p. 6).

Teachers who play the piano or feel comfortable about their own singing voices usually introduce songs by playing or singing them several times for the children and then encouraging children to sing along with them. Teachers who cannot play the songs can use recordings to introduce music quite successfully. (A bibliography of suggested recorded music is provided in Appendix E.)

After presenting the whole song several times, the teacher may want to sing a line if the children are having difficulty learning it, but each experience should end with the children singing the whole song through again. This routine will need to be repeated several times over a period of days before the children will be comfortable with a new song.

Musical experiences can be opportunities for problem solving, as children invent new words to songs or new ways of moving to music. Singing games such as "Hokey Pokey" and "Punchinella" lend themselves naturally to problem solving, as children must create their own movements. Children can also create new words to familiar songs. They might substitute any five-letter name in "B-I-N-G-O" and make up a verse about that person. Problem solving is encouraged when children are free to explore and play and when their efforts are supported (Hitz 1987).

Chants such as "The Bear Hunt" are also valuable in the music program, as children learn the rhythms and patterns of language. Many chants lend themselves to instrumentation or body percussion sounds: children can add claps, snaps, or clicks to the rhythm of the chant. Buchoff (1994) suggests that many poems and jump-rope rhymes are appropriate for classroom use. After the children have learned a chant, they can add physical accompaniments, such as clapping, snapping their fingers, tapping their fingers or toes, and so on. Putting the words to a chant on a poster or in a booklet or newsletter can also help children share the chant with their peers and parents.

Wolf (1994) offers the following "secrets for success" in presenting songs:

1. Have an expressive face.
2. Look at the children.
3. Be a participant and get involved.
4. Have fun!
5. Know the song well; learn it from a cassette, if necessary.
6. Start the song with a "Ready, go!"
7. Use visuals and props.
8. Choose success-oriented songs. (p. 24)

Playing Instruments

Today's approach to playing instruments with young children focuses on their exploration of sound and rhythm. Even very young children like to produce sounds by banging on pots and pans. Such interest usually continues, and they are eager to explore sound with drums, bells, xylophones, and shakers. Even though the focus is on exploration, the teacher can help individuals or small groups with instruction in how to hold an instrument or how to strike it to get a more satisfactory sound. As children become able to keep a beat, they can invent simple accompaniments to familiar songs. Primary children can begin to learn to play simple instruments such as recorders.

Studies of children's use of musical instruments and the implications for teachers can be summarized as follows:

1. Children should have many opportunities for free exploration with instruments before any structured activities are attempted.
2. Teachers should attend to children's interests and needs when providing any instruction on how to play an instrument.
3. Children need to express rhythm through physical movement before instruments are introduced.
4. Exploration with instruments can help children learn about pitch, timbre, rhythm, and melody.

Teaching should be focused on helping children achieve the technical skills needed to express creative ideas (McDonald and Simons 1989).

Listening Experiences

Children can be encouraged to listen to a variety of music. Guided listening experiences for younger children should be very short. As children mature, the pieces of music selected for listening can be longer and the children can be expected to hear more complex patterns. Teachers should select classical music, folk music, and music from a variety of cultures and ethnic groups. Listening experiences are most effective if the children are comfortable, both physically and psychologically, and if the experiences are based on the children's previous experiences. Children also need guidance in what to listen for, such as repeated phrases or passages that create moods or images.

Listening experiences can be created through games and other everyday experiences. Children can be encouraged to listen to environmental sounds, both inside and outside the room. Games can include guessing what produced a given sound, clapping back a pattern produced on a drum by the teacher or another student, or recognizing voices (as in "Doggie, Doggie, Who Has the Bone?").

Older preschoolers and primary children can benefit from listening to short, live performances. Often, local symphony orchestras or high school groups prepare special programs for young children. Some of these programs introduce the instruments of the orchestra and help children listen for their sounds; others present musical stories that children will enjoy. Suther (1993) found that introducing children to musical selections in advance of a program greatly enhanced their ability to listen to and appreciate the performance of an orchestra. To achieve this, teachers were provided with teaching kits consisting of plans for musical activities and recordings of the music to be played.

Whether to use music in the background when children are engaged in other activities is a question that teachers will have to answer for themselves. Some teachers argue that children ignore background music; this makes it difficult for them to learn to listen to music attentively. Others argue that providing carefully selected background music at quiet times of the day can be a way of exposing children to music when there might otherwise be no time to do so. No one advocates playing music that adds to the noise level when the children are engaged in noisy activities. Many teachers do choose to make records and tapes available for children to use at listening stations during the activity times of each day. Such stations allow children who wish to listen to music the opportunity to do so without disturbing other children.

Movement and Dance

Movement to music begins very early—children often sway and nod to music they hear. Emile Jaques-Dalcroze (1865–1950), a Swiss composer and teacher, believed that movement was the best way to help children learn to love and appreciate music. He believed that training in moving in response to music should begin in the first year of life (Jaques-Dalcroze 1921). (We will return to Jaques-Dalcroze in a following section on "Dalcroze Eurhythmics.")

Fundamental motor abilities are learned and mastered during the preschool years; it therefore makes sense to focus on the *process* of movement instruction during this time, rather than on the *product*. Most children have mastered the basic movements by the time they enter first grade, but as Malina (1982) notes, "The quality of performance continues to improve as the fundamental patterns are refined and integrated into more complex movement sequences" (p. 215). Seven- and eight-year-olds continue to gain skill and control in motor development. They can add a

TABLE 12.2

Listening and Moving to Music

Birth to four months	**Awareness of music starts almost immediately.** The baby may show his early awareness by responding differently to different kinds of music; he quiets himself to a soothing lullaby and becomes more active when lively music is played.
Four to eight months	**Musical awareness becomes more active.** The baby now enjoys listening intently to all types of sounds in his environment. He begins showing more active awareness of musical sounds by turning his head or face toward the source of the music.
Ten to eighteen months	**Expression of musical preferences begins.** The infant may begin indicating the types of music he likes best—many at this age prefer vocal to instrumental—as well as showing clear displeasure at music he does not like. He rocks or sways his hips to a familiar tune, although not necessarily in time with the music, and claps his hands to a pleasing song.
Eighteen months to two years	**Exploration of musical sounds increases.** Sounds in her environment continue to captivate the toddler. Her developing language skills and increasing mobility allow her to seek out sounds that please her most. She may especially enjoy music on daily TV or radio programs or commercials, and may watch with fascination as a family member plays a musical instrument.
Two to three years	**Dance begins.** The toddler now attempts to "dance" to music by bending his knees in a bounding motion, turning circles, swaying, swinging his arms, and nodding his head. He especially likes a marked rhythm, so band music, nursery songs, or catchy TV jingles may be favorites. He shows an increasing ability to keep time and to follow directions in musical games, which he loves. You'll also notice that he can now pay attention for longer periods. While easily distracted in the past, he can now lie or sit down quietly and listen for several minutes at a time.
Three and one-half to four years	**Self-expression through music increases.** At this stage, a very significant change takes place. As the child listens, she is increasingly aware of some of the components that make up her favorite music. She may love to dramatize songs and may also enjoy trying out different ways of interpreting music (for example, experimenting with different rhythms). She shows marked improvement in keeping the beat, although she is still not always entirely accurate. Music is now an important means for her to express and communicate ideas and emotions that may be beyond her developing language skills.
Four to five years	**Ability to discuss musical experiences expands.** By now the child can talk about what a piece of music suggests to him, and he is able to tell you in greater detail what he is hearing. This is the stage of the "active listener." With encouragement, the child's desire to listen to music will increase.
Five to six years	**Actual coordinated dance movements begin.** The child's increased motor control and ability to synchronize his movements with the rhythm of the music are evident as one watches his attempts to dance. He can actually synchronize hand or foot tapping with music and can skip, hop on one foot, and make rhythmic dance movements to music. This is the time when he may begin to show an interest in dance lessons.

Source: Music: A Way of Life for the Young Child, 4th ed., by K. M. Bayless and M. E. Ramsey, © 1991. Reprinted by permission of Prentice-Hall, Inc., Upper Saddle River, NJ.

beat to music, keep a beat with an instrument while singing, and learn simple folk dances. Table 12.2 presents Bayless and Ramsey's (1991) review of the basic sequence of motor development and implications for instruction in movement.

Movement experiences should be planned to include both creative and more structured movements. Creative movement activities are those in which children interpret instructions in their own ways; their movements may not necessarily match the beat of the music. Examples of creative movement activities are having children move in a given direction and then change direction when the music changes; use movements that are heavy or light; move fast or slow; and so on. More structured movement experiences include asking children to learn to keep a beat and move to a beat.

Weikart (1982) suggests that movement exercises to help children learn to feel and move to a beat should begin with speech activities and progress to keeping the beat to music. She recommends the following sequence in teaching children to keep a beat:

Step One: Say. No music is used. The learner is asked to repeat single words ("knee, knee, knee" or "walk, walk, walk") which will be matched with movements in the next step.

Step Two: Say and do. Learners are asked to match the chant with motions so that both occur simultaneously. The beat is kept by the chant of the words.

Step Three: Whisper and do. Learners are asked to whisper the chants while continuing the motions. After they are proficient, music is added.

Step Four: Do. Learners are asked to think the chant while continuing the movement. Music must have a strong beat that can be clearly understood. (pp. 18–19)

A typical structured movement experience is clapping to simple rhythms. Teachers often have children clap the syllables in their own and their classmates' names. Teachers might also ask children to walk to a drum beat or walk to the beat of music played on the piano or a recording. As children gain more control and are able to keep the beat more accurately, they may be asked to learn simple dance steps.

Sullivan (1982) recommends another simple movement exercise, "Clap, Clap, Clap Your Hands." With the children sitting down, the teacher plays:

C   C   G   F   E   C   C   D   E D   low G
Clap, clap, clap your hands. Clap your hands to-geth-er.

C   C   G   F   E   E   E   D   D D   C
Clap, clap, clap your hands. Clap your hands to-geth-er.

Children can be encouraged to think of other movements, such as tapping their knees, tapping their elbows, shaking their hands, shaking their heads, and so on.

Primary children can be encouraged to keep the beat and explore movement through such exercises as "Copycat." The children find their own space. The leader improvises a movement on the count of 1, and the children imitate the movement on the count of 2. A drum may be used to help keep the beat. In another exercise, the children stand in a long line across the room and are numbered off by threes. Together, they walk forward for eight counts, backward for eight counts, and then turn in their original spot for eight counts. When this pattern has been mastered, the "1's" perform the routine alone, followed by the "2's" and then the "3's." The whole pattern is repeated several times (Findlay 1971).

Approaches to Music Instruction

Four approaches to musical instruction for young children will be described briefly in the following sections: Dalcroze Eurhythmics, the Kodály method, the Orff approach, and Education Through Music.

Dalcroze Eurhythmics

Emile Jaques-Dalcroze developed an approach to teaching music based on the belief that rhythm was the fundamental force in music and that children should develop an awareness of music through body movement. Jaques-Dalcroze believed that sequence was very important in teaching children music and that the simplest of rhythmic experiences should be first, followed by more difficult and complicated activities, followed by instrumental study. This method—called *eurhythmics*—emphasizes the importance of an immediate physical response to music and of having children dramatize music with their bodies.

Findlay's *Rhythm and Movement: Applications of Dalcroze Eurhythmics* (1971) is a good source for teachers; it contains a brief explanation of the child's need for a rhythmic response and a wealth of ideas and activities that any teacher of young children will find interesting and helpful. Dalcroze training for teachers is also available at many universities across the United States.

The Kodály Method

Zoltán Kodály (1882–1967), a Hungarian composer, was a contemporary of Jaques-Dalcroze. He believed that the most important instrument in a child's music education was her own voice. Kodály relied heavily on children's games, nursery songs, and folk music in helping children learn to sing. He believed that accompaniments to songs should be very simple and that a child should learn to "appreciate music as a pure, unadulterated melody emanating from himself, this appreciation being achieved through ear-training exercises" (Bayless and Ramsey 1991, p. 218). The Kodály method is not complicated, and most teachers can implement the program without special training or special equipment.

The Orff Approach

Carl Orff (1895–1982), a German composer, developed his method from work with young dance students in his school. Orff is most commonly associated with the pitched instruments that bear his name. (Most catalogs of musical instruments for children include the Orff instruments.) The Orff program involves structuring a musical environment and then helping children improvise within the environment. Important elements of the Orff method include rhythm, body percussion (stamping, slapping the thighs, clapping, and finger snapping), dramatic movement, melody, and the use of instruments (both percussion instruments and pitched instruments). Orff advocated that activities progress from speech to rhythmic activities to song and then to playing musical instruments. Although they are fairly expensive, many schools use Orff instruments, and Orff training is available to teachers who are interested in learning the approach (McDonald and Simons 1989).

Crinklaw-Kiser (1996) found that the Orff-Schulwerk approach to music is very compatible with a whole-language or developmentally appropriate curriculum. (The word *schulwerk* in the title means "school-work.") This approach begins with what children like to do—sing, clap, dance, and so on. Starting with the rhythm of a song, the words are then added, and then activities are added to expand on that knowledge, such as word cards, charts, booklets, and so on.

Education Through Music

Mary Helen Richards developed the Education Through Music (ETM) program, which combines learning music, movement, singing, and exploration. As Richards (1969) explains, "Music is a catalyst and a leaven in the development of beautiful human beings. It is through the children's songs and games of our folk culture and through the children's natural love of movement that we can reach them with music" (p. 1). The approach advocates teaching children carefully selected songs; guiding them to understand the music (by discussing lyrics, analyzing rhythm patterns, and

Change is very evident in the creative arts. To extend our theme of change, the following are a few examples of activities:

Music

➤ Move to music, changing movements with each change in the music.

➤ Create a beat pattern and play it. Then change it and play it again. Repeat this sequence several times.

➤ While showing a short video, play one kind of music and then another. For example, show a video of children running and playing, first with happy, bubbly music and then with slower, sadder music (perhaps in a minor key). Does the change in music change the interpretation of action in the video?

➤ On a "cigar box guitar," change the width and length of the rubber bands and note the changes in pitch of the music produced.

➤ Play bar bells and determine the relationship between the length of each bar and the pitch of the music.

Art

➤ Mix colors to experiment with the changes that can be created. Use different materials, such as tempera paint, food coloring, acetate film, scarves of various colors, and so on.

➤ Experiment with changing shapes by cutting, tearing, and folding paper.

➤ Experiment with making lines that are very thin or very wide. Discuss the effects of using different thicknesses of lines in drawings.

➤ Experiment with changing textures by adding glue and sand to smooth textures or sanding rough textures until they are smooth. Think about textures in fabrics, and explore textures in paint by using a brush, a roller, and a sponge to apply paint to a surface.

Drama

➤ Move like something that is huge, and then change to move like something that is small. Experiment with the changes.

➤ Make big, expansive movements, working across the room; then change movements to fit a smaller space. Does it feel different to make large versus small movements? to watch them?

➤ Portray a character who changes from being very young to very old.

becoming familiar with melody patterns); and teaching other content areas, especially language arts, through music. Children sing, move to music, create patterns to represent music, and learn to listen carefully—what Richards calls "inner hearing."

Harper et al. (1973) report that kindergarten students who were exposed to the ETM program for twenty minutes each day showed growth on tests of auditory discrimination and on a screening measure when compared to children in a control group who received more traditional music instruction. ETM training is available through workshops and seminars for teachers wishing to learn the approach.

DRAMA

Drama in the early childhood classroom is defined as experiences in which children play, pretend, role-play, or create characters or ideas. McGregor, Tate, and Robinson (1987) state that the essential characteristic of drama is acting out. In acting out,

> there is an agreement to suspend the normal social roles with each other in identifying with the new imagined roles. There is an agreement to make a different use of the environment. In this case a desk becomes a dining table laden with food, a chalk box becomes a cigar box, and so on. This different use of the environment includes a shift in the conventions of time. Events may be telescoped to give them greater or less significance. The usual conventions of space and time may be suspended during acting out. (p. 12)

Drama in early childhood education is not the production of plays in which children memorize lines and act given roles. Such productions are often appropriate for older children but are not appropriate for the early childhood years. Creative drama usually refers to spontaneous productions in which children create or recreate stories, moods, or incidents without learning lines or practicing their roles.

Other aspects of drama include children's theater and participatory theater. *Children's theater* refers to productions designed for an audience of

Drama can be an aid to comprehension and an excellent vehicle for language learning.

children. The performers may be adults or children, but the production is aimed at the children in the audience. A newer form of theater for children is *participatory theater,* in which the audience is encouraged to participate in the production by contributing ideas or sounds or sometimes even by participating in the play.

Drama in the classroom can contribute to the general goals of early childhood programs in a variety of ways. It can foster:

1. The development of critical-thinking and problem-solving skills
2. An ability to work cooperatively with others
3. An increased ability to understand the perspective of others
4. An ability to communicate more effectively
5. The integration of ideas from many sources into a meaningful whole

Of course, drama experiences provide another avenue for self-expression and developing creativity that is as important as their contributions to other curriculum goals.

Encouraging Drama

Most experiences with drama occur spontaneously in children's play or in response to music, songs, stories, or other experiences. Teachers will want to encourage and support these dramatic activities, but they may also plan for specific experiences in drama. Teachers can encourage children's play and help them add or extend dramatic elements. For example, a teacher observing children choosing roles for dramatic play might help a child think of a role or imagine how someone might act in a given role or provide a prop or costume to help the child conceptualize the role more fully.

Most teachers of young children have observed that drama, like other creative arts experiences, is a natural response that arises in a supportive classroom environment with teacher encouragement. Children returning from a trip to the zoo often assume the roles of the people or animals they encountered there. After hearing a story, children will often act out the role of one of the characters. Even very young children can be heard imitating voices or observed pretending to be as sad or as scared as one of the characters in a story.

Planned drama experiences may be incorporated into movement, music, or literature experiences. If the children are exploring movement patterns, they might be asked to move in a way that represents a given character or mood—to tiptoe quickly to represent the movement of mice, for example. Children might also use drama to demonstrate their understanding of the lyrics of songs they are learning. (If they are asked to glide and they flap their arms, the teacher can assume that they do not understand the term *glide*.) After listening to a story, children often want to retell it through dramatic representations. If, after listening to *Where the Wild Things Are* (Sendak 1963), they can act out Max's anger, the power of the "wild things," and Max's relief when he returns to his very own room, there will be no need to ask them comprehension questions.

Other planned drama experiences can extend children's concept knowledge. Fox (1987, pp. 59–60) describes a dramatic activity that she calls "Caterpillars and Butterflies." (If the class were studying insects or caterpillars, these activities would not only add interest but would give the teacher a chance to observe the children's understanding of concepts.) Fox suggests that children begin by observing how real caterpillars move. After these observations, the children crawl around, imitating the movements of the caterpillars (perhaps to music). After hearing the teacher read *The Very Hungry Caterpillar* (Carle 1970), some children can form a tight circle to create an orange, and others can crawl through the orange (eating a hole in the orange). Then the children can think about what happens to the caterpillar after it has eaten all the food. They can curl themselves into cocoons and then pretend to nibble out and spread their butterfly wings. It is helpful if the children can observe the movements of a real butterfly or watch a film of a butterfly in slow motion before they imitate the butterfly movements. Children might also create butterfly wings with scarves or tissue paper and use them in their movements.

Dyer and Schiller (1993) suggest that dramatic performances be approached as problem-solving opportunities instead of the usual memorize-and-rehearse activities. Children should be allowed to figure out how to present to an audience different elements of a story or different interpretations of an event. When this problem-solving experience is part of preparing for a performance, the results will be children's intellectual growth as well as greater audience interest.

Cline and Ingerson (1996) provide the following tips for successful drama experiences:

- Keep story lines and sessions short.
- Focus initially on action instead of dialogue.
- Use many characters (even inanimate objects can be played). Create new ones if you need to.
- Encourage children to be specific ("If Humpty is fat, how can he move to show it?").
- Always keep a distinct physical boundary between the stage and the house (audience), even if it is just a line of tape on the floor. . . .
- Rotate players and audience frequently. . . .
- Narrate the stories during rehearsals and performances until the children become more proficient. . . .
- Interject comments or questions (side coaching). . . .

- Respect and encourage children's decisions. . . .
- Do not introduce the story with a movie, video, or play. These performances irrevocably become the "right" way and short-circuit the children's creativity. (p. 8)

ROLES OF SPECIALISTS

Teachers who are privileged to teach in schools that have specialists in art, music, or physical education on staff should not hesitate to call on these people. They can be excellent resources. However, specialists do not relieve classroom teachers of the responsibility for teaching art, music, or movement.

The best situation is for specialists and classroom teachers to work together to achieve mutual goals. Because art, music, and movement are integral to most content-area instruction, the classroom teacher's role is to inform the specialist of the concepts that she is seeking to help the children develop; the specialist's role is to advise the teacher of activities that would be appropriate for those concepts. For example, if the focus in the classroom is on small animals, an art specialist might suggest having children create torn-paper collages of animals or tempera paintings of animals.

An art specialist can help the classroom teacher not only by suggesting appropriate activities but also by helping the teacher recognize the language of art that is important for the children to learn and by helping the teacher develop other concepts. The art specialist is also a good resource person for the teacher who wants to present the works of other artists to young children. Exposure to fine art can serve as a stimulus to creative experiences and can increase awareness of aesthetic elements (Bowker and Sawyer 1988). The art specialist can also aid the classroom teacher in helping children learn to look at and talk about art. Unless the teacher and art specialist provide opportunities for this kind of art appreciation, it may never occur (Cole and Schaefer 1990).

Similarly, the music specialist can help the classroom teacher incorporate music into daily classroom activities. He can help the teacher select songs that are appropriate for the group and provide guidance in choosing movement experiences or instruments appropriate for the specific theme the teacher is using. For a theme of small animals, the music specialist might help the children learn songs about the small animals in the classroom; listen to animal sounds; distinguish pitch in animal sounds; and produce rhythm patterns to represent various animals.

The physical education specialist can also provide assistance for the classroom teacher of young children. The specialist can help select appropriate movement experiences and provide opportunities for motor activities that can contribute to children's learning in other areas. To extend the theme of small animals, the physical education specialist might help children reproduce the movement patterns of the animals in the classroom. These movements could further the objectives of the physical education program by promoting body control and integrating patterns of motor abilities.

The classroom teacher can take advantage of the expertise of specialists by keeping them informed about topics of interest in the classroom and needs that have been observed. Each specialist has much to offer that will expand children's experiences and further the collaborative development of the best program possible for each child.

CONNECTING THE ARTS AND OTHER SUBJECT-MATTER AREAS

Although the goals and objectives of a creative arts program are important enough to stand alone, the arts also contribute to other curriculum areas in powerful ways. Children learning concepts in science, math, health, and social studies can express their understandings through art, music, movement, and drama. The following sections provide a few examples of the many possible ways the arts can be integrated into different themes or subject-matter areas.

- *Shadows*—Movement possibilities include having children attempt to make their shadows move in certain ways, move without touching the shadows of the other children, and so on. Primary children can make shadow characters and produce a shadow play. Children might also create a stage for the shadow play from a large carton and decorate it. Children can select or create background music for their shadow plays.
- *Birds*—Children can imitate the movements of different birds on the ground and in the air. They can listen to bird songs and learn to recognize a few distinctive calls as well as melodic or repeating patterns. Birds can be represented through graphic art, collage, or sculpture. Bird nests can be made from natural materials. Primary children can note color patterns of birds and perhaps chart common colors or patterns.
- *Seashells*—Children can notice ocean sounds and the regularity of waves. Children can be challenged to represent the movements of different sea creatures, such as anemones or snails. They can sort shells by shapes and note the patterns of seashells. Paintings and drawings of seashells as well as objects (buttons, jewelry) made from seashells

It is hard to conceive of a developmentally appropriate program that fails to include the creative arts. For young children, the arts provide many opportunities to explore materials and techniques, to make choices, to express themselves, and to gain social and cognitive skills. Think about the arts in terms of:

- *Allowing each child to choose her own activity and within that activity, to choose how to complete the activity*—For example, a child might choose to paint at the easel and then choose which colors to use, how to place the elements of the composition on the paper, and how long to work on the painting.
- *Providing intellectual challenge*—A child can continue to learn new techniques and continue to explore new media. The arts are never learned in the sense of learning facts;

every experience with the arts is new and challenging.
- *Providing opportunities for growth in all domains*—While participating in the arts, children gain physical skill (control of body and fine motor skills), grow intellectually (making decisions, planning, organizing), gain social competence (work with others, have responsibility for materials, share space and materials), and develop emotionally (expressing feelings, gaining empathy for the feelings of others, and so on).

can be introduced. (Note, however, that the craft of making creatures from seashells is not art.)

- *Literature*—Children can dance like Sendak's (1963) "wild things"; recreate Peter's movements in *The Snowy Day* (Keats 1962); create costumes and make up a dance like the *Song and Dance Man* (Ackerman 1988); move as silently as the owl in *Owl Moon* (Yolen 1987); and dramatize folk tales.
- *Reading and writing*—After children have learned the lyrics to a song, they can put them on a chart or on sentence strips. Primary children can write new lyrics or substitute words in the lyrics.

THEORY INTO _Practice_

Choose a children's book, and plan an arts experience to deepen the children's understanding or appreciation of the book.

CHILDREN WITH SPECIAL NEEDS

Many experiences in the arts can be modified or adapted to make participation by children with special needs possible. Children with developmental delays may not be ready for group work or for some of the cognitive tasks in the arts program. Teachers will have to determine which experiences are developmentally appropriate for individual children and provide alternative experiences when necessary.

Because most art activities are planned for individuals, most children can participate in art at their own levels without adaptations; work surfaces or materials may have to be adapted for children with orthopedic disabilities. Examples of adaptations include providing work surfaces that are accessible for children in wheelchairs and providing sturdy materials that are easy to grasp so that children can draw and paint. Some children who do not have much control of their arms and hands might benefit from creating computer art; a computer program allows them to control color and so on. Children with visual impairments can paint, finger paint, create collages, and sculptures.

Teachers may need to seek expert advice about planning activities for children with specific types of hearing impairments. Some children are able to hear or feel many sounds—especially percussion or rhythmic elements. Gfeller (1989) provides several recommendations for adapting activities for children with hearing impairments:

1. Children who use hearing aids may hear better if background noises can be minimized.
2. If children use sign language, incorporate signing into singing activities.
3. Use visual aids to help children recognize patterns and other musical information that they may not be able to hear.
4. Placement in the group should make lip reading or watching or feeling instruments possible.
5. Using quality sound equipment that does not distort the sound helps children with some residual hearing.
6. Some children can hear better in the lower frequencies; therefore, instruments with lower pitches should be selected.
7. Rhythmic and percussive elements should be emphasized.

Children with delays in motor development may require instruments that do not have to be grasped, such as bells on a strap that can be fastened around the child's wrist or ankle; stands that hold instruments so that the child can play them are also helpful. During group movement sessions, children can be encouraged to move heads, arms, legs, or whatever body parts they can control; they need not feel left out just because they cannot manage whole-body movements.

Singing may be difficult for some children with speech disabilities, and teachers may need to use more chants and rhythmic speech experiences with them. The teacher may need to consult with a speech specialist to determine the best course of instruction for such children.

Brown (1991) suggests that signing can be added to many drama activities. She recommends that teachers use the following techniques for adapting drama for children with special needs:

1. Use pictures to visually represent new vocabulary and concepts.
2. Break the drama lesson up into a series of short segments.
3. Use repetition to reinforce new language and concepts.
4. Allow children to imitate as a starting point.

5. Sequence the activities, building from the simple to more complex.
6. Begin the activities with warm ups and end with a closing.
7. Introduce techniques to maintain focus and control. (pp. 173–174)

Brown (1991) goes on to suggest that signing during drama can help to involve those children who cannot physically participate in activities:

> While some children become frogs hopping from log to lily pad, other children may carry out the action with a puppet-frog and environment created from signs and gestures. Give children in wheelchairs a special role by using the chair as an integral part of the activity. Wheelchairs make great spaceships and train engines. Children with limited movement can be given the role of the tree in the middle that the other children's hand/leaves fall from, or the Indian chief who must call back braves from a hunt. (p. 178)

As with all children, exposing children with special needs to the arts is a matter of thinking about what the children can do, providing materials that are appropriate for them, and providing guidance in helping each child achieve his own goals.

PARENTS A N D **THE ARTS**

■ Encourage parents who are engaged in the arts—whether vocationally or avocationally—to share their art with the children.

CELEBRATING DIVERSITY

The creative arts offer teachers invaluable opportunities for celebrating the diversity of their classrooms and communities. When choosing examples of fine art to share with children, teachers should make sure that the pieces represent many cultures. Moreover, pieces should include traditional styles from various cultures, which may not be used by contemporary artists but will help children appreciate the various ways humans have represented forms that were important to them. For example, the traditional carvings of the Maori people of New Zealand represented the animals and plants around them; these patterns became stylized and were used in carvings and on fabric. The traditional art of the Native Americans of the Pacific Northwest represented the animals that were important in the stories of the tribes.

In addition to the visual arts, many cultural groups have rich histories of music, drama, and dance. Find videos or photographs of such arts.

THEORY

INTO *Practice*

Choose one of the cultures represented in your school. Find both traditional and modern examples of visual art, music, dance, and drama from that culture. Plan how to integrate these examples into the curriculum.

Learn some traditional songs and dances, with the help of local members of the culture, if possible.

Creative arts also offer children with language differences opportunities to be successful. Difficulties with a dialect or learning a second language will not affect a child's ability to create a painting or sculpture. Cultural and ethnic differences can be honored in musical and dance experiences and in sharing art from many cultures. It is difficult to think of any part of the curriculum in which cultural diversity can be celebrated more easily than in the arts.

CHAPTER SUMMARY

- The arts are very important in early childhood programs. Children need to learn to express themselves and what they know in a variety of ways; the arts provide multiple avenues for expression.
- Children's drawing develops through predictable stages: scribbling, preschematic, schematic, and drawing realism.
- Program goals in the visual arts include helping children explore a wide variety of materials, engage in pleasurable activities, gain control of fine muscles, express themselves, and learn about the work of other artists.
- Music is a basic mode of learning, experiencing, and communicating. The goals of a music program include helping children learn to sing and encouraging them to experiment with tempo, volume, and quality of sound; express themselves; listen to music; and appreciate many kinds of music.
- Young children's singing ability develops over time, as they gain control of their voices and learn to match the pitch of others.
- Songs selected by the teacher must be evaluated in terms of range of pitch, musical intervals, and content.
- Children should have many opportunities to explore simple musical instruments. Instruction in playing instruments should focus on helping individual children achieve their own musical objectives.
- Listening experiences are an important component of a music program. Children need guidance in listening and opportunities to listen to many types of music.

- Movement experiences should include both creative and more structured movements. Movement experiences can be planned to help children feel and move to a musical beat and to allow children to express their ideas.
- Drama in the early childhood classroom is a creative activity in which the children act out their ideas, impressions, and moods.
- Drama contributes to the overall goals of a program by helping children develop critical-thinking and problem-solving abilities, helping them work cooperatively with others, increasing their ability to understand the perspective of others, learning to communicate more effectively, and helping them integrate concepts from subject-matter areas.
- Specialists in art, music, and physical education can help classroom teachers achieve objectives in subject-matter areas and can collaborate with teachers in promoting goals specific to art, music, and physical education.
- Activities in the arts can help integrate topics of study from the sciences and the social studies and can extend literary experiences.
- Activities in the arts can be modified so that children with special needs can participate and benefit from the experience.
- Many opportunities exist to share the arts of other cultures with children. Even very young children can learn to appreciate that it is not only acceptable to express knowledge and feelings in many ways but desirable, as well.

A Successful Art Experience for Four-Year-Olds

Sand has become a source of great interest to our four-year-olds. We are building a new school nearby and have worked to develop a connection with the new site by bringing sand to our current playground from our future playground. The children have made elaborate sand structures on our playground, and we have put sand lightly shaded with colored salt into our sensory table inside. While the children are deeply engrossed in their play, we hear words like "gritty," "scratchy," and "rough."

In light of these experiences, I wanted to extend the children's interest in sand by integrating it into an art activity using sandpaper. I invited the children to sit with me at our large table to talk about the sand we have been using. I suggested we could try using sandpaper to create interesting pictures, and I showed the children the materials I had collected: sandpaper, crayons, scissors, colored construction paper, and an iron.

First, each of the six children folded a piece of coarse or fine sandpaper in half and opened it to cut along the folded line. The feel of the sandpaper stimulated conversation among the children. Jeremy felt cutting was hard because he could not remember which hand he used best to cut. Nathan thought he could smell dirt as he cut along the folded line. Sage cut successfully once she got help adjusting her fingers in the scissors. Kayla said this was easy for her because she cuts all the time at home, mostly coupons for her mom. Noah traced the underside of his upper lip with his tongue as he accurately cut along the fold of his paper. When we counted the pieces of sandpaper we had cut in half, the children discovered there were twelve.

I asked the children to rub their finger tips in the air and think about how they felt. The children said their finger tips felt "smooth," "cold," "sticky," and "wet." Then, when I asked them to rub their finger tips on the sandpaper, the children said it felt "scratchy," "prickly'" "bumpy," "rough," and "like my dad's face."

I invited the children to use crayons to draw on the rough side of the sandpaper. Sage said the crayons were smooth and the paper was scratchy. Noah said he was drawing a sailboat because sand is at the beach. Alexander made lots of colorful lines on his sandpaper and said each line was a pipe that was connected to the ocean. Kayla made a lollipop parade, and Nathan drew a scary pirate ship. Jeremy suggested that everyone make their colors dark, and he demonstrated how to lean on the crayon to produce a deeper color. Josh and Sage drew two fireworks displays. Charlie got excited and said that he was drawing a map that would lead Nathan's pirate ship to the buried gold. Nathan said it was a great map, and he sure would use it. Several children used many colors in their drawings, some used a few colors, and one child used only one color.

Next, I helped each child put his or her sandpaper drawing face down on a piece of construction paper, and together, we ironed the two papers together. The children watched the heat from the iron melt the crayon wax from the sandpaper onto the construction paper. As we lifted the sandpaper, a wonderful print was revealed on the construction paper. Noah thought it was probably magic. Kayla said that it smelled like dirt and a little like cereal and that she really liked the smell. Alexander said he was so happy and that he loved how his print looked. There was a lot of excitement as each print was revealed. The children appeared to have a great time with this sand art activity. Then we sat down to have tiny cheese SANDwiches for a snack.

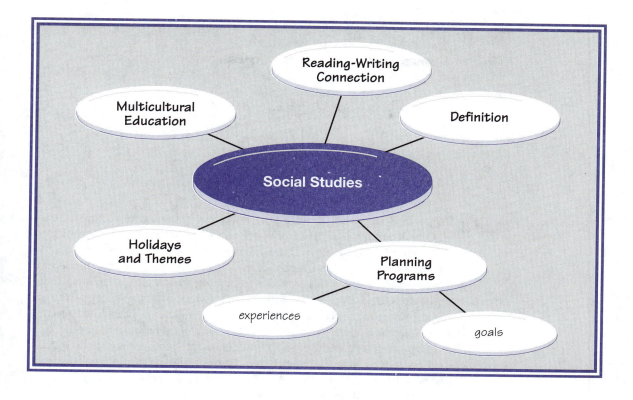

This week, your observations focused on social studies. You thought that you would recognize social studies activities in the classroom because you remember them from your own early schoolyears: memorizing the names of the presidents, the states and their capitals, and the imports and exports of various countries. However, what you saw was not what you expected. You found children working together to solve a problem with the playground materials and voting on what projects they wanted to do next. You also found children who were mapping their classroom and using cardboard cartons to build structures for their map.

When you returned to your class, some of your peers reported seeing young children answering questions such as "What is the name of our city? our state? our country? our continent?" Other of your classmates had seen children coloring pictures of George Washington and Abraham Lincoln and learning to say that they were famous presidents.

You and your peers have many questions about social studies. What *is* social studies? Is it learning to get along peacefully with others? Is it learning a set of facts? Is it a set of facts that are taught directly, or is it a set of concepts that are developed through living together?

Programs for young children use several approaches to social studies. One approach is to integrate social studies into the daily lives of the children. Proponents of this approach believe that social studies need not be a content area for young children. They believe that as children learn to settle disputes, work out systems for taking turns, and establish other arrangements for living and working together responsibly, they are learning the most important concepts of social studies. Another approach is to treat social studies as a content area with a body of knowledge that should be learned by all young children. Proponents of this view believe that social studies content is important and that young children could be learning much more than is commonly taught in preschools and primary grades. A third approach combines these two views of social studies, so that children learn content in social studies but do so while learning the skills of interacting in groups.

Proponents of all three views believe that social studies is important because world conditions are changing and citizens must be prepared to participate effectively in government and society. Education for participation in a democracy is not a new idea. The focus of American schools during the period following the Revolutionary War was on educating citizens to participate in the new democratic government. Thomas Jefferson (1743–1826) stated, "If a nation expects to be ignorant and free, in a state of civilization, it expects what never was and never will be" (Butts 1960). To be successful, a representative democracy requires a citizenry capable of examining the issues and making decisions that will benefit the nation.

John Dewey (1859–1952) also emphasized the importance of learning to live in a democratic society. He believed that classrooms should be democratic and that children should learn to participate in the decision-making process as part of their school experience (Dewey 1916). His thinking was considered to be radical in his time because schools of that era were so authoritarian.

The organizational pattern for social studies in elementary schools—called the **expanding curriculum**—was developed from the ideas of Lucy

Sprague Mitchell (1878–1967). The expanding curriculum typically begins in kindergarten or first grade with a focus on the individual; the focus then moves to the individual in a group, a community, a state, a nation, and finally, the world. Mitchell believed that children learn social studies by participating in real experiences. She described how children learn geography, for example, from field trips during which they can examine the real features of the region around them (Mitchell 1928). Mitchell believed that in order to learn, children must have experiences, see relationships, and make connections and generalizations. She expected teachers not merely to supply information but to arrange activities that would enable children to gain information through experience.

In recent years, the teaching of social studies has been widely criticized in the popular press. Critics have pointed to the lack of factual knowledge and skills exhibited by students, especially high school graduates, who lack geographic knowledge and often cannot even locate North America on a map. Critics also find that very few Americans have what they consider an adequate knowledge of U.S. history. According to some analysts, these problems have arisen in part because of the expanding curriculum. It is not the expanding curriculum itself that has caused problems, however. Rather, over the years, some teachers of young children have lost sight of Mitchell's emphasis on thinking and intellectual development and have presented so-called units on the home, school, and neighborhood. Critics have reason to be concerned with any curriculum that relies on units presented without active involvement by children and without consideration of what children already know.

DEFINITION OF SOCIAL STUDIES

What is social studies, and what is appropriate social studies instruction for young children? *Social studies* includes all the social sciences—anthropology, sociology, psychology, history, geography, political science, and economics—but neither teachers nor children should be expected to separate learning experiences into these categories. Social studies in early childhood classrooms should help children gain knowledge, skills, and attitudes that are important in the social sciences. Social studies, like other subject-matter areas, is best taught through an integrated approach that uses activities appropriate for the age and development of the children and is best learned through active participation.

In a position statement defining appropriate practice in the education of preschool children, the National Association for the Education of Young Children (NAEYC) describes social studies as integrated when children participate in meaningful activities: "build with blocks; observe changes in the environment; sing and listen to music from other cultures" (Bredekamp

1987, p. 56). The same document describes appropriate social studies instruction for the primary grades as follows:

> Social studies themes are identified as the focus of work for extended periods of time. Social studies concepts are learned through a variety of projects and playful activities involving independent research in library books; excursions and interviewing visitors; discussions; the relevant use of language, writing, spelling (invented and teacher-taught), and reading skills; and opportunities to develop social skills such as planning, sharing, taking turns, and working in committees. The classroom is treated as a laboratory of social relations where children explore values and learn rules of social living and respect for individual differences through experience. Relevant art, music, dance, drama, woodworking, and games are incorporated in social studies. (p. 71)

The National Council of Social Studies (NCSS) has also issued a position statement (NCSS Task Force 1989) that defines social studies and presents a rationale for including it in the curriculum:

> The social studies are the study of political, economic, cultural, and environmental aspects of societies in the past, present, and future. For elementary school children, as well as for all age groups, social studies have several purposes. The social studies equip them with the knowledge and understanding of the past necessary for coping with the present and planning for the future, enable them to understand and participate effectively in their world, and explain their relationship to other people and to social, economic, and political institutions. Social studies can provide students with the skills for productive problem solving and decision making, as well as for assessing issues and making thoughtful value judgments. Above all, the social studies help students to integrate these skills and understandings into a framework for responsible citizen participation, whether in their play group, the school, the community, or the world. (p. 15)

It is clear that teachers do have responsibilities in the area of social studies instruction other than to help children learn to interact in groups, but it is equally clear that social studies need not be a separate subject or divorced from other activities in children's experiences. An early childhood teacher must plan for experiences in which the children can be active and that will help children gain meaningful knowledge, skills, and attitudes important in the social studies.

PLANNING SOCIAL STUDIES EDUCATION

Goals

New goal statements have been developed for some subject areas within the social studies—namely, civics education, geography, and history. It seems, however, that at least the civics and geography standards fail to take into account the development of young children and knowledge about what children can learn in meaningful ways (Seefeldt 1995b). Therefore, the position statement of the NCSS (1989) seems to be the best available set of guidelines for creating social studies programs in which children gain the following knowledge, skills, and attitudes:

- *Knowledge goals*—Knowledge goals focus on concepts, including concepts that reflect the content of the social studies, such as:
  —Each person is unique.
  —People are interdependent.
  —The earth is covered with water and land.
  —Land forms determine where people live and affect how they live.
  —Social groups must solve problems.
  —Each person has responsibilities.

  Other knowledge goals focus on concepts based on the structure of the social science disciplines, such as:
  —We can learn about the past from evidence left by others.
  —Records can help us recall what has happened.
  —Groups can make decisions that affect each individual.
  —Individuals can help determine how problems are solved.

  Finally, some knowledge goals focus on concepts based on children's interests, such as:
  —Change is continuous.
  —Different social groups solve problems differently.
  —People in neighborhoods help each other.

- *Skill goals*—Skill goals are furthered by activities that emphasize the ability to record and communicate simple data; the ability to interact in socially acceptable ways with family, peers, and adults; and the ability to solve problems of a social nature.

- *Attitude goals*—Attitude goals emphasize helping children recognize the importance of each individual; respect the feelings of other individuals; and cultivate a continuing interest in learning about the people, places, and systems that are integral to the social studies.

Children can learn about democracy through many activities.

A relatively new concept in social studies for young children is *conflict resolution*. The goals of conflict resolution overlap several of the knowledge, skill, and attitude goals listed above. Drew (1987) identifies the major concepts of conflict resolution as "accepting self and others, communicating effectively, resolving conflicts, and understanding intercultural differences" (p. 1). Teachers who focus on conflict resolution will help children learn alternate responses to social situations, learn about other people, and learn how to communicate their feelings and expectations in ways that lead to peaceful solutions to problems. Luke and Meyers (1994/1995) suggest that using carefully selected literature, in which the characters solve their problems in a positive manner, is an effective means of teaching children about conflict resolution. Proponents of teaching conflict resolution skills hope that more people will learn to apply them and that eventually even nations will use the techniques to solve problems rather than resorting to violence or war.

Classroom Experiences

Threes and Fours

Appropriate experiences in the social studies, like any experience for children who are three or four, cannot be separated from play. Just as in math and science, teachers will want to provide not only play materials that help children learn some social studies concepts but also time to use them. In

Achieving DAP in social studies instruction, where topics are fairly abstract, may seem more complicated than in math or science instruction, where real things can be manipulated and observed. Teachers of young children will be especially challenged in planning appropriate social studies activities. In deciding what is developmentally appropriate, teachers should consider the following:

- Can children understand the concepts to be learned? If the concepts depend on being able to understand historical times or places far from children's experience, then children will not likely understand them.
- Are the concepts related to children's real-life experiences? Learning about a harbor may not be appropriate for children who live far inland.
- Can meaningful activities in which children are involved be planned around the concept? Field trips, resource people, and real objects to explore may bring concepts to life for young children; completing dittoed worksheets and coloring pages, however, will not promote concepts.
- Can the concept be integrated into other areas of the curriculum? For example, can the concept be developed through activities in which children sing songs, learn dances, read stories, and create art?
- Do the activities honor the diversity of the children and their families?
- Will stereotypes be reduced rather than increased through participation in social studies activities?

developing themes for organizing curriculum, teachers should make sure that social studies concepts are included when they are appropriate. The following descriptions may suggest other possibilities:

- Toys related to methods of transportation can be included in play areas. Trucks, cars, buses, trains, airplanes, and helicopters can be added to the block area, and boats and barges can be added to the water play area. The teacher can help children focus on the concept of the necessity of transporting goods and people.
- Children can take short walks in their neighborhood and identify structures (houses, businesses, churches, and so on).
- Children can be led to observe changes in their immediate environments, such as changes in the room, on the playground, or in the school building.
- Children can be encouraged to create structures with blocks that represent what they know of their neighborhood or community. They might construct a fire station if they live near one or if the school is near one, an airport if it is part of their experience, a gas station, a harbor, or other structures.
- Children can work together to move toys or materials that need to be moved or to clean up the materials and play areas.

- Teachers can keep a large scrapbook with records of important events in the children's experiences. Reviewing it with the children will teach them that we can keep records of events and that these records help us to recall the events accurately.
- Teachers can help children appreciate their growing skills and abilities by pointing out, for example, that they can run, throw a ball, walk on tiptoe, share materials, control the crayon when drawing, or use language more effectively than they could earlier.

Fives and Sixes

Social studies for the school beginner should continue to be based on play experiences and meaningful activities. The teacher will want to plan some experiences that help children develop specific concepts, but this does not imply that lessons in social studies should be isolated from other experiences. Suggested activities include the following:

- Children can continue to learn about change by observing any changes in the neighborhood or community (such as buildings being constructed or torn down). The children can record their observations in their journals, or the teacher can help them record their observations on experience charts. Photographs of the sequence of the changes can help children keep records. Children can also learn about change in themselves by bringing in baby pictures or baby clothes and comparing them with their current looks and clothing.
- Children can learn about the world of work by visiting workplaces in the neighborhood and then making models of the neighborhood. They can use hats and other pieces of clothing to create the roles of various workers. The teacher can then develop themes around different businesses or jobs (Borden 1987). The children's parents can be invited to class to describe their work and the tools they use. Teachers are urged to use their imaginations and invite workers of all kinds to the classroom—not just dentists or doctors. The parent workers who created the most long-term interest in one kindergarten (role-play, block play, sociodramatic play) were an athletic trainer, a telephone line person, and a shoe salesperson. People who work in the school can be asked to visit class and describe their work. Children will learn that the school cannot operate without many people making contributions.
- Children can celebrate the diversity of family structures in which they live. The teacher can find pictures to represent the family structures in the class, and the children can write or dictate lists of common features and positive attributes of families.
- Children can begin to explore racial and ethnic differences by examining differences in skin color, hair texture, and eye shape. After selecting paint chips or mixing paint to match their individual skin colors,

they can create a chart illustrating the range of colors in the class. They can create another chart of hair textures and eye colors. With guidance from the teacher, kindergarten children can discuss the advantages of physical characteristics under different environmental conditions—for example, dark skin provides more protection from the sun (Derman-Sparks and ABC Task Force 1989).

- Children can begin to categorize objects or goods as "wants" or "needs." They can develop the concept that people are paid for their work and that the money is used to acquire goods.
- Children can create three-dimensional maps of the classroom and of their neighborhood. Photographs can be attached to models of buildings or other structures in the neighborhood. These maps can be created with blocks, milk cartons, cereal boxes, and so on.
- Children can locate and label different kinds of homes in the neighborhood. They can look for single-family homes, apartment buildings, condos, homeless shelters, or whatever is part of their experience. They can compare and contrast living in each kind of house.
- Children can trace the route taken by the milk that is served every day in the classroom from the dairy farm to the dairy, the distributor, the delivery truck, and the cafeteria. They can make books of their observations and learn about the animals that provide milk and the people who process and deliver it.
- Children can survey the school neighborhood for problems. If they find litter, for example, they can try to find out who is contributing to the litter problem, find solutions to the problem, and report their findings to others at school or in the community. They could also pick up litter on a regular basis, thereby performing a valuable community service and contributing in a meaningful way to community life.
- Children can trace the route of a piece of mail. They can address a brightly colored envelope to themselves and then visit the post office and trace its progress: through the sorting machines, as it is sorted again by the postal worker on the delivery route, as it reaches the school, and as it is sorted yet again in order to reach their classroom.
- Children can invite their families to talk about family and cultural customs or holiday celebrations, food, clothing, or other cultural experiences with the class.

Sevens and Eights

Sevens and eights can do more with maps and learn more about economics and politics than younger children; however, they still need real experiences. Teachers should not expect sevens and eights to learn from textbooks or be able to handle abstract concepts that are not part of their experience. Activities for this age group include the following:

- Children can map their school and perhaps their neighborhood by constructing three-dimensional maps and then transferring the information to a two-dimensional form. They can create legends for the two-dimensional maps.
- Children can learn about elections and voting. They can visit a polling place and see how the records are kept and how the ballots are marked. They can invite people who are running for local office to visit and explain why they want to be elected. They might interview several different people to determine how people make decisions about voting or why they do or do not vote. They can participate in classroom and school elections and make classroom decisions by voting.
- Children can survey others in school to find out what kinds of jobs their parents hold. This information can be presented on charts and graphs. (The teacher can use the work done by parents as a source of themes—for example, factory production or service industries.) If some parents are unemployed, on welfare, on strike, or laid off from their jobs, teachers can help children learn some of the reasons for these conditions in their neighborhoods.
- The class can survey the community to determine local natural resources and how they are used. They can determine who in the community makes decisions about resources and interview those people about their long-term goals. The teacher can help children obtain information on conserving natural resources from books, speakers, films, and so on. Children can make lists of what they can do to conserve resources.
- Children can determine who is responsible for all the services provided in the community and create Venn diagrams of government and private responsibilities.
- Current events can provide learning experiences for this age group if they are related to the children's interests and experience. Interesting pictures or stories from newspapers can be posted on a bulletin board as a catalyst to spark discussion or further explorations.

CELEBRATING HOLIDAYS

Some teachers of young children center their social studies instruction around holidays. Many teachers move from one holiday to another, justifying the emphasis on holidays as important to the cultural heritage of the children. Such a rationale is logical only if the children share the culture in which the holiday originated. It is acceptable to celebrate holidays appropriately with young children, but social studies should certainly be more than completing worksheets about Lincoln's birthday.

Holiday instruction is complicated by the fact that many holidays are religious in nature and cannot be celebrated in public schools. When the religious meaning is removed from holidays, only the secular elements are left—a lot of red and green art and Easter bunnies. Another objection to the "curriculum-by-holiday" approach is the frenzy that surrounds most holidays. By the time children do holiday art for a month, see all the advertisements on TV, and see all the displays in the stores, the holiday itself seems rather anticlimactic. Finally, too often teachers do not consider the meaning of the holiday for individual children in a program, particularly in today's multicultural society. We have to wonder, for example, what meaning Native American and Hispanic children get from a week of cutting and pasting shamrocks and similar St. Patrick's Day activities.

Given all the problems just mentioned, teachers may begin to wonder whether to celebrate holidays at all—and if so, how. The following guidelines may be helpful:

1. Consider what the children will learn if the holiday is acknowledged in the curriculum. Each holiday should be evaluated in terms of the curriculum goals of the program (Dimidjian 1989; Timberlake 1978).
2. Determine what the children think the holiday means and what they know about it.
3. Remember that the children should have the most important role in deciding how the holiday should be celebrated. Involve the children in planning and implementing the celebration. Is the celebration something they can really do themselves, or is it so elaborate that an adult must do it for them?
4. Reduce the amount of hype over holidays to a minimum. One or two meaningful art projects should be enough—it is not necessary to plan fifteen.
5. Celebrate holidays of all the cultural groups in your class. Involve children's families, and learn about some of their traditions. Find common elements in how people celebrate holidays: food, family visits, religious ceremonies, gifts, and so on. Recognize different cultural views of holiday celebrations. Native Americans, for example, probably do not have the same view of Thanksgiving as those in the mainstream culture (Ramsey 1979).
6. Present information that is age appropriate for the children. Do not try to make children memorize and repeat meaningless information. For example, on President's Day, children often have to repeat lists of facts about Washington or Lincoln. It may be worthwhile to show pictures of Washington and Lincoln and explain that they were great presidents, especially if the children initiate the conversations, but fours and fives have no need to know many details about these men. Sixes, sevens, and eights may know more about the current president, be

able to understand that past presidents were very important, and be able to listen to short biographies of these men. Children who demonstrate interest in learning more about past presidents or other historical figures should be encouraged to do so, but having children memorize facts isolated from their reality is not appropriate.

The following suggestions for specific holiday celebrations are based on ideas in two books: *Anti-Bias Curriculum: Tools for Empowering Young Children* (Derman-Sparks and ABC Task Force 1989) and *Teaching and Learning in a Diverse World* (Ramsey 1987).

Thanksgiving

- The children can focus on the harvest aspects of the holiday by visiting a farm, harvesting their own garden, or finding evidence of harvest in the community.
- The teacher can help the children find information about other harvest festivals and how they are celebrated.
- The teacher can help the children relate the eating of a meal to the celebration of the harvest.
- The teacher should supply *accurate* information about contemporary Native Americans using books, pictures, and guest speakers. The teacher can help children critique greeting cards and TV specials for images of Native Americans and the authenticity of the portrayals of the first Thanksgiving. In the words of author and Native American rights activist Michael Dorris, "It must be communicated to educators that no information about Native peoples is truly preferable to a reiteration of the same old stereotypes, particularly in the early years" (cited in Derman-Sparks and ABC Task Force 1989, p. 88).
- The children can help cook some foods typical of Thanksgiving celebrations such as cornbread, squash, and cranberries.

Halloween

- The teacher can help children recognize the harvest aspects of Halloween (scarecrows, pumpkins, and so on).
- Children can learn to recognize the similarities between jack-o'-lanterns and other cultures' representations of human figures with food. They can create some "vegetable people" from squash, turnips, or ears of corn. The vegetable people can be washed and eaten after the activity.
- Children can explore costumes for different purposes (theater, other entertainment). Younger children can be encouraged to explore the concept of being the same person even though they look different in costumes.
- A maker of masks can be invited to share his collection and help the children understand some of the cultural uses of masks or show slides

THEORY INTO *Practice*

If possible, observe the same holiday celebration at a preschool and in a primary grade. Could you determine the goals of each celebration? Could you determine if the children actually learned what they were intended to learn? Use the guidelines in this chapter to evaluate each celebration.

of different masks from around the world. Involve the children in mask making. In order to avoid having them associate the color black with scary things, children can be encouraged to make masks that are scary but not black and others that are black but not scary.

- Teachers can help children explore scary feelings. Children can create paintings, songs, or dances that help them express their feelings. They can find scary things in books such as *Where the Wild Things Are* (Sendak 1963) and *There's a Nightmare in My Closet* (Mayer 1968) and talk about how the characters responded to being scared.

- Children in communities that still maintain the tradition of going from house to house at Halloween can explore how that tradition is carried on in other celebrations. Teachers can help children understand the trick in *trick or treat* by sharing "trickster" stories from the southwestern Native American tradition and inviting children to plan some tricks.

- Older children can trace the origins of symbols used in Halloween celebrations.

> **PARENTS AND SOCIAL STUDIES**
>
> ■ Ask parents to tell you how they feel about celebrating holidays at school. In your invitation to parents, make sure that you describe the cultural diversity of your school, so that parents can think about how others might feel about holidays.

SOCIAL STUDIES THEMES

As with other subject-matter areas, a thematic approach to social studies offers opportunities for children to do meaningful tasks that can help them acquire important knowledge, skills, and attitudes. A list of possible themes that would be useful for developing social studies concepts would be nearly endless. Teachers could focus on the family; justice; change; the neighborhood; the city; celebrations; historical places in the community; parks; interdependence; workplaces; bread—and this is by no means an exhaustive list. Suggestions for developing two such themes are described in the following sections.

Activities for a Supermarket Theme
- Learn vocabulary words: *shopping, bakery, produce, dairy, meat, canned goods, paper goods, cereals, spices* (and other words related to each of these categories).
- Have children write signs, shopping lists, advertisements for products, descriptions of new products, directions for using products, or an ABC book of the supermarket.
- Visit a local supermarket. List departments. Observe signs on aisles, shelves, and products. Observe workers and find out what each does: delivery people, stock people, butchers, bakers, custodians, checkers,

Social studies instruction must include experiences in which children can participate actively.

manager, deli clerk, florist. Purchase unfamiliar fruits or vegetables to taste later.

- Set up a supermarket in the classroom using as many props as possible: aprons, name tags, jackets, bags, shelves, a scanner or a cash register. Classify foods into departments (meat department, dairy case, frozen foods, and so on). Group foods that go together (Mexican foods, Chinese foods, and so on). Find other ways food items can be grouped.

- Use a map to find countries where imported products originate: crackers, cheeses, exotic fruits, and the like.

- Learn money concepts. Observe as the teacher pays for purchases. Discuss the concept "change." Depending on children's math skills, look at the costs of items in grocery ads. Compare costs at different stores. Give each child an amount of play money: What can she buy with the money? Will she get change? Discuss how families get money to purchase food. Talk about why packaged foods cost more than foods prepared at home by consumers. Compare the costs of making bread or applesauce, for example, versus buying it.

To continue our theme of change, think about the following possibilities in planning social studies activities:

➤ Read *The Little House* (Burton 1942), and make a list of the changes that occur in the environment surrounding the house.

➤ Ask children to collect toys and clothes that they once wore and used; then make a display of these items to compare the children's earlier sizes and interests to those of today. Read *You'll Soon Grow into Them, Titch* (Hutchins 1983), and compare the children's changes to those experienced by Titch.

➤ Collect photographs of your school or community from as many years ago as possible; make a book showing the changes over time. Read *Shaker Lane* (Provensen and Provensen 1987), and compare the changes described in the book with those observed in your community.

➤ Visit a museum to observe a household appliance that was commonly in use thirty or so years ago; present a report comparing the nature and purpose of that old appliance to those of the same or a similar appliance today. For example, compare a wringer washing machine with a modern machine, a flat iron with an electric iron, or a popcorn popper to be used over an open fire with an electric popper.

➤ Visit a museum to observe the clothing worn by children in various periods of history. Compare what children wore in the past to what they wear today; note the changes.

➤ Interview grandparents or other elderly relatives or friends about the significant changes that have taken place during their lives. For example, ask about changes in transportation, communication, work, shopping, and so on.

➤ Adopt a tree and keep a record of how it changes over the year. The following books can help children develop the concept of change in trees: *The Apple Tree* (Parnell 1987); *Sky Tree* (Locker 1995); *Someday a Tree* (Bunting 1993); *Have You Seen Trees?* (Oppenheim 1995); and *Red Leaf, Yellow Leaf* (Ehlert 1991).

➤ Encourage families to help their children develop family history books, which reflect both the changes in and continuity of family life.

➤ Help each child develop her own personal history book using photographs, height and weight records, family anecdotes, pictures of her home, and samples of her work.

Activities for a Neighborhood Theme

• Take a walk around the neighborhood of the school. Ask one group of students to record information about signs they see in the neighborhood: street signs, stop signs, business signs, and so on. Ask another group to record what types of buildings are in the neighborhood, such as multistory buildings, single-family houses, and so on. Have another group record the kinds of businesses in the neighborhood, such as grocery stores, hardware stores, drug stores, and the like. Have another group record the types of people observed in the neighborhood and

Plan activities for a specific age of young children around a theme related to social studies.

what they are doing. If appropriate, ask another group to record what is beautiful or decorative in the neighborhood.

- Have children interview people who live or work in the neighborhood. Interview questions should include how long each person has lived or worked there, where he lives or works (if it is not in the neighborhood), what he especially likes about the neighborhood, what he thinks is a problem in the neighborhood, and what (if anything) he would like to see changed about the neighborhood.
- Record the data from the interviews, and make decisions about how to share this information with others.
- When the children return to the classroom, have them begin to construct a three-dimensional map of the immediate neighborhood using blocks, milk cartons, and other materials. Children should include in their construction the signs and other print found in the neighborhood.
- Create a neighborhood newspaper, reporting stories about the various people who live and work in the neighborhood.
- Determine who is in charge of any problem areas in the neighborhood, such as poorly maintained streets; invite that person to speak to the class about plans for repairing or eliminating the problem.

MULTICULTURAL EDUCATION

Multicultural education and **antibias curriculum** are terms used to describe educational programs that attempt to teach children respect for all people and their cultures. Multicultural education involves learning about one's own and other cultures in an integrated way. A multicultural or antibias curriculum is not achieved by superficial lessons; it is achieved by sensitive and knowledgeable teachers who help children learn in a context in which all cultures are appreciated.

The National Council for Accreditation of Teacher Education (1987) defines *multicultural education* as a perspective that recognizes "(1) the social, political, and economic realities that individuals experience in culturally diverse and complex human encounters and (2) the importance of culture, race, sex and gender, ethnicity, religion, socioeconomic status, and exceptionalities in the education process" (p. 57).

The effort to eliminate racism and prejudice by making students and teachers more aware and accepting of the cultural diversity in the United States is relatively new. Recent U.S. demographic information indicates that cultural and ethnic minority populations are growing rapidly; consequently, multicultural education is also gaining importance.

Whaley and Swadner (1990) argue for beginning multicultural education in infant and toddler programs. Very young children learn to discriminate differences and classify things and feelings; they can also learn to be more

Learning about others is enhanced through the use of artifacts that children can explore or create.

empathetic than was once believed. Programs that support multicultural education are important as very young children begin to learn about people other than family. Teachers of preschoolers can make sure that materials (books, music, dolls, and so on) represent a variety of cultures, use pictures of different cultural and ethnic groups involved in a variety of experiences, and take every opportunity to help children learn to care for each other.

The basic assumptions of multicultural education have been articulated by Hernandez (1989):

1. It is increasingly important for political, social, educational, and economic reasons to recognize that the United States is a culturally diverse society.
2. Multicultural education is for all students.
3. Multicultural education is synonymous with effective teaching.
4. Teaching is a cross-cultural encounter.
5. Traditionally, the educational system has not served all students equally well.
6. Multicultural education is synonymous with educational innovation and reform.
7. Next to parents, teachers are the single most important factor in the lives of children.

8. Classroom interaction between teachers and students constitutes the major part of the educational process for most students (pp. 9–11).

Several classroom implications follow from these assumptions. One is that lessons limited to teaching children about a single aspect of one other culture are inappropriate. For example, teachers sometimes attempt to teach about Hispanic culture by making and serving tortillas. More appropriate experiences would continue over a period of several days, during which children would discover that each cultural group has bread of some kind and participate in making and eating bread from each cultural group represented in the classroom. These experiences could reveal to children that people of all cultures buy bread at markets, that some cultures do not have traditional breads at all, and that others bake traditional breads only on special occasions. Finding the common elements in how people from different cultures cook, eat, dress, live in families, and carry on daily activities is an important goal.

Multicultural education is not just learning about other cultures. Facts alone will never erase stereotypes and prejudice. As Phillips (1988) stresses:

> We must struggle to truly understand how culture is a source of group power and strength, and to examine how to allow groups to retain their cultural integrity while they gain the skills to function in the larger society. This perhaps is the central struggle we face as adults responsible for preparing today's children and tomorrow's leaders in a society that may de-value them by demanding that they give up their culture in order to achieve. (p. 46)

For too many children, success in school depends on learning in only one way and giving up other ways of learning and acting. Many Native American educators believe that Native American students drop out of school as soon as they can legally do so because they have to be "White" in order to succeed at school. Teachers of young children can provide students with many choices of learning activities and with many avenues for expressing what they know and are learning.

Another implication of Hernandez's (1989) assumptions is that effective teaching must be individualized, based on the child's development and relevant to the child's experience. Memorizing facts about other cultures, pasting a sombrero on a ditto sheet of a Hispanic man sitting under a cactus, and learning about Native Americans of long ago are activities that do not meet the criteria for effective teaching. Children will develop concepts about other people as they interact with real people at school and in their neighborhoods. Thomson (1989) suggests that experiences in which children can actively participate are the most valuable for helping them develop understanding and tolerance. She suggests that experiences such as role-playing Rosa Parks or discussing children's feelings upon encountering discriminatory signs foster the active learning that is necessary for young children.

A third implication of Hernandez's assumptions is that teachers must take individual responsibility for learning about the children in the class and for helping all children learn to appreciate each other. Children learn how to appreciate others from observing and participating in interactions with the teacher. No commercial multicultural education program can relieve the teacher of learning about the children, including their cultural backgrounds, and planning experiences that will help them learn about each other in positive ways.

As children learn about about others in their class and the world around them, teachers should respond to their questions in ways that reduce their fears (Baker 1994; Derman-Sparks 1993/1994) and help them understand individual and cultural differences. Thomson (1993) helped children understand discrimination by posting signs in various areas of the classroom that showed the international symbol for *no*. (These signs might forbid wearing things such as tie shoes, plaid clothing, or other non-personal, changeable items.) After experience, the children talked about how it felt not to be allowed to participate.

Education that is multicultural will be reflected in the teacher's choices of books and literature, in the signs posted in the classroom, in holiday celebrations, and in planned activities—in short, throughout the curriculum. For example, children can learn about different languages and different systems of writing through language arts activities (Saracho and Spodek 1983). They can learn about foods contributed to their diets by North and South American cultures (corn), Eastern cultures (rice), or European cultures (wheat). Children's families also are a valuable source of information and support for a multicultural or antibias curriculum. Teachers can bring families into the classroom to share traditions, expectations, and stories (McCracken 1993; Neuman and Roskos 1994; Swick et al. 1995; Swick, Boutte, and Van Scoy 1995/1996; Wardle 1996).

Teachers must plan all activities with an eye for including a multicultural dimension. Table 13.1 on page 426 is a checklist designed to help teachers analyze their classrooms and provide education that is multicultural. Another useful resource for teachers is an extensive bibliography of materials about cultural diversity in the United States, which can be found in the March 1993 issue of *Young Children* (National Association for Education of Young Children 1993).

PARENTS AND SOCIAL STUDIES

- After parents visit the classroom or contribute significant items from their cultures, be sure to acknowledge them in newsletters, on bulletin boards, and in displays.

TABLE 13.1

Multicultural Checklist

This checklist will help you focus on individual aspects of your classroom environment, take a closer look at your curriculum, and highlight areas that need improvement. Try to answer each question as it pertains to your classroom.

Curriculum Area	Questions
Language Arts	1. Does your classroom have a wide variety of age-appropriate and culturally diverse books and language arts materials? Look for examples.
	2. Are the cultures in your class and community represented in your books and materials?
	3. Are there any books that speak of people of diverse cultures in stereotypic or derogatory terms? What are they? Should they be removed, or is there a way to use them with children to broaden their concepts and encourage them to share their experiences?
	4. Are the pictures of people on the walls representative of a multicultural community?
Social Studies	5. Does the curriculum help children increase their understanding and acceptance of attitudes, values, and lifestyles that are unfamiliar to them? If so, how? If not, what can you do to change it?
	6. Are materials and games racially or sex-role stereotypic? If so, how can you change your collection to give strong, positive images?
Blocks	7. Are the accessories in the block area representative of various cultural groups and family configurations? If not, how can you change them?
	8. Are the people block accessories stereotypic in terms of sex roles? If so, how can you change them?
Dramatic Play	9. Is there a wide variety of clothes (everyday garments, not exotic costumes) from various cultural groups?
	10. Are the pictures on the walls and the props representative of a diversity of cultures?
	11. Are the dolls representative of the major racial groups in our country, not just in colors but in features?
Music and Games	12. Do music experiences reinforce children's affirmation of cultural diversity? How?
	13. Do you use fingerplays, games, and songs from various cultural groups?
Cooking	14. Do cooking experiences encourage children to experiment with foods they aren't familiar with?
	15. Are these experiences designed to give children a general notion of the connections between cultural heritage and the process of preparing, cooking, and eating food? If so, how?

Source: Adapted from Frances E. Kendall, Ph.D., "Creating a Multicultural Environment," *Pre-K Today* (November/December 1988): 34–39. Reprinted with permission of the author.

The ability of children now in early childhood classes to cope with life in the twenty-first century may well depend on the quality of their educational experiences. Quality education must include multicultural experiences.

CONNECTING SOCIAL STUDIES WITH READING, WRITING, AND LITERATURE

Social studies topics are interesting to children; they want to know about people and relationships in their world. Topics of interest can be introduced, explored, and summarized through meaningful literacy experiences using stories and poetry. Topics of interest in the social studies often emerge from reading aloud. The following books and stories, for example (adapted from Hennings 1982), relate to the themes of freedom, justice, interdependence, and power:

THEORY INTO Practice

Choose a social studies concept that you would like to introduce through literature to a specific age group. Find at least three books you could use to do so. Create a plan for using them. Will you read the books aloud, one by one? Will you present a media version of one or all of them? How will you guide the children in relating the books to the concept?

Freedom

Hawk, I'm Your Brother (Baylor 1976)
Hansel and Gretel (Lesser 1984)
Jorinda and Joringel (Grimm 1970)

Justice

Why Mosquitoes Buzz in People's Ears (Aardema 1975)
Once a Mouse (Brown 1961)
The Three Little Pigs (Zemach 1988)
Goldilocks and the Three Bears (Brett 1987)
The Three Billy Goats Gruff (Galdone 1973)
Roland the Minstrel Pig (Steig 1968)
Strega Nona (de Paola 1975)
Mufaro's Beautiful Daughters (Steptoe 1987)
The Talking Eggs (San Souci 1989)
Lon Po Po (Young 1989)

Interdependence

The Big Snow (Hader and Hader 1948)
Ox Cart Man (Hall 1979)
Building a House (Barton 1981)
Truck (Crews 1980)

Power

Fisherman and His Wife (Jarrell 1980)
The Stonecutter (McDermott 1981)
The Mouse Couple (Malotki 1988)

Participating in arts activities can help children understand others better.

Table 13.2 lists guidelines adapted from those of the Council on Interracial Books for Children (1974), which teachers may find helpful in evaluating literature for the classroom.

In addition to read-aloud experiences, there are many other opportunities for meaningful literacy experiences as children explore social studies topics of interest. For example, if children are studying the work of their parents or of school personnel, they could write reports of their findings from their surveys, read more about some of the occupations that especially interest them, write entries for an ABC book of jobs, write letters inviting speakers to class and thank-you notes to speakers who have shared information, and so on. The children might also create charts, reports, books of various kinds, narrative stories, and poetry. For example, if the children have been exploring the cultures of the children in their class, they could create journals in which they record their responses to foods they have tried, pictures of articles of clothing, or their personal responses to something they learned. The class might create a "big book" with photographs and reports they have dictated, which could be reviewed often.

There are many ways of recording and summarizing what children learn. Such documentation allows children to present and reflect upon what they learn. It is also useful to teachers in reporting to

PARENTS _{AND} SOCIAL STUDIES

■ Be sure to include information about social studies activities or themes in your parent newsletter. Also perhaps mention the names of some books that would be especially helpful in learning about specific social studies topics.

TABLE 13.2 A Checklist for Analyzing Bias in Children's Books

Guidelines	Points to Consider
Check the illustrations	a. Look for stereotypes. Some illustrations are blatantly stereotypical; others may be more subtle in ridiculing characters based on their race/ethnicity or sex. b. Look for tokenism. Check to be sure that the illustrator has not simply colored in characters who have white features and that all people of color do not look alike. c. Examine who's doing what. Are only white men active or in leadership roles? Are women and people of color in subservient or passive roles?
Check the story line	Watch for subtle bias in the following areas: a. Standards for success—Do people of color have to exhibit so-called white behavior in order to succeed? Must people of color be extraordinary in order to succeed? b. Resolution of problems—Are problems solved by white people? Are societal problems explained, or are they treated as inevitable? Are minority people considered to be the problem? c. Role of women—Are achievements of women and girls based on their looks? Could the same story be told if the sex roles were reversed and the characters were men or boys?
Look at the lifestyles	Are the contrasts between people of color and whites negative? Are people of color presented in settings other than barrios or ghettos? Does the author sincerely present an alternative lifestyle without negative value judgments?
Weigh the relationships among people	Are the whites in the story in control? Are the family structures stereotypical?
Note the heroes	If the heroes or heroines are persons of color, do they avoid all conflict with whites? Are they admired for the same qualities as white heroes or heroines?
Consider the effects on a child's self-image	Are standards established that limit the child's aspirations and self-esteem? Are there positive and constructive role models for children of color and girls?
Consider the author's or illustrator's background (if possible)	If the book is about people of color or women, does the author or illustrator have the experience and knowledge necessary to create nonbiased descriptions or discussions?
Check the author's perspective	Is the author's or illustrator's personal perspective limited? Does this view distort the story in any way?
Watch for "loaded" words	Some words carry insulting or derogatory connotations. Does the author avoid the use of such words as *savage, treacherous,* and *primitive* when describing people of given ethnic, cultural, or social groups?
Look at the copyright date	The copyright date is no guarantee that a book is nonbiased, but more recent books generally present a more authentic view of people of color and women than those published in the 1960s and before.

Source: Adapted from Council on Interracial Books for Children 1974.

parents and administrators the concepts that children are developing and their growing literacy abilities and understandings in the social studies.

CHAPTER SUMMARY

- Several approaches to social studies can be found in programs for young children. Some approaches stress learning facts, and some stress learning to live together successfully in group settings. Others attempt to combine these two approaches.
- Goals of social studies instruction focus on strengthening knowledge, skills, and attitudes. Children's experiences should help them develop concepts related to social studies, skills in collecting and presenting data, and attitudes that are important in a democracy.
- Teaching social studies as a series of lessons is not as effective as integrating it into a variety of classroom activities.
- Holidays are often the basis of the curriculum in social studies. When celebrating holidays, teachers should examine what children will learn from celebrations; include different cultural perspectives; involve the children in making decisions about holiday celebrations; reduce the amount of stress surrounding holidays to a minimum; and choose appropriate learning experiences for the age and developmental level of the children.
- An important strategy for integrating social studies with other curriculum areas is to use themes.

As always, teachers should select themes that are meaningful to the children and that provide real reasons to apply skills.

- Education that is multicultural is more important than ever in the United States and the world. Ethnic and cultural minority populations are becoming larger; it is imperative that groups work together.
- A multicultural point of view should permeate all instruction and not be limited to isolated lessons designed to teach one cultural group about another.
- Multicultural education should begin with infants and toddlers and should help children learn to respect and care for each other.
- Multicultural education is synonymous with effective teaching. Teachers must plan experiences that are appropriate to children's ages and developmental abilities.
- Social studies topics are interesting to children. Literacy experiences are a natural way of introducing, exploring, and concluding topics related to the social studies.

A TEACHER SPEAKS

EMILIE RODGER
Sedona Elementary School
SEDONA, ARIZONA

*S*ocial studies—or the study of societies and their interdependence on one another—by definition means learning about our place and the places of others in the world. In order for young children to make sense of this concept, we must start with that which is most important to youngsters: their families. They know their families, and they know they belong to their families.

As a teacher, I further promote the home/school connection in all other topics, as well, so that we—the children and I—may embark on our family discovery adventures together. I've used several methods of making the connections, including:

1. *Sending a family survey letter home to the parents and asking them to complete it together, if at all possible*—This survey letter includes questions relating to family names, number of people in the family, pets, occupations, interests, hobbies, and special traits of individuals in the family. Students are asked to return the surveys and share their information with the class. Translations of the letters are sent in the languages needed.

2. *Having children construct a bulletin board of the classroom "family," which is comprised of individual students' families*—This bulletin board includes any information the students desire to share about themselves and their families using any chosen media: poetry, artwork, songs, chants, pictures, and the like. Children's literature is used as a springboard for discussions about family configurations, dynamics, and traditions. Students develop skits about their roles in their families and/or their classrooms. Parents, grandparents, and other available family members are invited to the classroom to share stories about their cultures, or occupations. Many discussions occur about how families are the same and different, again illuminating the common bond of humanity.

3. *Encouraging students to keep journals*—These journals are used to record interviews with various family members, comments about what families do together, any traditions they have shared, as well as ideas the children would like to incorporate into the classroom community.

This unit or topic extends for approximately one month, culminating in a presentation to families about the discoveries students have made about themselves and each other. The presentation often includes songs, artwork, portfolios, and/or collages depicting each student in the middle of a sheet of paper, surrounded by the meaningful people, objects, or hobbies in her life. The success of this unit is due to young children's self-absorption and their need to make sense of the world around them. This unit on families is a simple, exciting, challenging way to incorporate and involve all youngsters in an awareness of the external world.

This unit is the central thread in the cultural tapestry woven throughout the year, as the children learn about themselves. Having this knowledge increases their self-esteem, and as their self-esteem increases, they learn and care about other cultures, their relation to them, and their interdependence on each other. The result is an understanding and clear awareness of the importance of each unique individual in the human family.

14

WELLNESS FOR THE YOUNG CHILD
Motor Development, Health, and Safety

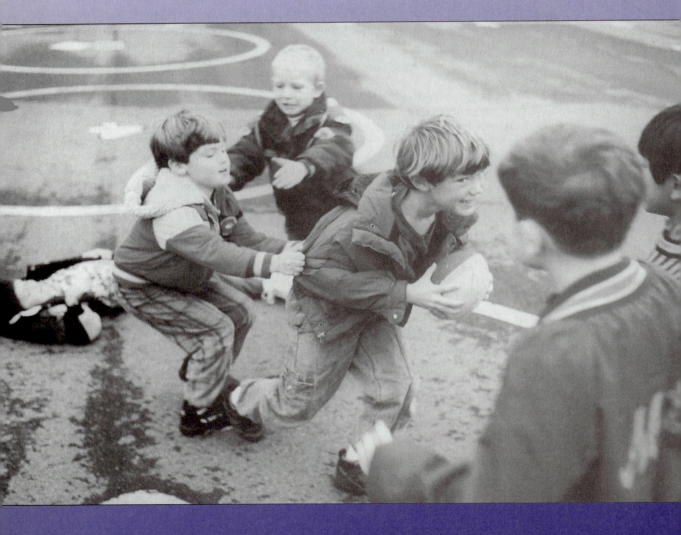

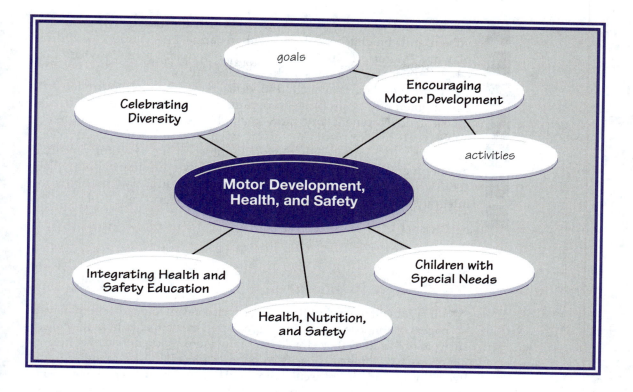

As you looked at your assignment sheet this week, you really wondered what you would see when you visited a child-care center near your university. Your assignment was to observe children's activities that related to issues of *wellness:* motor development, health and nutrition, and safety.

During your visit, you learned that the children in the child-care center played outdoors twice each day, weather permitting. As you observed this outdoor play, you found that most of the children were physically very active; they ran, climbed, pedaled wheel toys, jumped off a small bench, rolled down a hill, and dug in the sand. But a few of the children sat on the cement near the building and talked or played dolls.

When you returned to your own class and shared findings with your peers, you heard about many models of physical education: some in which every child did exercises, such as touch-

433

ing toes and jumping jacks; some in which the teachers were uninvolved and the children played without adult intervention (or didn't play at all), unless a safety issue was involved; and some in which the whole group played games such as dodge ball.

You believe that early childhood teachers who seek to implement developmentally appropriate programs should not ignore children's physical development any more than they should ignore children's intellectual development. Yet given what you and your peers have observed, different teachers obviously interpret the need for physical development in vastly different ways. You have questions about what activities are appropriate, how to encourage participation, and how to integrate learning about health and safety into every child's day.

In this era when physical fitness is of such concern to many adults, newspapers continue to report that U.S. children are neither as fit as they once were nor as fit as they should be. Many more children than ever before are obese, have limited capacity to perform physical tasks, or suffer from hypertension and cardiovascular disease. The solution to this problem lies in educating children to make more healthful choices in their lives—choices that include active exercise and a healthy diet. The list of fitness facts in this chapter emphasizes the need to develop the habit of healthy exercise in young children.

Young children need the opportunity to develop **fundamental motor skills.** That does not mean that they need a workout program that will make them physically fit as adults. Seefeldt (1984) advises caution in devising a program designed to develop fitness in young children, because not enough is known about the relationship between physical fitness and overall health at this age; obviously, young children are different from other populations on which fitness data have been collected. However, Seefeldt does suggest that a planned program of physical education can be beneficial to young children.

ENCOURAGING MOTOR DEVELOPMENT

Young children need a variety of enjoyable experiences to give them both a broad range of physical skills and a disposition to continue to participate in physical activities. Grineski (1988) states that a physical education program can accomplish the following:

As children develop physical skills, their self-concepts are often enhanced, as well.

1. Provide movement opportunities for children to explore and experiment with and in doing so allow them to express their pleasure in being a player or mover
2. Develop the psychomotor domain through a planned sequence of learning experiences designed to enhance body awareness, spatial awareness, balance, and fundamental motor skills
3. Promote the development of self-concept by providing more accurate perception of self through participation in a wide variety of success-oriented and appropriate physical education experiences
4. Develop minimal levels of physical fitness competence
5. Stimulate the development of imagination through game play, dramatic play, use of apparatus, tumbling, rhythmic expression, and movement exploration experiences
6. Promote the development of thought processes through participation in guided discovery and problem-solving activities
7. Facilitate the development of language skills through the use of movement-related terms
8. Enhance the development of social skills through experiences designed to promote positive interpersonal interactions with playmates (i.e., cooperative games) (pp. 92–93)

Teachers know that motor development is important and can contribute to children's development in other areas. The psychomotor domain is stimulated by activities that require thought and deliberate movement, such as bouncing a ball, hitting a target with a ball, or hitting a ball with a

ENCOURAGING MOTOR DEVELOPMENT

bat. This area of development includes fundamental motor skills such as walking and running, which are necessary for participation in games and sports throughout life. Seefeldt (1984) notes that "the rudimentary skills which make up the components of our games and sports can be learned by children in an enriched environment before they are six years of age" (p. 35). He goes on to state that both opportunities for practice and motivation are at their highest levels in the early childhood years.

Although physical fitness for young children is more difficult to define than fitness for older populations (Seefeldt 1984), with a minimal level of physical fitness, young children will be able to perform physical tasks such as walking and running. Fitness is also defined by cardiorespiratory function, relative leanness, abdominal endurance, lower-back flexibility, and upper-body strength and endurance (Gober and Franks 1988; Leppo 1993; Ross and Pate 1987). Because children younger than age ten have been included in national studies of children's fitness only recently (Ross and Pate 1987), fitness for young children cannot be measured against a national standard; it can, however, be encouraged by teachers.

Teachers must not overlook physical education activities in their efforts to balance a program so that every area of a child's development is fostered. Physical education activities can contribute to a child's social and intellectual development as well as to physical development. For example, through sports or games, children learn to interact with others in positive ways. Children may learn the importance of interdependence and the feeling of belonging that being part of a team can offer. A child's self-concept may be enhanced as the child becomes physically skillful. Children gain intellectual skill by creating games and movements, expressing themselves as they negotiate in games, and solving problems related to physical goals. Working puzzles, cutting, and pushing buttons to operate teaching equipment all require not only thinking but physical skills, as well. Omwake (1971) reminds us that children need both physical skills and cognitive abilities to feel good about themselves. Emphasizing only cognitive abilities may strengthen a child in one area while undermining his ability in another. Weiller and Richardson (1993) state the case well: "Regular, appropriate physical activity is the responsibility of all educators. It is crucial that children acquire appropriate skills, develop a sound fitness level, and feel positive about their movement abilities" (p. 137).

Goals of Physical Development Programs

The goals of physical development programs for young children include having children participate in a variety of activities that will foster motor development; helping children develop gross motor skills; helping children develop a positive attitude toward active movement experiences; and helping children develop fine motor skills. These goals, like goals in other areas of curriculum, are broad and can best be met by a balance of planned and spontaneous activities. Activities designed for specialized skill development should never overshadow, replace, or serve as the primary purpose of general physical education (Gallahue 1981). However, teachers must make a concerted effort to involve children in active physical experiences. One study (Miller 1978) found that children in free-play situations often spent the time playing quietly and spent very little time in vigorous physical activities. Participation in vigorous activity can be increased through planned activities, teacher modeling and participation, and careful observation of children to ensure their involvement.

A developmentally appropriate program of physical education is based on three principles: "(1) motor skill development is sequential and age-related; (2) children progress through similar sequences of motor development; and (3) the rates at which children progress through sequences of motor development varies" (Grineski 1992, p. 33). Gabbard (1995) agrees that children need to participate in age-appropriate activities and adds that gender should not determine participation in activities, that activities should be noncompetitive, and that equipment should match the size, confidence, and skill of the children. Primary-age children should be involved in activities designed to help them develop movement awareness and basic motor skills. As in any other area of the curriculum, the teacher has to observe the children carefully in order to know when to increase the difficulty of the task and when to provide more time for development of individual skills.

> **PARENTS AND WELLNESS**
>
> ■ Get parents involved in their children's physical activities by sending home descriptions of activities that the whole family can enjoy together—for example, bowling with a ball and empty soda containers.

Planned Activities

Physical education programs should include experiences with movement and games and activities that help to foster skill development. In each of these areas, activities must be matched to children's developmental levels and to the needs of individuals. Some children will be able to jump from a standing position or catch a ball while others will still be learning to walk backward or to go down steps by alternating feet.

When planning for individual differences, teachers can accommodate a wide variety of skill levels in the way that directions are given. For example, rather than ask all children to do headstands, teachers could ask all children to "find a way to balance using three parts of your body" (Petersen 1992, p. 37). As you read the following ideas for planned experiences, keep

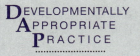

DEVELOPMENTALLY **A**PPROPRIATE **P**RACTICE
....

Think about your readings, your observations, and your experiences as you respond to the following statements about developmentally appropriate practice in physical education and health:

- A developmentally appropriate physical education program offers children a challenge at the level of their individual abilities.
- An outside play period is *not* sufficient for physical education in a developmentally appropriate program.

- Some areas of health education require direct instruction, which does not normally fit a developmentally appropriate program.
- The guidelines for DAP state that teachers of young children are responsible for children's total development, not just academic or intellectual development.

in mind that all activities must be evaluated in terms of their appropriateness for individual children.

Movement

In planning movement activities, emphasize the exploration of space and how the human body can move in space. Many movement activities can be enhanced with the addition of music or rhythmic accompaniment.

Jumping

Lay two ropes on the ground about ten inches apart, and allow children to practice a standing broad jump over them; as children's skills increase, move the ropes farther apart. Place hula hoops in a pattern across the floor or on flat ground so that children can jump from one to another. Position a sturdy bench or box so that children can jump off it safely. Encourage children to explore how they can turn while jumping or how they can stretch their bodies or make them as small as possible while jumping.

Climbing on Apparatus

Encourage children to think of different ways to hang, move, stretch, or curl and to find different ways to get on and off the apparatus safely.

Following an Obstacle Course

Build an obstacle course with materials in the classroom. For example, create a path to follow that requires children to crawl under a table, climb over a sturdy bench, jump through a series of hula hoops placed on the floor, and crawl through a tunnel created with a quilt and chairs. Invite children to move over, around, under, and through in as many ways as possible.

Rolling and Tumbling

If you have a grassy slope that children can roll down, use it. If not, encourage children to roll and find ways to turn their bodies on mats.

Using a Parachute

Preschool children can enjoy stretching a parachute and moving it up and down. They also enjoy getting under it. Older, more well-coordinated children can enjoy games in which they bounce objects on the parachute, take turns running under it, and use it in stretching and rhythmic activities.

Games

Games such as circle games in which only one person is "it" often require all other participants to sit or stand and wait for most of the play period. Better choices are games that involve the whole group. Teachers can invent games of Tag with multiple "its" for kindergarten and primary children.

For preschool children, one game that keeps everyone moving is Soap Bubbles, in which all the children move within a marked space without touching anyone else. If children touch, they "burst" and must make themselves as small as possible. (Children who have been touched can move outside the space and continue moving.) The game begins with a very large space, but the teacher moves the space markers so that there is less and less space until most children have been touched. This game can be accompanied by music (Pangrazi and Dauer 1992).

Many games for primary children involve an entire group in movement activities. One example is Back-to-Back, for which there must be an uneven number of children. Children pair off and stand back-to-back; the child left over claps her hands and calls out a movement ("run," "hop," "skip," "slide," "gallop," or "jump"). Following the command, each child must move forward a certain distance and then turn and find a new partner; the one left over becomes the leader for the next round. In a similar game called Stop and Start, the children are spaced far enough apart to move freely. The leader calls out a movement, such as "skip." All the children move until the leader signals them to stop. Any child who moves after that must wait on the sidelines for one round.

THEORY INTO Practice

Plan experiences in movement and physical skills development for a group of four-year-olds and for a group of seven-year-olds.

Skill Activities

Throwing and Catching

Very young children should practice throwing with relatively large, soft balls. Balls about six inches in diameter are easiest to catch. Threes and fours can begin to catch with their arms extended. A yarn ball or a Nerf ball is good for these children. Children can be encouraged to throw a ball as high as possible, to roll it on the ground, and to stop the ball with their feet or other body parts while it is rolling. Children can also toss the ball with two hands, with one hand, and play catch with a partner. Tossing bean bags or tossing or rolling small balls at a target (a bowling pin or an empty bleach bottle) are also appropriate activities.

Kicking and Batting

Primary children can begin to learn to kick a ball. To learn how, they should begin with a stationary ball and be encouraged to tap the ball with their feet, to tap it so that it goes to a partner, and to kick the ball to a target area. Batting a ball should also begin with the ball stationary, perhaps on a cone. Children should be encouraged to think of as many ways to hit the ball as possible.

Benelli and Yongue (1995) suggest making a bat from a two liter plastic bottle and a wooden dowel. They explain that the handles of most bats are too large for small hands and the hitting surfaces are too small.

CHILDREN WITH SPECIAL NEEDS

Children with special needs can participate in outdoor play and physical education activities with some adaptations in equipment and in activities. The teacher must consider the developmental level of the individual child and the child's abilities when planning for physical experiences. Children with mental retardation can participate in most outdoor activities, but they may need more encouragement and more praise than other children. Teachers may have to help children with retardation establish motor patterns by moving them into positions or by modeling behaviors over and over. These children may also make less rapid progress, and teachers should be aware that children may have to repeat activities many times before mastering them.

Children with visual disabilities can participate in many climbing, swinging, and sliding experiences without adaptations. For skill activities for these children, the teacher will need to be attentive to lighting conditions and equipment choices. For example, Pangrazi and Dauer (1981) recommend that when teaching a child with visual limitations to catch a ball, the area should be well lighted and a yellow ball should be used. In certain games, children with visual limitations can get help from other children; the teacher can make sure that tactile information is provided to help children identify home base, boundary lines, and so on.

Auditory disabilities rarely prevent children from participating fully in physical activities. Such children should be placed in front of the teacher so they can read lips and have the best opportunity for hearing directions. Children with auditory disabilities may need interpreters in order to follow the directions in games and may need visual signals to supplement some auditory signals. For example, if children were playing Stop and Start, described earlier, the teacher could wave a flag when the group was to stop moving.

Teachers who want to involve children with orthopedic disabilities in programs of physical education should first consult with the child's physician or case manager to determine the level of activity recommended. A physical education specialist can help the teacher make the adaptations that will benefit each child. Some will need modified equipment, for example, a bat with straps that enable the child to hold it. Others will need to use larger or softer balls or to participate in activities that involve upper-body strength if their legs are immobile. Every child needs to interact as much as possible with other children, and physical education should not be inaccessible to children with disabilities.

Pangrazi and Dauer (1992) recommend that teachers think about modifications for youngsters lacking strength and endurance by lowering or enlarging goals, softening balls, reducing the distance balls must be thrown, and using lighter balls and bats. If coordination is a problem, teachers should have children begin with stationary objects when learning to strike an object; throw for velocity without concern for accuracy when learning to throw; and use soft, lightweight objects for catching, such as beach balls and balloons. For children who lack ability in balance, teachers might increase the width on balance beams; suggest learning to balance with as many body parts touching the floor as possible; provide assistance with balance, such as a cane or chair; and think about play surfaces so that children are not playing on slick floors with slick shoes (pp. 133–134).

HEALTH, NUTRITION, AND SAFETY

Helping children develop their physical abilities and encouraging them to be physically active is certainly important. It is also important to help children learn to make good choices in health practices, nutrition, and safety. Young children, of course, do not make these choices without guidance from parents and teachers, but they can begin to develop healthy habits.

Health Education

Historically, health care was an important goal of early preschool programs. In today's world of more personal responsibility for health, education for healthful choices continues to be important; however, it tends to be overlooked in many programs (Bruhn and Nader 1982). Because children and young adults do not perceive themselves as vulnerable to illness (Gochman and Saucier 1982), health educators have recommended that programs in health education be developed and implemented for children as young as two or three (Kingsbury and Hall 1988).

Personal Routines

Health education is not a lesson to be taught on a schedule. It must be integrated throughout the day and made a part of many activities. Children learn about good health habits in many ways: observing parents and teachers (especially those who take time to explain why they are making the decisions that they make); listening to stories; and making regular visits to the doctor and dentist. For example, as children wash their hands after using the toilet and before eating, the teacher can mention the importance of cleanliness in staying healthy; as children brush their teeth after eating, the teacher may demonstrate how to hold the brush and point out that brushing down over the teeth is best. Brushing teeth can be encouraged if the children can reach their own toothbrushes and the sink so that they can be independent about the task. A visit by a dental hygienist to demonstrate the correct procedures for brushing and flossing will remind children to brush on a regular basis. The children might also visit a dentist's office and get a chance to sit in the chair and look at the tools and equipment. A flashlight and a chair will probably be all the children need to play "dentist" after such a visit. When a child loses a tooth, the teacher is given a perfect opportunity for discussing and reading about teeth—how they grow and the importance of caring for them.

A significant portion of health education in early childhood programs will be taught as daily routines are established. Children will learn to wash their hands after using the toilet or blowing their noses or before eating and to brush their teeth after eating. As they participate in these routines, they can be taught the reasons these behaviors are important. Although young children are not able to understand the causal relationships between germs and disease, they can understand that regular hygiene routines contribute to their staying well and feeling healthy.

Teachers also must be aware of sanitary procedures that will help prevent illness. Teachers of infants and toddlers must be careful to wash their hands thoroughly after diapering or assisting children at the toilet. Often teachers of young children must help them blow their noses or clean their faces after a sneeze. Teachers should scrub their hands after every such incident. Teachers must also model the importance of washing their hands carefully before either serving or cooking food. Changing tables and tables where food is served should be scrubbed and disinfected regularly.

Medical Procedures

The health education program should also include helping children become more comfortable and accepting of medical procedures, health care professionals, and hospitals. Parents should be involved in planning these particular activities, as they can provide specific information about their children's experiences and possible fears. Many activities in the classroom—such as playing with puppets, listening to stories, playing with toy medical equipment (or real equipment, if that is possible and appropriate), and meeting health care professionals—can help children understand and feel more positive about medical care. Field trips to the offices of health care professionals and to hospitals can also be arranged. These trips must be planned carefully, but most hospitals have programs for educating even very young children about being in the hospital.

Children can learn some simple first aid procedures. One program uses puppets to dramatize stories in which first aid is required (Marchand and McDermott 1986). Children learn first aid procedures and why they are necessary. They also learn to select the most appropriate procedure from the alternatives available and how to use the telephone to get help in an emergency.

Substance Abuse and AIDS

Two relatively new facets of health education for young children are substance abuse programs and programs to educate children about AIDS (acquired immune deficiency syndrome). In many public schools, such programs are now required. With so much about drugs and AIDS on television and in the conversations of adults, teachers in preschool settings must be able to answer children's questions and understand their fears. Early childhood educators are in a unique position to contribute to preventing drug abuse and educating the public about AIDS, because both problems affect many children's lives directly and because early childhood educators can work with parents in ways that have positive results over long periods of time.

In a longitudinal study that followed a group of children from the time they were five until they were eighteen, Shedler and Block (1990) found that young adults who were frequent users of drugs were relatively maladjusted as children of seven years old. The frequent users were described at age seven as

> not getting along well with other children, not showing concern for moral issues (e.g., reciprocity, fairness), having bodily symptoms from stress, tending to be indecisive and vacillating, not planful or likely to think ahead, not trustworthy or dependable, not able to admit to negative feelings, not self-reliant or confident, preferring nonverbal methods of communication, not developing genuine and close relationships, not proud of their accomplishments, not vital or energetic or lively, not curious and open to new experience, not able to recoup after stress, afraid of being deprived, appearing to feel unworthy and "bad," not likely to identify with admired adults, inappropriate in emotive behavior, and easily victimized and scapegoated by other children. (p. 618)

Based on these findings, Shedler and Block (1990) recommend that resources for prevention of drug abuse be focused on intervening in the development of the personality syndrome that underlies drug use, rather than on campaigns such as "Just Say No." The research highlights the importance of positive experiences for children at home and at school that will develop stronger self-concepts, more skill in social interactions, and more prosocial behaviors.

Even young children know about AIDS and may fear that they or people close to them will catch the disease. Children see programs, news stories, and commercials on television aimed at educating the public about AIDS, but they rarely understand what they see and hear. Teachers who feel the need to provide information about AIDS must consider the children's cognitive development and needs when making decisions about what to say. As Skeen and Hodson (1987) remind us:

> We do *not* want young children (who, as we all know, muddle the most carefully correct sex information) to get it into their heads that sex will kill you. We do *not* want young children (many of whom fear when they see blood oozing from a small cut that they will deflate like a balloon losing its air and cease to exist) to begin worrying about poisoned blood inside them. We do *not* want young children, for whom it is overridingly important to trust that grownups, most especially parents, will protect them, to be told that babies can be given AIDS through their mothers' blood! Information is not always good. (p. 69)

Teachers of young children can be prepared to answer children's questions in positive ways. For example, they can say that AIDS is a disease but that children who do not have it are not likely to catch it and that children cannot get it from touching a person who has it. Most children asking such questions are seeking reassurance that they are safe; they do not need a lesson on adult sexual behavior or drug use. Parents also may need guidance in what to say when children ask them questions. Primary-grade children are likely to encounter some sort of planned instruction that is aimed at making children aware of the dangers of AIDS. The goals of most programs for primary children are limited to having the children understand that they cannot contract AIDS by being with or touching someone who has AIDS.

When making a decision about what to tell children when one of their classmates has AIDS, teachers will have to exercise their own judgment, based on knowledge of the children and how much they have heard from parents. If the children know that a child is ill and ask questions, the teacher should answer as honestly as possible while helping children feel safe from the disease.

Even though young children do not need to know much about AIDS, teachers *do* need to know. The National Education Association has published a handbook of information entitled *The Facts about AIDS* (Bauer et al. no date). Because many teachers will have children who have AIDS in class or will know of parents who have AIDS, they will be faced with providing information to other parents; thus, teachers need accurate, up-to-date information. They also need to work together to determine the best alternatives for teaching children about AIDS and the best information to provide to parents (Fetter 1989).

Nutrition Education

Food is not only basic to life; it is also closely related to people's social and cultural lives. Food is an integral part of family, religious, and cultural celebrations. Many aspects of food are culturally determined: what people think is appropriate to eat; how they eat it (with fingers, pieces of bread, chopsticks, or forks); with whom they eat (with other men, with women and children, or in family groups); and when they eat during the day. How food is used socially is also culturally determined. Many people offer guests something to eat or drink as soon as they are in their homes, and food is often central to social gatherings. For years, business was conducted over lunch—now people even have "power breakfasts"! Teaching children to make healthy choices in the food they select is certainly a worthwhile goal and one that will affect their lives through adulthood.

Nutrition education is important because children commonly have problems related to nutrition. Although children do not often have control over what they are offered to eat, they do make choices from the food offered to them. The choices provided for them in a school setting should be nutritious and should help them learn about food and nutrition. Physical problems related to nutrition include tooth decay, obesity, iron deficiency anemia, and hypersensitivity to foods. Teachers need to focus on providing nutritious snacks; controlling the amounts of sugar, salt, and fiber in children's school diets; and establishing good food habits.

Appropriate goals for nutrition education with young children would include helping children learn to eat a variety of foods; increasing children's awareness of their reasons for selecting certain foods; and helping children develop positive attitudes about food.

Notice that these broad goals do not include teaching children to recite the four food groups on cue. Primary children might find it meaningful to classify foods according to their contributions to a healthy diet, but Herr and Morse (1982) believe that classifying foods into four groups requires more skill in generalization than should be expected from young children. They recommend that foods be categorized into ten groups: milk, meat, dried peas and beans, eggs, fruits, vegetables, breads, pastas, cereals/grains/seeds, and nuts.

The goals of teaching children sound eating habits can be achieved in the classroom by offering nutritious snacks and meals and through food preparation experiences. Teachers are responsible for the quality of food that children are offered; children can then choose if and how much they are going to eat. The following is a list of foods appropriate for snacks:

Raw Vegetables

Celery	Cauliflower flowerets
Peas in pod	Turnip sticks
Cucumber wedges	Jicama sticks
Tomato slices	Broccoli flowerets

Fresh Fruits

Apple wedges	Pineapple cubes
Orange segments	Pear or peach slices
Banana slices	Kiwi
Strawberries	Papaya
Blueberries	Mango

Other Snacks

Unsweetened fruit juice	Cottage cheese
Dried fruit	Peanut butter
Milk	Muffins
Milkshakes made from milk and fruit	Dry cereals (unsweetened)
Lowfat yogurt	Whole-grain crackers
Cheese	

In programs where children are offered lunch or both breakfast and lunch, teachers should follow the guidelines of the U.S. Department of Agriculture (USDA 1992, 1994) or the guidelines in the accreditation standards of the National Association for the Education of Young Children (NAEYC 1984) describing the nutritional and caloric requirements for children.

Teachers of children younger than three will want to be especially careful not to offer children food they cannot chew easily, such as raw carrots or peanuts, or bite-sized pieces of food that they can swallow without chewing. Foods such as raisins and popcorn can easily cause choking. Unless the children can be supervised carefully while they eat, other foods are better choices.

Teachers and parents must work together in order to achieve the goals of nutrition education. If parents know what teachers are trying to do with nutrition information, they can help reinforce the ideas. For example, teachers who work in schools where children bring their own snacks to school can ask parents to cooperate in sending only nutritious snacks for the children. A letter explaining the importance of reducing the sugar in children's diets (Rogers and Morris 1986) and a list of suggested snacks will aid parents in choosing snack foods that are appropriate.

One strategy for helping children learn to eat a variety of foods is to offer new foods at snack time. Rothlein (1989) suggests the following ways to make adding new foods to a child's diet relatively easy:

1. Introduce only one new food at a time.
2. Serve the new food with familiar foods.
3. Serve only small amounts of the new food—begin with one teaspoon.
4. Introduce new foods only when the child is hungry.
5. Talk with the child about the new food—taste, color, texture, and shape.
6. Encourage the child to taste the new food but do not force the child to eat it. If the food item is rejected, accept the refusal calmly and try again in a few weeks. As foods become more familiar, children more readily accept them.
7. If the child rejects the food, try to determine why she didn't like it. Often children will accept a food if it is prepared and presented in a different way. For example, raw carrots may be accepted although cooked carrots are refused.
8. Provide cooking experiences. When children are involved in preparing the food, they have more of an interest in tasting it.
9. Be a model! If children observe adults eating and enjoying new foods, they are more likely to enjoy them. Remember that young children often imitate the eating habits of their parents, and that the child's food habits—likes and dislikes—frequently reflect the parents'. Children can learn to accept foods disliked by a parent if they are presented positively and if Mom and Dad take a few bites themselves! Help parents see the wisdom of doing this. As a caregiver or teacher, model a curious approach to new foods yourself.
10. Finally, keep trying. . . . A child's fear of a new food can be reduced by simply increasing exposure to the food. (p. 34)*

To help older children learn to appreciate new foods, involve them in cooking experiences as part of their social studies or science studies, ask parents or volunteers to share special cultural or ethnic dishes, and taste foods that are mentioned in stories that they read or hear. For example, if the teacher reads the Paddington books aloud to the class, he could have children taste marmalade and could explain its place in a healthy diet.

* From Liz Rothlein, "Nutrition Tips Revisited: On a Daily Basis Do We Implement What We Know?" *Young Children* 44 (September 1989): 30–36. Reprinted with permission from NAEYC.

- If school snacks are supplied by parents, ask them to send nutritious foods. Be on the lookout for simple, healthy snack ideas that you can share with parents.

- If food allergies in some children make certain snack foods dangerous, contact parents and seek their cooperation. They can help reinforce the idea of not sharing foods or simply not send foods to school that are dangerous for some children.

Cooking Experiences

Many teachers involve children in preparing foods for snacks or meals to be eaten at school. Even very young children can spread peanut butter or cheese on their crackers, sprinkle topping on their toast, or make simple sandwiches. Older children can peel vegetables, cut fruit, squeeze oranges to make juice, make English muffin pizzas with cheese and pizza sauce, and cut up apples for applesauce. Kindergarten and primary children can read and follow simple recipes for a variety of foods. Teachers should be aware of certain guidelines for cooking experiences:

1. Cook only nutritious foods.
2. Let the children do the cooking. Watching while the teacher measures the ingredients and then getting to stir does not give children a feeling of being involved. In planning a cooking experience, consider the maturity and skills of the children. Can they do what is required— measure, cut, mix, and so on? How many children can participate in the activity? Experiences should be planned for individuals or very small groups.
3. Plan for the children's safety, particularly if an experience involves heat or cutting. Make sure children are carefully supervised when using sources of heat. Tape electrical cords of appliances to the wall so that children cannot trip over them and pull appliances off the table; position appliances so that spills land on the table rather than on the floor. Make sure that children understand how to use cutting tools and sources of heat safely.
4. Be attentive to cleanliness. Are the children's hands and the utensils clean? In some areas of the United States, hepatitis has been a problem and teachers have been asked not to cook at school. Check local policies before cooking in the classroom.

Teachers will of course want to anticipate the learning outcomes that will be possible from cooking experiences. Children will be able to relate content from other subject-matter areas to cooking experiences. The following are only a few examples of the possibilities:

- *Science*—Observing changes in matter such as melting, congealing, shrinking (greens before and after cooking), expanding (rice before and after cooking), and transformation of water into steam
- *Language*—Learning cooking vocabulary, such as *boil*, *simmer*, *roll*, *knead*, *dice*, *shred*, and *grate*, as well as the names of foods and utensils
- *Mathematics*—Comparing quantities, measuring
- *Social Studies*—Working cooperatively, learning about people involved in food production, preparing or tasting ethnic or cultural foods, and learning about food customs
- *Literacy*—Reading recipes or charts, connecting food experiences to stories (for example, making blueberry muffins after reading *Blueberries for Sal* [McCloskey 1948]), writing shopping lists, writing recipes, collecting and illustrating booklets of favorite recipes

Teachers can find many cookbooks containing nutritious and practical recipes for cooking experiences. The picture recipes in Figures 14.1 (below) and Figure 14.2 (on page 450) are from *Cook and Learn: Pictorial Single Portion Recipes* (Veitch and Harms 1981).

THEORY INTO Practice

Find a recipe for a nutritious snack. Plan for a certain age group to prepare this snack. Be sure to think about the skills necessary for success with this experience, given the age of the group. Construct an outline that would help a volunteer supervise this experience. What steps should be followed? What skills and vocabulary should be emphasized?

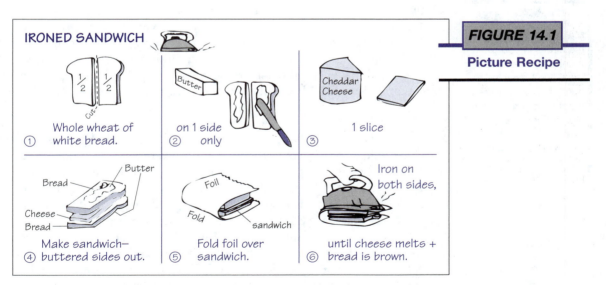

FIGURE 14.1

Picture Recipe

IRONED SANDWICH

① Whole wheat of white bread.
② Butter on 1 side only
③ Cheddar Cheese 1 slice
④ Make sandwich—buttered sides out.
⑤ Fold foil over sandwich.
⑥ Iron on both sides, until cheese melts + bread is brown.

Source: From *Cook and Learn*, by B. Veitch and T. Harms. Copyright 1981 by Addison-Wesley Publishing Company. Reprinted by permission.

FIGURE 14.2

Picture Recipe

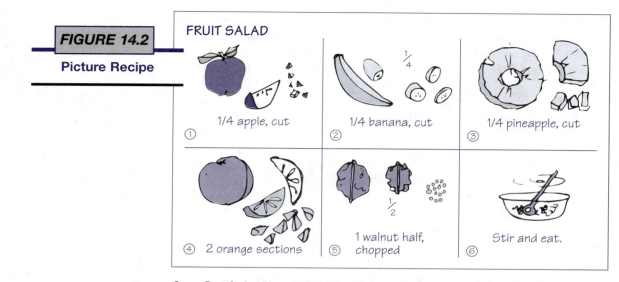

Source: From *Cook and Learn*, by B. Veitch and T. Harms. Copyright 1981 by Addison-Wesley Publishing Company. Reprinted by permission.

Safety Education

THEORY INTO Practice

Make a list of the resources in your community that can assist in providing safety instruction for young children. What programs do the fire and police departments have to offer? Do any other community groups offer safety programs?

Teachers of young children need to address questions of fire safety, traffic safety, water safety, poison safety, and personal safety. The teacher is responsible for checking the classroom and the play yard for any safety hazards, planning for emergencies, teaching children safe behaviors and what to do in an emergency, and supervising children closely. Pickle (1989) demonstrated that even preschoolers can benefit from instruction in safety education; primary children can also benefit from such instruction.

Fire Safety

Most elementary schools have a fire safety program that includes visits from local firefighters, poster contests about fire prevention, instruction about what to do if there is a fire, and regular fire drills. A fire safety program should help children recognize the danger of fire and learn to treat fire with caution; prepare children to respond appropriately during a fire through regular fire drills; and teach children how to call the fire department.

Every classroom should have a written plan of action in case of fire, which specifies the duties and responsibilities of each person (who will check the restroom, who will be responsible for children who are disabled, who will carry the class list, and so on), the exits to be used, and the point of assembly outside. Every teacher should practice fire drills on a regular basis. In some drills, selected exits should be blocked; drills should be planned to occur at unpredictable times such as meal times or nap times. Near each exit, teachers should post a map showing all exits and routes for evacuating the building and a class list to be used to account for the children after the building has been evacuated. Finally, teachers should provide parents with information about the fire drill procedures at school and encourage parents to plan regular fire drills at home.

Asking a local firefighter to visit the classroom can help promote children's awareness of fire safety. Most fire departments have an educational specialist who is responsible for teaching children fire prevention and fire safety. These people are usually talented in communicating with young children; they can teach children the "stop, drop, and roll" technique and demonstrate the pieces of equipment used by firefighters. Some firefighters encourage children to touch or try on equipment so that it does not frighten them when they see it on a firefighter. If children do try on firefighting gear, the firefighter can talk to the children about how different they look when they wear it. It is important that children recognize and not be afraid of firefighters in full gear in case they should ever have to be rescued from a fire. Teachers should preview any presentation to assure that it is appropriate for their children.

All children should be taught that in the case of a fire, they should leave the building or house first and then call the fire department. In the dramatic play area, a toy telephone and a large poster with the numbers to be dialed can help children practice dialing "0" or "911" to call the fire department in an emergency. Primary children might benefit from reading *The 9 Lives of El Gato the Cat* (Consumer Product Safety Commission 1983), a comic book that reviews the most common causes of fires and burns and explains what to do in case of fire. *Protect Someone You Love from Burns* is another publication of the Consumer Product Safety Commission (1978) that reviews fire safety.

PARENTS AND SAFETY
■ Keep parents informed about the safety lessons conducted at school so they can reinforce those lessons with their children at home.

Traffic Safety

Teachers must share with parents the responsibilities for teaching children about traffic safety. The most frequent accidents involving children are those in which the child darts into the street, usually in the middle of the block. Goals of a traffic safety program include teaching children to stop before entering a street; teaching children how to cross a street safely; and teaching children to interpret traffic signals.

With repetition and the cooperation of parents, teachers can impress upon children the importance of stopping at every curb. If there are no curbs on local streets, children should be taught to identify the boundary of the street and to stop there every time.

Children learn about traffic safety through both modeling and direct instruction.

Children need direct experience in looking and listening for traffic and then walking—not running—across the street. Often, very young children do not know what to look and listen for when they approach a street. With guidance from teachers and parents, they can learn to look and listen for approaching traffic and to cross carefully after the traffic has cleared. Children also must learn to make sure that drivers of stopped vehicles have seen them before crossing in front of the vehicles. Children may also need help understanding directions from crossing guards at school crossings. It may be prudent to teach children younger than four not to cross the street at all unless an adult tells them it is safe to do so.

Street crossings can be simulated in the dramatic play area so children can practice stopping, looking and listening for traffic, and walking carefully across the street. An area outdoors can be marked as a street, especially where children are riding wheel toys, and with guidance, the children can practice crossing these "streets" carefully. The teacher might also mark some streets on the floor inside with masking tape and have the children role-play pedestrians and drivers of vehicles as they practice traffic safety. Teachers can make or purchase replicas of traffic signals for the block center and help the children set up their own streets, complete with signals, and practice safety procedures.

The third goal, teaching children to interpret traffic signals, can be furthered by constructing paper traffic signals or wiring a simple signal to a battery. Games such as Mother, May I? help children learn to move when the signal is green and stop when the signal is yellow or red. Teachers can invent other games based on Follow the Leader or Tag in which children must respond to traffic signals.

With help from a police officer and volunteers, the children can be taken to an intersection and helped to cross the street with the signals provided. At intersections in some communities, children must learn to read symbols or the word *WALK*, rather than traffic signals. Pictures or posters of these words and symbols will teach the children to interpret them.

Involve parents by explaining what you are trying to teach in traffic safety and seek their help in reinforcing the same rules when they are with their children. Both parents and teachers must model safe traffic behavior if children are to learn it.

The NAEYC (1990) has published a curriculum package called *Walk in Traffic Safely*. The kit contains two storybooks, one for twos and threes and one for fours and fives; a teacher's guide that suggests discussion questions and learning concepts; a brochure for parents; and a poster to remind children about traffic safety. Two other NAEYC curriculum packets also relate to traffic safety. One is entitled *We Love You—Buckle Up!* and the other is called *Children Riding on Sidewalks Safely* (NAEYC 1987a, 1987b).

Water Safety

Discussions of water play in this book have stressed that such play should be carefully supervised. Water play is enjoyable and important for meeting program goals, and teachers should not hesitate to include water play in their programs—but it must be supervised. In some areas where backyard swimming pools are very popular, drowning has become the leading cause of death for young children. Children should never be left unsupervised when near swimming pools, lakes, or ponds. Even children in wading pools must have constant supervision.

No child should ever be allowed to swim alone, even if she is a capable swimmer. Swimming lessons do not make a child immune to danger, and supervision should not be relaxed simply because a child has had swimming lessons. The American Academy of Pediatrics (AAP) (1988) recommends that only children three and older be given swimming lessons. The AAP's view is that the risk of contracting infectious disease or swallowing dangerous amounts of water during swimming lessons are too great for children younger than three.

Poison Safety

Teachers have a responsibility to make sure that school environments are poison free. Anything poisonous, including ornamental plants, should be removed. Cleaning compounds or other hazardous materials must be stored in locked cabinets, out of children's reach. All such materials must be carefully marked with poison symbols and never stored in food containers.

Children must learn that they are never to eat any unknown substance or anything that is not food. Children younger than three or four cannot be expected to remember not to put objects in their mouths. Teachers of children this young need to take extra precautions to remove any dangerous items and to supervise the children closely.

Children should be taught to recognize the symbol for poison and to avoid containers that show it. Teachers should keep in mind that many household chemicals, such as automatic dishwasher detergent, are very dangerous if ingested yet are not marked with the poison symbol. Children must learn to recognize these dangerous items.

Personal Safety

Periodically, horror stories in the news remind us that the world is not always a safe place for children. Children must learn some rules of personal safety. In many police departments, officers are specially trained to communicate to children the importance of not talking to, accepting rides with, or taking treats from strangers. Many young children do not know

Helping children learn about safety is the responsibility of many people in the community.

what the word *stranger* means—they must be given practice in distinguishing strangers from people they know.

Identifying strangers might be made into a game, using pictures of familiar people and unfamiliar people so that children develop the concept that an unknown person is a stranger. Children might also role-play what to do if approached by a stranger offering treats or rides. Parents might be alerted to the dangers of having their child's name displayed on clothing or backpacks, which makes children identifiable; young children will be confused if a stranger knows their name.

Teaching children about "safe touching" from people they know is also very important. In many communities, groups present puppet plays that help children understand the difference between "good touching" and "bad touching." Films can also help teachers convey these messages to children, and children might role-play how to tell the appropriate person if they have been touched inappropriately.

Many primary-grade children are *latchkey children*, meaning that they stay alone after school until their parents return from work. Many communities offer special programs for helping these children learn rules for safety and for feeling more secure while they are alone. In the best of worlds, young children would not be left alone, but if they are, they need some guidance in answering the telephone and the door and in practicing fire safety and first aid. Efforts to keep children safe must involve the parents, the school, and the community.

PARENTS AND SAFETY

■ Hatkoff (1994) suggests that parents should be informed about what community resources are available to help their children. Teachers and schools can help provide this information by sponsoring programs such as Kids on the Block, which helps first- through eighth-graders learn self-protection strategies. (Kids on the Block is a national program; its address is listed in Appendix F, along with information about other safety resources.)

INTEGRATING HEALTH AND SAFETY EDUCATION

Many health and safety concepts can best be taught by establishing healthy routines, modeling healthy choices for the children, and incorporating discussions about health or safety procedures into the normal activities of the day. Children will learn nutrition lessons at snack and meal times by what is served and through conversations with the teacher. Traffic safety can be reviewed every time children go on a walk, although instruc-

➤ Observe the changes that occur in foods when they are not properly stored (for example, milk that sours or bread that molds).

➤ Observe the qualities of rice before and after cooking it. What causes the change in the volume of rice?

➤ Observe changes in the textures of raw versus cooked foods. Apples, carrots, and broccoli would make good examples.

➤ Weigh the children at the beginning of the year, again in January, and then again in May.

Determine each child's change in weight at each successive measuring period.

➤ Chart children's individual changes in abilities such as catching, batting, kicking, or rolling a ball.

➤ Record changes in children's individual abilities such as moving the length of the overhead bars by swinging hand to hand, walking the balance beam, and so on. Keep these charts in a binder so that each child can see only his own chart and there is no competition with others.

tion should not be limited to these reviews. Some safety lessons can also be incorporated into other experiences. For example, if the focus in literacy were on reading environmental print, then poison signs and traffic signs could be incorporated into the experience. However, some safety instruction should be included in the curriculum even if it cannot be integrated with other classroom experiences. Teachers may choose to present short lessons on safety once a week or so throughout the year; this approach is more effective than focusing on a safety theme and concentrating all the instruction in a one- or two-week period.

Physical education and nutrition experiences are easier to integrate into the classroom routine than safety instruction. If, for example, the current theme were animals, children could imitate animal movements, learn what animals need to eat to be healthy, compare human food to animal food, and so on. If the theme focused on the neighborhood, children could determine how food is obtained and distributed in the neighborhood and identify facilities for physical activities (parks, jogging trails, exercise stations, courts for basketball or volleyball, and so on). Science activities can include growing food and observing changes in foods as they cook. Social studies experiences can include visiting producers or distributors of food; learning about what manners are considered appropriate in different cultures (in some cultures, people eat with their fingers; in other cultures, people do so only with certain foods or at specific times, such as at picnics); and learning about who prepares food in different cultures (men, women, or both).

Goldberg (1994) describes a health program that addresses the special needs of children with asthma and food allergies. The entire class learned about the medical procedures used in treating asthma and allergies through activities in the dramatic play area, which was equipped with masks and other medical supplies. She recommends that teachers contact local health care professionals to collaborate with them in planning medically oriented dramatic play. Involving health care professionals in planning programs will help ensure that both parents and children understand the medical needs of others and live more comfortably with any conditions of their own, as well. This is particularly important in classes and schools in which students or staff may have life-threatening conditions.

Physical education and nutrition education can easily be integrated into literacy experiences. In addition to tasting foods mentioned in stories, children can create ABC books or reference books of healthy foods, learn to read recipes, find foods mentioned in stories, write stories about special times when food is served in their homes, and find food words used in conversation (for example, "That's peachy," "He's a ham," "That car is a lemon"). They can create movements to tell stories, describe movements after they do them, write about how exercise makes them feel, keep records of their exercise, and find examples of movements or exercise in the books they hear or read.

> **THEORY**
> *INTO*
> *Practice*
>
> Plan a literacy experience that incorporates physical education or nutrition activities.

> **PARENTS** A WELLNESS
> N
> D
>
> ■ Involve parents who work as health care professionals by asking them to share their work with the class.

CELEBRATING DIVERSITY

To involve families in health, nutrition, and safety programs, teachers can invite them to participate in field days or other such outings, in which adults and children can join in a variety of games and activities. Some of these might be traditional games of skill from the cultures represented in the classroom or games from earlier historical periods, such as rolling a hoop.

Families can also be wonderful resources for sharing foods that they enjoy or that are served at special times in their cultures. Teachers should help children understand that people from many cultures eat essentially the same things on a daily basis but that their special foods may vary. Having tasting parties with foods from different cultures may help make this clear. For instance, a study of breads from around the world might help children understand how all cultures have some special foods, even though they have many other foods in common, such as fruits and vegetables.

CHAPTER SUMMARY

- Planned physical education programs should include movement, games, and activities to foster skill development.
- Physical activities can be adapted to allow children with special needs to participate as much as possible. Adaptations might include modifying equipment and structuring experiences so that children can achieve goals.
- Children learn health concepts best when they are integrated with daily classroom routines, such as washing hands and brushing teeth.
- Children need to learn the importance of cleanliness and to become more comfortable with medical procedures and health professionals.
- Today's teachers must be prepared to help children resist substance abuse, to communicate with parents, and to answer children's questions about drug abuse and AIDS.

- Children can begin to learn about healthful foods through snacks and meals served at school. They can also learn about nutrition through cooking experiences.
- Teachers of young children must incorporate lessons on fire safety, traffic safety, poison safety, water safety, and personal safety into their programs. Parents should be involved in these efforts.
- Teachers should incorporate games, activities, and foods that are special to families from those cultures represented in the classroom. All children should know that their special family traditions are not only acceptable but important in the life of the school.

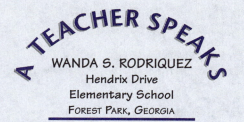

A TEACHER SPEAKS

WANDA S. RODRIQUEZ
Hendrix Drive
Elementary School
FOREST PARK, GEORGIA

Teaching Young Children about Health and Safety

Young children love to pretend. Having been a kindergarten teacher for over nineteen years, I have found that one of the best and most meaningful ways to teach health and safety is by letting my students use their imaginations and their love of drama. Together, in the safety of my classroom, we take a walk into the dangers of the world around us. As a group, we problem solve, test our theories, and choose the best solutions.

I begin by telling a story about a child or some children faced with a dangerous or potentially dangerous situation. I end the story at the point where the character has to make some kind of decision. The following is an example of a short safety story:

One cold winter day, Sara took a walk to the duck pond. When she got there, she was very surprised to see that the pond was frozen. Sara had always wanted to ice skate and thought that this would be a great chance to see what it would feel like to glide across the ice.

I end the story here and ask my class, "What would you do?" We discuss and record several ideas. Some responses to the story have been: "I would do it;" "I would step on the ice first to see if would break;" "If the ice was hard enough, I would skate on it;" and "I would go ask my mom if I could ice skate."

To help dramatize this story, I tape bulletin board paper over some of my big blocks to represent the pond, making sure to place the blocks far enough apart so that the weight of a child walking over these areas will cause the paper to break. I always play the role of the adult figure and choose the students to play the roles of the characters who make the decision. We act out each possible solution and discuss the results. Of course, when an actor or actress falls through, it always gets a big laugh, but the children really listen when we discuss what would happen if someone *really* fell through. I always take advantage of my adult role, so when my young actor or actress comes to ask for permission to skate on the pond, I have everyone's full attention as I tell about the dangers of a frozen pond.

This particular story is very important for the students in the part of the country where I live. Most winters are mild, but every once in a while, a pond will freeze over with a thin layer of ice. Using my method of teaching health and safety allows me the opportunity to teach what is truly important in the lives of my students. We reinforce the lessons by writing in our journals, using centers to recreate the story, and doing experiments with freezing water. It really helps students understand the dangers of a frozen pond when they see that ice develops around the *edge* of the bowl first.

Whenever possible, I use community resources to help with different areas of safety concerns: a firefighter for my stories about fire safety; a mother to help with stories involving babies; medical workers for stories about medicine, drugs, or accidents; a police officer for stories about getting lost or stranger dangers. This method of teaching health and safety integrates many other areas of the curriculum, but most importantly, it helps make safety real for my students.

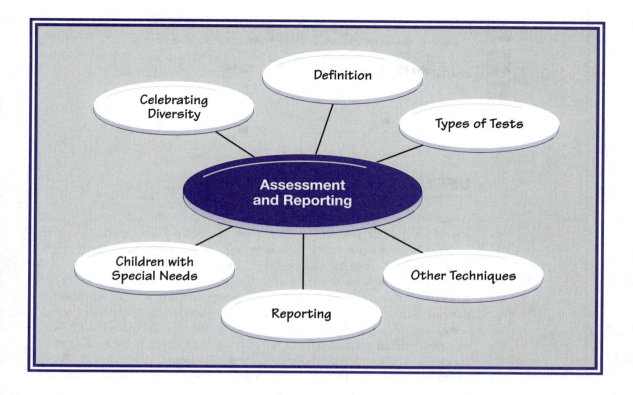

The local newspaper has just reported the test scores of children in area schools. Reading, mathematics, and writing scores are given by school and grade, with the percentages of increase and decrease since last year printed in bold type and the national averages highlighted. The almost full-page newspaper article is accompanied by an interview with the superintendent of schools, who emphasizes that the district will focus all future staff development efforts on raising those scores before the next test. Nowhere in the article is there any discussion about the match between the tests and the local curriculum, between the norming samples and the population of the community, or the appropriateness of using standardized test scores as the only measure of progress in area schools.

You are anxious to talk to your classmates about these test scores and other issues about evaluating young children. You cannot imagine giving the preschoolers you worked with last year a test that would require them to sit and answer questions. Yet you see from the newspaper article how much pressure there is from the community to prove that children are doing well in school. Is such proof available? How can teachers assess children appropriately?

DEFINITION OF ASSESSMENT

Assessment and *testing* are not synonymous terms. Although testing is only one of several components of assessment, in recent years, testing seems to be have been misused and to have become the major determinant of the value of schools and the abilities of children.

Assessment is more than just testing, however; it is using a variety of strategies in an effort to uncover the understanding and determine the development of individual children. Teachers assess children's social, emotional, and physical development as well as their intellectual growth—just as a pediatrician assesses a child not only by weighing and measuring him, checking his visual acuity, his hearing, and his reflexes but also by observing his ability to walk and his relationship to his parents. Similarly, programs are assessed by measuring not only the success of the children enrolled in them but also parents' satisfaction with their children's progress and teachers' feelings of accomplishment. Assessment is sometimes formal and sometimes informal. In contrast to testing, assessment is ongoing. A test is a sample of behavior or knowledge taken at a specific time. Assessment covers a much longer time frame and attempts to sample a much broader spectrum of behavior or knowledge.

Assessment is vital to good teaching; it is necessary to assess both the program and the progress of individual children. Good teachers would be involved in assessment even if there were no external requirements to do so; they want to know about how well children are doing, and they want to know about the effectiveness of their programs.

Assessment alone does not improve children or programs—just as measuring a child's height and weight does not make the child grow. Only when assessment has a purpose and is used to help make decisions about curriculum, about individual children, and about programs can it help a child or program grow.

Hills (1993) summarizes a strong assessment program when she states:

Assessment will serve the best interests of children when it is carried out as an integrated part of an overall program, when it contributes positively to children's self-esteem and developmental progress, and when it recognizes children's individuality and respects their family and community backgrounds. Assessment that will accomplish these ends is continuous, broadly focused on child development and learning, sensitive to children's diversity, integrated into their day-to-day activities, and designed to reap benefits for them, through teachers' knowledgeable planning and teaching and through clear communication between school and home. (p. 28)

Shepard (1994) also supports the concept of assessment as it "implies a substantive focus on student learning for the purpose of effective intervention" (p. 206). Assessment, then, cannot be limited to the administration of tests for young children. Assessment is most productive when it is an integral part of the learning process and the process is evaluated along with the product (Parker et al. 1995).

TYPES OF TESTS

Tests vary considerably in the purposes for which they were designed. The following definitions are based on the National Association for the Education of Young Children's (NAEYC) "Position Statement on Standardized Testing of Young Children 3 through 8 Years of Age" (1988):

Achievement test—A test that measures the extent to which a person has mastery over a certain body of information or possesses a certain skill after instruction has taken place

Criterion-referenced test—A test that evaluates a test taker in relation to a specified performance level (as distinguished from a test that compares the test taker's score to the performance of other people, which are norm-referenced tests)

Developmental test—An age-related, norm-referenced assessment of a child's skills and behaviors compared to those of children of the same chronological age; sometimes used incorrectly as screening tests

Norm-referenced test—A test that compares the test taker's performance to the performance of other people in a specified group

Readiness test—A test that assesses a child's level of preparedness for a specific academic or preacademic program

Reliability—The degree to which test scores are consistent, dependable, or repeatable; that is, the degree to which test scores can be attributed to actual differences in test takers' performance rather than to errors of measurement

Screening test—A test used to identify children who may be in need of special services; such a test focuses on the child's ability to acquire skills and may also be called a *developmental screening test*

Standardized test—A test composed of empirically selected items that is to be used in a specific way, is based on adequately defined norms, and is backed by data on reliability and validity

Validity—The degree to which a test measures what it is supposed to measure; also, the degree to which a certain inference from a test is appropriate or meaningful (p. 45)

THEORY
INTO
Practice

Examine a screening test and a readiness test. Study the information about reliability and validity that is furnished by the publisher of each test. Could the information that is gained from each test be gathered in other ways? Why?

As a student, you have probably had experience with all these kinds of tests. For instance, you probably took achievement tests while you were in elementary school, or you might have taken one in order to be admitted to the teacher education program you are in now. You might also have to take the National Teacher's Examination in order to become a certified teacher in your state. Generally, achievement tests are norm referenced and standardized. You have also likely taken tests in your college classes. These tests are usually criterion referenced, as the teacher determines the correct answers and, in theory, everyone could get a perfect score.

TESTING YOUNG CHILDREN

Young children are routinely given **screening tests.** Screening tests vary considerably, but most attempt to determine a child's ability to learn skills. Many of these tests ask children to identify objects, words, and numerals that are common in some environments. Developmental screening tests are designed to determine what children can do compared to other children their age. These tests often involve drawing geometric figures, bouncing balls, balancing on one foot, and repeating series of numerals or words. *Readiness tests* ask young children to recognize letters and numerals, to find objects that go together, and to recognize objects that are not the same as other objects in a set. These tests are supposed to predict a child's success in coping with an instructional program.

Meisels (1987) argues that in most cases, screening tests lack reliability and validity. Further evidence of the problems of reliability and validity comes from a large-scale study conducted in Minnesota (Thurlow, O'Sullivan, and Ysseldyke 1986), in which every preschool child in the state was given a developmental screening test. Some districts found a problem with every child, and some found no problems at all. These results probably reflect the inadequacies of the tests themselves, the way in which they were administered, or the way in which the results were interpreted. In sum, the study makes clear one of the real dangers of using standardized tests, which is that decisions may be made on the basis of faulty information.

Questionable reliability and validity are not the only problems associated with standardized tests. Meisels (1989) contends that testing changes teachers' perceptions of children, education, and instruction and allows test makers to control curriculum decisions. According to this view, if test results indicate that an individual child is not as capable as some other child, then teachers will treat the child differently. The child might not be invited to participate in some activities or might be stigmatized by being assigned tasks to help remediate the deficiency uncovered by the test. In some school districts, test scores are published in the local newspapers, which compounds the problem. As noted in the chapter-opening scenario, the scores by themselves are of limited value; other information about the local students, curriculum, and community is needed to view the scores in the accurate context. Publishing test scores also motivates some teachers to teach the information that will be tested so that their children's test scores look good. In short, the practice of publishing test scores is deplorable.

For example, one first-grade teacher had been teaching reading using literature and a whole-language approach that involved reading and writing. After some months, she was pressured by parents to tell them at which levels their children could read in the basal readers. She gave the children the basal tests and put them into three reading groups. She discovered after a month or two not only that the children felt differently about learning to read and about their abilities as readers but that she began to perceive the children differently. Before the tests, her perception was that all the children were capable of learning to read. After the tests, she began to feel that some were much less capable of learning to read. Happily, she realized what was happening, learned from her experience, and reverted back to her original strategies for teaching reading.

Standardized tests should be considered one of many avenues available for collecting information about a child, not the only avenue. Kamii and Kamii (1990) argue that standardized achievement tests encourage teachers to teach in ways that do not promote autonomous learning and that the tests do not tap children's thinking processes. Martin (1988) disapproves of the use of standardized screening tests to homogenize the children in any program. She maintains that a flexible program "can accommodate a wide diversity in children's backgrounds, maturity, temperaments, interests, talents, abilities, and skills" (p. 489). Screening tests, she believes, are symptoms of the schools' refusal to accept differences.

The report of a task force of the National Association of State Boards of Education (NASBE 1988) echoes this view. The authors state that "developmental or readiness tests should not be used to determine placement in what may be perceived as homogeneous groups. We think that early childhood classrooms should contain a heterogeneous mix of children with various levels of skills and abilities" (p. 14). It is true that pressures on schools to achieve are enormous and that some schools try to limit differences so that they can show more gains on tests. Only knowledgeable teachers, administrators, and parents can break this cycle.

THEORY INTO Practice

Review the brochure *Testing of Young Children: Cautions and Concerns* (NAEYC 1989). How can good information be disseminated to the public?

Before administering any standardized test, a teacher must think carefully about the purpose of the test and how the information from the test will be used. Standardized tests should *never* be used to deny services to any child or as the basis for placement decisions (retaining a child in grade, placing a child in special programs). Perrone (1990) states, "I cry when I read about young children 'held back' on the basis of a test, or placed in one or another of the schooling tracks that support various judgments about children's potential. And I wonder about those who believe that testing young children, then making placement, promotion, or retention decisions on the basis of such testing, leads to any constructive ends" (p. 1).

The following guidelines, which are based on the NAEYC's "Position Statement on Standardized Testing of Young Children 3 through 8 Years of Age" (1988), will help teachers determine if and when a standardized test should be used with young children:

1. Standardized tests must be used only for the purposes for which they were intended.
2. The use of standardized tests must be restricted to situations in which testing provides information that will clearly contribute to improved outcomes for children.
3. Test content should *not* determine the school's curriculum. Rather, the school's curriculum should guide teachers and others in the selection of tests.
4. Test givers must be qualified to administer the tests and sensitive to the developmental needs of young children.
5. Teachers and administrators must be knowledgeable about testing and able to interpret test results accurately and cautiously to parents, school personnel, and the media.
6. The younger the child, the more difficult it is to design tests that are reliable and valid. Nevertheless, all standardized tests used must be reliable and valid according to technical standards of test development.
7. Day-to-day instructional decisions must depend primarily on teacher observation. Standardized tests cannot provide information for planning day-to-day instructional activities.
8. Since standardized tests are not useful for day-to-day instructional decisions and student appraisal, taking time to administer the tests takes away from instructional time. Therefore, before teachers devote substantial classroom time to administering standardized tests, they should establish the purposes of the test data and determine whether the time and expense involved are warranted.
9. Student appraisal decisions should be based primarily on teacher observation and should reflect the goals of the classroom.

There are some valid reasons for using standardized tests, such as to collect data for research studies that allow broad-based comparisons that can help make schools better places for children. Some tests may also help in diagnosing children who need special services. The responsibility for using tests in ways that benefit children lies with teachers and administrators.

OTHER TECHNIQUES FOR ASSESSMENT

Anecdotal Records

When teachers observe children's behavior and record their observations, they produce *anecdotal records*. Kept over a period of time, these records are likely to reveal patterns of behavior that will suggest strategies for helping an individual child become more competent or supporting the child's obvious growth. Irwin and Bushnell (1980) state that anecdotal records help teachers "test hunches about reasons for a child's behavior or learning style, . . . identify what conditions may be reinforcing behavior, and . . . gain feedback about what children have learned from a particular curriculum unit or presentation" (p. 23).

One key to making an anecdotal record is to record the information without interpretation—just the facts, please! For example, if the teacher

Teachers can assess children's learning through observing them in many different experiences.

observes Sally push Leon so hard that he falls backward into the sandbox, then the teacher should record the act, not make a statement such as "Sally was aggressive." This may be the only incidence of pushing all year—Sally may be reacting to the fact that Leon pulled her hair. If Sally pushes several children and each incident is noted in the anecdotal record, then the teacher might interpret from the series of observations that Sally needs help in controlling her impulse to push people. A record that states that Sally was aggressive does not help the teacher focus on her behavior and find its causes. Any interpretation of behavior included in anecdotal records must be clearly labeled as such.

If possible, the teacher should record what happens just prior to an observation and also what happens after it. For example, if Leon pulls Sally's hair, that should be noted as part of the observation. What Sally does next should also be part of the recording. Knowing whether Sally runs away after pushing Leon, apologizes and helps him up, or sits down to play with him is valuable for the teacher in assessing Sally's behavior.

The bias of the observer is always an issue in anecdotal records. Even though the observer may record an incident exactly as it happened, with no evaluative or interpretive comments, the choice of incidents to record, the frequency of recordings, or the lack of recordings may all reflect the bias of the observer.

Another key to making helpful observations is to observe children in many different situations and activities. Children who never initiate conversation inside the classroom may talk nonstop outdoors and single-handedly organize half the class for an activity. Observations should also focus on the total development of the child. Records of the child's physical, social, emotional, and intellectual development help the teacher put together a clear picture of the whole child. Katz (1984) suggests looking at preschoolers in terms of their range of affect, variations in play, curiosity, response to authority, friendship, interest, spontaneous affection, and enjoyment of life.

Various educators' guidelines for collecting anecdotal records (Bentzen 1985; Boehm and Weinberg 1987; Irwin and Bushnell 1980) are summarized here:

1. Record the incident as soon as possible after it occurs.
2. Include the setting, time, and activity.
3. Record the exact words of the participants when possible.
4. Record the actions and words of other people in the incident.
5. Make each record as objective, accurate, and complete as possible.

Boehm and Weinberg (1987, p. 17) further recommend limiting discussion to one incident; recording incidents as soon as possible after they occur;

separating interpretive comments from factual reporting; and considering supportive information in order to accumulate the most useful records.

Making anecdotal records is time consuming. Unfortunately, this kind of information often stays in the teacher's head, rather than being put on paper. One technique for making note collecting easier is to prepare a loose-leaf notebook with a page for each child. The teacher might carry a pad of Post-it notes or computer labels in her pocket and jot down observations on individual notes; at the end of the day, these notes can be stuck on the appropriate child's page and the teacher won't have to recopy the information. Additional notes can be added as trends or patterns are observed (Hill and Ruptik 1994; Reardon 1991).

Teachers should make an effort to observe two or three children daily. Over time, they will have accomplished observations on every child. (Sometimes, a teacher may choose one or two children and observe them for a week or two. Usually, these are children the teacher feels need special help because they have either behavior or learning problems.)

If teachers develop the habit of observing carefully, they will have much information that is useful for planning and for sharing with parents. One study investigated the match between teacher assessments of children and the children's performance on tests. The teacher assessments were found to be very accurate predictors of children's performance on tests (Stoner and Purcell 1985). It is not surprising that qualified teachers are capable of making good assessments of young children.

Martin (1996) summarizes her beliefs about appropriate assessment by stating that it should include "the objective recording of the detail of the child's behavior; the necessity for ensuring that evaluation of observations is based on objective data rather than casual perceptions; and the belief that in the observation of behavior we reach the best understanding of each individual's development and richer appreciation of the patterns of the development of all children" (p. 8). Teachers can only develop good observation skills through practice and study, but the results will be well worth the effort (Benjamin 1994).

Checklists and Rating Scales

Teachers can use checklists to make quick notes of what children actually do in the classroom. This information is valuable for determining which children are interested in which activities or which children have accomplished given tasks. Teachers can use the information obtained from checklists for evaluating learning areas and for reporting to parents.

Most checklists are constructed by teachers and used in a variety of activities, although some may be supplied by the district, state, or other administrators. Consider a checklist of children's physical skills. The skills

Being able to keep good records is an important skill for successful early childhood teachers.

to be observed would be listed across the top of the page and the children's names down the side of the page. If skipping were one of the skills listed and a teacher observed a child skipping, she would enter the date beside the child's name. Other abilities are also relatively easy to record on a checklist: working puzzles, constructing patterns with beads or pattern blocks, cutting with the right or left hand, using counting as a problem-solving strategy, choosing a book and looking at it for five minutes, playing in a group for ten minutes, and so on. Most teachers who use checklists find that it is most helpful to have a variety of such lists in the areas where the activities would be most likely to be observed. Table 15.1 identifies possible skills and abilities that can be noted on checklists.

Checklists are appropriate for gathering factual information, not for determining the curriculum of the program. Some checklists include items such as counting to 10, tying shoes, and naming the letters of the alphabet. It is useful to know that children can do these things, but it is inappropriate to base the curriculum on a list of such skills and to engage the child in drill-and-practice exercises to master them.

Rating scales are similar to checklists except that the behavior is marked in terms of frequency (always, sometimes, never) or quality (above average, average, or below average). Rating scales can also provide useful information for teachers as they plan learning experiences. It is most appropriate to use rating scales to compare a child's current behavior to his

TABLE 15.1

Skills and Abilities That Can Be Noted on Checklists

Physical Development	Social-Emotional Development	Intellectual Development
• Develop large muscles: Run, hop, skip, gallop, balance, walk backward, throw and catch a ball	• Experience success at school	• Know and recite personal information: First and last name, age, address, birthdate, telephone number
• Develop small muscles: Cut, paste, clap, button, zip, tie, stack	• Interact with other children	• Explain simple pictures
• Manipulate tools	• Listen, follow directions	• Show an interest in print and a desire to read and write
• Copy simple shapes	• Make choices	• Differentiate between fantasy and reality
• Assemble puzzles	• Initiate and complete activities	• Speak in sentences of five or more words
• Draw, pretend write, write	• Accept responsibility	• Recognize colors
• Play games	• Express thoughts in a variety of ways	• Recognize numbers
• Wash, use the toilet, dress without assistance	• Show appreciation for, sensitivity to others	• Count
• Visually follow a line of print from left to right and top to bottom and return	• Explore and experiment	• Demonstrate one-to-one correspondence
• Distinguish sounds and symbols	• Practice social skills	• Recite the alphabet
	• Enjoy school	• Recognize upper- and lowercase letters
	• Maintain self-control	• Write first name
	• Talk	• Draw a picture of a person with ten recognizable body parts
	• Play	• Solve problems
	• Respond positively to adult authority	• Demonstrate resourcefulness and independence
	• Share	• Continue to expand vocabulary based on experiences
	• Help clean up	• Identify patterns and basic shapes
	• Approach tasks positively, stay with tasks	• Recognize likenesses and differences
	• Work independently	• Measure
	• Cooperate	• Paraphrase
	• Respond to humor	• Ask questions
		• Relate new information to previous knowledge
		• Brainstorm
		• Make lists
		• Remember a sequence or pattern
		• Classify objects and topics
		• Use reasoning skills
		• Participate in activities for aesthetic development

FIGURE 15.1

Rating Scale

Name	Frequently	Sometimes	Not yet
Uses language effectively			
Solves problems in arithmetic with sums to 10			
Participates in group discussions			
Participates in singing experiences			

previous behavior. Teachers can get caught in the trap of comparing children to each other if they are not judicious in their use of rating scales. Figure 15.1 shows an example of a rating scale.

Attitude and Interest Inventories

Information about how children feel about different activities and the things that interest them most is usually obtained by asking questions through an attitude or interest inventory. Often, these questions are intended to be open ended. For example, the teacher might ask "What is your favorite thing to do in the classroom?" or "What is your favorite thing to do outdoors?" Some inventories are designed to gather information by asking children to mark responses to given questions.

Figure 15.2 shows an example of the type of form a teacher might complete during an open-ended interview with a child. Figure 15.3 on page 474 is an example of one page of a five-page commercial attitude survey that would be used during an interview with a child; the format of the questions prompts the child to choose a response.

Attitude and interest inventories can help teachers make planning decisions. If the teacher determines that children are feeling uncomfortable about certain learning experiences, then those can be modified so that the children's attitudes about school might be improved. Interest inventories provide teachers with clues about experiences that would be of interest to the children and would therefore likely be successful learning experiences.

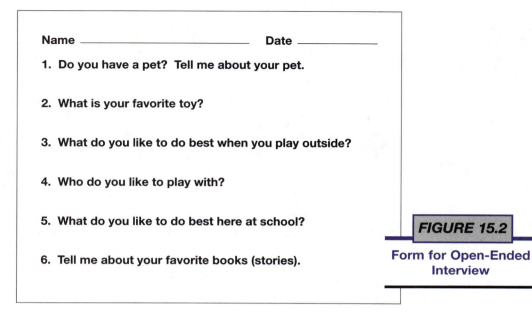

Name _____ Date _____

1. Do you have a pet? Tell me about your pet.

2. What is your favorite toy?

3. What do you like to do best when you play outside?

4. Who do you like to play with?

5. What do you like to do best here at school?

6. Tell me about your favorite books (stories).

FIGURE 15.2

Form for Open-Ended Interview

Time-Activity Samples

Another assessment technique is to record on a regular schedule the activities in which children are engaged. For example, for an entire day, the teacher would record each child's activity every thirty minutes. After a given period (a week, a month), the teacher would repeat the observation. These records would provide information about the child's choices over time and help the teacher determine each child's interests. Time-activity samples can also provide some clues as to the quality of the child's involvement but are most useful when accompanied by other information, as well. Figure 15.4 on page 475 is an example of a time-activity record.

Self-Evaluation

Even very young children can begin to evaluate themselves. They can describe orally what they learned while they were involved in the activities of the day, or they can tell how they learned to do something. Older children can decide with the teacher which things they are learning are most important and record those in a booklet or on a checklist that they have constructed.

Primary children might be encouraged to complete short, written evaluations of selected pieces of their work to share with others. For example,

FIGURE 15.3

**Elementary Reading
Attitude Survey**

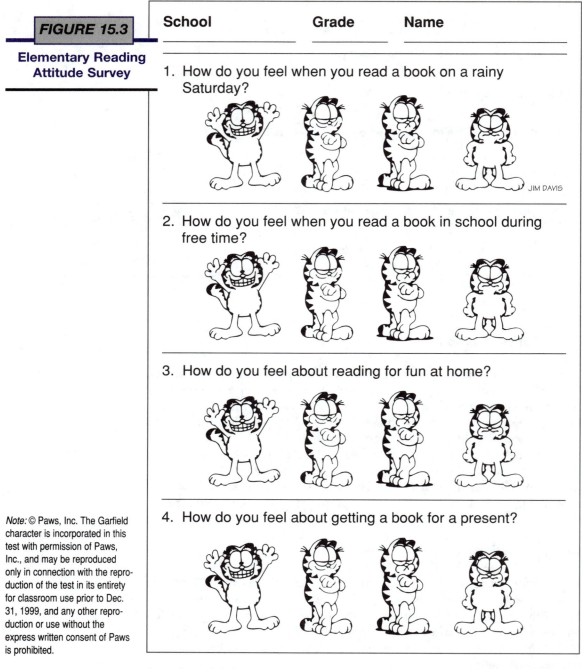

School   Grade   Name

1. How do you feel when you read a book on a rainy Saturday?

JIM DAVIS

2. How do you feel when you read a book in school during free time?

3. How do you feel about reading for fun at home?

4. How do you feel about getting a book for a present?

Source: Excerpt from the appendix from McKenna, Michael C., & Kear, Dennis J. (1990, May). Measuring attitude toward reading: A new tool for teachers. *The Reading Teacher, 43*(9), 626–639. Reprinted with permission of Michael C. McKenna and the International Reading Association. All rights reserved.

9:15 a.m.	Reading	Writing center	Sand/Water play	Art	Science
Juan	X				
Sara		X			
Addie			X		
Robert		X			

FIGURE 15.4

Sample Time-Activity Period

they might complete the sentence "I think this is my best writing because _____" or "I want to share this art because _____."

Part of the process of self-evaluation should include what needs to come next, so as children think about what they have done well, they should be encouraged to think about what they need to learn, too. For instance, if a child has learned to print his first name, he should be acknowledged for that achievement and then asked if he wants to learn to print his last name (or perhaps the name of a friend or some other word of interest). If a child can read a given text successfully, then he might be encouraged to read a more difficult text or a text from a different genre. Self-evaluation should be linked to personal goal setting.

Portfolio Assessment

Of the many types of alternative assessment, **portfolio assessment** seems to be the most popular with teachers. Paulson, Paulson, and Meyer (1991) define a *portfolio* as "a purposeful collection of student work that exhibits the student's efforts, progress, and achievements in one or more areas. The collection must include student participation in selecting contents, the criteria for selection, the criteria for judging merit, and evidence of student self-reflection" (p. 60).

Purpose
Before teachers decide to use a portfolio system, they must decide the purpose the portfolio will serve: Will it be used to communicate with parents?

THEORY INTO Practice

Prepare a presentation for your local school board in which you provide a rationale for eliminating standardized tests for young children and describe the measures you would recommend to take the place of standardized tests.

Teachers and children should conference frequently to review accomplishments and set new goals.

Will it be used to determine the child's individual progress? Will it be used for teacher accountability? Will it be used for all these purposes?

In deciding purpose, teachers should understand that a portfolio alone is not an assessment; rather, it is a collection of materials that can be used to assess progress. Thus, a portfolio is not especially useful until the materials have been evaluated by the teacher or others. A collection of materials such as writing samples and artwork, for instance, is only that—a collection. It becomes an assessment tool when it has been used to determine a child's progress and needs.

Graves (1990) suggests that teachers take an experimental stance toward portfolios, rather than treating them as permanent records. In this view, a portfolio is a dynamic, ongoing collection created by both teacher and child—either can contribute or remove items.

Portfolios can be invaluable in communicating with parents. When a child receives a letter grade of A or C for an entire year's performance in a subject, parents have no way of knowing exactly what the child has learned or how much progress she has made since the beginning of the term. Flood and Lapp (1989) suggest a comparison portfolio strategy that is especially helpful in communicating a child's growth to parents. They suggest selecting writing samples, reading samples, and other pertinent information (such as the number of books read, how often reading is chosen as a free-choice activity, changes in attitudes, and so on) that will demonstrate the child's growth in an area. Teachers should make sure that parents are aware of how pieces were selected for a portfolio: Are they the child's best work? work that demonstrates a particular competency? work that is in progress? Parents also should be invited to offer suggestions for portfolio entries or deletions.

Sometimes, portfolios are used to provide evidence for teacher accountability. For instance, items in portfolios could be used to document that given activities were provided for children. Teachers might also exchange three or four portfolios with peers in order to validate their own opinions about the instruction provided and the children's achievement. If teachers choose to exchange portfolios, the selection of the portfolios for examination should be clearly understood. For example, if four were to be exchanged, one might be from a child showing outstanding performance, two from children showing average performance, and one from a child having difficulties of some kind. Teachers might even want to submit portfolios of selected children's pieces to their administrators in order to demonstrate effectiveness in fostering children's achievement.

Content and Organization

Portfolios can be valuable for documenting children's growth, for communicating with parents, and for validating the quality of instruction. However, their usefulness depends on how and what materials are selected and how they are organized.

A variety of items could be included in a portfolio—drawings or paintings the child has made, photos of block constructions he has made, photos or videos of him climbing on outdoor equipment, notes about or videos of him throwing or catching a ball, records of books he has read (or listened to the teacher read), stories he has written or dictated, samples of his classification activities, and notes about his social growth.

Of course, portfolios may also contain teacher observations and notes. If, for example, a piece of writing is selected for inclusion in a child's portfolio, then the teacher might add some observation about the selection—perhaps noting that the child worked on the piece over a period of four days but was reluctant to make any changes after a conference with the teacher. The same sort of comment might accompany art samples or other work. Work samples, when used along with other information collected by the teacher, clearly demonstrate the child's growth and the effectiveness of the program.

The most logical organization for a portfolio that will be used to determine a child's individual progress is to create a section of the portfolio to match each of the major program goals. For example, Meisels (1993, p. 36) suggests the categories of personal-social development, language and literacy, mathematical thinking, scientific thinking, social studies, art and music, and physical development.

The High/Scope program (Schweinhart 1993) recommends the following categories:

- *Initiative*—expressing choices, engaging in complex play
- *Creative representation*—making, building, pretending
- *Social relations*—relating to adults, making friends
- *Music and movement*—exhibiting body coordination, imitating movements to a beat
- *Language and literacy*—showing interest in reading, beginning reading, beginning writing
- *Logic and mathematics*—sorting, counting objects, describing time sequences (p. 32)

Teachers of younger children might find different categories more appropriate for their students, whereas teachers of eight-year-olds might need more specific categories for mathematics, reading, and writing.

Once the major categories have been determined, one or two core items can be collected and dated in fall, winter, and spring. *Core items* are work samples that are common to all children. For example, all children in the first grade would be expected to complete some writing and reading. Other items can be added in each category that reflect the child's individual interests or activities.

Table 15.2 is a chart of goals for students that was developed in Missouri as part of the statewide Project Construct (Missouri Department of Elementary and Secondary Education 1992). The purposes of Project Construct were to establish a constructivist curriculum in all Missouri schools for young children and to assess these children in a manner consistent with constructivist thinking. A student portfolio based on these purposes would have four major sections and subsections as needed (see Table 15.2). Samples of work, photos, videos, and anecdotal records could be collected to verify the child's growth in these areas.

Another useful means of organizing a portfolio is to provide a table of contents or summary sheet, listing the materials included and the dates they were collected. Two or three times a year, it will be helpful to summarize the data in the portfolio. Such a summary will serve to help teachers determine where their information is too thin and to use what information they have more fully in planning learning experiences. Including some sort of summary will also help prevent the portfolio from becoming a jumble of materials over time.

Most teachers prefer to collect portfolio items in large, expandable folders or loose-leaf binders. However the materials are collected, they should be stored in a place that is easily accessible to both children and

TABLE 15.2

Project Construct Goals for Students

Sociomoral Domain

Social Relationships
- Build relationships of mutual trust and respect with adults.
- Build relationships with peers.
- Consider the perspectives of others.
- Negotiate and apply rules.

Dispositions
- Be curious.
- Take initiative.
- Be confident.
- Be creative.

Cognitive Domain

Logico-Mathematical Knowledge
- Construct classificatory relationships.
- Construct numerical relationships.
- Construct spatial and temporal relationships.

Physical Knowledge
- Act on objects and observe reactions.
- Act on objects to produce desired effects.

Conventional Knowledge
- Know personal information.
- Know about the community.
- Know conventional notations, manners, and customs.

Representative Domain

Symbolic Development
- Represent ideas and feelings through pretend play.
- Represent ideas and feelings through movement.
- Represent ideas and feelings through music.
- Represent ideas and feelings through art and construction.

Language Development
- Use language for a variety of functions.
- Expand and refine the form and organization of language.
- Construct meaning from language.
- Represent ideas and feelings through language.

Physical Development Domain

Motor Skills
- Develop motor skills for personally meaningful purposes.

Health and Safety
- Develop healthy living practices.

teachers. Often, children like to review what they have done already and add items that are especially significant to them. And teachers will certainly want to add to the portfolios on a regular basis.

A portfolio of work samples with careful summaries can be an accurate measure of a child's performance (Meisels et al. 1995). Since such a system is just as valid and provides much more information than achievement tests, it certainly seems reasonable to replace achievement testing with a well-developed portfolio system. Stone (1995b) summarizes the differences between portfolio assessment and more traditional testing in Table 15.3 on page 480.

PARENTS AND ASSESSMENT

- Make assessment the focus of one parent meeting. Provide parents with examples of various kinds of tests, and explain how each could best be used in a program for young children. Also provide examples of various tools of assessment, such as checklists and portfolios, and explain their use in your program.

TABLE 15.3 Portfolio Assessment versus Traditional Assessment

Portfolio Assessment	Traditional Assessment
Uses multiple forms of assessment	Uses one form of assessment
Gives complete picture of child's learning	Gives narrow view of child's learning
Makes assessment within contexts	Makes assessment in contrived learning context (i.e., test)
Is child-centered	Is curriculum-centered
Is ongoing	Conducts one-time test on particular task
Supports the process of learning	Represents isolated task separate from the process of learning
Focuses on what children can do	Focuses on what children cannot do
Evaluates child's past achievements and own potential	Evaluates by comparison to norms
Benefits children by supporting their growth	Labels, sorts, and ranks children
Provides teachers with information to extend child's learning	Provides little information teacher can use to help child
Provides opportunity for child to evaluate own learning	Uses only teacher evaluation

Source: From S. Stone, *Understanding Portfolio Assessment: A Guide for Parents* (Wheaton, MD: Association for Childhood Education International, 1995). Reprinted by permission of S. Stone and the Association for Childhood Education International. Copyright © 1995 by the Association.

Portfolios are most useful when they are built into the instructional day and help teachers make good instructional decisions (Stone 1995a). In schools and classrooms in which the use of portfolios for assessment is most successful, teachers and children work to describe good products. Then they think about how the portfolio entries demonstrate growth toward worthwhile goals. Finally, teachers, parents, and children use the portfolios to celebrate achievements, to set new goals, and to reflect on the process of learning together. Barclay and Breheny (1994) found that reporting to parents was much more effective when they kept portfolios of children's work to share at conference time.

REPORTING

Reporting to parents is an important aspect of the job of the early childhood teacher. Parents have a right to know about their child's performance and behavior in school. The teacher has an obligation to be as honest as she can with parents, but this honesty must be leavened with tact and sensitivity. Nothing is as important to a parent as his child; honesty does not have to be brutal or hurtful. Reports to parents usually take the form of report cards, conferences, narratives, telephone calls, casual conversations, newsletters, or videotapes.

Report Cards

Although many schools require report cards for children in kindergarten or the primary grades, report cards are frustrating to both parents and teachers of young children. Many parents and most educators question the information conveyed on report cards: What does a grade mean? Does an A in mathematics mean that the child knows a given set of concepts or that the child can complete a given number of computations correctly?

Many schools have done away with letter grades on report cards for kindergarten (and some for primary grades), but often letter grades have been replaced by checklists of skills mastered, such as "Speaks in complete sentences" or "Counts to 100." These checklists have some of the disadvantages of letter grades and leave the impression that the program consists of isolated skills.

A report card is not the best choice for reporting to parents. If teachers must use report cards, however, they should try to mediate the information for parents by enclosing written summaries of children's progress or at least comments that help parents understand the grades. Some schools have adapted their report cards so that they reflect more about what the child can do and depend less on letter grades. For example, rather than posting a grade in reading, some parts of a developmental checklist might be on the report card, such as "Self-corrects errors that change meaning." A report card might also have spaces for the child, teacher, and parents to record their goals for the next grading period. Another strategy is to have a conference with the parents to discuss the child's progress and to review the report card.

Conferences

The most effective way of reporting to parents is face to face, in a conference. A conference should not be conducted so that the parents sit passively while the teacher tells them about their child. Both parents and teachers (and sometimes children) should participate; each should learn from the other, and both should have the opportunity to share information.

Effective conferences require advance preparation. All the anecdotal records, information gathered from checklists, information from inventories or interviews, and portfolios of work will need to be assembled and organized. Teachers must not withhold information from parents; all records should be open to them. Preparation should also include writing a summary of the child's progress in all areas of development and thinking

THEORY INTO Practice

Interview two or three teachers of young children about how they assess children's progress and report to parents. Do they have control of these decisions? Are they required to use some specific techniques? Explain your findings.

about the implications of assessments for future planning for the child. The teacher's role is also to seek information from the parents by asking for their observations and their plans and expectations for their child.

During a conference, the teacher should be prepared to answer questions from parents. Parents will likely want to know what they can do at home to help their child, what interests and abilities the teacher has observed in their child, how their child gets along with other children, who are their children's friends at school, and what kinds of things are difficult for their child.

A conference may allow the teacher to share information about the program with parents as well as information about their child. The inverse of this sharing is eliciting the feelings and understandings of the parents about the program. A well-planned conference provides for sharing information and for keeping the lines of communication open between teachers and parents (Gelfer and Perkins 1987).

Effective follow-up to a conference will be helpful in planning the next conference and will increase the parents' trust. All agreements made during a conference should be summarized in writing, and copies should be made for both the teacher and the parents. If the conference ends with an agreement that the teacher will perform certain tasks, then these tasks should be completed promptly and the information should be entered in the conference file. For example, if the parents request that the teacher observe their child for a specific behavior in the next two weeks and report to them, then the teacher should make the observations, record them, and share them with the parents.

Evaluation of the conference is a component of follow-up activities. Canady and Seyfarth (1979, pp. 49–50) suggest some questions that will assist in evaluating the conference: Could the conference be described as a problem-solving session? Was there an equal distribution of power among all persons present during the conference? Was the emotional climate of the conference positive? Was the tone of the conference constructive? Were the goals of the conference understood by all persons present? Were the goals met? Were facts and all information related to the conference adequately handled? Follow-up should be considered as carefully as preconference planning.

THEORY INTO Practice

Participate in a simulation of a parent-teacher conference. Play the role of the teacher of a child with learning or behavior problems that must be communicated to the parent. What kinds of information would you gather before the conference? How would you arrange the physical setting for the conference? How would you conclude the conference? Would you include the child? Why or why not?

Narrative Reports

Another effective way of reporting to parents is through a narrative report. Narratives include basically the information that the teacher would share with parents in a conference. Statements in a narrative should be supported by evidence from the various records that the teacher has accumulated. One method of organizing the information is to focus on each area of development (intellectual, social, emotional, and physical). The narrative should also include what the teacher considers to be implications of the information and plans for the future.

A good narrative is a summary of the information from other records. For example, in summarizing a child's growth in social abilities, the narrative might read: "Since the beginning of the year, Denise has gained in her ability to communicate her needs and wants with words most of the time. On three occasions, she has been observed asking a child for a toy that she wanted. She is also able to share classroom materials. She has been observed willingly sharing toy trucks and blocks with other children. "

Note the objectivity of these remarks. They are specific observations, not judgments or generalizations. Statements such as "Jediah is unhappy" or "Samantha does not function at the level of her peers" have no place in a narrative report.

Telephone Calls

Generally, telephone calls are most useful for sharing with parents information about specific incidents. If, for example, Carly used words to express her frustration for the first time rather than hitting people, a telephone call to report that progress would be appropriate. Telephone calls should not be used to relay negative information about a child unless there is absolutely no alternative. Telephone calls should be brief and to the point and made at times that likely will be convenient for parents.

Casual Conversations

Sometimes, parents prefer to have casual conversations with the teacher when they are picking up or delivering their child. These conversations do not substitute for conferences, but teachers can help keep parents informed by reporting on progress or interesting anecdotes from the day. Again, these are not the times to report negative information. If a problem needs to be shared, a conference should be scheduled.

Newsletters

Although newsletters are not commonly listed as a means of reporting to parents, they can help keep parents informed about what is going on in the program. Some newsletters use reports that children write or dictate about field trips, visitors, or other events to provide interesting information to parents. Newsletters need not be formal productions that require a lot of time. Kindergarten and primary children can write items to be included in newsletters. Even threes and fours can write items (these may need to be translated for the parents) or dictate items to be shared with families. A review of the week's events and a list of plans for the next week will help parents know what their children are learning and doing. Many parents will engage their children in activities at home that relate to topics at school if they are kept informed through a newsletter.

Videotapes

Another general means by which teachers can keep parents informed about the school program is to make a videotape of a typical schoolday and encourage parents to check it out. After everyone has had a chance to view the video, the teacher should make a new one. The first video might provide general information about the program, and later videos might concentrate on specific topics: new themes, areas added to the classroom, classroom pets, storytime, music and movement activities, and so on. The teacher should ensure that every child is included in class videos.

PARENTS AND REPORTING

■ Ask parents to help create newsletters that include items specifically of interest to parents. You can also ask parents to help create or edit videotapes of school activities.

ASSESSMENT AND REPORTING

Assessment and reporting go together like graham crackers and milk. It is hard to fathom why any educator would bother to institute a comprehensive assessment program if the information was not to be shared with others—administrators, parents, and other teachers. It is also difficult to imagine attempting to report to parents about their children without having a strong, ongoing assessment program.

In the process of collecting information and preparing for reporting, teachers can evaluate their assessment programs: Are some pieces of information missing? Are there areas in the child's development about which more information is needed? Are there more effective ways of gathering the needed information? Parents, too, will offer assessment information. They may let the teacher know that the child is transferring the information being learned in school to other situations. Effective reporting and effective assessment go hand in hand.

PARENTS AND ASSESSMENT

■ Write a letter to parents in which you explain two or three of the principles presented in the Developmentally Appropriate Practice box (p. 485) that you think are critical to good assessment. Include examples from children's work to support and illustrate your explanation.

---

1. Curriculum and assessment are integrated throughout the program; assessment is congruent with and relevant to the goals, objectives, and content of the program.

2. Assessment results in benefits to the child, such as needed adjustments in the curriculum or more individualized instruction and improvements in the program.

3. Children's development and learning in all domains—physical, social, emotional, and cognitive—and their dispositions and feelings are informally and routinely assessed by teachers' observing children's activities and interactions, listening to them as they talk, and using their constructive errors to understand their learning.

4. Assessment provides teachers with useful information to successfully fulfill their responsibilities: to support children's learning and development, to plan for individuals and groups, and to communicate with parents.

5. Assessment involves regular and periodic observation of the child in a wide variety of circumstances that are representative of the child's behavior in the program over time.

6. Assessment relies primarily on procedures that reflect the ongoing life of the classroom and typical activities of the children. Assessment avoids approaches that place children in artificial situations, impede the usual learning and developmental experiences in the classroom, or divert children from their natural learning processes.

7. Assessment relies on demonstrated performance during real, not contrived, activities, for example, real reading and writing activities rather than only skills testing (Teale 1988; Engel 1990).

8. Assessment utilizes an array of tools and a variety of processes, including, but not limited to, collections of representative work by children (artwork, stories they write, recordings of their reading), records of systematic observation by teachers, records of conversations and interviews with children, and teachers' summaries of children's progress as individuals and as groups (Chittenden & Courtney 1989; Goodman, Goodman, & Hood 1989).

9. Assessment recognizes individual diversity of learning and allows for differences in styles and rates of learning. Assessment takes into consideration children's ability in English, their stage of language acquisition, and whether they have been given the time and opportunity to develop proficiency in their native language as well as in English.

10. Assessment supports children's development and learning; it does *not* threaten children's psychological safety or feelings of self-esteem

11. Assessment supports parents' relationships with their children and does not undermine parents' confidence in their children's or their own ability, nor does it devalue the language and culture of the family.

12. Assessment demonstrates children's overall strengths and progress, what children *can* do, not just their wrong answers and what they cannot do or do not know.

13. Assessment is an essential component of the teacher's role. Since teachers can make maximal use of assessment results, the teacher is the *primary* assessor.

14. Assessment is a collaborative process involving children and teachers, teachers and parents, school and community. Information from parents about each child's experiences at home is used in planning instruction and evaluating children's learning. Information obtained from assessment is shared with parents in language they can understand.

15. Assessment encourages children to participate in self-evaluation.

16. Assessment addresses what children can do independently and what they can demonstrate with assistance, because the latter shows the direction of their growth.

17. Information about each child's growth, development, and learning is systematically collected and recorded at regular intervals. Information such as samples of children's work, descriptions of their performance, and anecdotal records is used for planning instruction and communicating with parents.

18. A regular process exists for periodic information sharing between teachers and parents about children's growth and development and performance. The method of reporting to parents does not rely on letter or numerical grades but rather provides more meaningful, descriptive information in narrative form.

Source: From S. Bredekamp and T. Rosegrant, "Reaching Potentials through Transforming Curriculum, Assessment, and Teaching," in *Reaching Potentials: Transforming Early Childhood Curriculum and Assessment,* vol. 2, edited by S. Bredekamp and T. Rosegrant, 5–22 (p. 17). (Washington, DC: National Association for the Education of Young Children, 1995). Copyright © 1995 by NAEYC. Reprinted with permission.

CHILDREN WITH SPECIAL NEEDS

In planning assessment strategies for children with special needs, teachers must think about performance strategies that focus on the strengths of these children rather than the limitations. Lowenthal (1996) suggests that assessment for young children with special needs should involve much more than simply standardized tests. She notes, however, that some standardized tests have adaptations for children with specific disabilities. Teachers of special-needs children should use whatever means are available to help make the best decisions about each child's progress and future needs. Sampling systems, play observations, anecdotal records, and portfolio assessment can be invaluable in highlighting children's abilities.

Every child who has been identified as having special needs will have an *individualized education plan* (*IEP*) or *individualized family service plan* (*IFSP*), depending on her age. The development and implementation of these plans is specified by federal law. Each plan must contain the following information:

1. A statement of the child's present levels of educational performance, including academic achievement, social adaptation, prevocational and vocational skills, psychomotor skills, and self-help skills.
2. A statement of annual goals which describes the educational performance to be achieved by the end of the school year under the child's Individualized Education Program.
3. A statement of short-term instructional objectives, which must be measurable intermediate steps between the present level of educational performance and the annual goals.
4. A statement of specific educational services needed by the child (determined without regard to the availability of services), including a description of
   a. all special education and related services which are needed to meet the unique needs of the child, including the type of physical education program in which the child will participate, and
   b. special instructional media and materials which are needed.
5. The date when those services will begin and length of time the services will be given.
6. A description of the extent to which the child will participate in regular education programs.
7. A justification of the type of educational placement that the child will have.
8. A list of the individuals who are responsible for implementation of the Individualized Education Program.
9. Objective criteria, evaluation procedures, and schedules of determining, on at least an annual basis, whether the short-term instructional objectives are being achieved. (*Federal Register*, 41[252], pp. 56966–56998)

Each child's IEP or IFSP is written by a team of specialists, including his classroom teacher and parents, who specify what goals are to be achieved and how. But it is often the task of the classroom teacher to monitor the child's progress toward achieving those goals. Ongoing monitoring may lead to revisions in the initial plan and/or the curriculum. Assessment and curriculum are closely related for children with disabilities (Wolery and Wilbert 1994).

CELEBRATING DIVERSITY

It is common knowledge that many tests are culturally biased, yet the debate continues in the popular press about programs that accept students of color who have lower test scores than mainstream students who are turned away. Our job as teachers is not to resolve the debate but to ensure that assessment determines what children know and recognizes what their cultures value.

Good assessment for all students involves strategies that help students recognize their progress toward clearly defined goals and standards. In order to be culturally responsive, assessment must allow for variations in language, cognitive and communicative styles, and beliefs and values. For example, children who know about clipping grocery store coupons from newspapers might be asked to demonstrate how to group the coupons rather than to recall nursery rhymes that might be unfamiliar to them, given cultural differences. Adapting activities in ways like this allows children to demonstrate what they do know without being penalized for what they do not know about things that are culturally foreign to them.

A portfolio can be a valuable tool for encouraging dialogue with parents and community members about what children are learning and how it can best be assessed. Creating a culturally responsive portfolio requires that the curriculum also must be responsive to cultural differences and values. For example, what constitutes proper behavior for children may be defined differently in some communities than in others. To address these differences, parents and teachers can talk about the need to have certain behaviors in school. Parents also can help teachers understand how to help their children achieve certain goals or help the school modify the goals in light of cultural concerns. For example, suppose the school wants each child to attempt performing a new skill before having mastered it, whereas the cultural community advocates having the child observe the skill, practice it without an audience, and perform it only when he has decided that he is ready. In light of this cultural value, the school might need to think about curriculum and assessment differently. If each child is asked to cut on a line, create a poem, or the like, then classroom procedures should allow him to follow his own pattern of learning. Assessment would still evaluate the child's ability to perform the skill, but it would be initiated by the child. The work that is documented in a portfolio does not have to be the same for every child, nor does it have to be collected on the same schedule for every child.

CHAPTER SUMMARY

- Assessment is much more than testing; it involves ongoing data collection that leads to curriculum and planning decisions.
- Program assessment is achieved by looking at the progress of individual children, the opportunities for learning, and the curriculum. Like assessment of children, program assessment should be ongoing and should contribute to decision making about the program.
- Assessment of children should reflect as much information about them as possible, should serve a clear purpose, should be age appropriate, should be as much like the everyday work that children do as possible, should reflect the teacher's knowledge, and should be ongoing.
- Standardized tests are another tool for gathering assessment information about children. However, such tests should never be used to deny services to or make placement decisions about a child.
- The most common standardized tests given to young children are screening tests and readiness tests. These tests are often used inappropriately; critics of such tests also argue that they are not as valid and reliable as they should be.
- When testing young children, teachers should use tests only for the purposes for which they were intended and only when their use will clearly benefit children; select tests that are appropriate for the curriculum; allow only qualified people to administer tests; ensure that they and the school's administrators are knowledgeable about tests; choose only reliable and valid tests. Careful consideration should be given to the value of the tests in terms of the time consumed in administering them.
- Keeping anecdotal records is one method of collecting information about children. Such records should record exactly what happened and should be collected over time and in a variety of settings.
- Checklists and rating scales are quick ways of collecting limited information on children's skills. They can be used to document children's behavior in play situations, their physical skills, and a variety of other kinds of information.
- Attitude and interest inventories help teachers know more about what children are thinking and feeling. They can be open ended or require more structured responses.
- Time-activity sampling is a technique for periodically recording the location of each child (or selected children) and the activity in which he is engaged. These records provide information about how long children stay with activities and how often they choose the same activity.
- Portfolios of children's work are some of the most important assessment tools. These portfolios can include written work, video- and audiotapes, and photographs.
- Reporting to parents is an important component of the job of the early childhood teacher. The most common reporting methods include report cards, conferences, narrative reports, telephone conversations, casual conversations, newsletters, and videotapes.
- Report cards do not provide very meaningful information about young children. The best choice for effective communication between the teacher and parents is a conference. A written narrative is another effective approach.
- Telephone calls, casual conversations, newsletters, and videotapes can keep parents informed about day-to-day happenings and the general nature of the school program, but they are not appropriate for sharing in-depth information about individual children.
- Children with special needs may require types of assessment that are specified in their IEPs. The focus of assessment should always be on the strengths of the child.
- Some adaptations in assessment may be necessary in culturally diverse classrooms so that children will not be asked to perform tasks that are not relevant to their backgrounds and values. All children should be assessed through means that are fair and that demonstrate the value placed on each individual's culture and language.

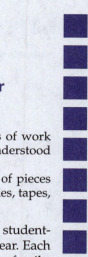

"Miss G., you always ask us hard questions. Now we ask ourselves and each other hard questions, too." —Ryan, age 7

Ryan is right: I do ask hard questions so that all of us in the class community will learn to think, question, and reflect on the learning we do each day. Now my "bottom line" is this question to myself: Why am I doing what I am doing?

Public school often has testing or assessment that is required. It sometimes helps me learn about my children, but more often, the evaluation and assessment decisions made by my students and me is more meaningful. It is productive for us to determine what will best capture our strengths, interests, and goals.

We keep portfolios. They are not collections of papers that sit in a file cabinet. The items placed in our portfolios are documents that represent what we can do and where we want to direct our attention. Last year, my class put together a portfolio checklist of documents that were important for us to consider for inclusion:

- *Reading:* Monthly goals, copies of running records (and a piece of writing that described what the reader did to change and improve the use of strategies), a list of the books the child read independently, and photos or samples of book projects (play, poster, letter to the author, etc.)
- *Writing:* Monthly goals, monthly writing samples with attached self-assessments that described what the samples demonstrated in terms of the writer's growth and change, self-edit checklists, writing samples from prompts, rubrics, and any other materials the student selected
- *Science:* Samples from science and nature logs, photos, written explanations, and samples of experiments/results
- *History/Social Studies:* Log entries, list of things studied/researched, photos, and samples

Assessment Practices for Primary-Aged Children

- *Math:* Math log entries, examples of work done, list of demonstrated concepts understood by the individual, goals, and interests
- *Physical Education/Art/Music:* List of pieces studied, strengths, interests, goals, samples, tapes, and written responses

Portfolios make it easy to organize student-led conferences held at the end of the year. Each child prepares a conference for his or her family. Other people may be included in the conferences (the Reading Recovery teacher, siblings, administrators, teachers from previous years, etc.). The portfolios and conferences represent the strong commitment to student involvement in the record-keeping and assessment procedures. The assessment model also keeps evaluation in sync with day-to-day learning and teaching.

I am busy maintaining records of children's academic, emotional, and social growth and change. My daily teaching plans come from what I observe the children doing as they work. Checklists do not work for me. They are more paperwork to transfer information. I now streamline my information to maintain a reasonable record-keeping system. Keeping folders or a notebook of running records helps me watch patterns and changes in students' reading behaviors over time. I also maintain notes on writing work, and I make conference notes as I work with individuals and groups. For work selected by students, I either concur with their choices or I pull other samples that I feel better represent their learning and work.

To be able to maintain the quality of teaching I want, my evaluation practices must be well thought out and simple. I observe the learners, evaluate their work, make teaching decisions, and reassess the growth. Assessment is ongoing, cyclical, and specific. To maintain that quality forces me to question my practices and get at the real issues.

Appendix A

NAEYC POSITION STATEMENT: TECHNOLOGY AND YOUNG CHILDREN— AGES THREE THROUGH EIGHT

Adopted April 1996

In this position statement, we use the word *technology* to refer primarily to computer technology, but this can be extended to include related technologies, such as telecommunications and multimedia, which are becoming integrated with computer technology.

Technology plays a significant role in all aspects of American life today, and this role will only increase in the future. The potential benefits of technology for young children's learning and development are well documented (Wright & Shade 1994*). As technology becomes easier to use and early childhood software proliferates, young children's use of technology becomes more widespread. Therefore, early childhood educators have a responsibility to critically examine the impact of technology on children and be prepared to use technology to benefit children.

Market researchers tracking software trends have identified the largest software growth recently has been in new titles and companies serving the early childhood educational market. Of the people who own home computers and have young children, 70% have purchased educational software for their children to use (*SPA Consumer Market Report* 1996). While many new titles are good contributions to the field, an even larger number are not (Haugland & Shade 1994).

Early childhood educators must take responsibility to influence events that are transforming the daily lives of children and families. This statement addresses several issues related to technology's use with young children: (1) the essential role of the teacher in evaluating appropriate use of technology; (2) the potential benefits of appropriate use of technology in early childhood programs; (3) the integration of technology into the typical learning environment; (4) equitable access to technology, including children with special needs; (5) stereotyping and violence in software; (6) the role of teachers and parents as advocates; and (7) the implications of technology for professional development.

NAEYC's Position

Although now there is considerable research that points to the positive effects of technology on children's learning and development (Clements 1994), the research indicates that, in practice, computers supplement and do not replace highly valued early childhood activities and materials, such as art, blocks, sand, water, books, exploration with writing materials, and dramatic play. Research indicates that computers can be used in developmentally appropriate ways beneficial to children and also can be misused, just as a tool can (Shade

* The sources cited in this appendix are listed in the References on page 496.

Source: National Association for the Education of Young Children, "NAEYC Position Statement: Technology and Young Children—Ages Three through Eight" (adopted April 1996), *Young Children* 51 (Sept. 1996), 11–16. Published by the National Association for the Education of Young Children. Copyright © 1996 by NAEYC. Reprinted with permission.

& Watson 1990). Developmentally appropriate software offers opportunities for collaborative play, learning, and creation. Educators must use professional judgment in evaluating and using this learning tool appropriately, applying the same criteria they would to any other learning tool or experience. They must also weigh the costs of technology with the costs of other learning materials and program resources to arrive at an appropriate balance for their classrooms.

1. In evaluating the appropriate use of technology, NAEYC applies principles of developmentally appropriate practice (Bredekamp 1987) and appropriate curriculum and assessment (NAEYC & NAECS/SDE 1992). In short, NAEYC believes that in any given situation, a professional judgment by the teacher is required to determine if a specific use of technology is age appropriate, individually appropriate, and culturally appropriate.

The teacher's role is critical in making certain that good decisions are made about technology to use and in supporting children in their use of technology to ensure that potential benefits are achieved. Teachers must take time to evaluate and choose software in light of principles of development and learning and must carefully observe children using the software to identify both opportunities and problems and make appropriate adaptations. Choosing appropriate software is similar to choosing appropriate books for the classroom—teachers constantly make judgments about what is age appropriate, individually appropriate, and culturally appropriate. Teachers should look for ways to use computers to support the development and learning that occur in other parts of the classroom and the development and learning that happen with computers in complement with activities off the computer. Good teaching practices must always be the guiding goal when selecting and using new technologies.

2. Used appropriately, technology can enhance children's cognitive and social abilities.

Computers are intrinsically compelling for young children. The sounds and graphics gain children's attention. Increasingly, young children observe adults and older children working on computers, and they want to do it, too. Children get interested because they can make things happen with computers. Developmentally appropriate software engages children in creative play, mastery learning, problem solving, and conversation. The children control the pacing and the action. They can repeat a process or activity as often as they like and experiment with variations. They can collaborate in making decisions and share their discoveries and creations (Haugland & Shade 1990).

Well-designed early childhood software grows in dimension with the child, enabling her to find new challenges as she becomes more proficient. Appropriate visual and verbal prompts designed in the software expand play themes and opportunities while leaving the child in control. Vast collections of images, sounds, and information of all kinds are placed at the child's disposal. Software can be made age appropriate even for children as young as three or four.

When used appropriately, technology can support and extend traditional materials in valuable ways. Research points to the positive effects of technology in children's learning and development, both cognitive and social (Clements 1994; Haugland & Shade 1994). In addition to actually developing children's abilities, technology provides opportunity for assessment. Observing the child at the computer offers teachers a "window" onto a child's thinking. Just as parents continue to read to children who can read themselves, parents and teachers should both participate with children in computer activities and encourage children to use computers on their own and with peers.

Research demonstrates that when working with a computer children prefer working with one or two partners over working alone (Lipinski et al. 1986; Rhee & Chavnagri 1991; Clements, Nastasi, & Swaminathan 1993). They seek help from one another and seem to prefer help from peers over help from the teacher (King & Alloway 1992; Nastasi & Clements 1993). Children engage in high levels of spoken communication and cooperation at the computer. They initiate interactions more frequently and in different ways than when engaged with traditional activities, such as puzzles or blocks. They engage in more turn taking at the computer and simultaneously show high levels of language and cooperative-play activity.

Technology extends benefits of collaboration beyond the immediate classroom environment for children in the primary grades who can already read and write. With the potential of access to the Internet or other on-line "user friendly" networks, young children can collaborate with children in other classrooms, cities, counties, states, and even countries. Through electronic field trips in real time or via diskette, children are able to share different cultural and environmental experiences. Electronic mail and telecommunications opportunities through the Internet facilitate direct communication and promote social interactions previously limited by the physical location of participating learners.

3. Appropriate technology is integrated into the regular learning environment and used as one of many options to support children's learning.

Every classroom has its own guiding philosophies, values, schedules, themes, and activities. As part of the teacher's overall classroom plan, computers should be used in ways that support these existing classroom educational directions rather than distort or replace them. Computers should be integrated into early childhood practice physically, functionally, and philosophically. Teachers can accommodate integration in at least five ways:

• Locate computers in the classroom, rather than in a separate computer lab (Davis & Shade 1994).
• Integrate technology into the daily routine of classroom activity. For example, a teacher might introduce musical rhythm with actions, recordings, and a computer used as an electronic rhythm-matching game. The children then would work in small groups with the computer program serving as one of several learning centers.
• Choose software to enrich curriculum content, other classroom activities, or concepts. For example, the program in the computer learning center might allow children to invent their own rhythms that they could simultaneously hear played back and see displayed graphically. They could edit these rhythms on the computer, hearing and seeing the changes.
• Use technology to integrate curriculum across subject-matter areas. For example, one group of children used the computer to make signs for a restaurant in their dramatic-play area (Apple

Computer Inc. 1993). The rhythm program helps children connect mathematical patterns to musical patterns.
• Extend the curriculum, with technology offering new avenues and perspectives. For example, exploring shapes on the computer provides opportunities to stretch, shrink, bend, and combine shapes into new forms. Such activities enrich and extend children's activities with physical manipulatives.

4. Early childhood educators should promote equitable access to technology for all children and their families. Children with special needs should have increased access when this is helpful.

Educators using technology need to be especially sensitive to issues of equity.

A decade of research on the educational use of computers in schools reveals that computers maintain and exaggerate inequalities (Sutton 1991). Sutton found gender, race, and social-class inequalities in the educational uses of computers, which Thouvenelle, Borunda, and McDowell summarize below.

• Girls used computers in and out of school less often than did boys.
• African American students had less access to computers than did White students.
• Presence of computers in a school did not ensure access.
• Teachers, while concerned about equity, held attitudes that hindered access—they believed that better behaved students deserved more computer time and that the primary benefit for low-achieving students was mastery of basic skills (i.e., drill-and-practice software).
• Richer schools bought more equipment and more expensive equipment. (1994, 153–154)

These findings identify trends that, unchecked, will almost certainly lead to increased inequity in the future. Early childhood educators must find ways to incorporate technology into their classrooms that preserve equity to access and minimize or even reverse the current trends. For example, anecdotal reports indicate that preschool-age boys and girls show equal interest in computers, but as they grow older girls begin to spend less time with computers than do boys. There are a number of ways educators can proactively work to maintain girls' interest in computers and technology: (1) consider girls' interests and interaction styles when selecting and evaluating software for classroom use; (2) model the use of the computer as a learning and productivity tool and invite children, especially girls, to observe and assist them in the work; and (3) promote equity by offering special times for "girls only" use of computers, which permits girls to explore the computer without having to directly compete with boys (Thouvenelle, Borunda, & McDowell 1994).

Considerations of equity in curriculum content require qualitative judgments. For example, research evidence indicates that children who are economically disadvantaged have less access to computers at home and at-home access is related to attitudes and competence (Martinez & Mead 1988). If schools wish to provide equity to children of low-income families, with respect to their confidence and competence concerning computer learning, these children need to be provided more in-school computer access (Sutton 1991). And that access must be meaningful, moving beyond rote drill-and-practice usage.

Preschool-age children spend time in a variety of diverse settings (e.g., homes, child care centers, family child care), which further complicates the issues of equity and access. Some of these settings have considerable access to technology while others lack the very basics. The more early childhood educators believe in the benefits of appropriate use of technology at the preschool age, the more responsibility we bear in ensuring equity and access to this important learning tool.

Efforts should be made to ensure access to appropriate technology for children with special needs, for whom assistive technologies may be essential for successful inclusion.

For children with special needs, technology has many potential benefits. Technology can be a powerful compensatory tool—it can augment sensory input or reduce distractions; it can provide support for cognitive processing or enhance memory and recall; it can serve as a personal "on-demand" tutor and as an enabling device that supports independent functioning.

The variety of assistive-technology products ranges form low-tech toys with simple switches to expansive high-tech systems capable of managing complex environments. These technologies empower young children, increasing their independence and supporting their inclusion in classes with their peers. With adapted materials, young children with disabilities no longer have to be excluded from activities. Using appropriately designed and supported computer applications, the ability to learn, move, communicate, and recreate are within the reach of all learners.

Yet, with all these enhanced capabilities, this technology requires thoughtful integration into the early childhood curriculum, or it may fall far short of its promise. Educators must match the technology to each child's unique special needs, learning styles, and individual preferences.

5. The power of technology to influence children's learning and development requires that attention be paid to eliminating stereotyping of any group and eliminating exposure to violence, especially as a problem-solving strategy.

Technology can be used to affirm children's diversity.

Early childhood educators must devote extra effort to ensure that the software in classrooms reflects and affirms children's diverse cultures, languages, and ethnic heritages. Like all educational materials, software should reflect the world children live in: It should come in multiple languages, reflect gender equity, contain people of color and of differing ages and abilities, and portray diverse families and experiences (Derman-Sparks & A.B.C. Task Force 1989; Haugland & Shade 1994).

Teachers should actively select software that promotes positive social values.

Just like movies and television today, children's software is often violent and much of it explicit and brutally graphic, as in most of the best-selling titles for the popular game machines. But, often, violence is presented in ways that are less obvious. In all its forms, violence in software threatens young children's development and challenges early childhood educators, who must take active steps to keep it out of their classrooms (see the *NAEYC Position Statement on Violence in the Lives of Children* 1994).

Some software programs offer children the opportunity to get rid of mistakes by "blowing up" their creations—complete with sound effects—instead of simply erasing or starting over. As a metaphor for solving problems or getting rid of mistakes, "blowing up" is problematic. In the context of a computer software experience, it is more troubling than in the context of television or video. Children control the computer software, and, instead of being passive viewers of what appears on the screen, with the computer they become active decisionmakers about what takes place on the screen. Software programs that empower children to freely blow up or destroy without thought of the actual consequences of their actions can further the disconnection between personal responsibility and violent outcomes.

Identifying and eliminating software containing violence is only one of the challenges facing early childhood educators. A related, opposite challenge is discovering software programs that promote positive social actions. For example, software has the potential to offer children opportunities to develop sensitivities to children from other cultures or to children with disabilities. Much could be done to help children develop positive responses to cultural and racial diversity by offering software programs that enable children to explore the richness within their own and different cultures.

6. Teachers, in collaboration with parents, should advocate for more appropriate technology applications for all children.

The appropriate and beneficial use of technology with young children is ultimately the responsibility of the early childhood educator, working in collaboration with parents. Parents and teachers together need to make better choices as consumers. As they become better educated on the appropriate uses of technology, parents and teachers are more likely to make informed decisions and to make it known to developers of technology when they are unhappy with products. Working together, parents and teachers are a large consumer group wielding greater influence on the development of technology for young children. Following are specific recommendations for early childhood professionals as they advocate for more appropriate technology applications for all children.

- Provide information to parents on the benefits and use of appropriate software.
- Advocate for computer hardware that can be upgraded easily as new technology becomes available.
- Encourage software publishers to make previewing of software easier for parents and educators.
- Advocate for a system of software review by educators.
- Promote the development of software and technology applications that routinely incorporate features that cater to the needs of learners with different abilities.
- Advocate for software that promotes positive representation of gender, cultural and linguistic diversity, and abilities. Software publishers should create a balance of programs that appeal to both boys and girls.
- Encourage software publishers to create programs that support collaboration among learners rather than competition. Fostering cooperative learning enhances the acceptance of the abilities of all learners.
- Encourage software publishers to develop programs that reflect appropriate, nonviolent ways to solve problems and correct mistakes.
- Develop formal and informal information sharing and support for teachers, parents, and appropriate organizations and community-based programs. Encourage free community access to technology through libraries, schools, and so forth.
- Support policies on federal, state, and local levels that encourage funding that supports equity in access to technology for young children and their families.

7. The appropriate use of technology has many implications for early childhood professional development.

As early childhood educators become active participants in a technological world, they need in-depth training and ongoing support to be adequately prepared to make decisions about technology and to support its effective use in learning environments for children.

To achieve the potential benefits of technology, both preservice and inservice training must provide early childhood educators with opportunities for basic information and awareness. These efforts must address the rapid proliferation and fast-paced change within the technology arena. Opportunities that emphasize evaluating the software in relation to children's development are essential.

Institutions of higher education and other organizations and groups that provide preservice and inservice education have a responsibility to

• incorporate experiences that permit educators to reflect on the principles of early childhood education and how technology can support and extend these principles;
• give teachers concentrated time to focus on how best to use educational technology and to develop a plan for the use of educational technology in a school or early childhood program;
• provide hands-on training with appropriate software programs to assist teachers in becoming familiar and comfortable with the operations and features of hardware and software; and
• provide on-site and school-based training on effectively integrating technology into the curriculum and assessment process.

At the classroom level, teachers need staff-development experiences (Kearsley & Lynch 1992) that permit them to

• use teaching techniques that fully use the technology;
• encourage parental involvement with technology;

• match technology applications to the learning needs of individual children;
• look for cross-curriculum/cross-cultural applications;
• facilitate cooperative interactions among children; and
• use technology to improve personal efficiency.

The potentials of technology are far-reaching and ever changing. The risk is for adults to become complacent, assuming that their current knowledge or experience is adequate. "Technology is an area of the curriculum, as well as a tool for learning, in which teachers must demonstrate their own capacity for learning" (Bredekamp & Rosegrant 1994, 61). As teachers try out their new knowledge in the classroom, there should be opportunities to share experiences and insights, problems and challenges with other educators. When teachers become comfortable and confident with the new technology, they can be offered additional challenges and stimulated to reach new levels of competence in using technology.

Early childhood educators should use technology as a tool for communication and collaboration among professionals as well as a tool for teaching children.

Technology can be a powerful tool for professional development. Software can provide accessible information and tools for classroom management, planning, and creation of materials. Telecommunications and the Internet can enable teachers to obtain information and new ideas from around the world and to interact with distant experts and peers. Early childhood educators can incorporate principles of cooperative learning as they assist distant peers in acquiring new skills; share curriculum ideas, resources, and promising practices; exchange advice; and collaborate on classroom and professional development projects. Providing training and support for access to services available via on-line networks and the Internet has the potential of opening the doors to worlds of additional classroom resources. With a responsive on-line system, mentors can assist novices in becoming more technology literate and more involved in actively using technology for professional benefits. As educators become more competent users of technology for personal and professional growth, they can model appropriate use for young children.

References

Apple Computer Inc. 1993. *The adventure begins: Preschool and technology.* Videocassette. (Available from NAEYC.)

Bredekamp, S., ed. 1987. *Developmentally appropriate practice in early childhood programs serving children from birth through age 8.* Exp. ed. Washington, DC: NAEYC.

Bredekamp, S., & T. Rosegrant. 1994. Learning and teaching with technology. In *Young children: Active learners in a technological age,* eds. J.L. Wright & D.D. Shade 53–61. Washington, DC: NAEYC.

Clements, D.H. 1994. The uniqueness of the computer as a learning tool: Insights from research and practice. In *Young children: Active learners in a technological age,* eds. J.L. Wright & D.D. Shade, 31–50. Washington, DC: NAEYC.

Clements, D.H., B.K. Nastasi, & S. Swaminathan. 1993. Young children and computers: Crossroads and directions from research. *Young Children* 48 (2): 56–64.

Davis, B.C., & D.D. Shade. 1994. Integrate, don't isolate!—Computers in the early childhood curriculum. *ERIC Digest* (December). No. EDO-PS-94-17.

Derman-Sparks, L., & the A.B.C. Task Force. 1989. *Antibias curriculum: Tools for empowering young children.* Washington, DC: NAEYC.

Haugland, S.W., & D.D. Shade. 1990. *Developmental evaluations of software for young children: 1990 edition.* New York: Delmar.

Haugland, S.W., & D.D. Shade. 1994. Software evaluation for young children. In *Young children: Active learners in a technological age,* eds. J.L. Wright & D.D. Shade, 63–76. Washington, DC: NAEYC.

Kearsley, G., & W. Lynch. 1992. Educational leadership in the age of technology: The new skills. *Journal of Research on Computing in Education* 25 (1): 50–60.

King, J.A., & N. Alloway. 1992. Preschooler's use of microcomputers and input devices. *Journal of Educational Computing Research* 8: 451–68.

Lipinski, J.A., R.E. Nida, D.D. Shade, & J.A. Watson. 1986. The effect of microcomputers on young children: An examination of free-play choices, sex differences, and social interactions. *Journal of Educational Computing Research* 2 (2): 147–68.

Martinez, M.E., & N.A. Mead. 1988. *Computer competence: The first national assessment.* Tech report no. 17-CC-01. Princeton, N.J: National Educational Progress and Educational Testing Service.

NAEYC position statement on violence in the lives of children. 1994. Washington, DC: NAEYC.

NAEYC, & NAECS/SDE (National Association of Early Childhood Specialists in State Departments of Education). 1992. Guidelines for appropriate curriculum content and assessment in programs serving children ages 3 through 8. In *Reaching potentials: Appropriate curriculum and assessment for young children, volume 1,* eds. S. Bredekamp & T. Rosegrant, 9–27. Washington, DC: NAEYC.

Nastasi, B.K., & D.H. Clements. 1993. Motivational and social outcomes of cooperative education environments. *Journal of Computing in Childhood Education* 4 (1): 15–43.

Rhee, M.C., & N. Chavnagri. 1991. *4 year old children's peer interactions when playing with a computer.* ERIC, ED 342466.

Shade, D.D., & J.A. Watson. 1990. Computers in early education: Issues put to rest, theoretical links to sound practice, and the potential contribution of microworlds. *Journal of Educational Computing Research* 6 (4): 375–92.

SPA consumer market report. 1996. Washington, DC: Software Publishers Association (SPA).

Sutton, R.E. 1991. Equity and computers in the schools: A decade of research. *Review of Educational Research* 61 (4): 475–503.

Thouvenelle, S., M. Borunda, & C. McDowell. 1994. Replicating inequities: Are we doing it again? In *Young children: Active learners in a technological age,* eds. J.L. Wright & D.D. Shade, 151–66. Washington, DC: NAEYC.

Wright, J.L., & D.D. Shade, eds. 1994. *Young children: Active learners in a technological age.* Washington, DC: NAEYC.

Appendix B

COMPUTER SOFTWARE AND YOUNG CHILDREN

This list brings together resources that suggest appropriate uses of computers with young children, and sources that provide software reviews for children from preschool age through age 8. Information on specific programs or companies is provided for information only; no endorsement of any specific product should be inferred.

Online and CD-ROM Resources

Parents, Educators, and Publishers (PEP).
http://www.microweb.com/pepsite/index.html

This Web site includes a directory of educational software publishers, hints on shopping for computer hardware and software for children, and excerpts from the *Children's Software Revue* newsletter.

How to Buy Educational Software.
http://www.adventure.com/WWW/ka_info/educational_software/index.html

This Web site presents tips, primarily from *Children's Software Revue* editor Warren Buckleitner, on purchasing software for children.

Parent's Guide to Children's Software 96.
1995 From the Editors of *Newsweek* Magazine. CD-ROM and paperback book. Available for Macintosh and Windows from Newsweek, 655 Montgomery Street, Suite 1010, San Francisco, CA 94111. For complete ordering information, call 800-634-3002.

This commercially available CD-ROM includes "multimedia reviews" which allow users to experience the sound, video, animation, and interactivity of 50 products receiving the "Editors' Choice" award from the editors at *Newsweek Magazine*. Includes educational and entertainment software for children ages 2–12.

Books and ERIC Documents

Hohman, Charles, Barbara Carmody and Chica McCabe-Branz. (1995). **High/Scope Buyer's Guide to Children's Software.** *11th Edition Ypsilanti, MI: High/Scope Educational Research Foundation. Not available from EDRS. Available from High/Scope Press, 600 North River Street, Ypsilanti, MI 48198-2898; 313-485-2000; ($19.95). 300p. PSO23914.*

This guide to software for children from 3 to 7 years of age is designed to help teachers and parents evaluate and choose computer software for home or classroom use. The guide includes software descriptions, ratings of educational software programs, listings of award-winning programs, a glossary, and a national directory of software producers.

Association of Library Service to Children. (1995). **Notable Films/Videos, Recordings, & Computer Software.** *(Reprinted from School Library Journal, April, 1995). Single copies available free from the American Library Association, Headquarters Library and*

Source: ERIC Clearinghouse on Elementary and Early Childhood Education, "Computer Software and Young Children," *Resource List* (Urbana: University of Illinois, December 1995).

Information Center, 50 E. Huron Street, Chicago, IL 60611; 312-280-2153). 7p.

This annual annotated listing of computer software and CD-ROMs is compiled each year from the previous year 's releases (the 1995 edition covers 1993-94 releases). For each product, an annotation and a complete list of distributors are included.

Wright, June L., and David D. Shade, Eds. (1995). **Young Children: Active Learners in a Technological Age.** *Washington, DC: National Association for the Education of Young Children. Available from NAEYC, 1509 16th Street, N.W., Washington, DC 20036-1426; 800-424-2460 (NAEYC Cat. No. 341). PS023167.*

Intended to address the issues of appropriateness of computer use with young children and how children and early childhood educators interact with the computer in early childhood settings, this book is divided into three parts. Part 1 discusses "Young Children as Active Learners"; Part 2, "The Role of Technology in the Early Childhood Curriculum," includes a section on "Family Choice at Home and School"; Part 3 describes "The Challenge for Early Childhood Educators" posed by computers and software use. A list of appropriate software for young children is included.

Newsletters

Children's Software Revue. *Bimonthly. $24/year; available from Children's Software Revue, 520 N. Adams St., Ypsilanti, MI 48197; 800-993-9499.*

This independent newsletter (with no advertising) uses a carefully evolved software review instrument to evaluate 100–130 educational software titles in each issue. Experts', parents', and children's opinions are considered. Free sample issues are available.

Children's Software: A Quarterly Newsletter for Parents. *$15/year. Available*

from: Children's Software Press. 720 Kuhlman, Houston TX 77024.

This newsletter is a joint project of Children's Software Press and the Department of Computing in Education at Teacher's College, Columbia University.

Journal Articles

Haugland, Sue. (1994). **Computers and Young Children: Selecting Software That Facilitates Developmental Gains.** *Day Care & Early Education, 21 (4, Summer): 45-46. EJ485390.*

Noting that much of the new instructional software has been disappointing in terms of appropriateness for young children, the authors review several programs notable for their developmental appropriateness in the area of creative arts, language arts, thematic approaches, and computer accessibility.

Wiburg, Karin, and Bruce Carter. (1994). **Thinking with Computers, Part II.** *Computing Teacher, 22(2, October). 6–9. EJ491484.*

Wiburg examines research on computers as cognitive enhancers, focusing on applications software that includes spreadsheets, graphing, and databases. Appropriate computer-based problem-solving environments for young children are reviewed.

Bennett, Hugh. (1994). **To Instruct and Delight: Children's and Young Adult's Literature on CD-ROM.** *CD-ROM Professional, 7(4, July-August), 84–86, 88–90, 92–94. EJ486811.*

This article reviews the work of seven companies that produce multimedia children's storybooks on CD-ROM. Characteristics of each company's approach to children's literature are given, and the use of nonprint media to develop the story is discussed. Platform compatibility for 59 CD-ROM titles and publisher information are provided.

Allen, Denise. (1994). **A Spring Software Sampler. Teaching with Technology.** Teaching Pre K-8, 24(8, June): 20–22. EJ482124.

Reviews five computer software programs for students 3 to 14 year old: (1) The Graph Club (Tom Snyder Productions); (2) Kid Cad (Davidson Associates); (3) Kid Keys (Davidson Associates); (4) Math Ace (Magic Quest); and (5) Busytown (Computer Curriculum Corporation). Prices, supplier addresses, and hardware requirements are provided.

Haugland, Sue. (1993). **Computers and Young Children: The Outstanding Developmental Software.** Day Care & Early Education, 21(2, Winter): 32–33. EJ482071.

Developmental Software Awards were presented to computer programs in several categories: (1) *art,* Kidpix (Broderbund Software); (2) *creative problem solving,* FaceMaker, Golden edition (Queue); (3) *language,* My Words (Hartley Courseware) and Paint with Words (MECC); (4) *math and science,* EZ Logo, revised edition (MECC) and Learn about Plants (Create and Worlds); and (5) *thematic focus,* The Farm (Mobius).

Buckleitner, Warren. (1993). **Kids and Computers Update.** Child Care Information Exchange, 93(Sep–Oct): 75–78. EJ471310.

This article answers nine common questions that daycare providers and parents ask about computers and young children, such as: (1) What can children learn with computers? (2) What are the advantages and disadvantages of having computers? (3) What types of affordably priced computers are best? and (4) What are the best software programs for young children?

Clements, Douglas H., Bonnie K. Nastasi, and Sudha Swaminathan. (1993). **Young Children and Computers: Crossroads and Directions from Research. Research in Review.** Young Children, 48(2, Jan): 56–64. EJ458126

Research suggests wide-ranging benefits of open-ended computer programs such as LOGO. This article considers the ways in which these programs develop young children's subject-matter knowledge and problem-solving and socioemotional competencies.

References with an ED (ERIC Document), EJ (ERIC Journal), or PS number are cited in the ERIC database. ERIC documents (EDs and PSs) are available in microfiche collections at more than 900 locations worldwide or can be ordered through EDRS: 1-800-443-ERIC, unless an alternate availability is cited. References with an EJ (ERIC Journal) number are available from the originating journal, interlibrary loan services, or article reproduction clearinghouses, such as UMI: 1-800-732-0616; or ISI: 1-800-523-1850.

Appendix C

PLAYGROUND RATING SYSTEM

Rate each item for existence and function on a scale from 0 – 5.

- 0 = not existent
- 1 = some elements exist but not functional
- 2 = poor
- 3 = average
- 4 = good
- 5 = all elements exist, excellent function

Divide final total score (out of a possible 300) by 3 to obtain final rating (out of a possible 100).

Score	Section I. What does the playground contain?
_____	1. A hard-surfaced area with space for games and a network of paths for wheeled toys.
_____	2. Sand and sand play equipment.
_____	3. Water play areas, with fountains, pools and sprinklers, and water play equipment.
_____	4. Dramatic play structures (playhouse, old car or boat with complimentary equipment, such as adjacent sand and water, and housekeeping equipment).
_____	5. A superstructure with room for many children at a time and with a variety of challenges and exercise options (entries, exits and levels).
_____	6. Mound(s) of earth for climbing and digging.
_____	7. Trees and natural areas for shade, nature study and play.
_____	8. Zoning to provide continuous challenge; linkage of areas, functional physical boundaries, vertical and horizontal treatment (hills and valleys).
_____	9. Construction area with junk materials such as tires, crates, planks, boards, bricks and nails; tools should be provided and demolition and construction allowed.
_____	10. A purchased or built vehicle, airplane, boat, car that has been made safe, but not stripped of its play value (should be changed or relocated after a period of time to renew interest).
_____	11. Equipment for active play: a variety of overhead apparatus, climbers, slides, balancing devices, swings, etc.
_____	12. A large soft area (grass, bark mulch, etc.) for organized games. A large concrete or asphalt area for organized games.
_____	13. Small semi-private spaces at the child's own scale: tunnels, niches, playhouses, hiding places.
_____	14. Fences, gates, walls and windows that provide security for young children and are adaptable for learning/play.

Source: J. L. Frost, *Play and Playscapes* (Albany, NY: Delmar, 1992), pp. 107–109. Reprinted by permission of Joe L. Frost, Parker Centennial Professor, University of Texas. © 1996 Joe L. Frost (revised).

Score	Section I. What does the playground contain?
_____	15. A garden and flowers located so they are protected from play, but with easy access for children to tend them. Gardening tools are available.
_____	16. Provisions for the housing of pets. Pets and supplies available.
_____	17. A transitional space for outdoors to indoors. This could be a covered play area immediately adjoining the playroom, which will protect the children from the sun and rain and extend indoor activities to the outside.
_____	18. Adequate protected storage for outdoor play equipment, tools for construction and garden areas, and maintenance tools. Storage can be separate: wheeled toys stored near the wheeled vehicle track; sand equipment near the sand enclosure; tools near the construction area. Storage can be in separate structures next to the building or fence. Storage should aid in children's picking up and putting away equipment at the end of each play period.
_____	19. Easy access from outdoor play areas to coats, toilets and drinking fountains. Shaded areas, benches, tables and support materials for group activities (art, reading, etc.).
_____	20. Accessibility, materials and equipment for children of all abilities/disabilities.
_____	**Subtotal Out of 100 points**

Score	Section II. Is the playground in good repair and relatively safe?*
_____	1. A protective fence (with lockable gates) next to hazardous areas (streets, deep ditches, water, etc.).
_____	2. Eight to ten inches of non-compacted sand, wood mulch or equivalent manufactured surfacing under all climbing and moving equipment, extending through fall zones and secured by retaining wall as needed.
_____	3. Size of equipment appropriate to age group served. Climbing heights limited to six to seven feet, or just above standing/reaching height of children.
_____	4. Area free of litter (e.g., broken glass, rocks), electrical hazards, high voltage power lines, toxic hazards.
_____	5. Moving parts free of defects (e.g., no pinch and crush points, bearings not excessively worn).
_____	6. Equipment free of sharp edges and broken, loose and missing parts.
_____	7. Swing seats constructed of soft or lightweight material (e.g., rubber, canvas).
_____	8. All safety equipment in good repair (e.g., guard rails, padded areas, protective covers).
_____	9. No openings that can entrap a child's head (approximately $3^{1}/_{2}$" x 9"). (See CPSC/ASTM for measurements and tests.)
_____	10. Equipment structurally sound. No bending, warping, breaking, sinking, etc. Heavy fixed and moving equipment secured in ground and concrete footings recessed under ground at least four inches.
_____	11. Adequate space between equipment—typically six to twelve feet, depending upon type of equipment (see CPSC/ASTM).

*This is an overview of relevant safety items. For details, refer to the United States Consumer Product Safety Commission's *Public Playground Handbook for Safety* and the American Society for Testing Materials' *Standard Consumer Safety Performance Specification for Playground Equipment for Public Use.*

Score	Section II. Is the playground in good repair and relatively safe?*
_____	12. No signs of underground rotting, rusting or termites in support members (probe under ground).
_____	13. No metal slides or decks exposed to sun. Use plastic components or place in permanent shade.
_____	14. Guardrail and protective barriers in place that meet CPSC/ASTM height and other requirements.
_____	15. No loose ropes, suspended ropes or cables in movement area.
_____	16. All balance beams, cables and chains at low heights—prescribed by CPSC/ASTM.
_____	17. Signs at entry alerting to appropriate ages of users, need for adult supervision and any hazards.
_____	18. No protrusion or entanglement hazards.
_____	19. No tripping hazards—exposed concrete footings, rocks or roots.
_____	20. No water hazards—access to pools, creeks. No traffic hazards—streets, parking lots, delivery areas.
_____	**Subtotal Out of 100 points**

Score	Section III. What should the playground do?
_____	1. Encourages play: • Inviting, easy access • Open, flowing and relaxed space • Clear movement from indoors to outdoors • Appropriate equipment for the age group (s)
_____	2. Stimulates the child's senses: • Changes and contrasts in scale, light, texture and color • Flexible equipment • Diverse experiences
_____	3. Nurtures child's curiosity: • Equipment that the child can change • Materials for experiments and construction • Plants and animals
_____	4. Supports the child's basic social and physical needs: • Comfortable to the child • Scaled to the child • Physically challenging
_____	5. Allows interaction between the child and the resources: • Systematic storage that defines routines • Semi-enclosed spaces to read, work a puzzle or be alone

*This is an overview of relevant safety items. For details, refer to the United States Consumer Product Safety Commission's *Public Playground Handbook for Safety* and the American Society for Testing Materials' *Standard Consumer Safety Performance Specification for Playground Equipment for Public Use.*

Score	Section III. What should the playground do?

<table>
<tr><td>_____</td><td>6. Allows interaction between the child and other children:
• Variety of spaces
• Adequate space to avoid conflicts
• Equipment that invites socialization</td></tr>
<tr><td>_____</td><td>7. Allows interaction between the child and adults:
• Organization of spaces to allow general supervision
• Rest areas for adults and children</td></tr>
<tr><td>_____</td><td>8. Adults and play environment support functional, exercise, gross motor, active play.</td></tr>
<tr><td>_____</td><td>9. Adults and play environment support constructive, building, creating play.</td></tr>
<tr><td>_____</td><td>10. Adults and play environment support dramatic, pretend, make-believe play.</td></tr>
<tr><td>_____</td><td>11. Adults and play environment support organized games and games with rules.</td></tr>
<tr><td>_____</td><td>12. Adults and environment support special play forms (e.g., chase games, rough and tumble, sand and water play).</td></tr>
<tr><td>_____</td><td>13. Promotes solitary, private, meditative play.</td></tr>
<tr><td>_____</td><td>14. Promotes group, cooperative, sharing play.</td></tr>
<tr><td>_____</td><td>15. Involves children in care and maintenance of playground.</td></tr>
<tr><td>_____</td><td>16. Involves adults in children's play—regular adult/child planning and evaluation.</td></tr>
<tr><td>_____</td><td>17. Integrates indoor/outdoor play and work/play activities—art, music, science, etc.</td></tr>
<tr><td>_____</td><td>18. Promotes interaction between children and nature—plants, animals, etc.</td></tr>
<tr><td>_____</td><td>19. Adults are trained in play value, playground maintenance and safety, emergency procedures.</td></tr>
<tr><td>_____</td><td>20. The play environment is constantly changing—growing in challenge and complexity.</td></tr>
</table>

_____ **Subtotal Out of 100 points**

_____ **Grand Total Out of 300 points**

Appendix D

SOURCES OF TECHNICAL ASSISTANCE FOR ADA AUXILIARY AIDS AND SERVICES

Region I
New England Disability and
Business Technical Assistance
Center
145 Newbury St.
Portland, ME 04101
207-874-6535 (Voice/TDD)
*Connecticut, Maine,
Massachusetts, New Hampshire,
Rhode Island, Vermont*

Region II
Northeast Disability and
Business Technical Assistance
Center
354 South Broad St.
Trenton, NJ 08608
609-392-4004 (Voice)
609-392-7044 (TDD)
*New Jersey, New York, Puerto
Rico, Virgin Islands*

Region III
Mid-Atlantic Disability and
Business Technical Assistance
Center
2111 Wilson Blvd., Ste. 400
Arlington, VA 22201
703-525-3268 (Voice/TDD)
*Delaware, District of Columbia,
Maryland, Pennsylvania,
Virginia, West Virginia*

Region IV
Southeast Disability and
Business Technical Assistance
Center
1776 Peachtree St.

Ste. 310 North
Atlanta, GA 30309
404-888-0022 (Voice)
404-888-9007 (TDD)
*Alabama, Florida, Georgia,
Kentucky, Mississippi, North
Carolina, South Carolina,
Tennessee*

Region V
Great Lakes Disability and
Business Technical Assistance
Center
1640 West Roosevelt Rd.
(M/C 627)
Chicago, IL 60608
312-413-7756 (Voice/TDD)
*Illinois, Indiana, Michigan,
Minnesota, Ohio, Wisconsin*

Region VI
Southwest Disability and
Business Technical Assistance
Center
2323 South Shepherd Blvd.,
Ste. 1000
Houston, TX 77019
713-520-0232 (Voice)
713-520-5136 (TDD)
*Arkansas, Louisiana, New
Mexico, Oklahoma, Texas*

Region VII
Great Plains Disability and
Business Technical Assistance
Center
4816 Santana Dr.
Columbia, MO 65203

314-882-3600 (Voice/TDD)
*Iowa, Kansas, Nebraska,
Missouri*

Region VIII
Rocky Mountain Disability and
Business Technical Assistance
Center
3630 Sinton Rd., Ste. 103
Colorado Springs, CO
80907-5072
719-444-0252 (Voice/TDD)
*Colorado, Montana, North
Dakota, South Dakota, Utah,
Wyoming*

Region IX
Pacific Coast Disability and
Business Technical Assistance
Center
440 Grand Ave., Ste. 500
Oakland, CA 94610
510-465-7884 (Voice)
800-949-4232 (TDD)
*Arizona, California, Hawaii,
Nevada*

Region X
Northwest Disability and
Business Technical Assistance
Center
P.O. Box 9046
Olympia, WA 98507-9046
206-438-3168 (Voice)
206-438-3167 (TDD)
*Alaska, Idaho, Oregon,
Washington*

Source: H. P. Parette, N. S. Dunn, and D. R. Hoge, "Low-Cost Communication Devices for Children with Disabilities and Their Family Members," *Young Children* 50 (Sept. 1995), 75–81 (p. 77). Published by the National Association for the Education of Young Children. Copyright © 1995 by NAEYC. Reprinted with permission.

Appendix E

A SAMPLER OF RECORDED MUSIC

Lullabies— traditional and original, American and multicultural
Baby's Morning Time (Judy Collins)
Daddies Sing Goodnight
Earthmother Lullabies l, Earthmother Lullabies ll (Pamela Ballingham)
Lullabies for Little Dreamers (Kevin Roth)
Lullabies of Broadway (Mimi Besette)
Lullaby—A Collection
Lullaby Berceuse (Connie Kaldor & Carmen Champagne)
Lullaby Land (Linda Arnold)
Nitey-Nite (Patti Ballas & Laura Baron)
Sleep, Baby, Sleep (Nicolette Larson)
Star Dreamer (Priscilla Herdman)
'Til Their Eyes Shine

Nursery tunes— songs for the very young
The Baby Record (Bob McGrath & Katherine Smithrim)
Baby Songs, More Baby Songs (Hap Palmer)
Baby Tickle Tunes (Tickle Tune Typhoon)
Lullabies and Laughter (Pat Carfra)
Mainly Mother Goose (Sharon, Lois, and Bram)
Shake It to the One You Love the Best: Playsongs and Lullabies from Black Musical Traditions (Cheryl Warren Mattox)
Singable Songs for the Very Young, More Singable Songs for the Very Young (Raffi)

American folk songs— children's chants, play songs, and singing games
Activity and Game Songs (Tom Glazer)
American Children
American Folk Songs for Children (Pete Seeger)
The Best of Burl's for Boys and Girls (Burl Ives)
Circle Time (Lisa Monet)

Come On In, Fiddle Up a Tune (Eric Nagler)
Doc Watson Sings Songs for Little Pickers (Doc Watson)
Eric's World Record (Eric Nagler)
Family Tree (Tom Chapin)
Grandma Slid Down the Mountain (Cathy Fink)
Let's Sing Fingerplays (Tom Glazer)
Peter, Paul, & Mommy (Peter, Paul, & Mary)
Stay Tuned (Sharon, Lois, & Bram)
Stories and Songs for Little Children (Pete Seeger)
This a Way, That a Way (Ella Jenkins)

Multicultural music— from different ethnic groups, from around the world
Beyond Boundaries: The Earthbeat Sampler
Celtic Lullaby (Margie Butler)
Children's Songs of Latin America, Cloud Journey (Marcia Berman)
Family Folk Festival: A Multicultural Sing-Along
Gift of the Tortoise (Ladysmith Black Mambazo)
I Got Shoes! (African American) (Sweet Honey in the Rock)
Magical Earth (Sarah Pirtle)
Miss Luba and Kenyan Folk Melodies (Muungano National Choir of Kenya)
Nobody Else Like Me (Cathy & Marcy)
Papa's Dream (Los Lobos)
Positively Reggae
Shake Shugaree (Taj Mahal)

Holiday, religious, and seasonal music
Chant (Benedictine Monks of Santo Domingo de Silos)
Holiday Songs and Rhythms (Hap Palmer)
Just in Time for Chanukah (Rosenthal & Safyan)
Leprechauns and Unicorns, Oscar Brand and His Singing Friends Celebrate Holidays (Oscar Brand)

Source: M. R. Jalongo "Using Recorded Music with Young Children: A Guide for Nonmusicians," *Young Children* 51 (July 1996), 6–14 (pp. 12–13). Published by the National Association for the Education of Young Children. Copyright © 1996 by NAEYC. Reprinted with permission. (Adapted by permission from J. P. Isenberg and M. R. Jalongo, *Creative Expression and Play in the Early Childhood Curriculum*, 2nd ed. [Englewood Cliffs, NJ: Merrill/Prentice Hall, 1996].)

Mighty Clouds of Joy (Reverend James Cleveland)
Mormon Tabernacle Choir
Songs for the Holiday Season (Nancy Rover)
Vienna Boys Choir

Contemporary children's music
All of Us Will Shine (Tickle Tune Typhoon)
Ants (Joe Scruggs)
Bananaphone (Raffi)
Collections (Fred Penner)
Hearts and Hands (Tickle Tune Typhoon)
Hug the Earth, Circle Around (Tickle Tune
Typhoon)
Little Friends for Little Folks (Janice Buckner)
1-2-3 for Kids (The Chenille Sisters)
Rosenshontz (Gary Rosen & Bill Shontz)
Sillytime Magic (Joanie Bartels)
Singin' and Swingin' (Sharon, Lois, & Bram)
Take Me with You (Peter Alsop)
Will You Be My Friend? (The Roches)

Popular music—rock, jazz, new age, pop-chart, electronic, movie, and show
Baby Road (Floyd Domingo)
A Child's Celebration of Broadway
A Child's Celebration of Show Tunes
Electronic Music ll (Jacob Druckman)
Fresh Aire I (Manheim Steamroller)
Fresh Aire II (Manheim Steamroller)
Peter and the Wolf Play Jazz (Dave Van Ronk)
Really Rosie (Carole King & Maurice Sendak)
"Rhythm of the Pride Lands" (from The Lion
King)
"Sebastian the Crab" (from The Little Mermaid)
Star Wars Trilogy Soundtrack (London
Philharmonic)

Classical music
Carnival of the Animals (Camille Saint-Saens)
Fiedler's Favorites for Children (Arthur Fiedler &
the Boston Pops Orchestra)
The Firebird (Igor Stravinsky)
G'morning, Johann: Classical Piano Solos (Ric
Louchard)
Happy Baby Classics
La Mer (Debussy)
More Fiedler Favorites (Arthur Fiedler & the Boston
Pops Orchestra)
Mr. Bach Comes to Call (Toronto Boys Choir &

Studio Arts Orchestra)
My Favorite Opera for Children (Pavarotti)
Nutcracker Suite (Tchaikovsky)
Peter and the Wolf (Sergio Prokofiev)
Sleeping Beauty (Tchaikovsky)
Sorcerer's Apprentice (Dukas)
Symponie Fantastique (Hector Berlioz)
Tchaikovsky's Children's Album (The Moscow
Virtuosi)

Music for dancing, patriotic and marching songs
Choo Choo Boogaloo (Buckwheat Zydeco)
Play Your Instruments (Ella Jenkins)
Sousa marches (Tchaikovsky)
Strauss waltzes (Tchaikovsky)
Swan Lake (Tchaikovsky)
21 Really Cool Songs (Sugar Beats)

Music from various historical periods
Dance of the Renaissance (Richard Searles &
Gilbert Yslas)
Harpsichord Music (Jean-Phillipe Rameau)
Shake It to the One You Love: Play Songs and
Lullabies from Black Musical Traditions
The Wild Mountain Thyme (John Langstaff)

Music by contemporary artists
Earthrise: The Rainforest Album
Midori Live at Carnegie Hall (Midori)
Songbird (Kenny G)
Sounds of Blackness
Who's Afraid of Opera? (Joan Sutherland—video-
cassette with Beverly Sills, Stevie Wonder,
Luciano Pavarotti)

Story songs for quiet listening
Burl Ives Sings Little White Duck (Burl Ives)
A Child's Celebration of Song, "The Ugly Duckling"
(Danny Kaye)
Family Folk Festival: A Multicultural Sing Along,
"My Grandfather's Clock (Doc Watson) and
"The Circle Song" (Maria Muldaur)
Follow the Drinking Gourd (Morgan Freeman)
The Manhattan Transfer Meets Tubby the Tuba,
"Frosty the Snowman" (Manhattan Transfer)
Peter, Paul, and Mommy, "Puff the Magic Dragon"
(Peter, Paul, & Mary)
Special Delivery, "Mail Myself to You" (Fred Penner)

Appendix F

SAFETY RESOURCES

It is our hope that the ideas presented in this volume will inspire action to create safer environments for children. Such efforts, however, are more likely to succeed if one consults the existing resources. Thus, this section provides a few of the many resources available for making environments a bit safer for our children and youth.

General Resources

Andrew Glover Youth Program
Manhattan Criminal Courts
100 Centre St., Rm. 1541
New York, NY 10013
212-348-6381

Children's Defense Fund
25 E St., NW
Washington, DC 20001
202-662-3589

Committee for Children
171 20th Ave.
Seattle, WA 98122

Education Development Center
55 Chapel St.
Newton, MA 02160
617-969-7100

ETR Associates
P.O. Box 1830
Santa Cruz, CA 95061-1830

*Institute for
Mental Health Initiatives*
4545 42nd St., NW, Ste. 311
Washington, DC 20016
202-364-7111

*Paramount Plan: Alternatives to
Gang Membership*
16400 Colorado Ave.
Paramount, CA 90723
213-220-2140

*Rheedlan Centers for Children
and Family*
2770 Broadway
New York, NY 10025
212-866-0700

*Shepard Pratt National Center
for Human Development*
6501 North Charles St,
P.O. Box 5503
Baltimore, MD 21285-5503

Urban Strategies Council
672 13th St., Ste. 200
Oakland, CA 94612
510-893-2404

Victims Services Agency
Project SMART
60 Court St., 8th Floor
Brooklyn, NY 11210
718-858-9070

General Violence

Alternative to Violence Project
15 Rutherford Pl.
New York, NY 10003
212-477-1067

Alternatives to Violence
524 West Exchange
Akron, OH 44301
216-864-5442

*National Crime
Prevention Council*
1700 K St., NW, 2nd Floor
Washington, DC 20006-3817
202-466-6272

*National Institute for
Violence Prevention*
1 Cleveland Park
Roxbury, MA 02119
617-427-0692

*Society for Prevention
of Violence*
3109 Mayfield Rd., Rm. 207
Cleveland, OH 44118
216-371-5545

Source: J. L. Hoot and E. T. Bartkowiak, "Safety Resources," *Childhood Education* 70 (1994), 287–288. Reprinted by permission of the authors and the Association for Childhood Education International. Copyright © 1998 by the Association. Reprinted with permission.

Violence, Non-Violence, and the 20th Century
American Friends Service
    Committee
2161 Massachusetts Ave.
Cambridge, MA 02140

Violence Policy Center
1300 N St., NW
Washington, DC 20005
202-783-4071

Gun Violence

Center to Prevent
Handgun Violence
1225 Eye St., NW, Ste. 1100
Washington, DC 20005
202-289-7319

Coalition to Stop Gun Violence
The Educational Fund to End
    Handgun Violence
100 Maryland Ave., NE
Washington, DC 20002
202-544-7190

Media Violence

Center for Media Education
1511 K St., NW, Ste. 158
Washington, DC 20005
202-628-2620

Media Scope
12711 Ventura Blvd., Ste. 250
Studio City, CA 91604
818-508-2080

National Foundation to
Improve Television
60 State St., #3400
Boston, MA 02109
617-523-6353

Drugs/Alcohol

Midwest Regional Center for Drug
Free Schools and Communities
1900 Spring Rd.
Oak Brook, IL 60521
708-571-4710

National Clearinghouse for
Alcohol and Drug Information
P.O. Box 2345
Rockville, MD 20852

National Drugs and
Crime Clearinghouse
1600 Research Blvd.
Rockville, MD 20850
800-638-8736

U.S. Department of Education
Drug Planning and Outreach
    Staff
Office of the Assistant Secretary
    for Elementary and
    Secondary Education
400 Maryland Ave., SW
Rm 1073
Washington, DC 20202-6123
202-401-3030

Child Abuse/At-Risk Children

Kid Helpline, 800-334-4KID

Kids on the Block
9385-C Gerwig Ln.
Columbia, MD 21046
800-368-KIDS

National Adolescent
Perpetrator Network
1205 Oneida St.
Denver, CO 80220
303-321-3963

National Committee for the
Prevention of Child Abuse
332 South Michigan Ave.
Ste. 1600
Chicago, IL 60604-4357
312-663-3520

National Consortium on
Alternatives of Youth at Risk
5250 17th St., Ste. 107
Sarasota, FL 34235
800-245-7133

National Council of Juvenile and
Family Court Judges
P.O. Box 8978
Reno, NV 89507
702-784-6012

National Institute of Justice
Office of Juvenile Justice and
Delinquency Prevention
633 Indiana Ave., NW
Washington, DC 20531
202-307-5911

National Resources Center for
Youth Services
202 West 8th St.
Tulsa, OK 74119-1419

Parenting Programs

Center on Families,
Communities, Schools and
Children's Learning
The Johns Hopkins University
3505 N. Charles St.
Baltimore, MD 21218
410-516-0370

National Association for the
Education of Young Children
1509 16th St., NW
Washington, DC 20036-1426
800-424-2460

Parents as Teachers:
The Parents as Teachers
National Center
9374 Olive Blvd.
St. Louis, MO 63132
314-434-4330

Community Service Programs

Community Relations Service
U.S. Department of Justice
5550 Friendship Blvd., Ste. 330
Chevy Chase, MD 20815
301-492-5929

District Attorney of
Kings County
Legal Lives Project
Municipal Bldg.
Brooklyn, NY 11201
718-802-2000

Harvard Negotiation Project
500 Pound Hall
Cambridge, MA 02138
617-495-1684

National Center for Service
Learning in Early Adolescence
25 West 43rd St., Ste. 612
New York, NY 10036-8099
212-642-2946

Young America Cares
United Way of America
701 North Fairfax St.
Alexandria, VA 22314
703-836-7100

Youth Service of America
1319 F St., NW, Ste. 900
Washington, DC 20004
202-783-8855

Leadership Programs

National Education Service
1610 West 3rd St.
P.O. Box 8
Bloomington, IN 47402-0008
812-336-7700

National Youth
Leadership Council
1910 West County Rd. B
Roseville, MN 55113
612-631-3672

Peer Counseling

National Peer
Helpers Association
P.O. Box 3783
Glendale, CA 91221-00783
919-757-4287

Youth Reaching Youth
The 3P Project
National Network of Runaway
    and Youth Services
1319 F St., NW, Ste. 401
Washington, DC 20004
202-783-7949

Conflict Resolution

Abrams Peace Education
Foundation
3550 Biscayne Blvd., Ste. 400
Miami, FL 33137
305-576-5075

Ann Arbor Public Schools
2555 South State St.
P.O. Box 188
Ann Arbor, MI 48106
313-944-2240

Association for Supervision and
Curriculum Development
1250 N. Pitt St.
Alexandria, VA 22314

Building Bridges
Harvard Negotiation Project
500 Pound Hall
Cambridge, MA 02138
617-495-1684

Children's Creative
Response to Conflict
Box 271
Nyack, NY 10960

Community Board Center for
Policy and Training
149 9th St.
San Francisco, CA 94103

Conflict Resolution and
Peer Mediation
Resolving Conflict Creatively
163 3rd Ave., #239
New York, NY 10003
212-387-0225

Educators for
Social Responsibility
11 Garden St.
Cambridge, MA 02138

Friends Conflict
Resolution Programs
1515 Cherry St.
Philadelphia, PA 19102
215-241-7729 ext. 7234

Interaction Book Company
7208 Cornelia Dr.
Edina, MN 55435
612-831-9500

Iowa Peace Institute
P.O. Box 480
Grinnell, IA 50112
515-236-4880

Martin Luther King, Jr. Center
for Nonviolent Social Change
449 Auburn Ave., NW
Atlanta, GA 30312
404-524-1945

National Association for
Mediation in Education
425 Amity St.
Amherst, MA 01002
413-545-2462

New Mexico Center for
Dispute Resolution
510 2nd St., NW, Ste. 209
Albuquerque, NM 87102
505-237-0571

Pittsburgh Peace Institute
139 Wrightman St.
Pittsburgh, PA 15217
412-682-2600

School Mediation Associates
702 Green St., Rm. 8
Cambridge, MA 02139
617-876-6074

Safety

American Academy of Pediatrics
601 13th St., NW, #400
Washington, DC 20005
202-347-8600

Children's Aid Society
IS 218, 105 E. 22nd St.
New York, NY 10011
212-949-4936

Concerned Educators Allied for a Safe Environment
17 Gerry St.
Cambridge, MA 02138
617-864-0999

National Center for Injury Prevention and Control
4770 Buford Highway NE, F36
Atlanta, GA 30341-3724
404-488-4690

National PTA
700 N. Rush St.
Chicago, IL 60611
312-787-0977

National Safe Kids Campaign
111 Michigan Ave., NW
Washington, DC 20010-2970
202-939-4993

National School Safety Center
4165 Thousand Oaks Blvd.
Ste. 290
Westlake Village, CA 91362
805-373-9977

TIPS Program
Teaching Individuals
  Protective Strategies/
  Education Information
  and Resource Center
606 Delsea Dr.
Sewell, NJ 08080

Glossary

Absorbent mind A phrase describing Montessori's belief that the child is able to absorb information long before he can be taught certain concepts.

Antibias curriculum A curriculum aimed at eliminating bias of all types by teaching children to respect people regardless of their sex, age, race/ethnicity, or other traits.

Assessment Use of a comprehensive evaluation system to determine the quality of a program or the progress of a child.

Assisted communication Communication through means other than speech or sign such as computers, special boards, and so on.

Autoeducation The child's ability to organize her own thinking when engaged in certain activities.

Behaviorist A theory suggesting that behavior can be shaped by rewards and punishments.

Child care Care for children in a group, usually for the entire working day; the term day care was used previously.

Cognitive development The development of the ability to think and reason.

Communicative competence The ability to use language to achieve your needs, regardless of the social correctness of the utterances.

Construct To build personal mental structures that organize information and knowledge.

Constructivist A theory suggesting that children learn by constructing their own understanding; based on the work of Piaget and Vygotsky.

Convention A rule of written language that is determined by social agreement, such as the use of capital letters.

Corporal punishment Physical punishment such as spanking, pinching, or slapping.

Creativity Purposeful behavior or ideas that extend beyond the present and are original and imaginative.

Cueing system What a reader uses to get information about print, such as the graphophonic system, the syntactical system, the semantic system, and the schematic system.

Curriculum A written plan for learning experiences.

Developmentally appropriate practice (DAP) Practice that is age and individually appropriate for each child in a program.

Dialect A systematic variation from the common language that is used regularly and shared by a social group. The variation can be in word order, meaning, or pronunciation.

Direct instruction Instruction in which the teacher presents information directly to the children.

Discipline Guidance aimed at helping children gain self-control of their behavior.

Egocentric thought patterns Thought patterns in which the individual fails to consider the viewpoints of others.

Emergent literacy The concept that children are learning about printed language beginning in infancy rather than at one point in time.

Emerging curriculum An approach to curriculum development in which the teacher follows the lead of the children.

English as a second language (ESL) A term describing speakers whose native language is not English.

Environmental print Print that occurs in the everyday environment, such as stop signs and candy labels.

Expanding curriculum An organizational pattern for social studies in which the focus of activities moves from the individual to the family, the neighborhood, the city, the state, the nation, and the world.

Freedom The principle that dictates that the child, not the teacher, should choose activities for learning.

Functions of print The purposes of print: to provide directions, pleasure, information, and so on.

Fundamental motor skills Basic motor skills such as moving, running, jumping, throwing, and so on.

Head Start A program started in the 1960s to help young children who were disadvantaged prepare for success in school.

Home visit A planned visit to a child's home by a school staff member, such as a teacher, counselor, or principal.

Incidental learning Learning that occurs in addition to what is written into the learning plan.

Instructional materials Materials selected to help children develop specific skills or learn specific concepts.

Language delay A delay in the development of an individual child's language ability that results in his skills not matching what is typical of his peers.

Learning areas Areas in a classroom where certain activities can take place and certain materials are stored.

Learning plan A comprehensive plan of learning experiences for children.

Least restrictive environment (LRE) The educational setting that is the least restrictive for an individual with given characteristics; the setting that provides the best educational opportunity for a child who is disabled.

Mainstreaming A placement approach in which children with disabling conditions are included in regular classrooms; now more frequently referred to as inclusion.

Mandated goals Goals set by a school director or written into the school curriculum.

Maturationist A theory suggesting that children will "unfold," or develop to their full potential, given optimal conditions.

Metaknowledge Knowledge of what one knows.

Multicultural education An approach to education that encourages children to understand and respect all people and cultures.

Nonjudgmental attitude An attitude of acceptance; a refusal on the part of a teacher to criticize parents

Operant conditioning A form of conditioning that rewards behavior that moves closer to target behavior.

Paraprofessional A paid assistant in the classroom.

Parent place A special area of the classroom or a room in the school set aside for parents.

Phonemic awareness The ability to examine language separate from meaning and manipulate its component sounds.

Portfolio assessment Assessment based on an evaluation of a collection of artifacts and anecdotes.

Practice play Play in which the player explores the nature of objects or materials with no other play goals.

Prepared environment A learning environment structured to promote the development of given concepts in a child's mind.

Punishment Removal of privileges or physical punishment designed to change children's behavior.

Reflective abstraction Thinking about the results of personal manipulations of objects.

Room arrangement The arrangement of furniture and materials to meet the needs of the children and teacher.

Scientific process A strategy for solving problems that includes making hypotheses, collecting data, testing hypotheses, and drawing conclusions.

Screening test A test designed to determine whether a child is eligible for a particular program or needs special attention.

Sensitive periods Times in a child's development when certain concepts are learned more easily.

Shared reading Reading in which the teacher does most of the reading, but the children are actively involved in the process.

Simple abstraction Abstracting a concept from repeated experiences with objects.

Sociodramatic play Play in which children assume roles and act out episodes, such as putting a baby to bed.

Sociolinguistics The study of language as it's used in a social context.

Stimulus-response theory A theory that organisms will respond to given stimuli based on previous experience with the stimuli.

Story structure The organizational pattern of printed material that is typical of its genre.

Teaching strategies Methods of presenting instruction, such as demonstrations, lectures, and simulations.

Thematic approach The organization of curriculum and learning experiences around a chosen topic.

Transitions Periods of time between activities in the classroom.

Volunteers Parents or community members who help in the classroom without pay.

Zone of proximal development The gap between what a child can do independently and what he cannot do even with assistance.

References

Note: This References section is divided into three parts. The first two—General Sources and Children's Books—contain listings of sources cited and discussed in the text. The third part, Information for Parents, lists publications and organizations that provide information specifically for parents.

General Sources

Administration for Child, Youth, and Families. *Project Head Start Statistical Fact Sheet.* ERIC Document Reproduction Service 395699. 1995.

Alger, Harriet A. "Transitions: Alternatives to Manipulative Management Techniques." *Young Children* 39 (September 1984): 16–26.

Almy, Millie. "A Child's Right to Play." *Childhood Education* 60 (May/June 1984): 350.

Ambron, Sueann R. *Child Development.* 2d ed. New York: Holt, Rinehart and Winston, 1978.

American Academy of Pediatrics. *Safe Swimming for Your Young Child.* Washington, DC: AAP, 1988. (This leaflet is one in a series called "TIPP: The Injury Prevention Program.")

American Montessori Society. *Standards and Criteria for AMS School Accreditation.* ERIC Document Reproduction Service 2523040. New York: AMS, 1984.

Andrews, Angela G. "The Role of Self-Directed Discovery Time in the Development of Mathematics Concepts." *Teaching Children Mathematics* 2 (October 1995): 116–120.

Anen, Judith. *Enhancing the Curriculum through the Addition of Rich and Diverse Language Development Activities.* ERIC Document Reproduction Service 329944. 1991.

Association for Supervision and Curriculum Development. *Developmental Characteristics of Children and Youth.* Alexandria, VA: ASCD, 1975.

Atkins, Cammie. "Writing: Doing Something Constructive." *Young Children* 40 (November 1984): 3–7.

Aylward, Kim, Scott Hartley, Tiffany Field, Jean Greer, and Nitza Vega-Lahr. "An Art Appreciation Curriculum for Preschool Children." *Early Child Development and Care* 96 (September 1993): 35–48.

Baker, Gwendolyn C. "Teaching Children to Respect Diversity." *Childhood Education* 71 (Fall 1994): 33–35.

Baker, Katherine Read. *Let's Play Outdoors.* Washington, DC: National Association for the Education of Young Children, 1966.

Barbour, Nita, Tupper Dooly Webster, and Stephen Drosdeck. "Sand: A Resource for the Language Arts." *Young Children* 42 (January 1987): 20–25.

Barclay, Kathy, and Camille Breheny. "Hey, Look Me Over! Assess, Evaluate and Conference with Confidence." *Childhood Education* 70 (Summer 1994): 215–220.

Barclay, Kathy Dulaney, and Lynn Walwer. "Linking Lyrics and Literacy through Song Picture Books." *Young Children* 47 (May 1992): 76–85.

Barnett, Lynn A. "Research Note: Young Children's Resolution of Distress through Play." *Journal of Child Psychology and Psychiatry and Allied Disciplines* 25 (1984): 477–483.

Barnett, Lynn A., and Joan Fiscella. "A Child by Any Other Name: A Comparison of the Playfulness of Gifted and Nongifted Children." *Gifted Child Quarterly* 29 (1985): 61–66.

Bateson, G. *Steps to an Ecology of Mind.* New York: Ballantine, 1977.

Bauch, Jerold P. "The TransParent School: A Partnership for Parent Involvement." *Educational Horizons* 68 (Summer 1990): 187–189.

Bauer, Nancy, Martin Botel, Helen O. Dickens, Kenneth D. George, Sol Levin, Aaron H. Katcher, and Irving E. Sigel. *The Facts about AIDS: A Special Guide for NEA Members.* Washington, DC: National Education Association Health Information Network, no date.

Bayless, Kathleen M., and Marjorie E. Ramsey. *Music: A Way of Life for the Young Child.* 4th ed. Columbus, OH: Merrill, 1991.

Benelli, Cecelia, and Bill Yongue. "Supporting Young Children's Motor Skill Development." *Childhood Education* 71 (Summer 1995): 217–220.

Benham, Nancy Barbour, Alice Hosticka, Joe D. Payne, and Catherine Yeotis. "Making Concepts in Science and Mathematics Visible and Viable in the Early Childhood Curriculum." *School Science and Mathematics* 82 (January 1982): 45–55.

Benjamin, Ann C. "Observations in Early Childhood Classrooms: Advice from the Field." *Young Children* 49 (September 1994): 14–20.

Bentzen, Warren. *Seeing Young Children: A Guide to Observing and Recording Behavior.* New York: Delmar, 1985.

Bereiter, Carl, and Siegfried Engelmann. *Teaching Disadvantaged Children in the Preschool.* Englewood Cliffs, NJ: Prentice-Hall, 1966.

Bergen, Doris. "Using a Schema for Play and Learning." In *Play as a Medium for Learning and Development,* edited by D. Bergen, 169–180. Portsmouth, NH: Heinemann, 1988.

Bergen, Doris. "Should Teachers Permit or Discourage Violent Play Themes?" *Childhood Education* 70 (Annual Theme 1994): 300–301.

Bergeron, Bette S., Sarah Wermuth, Melissa Rhodes, and Elizabeth A. Rudenga. "Language Development and Thematic Instruction: Supporting Young Learners at Risk." *Childhood Education* 72 (Spring 1996): 141–145.

Berk, Laura E. *Infants, Children, and Adolescents.* Boston: Allyn and Bacon, 1996.

Berk, Laura E., and Adam Winsler. *Scaffolding Children's Learning: Vygotsky and Early Childhood Education.* Washington, DC: National Association for the Education of Young Children, 1995.

Berk, Laura. "Vygotsky's Theory: The Importance of Make-Believe Play." *Young Children* 50 (November 1994): 30–39.

Berko-Gleason, Jean, ed. *The Development of Language.* Columbus, OH: Merrill, 1985.

Betz, Carl. "Beyond Time-Out: Tips from a Teacher." *Young Children* 49 (March 1994): 10–14.

Bigler, R. S., and L. S. Liben. "Cognitive Mechanisms in Children's Gender Stereotyping: Theoretical and Educational Implications of a Cognitive-Based Intervention." *Child Development* 63 (1992): 1351–1363.

Bigler, R. S., and L. S. Liben. "The Role of Attitudes and Interventions in Gender-Schematic Processing." *Child Development* 61 (1990): 1440–1452.

Bird, John. *Science from Water Play.* London: Macdonald Educational, 1983.

Bjorkland, Gail. *Planning for Play: A Developmental Approach.* Columbus, OH: Merrill, 1978.

Blackburn, Ellen. "Stories Never End." In *Breaking Ground: Teachers Relate Reading and Writing in the Elementary School,* edited by J. Hansen, T. Newkirk, and D. Graves. Portsmouth, NH: Heinemann, 1985.

Bodrova, Elena, and Deborah J. Leong. *Tools of the Mind: The Vygotskian Approach to Early Childhood Education.* Englewood Cliffs, NJ: Prentice-Hall, 1996.

Boehm, Ann E., and Richard A. Weinberg. *The Classroom Observer: Developing Observation Skills in Early Childhood Settings.* 2d ed. New York: Teachers College Press, 1987.

Bondurant, J. L., D. J. Romeo, and R. Kretschmer. "Language Behaviors of Mothers of Children with Normal and Delayed Language." *Language, Speech and Hearing Services in Schools* 14 (1983): 233–242.

Borden, Esta J. "The Community Connection—It Works!" *Young Children* 42 (May 1987): 14–23.

Bordner, Ginger A., and Mira T. Berkley. "Educational Play: Meeting Everyone's Needs in Mainstreamed Classrooms." *Childhood Education* 69 (Fall 1992): 38–40.

Bowker, Jeanette E., and Janet K. Sawyer. "Influence of Exposure on Preschoolers' Art Preferences." *Early Childhood Research Quarterly* 3 (1988): 107–115.

Bredekamp, Sue, ed. *Developmentally Appropriate Practice in Early Childhood Programs Serving Children From Birth through Age 8.* Washington, DC: National Association for the Education of Young Children, 1986.

Bredekamp, Sue. "Reflections on Reggio Emilia." *Young Children* 49 (November 1993): 13–17.

Bredekamp, Sue. "Twenty-Five Years of Educating Young Children: The High/Scope Approach to Preschool Education." *Young Children* 51 (May 1996): 57–61.

Bredekamp, Sue, and Carol Copple, eds. *Developmentally Appropriate Practice in Early Childhood Programs.* Rev. ed. Washington, DC: National Association for the Education of Young Children, 1997.

Bredekamp, Sue, and Teresa Rosegrant. "Reaching Potentials through Transforming Curriculum, Assessment, and Teaching." In *Reaching Potentials: Transforming Early Childhood Curriculum and Assessment,* vol. 2, edited by S. Bredekamp and T. Rosegrant, 15–22. Washington, DC: National Association for the Education of Young Children, 1995.

Bredekamp, Sue, and Teresa Rosegrant. *Reaching Potentials: Appropriate Curriculum and Assessment for Young Children,* vol. 1. Washington, DC: National Association for the Education of Young Children, 1992.

Bredekamp, Sue, and Teresa Rosegrant, eds. *Reaching Potentials: Transforming Early Childhood Curriculum and Assessment,* vol. 2. Washington, DC: National Association for the Education of Young Children, 1995.

Brett, Arlene. "Computers and Social Development of Young Children." *Dimensions of Early Childhood* 23 (Fall 1994): 10, 13, 48.

Brewer, Jo Ann. "Literacy Development When Children's First Language Is Not English." In *Literacy in the 90's: Readings in the Language Arts,* edited by Nancy Cecil, 221–230. Dubuque, IA: Kendall Hunt, 1990.

Brittain, W. L. "Some Exploratory Studies of the Art of Preschool Children." *Studies in Art Education* 10 (1969): 14–24.

Brown, Mac H., Rosemary Althouse, and Carol Anfin. "Guided Dramatization: Fostering Social Development in Children with Disabilities." *Young Children* 48 (January 1993): 68–71.

Brown, Nancy, Nancy Curry, and Ethel Tittnich. "How Groups of Children Deal with Common Stress through Play." In *Play: The Child Strives toward Self-Realization,* edited by G. Engstrom, 26–38. Washington, DC: National Association for the Education of Young Children, 1971.

Brown, Victoria. "Integrating Drama and Sign Language: A Multisensory Approach to Learning for Children with Special Needs." In *Early Childhood Creative Arts: Proceedings of the International Early Childhood Creative Arts Conference,* edited by L. Overby. Reston, VA: American Alliance for Health, Physical Education, Recreation and Dance, 1991.

Bruhn, John G., and Philip R. Nader. "The School as a Setting for Health Education, Health Promotion, and Health Care." *Family and Community Health* 4 (1982): 57–59.

Bruner, Jerome. *Child's Talk: Learning to Use Language.* New York: W. W. Norton, 1983.

Bruner, Jerome. *The Process of Education.* New York: Vintage Books, 1960.

Buchoff, Rita. "Family Stories." *Reading Teacher* 49 (November 1995): 230–233.

Buchoff, Rita. "Joyful Voices: Facilitating Language Growth through Rhythmic Response to Chants." *Young Children* 49 (May 1994): 26–30.

Bullock, Merry, and Rochel Gelman. "Numerical Reasoning in Young Children: The Ordering Principle." *Child Development* 48 (June 1977): 427–434.

Bundy, Blakely Fetridge. "Fostering Communication between Parents and Preschools." *Young Children* 46 (January 1991): 12–17.

Burnett, Gary. *The Assessment and Placement of Language Minority Students.* ERIC Document Reproduction Service 357131. 1993.

Burns, Marilyn, and Kathy Richardson. "Making Sense Out of Word Problems." *Learning* 10 (January 1981): 39–44.

Burton, Grace M. "Patterning: Powerful Play." *School Science and Mathematics* 82 (June 1982): 39–44.

Butler, Lester G. "Language Acquisition of Young Children: Major Theories and Sequences." *Elementary English* 51 (1974): 1120–1123.

Button, Kathryn, Margaret J. Johnson, and Paige Furgerson. "Interactive Writing in a Primary Classroom." *Reading Teacher* 49 (March 1996): 446–454.

Butts, R. Freeman. "Search for Freedom—The Story of American Education." *National Education Association Journal* (March 1960): 33–48.

Butzow, Carol, and John Butzow. *Science, Technology and Society as Experienced through Children's Literature.* ERIC Document Reproduction Service 294141. 1988.

Buzzelli, Cary A., and Nancy File. "Building Trust in Friends." *Young Children* 44 (March 1989): 70–75.

Byrum, Donna, and Virginia L. Pierce. "Bringing Children to Literacy through Theme Cycles." In *Bringing Children to Literacy: Classrooms at Work,* edited by Bill Harp, 105–122. Norwood, MA: Christopher-Gordon, 1993.

Cain, Sandra E., and Jack M. Evans. *Sciencing: An Involvement Approach to Elementary Science Methods.* 2d ed. Columbus, OH: Merrill, 1984.

Cairney, Trevor H., and Lynne Munsie. "Parent Participation in Literacy Learning." *Reading Teacher* 48 (February 1995): 392–403.

Calkins, Lucy. *The Art of Teaching Writing.* Portsmouth, NH: Heinemann, 1986.

Cambourne, Brian. "Toward an Educationally Relevant Theory of Literacy Learning: Twenty Years of Inquiry." *Reading Teacher* 49 (November 1995): 182–202.

Canady, Robert Lynn, and John T. Seyfarth. *How Parent-Teacher Conferences Build Partnerships.* Fastback 132.

Bloomington, IN: Phi Delta Kappa Educational Foundation, 1979.

Canter, Lee. *Assertive Discipline.* Seal Beach, CA: Canter and Associates, 1976.

Canter, Lee. "Assertive Discipline and the Search for the Perfect Classroom." *Young Children* 43 (January 1988): 24.

Caples, Sara E. "Some Guidelines for Preschool Design." *Young Children* 51 (May 1996): 14–21.

Carlsson-Paige, Nancy, and Diane E. Levin. "Can Teachers Resolve the War-Play Dilemma?" *Young Children* 50 (July 1995): 62–63.

Cattermole, Juleen, and Norman Robinson. "Effective Home/School Communication—From the Parents' Perspective." *Phi Delta Kappan* 67 (September 1985): 48–50.

Cazden, Courtney. "Environmental Assistance to the Child's Acquisition of Grammar." Doctoral dissertation, Harvard University, 1965.

Chaille, Christine, and Lori Britain. *The Young Child as Scientist: A Constructivist Approach to Early Childhood Science Education.* New York: HarperCollins, 1991.

Chaille, Christine, and Steven B. Silvern. "Understanding through Play." *Childhood Education* 72 (Annual Theme 1996): 274–277.

Chapman, Marilyn L. "The Development of Phonemic Awareness in Young Children: Some Insights from a Case Study of a First-Grade Writer." *Young Children* 51 (January 1995): 31–37.

Chapman, Warren. "The Illinois Experience: State Grants to Improve Schools through Parent Involvement." *Phi Delta Kappan* 72 (January 1991): 355–358.

Charles, C. M., and Karen Blaine Barr. *Building Classroom Discipline.* 3d ed. New York: Longman, 1989.

Children's Defense Fund. *The State of America's Children, 1996.* Washington, DC: CDF, 1996.

Chittenden, E., and R. Courtney. "Assessment of Young Children's Reading: Documentation as an Alternative to Testing." In *Emergent Literacy: Young Children Learn to Read and Write,* edited by D. Strickland and L. Morrow, 107–120. Newark, DE: International Reading Association, 1989.

Chomsky, Carol. "Write First, Read Later." *Childhood Education* 47 (March 1971): 296–299.

Chomsky, Noam. *Aspects of a Theory of Syntax.* Cambridge, MA: MIT Press, 1965.

Christie, James F. "Dramatic Play: A Context for Meaningful Engagements." *Reading Teacher* 43 (April 1990): 542–545.

Christie, James F., and Francis Wardle. "How Much Time Is Needed for Play?" *Young Children* 47 (March 1992): 28–32.

Christie, James F., E. Peter Johnson, and Roger B. Peckover. "The Effects of Play Period Duration on Children's Play Patterns." *Journal of Research in Childhood Education* 3 (1988): 123–131.

Clark, Patricia. "Culturally Appropriate Practices in Early Childhood Education: Families as the Resource." *Contemporary Education* 66 (Spring 1995): 154–157.

Clay, Marie M. "Introducing a New Storybook to Young Readers." *Reading Teacher* 45 (December 1991): 264–273.

Clay, Marie. *An Observation Survey of Early Literacy Achievement*. Portsmouth, NH: Heinemann, 1993.

Clay, Marie M. *What Did I Write? Beginning Writing Behavior*. Portsmouth, NH: Heinemann, 1975.

Clements, Douglas H., Bonnie K. Nastasi, and Sudha Swaminathan. "Young Children and Computers: Crossroads and Directions from Research." *Young Children* 48 (January 1993): 56–64.

Clements, Nancy E., and Edna W. Warncke. "Helping Literacy Emerge at School for Less-Advantaged Children." *Young Children* 49 (March 1994): 22–26.

Clewett, Ann S. "Guidance and Discipline: Teaching Young Children Appropriate Behavior." *Young Children* 43 (May 1988): 26–31.

Cline, Dusty B., and David Ingerson. "The Mystery of Humpty's Fall: Primary-School Children as Playmakers." *Young Children* 51 (September 1996): 4–10.

Cline, R. K. J. *Focus on Families: A Reference Handbook*. Santa Barbara, CA: ABC-CLIO, 1990.

Cochrane, Orin, Donna Cochrane, Sharon Scalena, and Ethel Buchanan. *Reading, Writing and Caring*. Winnipeg, Manitoba, Canada: Whole Language Consultants, 1984.

Colbert, Cynthia. "Connecting with Art in the Classroom." In "Nurturing the Expressive Arts," edited by Stevie Hoffman, Larry Kantner, Cynthia Colbert, and Wendy Sims. *Childhood Education* 68 (Fall 1991): 23–26.

Colbert, C., and M. Taunton. "Developmentally Appropriate Practices for the Visual Arts Education of Young Children." National Art Education Association Briefing Paper. Reston VA: National Art Education Association, 1992.

Cole, David A. "Facilitating Play in Children's Peer Relationships: Are We Having Fun Yet?" *American Educational Research Journal* 23 (1986): 201–215.

Cole, Elizabeth, and Claire Schaefer. "Can Young Children Be Art Critics?" *Young Children* 45 (January 1990): 33–38.

Cole, Martha L., and Jack T. Cole. *Effective Intervention with the Language Impaired Child*. 2d ed. Rockville, MD: Aspen, 1989.

Collier, Robert G. "Reading, Thinking, and Play: A Child's Search for Meaning." In *Claremont Reading Conference 47th Yearbook*, edited by Malcolm P. Douglas. Claremont, CA: Claremont Reading Conference, 1983.

Collins, Raymond C. "Head Start: Steps toward a Two-Generation Program Strategy." *Young Children* 48 (January 1993): 2531, 72–73.

Comenius, John Amos. *A Reformation of Schools*. 1642. Reprint, London: Scolar Press, 1969.

Connell, Phil J. "An Effect of Modeling and Imitation Teaching Procedures on Children with and without Specific Language Impairment." *Journal of Speech and Hearing Research* 30 (1987): 105–113.

Coopersmith, Stanley. *The Antecedents of Self-Esteem*. San Francisco: W. H. Freeman, 1967.

Copeland, Richard W. *How Children Learn Mathematics: Teaching Implications of Piaget's Research*. 4th ed. New York: Macmillan, 1984.

Council on Interracial Books for Children. *10 Quick Ways to Analyze Books for Racism and Sexism*. ERIC Document Reproduction Services 188852. 1974.

Crinklaw-Kiser, Donna. "Integrating Music with Whole Language through the Orff-Schulwerk Process." *Young Children* 51 (July 1996): 15–21.

Cross, T. G. "Habilitating the Language-Impaired Child: Ideas from Studies of Parent-Child Interaction." *Topics in Language Disorders* 4 (1984): 1–14.

Crosser, Sandra. "Managing the Early Childhood Classroom." *Young Children* 47 (January 1992): 23–29.

Cryan, John R. "The Banning of Corporal Punishment." *Childhood Education* 63 (February 1987): 146–153.

Cunningham, A. E. "A Developmental Study of Instruction in Phonemic Awareness." Paper presented at American Educational Research Association, New Orleans, LA, 1988 (as cited in Griffith and Olson 1992).

Curcio, Frances R., and Susan Folkson. "Exploring Data: Kindergarten Children Do It Their Way." *Teaching Children Mathematics* 2 (February 1996): 382–385.

Curry, Nancy E., and Sara H. Arnaud. "Personality Difficulties in Preschool Children as Revealed through Play Themes and Styles." *Young Children* 59 (May 1995): 4–9.

D'Angelo, Diane A., and C. Ralph Adler. "Chapter I: A Catalyst for Improving Parent Involvement." *Phi Delta Kappan* 72 (January 1991): 350–354.

Daniels, Marilyn. "The Effect of Sign Language on Hearing Children's Language Development." *Communication Education* 43 (October 1994): 291–298.

Davidson, Jane, and June L. Wright. "The Potential of the Microcomputer in the Early Childhood Classroom." In *Young Children: Active Learners in a Technological Age*, edited by June L. Wright and Daniel D. Shade, 77–91. Washington, DC: National Association for the Education of Young Children, 1994.

Davis, Jessica, and Howard Gardner. "The Arts and Early Childhood Education: A Cognitive Developmental Portrait of the Young Child as Artist." In *Handbook of Research on the Education of Young Children*, edited by B. Spodek, 191–206. New York: Macmillan, 1993.

Day, Mary Carol, and Ronald K. Parker. *The Preschool in Action: Exploring Early Childhood Programs*. 2d ed. Boston: Allyn and Bacon, 1977.

de la Roche, Elisa. "Snowflakes: Developing Meaningful Art Experiences for Young Children." *Young Children* 51 (January 1996): 82–83.

Derman-Sparks, Louise. "Empowering Children to Create a Caring Culture in a World of Differences." *Childhood Education* 70 (Winter 1993/1994): 66–71.

Derman-Sparks, Louise, and the ABC Task Force. *Anti-Bias Curriculum: Tools for Empowering Young Children.* Washington, DC: National Association for the Education of Young Children, 1989.

Dever, Martha T., and Elizabeth J. Jared. "Remember to Include Art and Crafts in Your Integrated Curriculum." *Young Children* 51 (March 1996): 69–73.

DeVries, M. W., and A. J. Sameroff. "Culture and Temperament: Influences on Infant Temperament in Three East African Societies." *American Journal of Orthopsychiatry* 54 (1984): 83–96.

DeVries, Rheta, and Lawrence Kohlberg. *Constructivist Early Education: Overview and Comparison with Other Programs.* Washington, DC: National Association for the Education of Young Children, 1987.

DeVries, Rheta, and Lawrence Kohlberg. *Programs of Early Education: The Constructivist View.* New York: Longman, 1987.

Dewey, John. *The Child and the Curriculum.* Chicago: University of Chicago Press, 1902.

Dewey, John. *Democracy and Education.* New York: Free Press, 1916.

Dimidjian, Victoria Jean. "Holidays, Holy Days, and Wholly Dazed." *Young Children* 44 (September 1989): 70–75.

Dinwiddie, Sue A. "The Saga of Sally, Sammy, and the Red Pen: Facilitating Children's Social Problem Solving." *Young Children* 49 (July 1994): 13–19.

Ditchburn, Susan J. *Patterning Mathematical Understanding in Early Childhood.* ERIC Document Reproduction Service 218008. 1982.

Dixon, Glen T., and Patricia Tarr. "Extending Art Experiences in the Preschool Curriculum." *International Journal of Early Childhood* 20 (June 1988): 27–34.

Doris, Ellen. *Doing What Scientists Do: Children Learn to Investigate Their World.* Portsmouth, NH: Heinemann, 1991.

Dreikurs, R., B. Grunwald, and F. Pepper. *Maintaining Sanity in the Classroom.* New York: Harper and Row, 1982.

Drew, Naomi. *Learning the Skills of Peacemaking: An Activity Guide for Elementary-Age Children on Communicating, Cooperating, Resolving Conflict.* Rolling Hills Estates, CA: Jalmar Press, 1987.

Dumtschin, Joyce Ury. "Recognize Language Development and Delay in Early Childhood." *Young Children* 43 (1988): 16–24.

Dyck, James A. "The Case for the L-Shaped Classroom. *Principal* 74 (November 1994): 41–45.

Dyer, Suzanne M., and Wendy Schiller. " 'Not Wilting Flowers Again!' Problem Finding and Problem Solving in Movement and Performance." *Early Child Development and Care* 90 (May 1993): 47–54.

Dyson, Anne Haas, and Celia Genishi. "Visions of Children as Language Users: Language and Language Education in Early Childhood." In *Handbook of Research on the Education of Young Children,* edited by B. Spodek. New York: Macmillan, 1993.

Dyson, Anne Haas, and Celia Genishi. *Visions of Children as Language Users: Research on Language and Language Education in Early Childhood.* Technical Report No. 49. ERIC Document Reproduction Service 335678. 1991.

Edwards, Carolyn, Lella Gandini, and George Forman, Eds. *The Hundred Languages of Children: The Reggio Emilia Approach to Early Childhood Education.* Norwood, NJ: Ablex, 1993.

Edwards, Linda C. *Affective Development and the Creative Arts: A Process Approach to Early Childhood Education.* Columbus, OH: Merrill, 1990.

Edwards, Linda C., and Martha L. Nabors. "The Creative Arts Process: What It Is and What It Is Not." *Young Children* 48 (March 1993): 77–81.

Eheart, B., and R. Leavitt. "Supporting Toddler Play." *Young Children* 40 (March 1985): 18–22.

Elam, Stanley M., Lowell C. Rose, and Alec M. Gallup. "The 28th Annual Phi Delta Kappa/Gallup Poll of the Public's Attitudes toward the Public Schools." *Phi Delta Kappan* 78 (September 1996): 41–59.

Elkind, David. "Child Development and Early Childhood Education: Where Do We Stand Today?" In *Curriculum Planning for Young Children,* edited by Janet Brown, 4–11. Washington, DC: National Association for the Education of Young Children, 1982.

Ellis, M. "The Complexity of Objects and Peers." In *Play and Learning,* edited by Brian Sutton-Smith. New York: Gardner Press, 1979.

Engel, Brenda. "An Approach to Evaluation in Reading and Writing." In *Achievement Testing in Early Childhood Education: Games Grown-Ups Play,* edited by C. Kamii, 119–134. Washington, DC: National Association for the Education of Young Children, 1990.

Engel, Brenda. *Considering Children's Art: Why and How to Value Their Works.* Washington, DC: National Association for the Education of Young Children, 1995.

Engel, Brenda. "Learning to Look: Appreciating Child Art." *Young Children* 51 (March 1996): 74–79

Epstein, Joyce L. "Paths to Partnership: What We Can Learn from Federal, State, District, and School Initiatives." *Phi Delta Kappan* 72 (January 1991): 344–349.

Epstein, Joyce L., and Susan L. Dauber. *Teachers' Attitudes and Practices of Parent Involvement in Inner-City Elementary and Middle Schools.* Baltimore, MD: Johns Hopkins University Center for Research on Elementary and Middle Schools, 1989 (as quoted in Olson 1990).

ERIC Clearinghouse on Elementary and Early Childhood Education. "Computer Software and Young

Children." *Resource List.* Urbana: University of Illinois, December 1995.

Erickson, Karen A., and David A. Koppenhaver. "Developing a Literacy Program for Children with Severe Disabilities." *Reading Teacher* 48 (May 1995): 676–684.

Erikson, Erik. *Childhood and Society.* 2d ed. New York: Norton, 1963.

Ernst, Gisela, and Kerri J. Richard. "Reading and Writing Pathways to Conversation in the ESL Classroom." *Reading Teacher* 48 (December/January 1995): 320–326.

Fagot, Beverly I., and Richard Hagan. "Aggression in Toddlers: Responses to the Assertive Acts of Boys and Girls." *Sex Roles* 12 (February 1985): 341–351.

Fallon, Irmie, and JoBeth Allen. "Where the Deer and the Cantaloupe Play." *Reading Teacher* 47 (April 1994): 546–551.

Federal Register, 18 June 1990, p. 24838.

Federal Register, 30 December 1976, pp. 56966–56998.

Ferreiro, Emilia, and Ana Teberosky. *Literacy before Schooling.* Portsmouth, NH: Heinemann, 1982.

Fetter, M. Patricia. "AIDS Education: Every Teacher's Responsibility." *Childhood Education* 65 (Spring 1989): 150–152.

Findlay, Elsa. *Rhythm and Movement: Applications of Dalcroze Eurhythmics.* Evanston, IL: Summy-Birchard, 1971.

Fine, Edith H., and Judith P. Josephson. "Footprints, Fireflies and Flight: Primary Science Magic." *Childhood Education* 62 (September/October 1984): 23–29.

Flood, James, and Diane Lapp. "Reporting Reading Progress: A Comparison Portfolio for Parents." *Reading Teacher* 42 (March 1989): 508–514.

Follis, Helen, and Gerald Krockover. "Selecting Activities in Science and Mathematics for Gifted Young Children." *School Science and Mathematics* 82 (January 1982): 57–64.

Ford, Sylvia A. "The Facilitator's Role in Children's Play." *Young Children* 48 (September 1993): 66–69.

Forman, George. "The Constructivist Perspective to Early Education." In *Approaches to Early Childhood Education,* 2d ed., edited by Jaipaul Roopnarine and James E. Johnson. New York: Macmillan, 1993.

Forman, George E., and David S. Kuschner. *The Child's Construction of Knowledge: Piaget for Teaching Children.* Washington, DC: National Association for the Education of Young Children, 1983.

Fox, Mem. *Teaching Drama to Young Children.* Portsmouth, NH: Heinemann, 1987.

Frank, Lawrence K. "Play Is Valid." *Childhood Education* 44 (March 1968): 433–440.

Froebel, Friedrich. *The Education of Man.* Translated by W. N. Hailmann. New York: D. Appleton, 1826.

Frost, Joe L. *Play and Playscapes.* Albany, New York: Delmar, 1996.

Frost, Joe L., and Joan B. Kissinger. *The Young Child and the Educative Process.* New York: Holt, Rinehart and Winston, 1976.

Frost, Joe L., and Barry L. Klein. *Children's Play and Playgrounds.* Boston: Allyn and Bacon, 1979.

Frost, Joe L., and Susan C. Wortham. "The Evolution of American Playgrounds." *Young Children* 43 (July 1988): 19–28.

Gabbard. Carl. "P.E. for Preschoolers: The Right Way." *Principal* (May 1995): 21–24.

Gabbard, Carl. *Playground Apparatus Experiences and Muscular Endurance among Children 4–6.* ERIC Document Reproduction Service 288190. College Station, TX: Texas A&M University, 1979.

Galen, Harlene. "Increasing Parental Involvement in Elementary School: The Nitty-Gritty of One Successful Program." *Young Children* 46 (January 1991): 18–22.

Galinsky, Ellen. "Parents and Teacher-Caregivers: Sources of Tension, Sources of Support." *Young Children* 43 (March 1988): 4–12.

Gallahue, David L. *Fundamental Movement Experiences for Children: A Developmental Skill Theme Approach.* ERIC Document Reproduction Service 211459. Paper presented at the annual conference of the Indiana Association for Health, Physical Education, Recreation, and Dance, Lafayette, Indiana, 1981.

Gandini, Lella. "Fundamentals of the Reggio Emilia Approach to Early Childhood Education." *Young Children* 49 (November 1993): 4–8.

Gardner, Howard. *Frames of Mind: The Theory of Multiple Intelligences.* New York: HarperCollins, 1983.

Gardner, Howard. "Reflections on Multiple Intelligences: Myths and Messages." *Phi Delta Kappan* 77 (November 1995): 200–209.

Gartrell, Dan. "Assertive Discipline: Unhealthy for Children and Other Living Things." *Young Children* 42 (January 1987a): 10–11.

Gartrell, Dan. "Misbehavior or Mistaken Behavior?" *Young Children* 50 (July 1995): 27–34.

Gartrell, Dan. "Punishment or Guidance?" *Young Children* 42 (March 1987b): 55–61.

Garvey, Catherine. *Play.* Cambridge, MA: Harvard University Press, 1977.

Gelfer, Jeffrey I., and Peggy G. Perkins. "Effective Communication with Parents: A Process for Parent/Teacher Conferences." *Childhood Education* 64 (October 1987): 19–22.

Gelman, Rochel, and Marsha F. Tucker. "Further Investigations of the Young Child's Conception of Number." *Child Development* 46 (March 1975): 167–175.

Genishi, Celia, and Anne Haas Dyson, eds. *Language Assessment in the Early Years.* Norwood, NJ: Ablex, 1984.

Gfeller, Kate. "Integrating the Handicapped Child into Music Activities." In *Musical Growth and Development: Birth through Six,* edited by Dorothy T. McDonald and Gene M. Simons, 113–140. New York: Schirmer Books, 1989.

Gilbert, Jean. *Musical Starting Points with Young Children.* London, England: Ward Lock Educational, 1981.

Ginott, Haim G. *Teacher and Child.* New York: Macmillan, 1972.

Glasser, William. *Control Theory in the Classroom*. New York: Perennial Library, 1985.

Glazer, Susan Mandel. "Oral Language and Literacy Development." In *Emerging Literacy: Young Children Learn to Read and Write*, edited by Dorothy S. Strickland and Lesley Mandel Morrow, 16–26. Newark, DE: International Reading Association, 1989.

Gober, Billy E., and B. Don Franks. "Physical and Fitness Education of Young Children." *Journal of Physical Education, Recreation, and Dance* 59 (September 1988): 57–61.

Gochman, David S., and T. F. Saucier. "Perceived Vulnerability in Children and Adolescents." *Health Education Quarterly* 9 (1982): 46–59.

Goldberg, Ellie. "Including Children with Chronic Health Conditions: Nebulizers in the Classroom." *Young Children* 49 (January 1994): 34–37.

Good, R. G. *How Children Learn Science: Conceptual Development and Implications for Teaching*. New York: Macmillan, 1977.

Goodman, K., Y. Goodman, and W. Hood. *The Whole Language Evaluation Book*. Portsmouth, NH: Heinemann, 1989.

Goodman, Ken. *On Reading: A Common-Sense Look at the Nature of Language and the Science of Reading*. Portsmouth, NH: Heinemann, 1996.

Goodman, Kenneth, E. Brooks Smith, Robert Meredith, and Yetta Goodman. *Language and Thinking in School*. 3d ed. New York: Richard C. Owen, 1987.

Goodman, Yetta. "Kidwatching: Observing Children in the Classroom." In *Observing the Language Learner*, edited by Angela Jaggar and M. Trika Smith-Burke. Newark, DE: International Reading Association/National Council of Teachers of English, 1985.

Goodman, Yetta, and Bess Altwerger. "Print Awareness and Pre-School Children: A Working Paper." Tucson, AZ: Arizona Center for Research and Development, College of Education, University of Arizona, 1981.

Goodman, Yetta M., and Carolyn Burke. *Reading Strategies: Focus on Comprehension*. Katonah, NY: Richard C. Owen, 1980.

Gordon, Ann, and Kathryn W. Browne. *Guiding Young Children in a Diverse Society*. Boston: Allyn and Bacon, 1996.

Gould, A. O. "Developing Specialized Programs for Singing." *Council for Research in Music Education* 17 (1969): 9–22.

Gowen, Jean W. "The Early Development of Symbolic Play." *Young Children* 50 (March 1995): 75–84.

Grangaard, E. M. "Color and Light Effects on Learning." ERIC Document Reproduction Service 382381. 1995.

Graves, Donald. Presentation at a conference of the International Reading Association, Atlanta, Georgia, May 1990.

Graves, Donald. *Writing: Teachers and Children at Work*. Portsmouth, NH: Heinemann, 1983.

Graves, Donald, and Virginia Stuart. *Write from the Start*. New York: New American Library, 1985.

Graves, Michael F., Bonnie B. Graves, and Sheldon Braaten. "Scaffolded Reading Experiences for Inclusive Classes." *Educational Leadership* (February 1996): 14–16.

Gray, Dianne E. *The Teacher's Role in Understanding Aggression and Dealing with It Effectively in the Preschool Environment*. ERIC Document Reproduction Service 200334. 1981.

Greabell, Leon C., and Sonia D. Forseth. "Creating a Stimulating Environment." *Kappa Delta Pi Record* 17 (February 1981): 70–73, 75.

Greenberg, Polly. "How and Why to Teach All Aspects of Preschool and Kindergarten Math Naturally, Democratically, and Effectively (For Teachers Who Don't Believe in Academic Programs, Who Do Believe in Educational Excellence, and Who Find Math Boring to the Max)—Part 1." *Young Children* 48 (May 1993): 75–84.

Greenberg, Polly. "Ideas That Work with Young Children: How and Why to Teach All Aspects of Preschool and Kindergarten Math—Part 2." *Young Children* 49 (January 1994): 12–18.

Greenberg, Polly. "Parents as Partners in Young Children's Development and Education: A New American Fad? Why Does It Matter?" *Young Children* 44 (May 1989): 61–75.

Greenwood, Deborah. "Home-School Communication via Video." *Young Children* 50 (September 1995): 66.

Griffith, Priscilla L., and Mary W. Olson. "Phonemic Awareness Helps Beginning Readers Break the Code." *Reading Teacher* 45 (March 1992): 516–523.

Grineski, Steven. "Teaching and Learning in Physical Education for Young Children." *Journal of Physical Education, Recreation and Dance* 59 (May/June 1988): 91–94.

Grineski, Steven. "What Is a Truly Developmentally Appropriate Physical Education Program for Children?" *Journal of Physical Education, Recreation and Dance* 63 (August 1992): 33–35, 60.

Grubb, Norton. "Young Children Face the State Issues and Options for Early Childhood Programs." *American Journal of Education* 97 (August 1989): 358–397.

Gullo, Dominic F., Carol U. Bersani, Douglas H. Clements, and Kathleen M. Ramsey. "A Comparative Study of 'All-Day,' 'Alternate-Day,' and 'Half-Day' Kindergarten Schedules: Effects on Achievement and Classroom Social Behaviors." *Journal of Research in Childhood Education* 1 (1986): 87–94.

Gunsberg, Andrew. "Empowering Young Abused and Neglected Children through Contingency Play." *Childhood Education* 66 (1989): 8–10.

Halliday, M. A. K. "Three Aspects of Children's Language Development: Learning Language, Learning through Language, Learning about Language." In *Oral and Written Language Development Research: Impact on the Schools*, edited by Y. Goodman, M.

Haussler, and D. Strickland. Urbana, IL: National Council of Teachers of English, 1982.

Halpern, Robert. "Major Social and Demographic Trends Affecting Young Families: Implications for Early Childhood Care and Education." *Young Children* 42 (September 1987): 34–40.

Harding, Nadine. "Family Journals: The Bridge from School to Home and Back Again." *Young Children* 51 (January 1996): 27–30.

Hardman, Michael L. et al. *Human Exceptionality: Society, School, and Family.* 4th ed. Boston: Allyn and Bacon, 1993.

Harlan, Jean. *Science Experiences for the Early Childhood Years.* 2d ed. Columbus, OH: Merrill, 1980.

Harms, Thelma. "Evaluating Settings for Learning." *Young Children* 25 (May 1970): 304–309.

Harp, Bill. *The Handbook of Literacy Assessment and Evaluation.* Norwood, MA: Christopher-Gordon, 1996.

Harp, Bill, and Jo Ann Brewer. *Reading and Writing: Teaching for the Connections.* Fort Worth, TX: Harcourt Brace, 1996.

Harper, Andrew, Marty Flick, Karen Taylor, and Renee Waldo. "Education Through Music: A Breakthrough in Early Childhood Education?" *Phi Delta Kappan* 54 (May 1973): 628–629.

Harsh, Ann. "Teach Mathematics with Children's Literature." *Young Children* 42 (September 1987): 42–49.

Harste, J., V. Woodward, and C. Burke. *Language Stories and Literacy Lessons.* Portsmouth, NH: Heinemann, 1984.

Harter, S. "Developmental Perspectives on Self-Esteem." In *Handbook of Child Psychology:* vol. 4. *Socialization, Personality, and Social Development,* 4th ed., edited by E. M. Hetherington, 275–386. New York: Wiley, 1983.

Hartle, Lynn et al. "Outdoor Play: A Window on Social-Cognitive Development." *Dimensions of Early Childhood* 23 (Fall 1994): 27–31.

Haskell, Lendall L. *Art in the Early Childhood Years.* Columbus, OH: Merrill, 1979.

Hatkoff, Amy. "Safety and Children: How Schools Can Help." *Childhood Education* 70 (Annual Theme 1994): 283–288.

Heath, Harriet E. "Dealing with Difficult Behaviors—Teachers Plan with Parents." *Young Children* 49 (July 1994): 20–24.

Henderson, Anne T. "Parents Are a School's Best Friends." *Phi Delta Kappan* 70 (October 1988): 148–153.

Henniger, Michael. "Learning Mathematics and Science through Play." *Childhood Education* 63 (1987): 167–171.

Henniger, Michael L. "Enriching the Outdoor Play Experience." *Childhood Education* 70 (Winter 1993/1994): 87–90.

Henniger, Michael L. "Planning for Outdoor Play." *Young Children* 49 (May 1994): 10–15.

Hennings, Dorothy Grant. "Reading Picture Storybooks in the Social Studies." *Reading Teacher* 35 (December 1982): 284–289.

Herlein, Woodie S. "Teaching Tips for Learning Centers: Providing a Safe and Educational Outdoor Environment." *NHSA Journal* (Summer/Fall 1995): 41–45.

Hernandez, Hilda. *Multicultural Education: A Teacher's Guide to Content and Process.* Columbus, OH: Merrill, 1989.

Herr, Judith, and Winifred Morse. "Food for Thought: Nutrition Education for Young Children." *Young Children* 39 (November 1982): 3–11.

Hester, Hilary. "Peer Interaction in Learning English as a Second Language." *Theory into Practice* 26 (1987): 208–217.

Heyman, Mark. *Places and Spaces: Environmental Psychology in Education.* Fastback no. 112. Bloomington, IN: Phi Delta Kappa Educational Foundation, 1978.

Hill, Bonnie C., and Cynthia Ruptic. *Practical Aspects of Authentic Assessment: Putting the Pieces Together.* Norwood, MA: Christopher-Gordon, 1994.

Hill, Carol B. *Creating a Learning Climate for the Early Childhood Years.* Fastback no. 292. Bloomington, IN: Phi Delta Kappa Educational Foundation, 1989.

Hill, David. "Order in the Classroom." *Teacher Magazine* (April 1990): 70–77.

Hill, Winfred F. *Learning: A Survey of Psychological Interpretations.* 3d ed. New York: Thomas Y. Crowell, 1977.

Hills, Tynette W. "Assessment in Context—Teachers and Children at Work." *Young Children* 48 (July 1993): 20–28.

Hirsch, Elisabeth S., ed. *The Block Book.* Rev. ed. Washington, DC: National Association for the Education of Young Children, 1984.

Hitz, Randy. "Assertive Discipline: A Response to Lee Canter." *Young Children* 43 (January 1988): 25–26.

Hitz, Randy. "Creative Problem Solving through Music Activities." *Young Children* 42 (January 1987): 12–17.

Hoffman, Stevie, and Linda L. Lamme, eds. *Learning from the Inside Out: The Expressive Arts.* Wheaton, MD: Association for Childhood Education, 1989.

Hohmann, Mary, Bernard Banet, and David P. Weikart. *Young Children in Action.* Ypsilanti, MI: High/Scope Press, 1979.

Hohmann, Mary, and David P. Weikart. *Educating Young Children: Active Learning Practices for Preschool and Child Care Programs.* Ypsilanti, MI: High/Scope Educational Research Foundation, 1995.

Holdaway, Don. *The Foundations of Literacy.* Portsmouth, NH: Heinemann, 1980.

Holt, Bess-Gene. *Science with Young Children.* Rev. ed. Washington, DC: National Association for the Education of Young Children, 1989.

Honig, Alice Sterling. "Compliance, Control, and Discipline." *Young Children* 40 (January 1985): 50–58.

Honig, Alice S. "Research in Review: Prosocial Development in Children." *Young Children* 37 (July 1982): 51–62.

Hoot, J. L., and E. T. Bartkowiak. "Safety Resources." *Childhood Education* 70 (Annual Theme 1994), 287–288.

Horn, M., and J. Sieder. "Looking for a Renaissance: The Campaign to Revise Education in the Arts." *U.S. News & World Report* 30 (March 1992): 52–54.

Hough, R. A., J. R. Nurss, and M. S. Goodson. "Children in Day Care: An Observational Study." *Child Study Journal* 14 (1984): 31–46.

Hough, Ruth A., Joanne R. Nurss, and Dolores Wood. "Tell Me a Story: Making Opportunities for Elaborated Language in Early Childhood Classrooms." *Young Children* 43 (1987): 6–12.

Howe, Ann C. "Science in Early Childhood Education." In *Handbook of Research on the Education of Young Children,* edited by B. Spodek, 225–235. New York: Macmillan, 1993.

Hranitz, John R., and E. Anne Eddowes. "Priorities: Parents and the Home." *Childhood Education* 63 (June 1987): 325–330.

Huffman, Amy B. "Beyond the Weather Chart: Weathering New Experiences." *Young Children* 51 (July 1996): 34–37.

Hughes, Fergus P. *Children, Play, and Development.* Boston: Allyn and Bacon, 1995.

Huse, Vanessa E., Nancy L. Bluemel, Rhonda H. Taylor. "Making Connections: From Paper to Pop-Up Books." *Teaching Children Mathematics* 1 (September 1994): 14–17.

Hymes, Dell. *Foundations of Sociolinguistics: An Ethnographic Approach.* Philadelphia: University of Pennsylvania Press, 1974.

Iatridis, Mary. "Teaching Science to Preschoolers." *Science and Children* 19 (October 1981): 25–27.

Ilg, Frances L., and Louise B. Ames. *The Gesell Institute's Child Behavior.* New York: Dell, 1955.

Irwin, D. Michelle, and M. Margaret Bushnell. *Observational Strategies for Child Study.* New York: Holt, Rinehart and Winston, 1980.

Isbell, Rebecca, and Shirley Raines. "Young Children's Oral Language Production in Three Types of Play Centers." *Journal of Research in Childhood Education* 5 (Spring/ Summer 1991): 140–146.

Isenberg, Joan P., and Mary Renck Jalongo. *Creative Expression and Play in the Early Childhood Curriculum.* New York: Macmillan, 1993.

Isenberg, Joan, and Nancy Quisenberry. "Play: A Necessity for All Children." *Childhood Education* 64 (February 1988): 138–145.

Isenberg, Joan P., and Teresa Rosegrant. "Children and Technology." In *Selecting Educational Equipment and Materials for School and Home,* edited by Joan Moyer, 25–29. Wheaton, MD: Association for Childhood Education International, 1995.

Jacobs, Heidi Hayes, ed. *Interdisciplinary Curriculum: Design and Implementation.* Washington, DC: Association for Supervision and Curriculum Development, 1989.

Jaggar, Angela. "Allowing for Language Differences." In *Discovering Language with Children,* edited by Gay Su Pinnell. Urbana, IL: National Council of Teachers of English, 1980.

Jaggar, Angela, and M. Trika Smith-Burke, eds. *Observing the Language Learner.* Newark, DE: International Reading Association/National Council of Teachers of English, 1985.

Jalongo, Mary Renck. "The Child's Right to the Expressive Arts: Nurturing the Imagination as Well as the Intellect. A Position Paper of the Association for Childhood Education International." *Childhood Education* 66 (Summer 1990): 195–201.

Jalongo, Mary R. "Using Recorded Music with Young Children: A Guide for Nonmusicians." *Young Children* 51 (July 1996): 6–13.

Jalongo, Mary Renck. "What Is Happening to Kindergarten?" *Childhood Education* (January 1986): 154–160.

Jalongo, Mary Renck, and Mitzie Collins. "Singing with Young Children! Folk Singing for Nonmusicians." *Young Children* 40 (January 1985): 17–21.

Jaques-Dalcroze, Emile. *Rhythm, Music and Education.* Translated by L. F. Rubenstein. London, England: Hazell Watson and Viney Ltd. for the Dalcroze Society, 1921.

Javernick, Ellen. "Johnny's Not Jumping: Can We Help Obese Children?" *Young Children* 43 (January 1988): 18–23.

Jensen, Mary A. "Story Awareness: A Critical Skill for Early Reading." *Young Children* 41 (November 1985): 20–24.

Johnston, Lynne, and Joy Mermin. "Easing Children's Entry to School: Home Visits Help." *Young Children* 49 (July 1995): 62–68.

Jones, Elizabeth. "Inviting Children into the Fun: Providing Enough Activity Choices Outdoors." *Child Care Information Exchange* 70 (December 1989): 15–19.

Jones, Elizabeth, and John Nimmo. *Emergent Curriculum.* Washington, DC: National Association for the Education of Young Children, 1994.

Jones, Hazel A., and Steven F. Warren. "Enhancing Engagement in Early Language Teaching." *Teaching Exceptional Children* 23 (Summer 1991): 48–50.

Jones, M. Gail "Family Science: A Celebration of Diversity." *Science and Children* 34 (October 1996): 31–33.

Jones, Vernon F., and Louise S. Jones. *Comprehensive Classroom Management: Motivating and Managing Students.* 3d ed. Boston: Allyn and Bacon, 1990.

Jorde, Paula. "Early Childhood Education: Issues and Trends." In *Early Childhood Education in the Schools,* edited by Jerold P. Bauch. Washington, DC: National Education Association, 1988.

Kagan, Sharon L. *When Parents and Schools Come Together: Differential Outcomes of Parent Involvement in Urban Schools.* ERIC Document Reproduction Service 281950. 1982.

Kamii, Constance. *Number in Preschool and Kindergarten.* Washington, DC: National Association for the Education of Young Children, 1982.

Kamii, Constance, and Georgia DeClark. *Young Children Reinvent Arithmetic: Implications of Piaget's Theory.* New York: Teachers College Press, 1985.

Kamii, Constance, and Rheta DeVries. *Group Games in Early Education: Implications of Piaget's Theory.* Washington, DC: National Association for the Education of Young Children, 1980.

Kamii, Constance, and Rheta DeVries. *Physical Knowledge in Preschool Education.* Englewood Cliffs, NJ: Prentice-Hall, 1978.

Kamii, Constance, and Rheta DeVries. *Physical Knowledge in Preschool Education: Implications of Piaget's Theory.* Rev. ed. Englewood Cliffs, NJ: Prentice-Hall, 1993.

Kamii, Constance, and Rheta DeVries. "Piaget for Early Education." In *The Preschool in Action: Exploring Early Childhood Programs,* 2d ed., edited by Mary Carol Day and Ronald K. Parker, 365–420. Boston: Allyn and Bacon, 1977.

Kamii, Constance, and Linda Joseph. "Teaching Place Value and Double-Column Addition." *Arithmetic Teacher* 35 (February 1988): 48–52.

Kamii, Constance, and Linda Leslie Joseph. *Young Children Continue to Reinvent Arithmetic—2nd Grade: Implications of Piaget's Theory.* New York: Teachers College Press, 1989.

Kamii, Constance, and Mieko Kamii. "Why Achievement Testing Should Stop." In *Achievement Testing in the Early Grades: The Games Grown-Ups Play,* edited by Constance Kamii, 15–39. Washington, DC: National Association for the Education of Young Children, 1990.

Karnes, M. B., A. M. Schwedel, and M. B. Williams. "A Comparison of Five Approaches for Educating Young Children from Low-Income Homes." In *As the Twig Is Bent . . . Lasting Effects of Preschool Programs,* edited by Consortium for Longitudinal Studies. Hillsdale, NJ: Lawrence Erlbaum Associates, 1983.

Karr, Jo Ann, and Elizabeth Landerholm. *Reducing Staff Stress/Burnout by Changing Staff Expectations in Dealing with Parents.* ERIC Document Reproduction Service 351128. 1991.

Katims, David S., and Patsy L. Pierce. "Literacy-Rich Environments and the Transition of Young Children with Special Needs." *Topics in Early Childhood Special Education* 15 (Summer 1995): 219–234.

Katz, Lilian. "Engaging Children's Minds: The Implications of Research for Early Childhood Education." In *A Resource Guide to Public School Early Childhood Programs,* edited by Cynthia Warger. Alexandria, VA: Association for Supervision and Curriculum Development, 1988.

Katz, Lilian. Keynote speech. Oregon Association of School Administrators conference of kindergarten teachers and elementary principals, Salem, Oregon, 1986.

Katz, Lilian. *More Talks with Teachers.* Urbana, IL: ERIC Clearinghouse on Elementary and Early Childhood Education, 1984.

Katz, Lilian, and Sylvia C. Chard. *Engaging Children's Minds: The Project Approach.* Norwood, NJ: Ablex, 1989.

Kean, Thomas H. "The 'Imperative' of Arts Education." *Excellence in Teaching* 7 (Winter 1989/90): 4–5.

Kellogg, Rhoda. *Analyzing Children's Art.* Palo Alto, CA: National Press Books, 1970.

Kendall, Frances E. "Creating a Multicultural Environment." *Pre-K Today* (November/December 1988): 34–39.

Kennedy, David K. "After Reggio Emilia: May the Conversation Begin!" *Young Children* 51 (July 1996): 24–27.

Kent, Judith F., and Jennie Rakestraw. "The Role of Computers in Functional Language: A Tale of Two Writers." *Journal of Computing in Childhood Education* 5(1994): 329–337.

Kieff, Judith. "Preferences of Mothers of At Risk and Peer Model Children for Parent Involvement Strategies." Doctoral dissertation, Oregon State University, 1990.

Kilmer, Sally J., and Helenmarie Hofman. "Transforming Science Curriculum." In *Reaching Potentials: Transforming Early Childhood Curriculum and Assessment,* vol. 2, edited by S. Bredekamp and T. Rosegrant, 43–63. Washington, DC: National Association for the Education of Young Children, 1995.

King, Martha L. "Language: Insights from Acquisition." *Theory Into Practice* 26 (1987): 358–363.

Kingsbury, Nancy M., and Joan C. Hall. "Provision of a Health Education Program for Preschoolers: A Demonstration Project Using Volunteers." *Early Child Development and Care* 36 (July 1988): 91–100.

Klesius, Janell P., and Priscilla L. Griffith. "Interactive Storybook Reading for At-Risk Learners." *Reading Teacher* 49 (April 1996): 552–590.

Kokoski, Teresa M., and Nancy Downing-Leffler. "Boosting Your Science and Math Programs in Early Childhood Education: Making the Home-School Connection." *Young Children* 50 (July 1995): 35–39.

Koste, Virginia G. *Dramatic Play in Childhood: Rehearsal for Life.* Lanham, MD: University Press of America, 1987.

Kostelnik, Marjorie, Laura Stein, Alice P. Whiren, and Anne K. Soderman. *Guiding Children's Social Development.* 2d ed. Albany, NY: Delmar, 1993.

Kostelnik, Marjorie, Alice P. Whiren, and Laura Stein. "Living with He-Man: Managing Superhero Fantasy Play." *Young Children* 41 (1986): 3–9.

Krashen, Stephen D. *Second Language Acquisition and Second Language Learning.* New York: Pergamon Press, 1981.

Kritchevsky, Sybil, and Elizabeth Prescott. *Planning Environments for Young Children: Physical Space.* Washington, DC: National Association for the Education of Young Children, 1969.

Kuehn, Christine. "Inventing: Creative Sciencing." *Childhood Education* 65 (Fall 1988): 5–7.

Labinowicz, Ed. *Learning from Children: New Beginnings for Teaching Numerical Thinking.* Menlo Park, CA: Addison-Wesley, 1985.

Labinowicz, Ed. *The Piaget Primer: Thinking, Learning, Teaching.* Menlo Park, CA: Addison-Wesley, 1980.

Labov, W. "The Logic of Non-Standard English." In *Language and Poverty,* edited by F. Williams. Chicago: Markham, 1970.

Laminack, Lester. "Mr. T Leads the Class: The Language Experience Approach and Science." *Science and Children* (February 1987): 41–42.

Lasky, E. Z., and K. Klopp. "Parent-Child Interactions in Normal and Language-Disordered Children." *Journal of Speech and Hearing Disorders* 47 (1982): 7–18.

Lasky, Lila, and Rose Mukerji. *Art: Basic for Young Children.* Washington, DC: National Association for the Education of Young Children, 1980.

Lazdauskas, Heidi. "Music Makes the School Go 'Round." *Young Children* 51 (July 1996): 22–23.

Leatzow, Nancy, Carol Neuhauser, and Liz Wilmes. *Creating Discipline in the Early Childhood Classroom.* Provo, UT: Brigham Young University Press, 1983.

Lee, Fong Yun. "Asian Parents as Partners." *Young Children* 50 (March 1995): 4–8.

Lehman, Jeffrey R. "Measure Up to Science." *Science and Children* 31 (February 1994): 30–31.

Leik, Robert K., and Mary Anne Chalkey. "Parent Involvement: What Is It That Works?" *Children Today* (May–June 1990): 34–37.

Leitch, M. Laurie, and Sandra S. Tangri. "Barriers to Home-School Collaboration." *Educational Horizons* 66 (Winter 1988): 70–74.

Leppo, Marjorie L. *Healthy from the Start: New Perspectives on Childhood Fitness.* Teacher Education Monograph 15. ERIC Document Reproduction Service 352357. 1993.

Levin, Diane E., and Nancy Carlsson-Paige. "The Mighty Morphin Power Rangers: Teachers Voice Concern." *Young Children* 50 (September 1995): 67–72.

Levin, I., F. Wilkening, and Y. Dembo. "Development of Time Quantification: Integration of Beginnings and Endings in Comparing Durations." *Child Development* 55 (1984): 2160–2172.

Lillard, Paula P. *Montessori: A Modern Approach.* New York: Schocken Books, 1972.

Lindfors, Judith Wells. *Children's Language and Learning.* Englewood Cliffs, NJ: Prentice-Hall, 1980.

Love, Ida H., and Daniel Levine. *Performance Ratings of Teacher Aides with and without Training and Follow-Up in Extending Reading Instruction.* ERIC Document Reproduction Service 349294, 1992.

Lowenfeld, Viktor, and W. Lambert Brittain. *Creative and Mental Growth.* 7th ed. New York: Macmillan, 1982.

Lowenthal, Barbara. (1996). "Teaching Social Skills to Preschoolers with Special Needs." *Childhood Education* 72 (Spring 1996): 137–140.

Luke, Jennifer L., and Catherine M. Myers. "Toward Peace: Using Literature to Aid Conflict Resolution." *Childhood Education* 71 (Winter 1994/1995): 66–69.

Lund, Kathryn A., and Candace S. Bos. "Orchestrating the Preschool Classroom: The Daily Schedule." *Teaching Exceptional Children* 14 (December 1981): 120–125.

Lunzer, E. "Intellectual Development in the Play of Young Children." *Educational Review* 11 (1959): 205–217.

McCarthy, Jan. "Reggio Emilia: What Is the Message for Early Childhood Education?" *Contemporary Education* 66 (Spring 1995): 139–142.

McClintic, Susan V. "Conservation—A Meaningful Gauge for Assessment." *Arithmetic Teacher* 35 (February 1988): 12–14.

McCracken, Janet Brown. *More Than 1, 2, 3—The Real Basics of Mathematics.* Washington, DC: National Association for the Education of Young Children, 1987.

McCracken, Janet B. *Valuing Diversity: The Primary Years.* Washington, DC: National Association for the Education of Young Children, 1993.

McDonald, Dorothy T. *Music in Our Lives: The Early Years.* Washington, DC: National Association for the Education of Young Children, 1979.

McDonald, Dorothy T., and Gene M. Simons. *Musical Growth and Development: Birth through Six.* New York: Schirmer Books, 1989.

McGregor, Lynn, Maggie Tate, and Ken Robinson. *Learning through Drama.* Portsmouth, NH: Heinemann, 1987.

McIntyre, Margaret. *Early Childhood and Science.* Washington, DC: National Science Teachers Association, 1984.

McKenna, Michael C., and Dennis J. Kear. "Measuring Attitude toward Reading: A New Tool for Teachers." *Reading Teacher* 43 (May 1990): 626–639.

McNairy, Marion R. "Sciencing: Science Education for Early Childhood." *School Science and Mathematics* 85 (May/June 1985): 383–393.

McNeill, David. "Developmental Psycholinguistics." In *The Genesis of Language,* edited by Frank Smith and George Miller. Cambridge, MA: MIT Press, 1966.

Malaguzzi, Loris. "For an Education Based on Relationships." *Young Children* 49 (November 1993): 9–12.

Malina, R. M. "Motor Development in the Early Years." In *The Young Child: Reviews of Research,* vol. 3, edited by S. G. Moore and C. R. Cooper, 11–229. Washington, DC: National Association for the Education of Young Children, 1982.

Malkus, Ulla C., David Feldman, and Howard Gardner. "Dimensions of Mind in Early Childhood." In *Psychological Bases for Early Education,* edited by A. D. Pellegrini. New York: John Wiley and Sons, 1988.

Marantz, Mady. "Fostering Prosocial Behavior in the Early Childhood Classroom: Review of the

Research." *Journal of Moral Education* 17 (January 1988): 27–39.

Marchand, Nancy E., and Robert J. McDermott. "'Mouse Calls': A Storytelling Approach to Teaching First Aid Skills to Young Children." *Journal of School Health* 56 (December 1986): 453–454.

Marshall, Hermine H. "The Development of Self-Concept." *Young Children* 44 (July 1989): 44–51.

Martin, Anne. "Teachers and Teaching." *Harvard Educational Review* 58 (November 1988): 488–501.

Martin, Bill, Jr. "Celebrating Language." Seminar sponsored by the School of Education, Oregon State University, Corvallis, Oregon, Summer 1986.

Martin, Sue. *Developmentally Appropriate Evaluation: Convincing Students and Teachers of the Importance of Observation as Appropriate Evaluation of Children.* ERIC Document Reproduction Service 391601. 1996.

Marxen, Carol E. "Push, Pull, Toss, Tilt, Swing: Physics for Young Children." *Childhood Education* 71 (Summer 1995): 212–216.

Mason, Jana M., and Shobha Sinha. "Emerging Literacy in the Early Childhood Years: Applying a Vygotskian Model of Learning and Development." In *Handbook of Research on the Education of Young Children,* edited by B. Spodek, 137–150. New York: Macmillan, 1993.

Masselli, David et al. "Aggressive Behavior of the Preschool Child." *Education* 104 (Summer 1984): 385–388.

Meisels, Samuel J. "High-Stakes Testing in Kindergarten." *Educational Leadership* 47 (April 1989): 16–22.

Meisels, Samuel J. "Remaking Classroom Assessment with the Work Sampling System." *Young Children* 48 (July 1993): 34–40.

Meisels, Samuel J. "Uses and Abuses of Developmental Screening and School Readiness Testing." *Young Children* 42 (January 1987): 4–6, 68–73.

Meisels, Samuel J., Fong-Ruey Liaw, Aviva Dorfman, and Regena F. Nelson. "The Work Sampling System: Reliability and Validity of a Performance Assessment for Young Children." *Early Childhood Research Quarterly* 10 (1995): 277–296.

Merrion, Margaret Dee, and Marilyn Curt Vincent. *A Primer on Music for Non-Musician Educators.* Fastback 270. Bloomington, IN: Phi Delta Kappa Educational Foundation, 1988.

Miller, Cheri Sterman. "Building Self-Control: Discipline for Young Children." *Young Children* 40 (November 1984): 15–19.

Miller, S. "The Facilitation of Fundamental Motor Skill Learning in Young Children." Doctoral dissertation. East Lansing, MI: Michigan State University, 1978.

Mitchell, Anne, and Judy David. *Explorations with Young Children: A Curriculum Guide from the Bank Street College of Education.* Mt. Rainier, MD: Gryphon, 1992.

Mitchell, Lucy S. "Making Young Geographers Instead of Teaching Geography." *Progressive Education* 5 (July/August/September 1928): 217–223.

Monroe, Eula E., and Robert Panchyshyn. "Vocabulary Considerations for Teaching Mathematics." *Childhood Education* 72 (Winter 1994/1995): 80–83.

Montessori, Maria. *Dr. Montessori's Own Handbook.* New York: Frederick A. Stokes, 1914.

Mooney, Margaret E. *Reading to, with, and by Children.* Katonah, NY: Richard C. Owen, 1990.

Morrow, Lesley M., and Muriel K. Rand. "Promoting Literacy During Play by Designing Early Childhood Classroom Environments." *Reading Teacher* 44 (February 1991): 396–402.

Murray, Paula L., and Richard E. Mayer. "Preschool Children's Judgments of Number Magnitude." *Journal of Educational Psychology* 80 (June 1988): 206–209.

Myhre, Susan. "Enhancing Your Dramatic-Play Area through the Use of Prop Boxes." *Young Children* 48 (July 1993): 6–11.

National Association for the Education of Young Children. *Accreditation Criteria and Procedures of the National Academy of Early Childhood Programs.* Washington, DC: NAEYC, 1984.

National Association for the Education of Young Children. "Educating Yourself about Diverse Cultural Groups in Our Country by Reading." *Young Children* 48 (March 1993): 13–16.

National Association for the Education of Young Children. *Helping Children Learn Self-Control.* Washington, DC: NAEYC, 1986.

National Association for the Education of Young Children. "NAEYC Position Statement: Technology and Young Children—Ages Three through Eight." *Young Children* 51 (September 1996): 11–16.

National Association for the Education of Young Children. "NAEYC Position Statement on Standardized Testing of Young Children 3 through 8 Years of Age." *Young Children* 43 (March 1988): 42–47.

National Association for the Education of Young Children. *Testing of Young Children: Concerns and Cautions.* NAEYC Brochure 582. Washington, DC: NAEYC, 1989.

National Association of State Boards of Education. *Right from the Start: The Report of the NASBE Task Force on Early Childhood Education.* Alexandria, VA: NASBE, 1988.

National Council for Accreditation of Teacher Education. *NCATE Standards, Procedures, and Policies for the Accreditation of Professional Units.* Washington, DC: NCATE, 1987.

National Council of Teachers of Mathematics. *Curriculum and Evaluation Standards for School Mathematics.* Washington, DC: NCTM, 1989.

National Council of Teachers of Mathematics. *Kindergarten Book.* Addenda series, grades K–6. Reston, VA: NCTM, 1991.

National Council of Teachers of Mathematics. *Professional Standards for Teaching Mathematics.* Reston, VA: NCTM, 1991.

National Council of Social Studies Task Force on Early Childhood/Elementary Social Studies. "Social Studies for Early Childhood and Elementary School Children: Preparing for the 21st Century." *Social Education* 53 (January 1989): 14–23.

National Education Association. "Resolution C-27." *National Education Today* 9 (September 1990): 17.

Neisworth, John T., and Thomas J. Buggey. "Behavior Analysis and Principles in Early Childhood Education." In *Approaches to Early Childhood Education,* 2d ed., edited by Jaipaul Roopnarine and James E. Johnson. New York: Macmillan, 1993.

Nelson, Katherine. "Structure and Strategy in Learning to Talk." *Monographs of the Society for Research in Child Development* 38 (1973): 149.

Neuman, Susan B., and Kathy Roskos. "Bridging Home and School with a Culturally Responsive Approach." *Childhood Education* 70 (Summer 1994): 210–214.

Neuman, Susan B., and Kathleen A. Roskos. *Language and Literacy Learning in the Early Years.* Fort Worth, TX: Harcourt Brace Jovanovich, 1993.

New, Rebecca. "Excellent Early Education: A City in Italy Has It." *Young Children* 45 (September 1990): 4–10.

Oken-Wright, Pamela. "Show and Tell Grows Up." *Young Children* 43 (1988): 52–58.

Olson, Lynn. "Parents as Partners: Redefining the Social Contract between Families and Schools." *Education Week* 9 (April 4 1990): 17–24.

Omwake, Eveline B. "We Know So Much—We Know So Little." In *The Significance of the Young Child's Motor Development,* edited by Georgianna Engstrom. Washington, DC: National Association for the Education of Young Children, 1971.

Pagni, David. "You're Never Too Old (or Too Young) to Use a Calculator." *Elementary Mathematician* 1 (December 1987): 10–11.

Pangrazi, Robert P., and Victor P. Dauer. *Dynamic Physical Education for Elementary School Children.* 10th ed. New York: Macmillan, 1992.

Pangrazi, Robert P., and Victor P. Dauer. *Movement in Early Childhood and Primary Education.* Minneapolis, MN: Burgess, 1981.

Parette, Howard P., Jr., Nancy S. Dunn, and Debra R. Hoge. "Low-Cost Communication Devices for Children with Disabilities and Their Family Members." *Young Children* 50 (September 1995): 75–81.

Parker, Emelie L. et al. "Teachers' Choices in Classroom Assessment." *Reading Teacher* 48 (April 1995): 622–624.

Parten, Mildred B. "Social Participation among Preschool Children." *Journal of Abnormal and Social Psychology* 27 (July/September 1932): 243–269.

Patton, Mary M., and Teresa M. Kokoski. "How Good Is Your Early Childhood Science, Mathematics, and Technology Program? Strategies for Extending Your Curriculum." *Young Children* 51 (July 1996): 38–44.

Paulson, F. Leon, Pearl R. Paulson, and Carol A. Meyer. "What Makes a Portfolio a Portfolio?" *Educational Leadership* 48 (February 1991): 60–63.

Pearlman, Susan, and Kathy Pericak-Spector. "A Series of Seriation Activities." *Science and Children* 31 (January 1994): 37–39.

Peck, Charles A., Tony Apolloni, Thomas P. Cooke, and Sharon A. Raver. "Teaching Retarded Preschoolers to Imitate the Free-Play Behavior of Nonretarded Classmates: Trained and Generalized Effects." *Journal of Special Education* 12 (Summer 1978): 195–207.

Pellegrini, Anthony D. *Applied Child Study: A Developmental Approach.* Hillsdale, NJ: Lawrence Erlbaum Associates, 1987.

Pellegrini, Anthony D. "The Relationship between Kindergartners' Play and Achievement in Prereading, Language and Writing." *Psychology in the Schools* 17 (October 1980): 530–535.

Pellegrini, Anthony D., and Brenda Boyd. "The Role of Play in Early Childhood Development and Education: Issues in Definitions and Function." In *Handbook of Research on the Education of Young Children,* edited by Bernard Spodek, 105–121. New York: Macmillan, 1993.

Perlmutter, Jane C., and Louise Burrell. "Learning through 'Play' as Well as 'Work' in the Primary Grades." *Young Children* 50 (July 1995): 14–21.

Perrone, Vito. "How Did We Get Here?" In *Achievement Testing in the Early Grades: The Games Grown-Ups Play,* edited by Constance Kamii, 1–14. Washington, DC: National Association for the Education of Young Children, 1990.

Perry, Gail, and Mary Rivkin. "Teachers and Science." *Young Children* 47 (May 1992): 9–16.

Pestalozzi, Johann Heinrich. *How Gertrude Teaches Her Children.* Translated by Lucy E. Holland and Francis C. Turner. Syracuse, NY: C. W. Bardeen, 1894.

Pestalozzi, Johann Heinrich. *Leonard and Gertrude.* Translated and abridged by Eva Channing. Boston: D. C. Heath, 1885.

Petersen, Susan C. "The Sequence of Instruction in Games: Implications for Developmental Appropriateness." *Journal of Physical Education, Recreation and Dance* 63 (August 1992): 36–39.

Phillips, Carol Brunson. "Nurturing Diversity for Today's Children and Tomorrow's Leaders." *Young Children* 43 (January 1988): 42–47.

Phyfe-Perkins, Elizabeth. "Children's Behavior in Preschool Settings: A Review of Research Concerning the Influence of the Physical Environment." In *Current Topics in Early Childhood Education,* vol. 3, edited by L. Katz et al. Norwood, NJ: Ablex, 1980.

Piaget, Jean. *The Child's Conception of Number.* London: Routledge and Kegan Paul, 1952.

Piaget, Jean. "Development and Learning." In *Piaget Rediscovered,* edited by R. Ripple and V. Rockcastle. Ithaca, NY: Cornell University Press, 1964.

Piaget, Jean. *The Equilibration of Cognitive Structures: The Central Problem of Intellectual Development.* Chicago: University of Chicago Press, 1985.

Piaget, Jean. *The Language and Thought of the Child.* 3d ed. London: Routledge and Kegan Paul, 1959.

Piaget, Jean. *The Origins of Intelligence in Children.* New York: International Universities Press, 1952.

Piaget, Jean. *Play, Dreams and Imitation in Childhood.* New York: W. W. Norton, 1962.

Piaget, Jean. *Science of Education and the Psychology of the Child.* New York: Orion Press, 1970.

Piaget, Jean, and Barbel Inhelder. *The Psychology of the Child.* Translated by Helen Weaver. New York: Basic Books, 1969.

Pickett, Anna L. et al. *Promoting Effective Communications with Paraeducators.* ERIC Document Reproduction Service 357586. 1993.

Pickle, Barbara. *Increasing Safety Awareness of Preschoolers through a Safety Education Program.* ERIC Document Reproduction Service 310880. 1989.

Piper, Terry. *Language for All Our Children.* New York: Merrill, 1993.

Potts, R., A. C. Huston, and J. C. Wright. "The Effects of Television Form and Violent Content on Boys' Attention and Social Behavior." *Journal of Experimental Child Psychology* 41 (1986): 1–17.

Prescott, Elizabeth, Elizabeth Jones, and Sybil Kritchevsky. *Group Day Care as a Child-Rearing Environment.* Washington, DC: Children's Bureau, Social Security Administration, Department of Health, Education and Welfare, 1967.

Price, Gary Glen. "Research in Review: Mathematics in Early Childhood." *Young Children* 44 (May 1989): 53–58.

"Prickly Problems #3: Parent Communications." *Child Care Information Exchange* 65 (February 1989): 15.

Ramsey, Patricia G. "Beyond 'Ten Little Indians' and Turkeys: Alternative Approaches to Thanksgiving." *Young Children* 34 (1979): 28–32, 49–52.

Ramsey, Patricia G. *Teaching and Learning in a Diverse World: Multicultural Education for Young Children.* New York: Teachers College Press, 1987.

Ransbury, Molly Kayes. "Friedrich Froebel 1782–1982: A Reexamination of Froebel's Principles of Childhood Learning." *Childhood Education* 59 (November–December 1982): 101–105.

Raper, George, and John Stringer. *Encouraging Primary Science: An Introduction to the Development of Science in Primary Schools.* London: Cassell, 1987.

Readdick, Christine A., and Patricia Bartlett. "Vertical Learning Environments." *Childhood Education* 71 (Winter 1994/1995): 86–90.

Reardon, S. Jeanne. "A Collage of Assessment and Evaluation from Primary Classrooms." In *Assessment and Evaluation in Whole Language Programs,* edited by Bill Harp. Boston: Christopher-Gordon, 1991.

Reifel, Stuart, and June Yeatman. "From Category to Context: Reconsidering Classroom Play." *Early Childhood Research Quarterly* 8 (1993): 347–367.

Rettig, Michael. "The Play of Young Children with Visual Impairments: Characteristics and Interventions." *Journal of Visual Impairment and Blindness* 88 (September–October 1994): 410–420.

Reutzel, D. Ray. "Breaking the Letter-a-Week Tradition." *Childhood Education* 69 (Fall 1992): 20–23.

Richards. Leah. "Measuring Things in Words: Language for Learning Mathematics." *Language Arts* 67 (January 1990): 14–25.

Richards, Mary Helen. *Mary Helen Richards Teaches: The Child in Depth.* Portola Valley, CA: Richards Institute of Music Education and Research, 1969.

Richardson, Kathy. "Assessing Understanding." *Arithmetic Teacher* 35 (February 1988): 39–41.

Richardson, Kathy, and Leslie Salkeld. "Transforming Mathematics Curriculum." In *Reaching Potentials: Transforming Early Childhood Curriculum,* edited by S. Bredekamp and T. Rosegrant, 23–42. Washington, DC: National Association for the Education of Young Children, 1995.

Richgels, Donald J., Karla J. Poremba, and Lea M. McGee. "Kindergarteners Talk about Print: Phonemic Awareness in Meaningful Contexts." *Reading Teacher* 49 (May 1996): 632–642.

Roeper, Annemarie. "Play and Gifted Children." In *Play as a Medium for Learning and Development,* edited by D. Bergen, 163–165. Portsmouth, NH: Heinemann, 1987.

Roff, Merrill, and S. B. Sells. "Juvenile Delinquency in Relation to Peer Acceptance-Rejection and Socioeconomic Status." *Psychology in the Schools* 5 (January 1968): 3–18.

Roff, Merrill, S. B. Sells, and M. M. Golden. *Social Adjustment and Personality Development in Children.* Minneapolis: University of Minnesota Press, 1972.

Rogers, Cosby S., and Sandra S. Morris. "Reducing Sugar in Children's Diets: Why? How?" *Young Children* 41 (July 1986): 11–16.

Rogers, Dwight L., and Dorene D. Ross. "Encouraging Positive Social Interaction among Young Children." *Young Children* 41 (March 1986): 12–17.

Rogers, Fred, and Hedda B. Sharapan. "Helping Parents, Teachers, and Caregivers Deal with Children's Concerns about War." *Young Children* 46 (March 1991): 12–13.

Rollins, Pamela R., Barbara A. Pan, Gina Conti-Ramsden, and Catherine E. Snow. "Communicative Skills in Children with Specific Language Impairments: A Comparison with Their Language-Matched Siblings." *Journal of Communication Disorders* 27 (June 1994): 189–206.

Roopnarine, Jaipaul, and Alice S. Honig. "Research in Review: The Unpopular Child." *Young Children* 40 (September 1985): 59–64.

Roopnarine, Jaipaul, and James E. Johnson, eds. *Approaches to Early Childhood Education.* 2d ed. New York: Macmillan, 1993.

Rosenthal, David M., and Julanne Y. Sawyers. "Building Successful Home/School Partnerships: Strategies for Parent Support and Involvement." *Childhood Education* 72 (Summer 1996): 194–200.

Ross, James G., and Russell R. Pate. "The National Children and Youth Study II: A Summary of Findings." *Journal of Physical Education, Recreation and Dance* 58 (November/December 1987): 51–56.

Roswal, Glenn, and Greg H. Frith. "The Children's Developmental Play Program: Physical Activity Designed to Facilitate the Growth and Development of Mildly Handicapped Children." *Education and Training of the Mentally Retarded* 15 (December 1980): 322–324.

Rothlein, Liz. "Nutrition Tips Revisited: On a Daily Basis Do We Implement What We Know?" *Young Children* 44 (September 1989): 30–36.

Rousseau, Jean-Jacques. *Emile.* Translated by Barbara Foxley. 1780. Reprint, New York: E. P. Dutton, 1950.

Routman, Regie, and Andrea Butler. "Why Talk about Phonics?" *School Talk* 1 (November 1995).

Rubin, K., G. Fein, and B. Vanderberg. "Play." In *Carmichael's Manual of Child Psychology: Social Development,* edited by E. Hetherington. New York: Wiley, 1983.

Ruiz, Nadeen T. "A Young Deaf Child Learns to Write: Implications for Literacy Development." *Reading Teacher* 49 (November 1995): 206–217.

Safford, Phillip L. *Integrated Teaching in Early Childhood: Starting in the Mainstream.* White Plains, NY: Longman, 1989.

Samaras, Anastasia. "Children's Computers." *Childhood Education* 72 (Spring 1996): 133–136.

Saracho, Olivia N., and Bernard Spodek, eds. *Understanding the Multicultural Experience in Early Childhood Education.* Washington, DC: National Association for the Education of Young Children, 1983.

Schickedanz, Judith. "Helping Children Develop Self-Control." *Childhood Education* 70 (Annual Theme 1994): 274–278.

Schickedanz, Judith. "Views of Literacy Development: Then and Now." Paper presented at the annual conference of the National Association for the Education of Young Children, Anaheim, CA, 1988.

Schickedanz, J. A., D. I. Schickedanz, and P. D. Forsyth. *Toward Understanding Children.* Boston: Little, Brown, 1982.

Schiller, Marjorie. "An Emergent Art Curriculum That Fosters Understanding." *Young Children* 50 (March 1995): 33–38.

Schiller, Pam, and Joan Townsend. "Early Childhood: Science All Day Long: An Integrated Approach." *Science and Children* 23 (October 1985): 34–36.

Schirrmacher, Robert. "Talking with Young Children about Their Art." *Young Children* 41 (July 1986): 3–7.

Schmidt, Patricia R. "Working and Playing with Others: Cultural Conflict in a Kindergarten Literacy Program." *Reading Teacher* 48 (February 1995): 404–412.

Schreiber, Mary E. "Lighting Alternatives: Considerations for Child Care Centers." *Young Children* 51 (May 1996): 11–13.

Schwartz, Sydney L. "Authentic Mathematics in the Classroom." *Teaching Children Mathematics* 1 (May 1995): 580–584.

Schwartz, Sydney L. "Calendar Reading: A Tradition That Begs Remodeling." *Teaching Children Mathematics* 1 (October 1994): 104–109.

Schwartz, Sydney, and Helen F. Robison. *Designing Curriculum for Early Childhood.* Boston: Allyn and Bacon, 1982.

Schweinhart, Lawrence J. "Observing Young Children in Action: The Key to Early Childhood Assessment. *Young Children* 48 (July 1993): 29–33.

Schweinhart, L. J., D. P. Weikart, and M. B. Larner. "Consequences of Three Preschool Curriculum Models through Age 15." *Early Childhood Research Quarterly* 1 (1986): 15–46.

Scott, Deborah, Brenda Williams, and Kathy Hyslip. "Mathematics as Communication." *Childhood Education* 69 (Fall 1992): 15–18.

Sears, N. C., and L. L. Medearis. "Educating Teachers for Family Involvement with Young Native Americans." Manuscript, East Central University, Ada, OK.

Sears, R. "Relation of Early Socialization Experiences to Self-Concepts and Gender Role in Middle Childhood." *Child Development* 41 (1970): 267–289.

Sears, Sue, Cathy Carpenter, and Nancy Burstein. "Meaningful Reading Instruction for Learners with Special Needs." *Reading Teacher* 47 (August 1994): 632–638.

Seefeldt, Carol. "Art—A Serious Work." *Young Children* 50 (March 1995a): 39–45.

Seefeldt, Carol. "Transforming Curriculum in Social Studies." In *Reaching Potentials: Transforming Curriculum and Assessment,* vol. 2, edited by S. Bredekamp and T. Rosegrant. Washington, DC: National Association for the Education of Young Children, 1995b.

Seefeldt, Vern. "Physical Fitness in Preschool and Elementary School-Aged Children." *Journal of Physical Education, Recreation and Dance* 55 (November/December 1984): 33–37.

Sgroi, Laura A. et al. "Assessing Young Children's Mathematical Understandings." *Teaching Children Mathematics* 1 (January 1995): 275–277.

Shade, Daniel D. "Appropriate Use of Computers with Young Children." Paper presented at the NAEYC National Institute for Early Childhood Professional Development, Minneapolis, MN, 1996.

Shedler, Jonathan, and Jack Block. "Adolescent Drug Use and Psychological Health: A Longitudinal Inquiry." *American Psychologist* 45 (May 1990): 612–630.

Shepard, Lorrie A. "The Challenges of Assessing Young Children Appropriately." *Phi Delta Kappan* 76 (November 1994): 206–212.

Shuy, Roger. "Language as a Foundation for Education: The School Context." *Theory Into Practice* 26 (1987): 166–174.

Shriver, Mark D., and Jack J. Kramer. "Parent Involvement in an Early Childhood Special Education Program: A Descriptive Analysis of Parent Demographics and Level of Involvement." *Psychology in the Schools* 30 (July 1993): 255–263.

Sigman, Marian, and Rhonda Sena. "Pretend Play in High-Risk and Developmentally Delayed Children." *New Directions in Child Development* 59 (Spring 1993): 29-42.

Skeen, Patsy, and Diane Hodson. "AIDS: What Adults Should Know about AIDS (and Shouldn't Discuss with Very Young Children)." *Young Children* 42 (July 1987): 65–71.

Smilansky, Sara. "Can Adults Facilitate Play in Children? Theoretical and Practical Considerations." In *Play: The Child Strives toward Self-Realization*, edited by G. Engstrom, 39–50. Washington, DC: National Association for the Education of Young Children, 1971.

Smith, Karen Clark. "Strand Model." Oregon State University, Corvallis, OR, 1988.

Smith, Robert F. "Early Childhood Science Education: A Piagetian Perspective." *Young Children* 35 (January 1981): 3–10.

Smith, Robert F. "Theoretical Framework for Preschool Science Experiences." *Young Children* 42 (January 1987): 34–40.

Sorohan, Erica G. "Playgrounds Are Us." *Executive Educator* (August 1995): 28–32.

Spidel, Jo. "Working with Parents of the Exceptional Child." In *Parents as Partners in Education*, 2d ed., edited by Eugenia Hepworth Berger. Columbus, OH: Merrill, 1987.

Spodek, Bernard. *Early Childhood Education.* Englewood Cliffs, NJ: Prentice-Hall, 1973.

Spodek, Bernard, Olivia N. Saracho, and Michael D. Davis. *Foundations of Early Childhood Education: Teaching Three-, Four-, and Five-Year-Olds.* Englewood Cliffs, NJ: Prentice-Hall, 1987.

Sprung, Barbara. "Physics Is Fun, Physics Is Important, and Physics Belongs in the Early Childhood Curriculum." *Young Children* 51 (July 1996): 29–33.

Standing, E. M. *Maria Montessori: Her Life and Work.* New York: Academy Guild Press, 1957.

Standing, E. M. *The Montessori Method: A Revolution in Education.* Fresno, CA: Academy Library Guild, 1962.

Steinfels, Margaret O'Brien. *Who's Minding the Children? The History and Politics of Day Care in America.* New

York: Simon and Schuster, 1973 (as quoted in Grubb 1989).

Stewart, Janice P. "Teacher-Mediated Learning for Young Readers: Successful Strategies with Predictable Book Reading." *Reading Horizons* 36, no. 2 (1995): 131–147.

Stipek, Deborah, Linda Rosenblatt, and Laurine DiRocco. "Making Parents Your Allies." *Young Children* 49 (March 1994): 4–9.

Stone, Janet I. "Early Childhood Math: Make It Manipulative." *Young Children* 42 (September 1987): 16–23.

Stone, Sandra J. "Integrating Play into the Curriculum." *Childhood Education* 72 (Winter 1995/1996): 104–107.

Stone, Sandra. "Portfolios: Interactive and Dynamic Instructional Tool." *Childhood Education* 71 (Summer 1995a): 232–234.

Stone, Sandra J. *Understanding Portfolio Assessment: A Guide for Parents.* Wheaton, MD: Association for Childhood Education International, 1995b.

Stoner, Sue, and Karyn Purcell. "The Concurrent Validity of Teachers' Judgments of the Abilities of Preschoolers in a Daycare Setting." *Educational and Psychological Measurement* 45 (Summer 1985): 109–116.

Sullivan, Molly. *Feeling Strong, Feeling Free: Movement Exploration for Young Children.* Washington, DC: National Association for the Education of Young Children, 1982.

Suthers, Louie. "Introducing Young Children to Live Orchestral Performance." *Early Child Development and Care* 90 (May 1993): 55–64.

Sutton-Smith, Brian. "The Spirit of Play." In *The Young Child at Play: Reviews of Research*, vol. 4, edited by Greta Fein and Mary Rivkin, 3–13. Washington, DC: National Association for the Education of Young Children, 1986.

Sutton-Smith, Brian. "The Struggle between Sacred Play and Festive Play." In *Play as a Medium for Learning and Development,* edited by Doris Bergen. Portsmouth, NH: Heinemann, 1988.

Swick, Kevin J. "Family Involvement: An Empowerment Perspective." *Dimensions of Early Childhood* 22 (Winter 1994): 10–13.

Swick, Kevin J., Gloria Boutte, and Irma Van Scoy. "Families and Schools Building Multicultural Values Together." *Childhood Education* 70 (Winter 1995/1996): 75–79.

Swick, Kevin J., and Shirley McKnight. "Characteristics of Kindergarten Teachers Who Promote Parent Involvement." *Early Childhood Research Quarterly* 4 (March 1989): 19–29.

Swick, Kevin J. et al. *Family Involvement in Early Multicultural Learning.* ERIC Document Reproduction Service 380240. 1995.

Sylva, Kathy, Jerome S. Bruner, and Paul Genova. "The Role of Play in the Problem-Solving of Children 3–5 Years Old." In *Play: Its Role in Development and Evo-*

lution, edited by Jerome S. Bruner, Alison Jolly, and Kathy Sylva, 244–257. New York: Basic Books, 1976.

Systems Development Corporation. *Effects of Different Head Start Program Approaches on Children of Different Characteristics: Report on Analysis of Data from 1968–69 National Evaluation.* Washington, DC: U.S. Office of Child Development, 1972.

Tatum, Pam S. *Promoting Wellness: A Nutrition, Health, and Safety Manual for Family Child Care Providers.* Atlanta, GA: Save the Children, 1994.

Taylor, Anne P., and George Vlastos. *School Zone: Learning Environments for Children.* New York: Van Nostrand Reinhold, 1983.

Taylor, Judy. "How I Learned to Look at a First-Grader's Writing Progress Instead of His Deficiencies." *Young Children* 51 (January 1996): 38–42.

Teale, W. H. "Developmentally Appropriate Assessment of Reading and Writing in the Early Childhood Classroom." *Elementary School Journal* 89 (February 1988): 173–184.

Temple, Charles A., Ruth G. Nathan, Frances Temple, and Nancy A. Burris. *The Beginnings of Writing.* 3d ed. Boston: Allyn and Bacon, 1993.

Thomas, A., and S. Chess. *Temperament and Development.* New York: Brunner/Mazel, 1977.

Thomson, Barbara James. "Building Tolerance in Early Childhood." *Educational Leadership* 47 (October 1989): 78–79.

Thomson, Barbara J. "This Is Like That Martin Luther King Guy." *Young Children* 48 (January 1993): 46–48.

Thurlow, Martha L., Patrick J. O'Sullivan, and James E. Ysseldyke. "Early Screening for Special Education: How Accurate?" *Educational Leadership* 44 (November 1986): 93–95.

Timberlake, Pat. "Classroom Holidaze." *Childhood Education* (January 1978): 128–130.

Tischler, Rosamund W. "Mathematics from Children's Literature." *Arithmetic Teacher* 35 (February 1988): 42–47.

Tracy, Dyanne M. "Using Mathematics Language to Enhance Mathematical Conceptualization." *Childhood Education* 70 (Summer 1994): 221–224.

Trawik-Smith, Jeffrey. "How the Classroom Environment Affects Play and Development: Review of Research." *Dimensions* 20 (Winter 1992): 27–30.

Tudor, Mary. *Child Development.* New York: McGraw-Hill, 1981.

Turkel, Susan, and Claire M. Newman. "What's Your Number? Developing Number Sense." *Arithmetic Teacher* 35 (February 1988): 53–55.

Twiss, Lindy L. "Innovative Literacy Practices for ESL Learners." *Reading Teacher* (February 1996): 412–414.

Ullmann, Charles A. "Teachers, Peers, and Tests as Predictors of Adjustment." *Journal of Educational Psychology* 48 (May 1957): 257–267.

Urzua, Carole. "Doing What Comes Naturally: Recent Research in Second Language Acquisition." In *Discovering Language with Children,* edited by Gay Su Pinnell. Urbana, IL: National Council of Teachers of English, 1980.

U.S. Department of Agriculture. *Food and Nutrition* 22 (December 1992), nos. 1–2.

U.S. Department of Agriculture. Leaflet 572, Human Nutrition Information Service. Washington, DC: USDA, August 1992.

U.S. Department of Agriculture. *Nutrition and Your Health: Dietary Guidelines for Americans.* Bulletin 232-8. Washington, DC: USDA, 1986.

Van de Walle, John A. "The Early Development of Number Relations." *Arithmetic Teacher* 35 (February 1988): 15–21.

Van Hoorn, Judith, Patricia Nourot, Barbara Scales, and Keith Alward. *Play at the Center of the Curriculum.* New York: Macmillan, 1993.

Veitch, Beverly, and Thelma Harms. *Cook and Learn: Pictorial Single Portion Recipes.* Menlo Park, CA: Addison-Wesley, 1981.

Vergeront, Jeanne. *Places and Spaces for Preschool and Primary (Indoors).* Washington, DC: National Association for the Education of Young Children, 1987.

Vukelich, Carol, and Mary Roe. "Imitations of Life: Authenticity in Classroom Literacy Events." *Contemporary Education* 66 (Spring 1995): 179–182.

Vygotsky, Lev. *Mind in Society: The Development of Higher Psychological Functions.* Cambridge, MA: Harvard University Press, 1978.

Vygotsky, Lev. *Thought and Language.* Cambridge: MIT Press, 1962.

Wachowiak, Frank. *Emphasis Art.* 3d ed. New York: Harper and Row, 1977.

Wadsworth, Barry J. *Piaget's Theory of Cognitive and Affective Development.* 4th ed. New York: Longman, 1989.

Ward, Christina D. "Adult Intervention: Appropriate Strategies for Enriching the Quality of Children's Play." *Young Children* 51 (March 1996): 20–24.

Wardle, Francis. "Proposal: An Anti-Bias and Ecological Model for Multicultural Education." *Childhood Education* 72 (Spring 1996): 152–156.

Wasserman, Selma. "Play-Debrief-Replay: An Instructional Model for Science." *Childhood Education* 64 (April 1988): 232–234.

Wasserman, Selma. "Serious Play in the Classroom." *Childhood Education* 68 (Spring 1992): 132–139.

Weaver, Constance. *Reading Process and Practice.* Portsmouth, NH: Heinemann, 1988.

Weikart, Phyllis S. *Teaching Movement and Dance.* 2d ed. Ypsilanti, MI: High/Scope Press, 1982.

Weiller, Karen H., and Peggy A. Richardson. "A Program for Kids: Success-Oriented Physical Education." *Childhood Education* 69 (Spring 1993): 133–137.

Weinstein, Carol S. "The Physical Environment of the School: A Review of the Research." *Review of Educational Research* 49 (Fall 1979): 577–610.

Wells, Gordon. *Learning through Interaction: The Study of Language Development.* Cambridge, England: Cambridge University Press, 1981.

Wells, Gordon. *The Meaning Makers: Children Learning Language and Using Language to Learn.* Portsmouth, NH: Heinemann, 1986.

Wenner, George. "Relationship between Science Knowledge Levels and Beliefs toward Science Instruction Held by Preservice Elementary Teachers." *Journal of Science Education and Technology* 2 (1993): 461–468.

Whaley, Kimberlee, and Elizabeth Blue Swadner. "Multicultural Education in Infant and Toddler Settings." *Childhood Education* 66 (Summer 1990): 238–240.

Whitin. David J. "Literature and Mathematics in Preschool and Primary: The Right Connection." *Young Children* 49 (January 1994): 4–11.

Whitmore, Kathryn F., and Yetta M. Goodman. "Transforming Curriculum in Language and Literacy." In *Reaching Potentials: Transforming Early Childhood Curriculum and Assessment,* vol. 2, edited by S. Bredekamp and T. Rosegrant, 145–166. Washington, DC: National Association for the Education of Young Children, 1995.

Wilson, Ruth A. "Nature and Young Children: A Natural Connection." *Young Children* 50 (September 1995): 4–11.

Winter, Suzanne M., Michael J. Bell, and James D. Dempsey. "Creating Play Environments for Children with Special Needs." *Childhood Education* 71 (Fall 1994): 28–32.

Wittmer, Donna S., and Alice S. Honig. "Encouraging Positive Social Development in Young Children." *Young Children* 49 (July 1994): 4–12.

Wolery, Mark, and Jan S. Wilbert, eds. *Including Children with Special Needs in Early Childhood Programs.* Research Monograph of the National Association for the Education of Young Children, vol. 6. Washington, DC: NAEYC, 1994.

Wolf, Jan. "Singing with Children Is a Cinch!" *Young Children* 49 (May 1994): 20–25.

Wuertenburg, Jacque. Speech to Northern Arizona Reading Council, Flagstaff, Arizona, April 1993.

Yarrow, L. "Should Children Play with Guns?" *Parents* 58 (January 1983): 50–52.

Yelland, Nicola J. "Encouraging Young Children's Thinking Skills with Logo." *Childhood Education* 71 (Spring 1995): 152–155.

Yespo, Jo Ellen, and Elizabeth O'Connor. *Social Sets and Social Status in Preschool Classrooms.* ERIC Document Reproduction Service 307065. 1989.

Yopp, Hallie K. "A Test for Assessing Phonemic Awareness in Young Children." *Reading Teacher* 49 (September 1995): 20–29.

Zaragoza, Nina, and Sharon Vaughn. "Children Teach Us to Teach Writing." *Reading Teacher* 49 (September 1995): 42–47.

Zigler, Edward F., and Matia Finn-Stevenson. *Children: Development and Social Issues.* Lexington, MA: D. C. Heath, 1987.

Zimmerman, Marilyn P. *State of the Art in Early Childhood Music and Research.* ERIC Document Reproduction Service 250068. 1984.

Zirkelbach, Thelma, and Kathryn Blakesley. "The Language Deficient Child in the Classroom." *Education Digest* 51 (January 1986): 52–55.

Children's Books

Aardema, Verna. *Why Mosquitoes Buzz in People's Ears.* New York: Scholastic, 1975.

Ackerman, Karen. *Song and Dance Man.* New York: Knopf, 1988.

Ancona, George. *Turtle Watch.* New York: Macmillan, 1987.

Andersen, Hans Christian. *The Ugly Duckling.* Retold and illustrated by Troy Howell. New York: Putnam, 1990.

Anno, Mitsumasa. *Anno's Counting House.* New York: Philomel Books, 1982.

Asch, Frank. *Turtle Tale.* New York: Dial Press, 1978.

Barton, Byron. *Building a House.* West Caldwell, NJ: Greenwillow, 1981.

Baylor, Byrd. *The Desert Is Theirs.* New York: Charles Scribner and Sons, 1970.

Baylor, Byrd. *Everybody Needs a Rock.* New York: Atheneum, 1974.

Baylor, Byrd. *Hawk, I'm Your Brother.* New York: Aladdin Books, 1976.

Brett, Jan. *Goldilocks and The Three Bears.* New York: Dodd, Mead, 1987.

Brown, Marcia. *Once a Mouse.* New York: Atheneum, 1961.

Brown, Marcia. *Stone Soup.* New York: Aladdin, 1947.

Buckley, Richard. *The Foolish Tortoise.* Natick, MA: Picture Book Studio, 1985.

Bunting, Eve. *Someday a Tree.* New York: Clarion, 1993.

Burton, Virginia L. *The Little House.* Boston: Houghton Mifflin, 1942.

Burton, Virginia. *Katy and the Big Snow.* Boston: Houghton Mifflin, 1943.

Burton, Virginia. *Mike Mulligan and His Steam Shovel.* Boston: Houghton Mifflin, 1939.

Carle, Eric. *The Grouchy Ladybug.* New York: Crowell, 1977.

Carle, Eric. *The Mixed-Up Chameleon.* New York: Crowell, 1984.

Carle, Eric. *The Very Hungry Caterpillar.* New York: Scholastic, 1969.

Chang, Monica. *The Mouse Bride: A Chinese Folktale.* Flagstaff, AZ: Northland, 1992.

Consumer Product Safety Commission. *The 9 Lives of El Gato the Cat.* Washington, DC: CPSC, 1983.

Consumer Product Safety Commission. *Protect Someone You Love from Burns.* Project Burn Prevention. Washington, DC: CPSC, 1978.

Cowley, Joy. *The Mouse Bride.* New York: Scholastic, 1995.

Crane, Walter. *The Frog Prince.* London: Windward, 1980 (reprint).

Crews, Donald. *Freight Train.* New York: Greenwillow, 1978.

Crews, Donald. *Truck.* West Caldwell, NJ: Greenwillow, 1980.

Davis, Alice V. *Timothy Turtle.* New York: Harcourt Brace Jovanovich, 1940.

de Paola, Tomie. *Strega Nona.* Englewood Cliffs, NJ: Prentice-Hall, 1975.

Eagen, Robynne. *Kid Concoctions.* Carthage, IL: Teaching and Learning, 1994a.

Eagen, Robynne. *Kid Creations.* Carthage, IL: Teaching and Learning, 1994b.

Ehlert, Lois. *Nuts to You!* San Diego: Harcourt Brace Jovanovich, 1993.

Ehlert, Lois. *Red Leaf, Yellow Leaf.* San Diego: Harcourt, 1991.

Galdone, Paul. *Over in the Meadow.* New York: Simon & Schuster, 1986.

Galdone, Paul. *The Three Billy Goats Gruff.* New York: Clarion Books, 1973.

Gardner, Beau. *The Turn about, Think about, Look about Book.* New York: Lothrop, Lee & Shepard, 1980.

Grimm, W. *Jorinda and Joringel.* New York: World, 1970.

Hader, Berta, and Elmer Hader. *The Big Snow.* New York: Collier Books, 1948.

Hall, Donald. *Ox Cart Man.* New York: Penguin Books, 1979.

Holling, Holling C. *Minn of the Mississippi.* Boston: Houghton Mifflin, 1951.

Hutchins, Pat. *Clocks and More Clocks.* New York: Macmillan, 1970.

Hutchins, Pat. *The Doorbell Rang.* New York: Greenwillow, 1986.

Hutchins, Pat. *You'll Soon Grow into Them, Titch.* New York: Puffin, 1983.

Jarrell, Randall. *Fisherman and His Wife: A Tale from the Brothers Grimm.* New York: Farrar, Straus and Giroux, 1980.

Jonas, Ann. *Reflections.* New York: Greenwillow, 1987.

Jonas, Ann. *Round Trip.* New York: Greenwillow, 1983

Keats, Ezra Jack. *Over in the Meadow.* New York: Scholastic, 1981.

Keats, Ezra Jack. *The Snowy Day.* New York: Viking, 1962.

Keats, Ezra Jack. *Whistle for Willie.* New York: Viking, 1964.

Kimmel, Eric. *The Greatest of All: A Japanese Folktale.* New York: Holiday House, 1991.

Kipling, Rudyard. *Just So Stories.* New York: Grosset and Dunlap, 1965.

Kohl, Mary Ann. *Mudworks.* Bellingham, WA: Bright Ring, 1989.

Kraus, Robert. *Leo, the Late Bloomer.* New York: Crowell, 1971.

Kraus, Robert. *Whose Mouse Are You?* New York: Macmillan, 1970.

Kraus, Ruth. *The Carrot Seed.* New York: Harper and Row, 1945.

Langstaff, John. *Over in the Meadow.* New York. Harcourt Brace Jovanovich, 1957.

Lee, Dennis. *Alligator Pie.* Toronto: Macmillan of Canada, 1974.

Lesser, Rika. *Hansel and Gretel.* New York: Dodd Mead, 1984.

Lewis, C. S. *The Lion, the Witch, and the Wardrobe.* New York: Macmillan, 1951.

Lloyd, David. *The Stopwatch.* New York: Lippincott, no date.

Lobel, Arnold. *Frog and Toad Are Friends.* New York: Harper and Row, 1970.

Locker, Thomas. *Sky Tree.* New York: HarperCollins, 1995.

Maccaulay, David. *The Way Things Work.* Boston: Houghton Mifflin, 1988.

McCloskey, Robert. *Blueberries for Sal.* New York: Viking, 1948.

McDermott, Gerald. *The Stonecutter.* New York: Penguin Books, 1981.

McGovern, Ann. *Stone Soup.* New York: Scholastic, 1968.

McGovern, Ann. *Too Much Noise.* New York: Scholastic, 1967.

McMillan, Bruce. *Time to . . .* New York: Lothrop, Lee & Shepard, 1989.

Malotki, Ekkehart. *The Mouse Couple: A Hopi Folktale.* Flagstaff, AZ: Northland, 1988.

Maris, Ron. *I Wish I Could Fly.* New York: Greenwillow, 1986.

Martin, Bill, Jr. *Brown Bear, Brown Bear.* New York: Holt, Rinehart and Winston, 1970.

Mayer, Mercer. *There's a Nightmare in My Closet.* New York: Dial Books, 1968.

Morgan, Pierr. *The Turnip.* New York: Macmillan, 1990.

National Association for the Education of Young Children. *Children Riding on Sidewalks Safely.* Washington DC: NAEYC, 1987a.

National Association for the Education of Young Children. *Walk in Traffic Safely.* Washington, DC: NAEYC, 1990.

National Association for the Education of Young Children. *We Love You—Buckle Up!* Washington, DC: NAEYC, 1987.

Navarra, John Gabriel. *A Turtle in the House.* Garden City, NY: Doubleday, 1968.

Oppenheim, Joanne. *Have You Seen Trees?* New York: Scholastic, 1995.

Parnell, Peter. *The Apple Tree.* New York: Macmillan, 1987.

Pearson, Tracey Campbell. *Old MacDonald Had a Farm.* New York: Dial Books, 1984.

Provensen, Alice, and Martin Provensen. *Shaker Lane.* New York: Viking Kestrel, 1987.

Reeves, Martha E. *The Total Turtle.* New York: Crowell, 1975.

Ross, Tony. *Stone Soup.* New York: Dial Books, 1987.

San Souci, Robert. *The Talking Eggs.* New York: Dial Books, 1989.

Sendak, Maurice. *Where the Wild Things Are.* New York: Harper and Row, 1963.

Shaw, Charles. *It Looked Like Spilt Milk.* New York: Harper, 1988.

Silverstein, Shel. *Where the Sidewalk Ends.* New York: Harper and Row, 1974.

Steig, William. *Roland the Minstrel Pig.* New York: Simon and Schuster, 1968.

Steig, W. *Sylvester and the Magic Pebble.* New York: Scholastic, 1969.

Steptoe, John. *Mufaro's Beautiful Daughters.* New York: Lothrop Lee and Shepard Books, 1987.

Stevens, Janet. *The House That Jack Built.* New York: Holiday House, 1985.

Stevens, Janet. *Tops and Bottoms.* New York: Harcourt Brace, 1995.

Stewig, John W. *Stone Soup.* New York: Holiday House, 1991.

Sumiko, Yagawa. *The Crane Wife.* Translated by Katherine Paterson. New York: Mulberry Books, 1979.

Switzer, Merebeth. *Nature's Children: Turtles.* New York: Grolier Educational, 1986.

Tolhurst, Marilyn. *Somebody and the Three Blairs.* New York: Orchard, 1990.

Tolstoi, A. *The Turnip.* Moscow: Malysh, no date.

Trivizas, Eugene, and Helen Oxenbury. *The Three Little Wolves and the Big Bad Pig.* New York: Macmillan, 1993.

Van Rynbach, Iris. *The Soup Stone.* New York: Greenwillow, 1988.

Waddle, Martin. *Farmer Duck.* Cambridge, MA: Candlewick Press, 1991.

Waters, John F. *Green Turtle Mysteries.* New York: Crowell, 1972.

Yolen, Jane. *Owl Moon.* New York: Philomel Books, 1987.

Yorinks, Arthur. *Hey, Al!* New York: Farrar, Straus & Giroux, 1986.

Young, Ed. *Lon Po Po.* New York: Philomel Books, 1989.

Zemach, M. *It Could Always Be Worse.* New York: Scholastic, 1976.

Zemach, Margot. *The Three Little Pigs.* New York: Farrar, Straus and Giroux, 1988.

Zolotow, Charlotte. *Someday.* New York: Harper and Row, 1965.

Zolotow, Charlotte. *Summer Is . . .* New York: Crowell, 1967.

Information for Parents

Monographs for Parents from the International Reading Association
These inexpensive booklets can be ordered from the International Reading Association (P.O. Box 8139, 800 Barksdale Road, Newark, DE, 19711):

Chan, Julie M. T. *Why Read Aloud to Children?* #877.

Glazer, Susan Mandel. *How Can I Help My Child Build Positive Attitudes Toward Reading?* #879.

Rogers, Norma. *How Can I Help My Child Get Ready to Read?* #876.

Rogers, Norma. *What Books and Records Should I Get For My Preschooler?* #872.

Rogers, Norma. *What Is Reading Readiness?* #870.

These brochures for parents are available from NAEYC (see address in following section):

Keeping Healthy: Parents, Teachers and Children. #774, 1990.

Media Violence and Children: A Guide for Parents. #585, 1990.

Ready or Not . . . What Parents Should Know About School Readiness. #554, 1992.

Information about Parent Involvement
Further information may be obtained by writing or calling any of the following organizations:

National Congress of Parents and Teachers
700 Rush Street
Chicago, IL 60611
312-787-0977

National Coalition for Parent Involvement in Education
National Education Association
1201 16th Street, NW, Room 810
Washington, DC 20036

NAEYC Information Service
1834 Connecticut Avenue, NW
Washington, DC 20009
202-232-8777 or 800-424-2460

Index

Note: Bold page numbers indicate topics that are key terms and defined in the Glossary.

National Council of Social Studies (NCSS), 410, 411–412
National Council of Teachers of Mathematics (NCTM), 303, 305, 306–307, 308, 309, 310
National Education Association (NEA)
on creative arts, 371
on AIDS, 445
National Teacher's Examination, 464
newsletters, 483–484
nonjudgmental attitude (of teachers toward parents), **164**–165
norm-referenced tests, 463, 464
number, 304–305, 311, 322–323, 326–327
nutrition education, 445–449, 450, 455

obstacle courses, 438
one-to-one correspondence, 320–321
open-ended materials, 120, 121. *See also* instructional materials
operant conditioning, 4–6 **(5)**, 46, 48
oral language
of children with special needs, 295, 402
communicative competence and, **228**–229
development of, 226, 228–229, 275, 276
reading and, 280, 285–286, 294, 428
Orff approach, 393, 394
outdoor learning environment, 93–97
outdoor play, 14, 97, 98, 128–130. *See also* play

painting, 380–381
paraprofessionals, 85–86, **183**–187
parent place, **175**
parent-teacher relationships, 163–179
communication, 166, 167, 169–179, 480–484
cultural diversity and, 186, 187
developmentally appropriate practice and, 184
encouraging, 166–172, 186, 187
nature of, 163–165
parents' roles in, 169–172
reporting, 480–484
teachers' roles in, 164–165
parents. *See also* families
attitudes toward education/ teachers, 165, 166, 167, 169
behavior management by, 139–140, 157
bilingual, 248
child care and, **36**
of children with special needs, 37, 38, 173, 178–179, 486–487
communicating with, 166, 167, 169–179, 480–484

conferences with, 169–171, 172, 481–482
cultural diversity and, 99, 165, 186, 187, 487
education levels of, 162, 166–167
health education and, 442–443, 444, 445, 457
home schooling by, 169
home visits to, 166, 169–171, **172**–174
home-learning activities and, 166, 171–172, 296
involvement in school, 99, 162–179, 186, 187, 205, 487
language development and, 233, 234–238, 246–247
letters/notes to, 172, 175–178, 483–484
nutrition education and, 446–447
portfolio assessment and, 475, 476–477, 448
reading by, 248, 258
relationships with teachers. *See* parent-teacher relationships
reporting to. *See* reporting
resources for, 175, 179
safety education and, 451, 452, 453
single, 163–164, 165
socioeconomic status of, 166, 169
visits to school by, 165, 166, 167, 172, 174–175
as volunteers, 85–86, 99, 179–180
working mothers, 36, 164
writing and, 266–267, 268–269, 270, 271
patterns/functions (in math), 319–320
pegboard systems, 86–88, 217
personal safety, 450, 454–455
personality, 15–16, 54–55, 443–444
phonemic awareness, 275, **277**–278
phonetic writing, 269, 270
phonics, 277
phonology, 227
physical development, 9–14
assessment of, 469–470, 471
behaviorist programs/theory and, 6, 8–9, 49
constructivist programs/theory and, 8–9, 54, 60–61
curriculum planning and, 13–14
fitness levels, 14, 117, 434, 436
learning environment and, 13
maturationist theory and, 6, 8–9
Montessori programs and, 43
motor skills. *See* motor skills
movement and, 390–391
patterns of, 9–14
physical education and, 84
play and, 14, 117, 129
physical disabilities, 2, 88, 130, 156, 295, 365, 401–403, 441

physical education, 434–441
activities for, 434, 437–441
for children with special needs, 440–441
curriculum planning for, 434–437
developmentally appropriate practice and, 437–438
games, 435, 436, 437, 438
gender and, 437
instructional materials for, 438, 440–441
integrated curriculum and, 399, 438, 456–457
intellectual development and, 436
language development and, 435, 436
learning areas for, 77, 84
literacy and, 457
motivation for, 434, 436
physical development and, 84
play and, 435, 436, 437
self-concept and, 435, 436
social development and, 435, 436
specialists in, 399, 400
teaching, 434–437
themes in, 456
physical fitness, 14, 117, 434, 436
physical knowledge, 8, 338, 350–351
physical science, 356–359
Piaget, Jean
on early childhood education, 54–55
on language development, 232
on learning, 7–8, 27, 34, 49–50, 51–52, 303
on learning mathematics, 303–304
on play, 106–107
on stages of cognitive development, 24–26, 27
on types of knowledge, 8
place value, 323–325
play, 102–133
academic achievement and, 114–115, 125–128
aggressive, 20, 109, 118, 130
analysis of spaces for, 70–74
assessment of, 111, 112, 123–125, 128, 129, 133
behavior management and, 108, 109
benefits of, 108–109, 119–120, 123–125
characteristics of, 110–111
child development and, 106, 107–108, 113, 117, 119, 120
for children with special needs, 130–132
children's roles in, 110–111
cultural diversity and, 99–100, 132
curriculum planning and, 112–113, 117–118, 121–123, 128, 129

room arrangements, **66,** 68–74, 88–89, 141, 142, 152. *See also* learning environment
rote memory, 8, 35
Rousseau, Jean-Jacques, 6, 34–35

"safe touching," 455
safety (in the learning environment). *See also* safety education
    allergies, 98, 173, 456
    assessment of, 97–98
    child release authorization, 97
    classroom hazards, 97
    drama and, 116, 452–453, 459
    emergency procedures, 97–98, 450–451
    fires, 97, 450–451
    first aid, 97
    food and, 446, 448
    instructional materials and, 75
    organizations concerned with, 507–510
    outdoor play and, 97, 98
    poisoning, 450, 453–454
    science and, 347–349
    water play and, 84, 94, 348
safety education, 450–457
    activities for, 287, 288
    for children with special needs, 450
    cultural diversity and, 457
    emergency procedures, 97–98, 450–451
    fire safety, 97, 450–451
    games in, 452–453
    integrated curriculum and, 451, 452–453, 455–457, 459
    literature and, 451
    parents and, 451, 452, 453
    personal safety, 450, 454–455
    poison safety, 450, 453–454
    "safe touching," 455
    telephone use, 98, 450, 451
    themes in, 456–457
    traffic safety, 450, 451–453, 455–456
    water safety, 450, 453
sand tables/play, 75, 83–84, 93, 94, 121
scheduling, 212–219
    activity time, 86, 214
    adaptations in, 89, 212, 217
    arrival time, 146, 147
    assessment of, 218, 219–220
    beginning of schoolyear, 217
    behavior management and, 141, 142, 146–147, 152, 218
    for children with special needs, 218–219
    children's ages and, 86, 88, 212
    departure time, 146, 147
    developmentally appropriate practice and, 217

examples of, 212, 213
factors in, 212
group time, 214–215
health education, 442
holidays. *See* holidays
integrated curriculum and, 200
kindergarten, 213, 218
learning areas and, 86–88
learning plans and, 209
mathematics, 308
preschool, 213
primary grades, 212, 213, 214
pull-out programs, 218–219
purposes of, 212
routine activities, 212, 216–217
school calendar, 172
sharing time, 214–215, 244
snack time, 215, 445, 446, 447, 448
systems for, 86–88, 101
transitions, 146, 147, **215**–216
schematic drawing, 373, 376
School for Constructive Play, 49, 55
science, 336–367
    activities for, 344, 356, 357, 350–361
    biological, 345, 353–356
    for children with special needs, 365
    children's enjoyment of, 349–350
    classifying/comparing, 343
    communicating, 343
    constructivist programs/model and, 338–339, 353
    content/balance in, 345–348
    cultural diversity and, 349–350, 366
    curriculum planning for, 341, 344–353
    definition of, 339–342
    developmentally appropriate practice and, 340, 352
    earth, 359–361
    experimenting, 343–344
    gender differences and, 349, 366
    instructional materials for, 346, 347, 353
    integrated curriculum and, 243, 339, 343, 345, 353, 357, 358, 359, 361–365, 370, 372, 449
    learning areas for, 77, 82–83, 353
    learning environment for, 347–348
    literacy and, 363, 365
    literature and, 360, 363–365
    logico-mathematical knowledge, 338, 350–351
    manipulatives used in, 338
    mathematics and, 302, 338, 361–362
    measurement, 343, 362
    observing, 342
    physical, 356–359
    physical knowledge, 338, 350–351
    play and, 127, 343–344, 361
    problem solving and, 339

readiness and, 342
reading and, 357, 358, 363–365
relating/inferring/applying, 344
requirements for, 361
safety issues, 347–349
scientific process, **339**–340, 342–344, 355
seriation, 361–362
teaching, 338–339, 341–344
textbooks, 361
themes in, 359, 361, 362, 363–365
understanding concepts in, 338–340, 346–347, 350
writing and, 343, 345, 357, 358, 363–365
scientific process, **339**–340, 342–344, 355. *See also* science
screening tests, 7, 463, **464**
scribbling
    as drawing, 373, 374
    as writing, 266–267
sculpture, 381
self-concept/self-esteem
    assertive discipline and, 151–153
    behavior management and, 138, 139, 146, 152, 154, 155
    behaviorist programs/theory and, 49
    development of, 15, 16–18
    gender differences and, 16
    health education and, 444
    parents' involvement in school and, 162
    physical education and, 435, 436
self-evaluation, 473–475
semantics, 228, 261, 280
sensitive periods, 39, **42**
seriation, 312–313, 321, 361–362
seven- to eight-year-olds. *See also* primary grades
    cognitive development of, 11
    emotional development of, 11, 23
    language development of, 234
    mathematics activities for, 312, 313, 314, 315–316, 317–318, 320, 322, 323, 325
    physical development of, 10, 13, 14
    science activities for, 355–356, 358–359, 360–361
    social development of, 10, 21
    social studies activities for, 415–416
sewing/weaving, 381–382
sex roles, 15, 20. *See also* gender
shared reading, **286**
sharing time, 214–215, 244
sight-word vocabulary, 259, 261, 294
sign language, 226, 238
simple abstraction, **303**
singing, 80, 248, 385–388